MW00608020

"Make visible what, without you, might perhaps never have been seen."
– Robert Bresson, *L´Argent*

"I think of a screenwriter as a sculptor. And I used to think that the screenplay is the sculpture, but I don't think that fully captures what we do. I'd say what's more accurate is that you're the sculptor, and the reader's emotional journey is the sculpture. Words are your chisel, and the screenplay is the act of chiseling. Everyone else's job on a film is to use magic to bring the sculpture to actual life."
— David Wappel, *Long Gone By*

$21.95 U.S.

SCREENWRITING
TRIBE

WORKSHOP HANDBOOK
FOR WRITING AND POLISHING
FILM AND TV SPEC SCRIPTS

SECOND EDITION

DANIEL JOHN CAREY
FOUNDER OF SCREENWRITING TRIBE

Screenwriting Tribe:
Workshop Handbook for Writing and Polishing Film and TV Spec Scripts:
Second Edition

Disclaimer:

This book is sold for information purposes only. How you interpret and utilize the information in this book is your decision. Neither the author nor the publisher and/or distributors will be held accountable for the use or misuse of the information contained in this book. This book is not intended as legal advice. Because of the way people interpret what they read, and take actions based on their own intellect and life situations, which are not in the author's, publisher's, and/or distributor's control, there is always some risk involved; therefore, the author, publisher, and/or distributor of this book are not responsible for any adverse effects or consequences from the use of any suggestions described herein.

ISBN 13: 978-1-884702-41-9   **ISBN 10:** 1-884702-41-4
Library of Congress Control Number: 2020933273
808.2'3-dc22   **CIP 98-4805**
First Edition: 2018
Second Edition: 2020
Oakonic, POB 1272, Santa Monica, CA 90406-1272
Cover: Design concept by the author. Graphics by Noel.
Editing by Rose Carey.

Copyright © 2018, 2020 by Daniel John Carey

All intellectual rights owned by Daniel John Carey and reserved in perpetuity throughout the universe. No part of the author's words in this book may be reproduced in any form or by any electronic, mechanical, or other means, including on the Internet, through cell phone and/or personal, educational, public, and/or business communication and technology systems, or through any and all information storage, retrieval, or reproduction systems, including book sample and publicity Web sites, without permission in writing from the author, and only the author, except by a reviewer, who may quote brief, attributed passages of the final published book in a review; and as fair use by those wishing to use short, credited quotations of the author's words.

"There's a giant group of people who want to be writers, and a smaller group who actually write, and an even smaller group who are actually going to strive so hard that someone's going to pay attention to them."
— Steve Koren, *Seinfeld*

THANK YOU, TRIBE!

This book is dedicated to the members of Screenwriting Tribe. It's been my privilege getting to know, working with, spending Sundays with, and being on this learning adventure with you while incubating your screenplays.

Thank you to Pam, the owner of the UnUrban Coffee House for being our sponsor, and for the important service that her venue provides to the artistic community of Los Angeles. The performance room of her indie coffee house is like a dream factory. Poets, comics, actors, singers, musicians (including Alec Benjamin), writers, and other artists have found and sharpened their talents there. Much of this book was written in UnUrban Coffee House.

Thank you to Tony, the owner of Sideshow Bookstore, for his continued support. His store, which is another dream factory, has been the morning location of Screenwriting Tribe. It is a wonderful place to find books of all varieties.

Thank you to my sister Rose for helping me to polish this manuscript.

Any errors in this book are my own.

"You can fail at what you don't like. So, you might as well take a chance on doing what you love."
— Jim Carrey, actor

"Find your tribe, brainstorm ideas that rile each other up, and take turns helping each other's work."
— Josh Ruben, *Scare Me*

"Word-work is sublime because it is generative; it makes meaning that secures our difference, our human difference – the way in which we are like no other life. We die. That may be the meaning of life. But we do language. That may be the measure of our lives."
— Toni Morrison, *Beloved*

"I don't think writers function because they have something they particularly want to say. They have something they feel."
— Stanley Kubrick, *2001: A Space Odyssey*

"I find writing to be the most difficult thing I've ever done. I find it much more difficult than directing, because it requires concentration, and I'm not the most concentrated of people."
— Seven Spielberg, *A.I. Artificial Intelligence*

"Movies are written three times: Once on paper. Once on film. And, once in the editing room."
— Christopher McQuarrie, *Jack the Giant Slayer*

TABLE OF CONTENTS

329 **NOTE 81:** The character names are too similar, and it is confusing.

329 **NOTE 82:** There are speaking characters with general names, rather than proper names, or nicknames that give a clue to their personalities.

330 **NOTE 83:** The dialogue is name happy as characters continually call each other by their names.

331 **NOTE 84:** There are numerous scenes of characters entering and greeting each other.

331 **NOTE 85:** There are unnecessary speaking roles of characters who do nothing for the story, but only increase the budget.

332 **NOTE 86:** The characters are overly described to a fault, and that would require a global talent search.

332 **NOTE 87:** There is tornado character description swirling with unnecessary details.

333 **NOTE 88:** The wardrobe description is over-the-top in complexity.

335 **NOTE 89:** The sets are over described.

335 **NOTE 90:** The description of the scenery is more like a grand novel.

336 **NOTE 91:** The vehicle description is excessively detailed.

336 **NOTE 92:** Exact song titles are listed.

337 **NOTE 93:** The script misuses V.O., O.S., and O.C.

338 **NOTE 94:** The script is filled with clichés.

338 **NOTE 95:** The script uses stereotypes that are insulting, over-the-top, and/or don't function for the genre.

339 **NOTE 96:** The character description is worded in a way that plays into the subjective and objective gaze.

340 **NOTE 97:** The script contains random or meaningless or blatant make-out scenes and/or nudity that does nothing for the story.

341 **NOTE 98:** The description is wordy to the point of being novelesque.

341 **NOTE 99:** The script contains scenes that would require an excessive budget beyond a likely return on investment.

342 **NOTE 100:** The script contains numerous flagged words (words in capitalization meant to flag the attention of the crew).

342 **NOTE 101:** The writer uses SFX before sounds, as if the sound, foley, FX, and other crew members are going to be reading the spec script.

343 **NOTE 102:** There is distractive capitalization.

344 **NOTE 103:** The opening is confusing as to the indications of words to appear/superimposed on screen.

345 **NOTE 104:** The script contains underlined words that are not necessary, are confusing or distractive, or meant for actor direction (micromanaging the actors).

346 **NOTE 105:** There are bolded words in description, dialogue, and/or parentheticals.

"Make no mistake, not only is story the true wealth of the world, but our world has never needed us to work more consciously with the magic of story than it does now. You probably have some sense of why I say this. The signs that we need to get a whole lot smarter are here. And story is at the very least how we mobilize intelligence."
– Amnon Buchbinder, author *The Way of the Screenwriter*

"With any content, it's always the story. If you're not invested in the story – which starts on the page – then, generally, you're not going to have the kind of enthusiasm you want in the result."
– Jennifer Salke, Amazon Studios

"We only have two hours to change people's lives."
– John Cassavetes, *A Woman Under the Influence*

"Good acting and writing are the oxygen and hydrogen of cinema. If you don't have either of them it will be hard to have a good movie."
– Francis Ford Coppola, *Tetro*

"Learn the rules like a pro, so you can break them like an artist."
– Pablo Picasso, artist

Vision Quest

Similar to a screenwriting workshop where there are numerous opinions given, with some contradicting each other, on a much more diverse level, this book contains the views of many writers and of other people in the film, TV, and other industries. Some of the opinions are not in alignment with what is expressed by others.

In the screenwriting profession, not everyone shares the same opinions, or writes by the same guidelines. Some follow rules that others don't. This book is a way to learn some of their rules, and consider which ones you might follow – or break.

As a screenwriter, your quest is likely to experience the reality of seeing your work on the big – or small – screen. This book has been composed to share ideas for consideration, to explore possibilities, and hopefully to inspire writers to create their best work so that their vision might end up on screen.

"Script is – by far – the most important thing in the film industry."
– Dov Simens, WebFilmSchool.com

Know this: Producers, directors, cinematographers, editors, actors, film crews, agents, managers, prop and film equipment company workers, theater employees and thousands of other people do not have jobs, unless screenwriters write scripts.

It is time to begin your writing adventures in the screen trade.

But first, there are beginning steps.

"Concerning all acts of initiative and creation, there is one elementary truth, the ignorance of which kills countless ideas and splendid plans: That the moment one definitely commits oneself, the providence moves, too. Whatever you can do or dream you can do, begin it. Boldness has genius, power, and magic in it. Begin it now."
– Johann Wolfgang von Goethe, *Faust*

While there are things about the industry that make it seem easy to advance in it, those who do establish solid careers prepare. They study, practice, and sharpen their skills to become ready to be part of productions that will engage audiences. You might end up being one of them.

"Although for some people cinema means something superficial and glamorous, it is something else. I think it is the mirror of the world."
— Jeanne Moreau, *The Birch-Tree Meadow*

As you write a screenplay, consider what you want the audience to feel, based on what they see and hear. What is it about the story that will make people want to engage, and watch every second of it?

Before you submit a screenplay to the industry, make sure it has an engaging story with sufficient components, and is ready to be presented.

Someone recently showed me part of their screenplay. They said a producer wanted to look at it. I said, "Don't show this to anyone, yet." I could tell by the first lines of that screenplay that it was absolutely not ready for anyone of relevance to read. I suggested that he take the time to put it through a workshop. He said he didn't have that time. Apparently, he dismissed me, and submitted it to the producer.

If you owned a restaurant, would you serve food before it is ready? If you made wedding cakes, would you assemble them when they were half baked? If you manufactured cars, would you put them in the sales showroom partially built? If you were installing a sewage system, would you allow sewage to run through it when there are unsecured connections? If you wanted to be a violinist, would you expect to be welcomed into an orchestra, before you displayed capable skills, but were only able to make screechy noises?

Many beginning writers have a script that is half baked, half assembled, and with leaking plot holes. They are eager to show it to anyone and everyone. They think that they are ready to go big, when their script isn't polished enough even for their grandmother to read it. Yet, they seem in a rush to submit it to contests, studio writing programs, managers, agents, directors, producers, and stars. To those with experience in the industry, reading unready scripts is like listening to someone try to play a violin when they don't know how.

Pick up a stringed instrument that you don't know how to play, and perform two hours of music on it. It will sound like what it is like for a film professional to read a screenplay that is not ready for industry submission.

This book is an attempt to help you to get closer to becoming someone who can write a relevant script that, after workshopping, editing, getting coverage, and otherwise polishing, will be ready for submission to the industry.

I hope your scripts will end up being illuminated on the screen.

"Part of the requirement for me to be an artist is that you're trying to share your personal existence with others and trying to illuminate modern life, trying to understand it."
— Francis Ford Coppola, *Patton*

"Words are sacred. They deserve respect. If you get the right ones, in the right order, you can nudge the world a little."
– Tom Stoppard, *Tulip Fever*

"Writers perform an extremely important role: They make others dream – those who are unable to dream for themselves. And everyone needs to dream. Could there be any more important job in life than that?"
– Felix J. Palma, *The Map of Time*

"Stories are a gateway to radical empathy, and the greatest ones are catalysts for action."
– Bryce Dallas Howard, actor

SCREENWRITERS ARE CULTURAL ENGINEERS

"The more we're governed by idiots and have no control over our destinies, the more we need to tell stories to each other about who we are, why we are, where we come from, and what might be possible."
– Alan Rickman, *The Little Chaos*

A film can alter the views of people around the planet.

A film can help get people to end abuse, neglect, bullying, racism, oppression, fraud, and atrocities.

A film can spark a revolution of thought that results in changed government and institutional policies.

A film can trigger actions that save endangered species, and that protect the environment needed for the survival of life.

In addition to being entertaining, films can inspire and reinvigorate movements, focus attention, open closed minds, give hope to the weary, enlighten, motivate, nurture, spotlight triumph, improve the human condition, and alter the path of humanity.

Film is art. Art is life. Life is reflected in film. Film can help generate the art that is life.

Screenwriting is the genesis of film, and can also be the origins of global change.

"Movies touch our hearts and awaken our vision, and change the way we see things. They take us to other places, they open doors and minds. Movies are the memories of our lifetime. We need to keep them alive."
– Martin Scorsese, *The Age of Innocence*

The eyes retain an image for a split second. The memory of it can last a lifetime, and alter a person's view of and interaction with the world. With that in mind, be conscious of what you are creating to put into the minds of others.

"Imagination is a force that can actually manifest a reality."
– James Cameron, *Avatar*

"If you doubt that storytelling can change the world, look at what happens when the techniques are exploited by evil people."
– Michael Hennessy, actor

"It is important that films make people look at what they've forgotten."
– Spike Lee, *Malcolm X*

"One of the great things about movies, interestingly, one of the things that separates them theatrically from some of the other mediums now is the cultural impact that films make. They make cultural impact. And I know for my own self, I like it when we're making a positive cultural impact. I think that's a really great thing. And one of the things that movies can still do, and still do on a worldwide basis."
– Tom Rothman, Sony Motion Picture Group

"We have a responsibility as artists to try and generate conversation."
– Liz Hannah, *The Post*

"There is no reason why challenging themes and engaging stories have to be mutually exclusive. In fact, each can fuel the other. As a filmmaker, I want to entertain people first and foremost. If out of that comes a greater awareness and understanding of a time or a circumstance, then the hope is that change can happen."
– Edward Zwick, *Thirtysomething*

"I don't think writers should write about answers. I think writers should write about questions."
– Paul Haggis, *Crash*

"Excavating, teaching, and celebrating the feminine through stories is, inside our climate emergency, a matter of human survival. The moment we start imagining a new world and sharing it with one another through story is the moment that new world may actually come."
– Brit Marling, *The OA; NYT: I Don't Want to Be the Strong Female Lead*

"We need to keep an eye on the other human experiences to give ourselves the fullness and the breadth of our own humanity. Our humanity is served back to us through the eyes of those who have diminished us. And they serve back to us a view of ourselves that is incomplete. If we don't look to the bigger picture, our view will narrow to that which is constantly fed to us."
– Sidney Poiteir, *For Love of Ivy*

"The screen is a magic medium. It has such power that it can retain interest as it conveys emotions and moods that no other art form can hope to tackle."
– Stanley Kubrick, *Full Metal Jacket*

"Hollywood is a film industry, a film business. I don't approach my career in that way. I see it as art, and I become involved in films that ring my bell."
– Sissy Spacek, actor

"Art is a special revelation of the higher powers of the human soul."
– Frederick Douglass, former American slave

FILMMAKING IS ART

"What is art? Like a declaration of love: The consciousness of our dependence on each other. A confession. An unconscious act that reflects the true meaning of life – love and sacrifice."
– Andrei Tarkovsky, *The Mirror*

"Writers are among the most sensitive, most intellectually anarchic, most representative, most proving artists. The writer's ability to imagine what is not the self, to familiarize the strange, and to mystify the familiar – all this is the test of her or his power."
– Toni Morrison, *Beloved*

Artists help define and design what society is and becomes. Their influence is everywhere.

"Art does not reproduce what we see. It makes us see."
– Paul Klee, Swiss German Artist

We have heard someone start a sentence by saying, "That movie made me feel…" Film triggers emotions, which are associated with body chemistry, mood, and feelings. Those who create films communicate energy into – and reformulate the energy of – the people who watch the films.

Artistic expression is communication. It is language. It brings one person's view or understanding into another. Films do that.

Filmmaking is and films are art.

"No art passes our conscience in the way film does, and goes directly to our feelings, deep down into the dark rooms of our souls."
– Ingmar Bergman, *Fanny and Alexander*

"Art invites us to know beauty and to solicit it, summon it, from even the most tragic of circumstances. Art reminds us that we belong here."
– Toni Morrison, *Beloved*

In the spring of 1968 there were riots and demonstrations in the streets of Paris, and later in other parts of France. This happened after the French minister of culture tried to close the Cinematheque Française run by Henri Langlois. The crowds and some well-known persons of the international film community rallied behind Langlois, who was famous for endless screenings of films he had spent decades collecting from all over the world, including from war-torn countries.

Langlois considered film to be its own country. His theatre was popular among people in the art community of Paris. It was because of Langlois that the Cinematheque existed, and it is because of his dedication that many films from throughout the world have been preserved.

Among those attending Cinematheque Française was a group of passionate film fans and creators known as *the Rats of Cinematheque* or *Children of the Cinematheque*. The Rats – including New Wave film directors Jean-Luc Godard, Francois Truffaut, and Jacques Rivette – spent many hours at the theatre and in social settings passionately discussing the films that they had watched at the Cinematheque.

The knowledge shared among those who frequented Langlois' Cinematheque altered the film world forever because it strengthened the concept that film is a form of art and a way for filmmakers and society in general to express and to be expressed.

"Poets and anarchists are always the first to go. Where? To the frontline. Wherever it is."
– Giannina Braschi, author *Empire of Dreams*

As film helps to formulate the thoughts of large numbers of people around the world, the Cinematheque Française part of film history is an example of how little things can affect larger things – including international culture.

To this day, the energy of the Rats of Cinematheque continues to saturate the film community.

"I think everyone whose response to the financial struggles of an artists is, 'Well, you should have gone into tech or something useful,' should have to go thirty days with no reading, no TV, no movies, no museum visits, no video games, no theatre, and have arts stripped from all of their other experiences. No music in restaurants, at sporting events, bars, stores, nothing. No audio books or podcasts or music on their commute. After thirty days deprived of all contributions of artists, I would be interested to know if anyone would still say artists are drains on society and unworthy of life."
– Denise Ivanoff, actor and director

No matter what stage of life you are in, it is never too late to recognize and engage in your talents, and to practice your art.

"I am always doing that which I cannot do in order that I may learn how to do it."
– Pablo Picasso, artist

Some of those who have been considered to be the greatest artists went through decades of learning about and/or misunderstanding themselves – and being misunderstood. Some were treated badly because of those misunderstandings – before they created their most celebrated works.

"There are some truths about life that can be expressed only as stories, or songs, or images. Art delights, instructs, consoles. It educates our emotions."
– Dana Gioia, poet

There are many examples of artists who created landmark works in their later years. For instance, Louise Bourgeois didn't create her famous steel and marble Maman spider sculpture until she was 87 years old. Another example is Anna Mary Robertson "Grandma" Moses, who didn't start painting until she was in her seventies. In the acting community, there are people like Estelle Parsons, who, at age 82 was on a national tour starring in Tracy Letts' play *August: Osage County*, in which she appeared on Broadway when it won both the 2008 Tony Award and Pulitzer Prize for Best Play.

"No matter how old you get, if you can keep the desire to be creative, you're keeping the man-child alive."
– John Cassavetes, *Gloria*

"You must be very careful, or without knowing it you can change the world."
– Vera Nazarian, *Pomegranate*

Just as there were opportunities in past decades for films and filmmakers to play roles in awakening the masses to their possibilities, as long as films can be produced and viewed their remains the chance that films will play roles in what society is and becomes. And with it, the artistic terrain for creative people to communicate messages.

"There are people who talk about the American cinema of the '70s as some halcyon period. It was, to a degree. But, not because there were any more talented filmmakers. There's probably in fact more talented filmmakers today than there was in the '70s.
What there was in the '70s was better audiences. And a lot of what was happening in the world had people in consternation. Women's rights. Gay rights. Sexual liberation. Drug liberation. Anti-war. All of these things were rolling on top of each other. And people were turning to the arts. Specifically:

movies. What should we feel about this? *Bob and Ted and Carol and Alice*, about wife swapping. And *Coming Home*, about Vietnam veterans. Or, *An Unmarried Woman*, about female liberation. So, almost one a week, films were coming out to address these things that were on people's minds. And when people take movies seriously, it's very easy to make serious movies. When they don't take it seriously, it's very very hard.

We now have audiences that don't take movies seriously. It's very hard to make a serious movie for them. So, it's not that us filmmakers are letting you down, it's you audiences are letting us down. Because if audiences are receptive to a quality movie, believe me, they will get it. We are all just waiting to make it.

So, at the same time, that period of about ten to twelve years there, every single week there was some kind of film coming out addressing some social issue in a fictional form."
– Paul Schrader, *First Reformed*

Films, television, plays, literature, music, and design create various forms of energy, they trigger and build concerns, which then influence culture. Including the culture of art that saturates society.

"The written word can be powerful and beautiful. But films transport us to another place in a way that even the most evocative words never can."
– Saoirse Ronan, actor

With film and TV shows, there are people sitting and watching something, and it might be for a half hour, an hour, or more than two hours. As you are a filmmaker, what is it that you are doing to the audiences? How are you impacting them? What are you making them factor and consider? How is what you are presenting to them going to alter their thoughts, behaviors, and their culture?

Film plays with feelings, hope, wants, needs, yearnings, anticipations, and, through the characters on screen, is often a conduit of vicarious expression and realization.

"I think raising consciousness – helping people see and understand how they're connected to these larger systems in the world around us – is an incredibly important thing. I think art can do this in ways that are provocative, meaningful and inspirational, deeply moving, beautiful, connected with history and culture and resonant. I think that's a big part of it. There's another part of it where I think artists have the opportunity to more than call attention to problems and preach, to really help solve problems. To help create things that work better, that are just more beautiful and right."
– Sam Bower, founding director of Green Museum

"There are no days in life so memorable as those which vibrated to some stroke of the imagination."
– Ralph Waldo Emerson, essayist and philosopher

"Every artist makes herself born. You must bring the artist into the world yourself."
— Willa Cather, author *O Pioneers!*

"I feed on other people's creativity. Photographers, artists of every kind. Sometimes a feeling that you get listening to a song can be so powerful. I've wanted to write whole scripts around what I felt when listening to a piece of music. I think music is important, and surrounding your visual field with stimulating things."
— James Cameron, *Terminator*

"Your life is a work of art. You are the designer of your life, the paint brush is in your hands and with every beautiful picture you paint and every opportunity you cease, will one day form into your masterpiece."
— Adam Taste, philosopher

"I believe that all great art holds the power to dissolve things: Time, distance, differences, injustice, despair.
I believe that all great art holds the power to mend things: Join, comfort, inspire hope in fellowship, reconcile us to our selves.
Art is good for my soul, precisely because it reminds me that we have souls in the first place."
— Tilda Swinton, *Here*

"We are nothing but the stories we live and die by."
— Nic Pizzolatto, *True Detective*

"Like going to temple, or a mosque, or church, or any other religious institution, movie going is in many ways a sacred ritual, repeated week after week after week. I'll be there this weekend, just like I was most weekends between 1996 and 1990, at the multiplex near the shopping mall about five miles from my childhood home in Columbus, Georgia."
— Franklin Leonard, founder of The Blacklist

You may never know who you will influence when a screenplay of yours is produced and released into the world. So, write something that will influence good.

"Everybody has something that chews them up and, for me, that thing was always loneliness. The cinema has the power to make you not feel lonely, even when you are."
— Tom Hanks, actor

"It is through art that we will prevail, and we will endure. It lives on after us, and defines us as people."
— Rita Moreno, actor

"Biochemicals are the physiological substrates of emotion, the molecular underpinnings of what we experience as feelings, sensations, thoughts, drives, perhaps even spirit or soul."
 – Dr. Candace B. Pert, author *The Molecules of Emotion*

"I don't do drugs, I am drugs."
 – Salvador Dali, *Improvisation sur un dimanche aprés-midi*

"Every trick that will induce emotion in the audience, you use. You use them all."
 – John Sturges, director

CONSIDER FILM A DRUG

"We don't go to the movies for plot. We go to the movies to feel something."
 – Franklin Leonard, founder of The Black List

"Movies are supposed to make you feel something. They are road maps to emotion."
 – Lindsay Doran, producer

"Neurocinematics is a term coined by Uri Hasson at Princeton University, who was among the first to investigate how the brain responds to the movies using an fMRI brain scanner.

His team looked at the similarity in the brain responses of a group of viewers to different types of films. When volunteers watched a section of Alfred Hitchcock's *Bang! You're Dead*, for example, they found that about 65 percent of the frontal cortex – the part of the brain involved in attention and perception – was responding in the same way in all the viewers. Only 18 percent of the cortex showed a similar response when the participants watched more free-form footage of the sitcom *Curb Your Enthusiasm*. The level of correlation between people indicates how much control the director has over the audience's experience, Hasson claims."
 – Jessica Hamzelou, *Brain Imaging Monitors Effect of Movie Magic*, NewScientist.com

"'I like to watch people's brains while they're watching movies,' admits Pea Tikka, a filmmaker, researcher, and scholar visiting Los Angeles this fall from Finland. She goes on to explain her growing fascination with brain imaging techniques that allow her to study how different kinds of images affect viewers. Together with neuroscientists in a research project called

10

aivoAALTO at Aalto University, Helsinki, she is exploring the avant-garde, such as Maya Deren's *At Land*, and, in the near future, animated films. 'Filmmaking and brain research are meeting,' Tikka continues, noting that the emerging field is known as 'neurocinematics,' a term coined by Uri Hasson in a 2008 essay titled *Neurocinematics: The Neuroscience of Film*, which considers films and their ability to control or affect the mind."
   – Holly Willis, *Neurocinematics: Your Brain on Film*, KCET.org

Similar to taking a drug, watching a film can alter brain and eye function, lower or heighten body temperature and blood pressure, dilate or restrict blood vessels, increase or slow breathing, salivation, and perspiration, and impact digestion and other gastrointestinal and organ activities – including skin tension and temperature. This is because watching a film can alter the hormonal and chemical production within the tissues, which change adaptive and physical conditions. The internally-produced substances are known as molecules of emotion, which are also tied in with cellular replication and the electrical fields within the person.

"People all over the world spend countless hours of their lives every week being fed entertainment in the forms of movies, TV shows, newspapers, YouTube videos, the internet. And it is ludicrous to believe this stuff doesn't alter our brains."
   – Charlie Kaufman, *Anomalisa*

"Brain activity was measured using functional magnetic resonance imaging (fMRI) during free viewing of films, and inter-subject correlation analysis was used to assess similarities in the spatiotemporal responses across viewers' brains during movie watching. Our results demonstrate that some films can exert considerable control over brain activity and eye movements. However, this was not the case for all types of motion picture sequences, and the level of control over viewers' brain activity differed as a function of movie content, editing, and directing style."
   – Neurocinematics: The Neuroscience of Film

The researchers at New York University who conducted the neuroscience of film study quoted above found that watching a film alters brain function, including areas that process specific types of information and communication, and those that trigger physical responses.

"Every decision about a movie, about cinematography, about light, about camera placement, is emotionally important. And, after all, what matters in life, I think, is what you feel."
   – Rodrigo Prieto, cinematographer

Among the areas of the brain that are activated when a person engages with a film are the frontal cortex, sensory cortex, motor cortex, and also the ventral visual areas and occipital lobe. But, it is a whole-body experience, as parts of the body are connected, including through the hormonal and neural chemicals created by expectations, perceptions, and other thought processes.

"It is an example of what films can do, how they can slip past your defenses, and really break your heart."
– David Gilmour, musician

"My lab wondered if we could 'hack' the oxytocin system to motivate people to engage in cooperative behaviors. To do this, we tested if narratives shot on video, rather than fact-to-face interactions, would cause the brain to make oxytocin. By taking blood draws before and after the narrative, we found that character-driven stories do consistently cause oxytocin synthesis. Further, the amount of oxytocin released by the brain predicted how much people were willing to help others; for example, donating money to a charity associated with the narrative.

In subsequent studies, we have been able to deepen our understanding of why stories motivate voluntary cooperation. (This research was giving a boost when, with funding from the U.S. Department of Defense, we developed ways to measure oxytocin released noninvasively at up to one thousand times per second.) We discovered that, in order to motivate a desire to help others, a story must first sustain attention – a scarce resource in the brain – by developing tension during the narrative. If the story is able to create that tension, then it is likely that attentive viewers/listeners will come to share the emotions of the characters in it, and after it ends, likely to continue mimicking the feelings and behaviors of those characters. This explains the feeling of dominance you have after James Bond saves the world, and your motivation to work out after watching the Spartans fight in *300*."
– Paul J. Zak, *Why Your Brain Loves Good Storytelling*; *Harvard Business Review*

The mind-altering molecules of emotion formed by our cells in correlation with our thoughts include endogenous opioids, such as neuropeptides and cannabinoids. Perhaps the most well-known are the endorphin opiate peptides associated with the euphoric runner's high. However, cannabinoids cross the blood-brain barrier, are produced by the neurochemical endocannabinoid system, and may be more responsible for exercise-induced elation.

"I recognize terror as the finest emotion and so I will try to terrorize the reader. But if I find that I cannot terrify, I will try to horrify, and if I find that I cannot horrify, I'll go for the gross-out. I'm not proud."
– Stephen King, *The Shining*

"What you are doing is feeling the emotions that your characters are feeling, and finding the best way to express those emotions in the most powerfully felt, truthful, effective, moving way."
– Ronald Bass, *Rain Man*

Substances produced in response to a dramatic experience include acetylcholine, dopamine, epinephrine, estrogen, gamma-aminobutyric acid, norepinephrine, oxytocin, progesterone, serotonin, and testosterone. These are in tune with which parts of the nerve system that are activated by sounds, images, smells, taste, feelings, desires, and memories.

"As a general rule, an engaged brain will have high levels of activity in areas involved in processing sound and images. And if a person is watching a good horror movie, for example, you'd expect to see more activity in the amygdala – the part of the brain that responds to threats. On the other hand, a scene which inspires compassion will activate the insula."
– Jessica Hamzelou, *Brain Imaging Monitors Effect of Movie Magic*, New Scientist.com

Seeing acts of kindness triggers the production of endogenous opioids and also hormones such as oxytocin, which signal cells to release nitric oxide, causing the dilation of the blood vessels, reducing blood pressure, stress, and the presence of free radicals, leading to a more relaxed mood, calmer breathing, and a less acidic body chemistry. Witnessing harm and meanness does the opposite.

"With a lot of films, people are sitting on the outside looking in, but I want the audience to get a bit more intimately involved with what's going on, so that they maybe can experience it a little bit more intensely."
– Andrea Arnold, *Fish Tank*

The brains and bodies of humans and other animals have been found to contain what are called mirror neurons. These are neurons that respond to the way those around us act and react.

To witness the engagement of mirror neurons, simply observe the anticipatory behavior of people at a sporting event. The spectators physically respond to the motions of the team members.

"The beauty of any artwork is that it becomes the person that's watching it. What do you take out of it?"
– Daniel Kaluuya, *Skins*

The nerves that control voluntary and involuntary movements engage when a person watches someone approach or go away from something that is desirable or undesirable. This is why we squinch our faces as we are repulsed when seeing a character taste something that is highly undesirable. It is also why we physically react when we see a character suddenly experience extreme danger or pain. It all has to do with how viewing a story alters the mind.

"I have this theory that acting is a lot physics, neuroscience. You can have a thought on stage and it can resonate with somebody in the back row. What is that? I think what we do is set up energy fields. You set up literally an

energy field, and you shoot that out into the audience. And they shoot things back. And then, it become this great exchange."
– Glenn Close, actor

"I like to disappear into a role. I equate the success of it with a feeling of being chemically changed. That's the only way I can express it."
– Chiwetel Ejiofor, *The Boy Who Harnessed the Wind*

An actor can become so involved in portraying a character that the actor's brain, intestines, and other tissues are tricked into producing molecules of emotion in tune with what the actor would produce if they were experiencing the staged events in real life.

Similarly, viewers of a film can be so engaged in the conflict and contention taking place on screen that their tissue produce molecules of emotion in tune with experiencing the drama. This process of identifying and engaging with story on a neurochemical level is called *neural coupling*.

"Storytelling at its best is a delivery system for emotion."
– David Rabinowitz, *BlacKkKlansman*

Interestingly, when audiences watch films in 3D, their neural responses can become even more engaged than when they watch a film without 3D glasses.

Film marketing companies that work with the major studios know all about this stuff, and they have worked with companies that use the technology that traces brainwaves and eye movements to gear films and their trailers, commercials, and other marketing images to be in tune with what is shown to illicit desired responses in the brains of viewers. The technology is also used to design political campaigns, and by so-called "news" companies.

"While we, as writers, are thinking about emotions and psychology, much of it apparently boils down to a chemical reaction in the brain.
So, think of engendering empathy. Work on creating tension. But, also be aware that the brain loves good storytelling – because it arouses emotions through the influence of a writer's best friend: Oxytocin."
– Scott Myers, GoIntoTheStory.BlckLst.com

"I want to have a relationship with the audience, which, in a way, invites them to be the last piece of the meaning of the film. Of course, the film is itself. It's a piece of work. It's finished – but they are the last piece. Until the audience is in front of it, the film doesn't have the full meaning."
– Rebecca Daly, *Good Favour*

"Jean-Luc Godard said, 'Cinema is truth twenty-four times per second.' Maybe. It's lying twenty-four times a second, too. All the time.
All story is manipulation.
Is there an acceptable manipulation? You bet. People say, 'Oh, I was so moved to tears in your film.' That's a good thing. I manipulated that. That's

part of storytelling. I didn't do it disingenually, I did it sincerely. I'm moved by that, too. That's manipulation."
– Ken Burns, documentarian

Just as people listen to music to get a feeling, they also go to a film to get a feeling. What they are feeling is their body chemistry changing.

"You know, we've gotten to this place where you go to a movie for one particular surgical fix. So, it's like I want the pulse-pounding action, or the insane falling off my seat comedy, or the devastating, heart-breaking drama.
– J.J. Abrams, *Super 8*

"The most amazing thing for me is that every single person who sees a movie – not necessarily one of my movies – brings a whole set of unique experiences. Now, through careful manipulation and good storytelling, you can get everybody to clap at the same time, to hopefully laugh as the same time, and to be afraid at the same time."
– Steven Spielberg, *High Incident*

Write a script so engaging that it is a sensory intoxicant. When the lights go dim, alter the chemical and hormonal states of the viewers. Manipulate their circuitry. Make it so that their cell membrane receptors become occupied by molecular structures that their tissues produce in tune with experiencing your film.

"The goal is not to dictate the audience's emotions. I look for the emotion in each scene, and let the audience decide what to do with it."
– Michael Starrbury, *When They See Us*

"Audiences want characters who are relatable on a primal human level. This makes the characters believable. As you know, people watch movies to feel emotion vicariously. Whether it is love, revenge, fate, anticipation, or what have you. You can only touch these moviegoers if they are able to relate to how your character feels."
– David Trottier, author *The Screenwriter's Bible*

"The movie business doesn't care about good screenwriting.
Contrary to everything taught in the craft of screenwriting, the movies being made these days favor cerebral concepts over the audience's emotional experience. Especially the 'hits.'
I keep leaving the theater (and my streaming couch) without having gone on any kind of emotional journey. With no feeling of catharsis, at all.
Even the most successful movies make me have to Google stuff just to understand what the movie was supposed to have been about.
As writers, we can deliver an emotional script – based on understanding and executing dramatic excellence – but the industry machine doesn't care, and will hack that emotion up to grind out to the audience something else:

Banal, visceral spectacle, cerebral symbolisms and social messages based upon current (temporary) politically-correct dogma.

But, in the end, no explosive thrills, sadness, fear, laughter, poignancy, or other emotion to purge the viewer's psyche like great stories (well told) have the power to do.

It's probably that the sales powers of the research and marketing departments supersede the story department's knowledge.

Yeah, I said it."

– Bruce B. Gordon, *Whole 'Nother Level*

"Get emotionally connected to your story so you can deliver it. You know, if you can't deliver the emotions to your script, there's no point to your story."

– Robert Redford, director/actor

"Story is a series of emotional impulses designed to separate the audience from their conscious reality. What I'm trying to do is not through scenes, lines, notes, words – it's through impulses. Instantaneous impulses. By impulses – shot-by-shot by frame-by-frame – I'm trying to involve you in my reality, and separate you from yours. I do that through engagement – by keeping you engaged, by keeping you engrossed. If I keep you listening to what is happening in my story, wondering what is happening next in my story, you're not thinking about yours."

– Christopher McQuarrie, Mission: Impossible 7

"A good story is a good story, and you don't need fifty million dollars and a Tom Cruise to tell it."

– Emre Sahin, *Rise of Empires: Ottoman*

"It's important to say that the more challenging a scene is, in a way, the more fun it is – because the more of my job I get to do."

– Daniel Radcliffe, actor

"I like to lead the audience, so when the audience thinks the film is over, that's when they're thrust into a whole new territory that heightens the emotional experience. If you, as a screenwriter, can create certain ground rules, and get the audience into your rhythm, you can get them right out to the end of the dock, then give them a big kick in the ass, and they're going to suddenly find themselves in a new place where they never thought the journey was going to take them."

– James Cameron, *Alita: Battle Angel*

"It is the power of memory that gives rise to the power of imagination."
— Akira Kurosawa, *The Hidden Fortress*

"Writing is perhaps the greatest of human inventions, binding together people who never knew each other, citizens of distant epochs."
— Carl Sagan, *Contact*

"All artists are anarchists, in some way. Some more extreme than others. But, it's something that I think artists are supposed to do. We're supposed to present a different angle on everything, and I certainly think it is art, as much as poetry, in my opinion."
— Robert Zemeckis, *Back to the Future*

THE GENESIS AND EVOLUTION OF SCREENWRITING

"To understand formatting is to understand the language of screenwriting."
— David Trottier, author *Dr. Format Tells All*

Screenwriting is scriptwriting. But, scriptwriting can also be for stage and for radio plays, radio commercials, and other nonscreen recorded productions.

Screenplays include the visual descriptions of what will appear on screen. Screenplays also contain the dialogue that the characters are to say, and sometimes the descriptions of some of the sounds that will be heard by the audience.

"A well-written script creates in the mind's eye of the reader the experience of watching a movie. In other words, the script picturizes the action."
— Michael Ray Brown, *Screenwriting Structure Checklist*

"Don't tell me the moon is shining; show me the glint of light on broken glass."
— Anton Chekhov, playwright

"The movies that influenced me were the movies that told their stories through pictures more than words."
— Sam Mendes, *Skyfall*

The recipe for writing an excellent screenplay is to use sharp, resonant description and clever dialogue to tell a compelling story weaved with enticing backstories played out by interesting characters. Those stories should be revealed not only through what the characters say, but what they don't say. That is: With strong, engaging subtext.

"What is subtext? Subtext is what is under the text. It's what is between the lines, the emotional content of the words, what is really meant. Dialogue is like an iceberg. The text is the visible part. The subtext is below. The text implies the subtext lying below.

Audiences seldom want to see the whole block of ice. Likewise, your characters should seldom say exactly what they feel.

Subtext is everything the dialogue says that is not spoken.

When an actor wants to know her motivation in a scene, she wants to understand the emotions going on within the character. She wants to know the subtext."
– David Trottier, author *The Screenwriter's Bible*

The longer you spend writing screenplays, the more you will understand what they contain in what they don't contain.

"You only learn to be a better writer by actually writing."
– Doris Lessing, *Maupassant*

The formula, structure, format, pacing, tension, conflict, contention, characterizations, subtext, setting, and other components of a screenplay is a literary art meant for being displayed on a screen that people can watch and hear. Preferably clever enough to hold the attention of the viewers.

"If all that's going on in your scenes is what's going on in your scenes, think about it a long time."
– William Goldman, *The Princess Bride*

"Structure is a symptom of a character's relationship with a central dramatic argument."
– Craig Mazin, *Chernobyl*

Screenwriting is a language done in many languages. It uses spare prose to describe setting mixed with stage direction telling actors what they are to do, and combines that with dialogue. Preferably, as mentioned, with strong, engaging subtext.

"It's not a radio play. We are actually dealing in pictures. So, if the pictures are narrative, that's good, right? Some of the best films tend to be more visual than wordy."
– Ridley Scott, *Blade Runner*

"An overturned tricycle in the gutter of an abandoned neighborhood can stand for everything."
– Stephen King, *Misery*

"One day I will find the right words, and they will be simple."
– Jack Kerouac, *On the Road*

While poetry, lyric, short story, and novel writing can include the thoughts of the characters, what screenplay description does not do is describe the thoughts of the characters.

Screenplay scene description contains descriptions of things and actions that can be filmed or recorded.

In a screenplay, character thoughts, including reasoning, motives, desires, anticipations, fears, and otherwise choices are displayed through visuals (how the characters dress, style their surroundings, what they do with things, what they own, and sometimes the non-language vocalizations that the characters make [Such as: Moans, laughs, screams, and giggles]), action, and dialogue.

"When I write a screenplay, I'm writing for myself. I'm the director and I need to create an emotional map. Not just plot, but a map of where these characters are, where they're going, and where they've been. A map from which I can direct the actor, direct the action, direct the production designer, direct the cinematographer. It helps me to have an emotional map and know what's going on in between the lines. I put that in there. There are pieces and nuances, of course, as we know, as filmmakers, that will never make it to the screen – or will never be spelled out visually. Yet, knowing that it's there, and knowing what the thing is about, helps the actor in an unspoken moment that may never make it to the theatre. It helps me. It's a guide."
– Ava Duvernay, *Queen Sugar*

"It's important not to get too flowery. Scripts aren't novels, and you don't have the word count or space to dive into extended metaphors in your prose."
– Evan Littman, GetMade

Including character thoughts in screenplay description is cluttering the script with "unfilmables" or "novelistic writing," which should be omitted from a spec script. If unfilmables are in your script pages brought to a workshop, you might get a note next to them that the description is novelesque.

That all being said, if you work on a series, you may notice the production script containing character thoughts and reasoning, as some shows tend to include those – and it might have to do with connecting details in past episodes to the present episode's actions and events.

You might also notice unfilmables in film scripts. If you are going to include them, do so quite sparingly. Limit them to being about things, like a character's satisfaction or dread that can be displayed, but not about things like a character's reasoning, memories, or plans that won't be visually displayed.

"Memories, thoughts, insights, knowledge, and realizations cannot visually appear on the movie screen, but you can describe actions, facial expressions, gestures, and reactions that suggest them. As a general rule, only describe what the audience can actually see on the screen and hear on the soundtrack.

Screenplay description should direct the mind's eye, not the director's camera."
– David Trottier, author *The Screenwriter's Bible*

If you are a successful filmmaker who is going to film the script that you write, you can write your script anyway you like. But, consider that you will be working with cast, crew, financiers, and producers who are used to standard formatting. The valid ones will notice if you don't write a sharp script.

Filmmaking engages group synergy. A script is the tie that binds the team.

No matter what language or country a screenplay is written in, certain established essentials are used.

"People who can help get your screenplay sold and/or made into a movie read a lot of screenplays. You must make it easy for them. Even minor deviations in format can be fatally distracting."
– Amnon Buchbinder, author *The Way of the Screenwriter*

For spec scripts, stick to what is the standard format in what you present to managers, agents, directors, studio readers, producers, and investors. And, don't muddle the script with overly wordy, novelesque writing.

"So, the writer who breeds more words than he needs, is making a chore for the reader who reads."
– Dr. Seuss

"My most important piece of advice to all you would-be writers: When you write, try to leave out all the parts readers skip."
– Elmore Leonard, *Stick*

"Screenwriting, as a whole, tends to be more objective. In a novel, you can have chapters of stream-of-consciousness writing that add depth to the plot and characters. Film doesn't allow for that by its nature, at least in the long form."
– Stephen McFeely, *The Life and Death of Peter Sellers*

"Screenwriting is always about what people say or do, whereas good writing is about a thought process, or an abstract image, or an internal monologue – none of which works on screen."
– David Nicholls, *Far from the Maddening Crowd*

I know that parts of this book contain what some consider basic, while, to others, it is new. I'm trying to be helpful. Read what helps, skim other parts. Even the familiar stuff might need to be reviewed to help sharpen your skills.

Unlike other literary arts, including poetry, lyrics, novels, and stage plays, screenplays are meant to be interpreted into visual and verbal art projected onto or through a screen.

"An artist is an entertainer, number one. A storyteller who takes people someplace, who gives them what they didn't know they wanted."
– Julie Taymor, *The Tempest*

Both stage and screen plays are meant to engage audiences for a length of time during which the viewers become psychologically invested in the stories in ways in which they likely will temporarily forget their lives, connect with the concerns of the characters, and become engaged in subjective perspective.

Watching actors play out a story is escapism.

"Give your audience no choice but to continue watching."
– Glen Dolman, *Bloom*

"Cinema should make you forget you are sitting in a theatre."
– Roman Polanski, *Rosemary's Baby*

When an audience watches a film, not everyone will interpret it the same way. Some viewers will connect more strongly with certain characters, others with the side stories, or the situation, setting, era, psychology, humor, or drama. Some will like the film more than others. Some will assume different conclusions of what the film was about. Some may think it is the best film they ever saw, while others have the opposite view, and each might say the other took the film out of context, or didn't realize what it was about, or that they are not intellectually capable of recognizing what they should have about the film. Maybe that is part of the magic of what screenwriters do.

"If a million people see my movie, I hope they see a million different movies."
– Quentin Tarantino, *Once Upon a Time... in Hollywood*

"Either a film has something to say to you, or it hasn't. If you are moved by it, you don't need it explained to you. If not, no explanation can make you moved by it."
– Federico Fellini, *La Dolce Vita*

The original screenwriters were called *scenario writers*. They were not writing the types of films we know today that play to global audiences. The original films were silent, simple, and short. Few people saw them. There were no movie theatres.

"The shot (an unbroken continuity of time captured on film) and the cut (an interruption, the termination of one shot and origin of the next) together constitute the initial, most basic, alphabet of cinema. The shot came first: The earliest movies consisted of an unbroken stream of time. The magic of this was sufficient to excite the audience. Soon, however, the cut was introduced, and that was the true beginning of cinematic storytelling."
– Amnon Buchbinder, author *The Way of the Screenwriter*

21

The first play written specifically for filming is considered to be that of the 1902 film by Georges Melies titled *A Trip to the Moon*. The script for the film was called a *photoplay* or *scenario*. Melies' script contained specific information about locations, scene description, and dialogue. Since then, screenwriting has turned into a sort of language with its own set of guidelines.

Edwin Porter was another early screenwriter. An associate of Thomas Edison, in 1903 Porter wrote and directed *The Life of an American Fireman*.

As is mentioned in Marc Norman's book *What Happens Next: A History of American Screenwriting*, by the 1910s, there were a variety screenwriting schools in Los Angeles, including one attended by Frank Capra.

Thomas Harper Ince: The Industrial Studio Revolution

Producer, director, writer, and former Broadway and Vaudeville actor, Thomas Harper Ince is credited with developing screenplay standards.

To avoid the legal reach of Thomas Edison's Motion Picture Patents Company that had been attempting to control the early filmmaking industry, Ince worked making films in Cuba for Carl Laemmle's Independent Motion Pictures Company.

In 1911, Ince landed financing from Charles O. Bauman, co-owner of the New York Motion Picture Company, which had been making films at a small studio lot located in what is now Echo Park in Los Angeles.

Dissatisfied with the limited facilities, Ince sought land to expand his concept of being able to make a variety of films on one property. He moved to a rented property in Pacific Palisades that is now occupied by the New Age spiritual center called the Self-Realization Fellowship.

In 1912, Ince purchased land high up in nearby Santa Ynez Canyon, which is now partially the residential development called Pacific Palisades Highlands. His Inceville studio property – officially named Triangle Ranch – took up thousands of acres. The studio is said to be the first to turn filmmaking into an industrial process with standardized practices on each set, with several films in production on the same day. Those disciplined processes included standardized screenplay formatting.

Ince's property included offices, a large dining hall/commissary, specially designed indoor "sound stages," a prop house, wardrobe facilities, and a variety of sets, including a Western town, a cattle ranch, horse corrals, a Japanese village, a village to resemble one in Switzerland, functioning cottages in a town with a church, facades of mansions, and a village of teepees occupied by Sioux and some other Native Americans who were featured in Ince's (racist) Westerns. The property also had working agricultural farms to grow feed grain for the hundreds of horses and cattle, and to grow fruits and vegetables to feed staff, crew, and actors.

By 1913, and using Ince's filmmaking conventions, the studio was producing dozens of films that were shown in theaters in many countries.

To improve access to skilled writers, Ince helped start the Photoplay Authors League, which eventually became the Screen Writers Guild.

Ince is known as "the father of the Western." But, he also may as well be known as the original movie mogul, as what he did changed the way films were made. Ince was the studio head in charge of directors, writers, production managers, actors, editors, and crew.

Ince made hundreds of films, including at Inceville, then after joining Mack Sennett and D.W. Griffith in Triangle Motion Picture Company in Culver City, which was located on the property that eventually became the MGM lot, and then the Sony Studios lot. He found that filming inland was better than close to the ocean in Pacific Palisades, where the marine layer of clouds or fog could shade most of the day.

After selling out to Sennett and Griffith in 1918, Ince and Adolph Zukor started Paramount-Artcraft Pictures, which became Paramount Pictures.

To regain control, in 1918 Ince purchased 14-acres of land in Culver City and named it the Thomas H. Ince Studios. The lot was expanded onto adjoining land and consisted of various sound stages, bungalows, a carpentry, props and wardrobe facilities, a commissary, medical facility, fire department, and a Western town. An administrative building designed to resemble George Washington's Mount Vernon mansion was built facing West Washington Blvd.

Once again independent, Ince approved the scripts written for and filmed at his studio, and he was the boss of the directors and other talent and crew who worked on the productions.

Ince's associates included William Randolph Hearst, who owned the yacht (The Oneida) where Ince apparently suffered a heart attack at age 42 in 1924. (Or, some say that Ince suffered a gunshot wound, when Hearst mistook him for Charlie Chaplin). The heart attack or bullet wound happened during a trip that included a variety of actors (including Charlie Chaplin and Hearst's mistress, Marion Davies – who may or may not have been having an affair with Chaplin), musicians, writers, producers, and celebrity gossip writer Louella Parsons. The gathering off San Diego – where the yacht had traveled – was meant to celebrate Ince's birthday during the era of alcohol prohibition (due to the workings of the petroleum industry to eliminate alcohol from the market so that petroleum could be established as the fuel for automobiles [Yes, that was the true reasoning behind alcohol prohibition – not health or morality issues.]), and when it was common for the wealthy to gather on yachts to drink without legal concern. During the gathering, Ince was also to form a business arrangement with Hearst so that Hearst's Cosmopolitan Productions would then use Ince's studio facilities. Whatever happened on The Oneida, it resulted in Ince dying days later at his home in Los Angeles.

Ince's wife, Elinor, dismissed the story about him being shot by Hearst. Ince's son, William, who eventually became a doctor, said that Ince's condition was more likely thrombosis (a blood clot).

The Peter Bogdonavich film *The Cat's Meow* is based around the yacht excursion.

Hearst's privileged granddaughter, the convicted armed bank robber and posey kidnapped revolutionary Patricia Hearst co-wrote a novel titled *Murder at San Simeon*, which is based on the Hearst/Ince story.

The original 14-acre Ince lot was sold to Cecil B. Demille, with offices rented by Howard Hughes. After Demille sold it, the lot became Pathe Culver City Studio, and eventually was renamed a variety of times, including Desilu Culver Studios, and then became Culver Studios.

While "The Mansion" façade of Ince's studio was preserved, the building was undermined for a large parking garage and the upper structure was overhauled to include modern offices. Today, many people think the mansion façade was built for *Gone with the Wind*, but that set was far back on the adjacent land, which is now a residential development.

In 2019, Culver Studios started being converted into Amazon Studios consisting of some of the original sound stages, the mansion office building, and a whole other set of structures built for Amazon's purposes. The entrance gates are on Ince Blvd.

Ince's original studio lot in Pacific Palisades was sold off, destroyed by various fires, and productions ceased there in the early 1920s.

Ince's original home on Franklin Blvd. at Bronson Avenue in Hollywood was demolished and Elinor had built the Château Élysée luxury residential apartment building styled to resemble a French-Normandy castle. In 1969, the hotel was taken over by the Church of Scientology, and is registered as a Historical National Monument.

Within several years of the dawn of filmmaking, theatres were being built specifically for people to gather as an audience to watch a film that told a story. That quickly grew into a popular form of entertainment. Within the first two decades of the twentieth century, tens of thousands of movie theaters were built in cities and towns across the planet. Most were owned by the studios, until the 1948 Supreme Court ruling against vertical integration (which, as I write this in 2020, is a law under reconsideration), which then required the studios to sell the theaters.

By the time that it became popular to use recorded sound in film, a standard way of formatting screenplays was necessary so that multiple people working collaboratively on a set could follow along with what was being filmed.

"Screenwriting is a collaboration in the end, no matter what. It has to be."
– David Magee, *Finding Neverland*

"The key is to work with people who are passionate about storytelling, and who have a similar sensibility of the type of nature of the stories that you want to tell."
– Patrick Lussier, *Trick*

It was popular in the early film industry for photoplay writers to be women.

One of the first books about screenwriting was written by playwright, author, screenwriter, and former child stage actress Anita Loos. Her husband, director and producer John Emerson, was credited as a co-author – but even Loos said that the book was largely her own work. The book, *How to Write Photoplays*, was published in 1921. It used the term photoplaywright to describe what we now call a screenwriter.

In May, 1914 Loos, along with Thomas Ince, Mary Hamilton O'Connor, Frank E. Woods, D.W. Griffith, and several others started the Photoplay Authors League. In the 1920s, it was renamed the Screen Writers Guild.

Loos wrote more than 200 screenplays, with over 100 being produced. She was perhaps the first ever screenwriter to be put on staff of a studio. That was when D.W. Griffith hired her to work for Triangle Film Corporation.

The early studios employed screenwriters under contract. The writers typically worked writing scripts on teams, rewrote what each other wrote, or specialized in polishing scripts in various genres.

Former Broadway actor and playwright Preston Sturges is credited with writing the first spec screenplay that sold to a studio, Fox Film Corporation. The film *The Power and the Glory,* starring Spencer Tracy, premiered in 1933.

Sturges was the first to arrange to get a percentage of the profits of a film he wrote. He had been a contract writer with the studios, but wrote other screenplays on spec, and famously sold *The Great McGinty* to Paramount Studios for $10, with the agreement that he would direct it. That film is landmark because it is the first for which a writer won an Academy Award for an original screenplay. When Sturges joined in a business arrangement with Howard Hughes, who agreed to finance his productions, Sturges became one of the earliest writer/director/producers.

Other writers, including John Huston and Billy Wilder, eventually sold spec scripts to the studios outside of being contract writers. Michael Kanin and Ring Lardner sold their spec script *Woman of the Year* to MGM. That film also starred Spencer Tracy, and co-starred Katherine Hepburn, who presented the script to the studio as a starring vehicle for her.

While many women were the original screenwriters, over the years, somehow, men became dominant in the field of screenwriting – and they won most of the screenwriter awards. Clearly, just as non-Caucasian screenwriters have not been formally recognized for their skills, were denied opportunities, and essentially were pushed away from screenwriting as a career choice, women have a history of the same.

Gender, age, color, culture, and nation of origin are not things that determine a person's ability to learn how to write excellent screenplays. The international film industry is evidence of that.

By learning the craft of screenwriting, and writing a variety of screenplays, you are as likely to write something as valid and producible as scripts written by people who are unlike you.

"Every story I write is different. Some are hard. Some aren't. *Chronical* was tremendously easy. I have a hard time comparing my process on different things, but I will say this: The more you write, the better you get at it. That's one of the few things that's markedly true."
— Max Landis, *An American Werewolf in London*

If you want a career in screenwriting, learn and follow the standard screenplay formatting guidelines, and understand when it is useful, clever, and not problematic to break the rules.

"A screenplay is really a blueprint. The words on the page are standing in for a moment that will be recorded later."
— Rebecca Miller, *Maggie's Plan*

"A script is equal parts creativity and logistical document. It serves as a blueprint for the movie. As such, there are structural guidelines screenwriters must abide by. Producers don't simply say that they want it formatted a particular way because they're picky, they do it because it's important for setting up the logistics of the film.

Anyone who went to film school should know this, but I'm amazed by how many people do not. Even simple things like changing the location if someone walks out into a hallway often gets missed."
— Ben Yennie, ProductionNext.com

"The spec script is not a blueprint for the eventual movie, but a guide to it."
— David Trottier, author *The Screenwriter's Bible*

"Screenwriting is a very strange hybrid kind of writing. It's not like prose writing — in fact, it's better if your prose isn't very good, or deep. You've got a whole crew who are going to be looking at it for suggestions for an architecture that they are there to carry out. So, you're very restricted. You don't bother to describe what your characters look like, for example, other than to say, you know, he's handsome and he's tall. An actor is going to be cast who might not look like that, so there's no point. Likewise, with locations and costumes. So, it's a very pared down, simple form, really, the screenplay. The only thing that goes directly on the screen is the dialogue and the narrative structure. You can be a terrible writer, but if you write good dialogue, and have a good sense of narrative structure, you can be a good screenwriter, and still be functionally illiterate, which a lot of good screenwriters in my experience are. Very different."
— David Cronenberg, *Naked Lunch*

"I always say when you write a book, you're a 'one-man band.' Whereas, when you finish a screenplay, it's just a sketch."
— Diablo Cody, *Raised by Wolves*

With so many people involved in making one project, the cast and crew of a film all need to be able to look at the script, recognize its elements, and know what their job is on the production.

As mentioned, by the time sound was used in films – and filmmaking was becoming more distinguished as the behind-the-camera talent sharpened their skills in the craft, and technology improved – it was important for screenplays to be written in a way that was standard across the industry.

As the need for screenplays to be written in a standard format grew, and film technology developed, so did a market to supply films to theatres packed with audiences increasingly reliant on film as a form of entertainment.

As the Great Depression set in, the elaborate "movie palace" theatres became an escape from the stressful reality of everyday life, and audiences came to expect certain qualities in films. The so-called glamour of Hollywood and the adjacent celebrity gossip industry fed by the studio publicity machines was also an escape.

Within a region featuring varieties of terrain in fairly dependable year-round tame weather, Los Angeles became the world center of filmmaking. Many of the films were produced inside the walls of the factories we call "movie studios," while other filming was done using locations in the nearby hills, canyons, mountains, beaches, lakes, deserts, cities, towns, neighborhoods, parks, and farms.

When already existing locations couldn't be found, or didn't exist, Hollywood craftspeople became skilled at creating locations, including by building lakes, structures, vehicles, and backgrounds, and recreating settings from different eras, or building sets to resemble distant lands – or versions of imagined settings on other planets, or of the future.

From the start of the filmmaking industry, and as it spread into other countries and cultures, it all depended on screenwriters.

With the introduction of television, the profession of screenwriting expanded globally to feed the growing popularity of television productions made in various large cities in many countries. With that, a different type of screenplay formed, that of the multi-cam sitcom filmed in front of a studio audience.

Lucille Ball and her 1951 *I Love Lucy* series became the first TV show to be done in the style that we now call situation comedy, or sitcom. It was the first to film in front of a studio audience, the first show to use a variety of adjacent settings, the first to use a system of largely static cameras set during rehearsal, and the first sitcom to be internationally popular. As that series and her eventual other sitcoms, *The Lucy Show*, *Here's Lucy*, and *Life with Lucy* went into what became known as syndication, she was the first person who was on TV somewhere on the planet 24 hours every day.

When Ball divorced Desi Arnaz, she bought him out of their Desilu Productions, and that made her the first woman of the modern era to head her own studio, which produced a variety of shows, including *Star Trek*.

The first women to head their own studios were French-American filmmaker Alice Guy-Blaché, in New York 1910, American filmmaker Lois Weber in California in 1917, and writer, producer, actor, model, and director Mabel Normand, who headed the Mabel Normand Feature Film Company, which operated out of other studios from the teens into the early 1920s.

In 1896, Guy-Blaché was working as a secretary at a camera supply company in France when she made the first ever narrative film.

Weber was discovered by Guy-Blaché and her husband Herbert, who employed Weber as a script writer, director, and actress at their Solax studios. Lois went on to write, direct, and act in other films at other East Coast studios, before moving West to run Rex Studios with her husband.

Normand began acting in films in New York in 1909, then moved to California by 1912, where she partnered with Mack Sennett in Keystone Studios. She had guided Charles Chaplin into his film career, sticking up for him when he was being dismissed by Sennett. Normand starred with Chaplin in 12 films, including some she wrote or co-wrote and/or directed. Marisa Tomei portrayed Normand in the 1992 film *Chaplin*. After leading a life rich in scandal, cocaine addiction, affairs, and on the fringes of two homicides committed by others, she died of complications of tuberculosis at age 37 in 1930. The character name Norma Desmond in *Sunset Blvd.* is a play on the name Mabel Normand.

By 1960, the combination of TV and film productions provided solid work for many people skilled in the craft of screenwriting. The vast majority of the work was based in Los Angeles.

"I could be just a writer very easily. I am not a writer. I am a screenwriter, which is half a filmmaker. But it's not an art form, because screenplays are not works of art. They are invitations to others to collaborate on a work of art."
– Paul Schrader, *Taxi Driver*

In the modern age, screenplays are used on TV, cable, streaming, and web series (serials, anthologies, limited series, procedurals, and episodics), sitcoms, films and short films, commercials, video games, and short form video made for cell phone screens. Production using standard format screenplays spread globally, with studios located in many different countries.

The modern spec-script market is considered to have begun in 1967, when William Goldman sold his spec screenplay of *Butch Cassidy and the Sundance Kid* to 20th Century Fox, which released the film in 1969. It took years for the spec script market to take off, as the studio contracted writers made their way into TV, or into the indie film market.

The 80s spec script market is most famous for spec scripts selling for hundreds of thousands. Then, in 1990, there was Joe Eszterhas' script *Basic Instinct*, which sold for $3 million, and Shane Black selling *The Last Boy Scout* for $1.75 million. Since then, the spec script market has fluctuated with some years being better than others for optioning or selling scripts. The wild prices sometimes paid for scripts has drawn an ongoing stream of people into the dream of becoming the next hot screenwriter – with relatively few experiencing that big pay reality.

The possibilities of making it big in screenwriting has also created a market for classes, seminars, retreats, weekend intensives, and schools teaching screenwriting. Some schools in Los Angeles have dozens of instructors teaching screenwriting, and the classes are filled with people who pay hundreds to thousands to take the courses. It's turned into a money grab, and many aspiring writers have been – and continue to be – taken advantage of.

One reason I started Screenwriting Tribe is because I saw so many people being taken advantage of, being given bad advice, and spending months – or years – stagnant, and not learning ways of writing producible scripts. I felt that I knew a way that was far less expensive, could charge about what it takes to keep the group running, and provide ways for screenwriters to help each other sharpen their skills in the craft, and – hopefully – advance in the field. I also had worked as a reader for producers and worked at a studio, and I saw how the unpolished scripts are quickly dismissed.

There are less expensive ways to learn the screenwriting craft than by paying thousands of dollars to a school, or for overpriced seminars, retreats, and coaches. While film schools have their advantages, including for networking and building camaraderie with others who soon might be succeeding in the industry, schools aren't the route that many of the most successful screenwriters took.

I had also read a wide variety of screenwriting books, and thought that I could write one that was more helpful, and more along the lines of a book that I wish I had when I was young. So, here is this book.

To succeed in the craft, you must learn standard formatting, and write valid, sharp, commercially viable scripts that appeal to talent, and that will pass up the ladder to those who have the ability to get projects funded, produced, and distributed – or who can hire writers. Or, you must produce your own scripts with the qualities that distributors and audiences seek. Even then, the scripts need to be correctly formatted.

Anyone who knows standard screenplay formatting can glance at a scene heading and know if that scene is interior, exterior, night, or day, dusk, dawn, sunrise, or sunset, and the setting.

By reading the scene description, they know what the visual should contain, including staging, decoration, props, FX, and actors.

"I think, in a weird way, the reason I was drawn to screenwriting and the reason I really love doing it is because I love writing dialogue."
– David Benioff, *Troy*

The dialogue in a screenplay conveys what is needed to be heard by audiences to progress the character concerns, reasoning, motives, conflict, and contention along the storyline.

As screenplay formatting has standardized, a person can go from studio to studio across the globe and see the same screenplay formatting, with only slight differences.

Even when a TV series will have been in production for years, and the staff writers and producers have developed their own ways of writing scripts for that production, the scripts remain within the same basic standard format. The differences are usually in the scene description, sometimes with reminders of what happened in previous episodes, or reasons of why things are being said and done in a particular scene, and sometimes with more actor direction and character detail than what is normal for a spec script. That could mean that the direction is more novelistic than what is seen in other scripts – certainly more than what is seen in spec scripts.

"The script, I always believe, is the foundation of everything."
– Ewan McGregor, actor/director

Without screenplays, there would be no feature films, or theatrical shows on TV, cable, or on the Web.

Without screenwriters, the film and TV industry wouldn't exist. Because of that, the industry needs an ongoing variety of screenwriters to supply scripts that will be turned into content.

"Work like hell! I had 122 rejection slips before I sold a story."
– F. Scott Fitzgerald, *Three Comrades*

"My big problem was finishing. I must've written twenty-five first acts. Abandon, and move on, abandon, and move on. This went on about three years. Funny thing, once I was able to finish a script, I was able to make a living at it right away."
– Walter Hill, *48 Hours*

Get busy. Study the craft of screenwriting. Finish, polish, workshop, and get coverage on your most marketable screenplays – before submitting the scripts to the industry.

Learn the industry. Read the trades (*Variety*, *The Hollywood Reporter*, and other print and online publications centered on the film and TV industry, such as *Sight & Sound* magazine published by the British Film Institute).

Be prepared for meetings with people who want to talk about your scripts, who are considering buying them, or who like your writing enough to pay you to write their scripts – or to pay you to polish or rewrite scripts that have been purchased.

Write a variety of screenplays so that you have a portfolio of at least several ready to show to managers, agents, and producers.

"If you already have three drama samples, why not write a 30-page comedy? I don't think it would hurt – and now you have that sample, as well."
– Matt Tinker, *Big Little Lies*

Perhaps you also want to star in a film that you wrote. Maybe you want to make your mark as a multi-talented person in Hollywood, which Billy Bob Thornton did with *Sling Blade*, which then won multiple awards – projecting Thornton into a solid film career.

Many well-known actors wrote projects that they also starred in, they include Tina Fey, Spike Lee, Ben Stiller, Ben Affleck, Sylvester Stallone, Tyler Perry, Emma Thompson, Julie Delpy, George Clooney, Miranda July, Albert Brooks, Tim Robbins, Steve Martin, Edward Norton, Justin Theroux, Christopher Guest, Ricky Gervais, Adam Sandler, and Rashida Jones.

If you are already a name actor, your name can help attract financing to make your project. As I'm writing this, I learned that actor Vivian Bang has done it with her film *White Rabbit*.

"Actors feel like we're always waiting for someone to give us the job. And that's not true. The idea that we have to wait and wait is a delusion. We have the power to create. And if someone sees it, you're a storyteller."
– Vivian Bang, *White Rabbit*

"For me, the problem is not the rejection, but the random factors of the industry. You can have a picture that's ready to go, and the star pulls out. Suddenly, there's no movie. They weren't going to make the movie because they loved the script, but because the star committed to it. You could have a movie ready to go, and the management changes. The bad news is that they want to reinvent the movie. One factor changes and the whole thing spins off in another direction. So, half the time it is a horrible experience because the movie gets cancelled, and the other half it's a horrible experience because the movie gets made anyway, completely reinvented."
– Steven de Souza, *The Running Man*

"You have to understand how the business works. Sometimes, I'm so mystified I can't believe this is a business. You have to understand the tide comes in, and the tide goes out. There's a constant shift of personalities. Some studios are more stable than others, and you have to note which ones are which.

The problem with reading the trades is that a lot of information is planted by publicists, so it seems everyone but you is making a big deal somewhere, or they're associated with some wonderful project that's just been announced. You can't help but get into a state of envy. It's good to pick up the trades every now and then, but not every day."
– Robin Swicord, *Memories of a Geisha*

"At the very least, you should have a working understanding of how the movie business works. Acquisition. Development. Production. Post.

Marketing. Distribution. Where you plug in. What journey your script has lying ahead of it."
  – Scott Myers, GoIntoTheStory.BlckLst.com

Screenwriting:
- The process or activity of writing screenplays.
- A writing technique known for the practice of refinement within a format free of distractive elements.
- A method of communication.
- Engaging in the creation of a written document used to tell a story rich in conflict and subtext as a blueprint for staged scenes to be filmed at a variety of angles and handed over to an editor for final assemblage.
- A way of spilling one's hopes, wants, fears, humor, charm, delight, love, lust, heartache, sorrow, pain, regret, embarrassment, confessions, paranoia, conspiracy, darkness, history, guts, and brains onto paper using an elegant and a minimalist economy of words.

For a more comprehensive history of the origins of the screenwriting craft, please read these books:
- *The Writers: A History of American Screenwriters and Their Guild*, by Miranda J. Banks.
- *What Happens Next: A History of American Screenwriting*, by Marc Norman.

"If you want to be a writer, write every day. You have the choice on what to write. So, choose wisely. Try to find an idea that has some scope to it, some core notion that's different and that will stand out. Don't start big. Start with a fantastic character, and then lead the character into the concept."
  – John Glenn, *The Lazarus Project*

"Those who dream by day are cognizant of many things which escape those who dream only by night."
– Edgar Allan Poe, *The Masque of the Red Death*

"A writer is a world trapped in a person."
– Victor Hugo, *Les Misérables*

"You write who you are, somehow. Even if you try not to, you can't help but write who you are."
– Simon Beaufoy, *The Full Monty*

"We suffer more in imagination than in reality."
– Seneca, Roman dramatist

SCREENWRITER INTELLECT

"Those people who know that they really want to do this and are cut out for it, they know it."
– R.L. Stine, *Goosebumps*

"I don't need an alarm clock. My ideas wake me."
– Ray Bradbury, *The Twilight Zone*

"Inspiration can hit you in the head at any time in any context. It could happen in a conversation. Talking to someone at a party, you can get an idea. But you've got to remember those inspirations."
– James Cameron, *Avatar*

"Writers are completely out-of-touch with reality. Writers are crazy. We create conflict for a living. We do this all the time, sometimes on a weekly basis. We create horrible, incredible circumstances, and then figure a way out of them. That's what we do."
– Joss Whedon, *Toy Story*

"What is in my heart must come out, so I write it down."
– Ludwig Van Beethoven, musician

It isn't unusual to hear screenwriters say that they wake up in the middle of the night to write down stories, to work on changes to their stories, or to write ideas from dreams.

"Movies share so much with dreams – which, of course, only deal with interior lives. Your brain is wired to turn emotional states into movies. Your dreams are very well written. I know this without knowing any of you.

People turn anxieties, crisis, longing, love, regret, and guilt into beautiful, rich stories in their dreams.

What is it that allows us the creative freedom in our dreams that we don't have in our waking lives? I don't know. But, I suspect part of it is that in our dreams we're not constrained by worry about how we will appear to others. It's a private conversation with ourselves. And, if we're worried about it, this becomes part of the dream."

– Charlie Kaufman, *Human Nature*

Rod Serling kept a tape recorder next to his bed so that he could record his ideas and dreams and nightmares whenever he awoke.

"I always kept two books in my pocket, one to read, one to write in."
– Robert Louis Stevenson, *Treasure Island*

"I tend to jot down moments, lines, interactions that don't really make any sense. I try and explain these scattered notes to my close friends, and they become more and more logical. I see screenwriting as a bit like a math equation which I have to solve."
– Asghar Farhadi, *About Elly*

"I always try to keep a small pad of paper in my pocket, and write down any idea that seems interesting. I also type notes into my phone and computer. I basically have ideas written down everywhere. I've spent my life reminding myself that, even though I always tell myself I'll never forget an idea when I think of it, I always forget it – sometimes a minute or two after I've thought of it. So, I always force myself to write down any idea."
– Paul Feig, *Spy*

"Writing is what I do. It is like breathing to me at a certain point."
– Nora Ephron, *When Harry Met Sally*

"Write while the heat is in you. The writer who postpones the recording of his thoughts uses an iron which has cooled to burn a hole with."
– Henry David Thoreau, *Civil Disobedience*

Screenwriters often have to stop throughout the day to jot down thoughts, scrambling for things to write on so that they don't forget an idea to add to or turn into a screenplay.

"I was in a bookstore one day, and I don't know what happened. It was just like, 'Pow!' I sat down and I tore blank pages out of a couple books, and I just started writing. I wrote the whole story of *The Bucket List*. Ultimately the story is these two guys each have their own list of things they want to do with the short time they have left, but the one thing that's not on either of their lists that's missing is a true friend. They find that. And that's what the movie is

all about. I wrote it very quickly, just in a few weeks. I gave it to my agents and they said, 'This is great, but nobody's gonna buy this.'"
– Justin Zackham, *The Bucket List*

I joke that screenwriting is a particular type of mental condition, and most screenwriters live in institutions with no caretakers.

"It's an accepted fact that all writers are crazy. Even the normal ones are weird."
– William Goldman, *Butch Cassidy and the Sundance Kid*

"I think it's fairly common for writers to be afflicted with two simultaneous – yet contradictory – delusions: The burning certainty that we're unique geniuses, and the constant fear that we're witless frauds who are speeding toward epic failure."
– Scott Lynch, *The Lies of Locke Lamora*

"Screenwriting is not an art form, it is a punishment from God."
– Fran Lebowitz, author *Metropolitan Life*

"I write entirely to find out what I'm thinking, what I'm looking at, what I see, and what it means. What I want, and what I fear."
– Joan Didion, *A Star is Born*

"Screenwriting and making movies is really playing make-believe, like most of us did as children."
– Gabriel Campisi, *The Law*

"I used to be a night writer. I'd start about eleven, and write to five, six in the morning. And that was kind of a cascade of alcohol, nicotine, caffeine, and cocaine. And you can get a lot of writing done. There were certain spelling errors, but for the most part, it was quite good.
Those little people who live inside the typewriter, they need some inducement to come out. They just don't come out on their own. So, you have to give them – say, 'Come on out. Come on out.' And then, they come out, and they climb out of the typewriter and start running around the desk."
– Paul Schrader, *Bringing out the Dead*

"Sometimes stories cry out to be told in such loud voices that you write them just to shut them up."
– Stephen King, *The Dead Zone*

"The masterful writer knows that writing is a process of revelation, of discovery, that grows out of collaboration with the invisible."
– Amnon Buchbinder, author *The Way of the Screenwriter*

"Write in the dark. Free associate with your clothes off. Be free, no one is watching. It's you. Don't be embarrassed. After half an hour, stop and put the light on, and read this goop you just wrote. The meaningless phrases, the

unattached words, all without thinking what's there. But, there will be something there, gold nuggets in the shaken sandy soil. Something will show up. I do that to get started. Unclear always leads to something that clarity misses because it's stable, ordered, assembled. I am one of the unassembled believers, like how snowflakes arrive unassembled before they can become snowmen."
  – Alvin Sargent, *Ordinary People*

"An idea, like a ghost, must be spoken to a little before it will explain itself."
  – Charles Dickens, *Great Expectations*

"The imagination is a place all by itself. A separate country. Now, you've heard of the French nation, the British nation. Well, this is the imagination. It's a wonderful place."
  – George Seaton, *Miracle on 34th Street*

"Limitations live only in our minds. But, if we use our imaginations, our possibilities become limitless."
  – Jamie Paolinetti, *Trickster*

"My problem is that my imagination won't turn off."
  – Steven Spielberg, *Poltergeist*

Writers speak of having voices and characters in their head playing out scenarios like a theater in their mind. It's as if their minds contain societies and subcultures populated by characters that nobody else sees, hears, or knows of. In their imagination, the writers can walk around unseen within those cultures, and not only observe them, but control everything about, around, and that happens to them.

"It's been said that writers invent people and environments to control, due to having no control in real life. Well, **** yes. All you non-writers find your own way to deal with no control – we've got ours."
  – Jim Uhls, *Fight Club*

A writer's mind can be afflicted with the conflict and contention in the drama and comedy of the imaginary life unknown to people around them.

"The writer is both a sadist and a masochist. We create people we love, and then we torture them."
  – Janet Fitch, *White Oleander*

"I never have searched for a subject. They always just come along. They never come by way of decision-making. They just haunt me. I can't get rid of them. I did not invite them."
  – Werner Herzog, *Rescue Dawn*

"Every human being has hundreds of separate people living under his skin. The talent of a writer is his ability to give them their separate names, identities, personalities, and have them relate to other characters living with him."
– Mel Brooks, *Silent Movie*

"For me, screenwriting is all about setting characters in motion and as a writer just chasing them. They should tell you what they'll do in any scene you put them in."
– Justin Zackham, *The Bucket List*

"The writer is an explorer. Every step is an advance into a new land."
– Ralph Waldo Emerson, essayist

The writer's condition is exemplified in the film *The Whole Wide World*. The film is about the fascinating and tragically short life of writer Robert E. Howard.

The son of a financially troubled traveling doctor, Howard was born in Texas in 1906, and began writing as a child. His obsession with writing was nurtured by his mother, and ruled his life.

By age nine, Howard was writing a variety of stories based in ancient cultures.

When he was thirteen, he read about the late Iron Age and early Middle Age Pict tribe that lived in ancient Scotland.

By the time he was fifteen, Howard was submitting his stories to pulp fiction magazines.

Howard wrote poetry, worked as a small-town newspaper columnist covering the oil industry, worked at a post office, and as a soda jerk, and at other odd jobs for low pay. All the while, he struggled to make his writing career into something that could support him.

Howard wrote of cavepeople, barbarians, werewolves, ghosts, swashbucklers, assassins, boxers, monsters, magic, and the adventures of mythical heroes in ancient cultures. He wrote of wars among the Picts and the invading Romans.

Howard centered some stories in societies of his own invention, including that of the character Kull, king of Valusia, which existed in the Thurian Age, first told in Howard's pulp fiction piece *The Shadow Kingdom*.

Howard is credited with originating the Sword and Sorcery genre that has entertained generations.

Howard became a member of a group of corresponding writers introduced to each other through H.P. Lovecraft. The group was known as the Lovecraft Circle. Many of the writers in the circle wrote for the pulp fiction magazine *Weird Tales*.

Howard did not experience the fame of his writing.

At the age of 30, when he heard that his mother was dying, Howard shot himself in the head.

Howard wrote the tale of *Conan the Barbarian*, which was turned into the international hit film.

"For me, screenwriting is all about setting characters in motion, and as a writer just chasing them. They should tell you what they'll do in any scene you put them in."
– Justin Zackham, *One Chance*

If writers don't write, the stories in our minds don't stop. So, we write. Often alone. Sometimes as our children play sports or do homework. Other times in places that provide the quiet we need. Sometimes we write in public places because we are tired of being alone, or we don't want to be around the people or neighbors at home. For some of us, the cacophony of voices and the visual stimulation of being out amongst the commotion of a library, a park, or a coffee café inspires us.

"The dull externals of the screenwriter's working life are well known: We are the people taking up too much table space at cafes."
– Whit Stillman, *The Last Days of Disco*

"I have a group of cafes and coffee shops that I go to regularly. They usually have an area where I can plug in my computer and have a corner seat where I can do a couple hours of writing or whatever. Even the noise of the surrounding people walking by, those things are the things that stimulate my writing."
– Bong Joon-Ho, *Snowpiercer*

"My process every day is to go out every day to a coffee shop. I walk and I think, and I write in the coffee shop. Sometimes in my notebook. Sometimes I bring a computer. And then I go home. I like being in an environment. It's a little claustrophobic being in the office by myself."
– Charlie Kaufman, *The Dana Carvey Show*

"You just have to sit down and put the work in. Too many people talk about writing. You always see around L.A. people sitting in Starbucks with Final Draft, pecking away. Writing is just lonely, brutal, dirty work, and there's no way around it. You have to sit in the chair and stare at the blank page."
– David Ayer, *Training Day*

"Failing a hideaway such as I possess, I can recommend hotel bedrooms as far removed from your usual life as possible. Your anonymity in these drab surroundings and your lack of friends and distractions in the strange locale will create a vacuum which should force you into a writing mood and, if your pocket is shallow, into a mood which will also make you write fast and with application."
– Ian Fleming, *Thunderball*

"I have a home office, and an office I go to. I also write in hotel rooms. I'll never equal the amount of time with other people that I've spent alone over thirty-plus years."
– Tony Gilroy, *Michael Clayton*

"I always wanted to be in the world of entertainment. I just love the idea of an audience being happy with what I am doing. Writing is show business for shy people. That's how I see it."
– Lee Child, author of books featuring *Jack Reacher*

Screenwriters are from diverse economic backgrounds, and are of a variety of intellectual capacities. Many screenwriters struggled through life in a variety of ways, dabbling in numerous occupations, before realizing what they truly enjoy, feel connected to, and excel in.

"The option was to continue working at the convenience store for the rest of my life, until I got fired. And if not that convenience store, some other convenience store. And I was just no good at labor. I was just a very lazy, lazy person, and still am to a large degree. But when it came to this, I never felt lazy because it didn't feel like work. It's my passion; it's what I want to do. So, I guess it was a gamble and when I told my parents, I think they figured, this'll get it out of his system. Now he'll settle down and get a good job like his bothers."
– Kevin Smith, *Clerks*

"You want to be a writer? A writer is someone who writes every day, so start writing. You don't have a job? Get one. Any job. Don't sit at home waiting for the magical opportunity. Who are you? Prince William? No. Get a job. Go to work. Do something until you can do something else."
– Shonda Rhimes, *Scandal*

"Stop finding the ways that you can't do something and find all the ways that you can, and just go for it."
– Issa Rae, *The Choir*

Some of us screenwriters grew up wealthy, others were poor. Some were raised in so-called ideal situations, others were abandoned or abused and neglected as children, or lost families to accidents, addictions, illness, crime, or war. Some of us were recognized as brilliant, multi-talented children, and were given scholarships to universities. Others of us were considered failures – or thought of as recalcitrant children, unable or unwilling to conform. Some of us didn't graduate high school, and some didn't attend traditional school. Some of us, including me, have been homeless.

"The person born with a talent they are meant to use will find their greatest happiness in using it."
– Johann Wolfgang von Goethe, *Faust*

Quentin Tarantino speaks of being held back to go through sixth grade two times, then dropping out of high school. He is in the company of other successful screenwriters who didn't finish high school, including Walt Disney, Elaine May, Damon Wayans, Mary Pickford, Seth Rogan, William Faulkner, John Landis, and Chris Rock.

"Art is a joy, and a responsibility. Being able to tell stories saved my life."
– Tim Robbins, *Dead Man Walking*

Many of us worked in other professions. Some have lived in poverty, or as unhoused addicts. Some have served time in the military, or in prison, or have been institutionalized. Our writing helps release us from our past, and gives us something to escape into and to express ourselves, and a reason to live.

No matter what your background, create a pathway to your comfort zone.

"When I moved to New York at the age of 22, my plan of action was to write anything that anyone would pay me to write. I wrote jacket-flap copy for Doubleday, I got a job with *The Encyclopedia Britannica*, I wrote everything. But I always wanted to write for movies and television. After four, five years in New York, I moved to L.A. and started developing story ideas on a Nickelodeon show called *Hey Dude*. After that show finished, I had some extra time and wrote *Speed*."
– Graham Yost, *Mission to Mars*

There is not one type of person who becomes a screenwriter. While screenwriters are often considered to be of some sort of liberal tilt, there are all varieties of political leanings among screenwriters.

Some writers are into fitness and health, do yoga, bike, swim, hike, do weights, run marathons, climb rocks, scuba dive, surf, and play contact sports. Some are or were pro athletes. Others get their exercise by walking from bed to their desk, and to the kitchen and bathroom, and back.

"I'm very disciplined about my writing. I get up early. At 6 a.m., I go to the gym. I come back and have a light breakfast and coffee, and I'm at my desk by 7:30. I work until mid-day without interruption. I then have a light lunch, and then a nap. The afternoon is either business, or if I'm really under deadline, I'm back at it again.

I got to a point where the five days turned into six days turned into seven days. I thought, 'This isn't very healthy.' So, now I don't do that anymore. I'm back at five days a week."
– Robert Schenkkan, *Hacksaw Ridge*

"I'm very physical. When I'm writing, I'm playing all the parts; I'm saying the lines out loud, and if I get excited about something – which doesn't happen very often when I'm writing, but it's the greatest feeling when it does

— I'll be out of the chair and walking around, and if I'm at home, I'll find myself two blocks from my house."
  — Aaron Sorkin, *The Social Network*

"Just write every day of your life. Read intensely. Then see what happens. Most of my friends who are put on that diet have very pleasant careers."
  — Ray Bradbury, *The Picasso Summer*

"When I go into writing mode, I schedule my whole life around protecting those hours. Discipline is critical. I go to bed at a certain time. I eat a certain amount. I do everything I can to keep my brain on and focused."
  — Peter Berg, *Friday Night Lights*

Probably the one thing that successful screenwriters have in common is that they have curious minds, they are likely to research and question things, and to seek answers.

"I think the deeper you go into questions, the deeper or more interesting the questions get. And I think that's the job of art."
  — Andre Dubus III, *House of Sand and Fog*

"If you need to do research because parts of your story deal with things about you know little or nothing, remember the word back. That's where research belongs: As far in the background and the backstory as you can get it. You may be entranced with what you're learning about the flesh-eating bacteria, the sewer system of New York, or the I.Q. potential of collie pups, but your readers are probably going to care a lot more about your characters and your story."
  — Stephen King, *Apt Pupil*

It is probably common for successful screenwriters to have done more reading than the average person.

"By the time I was being treated like an overnight success, I had been making films eight or ten years. There had been a closet full of short films. I'd done a feature on Super 8 the year before. So, by the time anyone saw *Slacker*, which was the first film (of mine) that got national distribution, and people were paying to see, I felt I had already put in my decade. I had put in exactly a decade of watching 600 movies a year, reading about cinema. I had dedicated ten solid years. Every waking second. So, I felt ready to go to whatever new level."
  — Richard Linklater, *Waking Life*

Perhaps screenwriters are more likely to be okay with being alone for long periods of time.

"When I'm working alone, the old, hard way. Longhand. Fountain pen. Legal pad. Thesaurus by my side. This last item, I'm not ashamed to say, is quite helpful. When you write screenplays, you don't have a lot of room, and

the stage directions can become onerously repetitive – if you don't work at fresh descriptions. Try to show a reader a new way to see it. Unless, of course, you are using repetition as a rhythm device in creating mood – which, I guess, is a perfect illustration of one of the things I like best about screenwriting: Whatever is true, the opposite can also be true."
– Walter Hill, *The Warriors*

"Keep a small can of WD-40 on your desk – away from any open flames – to remind yourself that if you don't write daily, you will get rusty."
– George Singleton, *Perfect Attendance*

"I'm very lucky. I actually like screenwriting. I rarely feel a sense of doom going to my desk."
– Simon Beaufoy, *Everest*

"The mind of a writer can be a truly terrifying thing. Isolated, neurotic, caffeine-addled, crippled by procrastination, consumed by feelings of panic, self-loathing, and soul-crushing inadequacy. And that's on a good day."
– Robert De Niro, actor

"I've discovered that sometimes writing badly can eventually lead to something better. Not writing at all leads to nothing."
– Anna Quindlen, *Blessings*

"I get up very early. I get up at four, because I found sort of the hush of silence and darkness very conducive to my writing – because the phone's not ringing, there's no distractions. It's just me and the whimsical characters moving about. So, I start very early. I write until I'm tired, and then I stop. If I'm writing the first draft, it's total immersion. I don't do anything else, and work for twelve hours a stretch, take a break, and go back to work."
– John Logan, *Alien: Covenant*

What all successful screenwriters have in common is that they have written stories that appeal to many people.

"I didn't write *Snow White (and the Huntsman)* for any class, but I got bitten by the screenwriting bug and wrote a couple of scripts in my spare time – instead of going to keg parties or something."
– Evan Daugherty, *Divergent*

If you want to be a screenwriter, don't worry if you aren't like anyone else. Your uniqueness may be your best quality.

"If you look at how long the earth has been here, we're living in the blink of an eye. So, whatever it is you want to do, you go out and do it."
– Jamie Foxx, *All-Star Weekend*

Don't worry if you aren't smart enough. Many successful screenwriters grew up being considered less intelligent than other people. Reveal your brilliance in your writing.

"I used to be embarrassed because I was just a comic-book writer, while other people were building bridges or going on to medical careers. And then I began to realize: Entertainment is one of the most important things in people's lives. Without it they might go off the deep end. I feel that if you're able to entertain people, you're doing a good thing."
– Stan Lee, *Spider-Man*

"The movie business is tough. I think if I had just been a screenwriter, I'd still be waiting around for my first script to be produced. I think it's only because of my success as a playwright that I've been able to get some movies made."
– Tracy Letts, *August: Osage County*

"Your present circumstances don't determine where you can go; they merely determine where you start."
– Nido Qubein, motivational speaker

"Don't let anyone tell you that you can't do something. Make your own victories. Make your own mistakes."
– Joan Jett, musician

"Career and life philosophy changes are overwhelming, but all it takes is one little step at a time, and you'll reach your goal. But sitting in the same situation that doesn't work week after week will lead you nowhere – and only wastes precious time."
– Jeanne Veillette Bowerman, screenwriter advisor

"When you want to become a filmmaker, no one's going to knock at your door and say, 'I want to hire you to be a filmmaker.' It's a self-appointed role. You have to will it into being."
– Sofia Bohdanowicz, *MS Slavic 7*

Don't consider yourself an outsider. Write yourself into the inside, even by creating a unique type of screenplay that others will want to emulate. What you might be doing is taking people from the outside and bringing them into your world.

"The one thing that you have that nobody else has is you. Your voice, your mind, your story, your vision. So, write and draw and build and play and dance and live only as you can."
– Neil Gaiman, *Lucifer*

"Humans are storytelling animals. Everything is a story. Everyone's got stories. We're perceiving stories. We're interested in stories. So, to me, the big nut to crack is how to tell a story – what's the right way to tell a particular story."
– Richard Linklater, *Where'd You Go, Bernadette*

"I was writing scripts when I was in fourth grade – attempts at screenplays."
– Lorene Scafaria, *Hustlers*

"Almost no one is good at everything, but we are not just the good parts of what we do; we are also the bad parts. Your style emerges out of the things you don't do well."
– Guillermo del Toro, *Trollhunters*

"Everything I've written is personal. It's the only way I know how to write."
– Charlie Kaufman, *Synecdoche, New York*

"Good writing is remembering detail. Most people want to forget. Don't forget things that were painful or embarrassing or silly. Turn them into a story that tells the truth."
– Paula Danziger, *The Book Tower*

Don't fret over what you have been, the entertainment profession is more about what you choose to – and what you do – become.

"The question is not what you look at, but what you see."
– Henry David Thoreau, author *Walden*

"Every secret of a writer's soul, every experience of his life, every quality of his mind, is written large in his works."
– Virginia Woolf, author *A Room of One's Own*

If your past was troubled, consider it a goldmine of material for writing. It's how you present it as an engaging story that will make a difference.

"Everything we shut our eyes to, everything we run away from, everything we deny, denigrate or despise, serves to defeat us in the end. What seems nasty, painful, evil, can become a source of beauty, joy, and strength, if faced with an open mind."
– Henry Miller, *Tropic of Cancer*

"There are no dull subjects, only dull writers."
– H. L. Mencken, *The American Language*

"All of the very weird things that I had done, all the weird jobs that I had, and not going to school – when I got into screenwriting, I thought, 'All these things are rewarded here."
– Tony Gilroy, *The Cutting Edge*

"All that happens to us, including our humiliations, our misfortunes, our embarrassments, all is given to us as raw material, as clay, so that we may shape our art."
– Jorge Luis Borges, *Invasion*

"And by the way, everything in life is writable about if you have the outgoing guts to do it, and the imagination to improvise. The worst enemy to creativity is self-doubt."
– Sylvia Plath, *The Bell Jar*

"You can't use up creativity. The more you use the more you have."
– Maya Angelou, *Georgia, Georgia*

Your past, of any variety, may be one of your best assets as a writer. The style and inflection you use to write what some people may have otherwise considered a boring life situation could be what turns your work into a landmark piece of cinema history.

"Write. Rewrite. When not writing or rewriting, read. I know of no shortcuts."
– Larry L. King, *The Best Little Whorehouse in Texas*

"We're the last living alchemists. We create something out of nothing, and change one form into another. I think that is fantastic, and it takes courage. People who aren't writers don't understand the courage and endurance of what we do. The rejection can be so personal. It's hard to pick yourself up, but we do."
– Melanie Marnich, *The OA*

Don't consider your age as a factor in being a screenwriter. Creating and writing is for every age.

"If it's quality writing, I don't care how old you are. I've seen a teenager sell a script, as well as someone in their 80s."
– Zach Cox, Circle of Confusion management

There is no age restriction on being a screenwriter. Some begin writing as children, and others don't start to write screenplays until late in life.

"Age is not important, unless you're cheese."
– Helen Hayes, actor

"There is no doubt Hollywood has an age bias, more so for TV, less so for feature films. Part of this is due to the fact that many of the people who work in the development side of things are young themselves – 20s and 30s. Part likely derives from Hollywood's decades-long obsession with teenagers and the 18- to 25-year-old target demo. The conventional wisdom seems to be that the people who best understand and can write for that age group are members of that age group. The assumption being that older writers cannot grasp the subtle nuances of what it means to be a young person nowadays.

That's bull shit, of course. It's like saying men cannot possibly write authentic female characters, or women cannot write men. That young writers can't write old characters. That white writers cannot write black characters,

and vice versa. By this logic, we would have no science fiction movies featuring aliens, because none of us could possibly imagine what it's like to be a member of a species from another planet."
– Scott Myers, GoIntoTheStory.BlckLst.com

"Freedom is the operative word. Fiction means freedom, and we have to fight for that. Writers must be free to travel. We have to have passports into every territory. If we'd pigeonholed ourselves by saying, 'I can only write about being a middle-aged white man,' Shakespeare would never have written about anything outside of England. We would never have had *The Merchant of Venice*. He was not a merchant, never went to Venice. We have to fight for that against some strong headwinds. There's opposition to writers who imaginatively journey into a world they don't know, but that they want to know, and they're not backup by people saying, 'You are not of that culture. Get back in your box.'"
– Anthony McCarten, *The Two Popes*

If you want to be a successful screenwriter, only you can make it happen by writing scripts that agents will want to sell, directors will want to direct, actors will want to star in, financers will want to finance, distributors will want to distribute, and large numbers of people will want to watch.

"You're looking for characters that are going to be attractive to great directors and great actors."
– Len Amato, President: HBO Films: miniseries and Cinemax

"An actor is somebody who communicates someone else's words and emotions to an audience. It's not me. It's what writers want me to be."
– Dame Maggie Smith, actor

"I write the movie that I would like to go see, as opposed to writing the movie that someone else would like me to write."
– Alan Ball, *True Blood*

Write every day. Finish, polish, and workshop scripts. Have them edited. Get coverage. Submit them. Create your career.

"We all have friends who we start with, and you know, it's: Who gets their first? Who gets to the finish line, and then there's a lot of our friends behind us and we try to find a way to help them, if we can.
One of my friends was a writer, and of course, I sent him on a lot of jobs, and every report that came back was he just pissed off everybody.
And, finally, he came over and he goes, 'You know, I hate Hollywood. I hate all you people.' And I said, 'You know what? I tried to help you, man, you know? And, some of these people you are talking bad about actually have become friends of mine. And I don't understand the whole thing about Hollywood. Even though a writer always thinks the last thing they wrote is the

very best thing they wrote. Maybe it's just not good enough.' And, he said one more thing to me, and it really crossed the line. And, he's a kid from the '60s, so to speak, and you know protest marcher and other things, and it's very easy to put Hollywood down. But, he crossed the line with a friend of mine, and I don't know what happened, but I had him up against the wall. And I said, 'Look, would you just quit putting everybody down?' I said, 'Quit writing things that are one-hundred-twenty pages long." In our vernacular, that means script. I said, 'If you really want to write, write something that's 88 pages, or 888." And I realized I had my hands on him. I set him down, and I thought probably we had lost our friendship.

Of course, a week later he says, 'Hey, I don't have a place to stay, could I stay at your house?'

So, he stays there a couple of months, and he's writing every night. He says, 'Will you read what I wrote today?' And I said '####, no.' This went on, and finally, he started reading to my daughter – who was like three – every night.

Finally, my wife said to me, 'Look, he's in his room reading, he has to go.' And I finally said, 'Yeah, too much, you got to go." So, away he went.

He left what he had written, and he went down to Arizona, and he was working in a Chinese restaurant washing dishes. He called me and said, 'Have you read what I wrote?' I said, 'No. I don't really even like you anymore.' He said, 'I'm cold, and I'm working at this place, and I'm having to kill raccoons, and work at this Chinese restaurant.'

So, I sent him a sleeping bag. I sent him stuff. And, he said, 'Did you read what I wrote?'

Finally, I read it. It was *Dances with Wolves*.

When you have that situation, somebody that you know, who you start with, I was never so proud of somebody. I said, 'You did it, man. You really, really did it.' I said, 'I don't know how I'm going to do it, but I'm going to make it into a movie.'

– Kevin Costner, about Michael Blake. *Dances with Wolves* won multiple awards, including Oscars and Golden Globes, and was nominated for many BAFTAs, and was nominated by and won awards from film festivals, film societies, guilds, and critics' groups around the globe. It grossed over $400,000,000.

"There are two of you. One who wants to write, and one who doesn't. The one who wants to write better keep tricking the one who doesn't."
– Maria Irene Fornés, *The Rest I Make Up*

"The best thing about writing has been the writer's life – the sense of being expressed, the ownership of the day, the entirely specious sense of freedom we have, however slave we are to some boss or other. I wouldn't trade it for any other life."
– Anthony Minghella, *Cold Mountain*

"Lock up your libraries if you like. But there is no gate, no lock, no bolt that you can set upon the freedom of the mind."
– Virginia Woolf, *Orlando*

"Even if it's not perfect, even if you know you're gonna have to go back into it, type to the end. You have to have a little closure."
– Joss Whedon, *Serenity*

"Screenwriting is no different than playing the violin. You have to practice."
– Aaron Sorkin, *Charlie Wilson's War*

"I believe that in life you know that everything prepares you for the next thing, whether it's a hit, whether it's not a hit. Your failures are your accomplishments, because it makes you prepared for whatever it is that you are going to do next."
– Lee Daniels, *Empire*

Write. Even if you feel as if you are not ready. Write. Every day.

"If writers had to wait until their precious psyches were completely serene, there wouldn't be much writing done."
– William Styron, author *Sophie's Choice*

"To me, the only real star of the movie is the writer. And I work with writers very closely, from outline to first draft, and on to the seventh draft – whatever it takes."
– Dino De Laurentiis, producer

"Writers aren't exactly people. They're a whole bunch of people trying to be one person."
– F. Scott Fitzgerald, author *The Great Gatsby*

Release the creatures of your mind by writing them into scenes so that they can play out their lives on the screen.

"The key is creating characters and performances that are compelling. They don't all have to be 'good people,' but they do have to be people you don't want to turn away from."
– Patrick Lussier, *Terminator Genisys*

"As an activist it is important for me to speak up and advocate for those who can't. I turned to my art which has always been a great way to process, to move through things and release, while allowing me to stand up for my community."
– Kelly Fyffe-Marshall, *Black Bodies*

"Above all, write. Read a lot of great scripts. Apply your knowledge. Edit your own scripts mercilessly. Write some more. Then, join a writing group. Learn how to give and receive notes. Find your voice: Why you're important in the writers' room."
— Gennifer Hutchison, *Better Call Saul*

"Just like writing, receiving feedback requires practice, experience, and skills. Many writers connect feedback too closely to their ego/self-worth. So, they ignore it, stumble through it, or worst of all, fight it. That last batch of scribes is doomed from a career viewpoint. Doomed."
— Tim Schildberger, *Borat*

Screenwriting Tribe
Script Incubation Workshop

"You need people who can honestly tell you what concerns them about your project. Someone who wants you to succeed. Someone who will understand and empathize with what you want to do."
— David O. Russell, *I Heart Huckabees*

I wrote this book to be the book that I wish I would have read years ago.

I have been around the film and TV industry since I was a teenager. I've seen some people become grandly successful, while the vast majority do not. Part of what leads to one or the other experience is talent, but also the information people get, or don't get, and what they tune into, learn, and use, how focused they are, how hard they work at it, opportunities, chance, and luck. Working at it every day is key.

Wanting to be a screenwriter, and actually writing and polishing scripts to get them to the point where they can be submitted to the industry, and produced, are two vastly different things. One is fantasy. You have to do the work to get the other. Part of that work includes learning the craft, sharpening your skills in it, understanding how the business works, and participating in it.

"Just know that everyone's writing is terrible. Until it's not. No one's stuff is right immediately. You gotta work it. Refine it. Shape it. Spend time with it. It's a relationship. Between you and what comes from you. Not easy. Gonna be terrible before it's not. And that's okay."
— Ava DuVernay, *Central Park Five*

Having honed sharp skills in the craft of screenwriting is not something that a person can fake. The work shows up on the page, or it doesn't.

"You know, when you first start writing you're going to suck. And so, it's good to keep it to yourself – until maybe you don't suck as much."
– David Sedaris, author *Calypso*

It's easy to factor who has studied and worked to gain the skills needed to write sharp, engaging screenplays rich in contention, conflict, and subtext with drama played out by interesting characters saying clever and relevant dialogue in settings and eras that serve the story. Their scripts reveal it.

It seems that there are several differences in the scenarios of whether or not a person succeeds, and that are unrelated to physical structure or origins. Those are:
• The information a person acquires
• What they do with it
• How they communicate
• Their attitude
• How well they take care of themselves
• If they keep themselves updated in their chosen field
• If they are relentless about working daily to make their life become what they want it to be.
• …Of course, there are many other factors.

With screenwriters, some of those factors include:
• If they stay focused to persevere and pursue their dreams
• And, of course, if they continue to practice the craft, and improve in it by writing a variety of polished, marketable scripts – that sell.

"Writing is both a pleasure and a struggle. There are times when it's really aversive and unpleasant, and there are times when it's wonderful and fun and magical, but that's not the point. Writing is my job.

I'm not a believer of waiting for the muse. You don't put yourself in the mood to go to your nine-to-five job, you just go. I start in the morning and write all day.

Successful writers don't wait for the muse to fill themselves, unless they're geniuses.

I'm not a genius. I'm smart, I have some talent, and I have a lot of stubbornness. I persevere. I was by no means the best writer in my class in college. I'm just the one still writing."
– Akiva Goldsman, *A Beautiful Mind*

As a way to help writers pursue the craft, I began Screenwriting Tribe script incubation workshop in 2016 as a group of writers helping each other to polish their spec scripts.

"There's nothing more important in making movies than the screenplay."
– Richard Attenborough, actor, director

I was naïve in thinking that Screenwriting Tribe would consist of a few dozen writers. In the first month, it surpassed 100 members. As I'm writing this, the membership is over 900. It relies on writers actively writing, studying, workshopping, and striving to improve their skills in the craft. It has formed into a good network of people who help each other.

"Screenwriters should try to find a network of writers and industry professionals whom they trust. Attending writers' conferences or participating in networking events and being constantly present will show representatives that the screenwriter is taking an active role in making themselves known."
– Daniela Gonzalez, Circle of Confusion management

"Writers should constantly be generating new ideas for material. It's a never-ending cycle. If screenwriters live in L.A., networking is also a huge plus."
– Jonathan Hersh, Housefire Management

Screenwriting Tribe workshops feature film, short film, anthology series, limited series, procedural series, and episodic series scripts. We also workshop single-cam sitcom scripts (those are not filmed in front of a studio audience [despite the name, single-cam sitcoms typically use more than one camera]). (Examples of single-cam sitcoms are: *Black-ish, American Housewife, Parks and Recreation, Single Parents,* and *Modern Family*.)

Screenwriting Tribe does not workshop multi-cam sitcom scripts meant to be filmed in front of audiences, as those are a slightly different format, pacing, and timing. (Examples of multi-cam sitcom shows are: *Frasier, Friends, Man with a Plan, Last Man Standing, Will and Grace, Mom,* and *Big Bang Theory*.)

Screenwriting Tribe also does not workshop soap operas.

All TV shows are "episodics" – because they are a series of episodes. But, as detailed above, there are different classifications of episodics.

Another script that Tribe does not workshop is musicals.

Tribe also doesn't workshop the genre of horror that is super violent, or that can be considered torture porn.

"Keep your hands moving. Writing is about rewriting. Trust me and see."
– August Wilson, *Fences*

"Give your script to others to read. Good feedback brings the writer to a deeper understanding, not only of the screenplay-in-progress's flaws, but of its very essence. Every step forward in the creative process represents a growth in understanding, as opposed to merely a technical 'fix,' and those who serve us by reading and responding to our screenplay drafts play a crucial role in the process."
– Amnon Buchbinder, author *The Way of the Screenwriter*

Before a writer can sign up to bring pages to the workshop, they have to attend the workshop at least three times, and own this book. They are also to study *The Screenwriter's Bible,* and *Dr. Format Tells All,* John Truby's book *The Anatomy of Story,* and books on directing, editing, and film history. They are encouraged to read a variety of other books, such as Buchbinder's *The Way of the Screenwriter,* and Egri's *The Art of Dramatic Writing.*

What the workshop should not be is a bunch of writers correcting the same common errors over and over in each set of pages presented by writers who have not done the homework.

"Good feedback is kind, thorough, and timely. It's professional and focused. It leaves the writer feeling challenged to do better, but great about their strengths."
– Julie Gray, *Script Magazine,* JulieGray.info

What happens during the workshop:

At each workshop, four writers bring copies of twelve pages from their screenplays. The pages are read aloud by the members in attendance, with one person reading the scene headings and description, and other members reading the various characters.

"If you are using dialogue, say it aloud as you write it. Only then will it have the sound of speech."
– John Steinbeck, *The Red Pony*

The writer whose pages are being read remains silent during the reading of their pages. They also are to remain silent during the verbal feedback.

The first round of verbal feedback is for the participants to tell what they like about the script. The second round of verbal feedback is for helpful constructive criticism and technical corrections.

At Tribe workshop, the writers also receive written feedback on their script pages. That is why we read from printed pages. Other workshops read the scripts off of their computers, which means those workshops don't give written feedback.

The feedback time of a workshop is not for the writer to speak up and explain their script, or to get defensive. It is time for them to listen, to take notes, and to consider the comments.

Part of the process is simply to listen and consider, despite what you think of the feedback, or of the person giving it.

Some of the feedback you receive when you feel like being defensive against that feedback might be the feedback that is the most useful.

As you listen to feedback, take written notes – including what you don't agree with.

Not getting defensive during workshop feedback is a good thing. It's practice for when you might meet with producers, directors, actors, financiers, and others who might be involved in filming your script. Film is a collaborative industry. Be good at that skill. People who are good in the craft like working with people who are good to work with. Be good to work with.

"Be willing to pivot and collaborate. That's what I'm looking for in the writers I've hired, and that's what's gotten me to where I am. Know what you don't know, and listen, and be present."
– Bryan Cogman, *Game of Thrones*

"If you show someone somethings you've written, you give them a sharpened stake. Lie down in your coffin, and say, 'When you're ready.'"
– David Mitchell, *Peep Show*

"I feel that if you have to explain something, it loses strength. It's like a magician trying to explain his magic, in a way. Those kinds of things make me feel like I've lost something special about the film. The film should explain itself."
– Alejandro González Iñárritu, *The Revenant*

Even if some of those at the workshop have not read the previous pages, it could be helpful for a writer to listen to feedback based on twelve pages of the script, and consider how the reader may have factored the conclusions. That feedback of only part of their script by someone who hasn't read any other part of it could be helpful for the writer – in unexpected ways.

"Notes on your screenplay are not a personal attack. They might feel like that. You have made an investment of self, and you love what you have created. It is you. But someone's reaction to your writing is not a reaction to you. It is a reaction of the person who read your screenplay. Same screenplay, different people, different reactions. So, the reactions are personal to the readers. Detach from the notes to the degree to which you can improve your screenplay. Their reactions are formed primarily from their lives, not your words. Which leads me to this:

Do not embrace the extremes. Listen to the ends of the spectrum of opinions, but do not wallow there. If someone thinks your script is the worst attempt at screenwriting on record, take what you can, but do not stay with this, toss it off as something off and wild. If someone thinks your script is so awesomely perfect and beautiful that there's really nothing to be changed, take what you can, but do not stay with this, toss it off as something off and wild."
– Gordy Hoffman, BlueCat Screenplay Competition

It could take several weeks to workshop a one-hour pilot script, and about two-to-four months to workshop a full-length film script.

"A professional writer is an amateur who didn't quit."
– Richard Bach, *Illusions*

The goal of the workshop is:
• For writers to improve their skills in the craft as they polish their scripts for presentation to managers, agents, producers, directors, stars, financiers,

screenplay contests, writing labs, studio writing programs, and fellowship and mentorship programs.

"To go from being a competent writer to being a great writer, I think you have to risk being – or risk being seen as – a bad writer."
– Toby Litt, *Rare Books and Manuscripts*

"Being a writer is like having homework for the rest of your life."
– Lawrence Kasdan, *The Big Chill*

I didn't want a workshop in which participants were not doing their homework, or attending so that they could feel pacified by getting flowery compliments about their half-baked scripts. I wanted a script incubation workshop in which the members get pushed to polish their scripts to the level expected by the industry.

"The only way you can do anything new or interesting is to open yourself up to the risk of failing. In that sense, I try to look at failure and success both as neutral things."
– Charlie Kaufman, *How and Why*

"You're going to fail so many times. Just fail better. You're going to mess up. You have to. And you're going to do work that is problematic politically and personally, and work that is devoid of spiritual engagement, and your job is to keep trying to find your place in that work every time. And everyone is, like, they just want to put it out there and get it done. Why don't you put it out there until you're sure? Because once it's out there, you have no control."
– Tarell Alvin McCraney, *Moonlight*

"A lot of writers try to get approval and love way too early. Get the script right, first."
– Allison Burnett, *American Night*

"Literature is strewn with the wreckage of men who have minded beyond reason the opinions of others."
– Virginia Woolf, *Orlando*

I aim for a workshop in which writers feel safe sharing their work, consider the feedback, feel that they are spending their time in a worthwhile manner, and also show improvement – and do their homework.

What I don't want is a workshop in which people not quite understanding how competitive the industry is spend the time fishing for only the feedback that gives them a false sense that they are ready to enter the industry.

"No matter the number, the simple fact is the odds are against you. Get used to it. Even when you break into The Biz by selling a spec, you will face odds against you at every turn of your screenwriting career: Odds against selling that pitch, odds against landing that O.W.A. (Open Writing

Assignment), odds against your project getting a green light, odds against the movie turning out well, odds against the movie being a hit, and on and on."
– Scott Myers, GoIntoTheStory.BlckList.com

"It took seven years from the time I wrote *Mad Men* until it finally got on the screen. I lived every day with that script as if it were going to happen tomorrow. That's the faith you have to have."
– Matt Weiner, *The Sopranos*

"That there's a constant need for fresh voices means that there will always be a market for spec scripts. I can't say whether it's more or less likely they'll win the lottery. All I can say is that you have to buy a ticket to play the lottery, and you have to write a solid spec to get optioned."
– Jerrol LeBaron, InkTip.com

"My biggest piece of advice is always write on spec. I spent so much time over my career taking meetings with producers, and working on their ideas, and trying to sell them. I've been successful at times, but never as successful as I've been doing my own stuff."
– Jeff Bushell, *The Bernie Mac Show*

The spec script market is not the easiest place to make money. Most people writing scripts would make more money if they worked a job paying minimum wage. Those who do sell a script are likely to only have that happen once in their lifetime. Most people who want to write a screenplay never do. Most people who start a script never finish it. Most scripts that are finished never sell. And many of the scripts that are optioned or sold never get produced.

However, there are people who make money by selling screenplays, rewriting screenplays written by others, adapting novels, biographies, and news stories into screenplays, and otherwise getting paid to turn the ideas of others into screenplays – including being staffed on a series.

"Scriptwriting is the toughest part of the whole racket. The least understood and the least noticed."
– Frank Capra, *It's a Wonderful Life*

What is it that makes the difference between those who establish a career in screenwriting and those who never sell a script? The ones who do make a living at it are likely to do their homework, to understand the business of the industry, and to make connections when they are ready. They self-educate to know what the industry expects to see in a script – including engaging, compelling stories, concepts of interest to millions of viewers, and screenplays that are written using the correct formatting, are clear of errors, and are free of distractive elements.

"You better start writing now, because you know how to write, and you have fingers, and you have this one life, and during this one life you should put

your words down, and make your voice heard, and then let others hear your voice. And the only way any of that's going to happen is if you actually do it. People can't read the thoughts in your head. They can only read the thoughts you put down, carefully and with great love, on the page."
– Dave Eggers, *The Circle*

"Writing, to me, is simply thinking through my fingers."
– Isaac Asimov, *I, Robot*

I have included a wide variety of quotations in this book so that you will get a range of opinions from various successful people in the film industry. Some of the people essentially disagree with each other, but they are as successful as anyone could hope to get in the profession.

It should be obvious that there is no one way to make it in the industry. What works for one person might be something that another considers unwise, or unlikely to be helpful.

"Don't second-guess the film industry. Earn your stripes, and don't skip a step. Don't bypass the film festival circuit because many of the films shown are obscure 'arthouse films.' There is no need to write mainstream movies right away. Focus on 'real human truth.' In doing so, take no prisoners."
Phil Volken, *Extortion*

Attending and participating in a screenwriting workshop is a way to go about polishing your scripts and improving your skills in the craft – including your table discussion skills. It is also a way to get to know the business of the industry, the types of conversations you might have with people in the screenplay trade, and the way others maneuver their way through it.

"If you genuinely want to make films, then write screenplays. All you need to write a script is a paper and pencil. It's only through writing scripts that you learn specifics about the structure of film and what cinema is."
– Akira Kurosawa, *The Hidden Fortress*

A screenwriting workshop can only work well if the members engage in learning the craft to improve their skills, work to have polished scripts, and prepare themselves to deal with entering the spec script market.

"Writing is finally about one thing: Going into a room alone and doing it, putting words on paper that have never been in quite that way before."
– William Goldman, *Dreamcatcher*

Screenwriting Tribe does not have a teacher working as the authority to teach students by yapping instructions at them. It is a facilitated workshop with the writers teaching each other through verbal and written feedback, and networking. It is a group of writers learning about screenwriting through practice, feedback, study – and loads of rewriting.

"All experienced writers know writing is rewriting. It is only in the intensive process of revision that a promising idea becomes a great screenplay."
– Ray Morton, *Brothers*

Attendees of Tribe are to give helpful feedback. It is our dreams that we are working on – dreams of becoming successful screenwriters. Because of how tender that could be, I advise people to be realistically encouraging. But, we are also not there to say a bunch of hollow compliments, pleasant things, and give false hope. We also are not there to praise people who don't do their homework, who keep bringing in pages with the same mistakes, or who treat the group simply as a social experience.

Tribe workshop is meant to spur writers to complete a variety of polished scripts clear of distracting elements.

"Every movie is an experiment, and the only way you can grow at what you're doing is to take chances. You can't stick with what worked last time."
– Judd Apatow, *Fun with Dick and Jane*

Some actors attend the workshop. That helps us get a flair for the dramatic and comical during the page reads. It also provides a way for actors to both sharpen their cold reading skills, while also learning about screenwriting – which can give actors an edge in their acting. Some of the writers are also actors. However, actors should not attend to get lavished with praise, to be validated, to seek the spotlight, or to get cast. The workshop is for screenwriters to learn and improve their skills in the craft.

"I enjoy acting and screenwriting, in completely different ways. You have more creative freedom with writing, because you can create everything that happens. But, as an actor you also have creative freedom, because you don't so much focus on what has to move the story along, and only on how your character is reacting to a situation."
– John Francis Daley, *Horrible Bosses*

Screenwriting Tribe workshop is specifically meant for those holding the goal of selling scripts and/or establishing a career in screenwriting.

"Become part of a writers group. Not your friends, family, or inexperienced writers."
– Scott Myers, GoIntoTheStory.BlckLst.com

The workshop is not for those who aren't going to take their writing seriously. It's not for those who are only interested in a social scene, or those who are not actively writing – or are not preparing to write – screenplays.

"Goals on the road to achievement cannot be achieved without discipline and consistency."
– Denzel Washington, actor

A screenwriting workshop will not teach a person everything that they need to know about screenwriting. To expect a workshop to provide that is unrealistic – to the point of self-failure.

Some show up to a workshop expecting to get things for the small price of being at the table, as if they are owed something for being there. That's not the spirit of a collaborative screenplay incubation workshop. Someone who isn't willing to take the steps to improve their skills in the craft will not be a strong link in the group. They are also not likely to continue attending – nor will they be missed if they stop showing up.

"I've talked to people and they 'kind of like' films, and they 'kind of' want to do this, or they're 'thinking about' that. Any artistic medium, you can't just dabble and be 'kind of' interested. You have to dedicate your entire life to it. Really, let everything else go to whatever degree you can responsibly do that. You gotta go all in."
– Richard Linklater, *Waking Life*

A screenplay incubation workshop is also not a place for a self-impressed know-it-all ego head to show up wanting to be lavished with praise about their script, as if they are the new hot thing. If it's not on the pages, it's not in the script – and it doesn't matter what type of person wrote it. They should be open to feedback, and willing to do homework, including studying the books. They should also know that not everyone will like their script – no matter how excellent it is.

"If you're not early, you're late."
– John Ritter, actor

Part of being a professional in the industry is arriving early. Treat the workshop as a professional meeting. Unless you have a good reason, or have cleared it with the facilitator, it is unprofessional to arrive late to a writing workshop.

"There's nothing worse than walking into a pitch late. With everyone gathered in the room waiting for you. That's one strike against you, before you even start."
– Carter Blanchard, *Bedbugs*

As I'm now approaching four years of running the workshop, I have been late once – because of a freeway closure. I did leave early one time as I had to go work on an all-night film shoot. There have also been several times where I was out-of-town, and other members of Tribe facilitated the group in my place.

One man who was repeatedly late to the workshop, including on days when his script pages were to be read, was told to not come back, and his membership was deleted. Apparently, he didn't care if he was unprofessional. He also seemed to think it was okay that he wasn't there for the read and feedback of pages by other writers who were then present for his pages. He also didn't follow other guidelines. If everyone behaved like he did, the workshop would be chaos. Arrogance, rudeness, and disrespect gets a person kicked out of the group. Luckily, very few people have been a problem.

When you RSVP to a writing workshop, be there. Be there for yourself, and be there for the other writers.

If you do arrive late, don't be disruptive. Don't interrupt the read or feedback with your arrival. Enter quietly, and take a seat.

"Treat the group as if they're all industry professionals taking time out of their day to see your work."
– Sean Thompson, What I learned in Film School, InkTip

If a screenwriter feels as if they are not getting enough out of Tribe, perhaps they are not pushing themselves to do their homework, including reading a variety of screenwriting books, watching numerous online videos about screenwriting, reading many articles about screenwriting, and studying award-winning screenplays and watching the films made from them. They should also write screenplays that reveal their improved skills in the craft, polish those scripts, have them edited (by a script editor), and get coverage (see the coverage chapter in this book).

"A good three quarters of the submissions that come in can be pretty easily dismissed as people who haven't done their homework."
– Matt Connell, agent

Screenwriting Tribe pushes for the writers to learn about the industry, and to explore their career-launching options.

It is blatantly clear when someone isn't pushing themselves to improve their skills: Their scripts reveal it. It's not something they can hide.

"As you navigate through the rest of your life, be open to collaboration. Other people and other people's ideas are often better than your own. Find a group of people who challenge and inspire you, spend a lot of time with them, and it will change your life."
– Amy Poehler, *Parks and Recreation*

There are more ways than ever to sell screenplays, or to get them produced and delivered to broad audiences. Windows into the screenwriting profession are opening, including through contests, fellowships, and labs, and the various forms of delivery, including network, cable, and online platforms.

"I came to Los Angeles not knowing anyone or anything. Never had written anything, I still thought if I didn't do it then I would never have the chance to do it. So, I immersed myself in the learning process. I took extension courses, I studied other scripts, and just sat down and wrote. In fact, I wrote 25 screenplays before I got my first job."
– John Wirth, *Nash Bridges*

"Successful people don't wait. They don't get stalled on one step, one issue, one project. They continuously go about the problem of creating value. They're not interested in struggling and waiting, they're focused on doing."
— Frank Darabont, *The Green Mile*

"Workshopping your scripts is definitely a helpful tool in the arsenal. You have to make sure your best work is out there."
— Glenise Mullins, *The Lord of the Rings*, member of Screenwriting Tribe

"What I do is I look at the emotion behind the note. I look at what emotion that note is searching for, and I find a way to do it on my own terms, instead of the terms that they are suggesting."
— Christopher McQuarrie, *The Underworld*

WHY WORKSHOP A SCRIPT?

"One of the things I try to do with anything I write is have it read out loud. I think, when we work by ourselves, and you do your own voice in your head while you're reading through what you're writing, sometimes it's you talking to you, and then you realize that there isn't enough diversity in your characters. So, if you can get people together to read it so that you can hear it, it's really very helpful."
— Pamela Ribon, *Samantha Who?*

"I spent an excessive amount of time in film school — six years to be exact. I can tell you what I think are the two most important things that I learned after all that time:
1) Writing groups are an incredible asset for your work.
2) You need to understand how to take notes."
— Sean Thompson, *What I Learned in Film School*, Inktip

"Writers, you never get a second chance to make a first impression. Even if you think your script is done, read it, revise it, think about it, read it again, revise it again before sharing. People's impressions not just of the script but of you can be cemented by that read."
— Melissa Hilfers, *Jagged Edge*

"I think storytelling is a thing of beauty, and also very difficult. It's a craft you have to continue to work at."
— James Gray, *Blood Ties*

Workshopping a script helps those in the room learn the rules of screenwriting, and how to apply them to various scripts. And, it helps them to understand what breaking the rules means in ways that can benefit a script.

"We know there are rules for eating, walking, and breathing; we know there are rules for painting, music, dancing, flying, and bridge building; we know there are rules for every manifestation of life and nature – why, then, should not writing be the sole exception? Obviously, it is not."
– Lajos Egri, author *The Art of Dramatic Writing*

Maybe don't think of the so-called screenwriting rules as rules, but think of them as helpful or standard guidelines. When you do something outside of those lines, people who read scripts for a living notice. It can be a distraction, taking them out of the script, and considering that the writer hasn't done their homework. However, there are times when going outside the lines can help.

"The job of the screenwriter is to run the film in the reader's imagination. And nothing should get in the way of that."
– Colin Higgins, *Silver Streak*

"Of the many supposed rules of writing, the only one that's legit is 'write every day.'"
– Brian Koppelman, *Rounders*

"I have learned the first rule of screenwriting is having no rules. Everyone has to find their own way of doing things."
– Guillermo Arriago, *21 Grams*

Workshopping a script heightens and sharpens the tension, conflict, and contention, improves subtext, and strengthens character psychology and logic.

"The bigger the issue, the smaller you write. Remember that. You don't write about the horrors of war. No. You write about a kid's burnt socks lying on the road. You pick the smallest manageable part of the big thing, and you work off the resonance."
– Richard Price, *The Wire*

"You don't start out writing good stuff. You start out writing crap and thinking it's good stuff, and then gradually you get better at it. That's why I say one of the most valuable traits is persistence."
– Octavia Butler, *Wild Seed*

Workshopping a script helps clear it of issues that slow the read, that dull and blur the story, and that can cost the production time and money.

"You need to have a point for every page of your script. You need to have a reason why it is there and how it is moving the story forward."
– Peter Chiarelli, *The Proposal*

"Often, feedback sessions are seen as a chance for people to give their input. Nothing could be further from the truth. The purpose of creative feedback is to move the project forward. Anything that does not fulfill that purpose – no matter who it comes from – has no place in a feedback session."
– Scott Myers, GoIntoTheStory.BlckList.com. In reference to Pixar co-founder Ed Catmull's description of the "brain trust" feedback group engaged in developing films at the company.

"A script's structure grows out of its own internal D.N.A. Your job is to assess what the organic rules are for that specific script. It's like parenting. Your job is not to turn your child into 'every child,' it's to help them grow to be the best manifestation of whoever they are."
– Ed Solomon, *Mosaic*

Workshopping a script helps to eliminate distractive, faulty elements that stop it from being represented, sold, financed, cast, staffed, and produced.

"The essence of dramatic form is to let an idea come over people, without it being plainly stated. When you say something directly, it is simply not as potent as it is when you allow people to discover it for themselves."
– Stanley Kubrick, *Full Metal Jacket*

"Writing doesn't just flow out of the pen or keyboard fully formed. Each work is built concept by concept, beat by beat, word for word. It's a process of discovery."
– Nell Scovell, *The Simpsons*

Taking a script through an incubation workshop helps to sharpen a writer's skills in the craft. Their future projects will benefit from the process. They will write better scripts faster, and with fewer errors.

"When you recognize what your talents are, a happy life is developing them to the greatest extent you can."
– Ellen Burstyn, actor

"There's no question that a great script is absolutely essential, maybe the essential thing – for a movie to succeed."
– Sydney Pollack, director

"The most important thing is the script."
– Martin Scorsese, *Casino*

To help unclog the industry of scripts that are not ready to be submitted:
It would be helpful for managers, agents, producers, directors, actors, financiers, screenwriting contests, labs, and fellowship programs to ask writers these questions:
- Has this script been workshopped?
- If this script has not been workshopped, why hasn't it been?

"As they say, 'If it's not on the page, it's not on the stage.' And I think we have found issues with a screenplay where we were forced to move on the film because of availability of stars, and all of that. And, found the same problems in the finished film that we saw in the screenplay."
– Alan Horn, Walt Disney Studios

"Bad movies often go wrong either with a faulty script, or rushing for a release date. But, of course, there are good movies that don't work, and there are bad movies that are hits."
– Toby Emmerich, Warner Bro's Studios

"You can often tell immediately when you're reading a very special screenplay that is undeniable. The same can be said for a script that needs a lot of development – poor formatting, lack of visual scene descriptions, overwriting, on-the-nose dialogue, etc. Regardless, I always read enough to get a sense of the story and the writer's voice, and then make a decision if the quality warrants further consideration. What often makes me want to stop reading more than anything is when the script starts to feel derivative and predictable. I want to read a script that pops and keeps me engaged and surprised."
– Matt Dy, Lit Entertainment Group

"Other people's ideas are good, right? That's not to say that sometimes I'd get notes and be like, 'Well, that wasn't quite what I'd intended,' but I think this is the balance for a writer – the balance between accepting that your draft isn't going to be perfect, and that other people will have good ideas – and hanging onto what you love about your script. As a writer, you need to say 'no' sometimes, if you feel passionately about it. People respect that, I think. You can't fight everything, and often the notes are good."
– Daisy Coulam, *EastEnders*, to ScriptAngel.com

"Screenwriting is pushing a rock up a hill, and directing is running downhill with the rock behind you."
– Christopher McQuarrie, *The Usual Suspects*

Whether it be the writer or their characters, what is in the heart? What concerns the soul? What is the motive driving the actions and words? What will psychologically play with the audience? Get that on paper, and refine it.

Do not expect everyone to like it. Not everyone will. And, that is okay.

"Making a film is like raising a child. You cannot raise a child to be liked by everyone. You raise a child to excel, and you teach the child to be true to their own nature. There will be people who dislike your child because he or she is who they are, and there will be people who'll love your child immensely for the very same reason."
– Guillermo del Toro, *Scary Stories to Tell in the Dark*

"You might not write well every day, but you can always edit a bad page, you can't edit a blank page."
– Jodi Picoult, *My Sister's Keeper*

"The dream and the film are the juxtaposition of images in order to answer a question."
– David Mamet, *Wag the Dog*

THIS BOOK

I wrote this book because I thought screenwriters would benefit by sharing what I have learned from years of running screenwriting workshops.

I didn't write this book to replace any other screenwriting book, or while thinking that it would be the only book someone would – or should – read about screenwriting. To think that would be absurd, pretentious, and limiting. Instead, I wrote this book to go along with studying other screenwriting books.

In addition to this book, writers who workshop their scripts with Screenwriting Tribe are to study these books:
- *The Screenwriter's Bible*, by David Trottier
- *Dr. Format Tells All*, by David Trottier
- *The Anatomy of Story*, by John Truby
- *What Happens Next: A History of American Screenwriting*, by Marc Norman

And, also study other screenwriting books, which might include:
- *The Art of Dramatic Writing*, by Lajos Egri
- *The TV Showrunner's Roadmap*, by Neil Landau
- *Story Maps: TV Drama: The Structure of the One-Hour Television Pilot*, by Daniel P. Calvisi
- *The Lost Art of Story*, by Adam Skelter
- *Screenwriter's Compass*, by Guy Gallo
- *Screenplay*, by Syd Field (and other Syd Field books)
- *Writing Screenplays that Sell*, by Michael Hauge
- *Screenplay Story Analysis*, by Asher Garfunkle
- *Shakespeare for Screenwriters*, by J.M. Evenson
- *Your Screenplay Sucks*, by William Akers
- *How NOT to Write a Screenplay*, by Denney Martin Flinn

If someone studies at least those books – along with this book – they will get a handle on the craft. The knowledge they gain will be revealed in the dexterity of their screenplays.

At first, I was writing this as a booklet for the members of Tribe. The goal was to get all of us on the same page – so that we could work together and progress on the path toward writing polished scripts that are ready to be presented to the industry.

"There is no libretto. We need wit and courage to make our way while our way is making us."
– Tom Stoppard, *Shakespeare in Love*

That booklet I was writing became so much more than what I had first intended. It turned into a book of nearly 300 pages, and that was published in the spring of 2018. I overhauled that into what has turned into the book that you are reading.

What I went through while writing the book helped me to realize that the craft of screenwriting is quite complex, engaging, and time consuming.

"I became a script writer with absolutely no idea of how to write a script whatsoever. I still feel a bit of an outsider in that regard. If I can maintain that approach to screenwriting, it can continue to be enjoyable."
– Nick Cave, *The Proposition*

The more I have studied screenwriting, the more I have grown to consider it as a language. I now know that screenwriting can be studied for years while a person can still feel as if there is more to learn.

"Screenwriting is no more complicated than old French torture chambers, I think. It's about as simple as that."
– James L. Brooks, *Terms of Endearment*

Because there is so much to learn about screenwriting, a person writing screenplays should not stop their study of the craft by limiting themselves to the books listed above.

"A lot of people think movies are just sort of, 'Anybody can do it. Anybody can be a screenwriter.' But, it's a tough, tough craft. It's like writing a novel. You have to study it. Not everybody can go to film school, I get that. But, you can do extension classes, like I did, or online, or read books. Especially, get some freaking screenplays for movies you admire and read them, study them. There's structure, there's craft to it. You can't just sit down and puke out a script and think you're a genius. Writing is a muscle you have to exercise. It's all about learning and doing and persevering, just like any other career path; but especially in the arts."
– Lindsay Devlin, *Devil's Due*

65

To become a skilled screenwriter fluent in the craft, there are a variety of other books that screenwriters would be wise to study, including books that help them to understand character psychology, story, reasoning, and the filmmaking business.

"Jung was a huge influence on Joseph Campbell. And Campbell was an influence on George Lucas when he was making *Star Wars*. Indeed, Luke Skywalker's journey reflects Jung's ideas."
– Scott Myers, GoIntoTheStory.BlckLst.com

To understand the possibilities of story and character, it is helpful for screenwriters to study the following books:
• *The Hero with a Thousand Faces*, by Joseph Campbell
• *Poetics*, by Aristotle
• *The Power of Myth*, by Joseph Campbell
• *The Writer's Journey*, by Michael Vogler
• *Man and His Symbols*, by Carl Jung
• *The Emotional Craft of Fiction*, by Donald Maass

Also, study William Shakespeare, including:
• *Hamlet*
• *King Lear*

It is helpful for screenwriters to understand the business of film and TV production – including post-production.

I encourage members of Screenwriting Tribe to go to their local library and study the books they find in the collection on screenwriting, film and TV directing, production, financing, distribution, and other aspects of the industry.

The more you know about the film and TV industry, the better you can manage a career in it – especially if you want to be a successful screenwriter.

"Though this be madness, there is method in it."
– William Shakespeare, *Much Ado About Nothing*

"I would advise anyone who aspires to a writing career that before developing his talent he would be wise to develop a thick hide."
– Harper Lee, *To Kill a Mockingbird*

"Talent is helpful in writing, but guts are absolutely necessary."
– Jessamyn West, *Summer Flight*

Know that those who prepare for and learn about a craft, and apply what they learn to their practice of the craft, are more likely to experience success in it.

"Before *Whiplash*, I'd had a string of failed scripts. I'd pour my blood, sweat, and tears into them, and no one would like them."
– Damien Chazelle, *La La Land*

"Rejection still hurts, and it's still very hard to take those knocks. I have written or co-written more than twenty screenplays. Anyone that has done that process knows that that's a lot of blood, sweat, and tears."
– Guillermo del Toro, *The Shape of Water*

"Be true to yourself creatively. Don't try to write like your heroes. Try to be better than them. To be good, you have an original or genuine voice in the creative arts, you have to love what you do. It doesn't mean it will be easy. In fact, I can guarantee you that it won't be – not if you really want to be good. But, you have to love it. You have no chance if you don't. So, if you don't love writing, quit writing now and focus on something else."
– John Glenn, *Hatfields & McCoys*

Open your mind. Read, study, listen. Do the process. Don't be afraid to make mistakes – and to learn from those mistakes.

"I think the unfortunate mistake many screenwriters make is they reach out to industry folks before they should. Before they are ready in terms of their craft. In other words, just because your screenplay is written, it doesn't necessarily mean it's ready to be read by agents and managers. Get feedback on your script. We in the film industry are big on vetting writers, whether by contests, or referrals."
– Andrew Kersey, manager

"An essential aspect of creativity is not being afraid to fail."
– Edwin Land, co-founder of Polaroid

"People think when it comes to a screenplay you start with absolutely nothing. But, the trouble is, you have a million ideas. You have to dramatize it by omitting, by simplifying, by finding a clean theme that leads someplace."
– Billi Wilder, *Irma la Douce*

I hope that this book helps you improve your skills in the craft, understand the business of the industry, and motivates you to formulate the work that manifests your dreams.

"Don't wait. Find a story idea, start making it, give yourself a deadline, show it to people who will give you notes to make it better. Don't wait until you're older, or in some better job than you have now. Don't wait for anything. Don't wait til some magical story idea drops into your lap. That's not where ideas come from. Go looking for an idea, and it will show up."
– Ira Glass, *Sleepwalk with Me*

"When I first started writing, and no one was paying me, in order to feel like I had a real job, I would get out of bed, put on a jacket and tie every morning, and sit down at my desk."
– Graham Moore, *The Imitation Game*

67

"My life, my reading, everything about me revolves around the cinema. So, for me, cinema is life, and vice-versa."
– Sergio Leone, *A Fistful of Dollars*

"The scene is not going to be shot the way you wrote it. After the producer and production manager determine the budge and location, the director blocks the scene and decides on the number of camera 'set ups.' He or she must also work with actors who may have their own 'contributions.' Thus, it's unlikely that your scene will be shot the way you wrote it. Your job is to present a clear vision of what you have in mind, so that other professionals 'get' your scene, even though elements of it may be changed."
– David Trottier, author *The Screenwriter's Bible*

SPEC SCRIPTS, DEVELOPMENT-STAGE SCRIPTS, SHOOTING SCRIPTS, PRODUCTION SCRIPTS, AND PUBLISHED SCRIPTS

People with badly formatted scripts often defend their choices by saying that they saw a script online that was formatted similar to how they formatted their script.

The screenplays that you will find online are likely NOT spec scripts. There are several types of screenplays that you will find online. They might be published scripts that were typed out after the movie was released. Published scripts contain many elements that do not go into a spec script, and often are not formatted in a way that is standard to either spec scripts, development scripts, shooting scripts, or production scripts. Published scripts also might be called *transcripts*, and often are so far removed from correct spec script formatting that they should not be considered as a template or guide for people wanting to learn how to write a screenplay.

Published scripts might have margins that are not correct for a spec script, development script, shooting script, or production script. This is done to save space and paper. Published scripts are published specifically to be read as a form of entertainment. I have friends who are not in the film or TV industries, and who read published scripts the way some people read novels. It's a form of entertainment for them.

Another type of script that you might find online is a development-stage script. That is a version of a script that has been purchased, and it is partway going through changes on its way to becoming a production script. A development-stage script might have partially-written scenes, notes of what a scene should – or should not – contain, repeated scenes written in different ways, and otherwise writing that is being changed in one way or another. A development-stage script is one that that might be undergoing a rewrite by the original writer, or by a writer who was not the original writer. Development-stage scripts can be kind of a mess, and they are only meant for very few people to see them. A development-stage script also might be a script that has been abandoned by a production company. Development-stage scripts are sometimes leaked and passed around, and end up on the Internet – then, some people who see them then think that is how a script should look. Those very same people have not done their homework.

"A screenplay is written to be read, initially. And then – once it's purchased – you go back and rewrite it to be filmed."
– Taylor Sheridan, *The Last Cowboy*

Another type of script that you might find online is a shooting script. A shooting script is formatted just before the script is to go into production.

A shooting script can also be called a breakdown script, as it is the version of the script that was used to break it down into how it will be filmed, what will be needed, how the filming schedule will happen, and how much all of the various things will cost in relation to what will be needed during filming – from cameras to props, locations, background actors, catering, trailers, child actor needs (classrooms, teachers, assistants, etc.), and even the bathrooms needed during filming on location.

A shooting script contains annotations that include scene numbers, camera angles, and specific formatting meant for the notice of various crew – such as the camera crew, sound technicians, FX (the special effects crew), art director, set decorator, set dressers, props department, wardrobe department, and the script supervisor. A shooting script might contain scenes that are not in the final film – or it might not contain scenes that are in the final film (because there often are scenes filmed that are improvised on set).

"The director and cinematographer sit with the shooting script and discuss their ideas and shot plan desired for the movie (or TV show). They line these scripts so that they know what kind of camera angles and movement they want in each scene. The shooting script is then broken into shots, featuring cinematography jargon such as close-ups, medium shots, and wide shots.

After a spec script is purchased, the director and cast are attached. Then the movie goes into pre-production. In television, episodes are sent to the network, given notes, rewritten, and approved. Then the scene numbers are added so they can break each down individually."
– Jason Hellerman, *What's a Shooting Script, and How Do You Create One?* NoFilmSchool.com

Shooting scripts are not spec scripts. There will not be a shooting script of your film, unless you first write a selling script that will dazzle the readers, and pull in investors, actors, a director, cinematographer, editor, and whatever else is needed to make it.

Another type of script that you might find online is a production script. That is largely the same as a shooting script, but it will contain changes that were done during the filming of the script. While a film is being shot, there could be many dozens of changes, and that means that there might be dozens of varieties of the script that could be considered the production script. A production script could contain scenes that were not in the spec script, the pre-production script, the shooting script, or the published script.

This book is specifically meant for those who are writing spec scripts: scripts written with the intent to sell them, or to be used as a writing sample.

"I'm part of the spec generation. Meaning: Writing on speculation. I started out writing on spec, and I'm still writing on spec. That is a different kind of screenwriting than (the type of screenwriting that is done by) people who write for hire, because you are responsible to no one but your own calculations."
– Paul Schrader, *The Mosquito Coast*

Spec scripts are speculative:

• Spec scripts are written speculatively. That is, on the speculation that they might win screenplay competitions, might help the writer be accepted into a fellowship, mentorship, lab, or studio writing program, might be sold, might be produced, and otherwise might help the writer establish a career in the industry.

"The spec script is the selling script. You write it with the idea of selling it later – or circulating it as a sample. Once sold, and it goes into preproduction, it will be transformed into a shooting script, also knowns as the production draft.

The spec style avoids camera angles, editing direction, and technical intrusions. You may use those tools, but only when necessary to clarify the story.

Scenes are not numbered in a spec script."
– David Trottier, author *The Screenwriter's Bible*

"If you're writing a screenplay, you need to be prepared to let go. There's a good chance the words you write aren't going to be the ones that end up on screen."
– Meg Cabot, *The Princess Diaries*

"We had actors who were kind of hanging around on set. We wrote extra scenes for them. We said, 'You're here, let's shoot something in the corner, we might use it.'"
– Olivia Wilde, director of *Booksmart*

Spec scripts should be written while knowing that the script is very unlikely to be filmed exactly as it is written. There will be changes during pre-production, production, and the post-production processes, including editing, color grading, scoring, and so forth.

"Only after post-production is complete do I feel like my script is finished."
— Bong Joon-Ho, *Parasite*

Only if you are directing and/or producing your script should you expect to have a say in how it is filmed. But even then, the financiers could make certain requests. Otherwise, once you hand your script over to the studios, or producers, director, and crew, don't expect to be on set.

"If you have someone on set for the hair, why would you not have someone for the words?"
— Louis Malle, *The Thief of Paris*

As far as to how much of your script as it is written makes it to screen is in the hands of numerous people, including the producers, director, DP, assistant director, actors, script supervisor, set and wardrobe designers, editor, and financiers.

There might be different edits of the film or series done for various regions of the world – including to avoid political or moral conflict. That might mean that additional scenes will be filmed to create a version of the production acceptable to foreign markets.

"I think the notion of writing a script that is complete and then you just shoot it exactly as written, I don't think so much happens. It's such a collaborative process. And I also think movies and any sort of collaborative venture, it takes on a life of its own at some point – and you have to be able to recognize that and step back. And I think you have to be willing to make changes along the way. And I think a lot of writing gets done in the editing room, too."
— Alan Ball, *American Beauty*

"I prefer collaboration, because it's not so neurotic-making. You can check things through and laugh. The other person can help you feel better when things go badly."
— Jane Campion, *The Piano*

"Collaboration is the most incredible thing. You learn about yourself because you have to put your own ego in a very special place, where you can be your best, but at the same time accept all the ideas of the other guys. It's tough to be able to throw all the mediocrity you have at others, and deal with the worst things they will say about it."
— Nicolas Giacobone, *Birdman*

"You can't fix a bad script after you start shooting. The problems on the page only get bigger as they move to the big screen."
– Howard Hawks, *Rio Bravo*

"The important thing is to make a different world, to make a world that is not now. A real world, a genuine world, but one that allows myth to live. The myth is everything."
– Sergio Leone, *Once Upon a Time in the West*

"A script can feel lacking in professionalism when it's full of typos. Also, at this point, shouldn't we all know the difference between 'to' and 'too'?"
– Kristin Burr, producer

Script Polishing

Someone asked me why it is important to polish a script so much. "Can't you just film it and fix things as you film?" Sure, you can – if you want to spend loads of money figuring out things as you film, having to take time to reconfigure, and then probably more time – and spend more money – doing reshoots.

The more that you change the scenes during filming, the more that you also might need different sets, locations, props, wardrobe, FX, sound, lighting, camera, makeup, and hair situations, differences in the actors, a variety of background actors, and all varieties of components that each require alterations in cast and crew. All of that costs money and time.

"One thing I know, after thirty years of doing this, is you can't work it out while you shoot. It always ends up just making things so much more difficult in post-production."
– Emma Thompson, *Nanny McPhee*

"There are three things that are important for a film. Number one is story. Number two is story. Number three is story. Good actors can save a bad script and make it bearable, but good actors can't make a bad script good, they can only make it bearable."
– Mark Strickson, *Modern Dinosaurs*

You want to polish your screenplay – before you show it to anyone in the business. You might only have one chance to get your script to a decision-maker who can send your script on the path to production. Don't waste that chance by sending out an unpolished script.

"We see films all the time, whether they have access to all kinds of intellectual property or artifacts, and the one thing that they don't get is story. So, I think whether you're talking about a biopic, or an action film, or a science-fiction film that has all the CGI in the world, if you're not trying to connect with an audience, it doesn't really matter."
– John Ridley, *12 Years a Slave*

Those who read scripts for a living (including for agents, managers, producers, studios, fellowship and mentorship programs, labs, contests, and coverage services) will be able to tell if you have NOT done your homework. They will notice if the formatting is standard, if the descriptions work, if the dialogue sounds fluent, if the conflict, subtext, tension, and risk registers, if the backstories play out, if the characters display their contention, are engaging, and have arcs, if facts and historical sequences are sufficiently correct, and if the script is ready for the industry. (But then, many films slip by with various issues, and are produced. They get the stars and are massively marketed. And they make hundreds of millions, internationally. And, they are awful. So, maybe you shouldn't listen to anything I say.)

"To me, great stories have multiple themes that resonate and are powerful."
– Josh Singer, *Spotlight*

If your script does get optioned, and goes into production – by people without much experience – do you think that it will be better or worse if you had taken that script through a workshop of your peers to polish it? Will the people who option the script know more about screenwriting than you? Do you think that they are going to magically correct errors when they film it? Will it be something that many people will want to watch? Will it get distribution? Or, will it end up being so flawed that people will consider it unwatchable trash?

Distribution is a topic that can fill another book. Distributors continually seek commercially viable productions that will stand out from the rest, and/or serve niche markets (martial arts, horror, teenage romance, religious, LGBTQ, etc.). One way they find product is by attending film festivals, and the American Film Market convention in Santa Monica. They also get involved with films in the various pre-production stages for pre-sales, including for the foreign region markets. Their readers and the development executives that they work with know what they are seeking, and can be quite dismissive in their hunt for scripts and packages that will satisfy the markets. Small (indie) distributors are competing with big distributors, and they offer a variety of options – not always to the advantage of filmmakers. Sometimes what they offer filmmakers can be deceptive. Consider what Rob Hardy of FilmmakerFreedom.com says about distribution:

"There are a lot of bottom-feeding distributors who use the festival circuit as a means to snatch up films for pennies on the dollar – if they even pay you anything upfront – which very often they don't.

And, despite the fact they'll talk a big game and make all sorts of promises about the money you'll make, far too often you won't see a dime on the back end – even if they're making money with your project. There are all sorts of creative accounting tricks they use to pull off that feat.

Granted, not all small distributors are bad, and you can indeed strike worthwhile deals – if you're careful, and do your due diligence.

Just know that it's a major uphill battle, especially if you're not privy to these shenanigans, and well versed in the various types of rights you can negotiated in a distribution deal."
– Rob Hardy, FilmmakerFreedom.com

Of course, many screenwriters won't get involved with distribution, as they will be selling scripts, polishing scripts, or working as a staff writer – and won't be directing or producing their scripts. All the stuff that happens in production and post production will be handled by other people. The main point of this book is for writers to sharpen their skills in the writing craft, and to be able to write sharp scripts that will have an above-average chance of being produced.

"With a good script, a good director can produce a masterpiece. With the same script, a mediocre director can produce a passable film. But with a bad script even a good director can't possibly make a good film. For truly cinematic expression, the camera and the microphone must be able to cross both fire and water. The script must be something that has the power to do this."
– Akira Kurosawa, *Seven Samurai*

Are you simply going to rely on friends and relatives – people unskilled in screenwriting – to help you to polish your script? Do you think they are going to get your script up to the quality expected among those who have spent decades working in the film industry?

"To me, a really good story is like a flower opening. There's an organic quality to it. It's not a mechanical thing."
– Daniel Knauf, *The Blacklist*

There are numerous reasons why it is good to take a screenplay through an incubation workshop – no matter who is going to produce the script. Including, if you are going to make it yourself.

"Ensure that your script is watertight. If it's not on the page, it will never magically appear on the screen."
– Richard E. Grant, *Gosford Park*

I have been paid to overhaul scripts before they have gone into production. One of those gigs happened after I went to an audition to act in the film. I noticed some – actually, many – issues with the script, and mentioned those to the producer. He agreed with me, and paid me to massively overhaul the script. I know that I saved them many production headaches, loads of time, and a whole bunch of money.

I don't think a producer or director should rely only on one person to go through a screenplay before it is put into production. It is good to get feedback from experienced writers, and from other industry professionals.

"I think all writers, all writers, novelists, poets, everyone needs a good editor. Just to be really good at knowing what's good, and what isn't. I read a lot of novels, anyway. But, I read a lot and I think, 'Mmm, where is the editor?' Editing in film is something that's very highly regarded. But, the editing of the screenplay is somehow always put in our hands, and I couldn't write a decent screenplay without a really good editor. I don't think I could."
– Emma Thompson, *Nanny McPhee*

Because I've seen the benefits of workshopping a script, I think that every script would improve by being put through the process. Certainly, spec scripts benefit. Especially before a writer submits the script to anyone in the industry.

"Give me a good script, and I'll be a hundred times better as a director."
– George Cukor, director of *My Fair Lady*

I know that not everyone considers workshops as valuable as I do. Most scripts are not put through a workshop, and they progress along toward production, securing funding, a director, a cast, locations, crew, and being filmed. And then, often, the filmmakers realize, "Hey, maybe there are some issues with the script." In some level of panic, they reach out to someone with experience in analyzing and polishing screenplays. That can cost a load of money. Including in reshooting scenes, and filming additional scenes not in the original script.

"I think writers are vastly underrated and underpaid. It's totally impossible to make a great picture out of a lousy script."
– Billy Wilder, *The Private Life of Sherlock Holmes*

Unfortunately, many people make a film without having enough eyes go through the script. The result is that there are vast numbers of films that end up not being good enough to land distribution.

Maybe the writers, directors, and producers think that someone might do too much rewriting, or that their script is a brilliant masterpiece, or they don't think they have the money to pay for a script consultant. If they don't have those funds, why then would they think that they have the money to take the time and hire a crew to do reshoots and to shoot additional scenes?

Pay now, or pay later. Or, perhaps end up with a film that is so flawed that it will never be watched by paying audiences.

"There's nothing without the writing. It's true. Screenwriters are often not treated or considered with the importance that they should be."
– Danny Boyle, *Slumdog Millionaire*

Producers can spend the money on a pre-production script overhaul. Or, they can spend the money on production delays. Or, they can spend the money on reshoots, and on filming additional scenes. Or, they can film the script with all of its faults, and then end up with something that is so flawed that no distributor will touch it. Fortunes are lost filming garbage scripts.

There are also screenwriters who are involved in the production of their scripts, producing and/or directing, and starring, editing, color grading, and scoring. Some will be successful.

Maybe all of the production rewriting, reshooting, and shooting additional scenes works out, and they end up with a film that goes on to win awards, and lands international distribution deals, and makes vast quantities of money.

"I usually work on the script throughout the whole process. I re-wrote whole sections of *Ida* in prep, during rehearsals, and even during the filming. It's not like there's a script and then I go and execute it. The script is always growing, evolving in my own peculiar method. It's not like the usual film made in the U.S. or even in Britain. It's more like an ongoing process based on a simple structure that then gets complicated, simplified again, complicated again, introduces some characters, takes them out, and slowly distills something in the end that's very simple."
– Pawel Pawlikowski, *Ida*

"I continue writing during the shoot. I don't like it, but it really helps. You get a good feeling about where to make the film shorter. I always like going into shooting with not too reduced a script. I believe there is always something to find out on the shooting day."
– Maren Ade, *Toni Erdmann*

"I consider my job as a screenwriter to pack a script with possibilities and ideas – to create a feast for the filmmaker to pick from."
– Jonathan Nolan, *The Dark Knight*

As a screenwriter, you can pretty much expect to never be done with learning technique and style, and with knowing what is going on in the various branches of the film industry. This is especially true with technology updates, and the changing ways that filmed entertainment is delivered.

"We are all apprentices in a craft where no one ever becomes a master."
– Ernest Hemingway, *The Old Man and the Sea*

If you consider yourself to be such a master of screenwriting that you don't need another set of eyes to go through the screenplay, consider that even Ernest Hemingway didn't consider himself a master of writing.

"If it sounds like writing, I rewrite it."
– Elmore Leonard, *The Moonshine War*

"Rewriting is when writing really gets to be fun. In baseball, you only get three swings and you're out. In rewriting, you get almost as many swings as you want, and you know sooner or later, you'll hit the ball."
– Neil Simon, *The Odd Couple*

Screenwriting is a craft requiring skills that can always be sharpened.

"The truth is, when I started making films, I was terrified. I had a huge difference in what I was writing in the screenplay and what was on the screen after. Now, the more I experience, the more I make movies, the more I feel that the dream is closer to the screen. It comes from experience."
– Denis Villeneuve, *Maelstrom*

If you are going to make screenwriting a career, be tenacious in learning to improve your skills in the craft so that your scripts are up to industry standards. Be sure to only present polished scripts to the people who can be key in getting the scripts produced, and make sure that those scripts are page-turners.

"Everything's always about page-turning, right? What's next? So, if you create questions for audiences, then they'll want to know the answer. Or they begin to formulate possible outcomes. That's the game we play when we're hearing a story unfold. That's the part of what sucks us into a movie."
– Ron Howard, *Grand Theft Auto*

Screenwriting workshops can be especially helpful for a screenwriter at the beginning stages of a career.

As you advance in your career, you can call in your talented network of friends to do table readings of your scripts. That is what many of those in the top of the field do.

Until then, connect with a screenwriting workshop, and use it to your writing – and rewriting – advantage.

"Tap into what you don't want to say. Tap into that secret place, despite the agony, despite the personal pain, over and above the fatigue."
– Arthur Penn, *Alice's Restaurant*

Visit Screenwriting Tribe and see how we do things.

If you are in a region that lacks a screenwriting workshop, consider starting a workshop, using this book and Trottier's books as texts. Other writers have done that.

"I think a writer is suspect if a script isn't spell-checked. I'm an ex-editor, so grammar is important – except, obviously, in dialogue."
– Linda Obst, producer

"Find yourself a sounding board who isn't a parent, sibling, or significant other. Someone who understands the industry, and whose opinion you trust, someone who is there for you 24/7 when you need to vent, pitch ideas, and work through problems. Also, always be working. If I get stuck on a script, I sketch other characters or scenarios, instead of staring at a wall. That's how *Dinner in America* was born."
– Adam Carter Rehmeier, *Henry and Marvin*

"If I could say anything, it is to keep going. Don't go back and fix that first scene. Don't go back and fix that dialogue. Write yourself a little note saying, 'Put in first scene such-and-such.' If you happen to think of something, then get a little stickum and stick that somewhere on the wall. But don't go back, because going back is a trap. It keeps you from going forward. It keeps you from going ahead. Your first enemy, of course, is yourself. Yourself is also that little critic that sits on your shoulder that says, 'This is terrible.' You have to wipe him off your shoulders and keep going. He's the one who says, 'Go back. Go back.' You must get it down on paper. You must sit down and write with no attachment to outcome. Try to distance yourself from what's going to happen to this. No attachment to outcome. I don't know where I ever heard it, but I put it on a little piece of paper, and I had it framed. I have it right in front of me. When I get bogged down, I say, 'No attachment to outcome. Don't worry about what's going to happen to this. Just write the next word.'"
– Anna Hamilton Phelan, *Gorillas in the Mist*

When you write a screenplay, and when you polish a screenplay, always be aware of one thing: the budget that will be needed to film the scenes. You might think that you will have such a large budget that it won't matter. However, if people like Christopher McQuarrie are concerned about budget when they are writing a script, then you would be wise to do the same.

"It used to be I would go in and try to maximize the scope of a given location. I look at a location now and go, 'How much of this can I shoot in the least amount of time?' Kind of get the beautiful, big scope shots of it, and then make sure that the stuff that I owe at the end is the small stuff that I can recreate back on the stage. And you watch *Mission: Impossible*, all of the exposition in the movie – all of the things that are the hardest stuff to figure out, which is the reason why things are happening – you learn all that information in cars and in phone booths, and in small restaurants. You learn them in locations that we can recreate and film that information again, and again, and again. You'll notice that when they're out running around the streets of Paris, they're not saying a lot."
– Christopher McQuarrie, *Mission: Impossible - Rogue Nation*

"Being a kid growing up with Kurosawa films and watching Sergio Leone movies just made me love what it could do to you, and how it could influence you – make you dream."
– Antoine Fuqua, director

"Having a vision for what you want to create is essential."
– Eric Haywood, *Empire*

"Every decision is a financial decision, and every financial decision is a creative decision. You have to marry those two things. So, we can't make movies independent of the (financial) return on that movie."
– Tom Rothman, Sony Motion Picture Group

WHAT STUDIOS WANT

"In Hollywood, story content of movies follows a hierarchy of power, not the relative quality of various ideas. Hollywood does not lack for quality writing. It's just that quality writing commonly has to be sacrificed in order to propel a film into production. A studio needs a star and a director to make a film, so those are the folk who will decide the content. If they don't have the same creative sensibilities, then the content will change."
– Terry Rossio, *Shrek*

While studios keep pumping out lame, repetitive, overbaked, mass marketed sequels, there are likely thousands of original screenplays that could go into production – and, that aren't sequels. They are gathering dust or stuck in hard drives in the homes of struggling screenwriters – and even some successful screenwriters who have had a variety of scripts produced, but they haven't been able to get their masterpieces made.

"I don't write any kind of sequel or remake."
– Bong Joon-Ho, *Mother*

Instead of finding and making spec scripts, studios try to play it safe by producing stuff that is similar to other stuff that has made money. It includes remakes, sequels, prequels, and turning old but successful TV series into films. In other words: Tested material that has proven to sell and has title, story, and image recognition. That is, in difference to untested spec scripts. There are also shequels, which is remaking a movie that formerly starred male actors, and putting female actors in the lead rolls (see the 2016 production of *Ghostbusters*).

"If you look at Hollywood and Broadway, about eight out of ten movies or shows are based on existing (branded) I.P. (intellectual property) – *Crazy Rich Asians, Hamilton, Harry Potter, Lego, Phantom of the Opera, Chicago,* every Marvel movie ever. Even other Tony winners like *Kinky Boots* and *The Band's Visit* are based on independent films. Intellectual property kicks the door down for you. It's a little dispiriting from a pure invention point of view, because you don't get to experience the same creative breakthroughs like *The Descendants* or *Sideways* or *Fargo, Raising Arizona,* or *Dear Evan Hansen* on Broadway. Now, almost everything is based on something. And writers have to acknowledge how the marketplace has changed."

– J. Todd Harris, producer

Because *Baywatch* was a hit TV series, some people thought that it could be made into a successful film – especially if they threw in the world's current biggest star (Dwayne "The Rock" Johnson), a young studly (Zac Efron), and some runway model-type women in bathing suits. The result of that thinking is what was the overhyped *Baywatch* movie released in 2017.

According to IMDb, the budget of *Baywatch* was $69 million. The U.S. box office take was under $60 million. The global box office was about $175 million. So, maybe it made money – depending on how much it cost to pollute Earth by marketing the thing.

For the money that it took to make *Baywatch*, a variety of smaller films could have been made. Likely, over the years, those smaller films would result in more money for the studio than what *Baywatch* brought in.

Consider that – according to IMDb – the budget of *Get Out* was about $5 million. The U.S. box office was about $175 million. And the global box office was about $255 million.

Get Out wasn't a sequel. It didn't have any major stars. It was an original script by Jordan Peele. That should teach the studios a lesson. But, don't count on it.

For the money that it took to produce and globally market *Baywatch*, a dozen or more of the following lower-budget movies could have been made: *I, Tonya, Get Out, Lady Bird, The Florida Project, Three Billboards, The Disaster Artist, Wonder, Drugstore Cowboy, El Mariachi, Hunger, Clerks, Moon, Y Tu Mama Tambien, The Brothers McMullen, Donnie Darko, Once, Milk, American Pie, Halloween, Slumdog Millionaire, Bronson, Billy Elliot, Moonlight, Lost in Translation, Memento, Best in Show, Son of Rambow, Little Miss Sunshine, Cinema Paradiso, Who's Afraid of Virginia Woolf, As Good as It Gets, Waking Ned Devine, Napoleon Dynamite, My Big Fat Greek Wedding, The Cement Garden, Night of the Living Dead, Boyhood, Juno, Rocky, In the Company of Men, The King's Speech, Paranormal Activity, Beginners, Open Water,* and *Lock Stock & Two Smoking Barrels.*

"Studios want to have the sequel without the risk of making the original movie."

– Dan Petrie, *The Assistant*

Like it or not, films for most people in the industry are about making money, not about making culturally relevant art. For most projects, everyone from the producers to the crew, financiers, and distributors are mostly interested in two things: Making money and advancing their careers. Sometimes they get to work on things that they want to watch. Other times, it's simply a job. If your script isn't commercial enough, it is unlikely to get an in-demand director, recognizable cast, the necessary financing, or adequate distribution. While some government funding in the U.S. is available for a limited number of films – through state incentive programs – most films won't benefit from that. Having funding campaigns for films will not bring enough money for most scripts to be produced.

Documentaries are funded differently. They can get grants and patrons, and be helped along financially in ways that theatrical productions aren't. They are made with far less money, and are more likely to benefit from an online funding campaign that gathers money from people who simply want the documentary made so that a concern of theirs will be understood.

Maybe there should be more staged readings of screenplays, acted out by talent, with live audiences. With so many thousands of screenplays, maybe that is one way they can be enjoyed – because the grand majority of them will never be produced, no matter how entertaining they are.

If you can figure out a way to film the project with a micro budget, few sets, and only focus on actors displaying a story through words and actions, perhaps that is the way to go. But, if it doesn't make the money back on the investment, even with a micro-budget, what then?

The Lars von Trier film *Dogville* was cleverly done, with few sets, but lines drawn on a floor to indicate structures. The budget listed on IMDb is ten million. Likely the largest chunk of that cost is related to the large cast of top actors brought to film it in Sweden.

In film, what is truly art, and what is done strictly for money? Can they be the same thing? Should there be a bigger push to support and appreciate truly art films, statement films, revelation films, experimental films, and micro-budget films? By whom, why, and how?

The reality is that if your script is going to be made, it will be subjected to some sort of combination of things that go on with other "commercial" films linked to the studios and established streams of distribution, and tying the project in with some sort of branded content situation, and products that can be sold in combination with the film, and/or a significant trendy music soundtrack, and recognizable "name talent" (now, that might include – cough – a questionably – or non-talented – "social media star") to increase its marketability (and the type of talent that can bring in audiences in many regions of the planet: Especially Asia), and maybe a sequel situation and/or a lead-in to a spinoff and/or bringing the characters into a series.

How will it play and will it get the right attention at the Sundance, Cannes, Toronto, Telluride, Tribeca, Berlin, Venice, and even the Palm Springs and Santa Barbara film festivals? Will it sell into the international market, and will it play on the streaming services? Will it bring in the money?

Not many films have the luck to become "cult" films with followings that last decades, and which then continues the revenue stream. (See: *The Big Lebowski, Erasurhead, Donnie Darko, Princess Bride, Monty Python and the Holy Grail, Get Out, Do the Right Thing, Harold and Maude, Mean Girls, The Rocky Horror Picture Show, Clerks, Labyrinth,* and so forth.)

"I was reading recently about *Apocalypse Now*, one of the one's we'd call one of the greatest films – and it is. They put it out, and, you know, it played in the theaters for fourteen months. Not fourteen weeks. It played for fourteen months. It was never a blockbuster, but it just becomes something you had to see, and they were able to keep it out. That isn't in the realm of possibility. Fourteen weeks isn't even in the realm of possibility anymore."
– Edward Norton, *Motherless Brooklyn*

Is it cinema, or is it spectacle media?

Some people hold the opinion that the large studios are vertically integrated multi-national media companies that are not interested in turning out independent films. Because the big studios are global entertainment companies centered on satisfying stockholders, they should not be expected to supply product for the indie film market. Instead, they are multi-national corporations that are using spinoff and sequel templates to churn out spectacle media that functions as advertisements for merchandise and theme parks, that spotlights off into sequels and spin-offs, and that some say caters to the computer game audience. Spectacle media companies are about creating products that make money to meet quarterly financial goals. They are not about helping to create and distribute films that are culturally significant or socially relevant.

"Many films today are perfect products manufactured for immediate consumption. Many of them are well made by teams of talented individuals. All the same, they lack something essential to cinema: The unifying vision of an individual artist. Because of course, the individual artist is the riskiest factor of all."
– Martin Scorsese, *Silence*

In late 2019, Martin Scorsese received loads of media attention after *Empire* magazine published his comments about the Marvel movies and franchise films with their huge budgets, massive publicity campaigns, and broad global distribution hogging theaters.

"Honestly, the closest I can think of them, as well made as they are, with actors doing the best they can under the circumstances is theme parks. It isn't

the cinema of human beings trying to convey emotional, psychological experiences to another human being."
– Martin Scorsese, to *Empire* magazine

In 2019, *Variety* reported: "The MCU (Marvel Cinema Universe) franchise of 23 films had made more than $22 billion."

"Comics and graphic novels, people have always laughed at them as not being real art or real stories. It's simply not true. Superheroes are our new mythology. At the end of the day, stories are either teaching us lessons, or helping us experience the human condition in different ways."
– Taika Waititi, *What We Do in the Shadows*

In response to the uproar about his comments to *Empire*, Scorsese wrote an opinion piece for the *New York Times* titled *Martin Scorsese: I Said Marvel Movies Aren't Cinema: Let Me Explain*. He wrote: "In many places around this country and around the world, franchise films are now your primary choice if you want to see something on the big screen. It's a perilous time in film exhibition, and there are fewer independent theaters than ever. The equation has flipped, and streaming has become the primary delivery system."
Ironically, Scorsese's film *The Irishman* had just hit theaters, and Netflix.

"We have a theatrical window, which is great. Would I like the picture to play on more big screens for longer periods of time? Of course I would, But, no matter whom you make your movie with, the fact is that the screens in most multiplexes are crowded with franchise pictures."
– Martin Scorsese, about *The Irishman* being a Netflix release.

If a person considers what the big studios release, it could be concluded that the studios don't want spec scripts. Sort of. At least, they don't seem to want to produce many spec scripts. What the large studios join in with to distribute in the form of smaller, indie films is another story.
While many ridiculed Scorsese, he is entitled to his opinion, many people agree with him, and many defend his stance.

"I grew up when I did and I developed a sense of movies – of what they were and what they could be – that was as far from the Marvel universe as we on Earth are from Alpha Centauri.
For me, for the filmmakers I came to love and respect, for my friends who started making movies around the same time that I did, cinema was about revelation – aesthetic, emotional, and spiritual revelation. It was about characters – the complexity of people and their contradictory and sometimes paradoxical natures, the way they can hurt one another and love one another and suddenly come face to face with themselves."
– Martin Scorsese, in *The New York Times, November 4, 2019*

In 2019, Francesca Scorsese wrapped her father's Christmas presents in Marvel character wrapping paper.

How do the studio choices play into the spec script market? It might mean that your spec script will never sell to them. Or, maybe it will. Maybe it will be produced by a smaller company, and then distributed by a large studio – which is one way that they function. Maybe the studio will option your script to take it off the market for a couple of years (a coption), because it is too much like a script that they plan to make – but they don't tell you that reasoning.

Maybe the big studios will do what some have done in the past, and staff departments meant to produce (or purchase and distribute) smaller films, and films for specialized markets: Films made from spec scripts.

What any studio, financier, or distributor is concerned about when considering a script or film is: Will it appeal to a broad enough market to bring in a significant amount of money?

"So many elements go into making a great screenplay. That's why it's so hard to write one. If you take a look at some coverage from a studio, you'll see a grid where the reader has rated the script excellent, good, fair, or poor in such categories as premise, characterization, dialogue, storyline, and production values. The most critical element, though, is jeopardy. Whether it is a physical threat to the protagonist's life (as in thrillers), or a threat to his happiness (as in love stories), danger is what drives the plot. It's what keeps us on the edges of our seats, wanting to know what happens next."
– Michael Ray Brown, *Screenwriting Structure Checklist*

According to Len Amato, President: HBO Films: miniseries and Cinemax, his selection process for a script includes:
• Originality
• A bold statement
• Standing out from the crowd
• Potentially a great role for actors
• Potentially a great story

There will always be audiences wanting romantic comedies, romances, films that families can watch together, inspiring smaller movies, religious films, road trip films, quirky teenage comedies, whodunits, haunting ghost stories, murder mysteries, New Age pieces, dark comedies, thrillers, horror flicks, hero films, and other smaller types of films.

Apparently, studios will always need people to polish and doctor scripts – before those scripts are produced. They will always need people to write scripts that are remakes, prequels, and sequels, and the films made from TV shows. They will need writers to script spinoffs, and to adapt novels, biographies, and nonfiction books into screenplays. And they will need writers to turn news events into screenplays.

That spec script you write might not sell. But, it might be the key to getting you work with the studios – as a writer of some sort, perhaps as a script doctor – maybe as a writer who punches up the drama or romance or comedy, or refashions a script to fit a certain actor. And, you might end up as one of the writers in a room working with other writers who are working on a series.

So, just because they might not buy your spec script doesn't mean that you will never work with the studios.

"The only practical use of a spec for an existing show are the studio diversity programs.

A spec pilot script can have two purposes: A pilot can be something for development, and it can live as a staffing sample – and live as a staffing sample its entire life, and never be developed."
– Marlana Hope, *Grey's Anatomy*

A spec script displaying your skills in the craft of storytelling may simply end up being a ticket into working with the studios on their projects.

"Be so good that they can't ignore you."
– Steve Martin, *Roxanne*

"It's all about putting yourself in a position where people eventually can't say no."
– Rupert Wyatt, *Captive State*

Maybe their interest in your script will somehow work into people noticing it, buying it, funding it, directing it, acting in it, or otherwise helping to get it produced.

"Give the reader what they want, just not the way they expect it."
– William Goldman, *Marathon Man*

"Write something that's going to slap the reader in the face, give them goosebumps, and make them forget they're reading a script."
– Jonathon Hersh, Housefire Management

"If the script does not catch my attention in the first fifteen pages, I stop reading it. This might be the result of bad dialogue, repetition, or derivative work. Especially in the horror genre. For example, I just got an almost carbon copy of *Halloween* on my desk."
– Markus Linecker, Dedicated Talent Management

The first person to read your script at a studio, agency, or management company will likely be a reader – often someone who is an assistant. But there also are people who strictly work as readers. Readers are like factory workers laboring at a conveyor belt. But, instead of inspecting products for flaws before the products get sent to distributors and stores, the readers inspect scripts – before the scripts get sent to their bosses.

"I'm first and foremost interested in the story, the characters."
– David Lean, *A Passage to India*

If you can keep the readers tuned into your script story, and entertained from beginning to end, you have passed one part of the test toward production. Or, toward establishing a working relationship with someone at the studio.

"I am always looking at contest winning scripts, film schools, The Black List website, and, yes, I have my circle of execs and producers who tell me when they have read something great that's unrepped. Also talking to and building relationships with assistants is key, because they are the ones reading a ton and most often the first line of defense when screenplays come in, so they are a great resource for new and undiscovered writers that have the goods."
– Jake Wagner, Good Fear Film + Management

"Beyond persistence, the only advice I ever give to young filmmakers is: Don't be shy in the way you tell a story. Be bold."
– Danny Boyle, *Shallow Grave*

Before you send your script to managers, agents, production companies, and studios, polish it so tightly that it bleeds conflict, contention, and subtext. One way to help get your script in that condition is to take every page of it through a screenwriting workshop.

No matter how polished your script is, if it gets made, do not expect it to be filmed exactly as you wrote it. Expect changes. Experienced writers know that some scenes will be cut, or altered, and maybe new scenes, or parts of scenes will be added or improvised. A character might be cut, or another character might be added. Or, two characters could end up becoming one character.

On set, when there are lines made up by the director, who asks the actors to then try the scene with those lines, it is called "doing alts," as in "alternative lines."

"If a producer asks you to rewrite your script for free before making any kind of deal, only do so if the script will be genuinely improved, and you retain 100% ownership of the material – even if you use some of their ideas. Get an agreement to that effect. Independent producers, in general, like to get some kind of writing credit."
– David Trottier, author *The Screenwriter's Bible*

"Well, improvisation, if I were trying to explain it, is a rehearsal tool. It's not really a method. I don't throw a bunch of people into an area, and say, 'Okay, improv,' and everybody does what they want to do. It just doesn't happen. Improvisation is something that occurs in the rehearsal process. Now, in scenes where actors have to interact, they all protect themselves and they all deliver. I mean, they all became actors in order to create. That's what they want, and so I just insist that they do the creating. What I want to see is something I've never seen before. So how can I explain what that is? It's impossible."

– Robert Altman, *Gosford Park*

"Even failures can turn into something positive, if you just keep going. I wrote a television pilot called *Head of the Family*. CBS didn't want it. It was considered a failure. But, we rewrote it. A year later, it became *The Dick Van Dyke Show*."

– Carl Reiner, *The Trill of It All*

"Whenever you're a screenwriter on other people's movies, sitting at the monitor watching an actor change a line, or do something differently than you imagined it, you think, 'They've just destroyed the scene,' and get depressed. But, as a director, I've found that I kind of enjoyed it, because it liberates the scene and adds an extra layer to the performance. And now I feel that if you shoot a scene exactly as written, it's dangerous, because it can be a little bit dead. You want the actors to improvise based on a mood or an atmosphere they're feeling on set. I wish more screenwriters were allowed in rehearsals and read-throughs, and allowed on set, because dialogue between a writer and an actor is incredibly rewarding."

– Hossein Amini, *Drive*

"The difference between the almost right word and the right word is the difference between the lightning bug and the lightning."
– Mark Twain, *The Adventures of Tom Sawyer*

"When you make a movie, always try to discover what the theme of the movie is in one or two words."
– Francis Ford Coppola, *Megalopolis*

THE LOGLINE

The origin of the term logline is from when studios started owning a variety of scripts. They kept log books containing brief descriptions of the storylines of the scripts that they owned.

A logline is not a page-long synopsis.

A logline is a clever, concise, one or two sentence description that summarizes your script. It is meant to entice people into reading your script.

A logline likely gives an idea of the screenplay's genre, era, setting, conflict, contention, tension, and stakes.

A logline is a marketing tool that teases potential producers, directors, investors, and others with the engaging, riveting, manipulative and/or ironic predicament of the screenplay's story centered around an interesting, watchable, clever character – or an ensemble of relevant characters.

A logline might raise a question that the reader then wants answered by reading the script. Or, it stokes a concern or offers a puzzle that the reader will by confounded by and factor and anticipate solutions to as they read the script.

A longline gives us an idea of who the protagonist is, and who or what they are up against. It gives us an idea of why the person must overcome or fight for something. It makes us want to read the script to find out how the protagonist works through the predicament, and if they accomplish that thing.

Yes, attempt to put that all in one or two sentences. Shorter sentences, rather than longer sentences. Even if it is few words that only imply the situation in a clever way that triggers interest.

A well-written logline is likely not going to be longer than any single one of the six previous paragraphs on this page.

What a logline is not is a drawn-out, wordy, detailed description of the story within the screenplay.

When writing a logline, try for one or two sentences. Less is more.

Example of a logline:

A woman awakes to find her city abandoned, other than for some suspicious, disease-ravaged survivalists. She has a memory of building a time machine, and realizes that she must find the machine to return to the past to prevent what caused the end of humanity.

I made up that logline as I was writing this. Maybe some would say it is too long.

Here's an exercise: Rewrite that logline into a shorter version.

The Nicholl Fellowship has posted a list of loglines from scripts that have placed high in that contest.

(Search: Screenplay loglines.)

"To get me actually writing, you have to strike something inside, you have to hit a power main to get the energy. You have to strike something you care about."
— Rian Johnson, *Looper*

THE SPEC SCRIPT MARKET

Screenwriters in the early decades of filmmaking were often under contract as studio employees. It was common for contracted screenwriters to produce a certain number of script pages per day.

Besides being hired to write scripts based on the ideas of others to keep Hollywood studios busy producing content for the increasingly global film theater market, contracted writers adapted novels, biographies, comic books, news and historical events, mythical stories, and even cultural situations, songs, and poems into screenplays.

"The wise screenwriter is he who wears his second-best suit, artistically speaking, and doesn't take things too much to heart. He should have a touch of cynicism, but only a touch. The complete cynic is as useless to Hollywood as he is to himself. He should do the best he can without straining at it. He should be scrupulously honest about his work, but he should not expect scrupulous honesty in return. He won't get it. And when he has had enough, he should say goodbye with a smile, because for all he knows he may want to go back."
— Raymond Chandler, *Strangers on a Train*

While employed screenwriters continue to this day (particularly on the staff of episodics, procedurals, anthologies, limited series, sitcoms, and serials), since the mid-20th century, a market developed for spec scripts. That is, scripts written by anyone who wants to write a screenplay with the speculative goal of selling the script to producers, studios, stars, or directors.

Most spec scripts are stories originating in the minds of the writers. Some spec scripts are based on true events. Others are a response to cultural or political situations. They might revolve around a setting that is in the world of business, technology, science, medicine, law, crime, gambling, underground clubs, the military, politics, religion, entertainment, news, sports, games, school, children, or family and friends. Others are based on mythology, or they are based on novels or biographies that the writers have the rights to.

"Interestingly, I never thought I'd do an adaptation. I've also been quite against them. I think trying to translate one medium to another is wrong. I never really felt that books fitted into film. Generally, people are disappointed, aren't they?"
– Andrea Arnold, *Wuthering Heights*

"Any novel has the advantage of being able to describe both external behavior and internal behavior. Screenplays don't have that luxury at all. It's watching external behavior. So, even if you're faithful to a novel, and a scene feels like its faithful to a novel, if it works on screen, you have made changes to it.

The thing that comes out with adaptations is, you have to work as hard as you do on an original script. If you turn in to a producer – or director or studio or exec – an ungodly mess that's really faithful to the novel, you're gonna be replaced by another writer."
– Jim Uhls, *Fight Club*

To those writing scripts based on the materials (intellectual property = I.P.) of other writers:

• Do not adapt a book into a screenplay – unless you own the rights to the book. Or the book is so old that the copyright has expired, and the rights are now public domain – such as a book written hundreds of years ago.
    (Search: Books in public domain.)

• Do not write a sequel or prequel to a novel or other piece of fiction – unless you own the rights to that material. Or, the rights to that fiction piece are in the public domain

• Do not write a sequel or prequel to a film – unless you have the rights to do so.

• Do not write a script based on an old TV show or film – unless you have the rights to do so.

• Consult with an intellectual rights or entertainment attorney to clarify any concerns relating to the above writing scenarios.

You can start to get an understanding of screenplay sales and legal issues by reading Breimer's *The Screenwriter's Legal Guide*. Also, read: *The Pocket Lawyer for Filmmakers*, by Thomas Crowell.

"Art Buchwald has shown that in the world of Hollywood the elusive term 'net profits' has often been interpreted as if seen through a funhouse mirror.

Indeed, Hollywood has historically held a rather cavalier attitude toward writers' services. For these reasons alone, writers and their agents need all the knowledge they can get."
  – Stephen F. Breimer, Esq., author *The Screenwriter's Legal Guide*

- If you are going to submit a script to a studio fellowship program, you may be asked to write a script based on an episodic, procedural, anthology, or sitcom series that has been in, or is in, production. Only then should you consider writing a script based on material that you do not own the rights to – and do it only for submitting to the studio fellowship program, in relation to their list of approved shows.

- If you want to adapt material (intellectual property) written by another writer – such as a book in the public domain – make sure there is not some sort of legal bind. It can be financially restrictive to obtain the rights to newer books. You might be lucky and get some new book just as it hits the market, and pay a relatively small amount to option the rights to adapt that. You might need connections within the publishing industry to know which book might become a hot property. Read new book reviews. If you are lucky, the new book you option will then become a hit, and win awards – which would make your script more valuable. In your favor with newer books is that authors often have an idea that their book can be turned into a film.

"The simple act of condensing around ten hours of filmable material into 90 to 120 minutes inevitably means that compromises have to be made. Screenwriting, compared to novel writing, is cave painting. You want the images that stand out boldest and tell the story. The HBO series *The Wire* is often referred to as 'novelistic.' In some ways, I feel that the series or miniseries may be the best way for the novel to be adapted for the screen."
  – Irvie Welsh, author *Trainspotting*

"I guess my approach to adapting books is to treat them with a deep respect on one level, and at another part them to one side and go, 'I'm doing something completely different here.'"
  – Simon Beaufoy, *Slumdog Millionaire*

"Whole subplots and characters were shed, and with them some of the subtleties of characterization and ambiguities in relationships. What it gained, however, was a focused, driven plot. The changes didn't bother me. Books – even simple, spare ones like *Girl with a Pearl Earring* – shuttle back and forth in time, repeat themselves, go in and out of their characters' heads, and leave gaps for the reader to fill in. No wonder the storytelling (in screenwriting) has to be different (than novel writing).'"
  – Tracy Chevalier, author *Girl with a Pearl Earring*

While some spec scripts are optioned or purchased, even fewer make it into production.

Some spec scripts that get produced never make it to the screen, fail to land distribution, or are abandoned sometime during the production process.

"Nobody ever set out to make a bad movie. Movies are comprised of tens of thousands of individual creative and financial decisions. Some of those decisions go awry along the way. But, it's never a matter of intentions.'"
– Tom Rothman, Sony Motion Picture Group

It is not unheard of for a film to be abandoned when it is part way through production. It may have lost its funding, or there were disagreements among the filmmakers, or there was a death or health problem among the key players in the production.

Your spec scripts could work as your tickets into the career that you want. Even if what happens to them is completely the opposite of what you would have expected.

"For me, it's a matter of principle that I have never directed other people's scripts, not even while I was working in TV. There were a few cases where scriptwriters would provide me with material, but I would always turn that into something else entirely. Those writers weren't very happy, unsurprisingly, but as a director I had the upper hand. That's also when I noticed that I'm not made for collaboration. There are people who can work together on a script – the Coen brothers, for example. To me, that's a complete mystery."
– Michael Heneke, *Happy End*

"I think screenwriting gave me more of an affinity for plot. My first novel, *Me and Earl and the Dying Girl*, doesn't have a very sophisticated roadmap. But screenwriting required me to learn a higher level of plottiness, and I tried to bring that to *The Haters*."
— Meg Cabot, *The Princess Diaries*

BOOK TO SCRIPT

"As a writer of both novels and screenplays, I can say that screenwriting is a vastly rewarding creative life – if you fight hard enough to do it on your own terms. Whether I write books or not, my screenwriting life has been creatively rewarding and remains so."
— John Fusco, *Young Guns*

"Write a lot. When I first came to Los Angeles, I was able to get an agent through writing two novels, and having a short story published. What she found useful about the way I worked was that I didn't just have one screenplay, I had three or four. Some were contemporary, some period stories, so that when somebody asked for a writing sample, she could send them the one that seemed to resemble what they were looking for the most. Plus, I got the exercise of having written those scripts. I didn't obsess about one story, I just kept moving on and wrote about what interests me."
— John Sayles, *Limbo*

"Sometimes we cling to a project because we don't want to admit we were wrong, or the idea isn't good enough. We try to force that square peg into a round hole. No matter how much we shove, it'll never fit.
Maybe the answer is to switch formats. I have friends who are adapting their feature scripts into TV shows, realizing these characters and circumstances are better suited for a hundred one-hour episodes than a single two-hour film. Or maybe your idea is best suited as a novel, one to be adopted after its Amazon or e-book success."
— Jeanne Veillette Bowerman, co-founder of ScriptChat

Some writers think that if they turn their script into a book, it will increase the chances of it being made into a film or series.

If you write the book, and the book doesn't sell, the producers will look at that as a fail. They want to be involved with winning projects. It is unlikely that your book that sold little to no copies will make them recognize it as a hot property. But, maybe someone will. Good luck with that.

"Writing a novel is one of my great pleasures – writing to find out what the book is about, writing pleases myself as long as my publisher likes my work – but I have seldom enjoyed writing screenplays. Whether an adaptation of one of my books or an original, it seems always to become work and not much fun. I supposed that's because it has to be revised so many times to meet everyone's perception of what the story is about."'
– Elmore Leonard, *52 Pick-Up*

Books that sell well, become known, and they get the attention of Hollywood. If the book was published by a major publisher, those companies have their network of people who bring the book to certain industry players. If the book is by an author who has already written one or more hit books, the process of selling it to the film industry is in the works by the publishing date.

"It never occurred to me that my novel *In the Cut* might one day be made into a movie. A friend had sent the manuscript to a Hollywood book agent, who said that the story was so offensive that he not only could not represent it, but recommended that it never be published. So, my expectations were not high. Consequently, some months later, when Nicole Kidman offered to buy the film rights, I was surprised. My first meeting was with Nicole and the director Jane Campion. Jane made it clear that, no matter how much work I might do on the screenplay, in the end it would be necessary for her to write her own draft. I thought that a very good idea."
– Susanna Moore, *In the Cut*

Sometimes a book is considered hot before it is published, and that is a whole other game – usually involving some established writer, or the book is about a relevant and topical issue: Such as a race within an industry to accomplish something, or the book is about a politician, a corporate leader, or a famous person, or some combination of a riveting and/or newsworthy situations.

But, who writes the screenplay version? Often, it isn't the author. The studio hires an established screenwriter to turn the book into a screenplay. Even then, the script might not make it into production. Maybe other writers are brought in to try to save it.

The process of turning a book into a film or series can take years.

"The movies are fun, but I'm a novelist. In many ways, screenwriting is much easier than writing novels. I find screenplays twenty times easier to write than a novel."'
– Nicholas Sparks, *The Last Song*

It is true that you can send a book to a production company without a manager or agent. But, will they read it? The relevance of the book, how well it is selling, the cover design, the quality of the writing, and many other elements play into if they will pick it up, or toss it.

Perhaps there is a book out there that has been selling well, or once did, and you can purchase the rights to that, and try to get that made into a film or series. That can also take years. However, it has been done, many times.

You can also consider old books that are in the public domain, and turn one of those into a script. Or, modernize the story, and make it into a present-day story, or use the story as the basis for a science fiction script.

(Search: Novels in public domain.)

"Screenwriting is a terrible way to make a living and I always try to talk anyone out of it. Until you sit in a story meeting with studio executives with no particular ability – or actors who haven't even graduated high school telling you exactly how to change your script – you haven't experienced what it's really like to be a screenwriter in Hollywood. Also, unlike novelists and playwrights, you don't own the copyright on your original material. It hurts when you sell a project you love and then suddenly the project you really cared about will never see the light of day."
– Amy Holden Jones, *Indecent Proposal*

As far as turning your script into a book: Do you want to be a screenwriter, or an author? Some people have been successful at both.

"But, here's the thing: What you do as a screenwriter is you sell your copyright. As a novelist, as a poet, as a playwright, you maintain your copyright."
– Beth Henley, *Crimes of the Heart*

"The more screenwriting you do, the more you become aware that particular scenes aren't going to end up in the movie – because they're too expensive. That has perhaps changed the way I think about writing novels, actually, because I now write expensive scenes whenever I can."
– Nick Hornby, *Brooklyn*

"There are so few social model novels or stories for men. For women, every season there's a new *Joy Luck Club* and a new *How to Make an American Quilt*. Just all of these different models in which women can come together and talk about their lives. And, if you are a man, you've got either *Fight Club* or you have *The Dead Poet's Society*. And that is really it. So, we don't really have a lot of narrative that depict to men a role or a kind of script in which to come together and talk about their shit."
– Chuck Palahniuk, *Fight Club*

"The creation of an idea, the following of a story germ, the building up of plot, the creating of people of flesh and blood character: These are not easy things. They are extremely difficult. But, conversely, don't be put off by the fact that this month you can't do it, and next month is maybe even harder. This is, if not a lifetime process, it's awfully close to it.

The writer broadens, becomes deeper, becomes more observant, becomes more tempered, becomes much wiser over a period of time, passidly. It is not something that is injected into him by a needle. It is not something that comes up in a wave of flashing explosive light one night, and says 'Eureka! I've got it!' And then, proceeds to write the great American novel in eleven days. It doesn't work that way. It's a long, tedious, tough, frustrating process. But never, ever be put aside by the fact that it's hard. It if weren't hard, everybody would be a writer, and we'd have nothing but books – slovenly, grubby, filthy, heavy, grungy books weighing down our world. The fact is that it is a very selective process, unique to a few is what makes literature so valuable and so wonderful."

– Rod Serling, *The Storm in Summer*

"You can't clobber a reader while he's looking. Divert his attention, then clobber him and he never knows what hit him."
– Flannery O'Connor, *A Good Man is Hard to Find*

"Don't think about it as a spec script marketplace. Think of it as a writer marketplace. Rather than chasing the sale, continue to write your stories in your voice. Create a library of quality material. Build your network of relationships, and look for writing assignments."
– Stephanie Palmer, screenwriting coach

"The pitch deck/video being good and the script being good are two separate things. Could be a bad pitch deck and a great script, could be a great pitch deck and a bad script. One isn't necessarily an indicator of the other."
– John Zaozirny, producer and manager at Bellevue Productions

TV Spec Scripts

"Write! I know it sounds daft, but you'd be amazed at how many people tell me they'd love to be a TV writer, but when I ask them what they've written, they say 'not much.' In order for agents and producers to be willing to take a risk on you as a new writer, you need to have a good number of exciting, original, full-length screenplays under your belt. Having at least three or four scripts that show off your skills at creating fresh stories, exciting characters, and smart dialogue is vital.

P.S.: Don't write fan fiction versions of existing shows. In the U.K., producers only want to read your own original ideas."
– Chris Lindsay, *Casualty*

While spec screenplays for film can be sold to producers in a number of countries, the TV market is largely limited to places like Los Angeles, New York, Atlanta, London, and some other large cities where TV shows are produced. Because of this, it is most likely that those writing TV scripts would increase their chances of selling their script if they lived in one of those cities. L.A., New York, and Atlanta are where TV writers can network, hold meetings, attend seminars, workshops, and events, and otherwise be engaged in the industry. Video conferencing helps, and will be more and more common.

Of course, with new technology, lower-cost digital cameras, and smart phones, a person can make a TV series anywhere. Children using smart phone cameras make and post videos on YouTube that are more entertaining than some studio productions.

While in the past it was common for people to write spec TV scripts based on shows that are already in production, today it is more common to write an original spec TV script, and try to sell it, or to get investors to help fund the making of it – even if only a short version of a pilot episode to use as a sample to draw in talent, money, and producers. One reason this is so is because show producers, directors, writers, and even stars could be contractually forbidden from looking at scripts written on spec for the shows that employ them.

Many writers aim to have scripts ready for the TV "pilot season." In years before the start of Netflix, Amazon, Hulu, DisneyPlus, The Criterion Channel, and other online streaming platforms (direct to consumer = DTC platforms), pilot season was in the earlier part of the year, including when pilots were cast, filmed, and sold. Pilot season has become diluted, with pilots being cast and filmed year-round.

"If you go to streaming services and you pitch an idea that sounds like it could be on network TV, they don't want it. The streaming services say, 'Bring me something that is new and exciting and something we haven't seen before – bring me characters we haven't seen before.' And I think this speaks to, in the 500 television services universe we live in, how you've got to go to new, exciting, scary places if you're going to get any kind of attention whatsoever."
– Marc Cherry, *Why Women Kill*

"You can't control whether your show is going to resonate with people. All you can do is put your nose to the grindstone, write the best script you can – and hope that someday one of your stars grows up to marry the Prince of England."
– Aaron Korsh, *Suits*

Some writers are in the position to adapt the all-or-nothing attitude during pilot season, diving in full force with their spec script, trying to get the right parties interested, making the connections, getting the financing, casting the right actors, and so forth on their way to filming the thing. Then, presenting it to the decision-makers who can order a full season. There might be an order for half a season, with the thought being that if the show shows promise, the rest of the season's episodes will be ordered, then filmed. Fortunes are spent – or wasted – during the process.

Pilots are often filmed on location, rather than on a sound stage. I've worked on pilots that are filmed around Los Angeles. If the show lands a season (or half-season) order, some of those locations are then recreated on a sound stage – including lobbies of buildings that were filmed in during the pilot, offices and school hallways that were filmed in during the pilot, hospitals, police stations, courthouses, cafes, and houses that were filmed in during the pilot, and so forth. It's an expensive process. Your script has to be so good that someone or some company will want to put up the millions for all of that stuff. A script is an investment proposal to the money people.

One thing that also happens during the transition from a pilot episode to full production of the series is that some of the actors who appeared in the pilot may lose their jobs, other actors with more recognition may take on those roles, and parts of – or all of – the pilot may be refilmed using those actors. The actors who appeared in the pilot might be excellent actors, but then a new star actor is brought in, and the casting has to be done to play along with the dynamics and look of that actor. If an actor who played the mother in the pilot is replaced, the actor who played the son might also be replaced, simply based on appearance – unless adoption is part of that story.

Things about the pilot that also might be changed are locations, including moving the setting to another city. The pilot may have been filmed in Toronto, Atlanta, Cleveland, Vancouver, Albuquerque, or Los Angeles, but then – for any number of reasons – the series ends up being filmed in a different city. The move could also trigger changing the color palette and tone of the show.

I worked on one struggling show that was brought back for a second season. Prior to the start of the second season, the set was repainted with darker colors. Furniture was brought in with darker colors. The wardrobe of the actors was darker and more textured than the first year. The hair and makeup palette of the actresses was changed. The tone of the scenes was more serious. It made it halfway through the second season, then the network canceled the show.

To sell a TV spec script, it is likely that you already have to be in the TV industry, such as anything from a writer's or producer's assistant who worked up the career ladder, or have some other *in*. There is a matter of random selection in any spec script sale. To increase your chances, get work in some area of TV, and use your contacts to network with those in the industry.

"Thinking that you're going to write one script and become an overnight sensation is naïve. It happens to only the smallest percentage of writers. Most of us devote years and years of time to building our career. I've also learned that as much as I love being a writer, it's equally important to have a life outside of the business."
– Hollie Overton, *Shadowhunters*

It is likely that you have to be a successful person in Hollywood – or own the rights to an extremely hot project with relevant talent connected to it – to get a pilot script picked up to go straight-to-series. That is when an entire season gets funded on the presumption that it is going to be a good investment as it will be a reasonably popular – or a massively hit – show.

If you are someone who has had major success in Hollywood, such as a writer, director, star, comic, or "social media star" (who hasn't done something globally shameful [see: Logan Paul sued over forest video]) with an international following, you are more likely to get a straight-to-series deal.

To increase your chances of making it as a TV writer, write more than one script. Write the scripts for several pilots for several original shows created in your brain. Decide which one is the most commercially viable.

"If you're looking for your first break, newer scriptwriters should focus on something a little more out there, to stand out and get in the game."
– Zach Cox, Circle of Confusion management

Consider writing the first three episodes of your most promising spec. But, also consider that what will sell your series is the script of the first "pilot" episode. It is likely that the pilot is what they will use to judge your series, your concept, your writing skill, and your talent in the craft. What they may only want to see in addition to the pilot is an outline of one or more episodes. But, do not go overboard with your presentation by shoving a whole stack of episodes – or outlines of them – in front of their face. Maybe they will like to see the other scripts or what you have as the show's pitch bible.

Write the first episodes of two more ideas that you have for other shows. And, have ideas of what you would do with the second and third episodes of those shows.

As an exercise, outline a show bible for the most commercially viable pilot that you have written.

Some would say that it isn't much use to have a full series "bible" for your TV spec script. But, it probably isn't a bad idea to know what a show bible is, and to at least outline one for your show. It could help you to know your show by creating a series bible. There might also be people who want to see your pitch bible, or at least know that you have one outlined. (Search: TV series bible and TV pilot pitch bible.)

Read a variety of books about TV production and about writing for TV (such as *Story Maps: TV Drama: The Structure of the One-Hour Television Pilot*, by Daniel P. Calvisi and *The TV Showrunner's Roadmap*, by Neil Landau). Also, consider the books on TV writing that are in the collection of your local library.

If you are in LA, get to the WGA Library at 3rd and Fairfax, and read a variety of scripts, pitch decks, and other material from TV shows. Also, get to the Margaret Herrick Library at the Academy of Motion Picture Arts & Sciences on La Cienega and Olympic.

The more you understand about the specifics of writing and production, the more prepared you will be to deal with professionals in the industry.

Polish your scripts. Make sure they are correctly formatted, and as sharply written as you can possibly make them. Workshop them with other writers who are also writing TV spec scripts.

A script for a specific show currently on air should only be written under contract. That is, as a hired writer for that show. If you don't own the rights to it, you won't be able to do anything with it.

However, there is one specific reason to write a spec script of a series that has been or is currently in production. That is, to write a script to be used for submission to a fellowship program, which I explain later.

Don't write a spec script on a show presently in production and try to get it to people involved with that production.

You likely don't want to write a spec script for an old show that might end up going back into production, as shows like *Will and Grace*, *Full House*, *Arrested Development*, and *Rosanne* did.

Otherwise, a TV spec script should only be written for submission to the various studio fellowship programs – if that is what they want.

A studio writing program might ask you to write a script based on a show with which that particular studio is not involved. They may ask you to submit a script based on a show produced by a different studio. That way, they are not looking at scripts based on their shows. Looking at scripts based on their shows could place them in a legal bind.

In other words, the reason people write spec TV scripts based on shows that are currently in production is that some studio fellowship programs ask that writers submit scripts based on existing shows. That way, when the judges for – or the administrators of – the fellowship program read the submissions, they will be able to tell if the writer has what it takes to write a relevant script for a show. They want to know that the writer understands and can write guided by the dynamics of a show. If so, the writer can be hired to help write for a new show that is about to go into production, or can be placed on staff of an existing show.

Or, they might want to see your original spec scripts (not based on a show that has already been produced – but based on your own creation).

Before you are hired as a staff writer, it is likely that you will need to go through the fellowship program, or work your way up the ladder in the field in some other manner. Be creative in carving your path.

Because writing fellowships might ask for scripts based on existing shows, and a writer who wants to make it in TV would be expected to discuss various TV shows with people who are in the position of hiring, it is good for writers wanting to write for TV to follow recent hit shows, and understand the story and character dynamics of a variety of shows. Writers should have ideas for current shows – and not only shows that have been out of production.

The days of writing a spec script of an existing series, and selling that to the producers of that show, and perhaps getting on staff of that show are said to be as over as landline home phones. But, maybe you will be someone who will break through that way. While I would advise a writer to not count on it happening, I'm no prophet. Especially if you already have major connections, you can create your own path to success that perhaps others can't follow.

Other than for submitting to studio writing programs, if you are going to write a TV spec script, base it on your own ideas, your own concept, on characters you created in your mind, and strictly on your own imagination. Do not base it on a show that has been on, or currently is on the air.

Keep your eyes and mind open to the possibilities of taking non-traditional pathways to success in the TV and film writing profession.

"I think that the Internet is going to affect the most profound change on the entertainment industries combined. And we're all going to be tuning into the most popular Internet show in the world, which will be coming from some place in Des Moines."
– Steven Spielberg, *Poltergeist*

"It was so much easier for guys of one generation, because I don't have to go to L.A. I could make my own. I didn't have to make an exploitation film or to prove I was a filmmaker, and had some value. I made a film from my own backyard that actually got a national audience. That would have been unthinkable ten years before, twenty years before. I didn't have to move to L.A., New York, or San Francisco, or anywhere. I kind of stayed where I was, in Austin. The next film I had, *Dazed and Confused*, was set in Austin, or in Texas. So, it just made sense for me to shoot there. It was cheaper."
– Richard Linklater, *A Scanner Darkly*

Because of the vast number of ways that content is being produced for network TV, cable TV, streaming services, web channels, and specialty markets, the need for screenwriters to write content has expanded. The number of scripts being registered with the WGA and the U.S. copyright office has increased. It doesn't seem to be slowing down.

"To survive, you have to withstand the changes in the business. This business has gone through so many changes since I was young, and now it is on to something else. It is all weird today, for me, because I'm from the old times. You just have to keep adapting. Isn't that Darwinism? The creature that adapts to its environment survives."
– John Carpenter, *Village of the Damned*

Those writers who sharpen their skills, and who write clever, correctly formatted, broadly commercial scripts, and who pay attention to the industry are likely to be the ones to get the work.

Read the industry trades (*The Hollywood Reporter* and *Variety*, and the WGA magazine: *Written By*), and learn about the industry, who the power players are in it, and who might be interested in your type of writing.

"My movies are based in genre, which is a universal language. Everybody speaks it."
– Bong Joon-Ho, *Parasite*

Rather than try to chase a genre that you think is selling, consider what you might be naturally attracted to as far as a genre and tone, and write that script.

"Saying that Hollywood is buying thrillers, I have never written a thriller. Guess what? Next week they will be buying romantic comedies. You can't chase them hard enough and it is soul crushing to do that. You lose track of yourself.
Your job in life is to find your voice as a writer. If you lose your voice, you know, then what is the point?"
– Caroline Thompson, *The Addams Family*

An experience I had with a studio writing program was submitting a script, and they liked it. I met with them, and they told me that they liked it, and they described things about it that they liked, including that I wrote a strong female character. They clearly read my script. But, when we were alone, I was told by the person who ran the program, "You know, we aren't looking for Caucasian men." Awkward. I wanted to ask, but I didn't ask: "How about if you simply look for talented writers?" I understand their goal: To give opportunities where opportunities were denied. They are trying to correct the many wrongs of certain people being overlooked, ignored, and oppressed for generations.

If you are one who can write what content providers (networks, streaming services, etc.) are seeking, and you make the connections, but also have a variety of scripts ready to be submitted to agents, managers, producers, directors, stars, and others: Take aim and make the moves. That is especially so if you are a woman, a non-Caucasian writer, or among the denied, as there are opportunities open to you that have barely – or never – existed – including with fellowship and mentorship programs, production companies and studios, and contests and writing labs seeking to discover talent. Get on it!

"I feel this market has welcomed female directors and producers with meetings, but then you start to think, 'Am I getting this meeting just because I am a woman? I want to be in these meetings because I have something strong I am selling, not just because I am a woman.'"
– Tiffany Pritchard, casting director

No matter what the reason is for getting a meeting with the decision-makers, work it. Be confident in your talent, without being a braggart. Perhaps the business relationship will develop into something pleasantly unexpected for your career. Even if you don't sell your script, holding a meeting as a writer with a producer, development executive, director, or other person established in the business could open opportunities to be a writer for hire – or a writer who has their script produced.

"A lot of writing jobs come along because someone, somewhere is suddenly under the gun and needs someone they know and trust to come in and deliver. You want to be the name that jumps into their mind first, and you don't do that by hustling them, you do it by building that credibility with your work."
– Nicholas Thurkettle, *Black Friday*

"This over used term: Passion. I'll just say that there is a reason that some clichés are true, and passion is really important – whether it's a limited series, or a continuing series. It is important when you get in front of executives that you show a real, genuine passion, and I know that's what all of us look for at HBO. Story is king. The creators are kings and queens, and we are just looking for something that is really meaningful to filmmakers, and that we think that can connect to an audience."
– Len Amato, President of HBO Films: miniseries and Cinemax

"General meetings are incredibly important. You have to impress and nail them every time – even if they don't lead to a sale. Because the more people calling back to your reps to tell them how wonderful you are the more doors they will open for you."

– Moises Zamora, *American Crime*

"A lot of screenwriters have a drawer of unsold scripts that they cut their teeth on. I don't have one. Everything I've written – after my first spec – I wrote on assignment. Everything I've written was work."

– Jon Spaihts, *Doctor Strange*

A producer or production company with funding for an unwritten script may hire you to write the script. You will then be a commissioned writer.

It is a good idea to have contracts looked over by an industry-experienced entertainment attorney, before you sign. Doing so with an intellectual rights attorney who does not live in L.A., New York, Atlanta, London, or other major TV production capital, could end up being more problematic than a solution. So, if you look for an attorney for your writing contracts, consider those with experience in the field. You can find them by going to IMDbPro, searching for successful writers, and see if their page lists their legal representation. Even if those law firms won't take you on, they might be able to refer you to a different attorney who represents writers.

Another writing assignment scenario is that a producer or production company already has a script written, but they need someone to overhaul it, and incorporate a list of ideas that the producers have – and/or director has – for the show. Maybe they hired a star actor, and they need the script to be restyled in tune with what that star can do – or agrees to do. (The talent who become "attached" to a project are known as "elements." They can include an established or a promising director, producer, D.P., actor(s), and writer(s). Financiers and studios consider the elements when they look at which projects they want to fund or green light or give a "go.")

"As far as the filmmaking process is concerned, stars are essentially worthless – and absolutely essential."

– William Goldman, *Wild Card*

"If you want to attach a star, then you really need to have a great protagonist. A protagonist who is really active, who is really initiating the action of the movie, who's responsible for the forward momentum of the narrative. And perhaps there's a transformational arc there – because that's what actors want to play."

– Christopher Lockhard, *The Inside Pitch*

If you are hired under contract to write or overhaul a script, do read up on the WGA pay and other compensation and credit minimums for that type of work agreement. Don't depend on agents, managers, or attorneys to explain everything to you. They won't.

Be the one who does your research and looks out for yourself.

Even if you do not belong to the WGA, familiarize yourself with the WGA's Minimum Basic Agreement contract (MBA contract). Use their base rates as minimums for how you will expect to be compensated for work. However, as you are starting out, you might expect to be paid less – far less.

Don't agree to "sell" your script for "deferred pay," or for "net points." That is basically giving it away. Get paid up front, and don't expect to get paid after it is made. It is also unlikely that you will be getting residuals – for most screenwriting gigs. If any producer tells you that you will get IMDb credit, that is nonsense and tells you they are a bit scammy. Don't concern yourself with getting IMDb credit.

Have an entertainment attorney and your manager look over your contract.

You can find the WGA contract on the WGA website. Study it – especially if you want a career in screenwriting.

If you are dealing with a script sale offer from a party who is not a signatory of the WGA, it is even more important that you have any contract looked over by an intellectual property (I.P.) rights attorney. Do not sign a contract under pressure. Producers word contracts in their favor – likely with the help of their attorney. Make sure that the contract is also worded in ways that are in your favor. An I.P. attorney can help you negotiate the wording of the contract.

The more you know about what you will be dealing with as a pro screenwriter – including contracts – the more prepared you will be.

Do write a variety of your own scripts. Format them correctly – according to if they are film or one-hour episodics, anthologies, limited series (mini-series), single-cam sitcom, or the slightly different type of formatting used for multi-cam sitcoms.

For one-hour commercial TV, you can format the script as a film script. Labeling the teaser, acts, and tag in a one-hour spec script can be more of a distraction (however, it's not wrong – and might be a good idea as it could help position the script in the reader's mind as a TV show). Also, consider that with the popularity of commercial-free streaming, there are no commercial breaks (but, that can be different depending on the streaming service – as some have an option for subscribers to pay more to have commercial-free programming), so it may not be necessary to indicate the commercial breaks – which is basically where the act breaks would be labeled.

If you are going to indicate the teaser, acts, and tag in a spec script, those would fit better in a half-hour script – especially in a single-cam or multi-cam sitcom script. TV scripts also have what are called "buttons" in scenes, which is a clever bit of dialogue or action that can turn audience focus, and cue interest in what will happen in the next scene. That button might also be a "McGuffin," or "MacGuffin," also known as a "plot coupon" that is a device used to tilt the story or plot, and has something significant for a character to trigger their action (such as they want to find a certain thing, that then ends up sending them on their adventure, during which all sorts of stuff happens, which is what engages us), but is meant for only the character trigger, and doesn't have much of any other use. That also might be considered "Schmuck bait" – an obvious but cheap twist, event, dialogue, and that has to do with a turnoff, or want, or hunt that is meant to trigger audience focus, interest, hope, anticipation, or reaction. (The term MacGuffin is often attributed to Alfred Hitchcock, but the term reportedly was made up by screenwriter Angus MacPhail.)

For sitcom formatting specifics, see *The Screenwriter's Bible*.

As mentioned elsewhere, the Tribe workshop doesn't workshop multi-cam sitcom scripts. Multi-cam scripts are a different format than single-cam scripts, one-hour scripts, short film scripts, and film scripts. Some of the many differences are that in multi-cam sitcom scripts the sounds are sometimes given their own line, parentheticals are on the same line as dialogue, certain things are underlined and/or capitalized, acts are labeled, and so forth.

"We wrote over thirty screenplays before selling one professionally. Every early script was challenging and painful. Each one ended in disappointment. But we didn't stop writing – because it's a joy to create. No matter the outcome. The work is always the reward."
– Scott Beck and Bryan Woods, *A Quite Place*

If you feel stalled in trying to get a career in order, try producing one of your scripts – for as little money as possible. The creators of the series *It's Always Sunny in Philadelphia* shot their pilot for less than $1,000.

"The key is never to look to others for permission. Do it yourself, at whatever level you currently find yourself. You can buy a great camera for cheap. Get Avid on your computer, and distribute your work on YouTube. You are your voice. You don't look for it, you don't find it, you are it. So just do it. Get out of here. Start making a film."
– Alexander Payne, *Sideways*

Pitch Deck Creation
If you are making a pitch deck, you can use images that are copywritten, because you aren't selling or reproducing your pitch deck as a product. The images are only going to be used in the pitch deck for your presentation. Many people use images from Pages on the Mac, or Canva.com, Film-Grab.com, and ShotDeck.com.

There are also graphic designers who specialize in creating pitch decks. You can find them by searching online (try Stage32.com).

"I think *Schitt's Creek* is the perfect example of a show that proved TV needs time and space to grow. Some shows require more real estate to tell their stories properly, to earn the character arcs, to slow-burn their audience. I'd love to see more patience given to TV shows."
   – Dan Levy, *Schitt's Creek*

TYPES OF TV SHOW FORMATS

As you develop a series script, once you have an idea of the story, and have written a logline:

• **Know the format you are aiming for.**

There are seven formats of scripted TV shows:

Episodic series: Contains a story that plays out within that episode, involving characters that appear in each episode. There also are storylines that continue throughout many episodes, or that play into the entire series run.

Procedural series: Can be classified as episodics, but some classify procedurals as those with episodes that can be watched out of order, since each episode is self-contained – and usually as a science, or crime and/or courtroom drama. A typical procedural series is a *police procedural*. If they contain story and character arcs that stretch over several episodes, that means they would be better to watch in order, and that would classify them more as an episodic.

Limited series: This is the modern-name for what was formerly known as a miniseries. But, a miniseries typically had fewer episodes than what we now call a limited series.

In Europe, a serial could be what the U.S. television market refers to as a miniseries – or whatever you want to call it.

I'm all for keeping the classification of a miniseries as something that has two to five episodes, and a limited series as something that has more than five episodes. But, not everyone follows that.

A limited series takes place in several episodes, and is not meant to go for more than one season. Some storylines would only work as a limited series, such as a show about a real-life person. An example is a limited series based on John F. Kennedy.

A limited series also might also take place over two or three seasons, with it meant to end after the story plays out. One example is a series based on generations of one family, such as the royal family. It's not like you can go beyond the current year with that family, unless you take it into some sort of surreal futuristic oddity predicting what might happen with the royal family in future decades – when they lose their money and end up as bickering addicts in the future slums of post-apocalyptic London. (You read it here, first.)

Anthology series: This is a series that changes themes from season to season. One season may be based in a certain location with particular actors cast specifically for that season. An example of this is *American Horror Story*, in which the main actors take on completely different characters in each season.

Serial / serialized series: Plays out with each episode carrying on a story playing out through the entire season. To understand an episode, it is likely that you need to have watched the previous episodes.

In Europe, the serial can be what the U.S. calls a miniseries – or, something like that.

Single-cam sitcom series: These are sitcoms that are not filmed in front of a studio audience. They might film in a studio, on location, or both. While they are called "single-cam," they are usually filmed with more than one camera. Oftentimes the cameras move, and they are not stationary. The show might use tracking shots, crane shots, drone cameras, shoulder-mounted cameras, Steadicams, and other cameras that are not stationary.

Multi-cam sitcom series: These staged shows are filmed in front of an audience using stationary cameras. Usually four cameras are positioned in place for each scene, and each is operated by a camera person. The actors know how to play to each camera. The style is closer to a stage play than to a film.

On sitcoms, the scenes are often rehearsed one day, then filmed another day without an audience. On another day the scenes are acted again while being filmed in front of an audience. Whatever scenes work the best are then used in what airs on TV. On audience night, a warmup comic is there to keep the audience engaged and energetic between the scenes.

"To me, a story can be both concrete and abstract, or a concrete story can hold abstractions. And abstractions are things that really can't be said so well with words."
    – David Lych, *Twin Peaks*

TO SHAPE YOUR SERIES

- **Plot out the storyline...**
- With the scenes revealing the relevant information...
- That drives the story within the action and drama...
- Within the needs and wants of the characters...
- Who faultily and comically or dramatically – or some combination of those – stay on some sort of path toward their goals...
- Within some sort of timeline: Hours, days, weeks, months, or years...
- All with an eye on the climax of the episode...
- Which all plays along with the character arcs.

- **Plot out the character arcs...**
- Mixed within the plot points...
- In ways that use each character's background...
- Mixed with their needs and wants...
- Which guides their reasoning and motive...
- Which drives their actions and words...
- In combination with what halts, reverses, or advances them in relation to their goals.

- **Plot out the act breaks** within the mix of the storyline twists and character arcs.

"The more subtle and elegant you are in hiding your plot points, the better you are as a writer."
    – Billy Wilder, *Ocean's 11*

"Plot does not drive characters. Characters drive plot. Characters want, fear, need, act, react. This creates plot."
– Chuck Wendig, *Pandemic*

"Every scene should be not just there. I think someone gave me a good tip about this. It's 'then,' 'because,' 'but.' So, at the end of the scene, you go: 'But.' It's like the end of a sentence, or the end of a chapter. It's really, um – there should be an event in every scene, really. What's the event? That's what Mike Nichols always says: 'What's the event here?'"
– Emma Thompson, *Effie Gray*

If you are developing a series for broadcast TV, it is good to...
- Pay attention to the commercial breaks. Usually, that means...
- An opening teaser scene (containing usually two events) that...
- Hooks viewers, plus...
- Three acts, each with...
- An event or two, with...
- Act 2 ending in a climatic event that trips up what was in...
- Act 1, and what is then responded to in...
- Act 3. And then a...
- "Tag" ending scene, which is a wrap-up of the agreement of what was reached, or solution action or agreement that was aimed for as a conclusion at the end of Act 3.

Or, something like that – all in an engaging story rich in conflict and contention and played out by interesting characters.

Add up that, and you likely have a list of no less than nine main twists and turns, and various other points that are pertinent diversions and accelerants that play with the main story points and character arcs.

The diversions and accelerants consist of...
- Actions and/or things...
- Or dialogue. But, together, because... how could they not mix?

Which are always driven by...
- Character reasoning...
- Which is always based on needs and wants. As in: Motives.

But, diversions and accelerants can also be...
- Physical blocks or constructs, such as...
- Some person, or thing...
- Causing a twist or turn...
- That then plays into the character reasoning that is driven by what they want and/or need...
- Which always plays into character arcs within the goals of the storyline...
- With a conclusion to the episode...
  - But with enough left unsaid... and/or undone...

111

- To keep the character and story situations…
- Open for the audience to want another episode…
- Revealing more of the adventure of the characters…
- With them playing out their wants, needs, and contentions in every scene they are in – which are…
- Rich in subtext and conflict…
- Within the setting and theme of the story.

It is likely that as you are writing Act 1 (which plays off of the teaser scenes that introduced us to the setting and at least one character's issues that formulate their wants and needs), you already know what Act 2 and Act 3 will be, and what the ending tag scenario will be.

"The challenge of TV is to have your character take two steps forward and one and seven-eighths steps back. You want to see them striving to grow."
– Mike Schur, *The Office*

Because you outlined it, you know what the main plot points and character arc issues will be throughout all stages of the episode.

With streaming series, there are (probably) no commercials, so you can be less rigid with the act breaks – even to the point of not paying attention to them as you write it, and letting the story and character arcs play out in whichever way they will. Then, adjusting as you polish the script.

- **Plot out a season of episodes…**
- With each roughly following the above guidelines.

- **On the internet research…**
- Series pitch bible and pitch deck
- TV series writing books

If you are torn between whether you want to write a one-hour drama, a dramedy, a multi-cam (live audience) sitcom, a single cam (not filmed in front of a studio audience) sitcom, a kids' show, or other type of format, consider what it is that you like to watch. If you are not a sitcom person, maybe consider writing a sitcom that would make you laugh.

Rather than staying away from the type of show that you have not watched in the past, consider fixing that situation by writing what you want to see. You may be the revolutionary who changes the medium and brings in a variety of viewers who also had not watched that type of format.

"More than ever, we need good storytellers. Put a human face on the other. Shed light on the deeper truth. Engender empathy. Fan the flames of hope. Motivate people to act. Make us laugh. Make us cry. Make us thrilled. Make us think. But mostly, make us feel our shared humanity."
– Scott Myers, GoIntoTheStory.BlckLst.com

Any type of series could result in a film version being made. Shows that have been turned into films include everything from *The Brady Bunch* to *Charlie's Angels*, *Star Trek*, *Baywatch*, *Downton Abbey*, and *Breaking Bad*. So, be aware of the possibilities of the series that you write.

"There are no hard and fast rules for writing, and no secret tricks, because what works for one person doesn't always work for another. Everybody is different. That's the key to the whole business of writing: Your individuality."
– Judy Blume, *Tiger Eyes*

Some people write books in response to other books – including to give a completely different opinion or view of what another book presents. Consider doing the same with a pilot – by writing a pilot to contrast with a current or former TV series. It might be a series that you don't like or that you disagree with. Write the opposite show, using different characters with different names and different careers, and contrast them in a way that doesn't resemble the show you are using as a starting base. You might be someone who hates a certain detective show, and you have experience being a detective, and so you then write a detective show that is more real, or maybe more comical and/or completely wrong in a comical way.

"The origin of *The Apartment* was my seeing the very fine picture by David Lean, *Brief Encounter*. It was the story of a man who is having an affair with a married woman and comes by train to London. They go to the apartment of a friend of his. I saw it and said, 'What about the guy who has to crawl into the warm bed?' That's an interesting character. Then I put that down, and put down some other things in my notebook. The hero of that thing was the guy who endured this, who was introduced to it all by a lie. One guy in his company needed to change his clothes, he said, and used the apartment. And that was it."
– Billy Wilder, *Witness for the Prosecution*

"You don't have to know everything about the business, but the more you understand the world that a studio exec, producer, or director lives in, and the innumerable hassles and issues they have to handle, the less likely you will have a script notes moment like this: 'Lemme get this straight: You want to have a scene that involves boats with children, animals, snow, and a helicopter?' – eyes bugged out, glaring at you for not having a clue about what it takes to produce a movie."
– Scott Myers, GoIntoTheStory.BlckLst.com

Whatever type of TV script you write, always write with a financial eye. One thing TV is limited by is budget. An army of a thousand soldiers might work really well in a big-budget film, but a TV series is highly unlikely to have the sort of budget to use one thousand background actors in full uniform and engaged in battle in a mountain valley. So, be sure to be financially realistic with each and every single scene in your pilot. Many TV shows take place in few locations, with a handful of principal actors, and a scattering of other actors. Consider that angle when writing your pilot. However, you might be the one who writes some sort of big-budget TV pilot that works.

If you are in Los Angeles, New York, Atlanta, Vancouver, Toronto, London, Dublin, Berlin, Sydney, or other major city where TV and film production is common, or somewhat common – or even in Cleveland, Albuquerque, Honolulu, Paris, Perth, or Mexico City – consider writing a low-cost pilot, and filming it with local cast and crew talent. If anything, you might learn things that will help you transition into higher-budget productions.

"I want to see three scripts. Not because I care that they're all good. What I care about is that I know that you have enough energy, effort, and focus to keep writing. Because, that's TV. We did it last week. Now, we got to do it again this week.

Can you sustain the process of constantly coming up with stuff that nine times out of ten is not gonna be used? That's the job. Get used to it. It's not about rejection. It's just about culling all of these sources to get to the thing that is going to be the best thing that you can think to use at the time you are going to do it."
– Ali LeRoi, *Everybody Hates Chris*

"I prefer original work – pilot, short stories, whatever. Sometimes a spec of an existing show only tells you whether the writer is a good mimic. I don't think there's a number of pieces of writing one should have, per se. But, when I was starting, someone advised me to have variety – half-hour spec, hour spec, late-night packet, and so on. The idea was that if someone reads your work but is looking for something with a different tone, you can just say, 'Here, have that, too.'"
– Mike Schur, *The Good Place*

"All our dreams can come true if we have the courage to pursue them."
– Walt Disney, *Jack the Giant Killer*

"Nobody knows anything. Not one person in the entire motion picture field knows for a certainty what's going to work. Every time out it's a guess and, if you're lucky, an educated one."
– William Goldman, *The Princess Bride*

When considering your script, ask yourself, "Why would someone invest millions of dollars in this script?" And, "What is the likelihood of this becoming a series that millions of people would care to watch an entire season of, and then another season, and another?"

Write with the mind of an investor, a development executive, a producer, a director, a director of photography, and a star. All of those people want to be involved in projects that will advance and solidify their careers.

"I followed one of the most important pieces of writing advice you can get: Write the show or movie you would want to watch."
– Mickey Fisher, *Extant*

SERIES PITCH BIBLE

As you write the spec pilot episode: Do come up with ideas for what will potentially happen in future episodes. That is: Write a "series pitch bible," or "show bible." That series pitch bible document is in addition to a treatment. (A treatment is a two- or three-page document that describes the story in a way that entices someone to want to watch the show.)

TV shows that are on the air have a "bible" that keeps growing to include what the show presents in each episode, such as character backgrounds, which character is related to, or has dated, or was married to which other; major events that happened in the stories; reasoning behind the events; how those events were dealt with – and other matters.

Elements that are so established that they can't be ignored or dismissed (such as if a character has been established as having murdered someone) are considered "hard ground." Those would be in the show bible.

The series pitch bible you write to go along with your spec script is much less complicated than a series bible kept by an existing show.

The bible you write for your spec script is to give an idea of what the series is about, the setting and conflict, an idea of the character backgrounds and their contentions and arcs, and what can happen in future episodes.

A series pitch bible is largely about getting the series sold. Likely, it would include brief but enticing details about what you see happening over at least the next few episodes, and likely throughout the entire first season.

A series pitch bible should answer the question: Does this pilot episode have what it takes to lead into nine to twenty-four more episodes rich in conflict, contention, interesting characters, a good setting for the storyline, and other elements that will engage viewers enough to keep them watching for an entire season, and longer?

You might choose to put the pages of your series pitch bible in the following order:

The cover page of the series pitch bible includes the basic information:
- **Title of the series**
- **Name**(s) **of writer**(s)
- **Contact details:** Writer email and phone number, or manager/agent contact.

"World building is not story building. It is the landscape in which the story occurs. Too many details focusing on the world and its rules can detract from the story itself. It's the job of the screenwriter to bridge the realms of character and world."
– Kira Snyder, *The Handmaid's Tale*

The second page of the series pitch bible includes more basic information that is a window into the world you created:

- **Title of the series** (again)
- **The format/slot:** 24 episodes x 60 minutes. 12 episodes x 60 minutes. 10 episodes x 60 minutes. 8 episodes x 60 minutes. 6 episodes x 120 minutes. 4 episodes x 120 minutes. 3 episodes x 120 minutes. 2 episodes x 120 minutes. 24 episodes x 30 minutes. 12 episodes x 30 minutes. 10 episodes x 30 minutes. 8 episodes x 30 minutes. Or whatever number of episodes the series will go x the number of minutes per episode.
- **A tagline:** This is a clever line that could be used to market the show.
- **The format of the series:** Episodic, crime procedural, serialized drama, anthology, limited or miniseries, multi-cam or single-cam sitcom
- **The genre.**
- **The tone.** This could also be called the subgenre.
- **Visual realization.** If you are aiming for a certain look or texture to the series, mention it. Especially if it is something that could be considered unusual, as in black and white, or there are some scenes that – or characters who – will be animated. Or, certain characters or settings that will be black and white, while the rest of the cast is or settings are in color.
- **Compatible or transmedia formats.** Will the series also have an accompanying Website or app where people can gather more information to understand the episodes, characters, or other matters of the show?
    Perhaps the show will have interactive elements, such as it prompts the viewers to accomplish something before the next episode.
- **The setting, world, arena:** Where the series is set, and the year or era.
- **A logline:** One- or two-sentences giving an overview of the theme, setup, world, conflict, contention, and irony of the show and its main characters. Yes, attempt to put that all in one or two sentences. Shorter sentences. Not long, rambling sentences. Sentences that can be easily understood.
    When you eventually meet with producers, you might get their attention for less than five minutes. If they are enticed by the story, they might ask for

more information. Their decision to purchase your script might be based on that small window of attention.

The third page of the series pitch bible is likely going to be a one-page thematic pitch/treatment giving more details about the world of your creation, setting the tone and mood of the series.

Don't clog the entire page with dense writing.

Do focus on the world and conflict and contention of the show.

Play into the hooks, arcs, turning points, cliffside drama, ticking time bomb, and the antagonist and protagonist.

Write it in a way that teases the reader to want to see the show played out on screen.

And write it in a way that will interest actors to star in it.

The fourth page of the series pitch bible will contain the character names and short biographies that include an idea of their visual as well as their wants, needs, and conflicts, economic situation, and relationship to other characters.

If certain characters only exist in one – or chiefly in one – location in the series, you can list them as side characters at the various locations. That means, you list all of the coworkers under the `Workplace`, or use the workplace name: `Eria's Music Academy Office`. All of the neighbors under `Neighborhood`, or if the street has a name: `Willowbrook Drive Neighbor's`, or an element or thing specific to a group of characters: `Grandmother's Nosey/Gossipy Neighbors`. Or characters who only exist in another location: `Tanji's Homeless Encampment Jungle`.

Assigning the side characters to where they chiefly exist could help give flavor, tone, and visual to your script and the characters in it. That doesn't mean that those characters are only seen in those locations, but the locations are where we are most likely to see them.

Follow the series pitch bible character biography pages with a short episode synopsis that briefly details enticing information about what happens in each episode.

Each episode will likely be one to three short paragraphs.

Don't include one episode per page. Simply list then one after the other.

You can give each episode a name so that when you discuss them with people, you will know which episode is being referenced.

That list of episodes might only take up one page, or two.

Don't go more than two pages with the episodes synopsis (three pages, at most – fewer is better).

After the series pitch bible page(s) containing the episode synopsis, include a page containing a short description of what could happen in future seasons.

If you follow that advice, your entire series <u>pitch</u> bible will likely be 6 or 7 pages.

Make them clean, sharp, detailed, but sparse, enticing, clear, clever, and easy to read.

(Search: Pilot episode pitch bible.)

What you might find online when doing that search is a <u>series</u> bible from a show that has been produced and broadcast.

Know what a <u>series</u> bible looks like for a show that has been in production. See how wordy and complicated it is. Know that it is NOT what you will be doing with your spec script <u>pitch</u> bible.

While a series <u>pitch</u> bible will likely be less than eight pages, a <u>series</u> bible could be fifty to one-hundred pages per season.

Practice your pitch.

Practice how you would tell producers about your show – if they were to ask you during a one-minute elevator ride.

And, practice how you would pitch the series, including information from the pitch bible that you outlined.

"Don't start your pitch by saying how nervous you are. Or how you hate pitching. Most writers are nervous and hate pitching. Projecting confidence in that moment may feel like a total lie, but they don't need to know that. Go in strong, and command the room.

When they say thank you for coming in, say thank you for having me and that you appreciated the opportunity, and then get the hell out of there. Don't linger and keep talking. That's never good. Leave on a high note with a confident smile.

Don't act desperate. Maybe you're three months late on your rent, and this job will literally save you from eviction. Don't tell them how much you need this job, and how hard you'll work if they only give you a chance. Be confident."

– Carter Blanchard, *Glimmer*

"The work never matches the dream of perfection the artist has to start with."
– William Faulkner, *To Have and Have Not*

"This agent once told me that you have to write your way into the movie business. No one's going to let you direct, so you have to write your way in with ideas. And that was good then and it worked."
– John Carpenter, *Escape from New York*

THE STANDIN

I have been a standin and/or photo double on many TV shows and films, including for Bryan Cranston, Kevin Bacon, Matthew Morrison, Greg Kinnear, Dennis Quaid, Bob Odenkirk, Michael Hitchcock, Luke Perry, Paul Rudd, Mark-Paul Gosselaar, Sean Hayes, Dougray Scott, Jeffrey Tambor, J.K. Simmons, David Harbour, George Segal, Chris Cooper, Titus Welliver, John Benjamin Hickey, and many others – to the point of it turning into a blur.

On some of the TV shows and films, I was on set five days a week, for many weeks, and sometimes for several months in a row. On some TV shows, I was on set more than any of the writers, stars, directors, and producers.

Days working on network shows can often be 15 – or more – hours long. You can feel as if your life during those months revolves around the show. You are either on set working with the cast and crew, or you are sleeping, showering, exercising, or driving or biking back and forth to and from work, where you also eat most of your meals. That is about all you do – for months.

On one show, I pretty much knew every detail of the show that a person on set could possibly know. Not only did I standin for and photo double the star, and do his hand inserts, and often dressed in his character's wardrobe to do his over-the-shoulder shots, I also stood in for other male actors on the show when the main actor wasn't needed in the scenes. When the actor was busy with meetings, or doing publicity for the show, or otherwise couldn't be on set, I also did the rehearsals with the other actors. Sometimes, to save time, those rehearsals were filmed so that when the main actor became available, he could watch the video playback of me acting out the scene, and he could step in to do the scene without doing a rehearsal. It was fun. Luckily, the actor was cool.

As the sleep-deprived months went by, I knew what every character did and every word they said in every episode of that series. I knew how each scene was filmed. I saw how the scripts were continually being rewritten with new pages handed out throughout each day to update cast and crew on what was going to be filmed that week, day, or hour. Sometimes, part of a scene was filmed, and then it was refilmed on the spot, or later that day, or in the following days, or weeks. That's how network shows go. You adjust to the changes. And, you never complain (because many people are working as hard – or much harder – than you). Simply, show up on time, know your place and job, stay in your lane, respect the jobs of others, keep a good attitude, and pay attention so that you can do your job to help film the material.

Eventually, I wrote a script for that show. Because, you know, why not? I was there all damn day, helping to film the thing. For months, and months. And months.

I quickly found out that nobody in power on that show could look at my script – even if they wanted to. Several of the power players told me in person, or through texting or email that they wanted to read my script. But, they couldn't. Nor could I tell them any details about the episode that I wrote. A few of the higher-ups told me what they thought of the show, and they weren't compliments. Eyes opened. I also knew that some did read – but couldn't say that they read – my script.

I didn't know about the legal situation of why my script couldn't be read by the producers, stars, directors, or writers. Luckily, the producers were kind and explained it to me, with some humor – knowing how ironic it was that the person who worked on the show more than anyone could not have his script for the show read by any of the producers, writers, directors, or stars.

In modern-day Hollywood, there are contracts all over the place – especially among the key players on a network TV series. Those contracts control everything.

The creator of the show controlled the content of the show. It was in his contract. The series writers wrote out his vision of how every episode should be.

When I mentioned to some crew that I had written a script for the show, they asked to read it. As word got out that I wrote a script for the show, and that it didn't suck, more crew wanted to read it. Various crew read it bit-by-bit. Some laughed out loud as they read it – especially because of what happens in my script to a certain character. One crew said, "This is what we should be filming."

We had the best crew on that show. It was great spending time with them every day. It was a bummer when it ended. But, it wasn't unexpected. The ratings were awful.

The producers told me that I should change the script, give the characters different professions, change the city, get rid of a few characters, write some new characters into the story, and use it as a writing sample – and possibly sell it as a spec script (unlikely, but not impossible).

Use the lessons learned, and keep writing.

"There is the cult of the actor, and of the director, and there's even been the cult of the celebrity chef and gardener, but there has never been a cult of the screenwriter. But I'm happy about that, because what I crave – in a completely venal way – is creative opportunities, not recognition."
– Anthony McCarten, *The Theory of Everything*

THE IDIOTIC SCRIPT

When I was young and naïve about how the screenwriting biz worked, I had two guys call me who had been working on producing small films, and other stuff. They had read a script that I wrote and that was being passed around Hollywood. When they called me, I thought they were interested in producing my script. I went to meet them. They had a situation. They had written a nine-page story, landed some funding, could easily get the rest (including from family wealth), and needed a script written. They wanted to know if I could write a script based on their nine-page treatment. After reading the pages, I agreed to write it.

They were going to make me one of the producers. I didn't ask for money.

Yes, I was naïve. I had no idea how things worked.

They were so new that I don't think they understood the situation, either.

Their story was so clear and obvious that I wrote the script in a few weeks. I brought it to them and one of them seemed to be amazed. He held the script and asked, "How did you write this so fast?" I said it was easy. I simply sat down every day and wrote.

I often write fast. I interned at a radio station writing the news. I worked for newspapers and magazines. And I helped so-called "authors" write their books.

To tell you the story, I'll give the script a fake name. I'll title it *Idiotic*.

Some of the casting had been done. Locations were set. Then, there was some mess that happened with the two guys and the financier and distributor and other stuff that I had nothing to do with – based on their other projects. Weeks away from what was supposed to be the start of filming, everything collapsed. The guys went their separate ways. And I never got a dime.

They eventually told me that I could have the screenplay. It isn't the sort of story or screenplay that I would have dreamed up or written.

Because of another script I wrote, I got with an agent. I gave the *Idiotic* script to the agency. They said it should be easy to sell.

It never has.

One of the producer guys took my concept to heart. "Simply sit down and write." He ended up on the staff of a TV series, then wrote a variety of film scripts, including a few that went big. He has made major money.

Never write a script for free. Especially if it already has funding. That script had hundreds of thousands behind it.

"I've come to view screenwriting assignments as playwriting grants, because they provide a considerable financial cushion. However, they can also be extremely time-consuming. Film projects tend to drag on and on, which takes me away from the theatre, and then they don't get made. At the same time, the screenplays that have come my way have been quite challenging, for the most part, and even enjoyable."
– Donald Margulies, *Once and Again*

If you get writing assignments, make sure that you know what you are doing. Even if you aren't union, understand the WGA contract, and aim for making at least the WGA minimum on your writing assignments.

If you are hired by a studio and work for them as a writer to convert an idea into a script, you will make at least WGA minimum.

If someone claims to be a signatory of the WGA, call the WGA and clarify that.

As a beginner, you might get a studio meeting based on a spec you wrote, which might have placed high in – or won – a contest. As those producers did with me, the studio might really like your script, but the studio doesn't buy your script. They bring you in for an O.W.A. (open writing assignment), and you then write a script based on an idea they have, or as a sequel or prequel to something they already produced. Or, you are to overhaul a script that they own to sharpen it, or only to redo the dialogue, or restyle it for a particular actor, or to place it in a different era, or budget range, or make it funnier, or more dramatic, or twist it into a different genre. After you work on their script, they still might not film it. Or, another writer could then rewrite what you wrote. Studios spend loads of money on things like that. It's called "development." Some people call it "development hell."

The numerous scenarios relating to script sales, rewrites, writing for hire, and other writing situations are a tangled web.

As mentioned elsewhere, you can get an idea of option, sales, and writing for hire agreements by reading *The Screenwriter's Legal Guide*. Do read that book, and *The Pocket Lawyer for Filmmakers*, by Thomas Crowell.

"The reality in Hollywood is that very few screenplays that are optioned actually get purchased and/or made. I don't know if anyone could give you an exact percentage, but it is fairly low. Given that reality, the question you should be asking yourself is: 'What happens to my rewrite if my script is only optioned and not purchased?' Remember that writing services fall under the category of 'work-made-for-hire.' In other words, the person who pays for it owns it. Thus, if your script is optioned, but it is not purchased (that is, the option expires), you get your original script back, but the person who commissioned the rewrite owns the rewrite!"

– Stephen F. Breimer, Esq., author *The Screenwriter's Legal Guide*

"I have written a bunch of scripts that have not gotten produced, much more so early in my career than later. I think that ten or twelve years ago I decided to try to make that happen, that I wrote fewer scripts that didn't get made. I do some very conscious things to make that happen. They are not the thing a first-time screenwriter would be able to do. I only do one project at a time. When I start something, I know people I am working with, it's a project they're interested in. It also means I can be working for a studio or the executives who will still have their jobs when it's time to make the film. Developing films with directors, developing films with actors, is a poor percentage play for a screenwriter. If that person happens to not be ready, changes their mind, loses attention, whatever, your script sits there. So, I don't take those jobs anymore."

– Tony Gilroy, *The Bourne Identity*

"I've enjoyed some of the acting I've done, *North and South* and the movie *The First Great Train Robbery*. But, I've done a lot of stuff that I didn't enjoy. Part of that was because of all the lecherous men – studio executives, producers, directors. There was a lot of running away and hiding under tables. They made everything uncomfortable."
– Lesley-Anne Down, *Seven Days of Grace*

DON'T GO THERE

Twenty years ago, I was helping people polish screenplays, and I had written a dark comedy script that was being passed around town. I got invited places. There were parties, events, screenings, lunch meetings, evening gatherings at restaurants, being introduced to people. Power plays of some sort and wannabes were all around.

One thing that became clear is that some of the people I met were using their standing in the business to try to make other things happen with people much younger and/or perceived to be physically appealing.

One successful person was looking at my script, and another found out. He was a studio producer.

I got a call from Mr. Producer wanting to talk with me about my script. He asked me if I would be around that night, and if I could stop by his place.

Sure. Why not?

Yes, this is about that.

I was naïve.

What could possibly go wrong?

I get to the house that Mr. Producer had just moved in to. Apparently, for some reason, he wanted to show his house to me. It was like a private resort hotel with every luxury. High-tech, with buttons that controlled things: Various sorts of lighting, floor heaters, a screening room, a big pool with fountains, misters around the patio for hot days, security cameras. All, future trash.

I didn't care about any of it.

Posh mansions are ego-driven, rather than need-driven, and result in a tremendous amount of pollution to serve a few people. Los Angeles has massive numbers of outlandish resort homes – and an enormous population of people sleeping on sidewalks and beneath bridges.

I didn't know why I was being given a tour of the place. I was there to talk about my screenplay. Was it some sort of game?

So, as the awkward tour of the resort-like home went on, Mr. Producer and I finally made it to his office. We briefly spoke about my script. Then, he asked if we could speak more about it tomorrow. That was perplexing. Why was I there?

We walked down the long, dark hallway.

As we got to the dark foyer.

I thought he tripped on the rug.

He grasped hold of me. I thought it was so that he could avoid falling. I grabbed on to him to – I thought – help steady him.

Or, was he hugging me goodbye? Awkward.

Then, I felt his beard stubble against my face, and his lips, and tongue.

I shoved him away, and asked, "Dude, what are you doing?"

He said, "I thought."

I said, "You thought wrong. I'm here because you said you wanted to talk about my script."

I walked out of there disgusted, repulsed, and frustrated. Not only with that incident, but with some other nonsense I dealt with from other people in the industry – male and female – who misused their positions.

Over the following years, I didn't do much screenwriting, and I had stopped helping people polish their screenplays. Instead, I continued doing freelance work for magazines, newspapers, and book publishing companies, and helped so-called authors write their books. I also spent those years doing massive amounts of standing in for stars, photo doubling stars, and doing background acting work, and filling in for unavailable actors during rehearsals and table reads with other cast members on too many TV shows and films to count, some acting, and hand modeling (until my hands aged out of that).

By spending years at the center of the action on so many TV and film sets, on a daily, hourly, minute-by-minute basis, I saw the intricacies of how films and TV shows are made. I worked with and – while spending massive amounts of time with them – got to know many terrific crew people. I also learned how many of the successful people are good to work with, and I learned how several specific others are not. I can't watch movies or TV shows staring a few certain actors – because I know their bad behavior. Luckily, most aren't so heinous.

In 2014, I was injured on the set of *Teen Wolf* when I quickly reached out to catch a falling actress. The surgery and many months of recovery to relearn how to use my arm, wrist, hand, and fingers while I couldn't work, and the years of sleep deprivation caused by pain brought me back to writing. I pulled out my old scripts, began new ones, accepted gigs polishing scripts, and started helping writers with theirs. That lead me to start Screenwriting Tribe.

Learn that lesson that I learned the hard way. Protect yourself.

If someone wants to meet with you about your script, or about working in the industry – or for any job – there are places that are acceptable to meet.

1) Online. Do a virtual meet on Zoom or on another platform. More and more meetings are held this way.
2) An office with the door open. Or, an office or meeting room that has windows or glass walls open to other areas of the office space.
3) An office lobby, or open office lounge area – perhaps at one of those rented shared office spaces.
4) A public place, which might be a restaurant, a coffee house, a library, an office building courtyard, or – for film school situations – a college campus classroom, lobby, department lounge, or courtyard.

Don't agree to meet them alone in a hotel room, in a house, or in a vehicle (no matter who they are, how successful they are, or how famous they are), where things could quickly escalate into what you don't want.

Be safe.

"You've got to have heart, and you've got to have drive. And when you get knocked down, put your hands up on the ropes and pull yourself to your feet. Because, if you can't take a hit, you're not going to last long. That's for sure."

– Spike Lee, *Da 5 Bloods*

"Writing on a team for a showrunner is about generating story and serving the showrunner's writing process."
– Monica Beletsky, *Parenthood*

"When given an opportunity, deliver excellence – and never quit."
– Robert Rodriguez, *El Mariachi*

"My Mother was an actress. My Father was an actor and director. I am the son of filmmakers. I was born with this bow tie made of celluloid on my collar."
– Sergeo Leone, *The Good, the Bad, and the Ugly*

GETTING IN

Here is how it worked for one of the writers in Screenwriting Tribe. First, she already had experience in other parts of the industry, having had directed shorts, and developed her skills as an editor to the point that she was working as an editor on films and TV shows. She attended the Tribe workshop many times, and workshopped every page of two scripts – a TV pilot and a feature film. She then entered the pilot script into one of the main screenplay competitions, in which she placed in the top ten. That brought her to the attention of a top management company, which she signed with. Then, she signed with a top agency. She was sent out on meetings with showrunners to see if she would be a good fit in one of their writing rooms. Within a few months of signing with the management company and agency, she ended up being hired by a major studio to work as a writer on their biggest project.

Just weeks before she landed that great job, she had experienced disappointment when a mentorship program rejected her script. That goes to show that even if your script can win in some circles, others might reject it.

Do not get disappointed by rejections by screenplay competitions, mentorships, fellowships, managers, agents, directors, actors, and others.

Know that rejection is part of the process. No matter how hot and sharply written and clever your scripts are, they will be rejected by someone. Sometimes because they only work with certain genres, budgets, stars, talent, or with certain companies that have a set of criteria that they go by.

Keep polishing your scripts, do your homework, write more scripts. Push along and see who may accept your creations – while keeping your day job to support you as you improve your skills in and expand your network in the craft.

Because of her success, more people started attending Screenwriting Tribe – even though we already had more than enough people. How many of those people will do the work: Study the books, improve their skills in the craft, write sharp scripts, workshop every page, listen to and utilize the feedback, adjust their script more to sharpen it, have it edited, get feedback from a coverage service (see the coverage chapter in this book), and send it out to contests, fellowships, and mentorships, and get recognized? It's up to them, their skills, commitment, intellect, creativity, drive, personality, charisma, manners, ability to get it done, being in the right place at the right time, and luck.

"Stand out from the crowd. Entering competitions and schemes is the best way to do this – it tells producers that someone else has taken you seriously. By winning or being a runner-up in a well-regarded scheme, your work will get noticed and will help producers feel more confident about employing you. Keep an eye on schemes like Shore Scripts and the BBC Writersroom (bbc.co.uk/writersroom/opportunities) – as that lists a ton of entry schemes into the industry."
– Chris Lindsay, *Ghostwoods*

Some people say that the most important thing to do at first is to get a script fully produced in the quality needed to be entered into film festivals, and to get distribution deals. That means, simply doing whatever it takes to get a script made with high quality production standards. Then, use that produced film to prove what you can do.

But, if the film is lousy, it could work against you.

How do you make sure that your film is high quality? Here is one of many answers in the puzzle: Take every page of the script through a workshop, then have it edited and covered. Study this and other screenwriting books.

In addition to an excellent, compelling, engaging script, for a film to get accepted into festivals, and for it to land distribution deals (including distribution to various regions of the planet), it needs to have good quality camerawork, sound, lighting, acting, and other essentials that audiences expect.

Don't make worthless garbage.

Don't write an excellent script, then film it in a low-quality way, with actors who are lousy, with screwed up lighting, with bad sound, and with inadequate and distractive camerawork, and a disappointing soundtrack. It will waste your time and money, and end up only as a learning experience.

If you want to be a TV writer, as mentioned earlier, pay attention to the studio and other writing fellowship programs – and submit to them with a spec script from the list of approved shows that are listed on fellowship sites, or, if they require it, with your original spec scripts.

If you get accepted into a fellowship or mentorship or studio writing program, dive in, engage, and do what they require. With a studio writing program, it likely will include access to the writers' room on a current series, but also working under a mentor.

Each writing program has their own way of doing things.

(Search: Studio writing fellowships.)

Screenwriting Fellowships
- Academy Nicholl Fellowship
- BBC Writersroom Script Room
- CBS Writer's Mentoring Program
- Disney/ABC TV Writing Program
- HBO Access Writing Fellowship
- Humanitas New Voices
- NBC/Universal Writer's on the Verge
- NHMC TV Writer's Program (National Hispanic Media Coalition)
- Nickelodeon Writing Fellowship
- Producers Guild Power of Diversity Master Workshop
- Sundance Institute Episodic Story Lab
- Sundance Institute YouTube New Voices Lab
- Universal Writers Program
- Warner Bros Writer's Workshop

Keep an eye on ScriptMag.com and Creative Screenwriting Magazine to find out more about those and other opportunities.

Also, access: wga.org/the-guild/advocacy/diversity/writing-programs-conferences-festivals

As mentioned, another way of getting into a screenwriting profession is to enter your polished scripts into screenwriting contests. If you win, you can end up meeting agents, managers, producers, and others who can help you gain a career. (Search: Screenwriting contests.)

Know that many of the scripts that win contests don't get produced. They may be entertaining to read, but are not broadly commercial. Consider the script to be a writing sample, and a ticket for getting other screenwriting work.

There are heavily marketed pitch fests. These are where you pay to briefly meet producers and others in the industry and tell them about your script. Or, maybe they aren't producers, but assistants to someone, or they are someone hoping to be a producer, manager, or agent. Maybe pitch fests aren't what their hyper marketing presents them as being. Study up on what other people say about pitch fests, and consider if it is something that you want to pay to attend. Or, would your money, time, and focus be better used elsewhere. (Search: Screenwriting pitch fests.)

At some point, get to the Austin Film Festival. It is very much a writers' gathering.

Consider if putting your scripts on The Black List is something you'd like to try (Access: BlckLst.com). Do your research about The Black List, and read what people say about the site – pro and con.

Also, familiarize yourself with Coverfly (Access: Coverfly.com). Consider if Coverfly is also a tool that you would like to use to advance your career.

Join Stage32.com, and establish a profile. Network.

"Turn off your cell phone. Honestly, if you want to get work done, you've got to learn to unplug. No texting, no email, no Facebook, no Instagram. Whatever it is you're doing, it needs to stop while you write."
– Nathan Englander, author *Dinner at the Center of the Earth*

Don't be a social media addict. Do you think that the top screenwriters sit around for hours every day looking at and posting on social media? They are busy writing marketable scripts, networking, sharpening their skills in the craft, and knowing the business of the business.

Don't turn into a social butterfly – doing nothing but socializing in the field, while not writing and polishing scripts to build up an impressive portfolio of producible screenplays.

To be a screenwriter, you must write scripts. Write a variety of them. Finish them. Workshop them. Have an editor help you to polish them. Send them out for professional coverage. Get them to a manager who will connect you with an agent who has the contacts needed for selling your scripts.

Write scripts that can be produced into films and TV shows that will satisfy large numbers of people. That is what the money people want.

It could be fun and adventurous to be ambitious and write some grand screenplay that would cost hundreds of millions to make. Do that if you want, and maybe it will sell. But, also write scripts that would cost less than a few million, or less than a million to produce. (Search: Low-budget hit films.)

"I used to love to shoot my mouth off and say if you can make a film for less money you don't have to please as many people. While that statement is factually true, the problem is it's very hard now to make a film for less money. Way under five million is not easy to pull off, and still pay people the wages that are considered standard or obligatory."
– Debra Granik, *Winter's Bone*

"I think there's only one or two films where I've had all the financial support I needed. All the rest, I wish I'd had the money to shoot another ten days."
– Martin Scorsese, *I Call First*

No matter what the budget, you might want to work toward writing scripts that fall into this category: Commercial for its budget. That phrase means the film will appeal to a large enough number of people to bring in a significant return on investment.

"You can actually end up telling a more universal story the more you really burrow into a specific world."
– Damien Chazelle, *10 Cloverfield Lane*

If you can keep churning out scripts that satisfy the money people, you will be more likely to keep selling your work and/or be a hired writer.

You have to be a writer who not only understands the language of screenwriting, you also need to understand the business. Know the jobs of the various people with whom you will be dealing. Know how to conduct yourself in meetings. Be open and mannerly. Be the one who considers the ideas of those in the room, and who doesn't come off as dismissive, flip, elusive, arrogant, pretentious, or difficult to work with. You must make good business decisions, and you should be able to collaborate with a variety of people so that the projects you work on – and your career – move forward.

"Collaborate with each other. That's the old adage: Network horizontally rather than vertically, because you would be stunned by what kind of power you have at your disposal."
– Kay Oyegun, *This is Us*

You need to be a good client for your manager and agent. First, they want writers who write scripts that will sell. Be that writer.

Always remember, when you meet with producers and others in the industry, you might not sell your screenplays. But, you might be establishing a relationship that can lead to collaborations and writing assignments in future months or years.

While it is important to have an agent and manager who are good fits for your career, you also have to maintain a position that continues leading you into greater successes. Be engaged in promoting yourself. Be your own best advocate.

Make your screenwriting career happen. Nobody will do it for you. Write, and polish a variety of original scripts, and have them ready for when opportunities appear.

"I wrote my first screenplay when I was 15. And then I got to the top three of a screenwriting competition. My project wasn't chosen, but out of seven and a half thousand entries, I was in the top three. From the success of that, I was accepted into film school two years younger than most people. And so, I've been very, very furiously wanting to be a filmmaker since I was 15. I've sold four screenplays to major studios over the last 15 years, none of which have been made. And the problem is that it takes a Herculean effort to shepherd something through to actual production."
– Charlie Hunnam, actor

"Go into the arts. I'm not kidding. The arts are not a way to make a living. They are a very human way of making life more bearable. Practicing an art – no matter how well or badly – is a way to make your soul grow, for heaven's sake. Sing in the shower. Dance to the radio. Tell stories. Write a poem to a friend, even a lousy poem. Do it as well as you possibly can. You will get an enormous reward. You will have created something."
– Kurt Vonnegut, *Slaughterhouse-Five*

Writing Assignments

"Depending on the mandate from the producers hiring me, I either forget about the previous drafts, and go back to scratch with the original concept, as in *Piranha* or *Alligator* or *The Howling*, or I try to improve or change the existing script in the direction they want to take it."
– John Sayles, *Sunshine State*

You can write for hire, for people who or companies that have the kind of money that is needed to make a high-quality film. That can advance your career – if your script is excellent, if the actors do a fine job, if the camera, sound, lighting, sets, makeup, and wardrobe and other things about the film are done right, and if the other essentials fall into place.

"I'm not a very good employee. I wish I was – because there's a lot of money to be made by being a good employee.

I wrote four scripts for Scorsese, but we never talked about it. I would do it, he would talk, I would do it again, but there was only one person in the room when I was writing. And the last film we did together, *Bringing out the Dead*, I realized that we would not work together again, that it was over – because there were now two directors in the room, and one of them was calling himself a writer. And the other one was sort of pissed off. And so, I realized, you know, there can only be one director in Scorsese's script development, and that has to be him – and it's not me. So, um, I have not been very good at cooperating.

I've never held a job in my life. Every single job I've had, I got fired from. And it's always at some point where somebody says, 'Do it this way.' And, I say, 'No, that's not the way you do it, you do it this way.' Then they say, 'Who's the boss?' And you get fired. That's probably the reason that I've

worked on spec all these years. Because, I used to get jobs, but I always got in trouble, and I got a bad reputation as somebody who is not cooperative, who is not a team player. So, I sort of realized that the only way I can make a living is just do my thing, and then go out and find somebody to finance it."
– Paul Schrader, *The Jesuit*

One thing you might want for your screenwriting career is to get writing assignments. Managers want to represent writers who can write on assignment, and who can get paid to overhaul or otherwise doctor scripts that already have funding. That is also a competitive market. So, sharpen your skills.

Writers make more money writing on assignment and for hire than they do from selling their spec scripts.

Many screenwriters who have never had one of their spec scripts sold or produced make money by doing writing assignments, by doctoring other writers' scripts, or by being staffed on a series.

"You can have a situation where you are writing a project, and suddenly someone drops out – a director drops out – and the production company says, 'Actually, we need it to be this actor,' or, 'This has to be a man.' And you have to rewrite the whole thing – because it's a whole other story. I mean, there's that. Then, there's your studio notes, some of which can be very good, and some of which can be really not very good at all. And can be very irritating, actually. I mean, I have been known to break things and sob. But then, you have to just buckle down and suck it up, because you do want to get it made, sometimes you have to make compromises, as well."
– Emma Thompson, *Nanny McPhee*

Don't plan on a screenwriting career in which all you do is write and sell scripts. If that happens, wonderful (if that is what you want). But, more than likely, if you are going to have a career in Hollywood, you are going to be doing writing assignments and/or you are going to be on the staff of a series.

As mentioned, writing assignments can involve adapting a book that a producer owns the rights to, writing a script based on an idea by another person, turning a historical or other event into a screenplay, turning a song or some sort of pop cultural thing into a screenplay, or turning a mythological or otherwise another person's idea into a script. For pay.

"Emotional authenticity is more important than historical. We can't recreate a world, but we can recreate the emotions of it."
– James DiLapo, *Odysseus*

If you are hired to write a script, consider:
• What they like about the story.
• The productions that are similar in genre, era, setting, tone, and mood.
• What part of the story that first appears most important, and which part is less important. Consider the opposite.
• Asking which characters the producer connects with.

- What the rating will be.
- What the budget will be.
- Where it will be – or can be – filmed.
- When it will be filmed.
- If any recognizable actors are interested in – or attached to – the project.
- For yourself, think of what the film poster or show ad would look like.
- If it is the kind of project that would have a sequel, prequel, or spinoff.
- If it is a response film = a film done in response to another film. Such as, aiming for that setting, conflict, contention, reasoning, characterizations, era, view, tone, mood, genre, and market.
- A timeline of when they would like to see the first copy of the script.

Know that you will do research for free, and maybe even an outline of your concepts to reveal to the producers that you are the right hire for the gig.

Remember that what you are writing is a "work for hire," and you do not own the intellectual property (I.P.). It's all theirs.

You will likely be limited in how you can talk about it to anyone. You should not tell the details of the script to anyone outside of the company.

On social media, do not post the name of a project you have been hired to write. If the producer, production company, or studio want to announce it, leave it up to them. It is likely that they will be clear that you are to get their approval before you mention the project on social media.

Eventually, the company might do a press release, or other publicity, announcing the project and the names of the writers who are working on it. Until then, get approval before mentioning to anyone that you are being paid to work on a film or series. Of course, your manager and agent are okay for you to speak with about it. They should know to keep it quiet.

A written for hire script is not one that you would take through a workshop. Do not send it to a coverage service. Do not enter it into a contest, fellowship, mentorship, or studio writing program, or a lab. The only people you show the script to is who hired you to write it, and anyone else in the company assigned to work with you on the project, including the producer(s), development executive(s), other writers, and director(s).

"Writing assignments, or O.W.A.s (open writing assignments) represent the brass ring for many a screenwriter. Sure, every feature writer would love to sell spec after spec, but in a shrinking spec market that is not always a highly accessible or widely achievable reality. Similarly, in television, where getting staffed or selling an original pilot both seem like tall mountains to climb, writing assignments can be an entirely attractive position. Many TV writers partake in feature writing assignments in their off seasons. Television writing assignments are becoming more prevalent as well, specifically when a production entity seeks to develop new material based on a concept generated within."

– Lee Jessup, screenwriting career consultant, LeeJessup.com

"When you manage to express something with a look and the music, instead of saying it with words, or having the character speak, I think it's a more complete look."
– Sergio Leone, *For a Few Dollars More*

"Sound and music can be used to tell a story. We had an amazing composer. Sometimes you watch a scene and it doesn't quite hit you emotionally, but as soon as the music goes in it lifts it. It's just incredible. Every little piece together tells the story."
– Daisy Coulam, about *Deadwater Fell*

GETTING PAID TO DOCTOR SCRIPTS

You can be hired to doctor or overhaul a script that has already been purchased, budgeted, or otherwise is on the path to being put into production. I do that. I like doing it – so far.

As mentioned earlier, I once went on an acting audition for a film. While reading the few pages of the script that I was to use for the audition, I made note of a number of errors or ways those pages could be rewritten. After the audition, I mentioned to the director that I noticed some issues with the script. I ended up being paid to rewrite the script. I didn't get the acting role. I didn't want to be credited as a writer. It was simply a script doctoring job – amounting to a massive overhaul.

Probably the vast majority of scripts that are produced by the studios have been rewritten or doctored by one or more writers.

"The biggest problem with most rewrites is that you start at page one, which is already probably the best written page in the script. You tweak as you go, page after page, moving commas and enjoying your cleverness – all the while forgetting why you're rewriting the script. Instead, you need to stop thinking of words and pages, and focus on goals."
– John August, *Big Fish*

When a script is completely overhauled, it is called a *page-one rewrite*. Other scripts have specific things that are changed by specialty writers. There are writers who get paid to improve dialogue. Other writers are hired to make scripts funnier (referred to as a "punch up" of the humor). Some writers are hired to improve or correct the psychology of the characters.

There are scripts that are overhauled by people with experience in certain professions.

135

I knew someone who was an airline attendant and was hired to overhaul a screenplay that takes place on a jetliner.

Someone who has been in the military might be hired to overhaul a script featuring characters who are in the military.

Someone who knows about a certain type of wildlife might be hired to help overhaul a script that takes place in the wild.

If you are a writer who also happens to have a specialty profession, put that on your resume. Even if it is that you once worked at a morgue, or on an oil rig, or in the salt mines beneath Lake Erie. Also, if you have some unusual life experience, list that on your resume, even if it is that you are into spelunking, you sailed a boat across an ocean, you ran a restaurant, you build bikes from scratch, you know sign language, you grew up in a war zone, you're a piano teacher, you were a pig farmer, or you worked for a politician. You might find yourself being hired to polish some screenplay so that it is more factually accurate.

If you are hired to overhaul or doctor a script, don't expect to receive writer credit. You might get credit if you rewrote or changed at least fifty percent of a script. You might be one of a dozen – or more – writers who worked on the script. The WGA has guidelines relating to who receives credit for a script. Study the WGA contract.

"Be open to improvement, because your screenplay is only finished after it's produced."
– Markus Linecker, *Dedicated Talent Management*

"I don't want to rain on your parade, but I want you to know and I want you to hear it from somebody. The reason I didn't go the traditional route – I couldn't afford to. Those assistant jobs don't pay enough for the cost of living in L.A. They just don't."
– Wendy Calhoun, *Justified*

"Part of the job of any TV writer is to mimic the show that you're writing. That's a really important skill."
– Terence Winter, *Boardwalk Empire*

GETTING ON STAFF

"There's something about the schedule of working in TV that's attractive. You know exactly what the next six months are going to be like. You'll work Monday through Friday, and have the weekends off, and then there's going to be a hiatus here, so you can kind of plan a little bit."
– Nat Faxon, *The Descendants*

"I started as an actor, doing comedy (improv and sketch) in New York City. During that period of time, I helped produce the shows we created, and had an active role in developing the content. When I decided to change career paths, I started as a script reader, as I found it combined my love of literature and criticism, and film/performing."
– Betsy Beers, producer of *Grey's Anatomy*

"There's a fantastic writers' room working under lock and key. They're already generating really exciting material. They're down in Santa Monica. You have to go through such clearance, and they have all their windows taped closed. And there's a security guard that sits outside, and you have to have a fingerprint to get in there, because their whole board is up on a thing of the whole season."
– Jennifer Salke, Amazon Studios chief, about the *Lord of the Rings* series

If you end up being hired to write an individual episode – or any episode – of a TV series, study each previous episode so that you know the twists and turns and histories of the backstories and characters and their conflictions. Know the inflections of the lead actors. Don't expect the people on the show to explain it to you. Do your homework.

"There are many great writers out there who are, say, amazing at writing specific characters and killer dialogue, but who are shaky at building plot. And that's okay. We need the writers' room as a whole to be able to do everything, but not every writer. So, if you are really good at one particular aspect of storytelling, that sample script should really showcase that."
– Liz Flahive and Carly Mensch, *Glow*

The production will likely give you access to previous episodes.

If you are called to a meeting with a particular show, be prepared by doing research about the show, including by watching episodes.

If you are in L.A., you can check out old TV series by going to Cinefile Video in West L.A., or Videotheque in South Pasadena.

Some large libraries in L.A., such as the main library in downtown, or the Hollywood branch, and the main library of Santa Monica have collections of old TV shows on DVD.

Also, check the WGA Library on Fairfax, where you can read scripts from various shows. The library also has a collection of show bibles, pitch decks, note cards, outlines, correspondence, and handwritten drafts from certain shows.

"I think working in a writers' room is like a muscle: The more you do it, the stronger you become at it."
– Nahnatchka Khan, *Fresh off the Boat*

Even if you write a TV episode, don't expect it to be approved and filmed off the cuff. They will likely take it through rewrites and punch up the drama, comedy, characters, backstories, and foreshadowing of what is to happen in future episodes.

That is, unless your show is filmed in a different way than the typical American TV series. In 2019, Danna Stern, the head of Yes Studios in Israel, described to *The Hollywood Reporter* how their shows usually don't have writers' rooms, and an entire series may be written and directed by one person.

"Television producers, also known as show runners, don't buy scripts, they hire staffs. What they want is you and the craft and talent you can bring to their writing tables. Therefore, your script is more of an audition piece, an introduction to you as a writer, then a product for sale, and you will need to have more than one script for consideration."
– Ellen Sandler, *Everybody Loves Raymond*. Author *The TV Writer's Workbook*

"If you find yourself in a writers' room, concentrate and pay attention. If your idea gets shot down, don't sulk. Move on and don't be too sensitive. You'll learn that in a writers' room you can get somewhere in 20 minutes that it would have taken you weeks on your own because you've got all these genius minds at work. Check your ego and watch what established writers do."
– Christian White, *Clickbait*

If you are hired as a staff writer on a series, be prepared for the collaboration that will take place with the other writers, and also the producers, directors, showrunner, and stars. Don't be surprised if they want to meet with you individually. Listen and consider. Don't take things personally. Don't expect all of your ideas to be used. Do expect them to be changed to fit into the needs of the episode. Do expect rewrites of the script – even up to the minutes before filming. Even after scenes are filmed, they might be rewritten, recast, and refilmed – and still not used. Don't be a problem. Be a solution. You may be bumped up from staff writer to story editor, and (depending on the show) to executive story editor, and the bigger money of co-producer, producer, supervising producer, co-executive producer, executive producer. and consulting producer.

"I'm not going to take on a project if it's something that's not going to compel me at that time. When I joined *Big Love*, I had just gotten married. When I joined *The Big C*, my Father had recently passed. That's my barometer and that's how I connect to the material. I don't know how I would write if I couldn't connect on an emotional and intellectual level."
– Melanie Marnich, *Low Winter Sun*

Maybe one day you will be the showrunner or creator of a series. Be open to learning, listening in patience to the varieties of people who you work with, and altering your views.

"I feel like what it comes down to at the end of the day is this essential belief I have that there is something inside of you that you uniquely have to offer, and it takes a long time to identify as an artist."
– Mark Duplass, *Paddleton*

Days that are 15 – or more – hours long are not unheard of on set. Sleep deprivation can play with people's moods. And some rely on artificial stimulants to get through the day.

Substance abuse:
If you become known for substance abuse, word will spread – quickly. People in the industry network (gossip) – especially in the age of texting and social media.

Drug and alcohol addiction can quickly ruin your career – and you.

If you think you have a drug or alcohol problem, you probably do. Don't be foolish, seek help. Hiding it from others isn't a solution, but can greatly magnify the problem.

Explore 12-step programs, professional help from a psychologist, a sobriety house, a rehab center, or other ways of staying sober.

Include high-level, fresh, plant-based nutrition as part of sobriety. (Access: ForksOverKnives.com, NutritionFacts.org, and InfinityGreens.com) Drink water, instead of other things.

When most people think of being a TV writer, they might only consider weekly episodics, procedurals, situation comedies, limited series (mini-series), and anthologies. They might be thinking of the series on streaming services like Netflix, Amazon, Hulu, and others, which are one of those categories. But, there are also soap operas that produce daily episodes, and those productions also need writers.

Soaps (in some countries, they are called continuing dramas, which also go by the abbreviation C.D.) can have levels of writers who work to quickly churn out scripts that continue storylines that may have been going on for many, many episodes stretching months, and years. Some writers may only work on the outlines, and others write the dialogue in tune with those outlines, adhering to specific character, contention, and conflict arcs. Then, the main writers give the scripts a polish, before the scripts are filmed. And so on, doing what it takes to crank out episode after episode of the soap opera filmed quickly on a daily basis.

In addition to the usual small screen material, there is the video game market, which is a whole other thing to break into – and can't be covered in this book. But, consider that market as an option for writing. It likely would require massive focus, considering that video game scripts can run hundreds of pages, and contain tremendous amounts of dialogue.

If you want to be a staff writer on a TV show:
- Read a variety of books about TV production.
- Know the business processes.
- Make a list of all of the current shows that are in the genre you like.
- Research who the producers and writers are on each of those shows.
- On IMDbPro, search for those writers, and see who their managers and agents are. You will get ideas about which agents and managers you want representing you. (Yes, it is good to pay for IMDbPro – if you want to work in the industry. IMDbPro has details not contained on IMDb.)
- Get copies of the scripts from your favorite current shows, and study them.

It is interesting to see what has happened with TV. Decades ago, there were many "movie stars" who would never appear in a television show. That has changed. Now, many of the highest paid people in screen entertainment aren't in the movies. They are doing limited series (mini-series), anthology series, procedurals, sitcoms, and episodics. They are in TV. They are getting paid more for a single episode than most Americans earn in several years. Of course, their agents and managers – and taxes – take a percentage, but they still make bank.

The days of movies being where the so-called A-listers dwelled are over. While there are still those who will only work in film, the pull of the high-paid – and steady –TV acting gigs is strong.

"Movie stars like to shine. They like to have their movie star moments."
– Ron Shelton, *Blaze*

The story is what rules TV and film. It is best that the story appears on the size of screen that most effectively serves the story.

"Whatever story you want to tell, tell it at the right size."
– Richard Linklater, *Dazed and Confused*

"In my view, the only way to see a film remains the way the filmmaker intended: Inside a large movie theater, with great sound, and pristine picture."
– Ridley Scott, *Boy and Bicycle*

At Tribe workshop, most attendees say they write for both TV and film. But, even then, there is a strong focus on TV. The money is in productions made for the small screen. It is where talent is being drawn in – including actors who previously would have limited themselves to doing film. It is where writers know that they can write consistently – and get the steady paycheck.

Rather than occasionally selling a film script, screenwriters can enjoy regular employment by writing for the small screen – although maybe for less pay than what TV writers had made in prior years, and with fewer episodes to work on.

There is talk of how much work the writers have to do while developing characters that may only appear in about ten episodes of a cable or streaming series. Network TV was typically more than 20 episodes per season, which brought in more money, made it easier to get the union pension and health benefits, and provided more on-the-job experience per concept, which improves skill.

Whatever industry you work in, there is always give and take.

"I have been successful probably because I have always realized that I knew nothing about writing, and have merely tried to tell an interesting story entertainingly."
– Edgar Rice Burroughs, *Tarzan*

WRITING SAMPLES AND UNSOLD SCRIPTS

"If you want to make independent films, it's so competitive, and it's so hard. You've got to keep at it. Times in my career where I've become lazy or distracted, not only did I feel dissatisfied, like when I go two or three years without a film. But there is a definite 'out of sight out of mind', 'what have you done for me lately?' thing that happens. So, I think it's important to keep working for the more practical and financial reasons, and it helps to keep you fresh. I throw out a lot of what I write. Since *The Brothers McMullen*, I probably have twenty-five unproduced screenplays that I will probably never do anything with. But they had to be written in order to write the one that followed it."
– Edward Burns, *The Brothers McMullen*

Along the path to becoming a professional screenwriter, you will likely write a number of scripts that you might be better off thinking of as practice – even if you thought they were brilliant enough for producers to scoop up, and that actors would wrestle with each other to have the chance to star in the things. Reconsider. That is one way a screenwriting workshop can help you.

It takes other artists years of practice to achieve excellence. A musician practices for years, before giving any sort of significant stage performance. Painters and sculptors have to learn techniques. Athletes spend many days, and weeks, and months – and years – before they become top competitors. Should a screenwriter expect anything less to attain excellence, other than also having to spend months – and years – learning the craft – including by writing some scripts that never sell?

"Songwriting and screenwriting aren't that different to me."
– Billy Bob Thornton, *Sling Blade*

Some of the scripts you write that never get made might be used as "writing samples." That is: Scripts that you can show to people as examples of what you are capable of writing.

A producer, star, or director might read one of your scripts, and like it so much that they hire you to finish a script that is their creation, or that is a story by someone else, and it is a story that they own the rights to. Or, they will hire you to overhaul a script that is about to go into production.

"If you want a career as a writer, you must remember that screenwriting is a business. As a businessperson, you should find out everything about the person with whom you are going into business. Ask questions. Find out the reputation of the producer. Do you know anyone who has worked with him, knows him, or knows of him? Do your research, and, most important, avoid the sleaze factor in Hollywood, the wannabe's who can only be someone by virtue of the 'glue factor' and not by virtue of their own experience or talent."
– Stephen F. Breimer, Esq., author *The Screenwriter's Legal Guide*

After you option a script, it might not get made. The option expires, you keep the option money, the rights return to you, and you can option it to someone else. (There may be all sorts of complications in that scenario. Read: *The Screenwriter's Legal Guide*.)

Maybe that brilliant script of yours may never be optioned. Or, maybe many years will go by, and then you sell it, and then it gets made. Maybe after other writers have reworked it.

If people like Edward Burns and Emma Thompson can write scripts that never sell, including because the scripts might not be perceived by investors as what will fill theaters, don't be surprised when some of your scripts never sell.

"Last year, somebody tried to buy the first script I ever wrote for a lot of money, but I couldn't find a copy of it."
– Jack Nicholson, *Drive, He Said*

Whatever happens, don't stop at writing one, or two, or three, or five – or many more – scripts. It could be your seventh – or seventeenth – script that finally generates a screenwriting career. Then, maybe people will be interested in the other scripts you wrote. Or, you might realize that your first scripts are not as good as you once thought they were – and you will go about overhauling them, before you show them to anyone.

"Quantity produces quality. If you only write a few things, you're doomed."
– Ray Bradbury, *Moby Dick*

"I just hope these people stay persistent because sometimes it's six or eight scripts before they have that great script. All the people they admire went through these things and had adversity. Oliver Stone wrote ten scripts before he wrote *Platoon*, which got him all of his first jobs, which got him *Midnight Express*, and then he waited ten years to get *Platoon* made."
– Shane Salerno, *Aliens vs. Predator: Requiem*

Write seven screenplays. You might say that is difficult. So, you want to be a screenwriter, but you don't want to write screenplays? Reconsider what you think the career entails.

"I became quite successful very young, and it was mainly because I was so enthusiastic and I just worked so hard at it."
– Francis Ford Coppola, *The Godfather*

"Writers can self-generate, which will keep your career alive. You have all the power."
– John Ridley, *12 Years a Slave*

"I made a startling discovery. Time spent writing equals output of work."
– Ann Patchett, *Bel Canto*

"Write as if someone is waiting for it."
– Elizabeth Berger, *Love Simon*

"If you write one story, it may be bad; if you write a hundred, you have the odds in your favor."
– Edgar Rice Burroughs, *Tarzan*

"Write a script. Then write another script. And then, write another script after that. Don't think that whatever you wrote is so good that you could just stop writing and focus on doing that.
If you wrote it, finish it. Whatever you start – as best you can – finish it. Then, let some friends read it, whatever it is. And then, move on.
Whatever you think you've written now that probably feels good might be good. But, I absolutely guarantee you, whatever the next thing you do is will be better. So, write.
  Keep writing.
Don't stop writing."
– Ali LeRoi, *Everybody Hates Chris*

Write seven screenplays. As you do so, you will learn formatting, various types of story structure, ways of keeping the stories interesting with hooks and cliffhanger angles mixed with contention and conflict and clever, watchable characters. Along the way, you will factor what might be more likely to satisfy producers, directors, stars, financiers, distributors, and audiences.

"Our doubts are traitors, and make us lose the good we oft might win by fearing the attempt."
– William Shakespeare, *Macbeth*

"Writers should always have the market in mind. You should be aware of what's been sold and what's been made."
– Phil Volken, *Extortion*

"I don't think about audiences. I really, truly don't. I think about me. Me. I'm the audience. Is this something I want to see in a movie? Is this something I think is cool? Is this something I think is funny, or sad? Because otherwise you're kind of doing this tap dance for people. Why bother?"
– Charlie Kaufman, *Synecdoche, New York*

Allow yourself to write a script that is lousy. Finish it. It's a brain process. Put it away. Maybe one day you will realize how you can overhaul it and make it marketable.

Write a short film and direct it. Even though there typically is no money in shorts. You might realize that it could be expanded into a TV pilot, or a film. Or turned into a web series (with webisodes), or mobile series (with mobisodes) meant for watching on a cell phone or pad or ebook, which could lead to other screenwriting adventures. You might enter it into short film contests, and win awards – which can lead to other adventures in the screen trade. You might use the short for gaining interest to raise funds for the longer format. Someone in power might see it, and hire you to be involved with their projects (Search: Vin Diesel, *Multi-Facial*). Know that short films are usually for consideration of the director's skills.

Unless you are the writer/director of the short film, and not limited to being the writer while someone else directs it, there might not be much of a career boost there for you – but that's not a rule set in stone. If you do want to direct the full-length version, proving yourself with the short film can be one way to gain confidence – if you do an excellent job with it (and the camera work, sound, lighting, editing, and other "production values" are solid).

"The best way to get an agent? Write a good script. If your first one isn't good enough, make it better. If it still isn't good enough, write a new one. Once you write a good script, the rest will work itself out."
– John Swetnam, *Into the Storm*

Write a TV pilot. Or a few, or several pilots. Build up the arsenal of your portfolio of pilots so that when you finally hold meetings with managers, agents, producers, directors, and stars, you will have other scripts that might interest them – or can be refashioned for them.

"It's none of their business that you have to learn to write. Let them think you were born that way."
– Ernest Hemingway, *The Sun Also Rises*

145

Take every page of your favorite original script of your own creation through a screenwriting workshop. Listen to the feedback – even if you get the feeling that nobody likes it. Their feedback could help you in unexpected ways – including by helping you learn skills that you will use on another screenplay. We learn from mistakes. Maybe that script that you realized was filled with problems will be the one you will transform into your masterpiece.

"Chapter 9. *Goblet of Fire*. Nearly finished me. I rewrote it more times than I can now remember. You'll get there."
– J.K. Rowling, *Harry Potter*

Write a web series consisting of several – or more – short episodes with each being less than ten minutes. Plan on something you can film using cell phones and the film gear made for cell phones. (Search: Smart phone film attachments. Search: Mobisodes.)

The pilot episode of *It's Always Sunny in Philadelphia* was made by some struggling actors for something less than $1,000. FX picked it up. As a favor to an FX executive, Danny DeVito got involved in the second season as a guest actor. DeVito's children liked the show, and he ended up staying on as a regular cast member.

Write what will entice and captivate viewers.

"A movie is a spectacle – you are entertaining. The challenge is not to lose your audience. You have to hold on to them the whole time."
– John Krasinski, director/actor *A Quiet Place*

The idea for the film *A Quiet Place* was turned down by all of the top agencies. After several years of languishing as a concept and script, the film eventually was made. It quickly became an enormous global hit. The script's writers, Scott Beck and Bryan Woods then became the new in-demand wonders of the industry.

If you fall down, learn what got you there. Get up. Use the lessons learned, and keep on your desired path. That's what people do who go on to succeed – they learn from mistakes, they keep rising, and they propel themselves forward.

"If the material is challenging, it forces you to challenge yourself when handling it."
– Joel Coen, *No Country for Old Men*

Consider the story of Sylvester Stallone. He was so poor that he sold his dog. He wrote a script that people wanted to purchase, but he wouldn't sell it – unless they agreed to have him star in it. He turned down money that would have gotten him out of his financial rut of living in an apartment so small that he could close the door and open the window without getting out of bed. Eventually, his script was purchased with the agreement that he would star in it. He found the guy who he sold his dog to, repurchased the dog for more money than he sold it for, and used the dog as his co-star in the movie, *Rocky* – which went on to win numerous awards, and lead to many sequels.

"There are always goals. If you don't have a mountain, build one, and then climb it. And after you climb it, build another one. Otherwise, you start to flatline in your life."
– Sylvester Stallone, *Rocky*

"I devoted myself to writing for years without representation or a promise of anything. And there were times when I felt quite down about my prospects."
– Geoffrey Fletcher, *Precious*

Being down is part of the process of rising.

Practicing and learning from mistakes are part of improving your skills in a craft.

Write scripts. Workshop them. Have a script editor help you to polish them. Send them out for coverage. Only after all of that, get them to the right people.

"We all get knocked down in the business in every form. When you do something creative and put it out there, you expose yourself to criticism and rejection. Even as successful as I am, I get rejection all the time."
– Doug Liman, *Luna Park*

"Instead of the $250,000 expense of renting a private plane in which your lead finds redemption mid-turbulence, turn the plane into a shaky elevator. Congratulations, you have just saved $250,000, and brought yourself that much closer to making your movie. Allow the lack of money to fuel your creativity."
– Bianca Goodloe, managing partner at Goodloe Law and Kines Global; *The 7 Dirty Secrets to Film Financing*, IndieWire.com

Even Successful writers Don't Repeatedly Get Their Scripts Made

"When you're in the dumps at the end of your rope, ready to throw yourself off a cliff because you're convinced no one gives a shit about your stories, just remember that no director, no actor, no cinematographer, no set designer, costume designer, sound mixer, no SFX guys, no editor, no caterer, no driver, nobody, nobody has a job until you type 'The End.'"
– Frank Pierson, *A Star is Born*

It isn't unusual to hear those who you might consider to be successful screenwriters/directors talk about how they spent years trying to get one of their scripts made – even after they have proved themselves as writers who can deliver at the box office.

"Most of the screenplays I've written have not been made. And the ones that haven't been made I've worked very, very hard on, believed in, and loved, and thought they were good. But, they haven't been made. Or, I've handed them in, and then somebody years later has made it with a different script, and said, 'Oh, yeah, we just left yours.' So, I'm often left completely on the scrap heap without anyone even telling me. So, I don't get very well treated as a writer, either. So, that's comforting, isn't it, really?"
– Emma Thompson, *Bridget Jones's Baby*

Does the Film Have Good Roy?
When I first heard the term "good Roy," I was at a studio and thought it had something to do with a man named Roy. I was wrong. I heard someone say, "The Roy wasn't good on that one." Who is this Roy? What is he doing

that makes him not so good? But, they meant that the film didn't make money. It's not a person.

To get investors and distributors to back the production of a script, those money and business people have to see some sort of promise that they will get what they want out of the situation: A good return on investment (R.O.I.). Also known as "Good Roy."

"The first thing you want to do with your finished film is get it in front of distributors. You should be interested in getting a return on your investment."
– Jonathan Wolfe, Managing Director, American Film Market

"The amazing thing about any movie is not whether it's good, but that it got made at all."
– Frank Darabont, *The Walking Dead*

"You sell a screenplay like you sell a car. If someone drives it off a cliff, that's it."
– Rita Mae Brown, *The Slumber Party Massacre*

Being famous, and being a successful writer and/or director doesn't guarantee big returns at the box office. Many big names have been involved with films that have bombed and TV shows that have been canceled.

"Don't give up. You're going to get kicked in the teeth. A lot. Learn to take a hit, then pick yourself up off the floor. Resilience is the true key to success."
– Melissa Rosenberg, *Dexter*

If you are a writer wanting to sell scripts, write scripts that are broadly commercial, or that will be able to pull in a significant number of people from a target audience.

However, don't only write scripts that you think will appeal to the market. Write the films that you would like to see. Your script written with strong passion may turn out to be what speeds you into the career you would like to own.

If your script is going to appeal only to a narrow market, investors are going to want to have a strong feeling that the cost of producing that script will likely be recovered when that film hits theatres, or is otherwise distributed and viewed by audiences.

Budget.
Write within a realistic budget. Understand which scenes will cost more to film, and which scenes will cost less to film.

Locations: Filming in, on, around, or otherwise using bridges, highways, city streets, neighborhood streets, mountain tops, ski resorts, boats, beaches, piers, amusement parks, stadiums, museums, schools, military facilities, hospitals, airports, hotels, mansions, sky scrapers, tourist zones, landmarks, exotic locations, and islands requires permits, and perhaps certain specialists, safety experts, location managers, police, and others.

The greater distance you film from where the cast and crew live, the more your expenses will increase – including because of transportation and hotel costs.

Exterior locations are usually more expensive than interior locations.

Food: Wherever you film, food will be needed to feed everyone breakfast, lunch, dinner, and craft service: snacks, coffee, tea, juice, etc.

Night or day: Night shoots are usually more expensive than day shoots.

Weather: Scenes with fire, rain, snow, sleet, tornadoes, typhoons, and so forth all can be expensive to film.

Water: If you film in or on water, you will need certain equipment, and cast and crew will need things they won't need if you filmed on dry land.

Animals: The more animals, and the more high-maintenance those animals are, the more it will cost to film with them. They need to have caretakers, food, water, and a safe place to rest. They need to be transported. They need to be cleaned up after. However, many films now use CGI to create animals of all sorts, which can then be manipulated to do whatever is needed for the script. I worked on the Harrison Ford version of *The Call of the Wild*, the dog is CGI.

Principal actors: The more speaking roles you have, the more things will cost. Consider getting rid of some characters, combining multiple characters into one character, and using featured background actors who don't speak.

Children: Child actors require a parent or guardian, a teacher, a class room space, and they can only work for a certain number of hours. There needs to be a medic present or accessible. Studio lots have a medic office. Location filming will require a medic with their own supply kit.

Crowds: The more people you need, the more money you will need.

Wardrobe: Period pieces require more money for dressing, props, vehicles, wardrobe, and sets. Modern day productions require less money. If there are background actors in the project, and they need special wardrobe, it could mean having a day when they are called in for a fitting. That is more staff, and storage, and wardrobe rental and cleaning costs.

If you have scenes that require the background to wear tuxedos and gowns, and it is modern day, you can likely get enough people who can wear their own formal clothing, and pay them additional for their outfits. If you have a period piece, all of those clothes will need to be rented.

In Los Angeles, many productions rely on Western Costume to supply specialty wardrobe from their enormous warehouse in North Hollywood.

If there are characters who have their clothing damaged as part of the scene, those actors will need to have multiple identical outfits.

Props: The more props you need to film, and the more difficult they are to find and take care of, the more expensive the shoot will be.

Vehicles: The more vehicles you will need, the more it will cost to film. Cars usually need a variety of drivers. Productions often simply pay background actors for the use of their cars. If you need cars from a certain era, or expensive vehicles, you will also need more money.

Trains, planes, helicopters, motorcycles, tractors, bulldozers, tanks, submarines, yachts, speed boats, and other specialty vehicles come with their own variety of expenses, specialists, and safety issues.

Chases: Car chase scenes, or any scenes filmed with moving vehicles, can easily get expensive, especially if they are done in a city, on a highway, or a location with complicated terrain.

Crashes: Cost money. Require specialists, a stunt crew, equipment, safety procedures, and perhaps a variety of identical vehicles.

Stunts and fight scenes: Cost money. A stunt coordinator and other staff will need to be present. Safety precautions will need to be followed. Stunts also play into the cost of production insurance. A medic with a full medic kit must also be on set.

Explosions, pyrotechnics, and weaponry: These require safety procedures, permits, and specialists.

Prosthetics, molds and models, aging, wounds, blood, dismemberment, fake dead bodies, CGI: All of those cost money, and – depending on how complicated your scenes are – require specialists.

Etc.

Films aimed at target audiences are usually easier to market. Films that fall into this classification include those centered around sports, spring break, faith, fairy tales, vampires, zombies, super heroes, woman/child/man in peril, Halloween, Christmas, Valentine's Day, and wedding season. Even films based on a defined culture, such as motorcycle clubs, can be easier to market.

If there is an underserved but large population that is likely to welcome a film that they identify with, that could work out at the box office. An example: *Crazy Rich Asians*.

Consider what happened with the superhero film *Black Panther*, and how it was an instant global hit. There surely was a blatant absence of films featuring African-American actors playing comic book characters. Within weeks of its release, the film made several hundred million dollars domestically, and over a billion dollars internationally. That is a tremendous return on investment for a film that had a budget of about $200 million. Yes, that is an enormous budget. But, it paid off.

"Don't pitch stories, write spec scripts. Why try to convince a roomful of unread egomaniacs that you can write a good script about something? Just sit down and write the damn thing. It's much more honest to do it well than to promise to do it well.

151

Don't let the bastards get you down. If you can't sell your script, or if you sell the script and they bring in another writer to butcher it, or if the director claims in interviews that he really wrote your script, or if the actors claim that they improvised all of your best lines, or if you're left out of the press junket, simply sit down and write another script. And if the same thing happens to you on that one, write another and another and another and another, until you get one up there that's your vision translated by the director to the big screen."
— Joe Eszterhas, *Flashdance*

Visualize the poster for your film. Could the poster entice a paying public?

If you are in the industry long enough, you might hear the stories of people who bring movie posters to the annual American Film Market convention that is held in Santa Monica, California (AmericanFilmMarket.com. [Hint: AFM produces a directory listing the companies that attended the convention.]). They are posters for films that have not yet been made, or that exist in script form, or only in treatment form. The producers test what the international distributors are interested in. If the distributors are enticed by a certain poster, the producers then aim to finish the film, or write a script for that poster and film it, selling the rights to various regions of the planet to help pay for production. Are the stories of this happening true, or myth? It's not difficult to believe that there is some truth in it. With so many ways of delivering content to the global market, it isn't unreasonable to consider it a possibility that a film was financed and produced based on a concept poster and a pitch.

Consider sports films. They attract a particular audience – not only people interested in sports, but also family audiences (if the rating is family-friendly).

A film poster featuring a basketball player making a strenuous shot into a hoop as other players fail to block the shot can get the attention of the millions of people who play and/or follow basketball. By targeting that basketball fan market, the film should get a reasonable return on investment – especially if the script, acting, and production qualities are of high quality.

Sports films can be made for low cost, if they take place in a small setting, like a town park, or a small college – and not in a major arena. Compare what it cost to make *Hoosiers* (about $6 million) to what it cost to make *White Men Can't Jump* (about $30 million). Targeting advertising of such sports films to specific audiences can be key to attract a sufficient number of people to cover the costs of the film, and bring in a profit for investors.

"That's why I went with *Terms of Endearment*. It was the most human script I'd read in years, and I just knew it would be successful. Why? Product difference. To a studio executive who's in a more intense flow, product difference looks like danger. But to someone like myself, who is one step removed, that's what you're looking for. That wave is going to break, believe me. A lot of good things will get made that haven't been done yet."
— Jack Nicholson, *Ride in the Whirlwind*

While some would advise screenwriters to avoid writing for a specific market, that advice could be a bit unrealistic. It is common for producers to search for films that they can market to people with specific interests, including vampire films, superhero films, romantic comedies, horror films, creature features, faith-based films, wedding comedies, and so forth.

While it is likely a good idea to write a script based on something that you are passionate about, it wouldn't be a bad idea to write some screenplays that could be of interest to producers and distributors who specialize in niche films targeted to specific audiences, and that are sold into particular regions.

"If you've got craft, you got game. If you got game, you can write your way in and out of anything. Writing is the best gig in the whole business, as far as I'm concerned. It's the only job where you don't have to wait for someone to tell you what to do. You just sit down and make shit up."
– Robert Mark Kamen, *The Power of One*

"In the end, scripts are actor bait, plain and simple – no matter what medium. So, it all starts with character and concept, and my advice right now is to think small for your first few projects. What can be made? What can I actually get produced, or produce myself?"
– Brad Riddell, DePaul University, and USC School of Cinematic Arts.

Do write your passion projects. But, cover your bases, and write some scripts of different genres – and that can be produced with low budgets. You might find that you like writing about something you previously had no interest in. It could end up more financially rewarding than what you first thought would be your specialty.

"A lot of the scripts you write don't get made, and the ones that do get made are certainly – as a writer, they're not your vision."
– Dan Gilroy, *The Fall*

"I love writing, but I stopped because I felt I was more effective approaching filmmaking from a different vantage point. At this moment, I supposed I can do more for a script as an actor than as a writer – in the film sense. I wrote right up to *Easy Rider*, at which time I became someone who could add fuel to a project as an actor. I've always approached film as a unit, but you have to work your own field."
– Jack Nicholson, *Head*

"It is only in his work that an artist can find reality and satisfaction, for the actual world is less intense than the world of his invention – and, consequently his life, without recourse to violent disorder, does not seem very substantial. The right condition for him is that in which his work is not only convenient, but unavoidable."
– Tennessee Williams, *Cat on a Hot Tin Roof*

The House Un-American Activities Committee: Suspicion and Ruin

There was a politically dark time when a group of established screenwriters not only had problems trying to get work, they were blocked from working in the American film industry. It was so because, in 1947 they refused to testify before the notorious House Un-American Activities Committee, which was investigating potential Communist activity among Americans.

In July, 1946, *The Hollywood Reporter* named people in the industry who were considered to be Communist sympathizers.

Screenwriter Dalton Trumbo was on the list. He was known for his political views. He authored the popular anti-war novel *Johnny Got His Gun*.

Using the list, the HUAC summoned Trumbo and nine other writers to find if Communist messages had been hidden in studio films.

The Hollywood Ten were convicted of contempt of Congress for refusing the testify and refusing to name names of possible Communist sympathizers.

Trumbo served about ten months in a federal penitentiary in Kentucky.

More than 300 people, including actors, directors, producers, and screenwriters, were blacklisted, including Charlie Chaplin and Orson Welles.

The Motion Picture Association of America banned Trumbo and others from getting work in the film industry.

In response to the HUAC, and in attempts to prove allegiance to the U.S., most studios made films with anti-Communist themes. They also banned the blacklisted people from entering the studio lots. Careers were ruined.

Over the years that those blacklisted were denied work, some had died, some had moved away, including in other countries, and many never worked again in the film industry. (Search: Paul Robeson blacklisted.)

Some of the writers on the list did get work during the Blacklist years, but did so for low pay. They had to use pseudonyms on their scripts, or they used the names of other writers sympathetic to their situation.

Scripts Trumbo wrote under different names won Academy Awards for their screenplays, including *Roman Holiday* (1953) and *The Brave One (1956)*.

When Kirk Douglas had optioned Howard Fast's book *Spartacus*, he had the author write the screenplay. Finding the script inadequate, Douglas hired Trumbo to write the script. Trumbo was to use the pseudonym Sam Jackson.

On January 20, 1960, the *New York Times* published an article saying that Trumbo had been hired to pen a studio script. After columnist Walter Winchell revealed Trumbo as the writer of *Spartacus*. Douglas told Trumbo that he was going to give Trumbo full screen credit for *Spartacus*.

Universal-International Studio was the one studio that defiantly did not make the anti-Communist propaganda films, and they agreed with Douglas. In October, 1960, *Spartacus* premiered with Trumbo credited as the writer.

Trumbo also received writing credit on director Otto Preminger's film *Exodus*, which premiered in December, 1960.

Trumbo's situation helped to start the end of the terrible Hollywood Blacklist era. (Search: Director Elia Kazan turns in actors to the HUAC.)

"I was put on earth to face a blank page. Find whatever story or genre I want to deal with, and do my own little version of it."
– Quentin Tarantino, *Kill Bill*

"You want a drama to center around a small number of conflicts, and work through those."
– Tony Kushner, *Munich*

"I think you're only going to get noticed by following your own instincts and doing original work, and writing the thing that only you can write."
– Nancy Meyers, *Father of the Bride*

How to Choose a Story to Write

"I'm looking for some things that are different. You want relatability and you want a story that has an opportunity to first break out of the crowd, and have some emotional resonance with an audience. I mean, for me emotional resonance is one of the most important things

You have to spend years on a project, so you better relate to it on a very fundamental way, from the inside, or else it's not going to be a fun experience."
– Len Amato, President of HBO Films: miniseries and Cinemax

"If you genuinely want to make films, then write screenplays. All you need to write a script is paper and a pencil. It's only through writing scripts that you learn specifics about the structure of film and what cinema is. That's what I tell aspiring directors, but they still won't write. They find writing too hard. And it is. Writing scripts is a hard job."
– Akira Kurosawa, *After the Rain*

"I like to begin every screenplay with a burst of delusional self-confidence. It tends to fade pretty quickly, but – for me, at least – there doesn't seem to be any other way to start writing a script."
– Michael Arndt, *Star Wars: The Force Awakens*

"What helps me to choose what to write is knowing how it ends. You gotta know how it ends."
– Taylor Sheridan, *Hell or High Water*

155

"The hardest thing, I think, to do as a filmmaker is to choose your subject. What are you going to do? Kind of like being a painter. What are you going to paint? And when you first begin, there's a million options."
– Ridley Scott, *Blade Runner*

"I think if you stay nimble and connected to why you're telling stories, and keep looking for stories that resonate for other people, then there will always be a way, because people are hungry for it."
– Edward Norton, *Motherless Brooklyn*

"If it's an idea and I pretty much know the idea, but I feel really blocked about how to shape it, I start thinking about: Well, what are some key scenes that I feel like would be in this project? Whether it's the climax, or some other part of the film. And I try to write those scenes, first, out of order. What happens is, I call it the 'scent of blood.' What happens is you are in it now. And you didn't start on FADE IN: But you're in the script and it can kind of grow out from inside, instead of page one. Go over to this part where you really have some feeling, and write that. Because, at some point, if you don't let yourself stop, you're going to get into it."
– Jim Uhls, *Fight Club*

"Most aspiring screenwriters simply don't spend enough time choosing their concept. It's by far the most common mistake I see in spec scripts. The writer has lost the race right from the gate. Months – sometimes years – are lost trying to elevate a film idea that by its nature probably had no hope of ever becoming a movie."
– Terry Russu, *Shrek*

"You should follow your heart, and write what you're passionate about."
– Phil Volken, *Extortion*

"All fiction has to have a certain amount of truth to it to be powerful."
– George R.R. Martin, *Game of Thrones*

"I don't want to imitate life in movies; I want to represent it. And in that representation you use the colors you feel, and sometimes they are fake colors. But always it's to show one emotion."
– Pedro Almadovar, *Talk to Her*

"If a story is in you, it has got to come out."
– William Faulkner, *The Long, Hot Summer*

"It seems to me it's the hardest thing because you're starting from nothing and creating something. Everybody else is interpreting what you've written. Everybody else is an interpretive artist. Even the best of them. Stanley Kubrick was an interpretive artist. The best actors in the world are interpreting what's on the page, and they use it as a springboard to something else, but if it's not there, there's nothing to spring from. So, the writer is the only person who's

taking absolutely nothing, and 120 pages of it, and dirtying it up in such a way that it's gonna gross hundreds of millions of dollars and make a lot of people happy."
– Paul Guay, *The Little Rascals*

"A writer has to be driven crazy to help him to see."
– Philip Roth, *A.P.E.X.*

"Only write the script that you would pay to see on opening night."
– John August, *Corpse Bride*

"As far as chasing trends, what a writer needs to keep in mind is if a movie comes out and it's a hit in a particular genre or subject matter, there are already dozens of projects in development sitting behind that. The studios and financiers are all too ready to catalyze those projects – for better or worse. I'd rather zig when everyone else is zagging, for those reasons. When everyone is fishing in one pool, I want to go fishing in another hole. But that can sometimes bite you. If you're doing something that's so different from what everyone else is doing, it sometimes doesn't get any traction – because it's so different."
– Chris Salvaterra, producer

If you write a script based on what was a trend when you first started writing it, what you might find is that you set yourself up to play a game that has ended, and you can't even chase the goal post, because it has been dismantled and taken to a scrap heap. You also might have written something that is only a recap of a screen game that has already been played.

"Don't pay attention to the industry. Do your own thing. Make your own industry. Break open the form."
– Martin Scorsese, *Boardwalk Empire*

"I just realized that nobody knows what they're doing. Our business says, 'Give me the script that checks all the boxes.' But the films that resonate usually don't do that. Think about *Goodfellas*, it could be a textbook on how not to write a screenplay. It leans on voiceover at the beginning, then abandons it for a while, then the character just talks right into the camera at the end. That structure is so unusual that you don't have any sense of what's going to happen next. And, to me, that's the goal of a screenwriter: To allow audiences into a world where they can't predict what's going to happen."
– Taylor Sheridan, *Fast*

"I started writing down scenes that I thought were interesting – not always with the intention of writing a script that I would then sell or produce – simply as a way of memorializing moments I'd seen. Those moments became a collection of scenes that started to become a movie."
– Casey Affleck, *Light of My Life*

A script story can originate from anywhere. Choose any film, and you can find a writer who somehow was inspired to write a script based on any number of things. Some fictionalize people they know, or situations they have been in. Others came up with an idea triggered by a news story, some may have been inspired by events in their life, others write scripts based on fantasy, sports, history, politics, inventions, events that are paramount to revolutionary thought or cultural changes. Some writers are motivated to expose mistruths, tragedies, corruption, and evil ways. Some write scripts simply to entertain, motivate, inspire, enlighten, or get people to escape their daily problems.

"I write only when I'm inspired. Fortunately, I'm inspired at 9 o'clock every morning."
– William Faulkner, *The Big Sleep*

"My stories run up and bite me on the leg. I respond by writing down everything that goes on during the bite. When I finish, the idea lets go and runs off."
– Ray Bradbury, *Curiosity Shop*

"Some of the best ideas come from sheer discovery, and not by some masterminded, preconceived genius."
– Spike Jonze, *Her*

"That first real flash of excitement is always when I'm writing something that should do this way, and then all of the sudden inspiration happens, and it goes somewhere else – and I'm party to it."
– Quentin Tarantino, *Once Upon a Time… in Hollywood*

"Whether in painting, poetry, performance, music, dance, or life, there is an intelligence working in every situation. This force is the primary carrier of creation. If we trust it and follow its natural movement, it will astound us with its ability to find a way through problems – and even make creative use of our mistakes and failures. There is a magic to this process that cannot be controlled by ego. Somehow, it always finds the way to the place where you need to be, and a destination you never could have known in advance."
– Shaun McNiff, author *Trust the Process: An Artist's Guide to Letting Go*

"You have to take risks. If there's something that's calling you, you have to answer. It's a gift when you have a feeling about something. It's a gift when you have a desire – a dream. That is something – a seed that has been planted. Our responsibility is to answer in some way. So, that's how I thought. I kept having this nagging thing that I wanted to make a film, to tell stories. And so, I decided to answer the call."
– Ava DuVernay, *Central Park Five*

"It's a bit cliché, but you can't go wrong by writing what you know. Even if you're a horrible writer, your own knowledge and experience is unrivaled. Nobody knows what you know like you know what you know."
– Issa Rae, *The Choir*

"People always say, 'Write what you know,' and I think it's 'Write what you know, emotionally.'"
– Spenser Cohen, *Extinction*

"People ask, 'Are your things autobiographical?' and I think, no, they're not autobiographical directly, but of course my life has informed my work."
– Andrea Arnold, *American Honey*

"As a writer, whenever we take up a new story, we embark on a creative journey, leaving our ordinary world and venturing into the extraordinary world of our imagination."
– Scott Myers, GoIntoTheStory.BlckLst.com

"Pivot into your own voice. Even when you're a little unsure about that, just go in that direction, and be confident about your own voice. That's what people are looking for. Keep yourself inspired, because it's a difficult job to face a blank page, and a vulnerable space to send it out into the world. But you always have to tell yourself there is a place for your voice, and keep digging deeper into your point-of-view."
– Gordon Chism, *What Women Want*

"Anyone who has survived childhood has enough information about life to last them the rest of his days."
– Flannery O'Connor, *Black Hearts Bleed Red*

"The more specifically you write to your experience, the more compelling your story will be. But, if you're trying to stand back and write to an idea or a movement, it will be trash, it will be flat. Write to what moves you, and craft it well. Tell a great story."
– Jane Anderson, *The Wife*

You can simply do what some people have done to get ideas of what to base a script on: Take a few different news stories from the daily swirl of mud in the media, and mix them together. Choose an era, setting, and theme. Choose some names for the characters that don't sound the same. Create some back stories. Formulate a story that has a beginning, middle, and end, and that is infused with tension, concern, perplexity, twists, arcs, challenges, and payoffs.

"I always work backwards from theme. I know some people are driven by story first, or by character first. I'm driven by theme first. Every movie is about something."
– Audrey Wells, *The Hate You Give*

"I never really define the genre that I want the story to be in, or what metaphors or symbols I should place within the story. I always just want to depict very interesting and entertaining situations. I move through impulses."
— Bong Joon-Ho, *Parasite*

"Each writer starts differently, but the only valid way is start with character. Character is plot. Character is story."
— Eleanor Perry, *The Man Who Loved Cat Dancing*

"I've gotten ideas for movies from things that happened to me, from things I've read in newspapers, and in the case of *The Brother from Another Planet*, from dreams I've had."
— John Sayles, *Django Lives!*

"The creative process is mysterious. A conversation, a ride in the car, or a melody can trigger something."
— Alejandro González Iñárritu, *Birdman*

"A storyteller is an observer of life. Watch people around you every day of your life. You pick up instant stories wherever you go and refashion them into screenplays."
— Julian Fellowes, *Separate Lies*

"Ideas come from the Earth. They come from every human experience that you can either witness or have heard about, translated into your brain, in your own sense of dialogue, and your own language form. Ideas are born from what is smelled, heard, seen, experienced, felt – emotion wise. Ideas are probably in the air, like little tiny items of ozone. It's the easiest thing on earth is to come up with an idea."
— Rod Serling, *The Twilight Zone*

"Everybody walks past a thousand story ideas every day. The good writers are the ones who see five or six of them. Most people don't see any."
— Orson Scott, *Ender's Game*

Ideas for a screenplay can be from:
- Distorting your life experiences
- Your childhood journal
- Looking through family photos
- Letters you've sent or received
- Your day job
- Twisting the truth
- Inheritance issues
- Embellishing everything about your life
- Personal tragedy
- Undergoing psychotherapy
- Dreams, nightmares, night terrors

- Altered mind experiences
- Hypnotism
- Child abuse and neglect
- News stories
- What you think is horrible
- What you fear
- What makes you laugh
- What you wish to achieve
- Writing in response to something that happened to you
- Local myths
- Gossip
- Ideology
- Walking around graveyards
- Local old buildings, bridges, and other structures
- Trash found on streets and in alleyways
- Speaking with military veterans
- Speaking with civil servants
- Speaking with farmers and others
- Volunteering at a homeless shelter
- 12-step support groups
- Going to court hearings
- Observing people in public
- Going to museums
- Local, national, or global politics
- Exercising, gyms, yoga studios, fitness clubs
- Watching sports
- Sports heroes
- Being a member of a sports team
- Talking with children (always get parental permission)
- Books in a library
- Photography books
- Going to garage sales and second hand stores
- History
- Modern inventors
- Conspiracy theories
- Medical mysteries
- New diseases
- Travel
- Reading a book or watching a film you hate
- Environmental catastrophes
- Being involved in environmental causes
- Camping, hiking, kayaking, canoeing, and outdoor activities
- The person who at first doesn't interest you
- Local artists and musicians

- Listening to music
- Murders and other crimes
- Local businesses
- Extended metaphors
- Roman/Greco mythology
- Old novels
- Writing the opposite story of a popular book
- Writing the opposite story of a popular film
- Listening to radio theatre
- Attending live theatre
- Hypothetical questions

"Ideas will come to you more quickly if you've been putting in the time at your chosen craft."
 – Twyla Tharp, choreographer

"Knowing what you are going to write is a huge part of it. Knowing what you want to write, knowing the story you want to tell. And then, in writing, leaving yourself open to the discovery and exploration that process provides."
 – Billy Kelly, *Enchanted*

"Be pioneers. Find stories that are risky, but speak volumes of who you are as a writer."
 – Stephen Spielberg, *Close Encounters of the Third Kind*

"I have been interested in dreams, really since I was a kid. I have always been fascinated by the idea that your mind, when you are asleep, can create a world in a dream and you are perceiving it as though it really existed."
 – Christopher Nolan, *Inception*

"I listen to a lot of music. I use music to help me work, and put my mind in the moment. It helps me pick the tone, and helps when I need ideas. So, that's kind of my ritual."
 – Armando Bo, *Birdman*

"When I write a screenplay, I am usually just putting a road map for a film that has been bouncing around in my head down on paper so that other people can read and see it."
 – J.C. Chandor, *A Most Violent Year*

"I see the movie in my mind. Before I make the movie, I watch the movie. I've got a genuine vision that is how I see it."
 – Quentin Tarantino, *Once Upon a Time… in Hollywood*

To be a screenwriter, you don't have to be a college graduate who attended Harvard or Princeton. You might be from a poor part of Chicago, where you were raised by a single mom, as was Robert Townsend. You might have been from an impoverished family in China, who at times had no home, as did John

Woo's family. You can be a stripper who named yourself an after-market name, and became a blogger who then worked your way into becoming an award-winning screenwriter, as did Diablo Cody. You can be an oil rig worker who goes on to write and direct a wide variety of award-winning films, like Richard Linklater.

"Songwriting and screenwriting aren't that different to me."
– Billy Bob Thornton, *Sling Blade*

You can be a songwriter and singer who also happens to win multiple awards for acting, writing, and directing, as Billy Bob Thornton has.

"I'm more influenced by novelists than I am by filmmakers."
– Billy Bob Thornton, *Jayne Mansfield's Car*

When he was starting out in Hollywood, Thornton worked at a pizza parlor, where he allowed me to eat for free when I was completely broke as a result of multiple health problems. I don't know him, but, like me, I read that he ridded himself of serious health problems by adapting a plant-based diet.

"Somewhere along the line we stopped believing we could do anything. And if we don't have our dreams, we have nothing."
– Billy Bob Thornton, *The Last Real Cowboys*

Thornton famously worked as a waiter at an event attended by Billy Wilder, who suggested that Thornton try screenwriting.

"Usually, with film writing, I start with characters, and set about writing their story."
– Billy Bob Thornton, *A Family Thing*

If you want to be a screenwriter, write. Write daily. Wake up early and write before you go on with the day. As you go about doing whatever it is that you do each day, keep a pen and note pad handy to write down your ideas. Formulate stories that are engaging, filled with concerns that people can relate to, and that are rich in subtext that triggers audiences to factor, anticipate, and reconfigure.

"One of the few things I've discovered about writing is to form a habit that becomes an addiction."
– Frank Pierson, *The Good Wife*

"Let your characters talk to each other and do things. Spend time with them – they'll teach you who they are and what they're up to."
– Greta Gerwig, *Lady Bird*

If you write some script pages every day, and work to make it into a script that can then be polished into something worth filming, you will be far ahead of the people who only want to be screenwriters, and who never write one.

"You don't write because you want to say something; you write because you've got to say something."
– F. Scott Fitzgerald, *The Last Tycoon*

"My films are basically silent films. The dialogue just adds some weight."
– Sergio Leone, *The Seven Revenges*

"Take your absolute strongest idea, find the niche where it best fits in culture, and focus like a laser on creating the most expressive visualization of that concept possible."
– Brian Andrews, *Hominidae*

What your screenplays are about and how the stories play out is up to you. No matter what they are about, make them intriguing, and something that actors will want to act in, directors will want to direct, investors want to put money into, and large numbers of people will want to watch.

"Serious writers write. Inspired, or not. Over time, they discover that routine is a better friend than inspiration."
– Ralph Keyes, author *The Courage to Write: How Writers Transcend Fear*

"I've never understood writers who claim it's agony and claim to bleed every sentence. For me, it's a joy and a release, if it's going well. It's all I really know how to do with any competence."
– Gerald Nachman, author *Raised on Radio*

"There is nothing to writing. All you do is sit down at a typewriter and bleed."
– Ernest Hemingway, *The Killers*

"There is a Swedish expression, it translates to, 'dig where you stand.' Go for telling stories you know. The changes are those are the ones that will be most interesting to an audience."
– Levan Akin, *And then We Danced*

"Nothing is original. Steal from anywhere that resonates with inspiration or fuels your imagination. Devour old films, new films, music, books, paintings, photographs, poems, dreams, random conversations, architecture, bridges, street signs, trees, clouds, bodies of water, light and shadows. Select only things to steal from that speak directly to your soul. If you do this, your work – and theft – will be authentic.

Authenticity is invaluable; originality is non-existent. And don't bother concealing your thievery. Celebrate it, if you feel like it. In any case, always remember what Jean-Luc Godard said: 'It's not where you take things from – it's where you take them to.'"
– Jim Jarmusch, *Dead Man*

"Make the character emotionally true in everything he says, whether it's meant to be funny or not. That way – step-by-step, line-by-line – the audience believes this character."
– Kristina Reed, producer

"Rather than tell the audience who a character is, I like to show the audience what a character wants."
– Aaron Sorkin, *Lucy and Desi*

"I appreciate the craft that goes into action and fight sequences, but it seems the stream of assassin-character scripts tend to celebrate violence and destruction without purpose of repercussion."
– Kristin Burr, producer

Characters

"The most important thing to know before sitting down to write is the nature of each of your characters. Know them inside and out, through and through, as if they're real. Know them better than you know yourself."
– Diana Ossana, *Brokeback Mountain*

"I imagine them very clearly, and then attempt to describe what I can see. Sometimes, I draw them for my own amusement."
– J.K. Rowling, *Harry Potter*

"You love all your characters, even the ridiculous ones. You have to on some level; they're your weird creations in some kind of way."
– Joel Coen, *Toy Story*

"I think people who have faults are a lot more interesting than people who are perfect."
– Spike Lee, *Red Hook Summer*

"My favorite characters are ones who are desperate to be liked. Or to be loved and to be accepted, or cool and who are overcompensating so much that they become horrible. I like writing horrible people who aren't necessarily villains, but are trying hard to have an opinion. I find them really fun to write,"
– Taika Waititi, *Jojo Rabbit*

"What inspires me the most is people. Both real and fictional. If you need an idea for a character have a five-minute conversation with anyone. Character is always the thing that draws me to the page."
– Lesley Arfin, *Brooklyn Nine-Nine*

"I like to do what I like to call writing outside the script. And sometimes there are scenes that would come before the story of where the script starts. And sometimes I interview the characters. I try to goad them, provoke them, get them angry, then get them suddenly talking in a sentimental way about some memory, or something. And then get them joking and laughing, and basically get them all over the range with questions. It's very mechanical at first. But, they sort of start to come alive in an interview."
— Jim Uhls, *Fight Club*

"Characters do not come out of thin air. I think writers acquire characters by living a life in which something is risked. It's only by being defeated, rejected, exalted, by going through all the peaks and valleys, that you can acquire anything worth writing down."
— Michael Blake, *Dances with Wolves*

"Each character faces a dilemma in her life, and as an actor you're able to step into that character's skin, look through her eyes. You leave transformed, a different person, because once you live a little bit of someone's life, it changes you."
— Sally Field, *The Christmas Tree*

"Even if you have two lines, you have to do the same complete work as if you're number one on the call sheet. All characters have memories, they have people, they have a life. We live in our own close-up all the time."
— Alfre Woodard, actor

"Some of the most intense affairs are between actors and characters. There's a fire in the human heart, and we jump into it with the same obsession as we have with our lovers."
— Sigourney Weaver, actor

"Develop a clean line of action for your leading character."
— Billy Wilder, *Witness for the Prosecution*

To help your character development: Learn about archetypes.
Introduced by Swiss psychologist Carl Jung, the concept of archetypes has to do with the essential essences, tendencies, instincts, or personalities that are displayed in the way people function and behave, their motives and values, the positions they take, and the roles they play in their culture and society.

Archetype is a combination of the Greek words archein, the ancient or origin, and typos, the model or pattern. The archetype theory is that each person is an emulation or echo of their model or original pattern.

"Archetypes are the living system of reactions and aptitudes that determine the individual's life in invisible ways."
— Carl Jung, psychologist

According to Jung, archetypes play into the three components of psyche, including the ego, the unconscious mind, and the conscious mind. And that plays out in what the person has experienced, and what is expressed or suppressed.

Life experiences, culture, and community norms and expectations play roles in what a person expresses and suppresses, the façade or social mask they carry or agree to, and how they role play according to who and what they are surrounded by.

Then, there is the whole other level to all of this archetype thing: What a person dreams of – both in nocturnal dreams, and in day dreams. Those imaginary visualizations have to do with their hopes, wants, needs, and other impulsive urges and cravings. All of those are expressed, repressed, suppressed, or guided in some way – consciously or unconsciously through passive or aggressive intentions, or some mix of those that reveal base personal values.

There are books, articles, and videos about archetypes. All of it can't be covered in this book. Do your homework.

Jung details archetypes in the book *The Structure and Dynamics of Psyche*, which is the 8th volume in *The Collected Works of C.G. Jung*, published by Princeton University Press.

"It is the function of the consciousness, not only to recognize and assimilate the external world through the gateway of the senses, but to translate into visible reality the world within us."
– Carl Jung, author *The Red Book*

Another helpful book covering archetypes is *King, Warrior, Magician, Lover*, by Robert Moore and Goulas Gillette.

Caroline Myss has published a deck of 80 archetype cards. They are simple, but they might trigger ideas for character development.

12 archetypes and their 4 motivating orientations:
Do not consider these to be static or fixed. While they may be core to the person, there may be some fluidity in how their conscious or subconscious holds to their base archetype within their social orientation.

Freedom orientation
- Explorer
- Jester
- Rebel / outlaw

Ego orientation
- Alchemist / magician
- Creator
- Hero

Social orientation
- Caregiver
- Every person

- Lover

Order orientation
- Innocent
- Ruler
- Sage

You might also have your own observations as to what could make up the main base and life experience traits of a character.

These combinations could include:
- **Achiever** or **succeeder**
- **Activator** or **instigator**
- **Addict** or **substance abuser**
- **Advocate** or **promoter**
- **Angel** or **spirit guide**
- **Artist** or **creator**
- **Beggar** or **burden**
- **Bully** or **meanie**
- **Challenger** or **confronter**
- **Closet case** or **suppressed**
- **Companion** or **spouse**
- **Coward** or **wimp**
- **Deceiver** or **trickster**
- **Deceived** or **cheated**
- **Destroyer** or **demolisher**
- **Detached** or **scarred**
- **Do gooder** or **validation seeker**
- **Doubter** or **disbeliever**
- **Empress** or **emperor**
- **Enabler** or **aid**
- **Enthusiast** or **extrovert**
- **Fixer** or **corrector**
- **Follower** or **sheep**
- **Gambler** or **risk taker**
- **Glutton** or **self-harmer**
- **Healer** or **helper**
- **Hero** or **savior**
- **Individualist** or **non-conformer**
- **Investigator** or **seeker**
- **Liar** or **deceiver**
- **Loner** or **introvert**
- **Loyalist** or **fanatic**
- **Martyr** or **sufferer**
- **Matriarch** or **patriarch**
- **Mediator** or **middle-person**
- **Mentor** or **uncle/aunt**
- **Messenger** or **informant**
- **Needy** or **lowly**
- **Observer** or **spectator**
- **Orphan** or **abandoned**
- **Peacemaker** or **negotiator**

- **Performer** or **exhibitionist**
- **Pirate** or **thief**
- **Prophet** or **forecaster**
- **Protector** or **guard**
- **Rebel** or **resistor**
- **Recalcitrant** or **stubborn**
- **Reformer** or **motivator**
- **Renunciate** or **non-conformist**
- **Rescuer** or **advocate**
- **Rookie** or **trainer**
- **Scribe** or **informant**
- **Servant** or **supporter**
- **Sickly** or **downtrodden**
- **Teaser** or **flirt**
- **Traitor** or **treasonist**
- **Tyrant** or **sadist**
- **Student** or **learner**
- **Vampire** or **taker**
- **Victim** or **assaulted**
- **Visionary** or **seer**
- **Visitor** or **tourist**
- **Warrior** or **soldier**
- **Weakling** or **self-deceiver**
- **Wizard** or **Sorcerer**

… and so forth and so on.

Make up your own list of base personality traits, according to the needs of your story and the characters you need to formulate the story.

Each character might be triggered to turn into another as they learn, grow, gain wisdom, are influenced, are manipulated, and otherwise play out their lives in response to what they experience.

Don't label the characters in your script with the name of the archetype that you have decided they will be. Simply allow that to be displayed through their actions, responses, words, façade, and place. Have it attached to their apparent life philosophy and how they have to function within it, or to decide to recalculate it and factor their life within a newly adapted philosophy.

The gods and goddesses of Greek mythology also play into the personality types. You can research that to consider how those shade your characters and storyline.

"Marry the character elements to the story elements, which I think is what makes the character elements resonate."
– Lawrence Kaplow, *House*

Your characters: Considering the possibilities

"We get into each character's head, and ask: What do they want, what do they need, and what are they going to do next?"
– Thomas Schnauz, *Better Call Saul*

169

- Is each character **multi-dimensional**?

    Consider your character's past, present, or potential.

    Each of your scenes can have a character expressing one or more of these through words and/or actions.

    Sometimes, what the character says might be the opposite of what they verbalize = they are lying, deceiving, manipulating, hiding, strategizing, or otherwise expressing themselves in a way in tune with their intentions.

    Some actors go through scripts and, to consider what their character might be feeling in each scene, the actor writes a word on the side of each scene indicating what their character's chief concern, feeling, motive, and/or expression might entail for that scene.

    For each of the following, there is the opposite. Use a thesaurus to factor what one character might feel as opposed to their antagonist or manipulating factors, and how it conflicts with their philosophy.

- Adaptation
- Addiction
- Agitation
- Alienation
- Ambition
- Anger
- Anticipation
- Anxiousness
- Apathy
- Apprehension
- Audacity
- Beauty
- Belief
- Bitterness
- Cleverness
- Compassion
- Complicitness
- Confidence
- Conformity
- Confusion
- Contradiction
- Conversion
- Courage
- Deception
- Despair
- Desperation
- Destitution
- Devotion
- Disappointment
- Disgust
- Dismay
- Doubt
- Eagerness
- Embarrassment

- Entitlement
- Envy
- Faith
- Fear
- Foolishness
- Frustration
- Greed
- Guilt
- Happiness
- Hate
- Hesitation
- Honor
- Hostility
- Humor
- Hypocrisy
- Indifference
- Inferiority
- Initiative
- Irony
- Irrationality
- Isolation
- Jealously
- Liberation
- Limitation
- Love
- Lust
- Manipulation
- Mistreatment
- Needs
- Obligation
- Obsession
- Passion
- Philosophy
- Prejudice

- Pretentiousness
- Provocation
- Rage
- Reasoning
- Rebellion
- Regret
- Rejection
- Reluctance
- Resignation
- Resistance
- Restraint
- Reversal
- Revolt
- Revulsion
- Sensitivity
- Shame
- Shyness
- Strength
- Suffering
- Suppression
- Suspicion
- Sympathy
- Temptation
- Terror
- Theology
- Threat
- Uncertainty
- Vengeance
- Victimization
- Vindication
- Vulnerability
- Weakness
- Worthlessness
- Zeal

"I don't want to be at the mercy of my emotions. I want to use them, to enjoy them, and to dominate them."
– Oscar Wilde, *Dorian Gray*

"The emotion that can break your heart is sometimes the very one that heals it."
– Nicholas Sparks, *Welcome to the Basement*

"One thing you can't hide is when you're crippled inside."
– John Lennon, musician

"Your emotions are the slaves to your thoughts, and you are the slave to your emotions."
– Elizabeth Gilbert, *Eat Pray Love*

"Blushing is the most peculiar and most human of all expressions."
– Charles Darwin, biologist

• Look up: **Emotions wheel**. You will find a variety of them on the Internet. Consider the emotions each character might express because of their past or present predicament, and how their hope and intentions play into – or are impacted by – those.

"A screenplay is about distilling the essence of a story and its characters. You really have to find the heart and soul of your story, and hew to it."
– Ron Bass, *The King's Daughter*

• Are there any **flat** characters?

"When in doubt, make trouble for your character."
– Janet Fitch, *Dear Rita*

• Are the characters **overly described**?

• Does the description or dialogue state **the obvious** about a character that the script reader would already know?
     Obvious things in a script can be called **bald elements**. They should be worked out of the script, or reworded so that they aren't blatant or unnecessarily obvious.
     The **opposite of a "bald" element is** something that is in the script that needs to be highlighted or "stepped out," as in brought to light so that the readers will notice it more, because it is that important, so **step it out** to be more forward and obvious in the scene.

• Are there characters who you can **combine**, or who you can simply **delete** – without negating the story?

• Go through each scene and identify what each character is likely **feeling**, and how that plays out in their **actions and words driven by motive**.

171

- What are the characters **thought processes**, and how are those **displayed through actions**, including their reactions?

  "It is only because a thing contains a contradiction within itself that it moves and acquires impulse and activity. That is the process of all motion, and all development."
  – Georg Wilhelm Friedrich Hegel, author *The Science of Logic*

  Even the simplest characters have an **undercurrent of conflict working for or against various aspects of them** within some combination of **life theory dimensions** caught up in tolerance, acceptance, defiance, arrogance, shyness, humbleness, shame, pride, inferiority, superiority, ambition, retreat, frustration, regret, motivation, repulsion, love, resentment, inadequacy, pride, heredity, hope, curiosities of the unknown, and many other **contentious aspects of their being that ensnare, thwart, drive, escort, progress, or free them**.

- Are the **actions and dialogue** of the characters **consistent with reasonable motives** in tune with **wants and needs**, and the **conflict and contention** of their contradictory predicament?

- Are the **emotions displayed** in tune with the **predicament** and the **apparent life philosophy of the characters**?

- Are the characters not **reacting** to things that they would react to in real life?

- Are the characters **overreacting** to events or other people?

- Is the character's **life philosophy displayed** in how they deal with who and what they have – or have not – chosen to be around?

- If the characters are **conflicted with doubts and fears** (which they likely should be), is the **audience in tune** with that, while also **wanting and anticipating** the characters to get some guts and take actions to break through the **hurdles** preventing them from **accomplishment**?

  The character, with their **struggle of faults, fears, and doubts**, must gain the **confidence** and become **brave** enough to **take the actions** and **say the words** necessary to **formulate a solution**.

- Who amongst the **character's inner-circle** is **untrustworthy**, or at least **faulty**, and therefore a **threat** to the character accomplishing what needs to be done?

  Why is that person untrustworthy, or what are their **faults that might cause problems** for the main character?

- **Does the audience know** something that the character absolutely **needs to learn** about **to get** what the character **needs**?

In that way, the **audience** could be on the edge of their seats, **hoping** that **character realizes** what they **need to know** – and **act on that knowledge** – before that thing could badly **alter the life of the character**.

- What is the **character personally battling** in various aspects of their life?

- What is it about the **villain** that is **noble and good**, even with their evilness intact as they work **against the protagonist**?

    A one-note villain can come off as **flat, stale, static, cartoonish, or uninteresting**.

    "The thing is, when you paint somebody in all of their colors, they're never all bad or all good. Even the worst person has humanity in their somewhere."
    – Terence Winter, *The Wolfe of Wall Street*

    "Every villain can smile and every hero can frown. I mean, none of us do just one thing. Except politicians."
    – Robert Altman, *The Delinquents*

    Even the people who do the vilest things have something about them that reveals some form of **compassion and empathy**.

    "I love to start characters in a place where you think you know them. We can make all kinds of assumptions about them, and think they have no redeeming qualities. But, like everyone, they're complex."
    – Callie Khouri, *Blue Moon of Kentucky*

- Are the character's **dramatic needs** clear and is that **communicated to the viewers**?

- **Actions speak louder than words**.
    You might have characters **saying one thing, but doing the other**. That is similar to real life. Someone says they are going to do something, but they don't – and could do the opposite. That can lead to behavioral patterns.
    The **impressive people** in life **accomplish** things. The **less impressive waste their time**, energy, and resources, as their life passes by.
    People also **mislead and deceive**, getting people to think they are up to one activity, when they are doing the opposite, which might be **good, or evil**.

- Where is the character's absolute **crisis point** that pulls out their **emotions**, or during which they absolutely must hide their emotions, regroup, and force themselves forward toward what they think should be a **solution**?

- If the **viewers are indifferent to the characters**, not caring what they do or don't do, the **script is flat**.
    The **audience must want and hope** for something to happen, and **cheer** for and **anticipate** it happening.

    Get the audience to want to go into the film and **fight for what they want**, but do it by having the **main character act in proxy for the audience**.

"If you see a movie that successfully puts you in the shoes of somebody different than yourself, you see the world differently. So, I think the power of story is greater than the power of conversation, in a way."
– Jordan Peele, *Get Out*

- What is **pushing the character** to do what they do? Must they find **a cure** for a loved one? Must they **rescue** someone? Must they **save themselves**? Are they the **hero**?

- Does the character have to **attain something** by a certain point as the audience is aware that there are **time limits** as a **clock is ticking in the collective audience mind? Imply the silent time bomb.**

- Is **something amazing going to end** if the character doesn't **interfere**?

- Is there **a crack in a dam** that nobody but the character knows about, and the **character is the only** one who can notify everyone to evacuate, or perhaps release pressure to prevent the damn from causing a **surge that will kill everyone downstream**, including the character's family, the love of their life, their dog, cat, pet lizard, and ruin their potted plant collection?

- Must the character **keep something or someone hidden**, or else **something awful will happen**?

"Be a sadist. No matter how sweet and innocent your leading characters, make awful things happen to them – in order that the reader may see what they are made of."
– Kurt Vonnegut, *Slaughterhouse-Five*

- Is **some awful someone** trying to find the character based on a **misunderstanding**, and so the character must **stay steps ahead** of that awful person and accomplish something to **prove the awful person wrong**?

- Has the character been **falsely accused**, and must **prove their innocence**, or face the **ultimate punishment** or **lose their birthright**?

- What does the **character care about** that the **audience also will care about**?

- In which ways is the character **living undercover** at times, depending on who they are around or communicating with in their **daily role play of dealing** with their life and their surroundings – in clever ways to reach a goal?

- At each **intersection of the characters**, are they **manipulating each other** in ways that have to do with what they **need and want** in reaction to the **conflict and contention and contradictions**?

- In which ways are the character **bluffing each other in the game to get what they want and/or need**?

- What do the **characters learn from each other, take from each other, need from each other, want from each other, give to each other, love about each other, despise about each other**?

- What does your **main character truly, absolutely crave**, and how does that play into their **goal** and **how hard they work** for that thing so that there is a **through-line of action and emotion**?

  Through-line is the **dramatic crave** of the lead. It is **what is driving them** to get through what they are going through **to get what they want**.

  "The key is to find the spine, and that's not easy; you have to look and look and look, and it may take months. But, once I do, I put a piece of paper on my wall with about twenty-five or thirty words that describe what the movie is about."
  – William Goldman, *Dreamcatcher*

- Do the characters display **emotional tracking** from scene to scene in a way that **likely ultimately builds, wavers, possibly nearly falters as it is undermined by doubts** (or the actions and words of their contender), **and then regains momentum as they become determined to get what they want and/or need**? How do the characters attempt to **reign over** all of that?

- Do the **secondary characters** live, act, react, and talk in ways that display an **internal voice** that is playing out **beneath their surface**? Or, are they **flat, one-note**, and **only existing to fill a plot function**?

- Are the **obstacles** you created the types of things that make the **character learn and grow** as they get through, over, under, or around them?

- What is the **fantasy of each of the characters** – the **ideal life** they would like to experience?

  Is the **audience likely to be in tune with that fantasy** so that they will be **emotionally invested in the ride**?

  "To me, watching a movie is like going to an amusement park. My worst fear is making a film that people don't think is a good ride."
  – Darren Aronofsky, *Requiem for a Dream*

- Besides the main **hurdles**, what in your script is **working against or working with** the **side stories** that are **intertwined** in ways with the main story?

- How does the character **overcome those obstacles** in **proactive, aggressive, manipulative, eager, intentional** ways in tune with their **life philosophy** that they have to **reconfigure as they go through the adventure**?

  "One of the biggest mistakes rookie screenwriters make is not having a strong intention or obstacle. Intention and obstacle is what makes drama.

175

Somebody wants the money, they want the girl, they want to get to Philadelphia. It doesn't matter, they just need a strong intention, and then there needs to be formidable obstacle. The tactic that your protagonist uses to overcome that obstacle is going to be your story."
  – Aaron Sorkin, *Malice*

- What is the **essence of each character**?
  Can you state the character's essence in four words, or fewer?

- Does the **carrying out of the goal** of the character play into the **rhythm of the pacing** and **through-line** and **scene to scene emotional tracking** of the script?

- Does the script **approach and challenge** the **most relevant aspects of the characters**, and issues that were **paramount in forming their life choices and chosen philosophy? How does that play into their motive?**

- Are the **characters holding onto their reality** by displaying **reactions in tune with who they are** and **what they have experienced** in life? (See backstories, below.)

  "Minute physical differences between the individuals, and their psychological development, will influence their reactions to the same sociological conditions. Science will tell you that no two snowflakes have ever been discovered to be identical. The slightest disturbance in the atmosphere, the direction of the wind, the position of the falling snowflake, will alter the pattern. Thus, there is endless variety in their design. The same law governs us all. If one's father is always kind, or only kind periodically, or kind but once, or never kind at all, he will profoundly affect one's development."
  – Lajos Egri, author *The Art of Dramatic Writing*

- Do the characters display **desires, needs, purposes, goals, reasoning, drive, motives, voice, anticipation, conflict, and contention**?

- Do the characters **speak with their own purpose**, or are you having them say stuff simply to **display a story? Don't "talk at" the audience.**

- Is the character **gliding along too easily** without much of any **problems and potentially undermining conflict**, and not having to **deal or contend with obstacles** that prevent them from **obtaining what they want**?
  If things are **too easy for the character**, you must **hype up the drama, tension, concerns, and challenges** or you will be left with a **flat script**.
  Make watching the film a **roller coaster ride of emotion and sensations for the audience**.
  Play with the **senses and emotions of the audience**.

- Are the main characters **the most intriguing ones** in the script?

Consider that your **main character might not be the most interesting character** to focus on. There might be another character who is **more interesting**, and **in a situation that is more engaging to watch**, including because of their **apparent or alleged life philosophy or belief system**.

"I think once we fall in love with the characters, then it's really just about the characters for us. We have the best time writing when the characters are leading us somewhere, and we're not so much trying to write about some theme."
– Jim Taylor, *Sideways*

"It's the characters. That's what I spend most of my time with. Once I've done that, character will speak to plot and story."
– Craig Borten, Dallas Buyers Club

Character backstory has to do with what formed their:
- basis of existence or chosen lifestyle
- festering concerns
- defenses
- imperfections
- philosophy
- family position
- relationships
- socioeconomic status
- rise or fall
- state of or loss of innocence
- disappointments
- fears and avoidance
- skills and dexterity
- consciousness or level of education
- collection of scars, wounds, and pain
- irony
- joy
- humor – has seen it before, and wants more of it
- impatience – has dealt with it before, and is tired of it
- coping skills or reasoning – even if relating to their self-delusion and/or mental escape mechanisms/denial
- motives
- emotions or responses to current stimulus or stressors
- state of being

Some writers choose their character's personalities and how the characters deal with life situations based on astrological signs. Whether or not you are into astrology, maybe it can give you some ideas about your characters. You might think that astrology is too crazy, unscientific, or whatever view you have of it. But, it might be a helpful tool to use in developing your characters.

Water responds to the position of the moon and planets. If you don't think so, spend a weekend by the ocean, and you will see how the ocean responds to the position of the moon. Humans are mostly made up of water.

It could also be helpful to read books about psychology, even mass marketed so-called pop psychology books, like *How to Cope with Difficult People*, by Alain Houel and Christian Godefroy.

As an exercise, take a notebook and write backstories for each character.

- Where they were **born**?

- Who were their **parents**?

- What was or are their **parents' origins, education, careers, hobbies, and fitness, mental health, economic, and social status**?

- Did they **lose a parent**, and at what age?

- Were they **raised by a parent or guardian**, or did they have to **fend for themselves** from a young age?

"I think I'm most interested in parental relationships. *Wild Bill* was certainly about that, and *Eddie the Eagle*, too. That's definitely present in *Rocketman* as well, so it's starting to become a recurring theme. What is interesting for me about that is we've all got a mum and dad. That's the minimum requirement for being alive. Whether they're absent, or dead, or overbearing, or whatever their role is, they're there."
– Dexter Fletcher, *Wild Bill*

- Did they have **siblings**?

- How did they **relate to their siblings**?

- What role did they play in their **family dynamics**?

- What **languages** do they speak?

- What was their childhood **financial situation**?

- What type of **formal education** did they experience?

- Was their **education more from the streets, self-education**, and **school of hard knocks**?

- Do they play any **musical instruments**, and is that self-taught, or from formal training?

- What sorts of **sports** do they play?

- What were their **interests as children**?

- What was forced on them during childhood, in the way of **expectations from their elders and society**? How does this **echo into their current life**?

- What has their **love life** been like?

- Who did they look up to – if anyone at all – as a **role model** during childhood?

- Do they have any current **idols**?

- What was their **greatest loss during life**?

- Have they been **victimized**, and in which way? How did that shape them?

- Have they **done wrong to others**, and who were the people, why was it done, and how do they currently relate to that history?

- What has been their **greatest health challenge**?

- **What in their history is helping to propel them forward**, even if it is something they are trying to **escape**, or **avoid experiencing** ever again?

- How did they get into their **current predicament**?

- What do they **desire in life**?

- What is **holding them back** from getting what they want?

- What have they **missed out on** in life that they wanted?

- How have they **dealt with major unwanted changes** in their life?

- **How have they evolved** to be what they are?

- What is **relevant in the essence of the character** that would be helpful to reveal in relation to what they boldly or subtly do and say in tune with their **intellect, skills, and talents** and within the **conflict and contention**, in combination with their **needs and wants** – and what they **truly crave**?

- How does their **past play out in their current reality**, relationships, motives, words, actions, and reactions?

Open any news site, local, national, or global, and see the stories about how people are living, their professions, life choices, assaults, victimization, social structures, economic realities, family relations, educational backgrounds, loyalties, disloyalties, beliefs, denials, goals, victories, crimes, exploits, perversities, and other matters.

Even the most gigantic news stories hold onto a base structure of reality. Otherwise, it turns into fantasy and unrealistic distortion.

Look for ways of keeping the dialogue, actions, motives, relations, and expectations of your characters believable within the distinct realities of life within the cultures they experience.

179

Even when deviant, there is a base from which characters deviate.

"As a writer, you can't judge the character. You have to be able to find something about them that you can identify with that's like you."
– Aaron Sorkin, *Molly's Game*

"You want to write your world to oppose your character's desires. You're going to reinforce their need to get back."
– Craig Mazin, *Chernobyl*

"I just feel like a character has to say something, even if it's a stupid something. A character has to stand for something, and has to risk saying the wrong thing, even if it's just so somebody can step forward and say, 'Oh, that's full of shit.' At least they are saying something, you know – taking responsibility for their viewpoints, which is really what Tyler's speeches were about (in *Fight Club*) – expressing himself. Even more so than sort of coming up with a vision or a dream."
– Chuck Palahniuk, *Fight Club*

"If you want to be a screenwriter, take an acting class to get a sense of what you're asking actors to do. Learning other skills will help you communicate with people, and respect what they do."
– Tina Fey, *30 Rock*

"I say dialogue out loud. If I can't say it and make it sound convincing and not clunky, then no poor actor will be able to make it any better. It's all about being in a character's head.
I do like to sit in places by myself and eavesdrop on people's conversations. I'm fascinated by people's turns of phrase and their sometimes odd takes on the world.
I'm more interested in writing real characters with interesting personalities, and then readjusting the dialogue once I've cast the actors who will play these roles. I'd rather use whatever odd energy they bring naturally, rather than dictate to them some quirky way of talking."
– Paul Feig, *Spy*

"I'll declare that I agree with old F. Scott Fitzgerald. I often say that action is character. But it's true that, to be more precise, I say, 'Clack! Action and character, please.' Certainly, we must mean the same thing."
– Sergio Leone, *Sheba and the Gladiator*

"The most time I devote to is characters. I think that plots develop out of character needs and wants. I think the most fun comes from watching people do something and spend time with them. Once I have a kernel of where I want the story to go, or the kind of story I want to tell, I ask myself, 'Who is it that propels this plot forward the most?'"
– Barbara Stepansky, *Flint*

"I think a lot about E.M. Forster's delineation of round and flat characters: A round character acts and speaks as a real person would, and increases in complexity throughout the story; they're capable of contradiction and change, and we see their emotional and psychological development as the story progresses. I think a lot of unlikability for the audience is born out of flat characters."

– Helen Estabrook, producer

"From a writing standpoint, the things that interested me the most were the characters."

– James Cameron, *True Lies*

"It is true, of course, in an important sense, that a character exists only in his emotions and sensations. Without the expression of feeling, he no more represents a living person than does a fleshless skeleton. If he does not realistically express some credible emotion himself, he will not be likely to arouse feeling in those who watch him. His own characteristics and the plot of arrangement should set him in situations that plausibly arouse his own fear, hope, passion, desire, anger, love, jealousy, or other emotion, and his own feelings should be expressed so realistically as to arouse emotion in the beholder."

– Francis Marion, actor

"The most important thing in your story isn't going to be someone's sexual orientation, their skin color, their religion, whether they are able bodied, or disabled. The most important thing in your story is going to be intention and obstacle. What does this character want, and what's standing in the way of getting it?"

– Aaron Sorkin, *West Wing*

"I really like taking my story, what I have to say, my tale, my little autobiographies, but sticking them in crazy genre world."
– Quentin Tarantino, *Reservoir Dogs*

"You have to go into the script with as many complementary flavors as you can in the pot, and the more you get in there, the richer the end result."
– Drew Pearce, *Iron Man 3*

SCRIPT GENRE

"I really don't think genre is that important. It's more: 'What am I going to do with this?' 'What are the genre rules?' So, you look at the genre rules, and decide whether you're going to keep them or break them. 'What are the genre expectations of the audience?'"
– John Sayles, *Silver City*

You will be asked which genre your script fits into. The most simplistic answer, which doesn't tell much about the script, is either "drama" or "comedy." Other common answers are "romantic comedy," "murder mystery," "action flick," "horror movie," "political drama," and "sports movie." There are numerous subcategories or subgenres. Make up your own.

"I really like cross-pollinating movies. Is *Broadcast News* about friendship, or is it about ethics in journalism? Is *Jerry Maguire* about sports management, or love? Is *His Girl Friday* about a newspaper, or divorce? I just think that those movies I really like are about a number of things."
– Edward Zwick, *American Assassin*

Watch award-winning films or shows in your chosen genre.

"Once I know what that theme is about, then I percolate on different ways to illustrate the theme. And every scene in the movie will be in service to supporting the theme.
Under the Tuscan Sun was supposed to be about what happens between the day you wish you were dead and the day you're glad you're alive again. And everything I put in the movie was supposed to illustrate that journey and build towards that moment of being glad you're alive again."
– Audrey Wells, *Over the Moon*

As far as writing a genre, consider not getting caught up in having the males playing the traditionally male roles, and the women playing the traditionally female roles. Mix it up.

After writing your script, consider making one version of it in which you turn all of the male roles female, and all of the male roles female. See what that does to your story. A female can be a fighter jet pilot, or the owner of a sports team, car repair shop, lumber yard, or roofing or construction company. A male can be a househusband/father as the wife is the money-maker. In reality, a macho, straight man can run a dress or flower shop, and a woman can play a firefighter, welder, farmer, body building gym owner, or a car mechanic.

If you are only going to present the same stereotypical roles, maybe you are not being creative enough, or even challenging your ingrained – or society-induced – perceptions and expectations.

"I have complex feelings about genre. I love it, but I hate it at the same time. I have the urge to make audiences thrill with the excitement of a genre, but also I try to betray and destroy the expectations placed on that genre."
– Bong Joon-Ho, *Okja*

"I tend to do a lot of drafts, which has the effect of making the script more and more specific, because it gets more specific each time. Usually by the time I give it to the producer or director, I'm six or seven drafts in – and that's when the script really begins to open up and take shape as a film."
– Frank Pierson, *In Country*

How Many Drafts?

"I don't know how to count drafts. People always ask, 'How many drafts did you do?' I'm just always writing and revising. And I don't know what you call a draft at all. I occasionally turn the script in to get paid, but I'm just constantly working on it. There's all this time before the movie gets green lit, and then I'm continuing to work on it once it's green lit and we're rehearsing it – and then even during shooting I'm doing some work on it – if there's stuff that needs changing."
– Scott Frank, *Minority Report*

You might hear a writer say how many drafts they wrote of a script. I've heard people say they wrote five drafts, or some random number. But, what are they counting? Is that the number of drafts that they printed out during the months or years that they were writing it? Is it truly the number of drafts that were written before they sold it? Does it not take into account the numerous overhauls that they did of the script?

No matter how many drafts you have, keep a record of them. Back them up. Email them to yourself, and to someone who you absolutely trust. Put them on a thumb drive. Consider having a fireproof safe and/or a bank vault to store important documents, including the latest drafts of your screenplays.

"I feel like – when you are starting out – if you're writing an outline, before you've thought about this thing, then you're kind of committing yourself to something you don't yet know. Sometimes – always – I'll come upon something a month into writing that will change everything. I don't like to feel like I'm bound to something that's preconceived."
– Charlie Kaufman, *Chaos Walking*

"When working out a story, I try to stay away from traditional outlines. Trying to sit down and begin by listing the scenes in order seems overwhelming. My answer is to use notecards that I spread out on the floor."
— Jeff Nichols, *Take Shelter*

"When I write a screenplay, I create an emotional map where the characters are, where they're going, and where they've been."
— Ava DuVernay, *Battle of Versailles*

"Before I sit down to write, I have all the scenes listed, what happens in each scene, how many pages I anticipate each scene will take."
— Paul Schrader, *Taxi Driver*

"I'd write it to the end, and go back and write it all over again. Go back and write it all over again. I think I probably wrote — without exaggeration — about twenty drafts of *A Few Good Men*."
— Aaron Sorkin, *West Wing*

What counts as a draft?

Does the outline with various scenes detailed and some dialogue written count as a draft?

Does the first several pages you wrote of the script that contains a beginning, middle, and end with some dialogue and fleshed-out characters count as one draft?

Does the copy that had all of the punctuation, grammar, tense, and spelling errors count as one draft?

Or, does it count as a draft only if you overhauled the entire thing with things like a new character, new scenes, deleted scenes, rewritten dialogue, and some renamed characters with different intentions, contentions, conflict, subtext, backstories, concerns, and attitudes?

"The first draft is just you telling yourself the story."
— Terry Pratchett, *Good Omens*

Who is to say what counts as a draft? There are no draft police or a draft approval and certification organization. It's your decision.

"Every script you write (that gets made) will take 70 drafts. First 10 are before anyone sees it. Next 20 are before it gets green-lit. 30 more before you start shooting. And the last 10 happen along the way. Some drafts are a page, some are 50 pages. But, there will be 70."
— Jeffrey Lieber, *Lost*

"We (he and Oliver Stone) did twenty-six drafts of *Any Given Sunday*, one right after another, so I learned everything about the form from him. He was patient. I'd go to his house. He'd say, 'Pick up that Oscar. Hold it. It'll feel good. You'll enjoy it.' And then, we'd work."
— John Logan, *Penny Dreadful*

When someone asks me how many drafts I wrote of a script, my typical answer is, "A bunch." I don't count how many times I overhaul a script. What is the point?

"If you want to make a feature film, you get ideas for 70 scenes. Put them on three-by-five cards. As soon as you have 70, you have a feature film."
– David Lynch, *Inland Empire*

While studying the books, get the script up to the quality where you feel you can do the best you can. Then, workshop it.

After you take every page of the script through a workshop, you will end up with the workshopped draft.

Send the workshopped draft to a script editor. (A member of Screenwriting Tribe is a script editor, and many of the writers use her service.) Go through the suggested edits, and do another wave of polishing.

Send the edited draft to get professional coverage. Read the coverage, and consider what you want to alter.

Do all of that, before you share the script with the industry (contests, fellowships, mentorships, labs, agents, managers, directors, producers, financiers, actors).

Perhaps simply name that submission draft the "writer's draft 1.0." Do that, because there will certainly be other drafts done before the script ends up being made. Those are the development drafts or pre-production drafts. Then, there will be the breakdown draft and shooting script containing a wide variety of annotations in tune with the shot list and schedule that will also be created.

As the script is filmed, there will likely be numerous changes during the filming with scenes rewritten, improvised, or cut. Those will be the various production drafts.

Then, the editing of the footage is done, which can be a form of rewriting the scenes in ways that the writer had not considered. There will be the editor's cut – or assemblage – of the film. Then, there will be the director's cut of the film. And a cut done that satisfies producers.

The film might be recut to stylize it for foreign markets, network TV, and other forms of distribution.

Then, there could be a published script that might be the original writer's draft, or it might be a draft that includes all of the changes that were made during filming, and reflects the final film.

By the time all of that is done, how many "drafts" of the script and cuts of the film have there been? A bunch.

"The artist is the medium between his fantasies and the rest of the world."
– Federico Fellini, *La Strada*

"The most important element of any story is to make the reader want to know what happens next. Period."
– Lisa Cron, *Butterscotch*

"The sooner you start to connect empathetically and emotionally with your audience, the sooner you'll be communicating with them."
– Christopher McQuarrie, *Mission: Impossible 8*

Your First Draft

"Sometimes you're swinging your way through a first draft like a blind miner with a pick-axe. That's okay, just get it done."
– Justin Marks, *The Jungle Book*

"You can't think yourself out of a writing block; you have to write yourself out of a thinking block."
– John Rogers, *American Outlaws*

"Almost all good writing begins with terrible first efforts. You need to start somewhere."
– Anne Lamott, author *Bird by Bird*

"How do I know what I think, until I see what I say?"
– E.M. Forster, *A Room with a View*

"Get it down. Take chances. It may be bad, but it's the only way you can do anything really good."
– William Faulkner, *As I Lay Dying*

"No matter what you write, good or bad, it's an improvement to a blank page."
– Chris Sparling, *Greenland*

"The first draft is nothing more than a starting point, so be wrong as fast as you can."
– Andrew Stanton, *Finding Nemo*

"I always try to alternate writing between two phases. There's one phase where I don't censor myself. I just brainstorm. Follow my fantasy. No art

police allowed. I am emotionally open to the topic, and also try and follow everything that comes into my mind."
— Maren Ade, *The Forest for the Trees*

"This is how you do it: You sit down at the keyboard and you put one word after another until it's done. It's that easy, and that hard."
— Neil Gaiman, *Beowulf*

"The first draft is just you telling yourself the story."
— Terry Pratchett, *Johnny and the Dead*

"My one note of screenwriting advice is: Make sure you can see the movie, before you start writing the actual script."
— Arash Amel, *Grace of Monaco*

"Then comes the great leap which is the first draft, I call it 'the muscle draft,' where you just muscle it out. You don't worry about what you're missing, you just get through it, get to the end."
— Darren Aronofsky, *Requiem for a Dream*

"One rule for first full working drafts: Get them done ASAP. Don't worry about quality. Act. Don't reflect. Momentum is everything. Get to the end as if the devil himself were breathing down your neck and poking you in the butt with his pitchfork."
— Steven Pressfield, *Above the Law*

"There's a lot of pressure on writers now to be shocking on the first page. I understand that, but that doesn't necessarily make for a great story. It often cheapens the story. It doesn't let it ripen or evolve. It doesn't let us get to know the characters."
— Melanie Marnich, *The Affair*

"There are two simple mistakes that are easy to make:
1) Not making your lead character proactive. Your hero can't go through the script just reacting to things. He has to move the action. The audience has to be wondering, 'What is he going to do now – or next?' Audiences don't pay to see reactive characters. The hero has to be the master of his destiny – which also helps attract a star.
2) Forgetting that your scenes have to be about conflict. In any script, on any page, in any scene, you should be able to ask, 'Who is the hero? What does he want? What's preventing him from getting it?' This is a key concern to keep in mind. Even scenes that are primarily about advancing the story or laying out exposition must have an underpinning of conflict.
Keeping these two things in mind makes all the difference between a good first draft and a really good second draft."
— Bruce Feirstein, *Tomorrow Never Dies*

The first step to being a successful screenwriter is to write scripts. Otherwise, all of the thoughts and talk of writing scripts are simply ideas, fantasy, and commentary, and you will not have anything to work on polishing into what you can then workshop, have edited, get covered, and submit to contests, fellowship and mentorship programs, agents, managers, producers, directors, actors, and financiers.

"A screenwriter friend of mine said your number one goal is to get to the end. So, write it fast. Don't look back. If you have to have characters yak about something and you don't have a solution, do it anyway and let it suck. Then go back over it in a couple of weeks, and you'll be much clearer on what's strong and what's not strong and then attack the ones that are too verbose. At least you'll have a laundry list of things the audience needs to know – but don't hang up on finding the visual solution and not move forward on your screenplay."
– Brad Bird, *The Incredibles*

There are people who attend Screenwriting Tribe who want to learn about screenwriting because they have ideas for scripts, but haven't started writing a script. I tell them to read the books *The Art of Dramatic Writing*, *The Emotional Craft of Fiction*, *The Anatomy of Story*, the formatting section of *The Screenwriter's Bible*, and *Dr. Format Tells All*, and study this book. And do so while writing a first draft – even if they think it is the worst script ever written.

"What are you going to do? Everything, is my guess. It will be a little messy, but embrace the mess. It will be complicated, but rejoice in the complications."
– Nora Ephron, *When Harry met Sally*

"It's not until you really throw your character into the story that you can genuinely understand who they are."
– Elijah Bynum, *Hot Summer Nights*

Don't judge the first draft of your script as you write it. Simply write it. Allow for mistakes as you write, and keep writing.

"So much of writing is being wrong. The trick to being a good writer is to be a terrible writer at the beginning, and just keeping at it until you fix it."
– Krysty Wilson-Cairns, *1917*

"First drafts are for learning what your story is about."
– Bernard Malamud, *The Natural*

"I'm the kind of guy who wants to know the entire movie before I write it."
– Jordan Peele, *Us*

"I start thinking about key scenes. I write those scenes first, out of order. I call it 'the scene of blood.'"
– Jim Uhls, *Jumper*

"I don't do outlines. I don't plant where I'm going, because I like to be surprised when I'm writing."
– Ol Parker, *The Best Exotic Marigold Hotel*

While some say that they don't outline, it is likely more important to do for some films than it is for others. For instance, a writer working on a murder mystery, political drama, or police procedural likely would likely benefit by doing an outline. Rian Johnson was sure to do an outline for *Knives Out*.

"I always diagram stuff out, before I start writing."
– Rian Johnson, *Knives Out*

"I take off and write out a of a sense of desperate compulsion. I always write as if I've just gotten my x-ray from the doctor on Monday, and he best check with the insurance man and see whether or not the house is free and clear.

I always write with a sense of desperate urgency. Now, I don't think this is necessarily a preoccupation with my own demise. I think I'm good for another eighteen months – at least. But, I always write as if, 'Gee, get it down.'

Now, other writers, and many fine writers, and many writers finer than I, I might add, are very craftsman-like – meticulous delvers into structure, scenes, costumes, biographies of their people. They have everything down in note form, before they begin. They also have a very good idea of sense of, if it is a play, their acts, if it is a novel, their chapters. I don't at all. I just have a rough sense."
– Rod Serling, *The Planet of the Apes*

"Before I start writing scenes, I'm very careful to do a step outline where I try to find what the structure of that particular movie is going to be."
– John Sayles, *Piranha*

"Outlining is necessary work, but you have to have something left to discover during the writing, or you won't be inspired."
– Liz W. Garcia, *Cold Case*

"I don't start writing a script until I can see it all in my head, then it's a matter of getting it down in white heat."
– J. Michael Straczynski, *Sense8*

"The outlining part is a powerful moment in the process, because you can train yourself to see the true structure that lies there, before you fall in love with dialogue and your execution."
– M. Night Shyamalan, *Lady in the Water*

"For me, if I'm really struggling with the scene and writing three scenes to justify this one thing, I know that I'm not listening to the story. There's a story that wants to be told, and if you listen, then it tells itself really easily.

Hell or High Water, I wrote it in three weeks. And they shot that draft. There was no rewrite. It was because it was a story that I felt very close to, and knew exactly what I wanted to say – in the way I wanted to say it. And the characters were mirroring things I'd experienced in some form, or were terrified of experiencing, or had witnessed other people experience. So, it was a very visceral writing experience for me, and very instinctive. And not structural and outlined and planned and thought out."

– Taylor Sheridan, *Fast*

"My only conclusion about structure is that nothing works if you don't have interesting characters and a good story to tell."

– Harold Ramis, *Groundhog Day*

"Structure, I'm here to tell you is a total trap. Yes, screenplay is structure. But, structure isn't what you think it is. Structure doesn't say this happens on this page, this happens on that page, here is a punch point, here is a story point, here's a midpoint. Structure doesn't tell you what to do.

If you follow strict structural guidelines in all likelihood, you will write a very well-structured, bad script.

Structure isn't the dog, it's the tail.

Structure is a symptom. It's a symptom of a character's relationship with a central dramatic argument.

Structure isn't something you write well. It's something that happens because you wrote well.

Structure is not a tool. It is a symptom."

– Craig Mazin, *Chernobyl*

Amen to what Craig said there. And, also to what Charlie says here:

"I don't think there is any distinction between structure and story. I think they are two parts of the same thing. And I think if your story and your structure don't reflect each other, then you're not doing your job. I don't believe in the idea that there is a structure that movies have, and that need to adhere to it. I think you look at what it is you're trying to express, and figure out how to use it. I mean, the structure of something obviously is enormously important. But it's not different than trying to figure out a character or the time frame, or anything like that. They're all the same thing. I don't work in a scientific way. I think a lot about themes and relationships and things that I'm worried about in my life. I spend a lot of time before I ever write anything. I take notes, but I don't try to then write a script. That comes really late in the process for me."

– Charlie Kaufman, *Confessions of a Dangerous Mind*

"I try to step into a drama knowing, from the very beginning, what the last scene is going to be."
– Shonda Rhimes, *Private Practice*

Don't be neurotic and get stuck on rewriting the first pages over and over again. That's like preparing the soil for a garden over and over again, but never planting the plants that form the garden, and you'll still only have dirt.

Sometimes you won't know what the first pages should end up being, until you get to what could be the final pages – then adjust the first pages.

"Start by making the script a good read. What's that mean? It means you want the reader to read it relentlessly. You want the reader to read it fast, to be a page turner, a teaser, a heartbreaker, or a laugh a minute. It means – for screen direction – you want the script to read vertically, to give white space, to not have more than five lines in a paragraph. You want to pick strong, active verbs; ditch all weak adverbs and adjectives. You want to avoid all unnecessary detail. You want to get in late, get out early. Accomplish what the scene needs to accomplish, and get out."
– Paul Peditto, Script Gods Must Die

It might be helpful for you to write with certain actors in mind – or, not. Do whatever it takes to visualize the characters as you write the scenes and dialogue. Perhaps it will help make each character their own person so that they don't sound like each other.

"I never write with an actor in mind – never."
– Andrea Arnold, *A Beetle Called Derek*

"Very often, one of the problems with strong writers who deal in dialogue above plot – which happens to be, I think, more my forte than plot – is dialogue. If you look at some of the pages of the stuff I've written, and even some of the good things, shut your eyes, and you won't know who is talking, because they all talk alike. And, who do they talk like? Me. Now, that's wrong. And it's something I've got to lick over the years. But, it's the most common literary problem, I think, of a strong dialogist."
– Rod Serling, *Night Gallery*

"Thinking about actors makes you a lazy writer, because you're no longer thinking about a character, you're thinking about a specific person. So, you write a speech, and you think about Al Pacino reading it, and you say, 'Wow, that's a terrific speech!' Well, it's not a terrific speech. Al's a terrific actor, and you shouldn't confuse the two."
– Paul Schrader, *City Hall*

Consider making a character wall board on which you have the photographs of certain actors – or of people you have seen in magazines, in the news, or other places. Perhaps keeping in mind what they look like while you write might help you to apply a particular voice and tone for each character.

"I often write with an actor in mind, and then I never get them."
– Emma Thompson, *Last Christmas*

"I learned to not write with actors in mind. Because I find that you always get your heart broken, because they're not available when it comes time to shoot."
– Rian Johnson, *Looper*

"When I write, I don't think of actors. I intentionally don't think of actors, because I feel like, if I were to think of Jim Carrey then, for example, for that role in *Eternal Sunshine*, then I would write Jim Carrey, which isn't really the character. That's Jim Carrey. So, the ideal situation is that – for me – is that I write a character, but I feel like is realized in some way that expresses some traits that I think are important. Then, the actor comes and embodies it and brings Jim Carrey to it – rather than bringing it to Jim Carrey."
– Charlie Kaufman, *Eternal Sunshine of the Spotless Mind*

If it is a half-hour pilot, get past page 20. If it is an hour TV pilot, get past page 40. If it is a feature film, get past page 80. Do it as a brain exercise, a personal challenge, and don't be hypercritical of your writing. Don't be wimpy about it. Win the battle against the blank pages.

Don't talk about what you are writing, nobody wants to hear you say what you are going to do. Actions and completion are more impressive and interesting than talk.

"Write about what you love and don't ever talk about it, something I'm tempted to do, but it takes all the energy out of it. Have it be separate – because the energy will build up inside you and you'll go and write it."
– Casey Affleck, *Light of My Life*

Don't be the person who disperses all of your energy talking about what you are going – or hoping – to do. Talk less. Work harder. Be the one who stays focused, takes actions, and intentionally gets things finished.

"I don't outline extensively, I kind of just write – I kind of vomit it out when I'm writing. I tend to write a little too sporadically in terms of what I write – but what I write is kind of short, focused bits of writing. Then I just write a lot quickly and kind of work on fixing it after."
– Dan Fogelman, *Honeymoon with Harry*

"There's a magic in being present when you're writing a character. Just spit it out, then go back and edit it later."
– Reid Carolin, *Gambit*

"What I try to do at the beginning is just get to the end. Once I've gotten to the end, I know a lot more about the piece, and I'm able to go back to the beginning and touch stuff that never turned into anything, and highlight things that are going to become important later on. And I go back, and I keep doing

that, and I keep doing that, and I'll retype the whole script, over and over again – just to make things shaper and sharper."
   – Aaron Sorkin, *A Few Good Men*

"One of the biggest things about writing your first screenplay is that you actually finished a screenplay. It's a very important milestone just to have done that – even if it sucks."
   – Charlie Kaufman, *Chaos Walking*

"It's always easier to revise a script, even a truly awful one, than face the tyranny of the blank page."
   – Stan Chervin, *Space Warriors*

"You've got to write badly. If you write badly, at least you've got something to rewrite. If you're scared to write badly, then you've got nothing."
   – Tony Grisoni, *Fear and Loathing in Las Vegas*

"A writer who waits for ideal conditions under which to work will die without putting a word on paper."
   – E.B. White, author *Elements of Style*

"Get it down. Take chances. It may be bad, but it's the only way you can do anything good."
   – William Faulkner, *Land of the Pharaohs*

Some people call the first draft the vomit draft. Whatever you call it, at least you will have something to work with.

"Writing the last page of the first draft is the most enjoyable moment in writing. It's one of the most enjoyable moments in life, period."
   – Nicholas Sparks, *A Walk to Remember*

"Writers who sit down and write might judge what they're putting down. But I always just try to barf it out. I'm writing crap, but I'll put it down."
   – Kay Cannon, *Pitch Perfect*

"I start at the beginning, and keep going until I write 'The End.' I then go back and rewrite practically everything.
   Until there is a full script that exists, it's all a sort of dream. It doesn't feel real until you have a screenplay on paper that covers the whole story. After that, rewrite as much as you like. It's like carving in wood – where the wood is the screenplay."
   – Julian Fellowes, *Gosford Park*

"I think a badly-crafted, great idea for a new film with a ton of spelling mistakes is simply 100 times better than a well-crafted stale script."
   – Alexander Payne, *Sideways*

"I like to have order. I like to know what my scene list is, and have my tent posts that I want to try and hit. Then, I do a vomit draft."
– Joe Robert Cole, *Black Panther*

"If I can force myself to crank out a first draft, it becomes a lot easier for me to go back and assess it in an analytical way."
– Michael Werwie, *Extremely Wicked, Shockingly Evil, and Vile*

"Write freely and as rapidly as possible and throw the whole thing on paper. Never correct or rewrite until the whole thing is down. Rewrite in process is usually found to be an excuse for not going on. It also interferes with flow and rhythm, which can only come from a kind of unconscious association with the material."
– John Steinbeck, *Of Mice and Men*

"When your characters are really living, they tell you what they do."
– Andrea Arnold, *American Honey*

"I think imperfections are important, just as mistakes are important. You only get to be good by making mistakes, and you only get to be real by being imperfect."
– Julianne Moore, actor

Just as a pianist can't perform a concert piece on the first sitting, you should not be so harsh on yourself to expect to write a perfect first draft of a screenplay. Be realistic. Write every day. Practice might not make perfect, but it makes better.

"Don't wait until everything is perfect, because I don't think anyone's looking for a perfect script or perfect manuscript. They're looking for something that they can add their own voice to – something they can help make better. That's something I've learned on the other side of things. I wish I'd known that, because I wasted a decade not showing anyone anything, because it wasn't perfect."
– Christian White, *Clickbait*

"The most important gift a young writer can give themselves is the discipline of simply writing."
– Robin Swicord, *Matilda*

"Everyone who tells me they don't have time to write, I just say, 'One scene a night for three months, and you'll have a movie. You can even use the weekend.' It's possible to be a writer if you want to be a writer, even without all the time in the world. After doing the dishes, instead of turning on the television, or reading a book, or going to the movies, write one scene. Whatever you do write one scene."
– Bruce Joel Rubin, *Jacob's Ladder*

"It is better to write a bad first draft than to write no first draft at all."
– Will Shetterly, *Pocket Dragon Adventures*

Do save the various drafts of the script as you are writing it. Many writers email it to themselves every day as they write it. I have an external hard drive. I also store drafts on thumb drives. I also have a bank vault where I put the thumb drives. I also will print out a copy, and have a safe location where I have those. I don't want to be one of those writers whose house burned down and lost all of his work. (My family's house was gutted by fire when I was a child, so I know about that experience.)

Never simply have all of your work in your computer. Have backup copies. Every day you work on it, back it up. Why? Because I have known numerous people who have lost their work because their computer was lost, stolen, or damaged.

"I wrote *Swingers* if I recall in about two weeks, and I wrote *Chef* just as quickly. I get scared that I'm going to stop writing, and I have a lot of unfinished screenplays that I've said, 'Let me take a day off…'" And with *Chef* and *Swingers* I kept myself writing every day until I got a first draft out. Because there's not a lot of big plot points in any of them, it's all character and situational, so I wanted to make sure I had a first draft done – even if it was terrible. You know, when you re-write it's a different part of your brain, but when you're writing you just want to get it out and get through it. It's a real endurance, wind-sprint all the way through."
– Jon Favreau, *Chef*

After you have that rough draft, read through it. On one piece of paper, make a simple outline of the main story, including the beginning, middle, and end. On a separate piece of paper, make a list of the back stories, and their beginnings, middles, and ends.

Write a one paragraph description of each of the characters, including what they want and what they need, and how they help or hold back the progression or goals of other characters.

A side character might help in the progression of what we see in the main character simply by being the person in the way, or the person who is helped – or hurt – by the main character. The side character might only be someone who triggers a reaction or argument. They might lead to a twist in the thinking of the main character, and realign them onto a path more likely to lead to where they want to get – or, not.

"Filmmaking is a chance to live many lifetimes."
– Robert Altman, *Kansas City*

Write a sentence about each of the lesser characters.

Go through each scene and decide what each scene is meant to reveal about conflict, contention, tension, and character want, need, reasoning, anticipation, and motive. Aim for what is compelling.

"Screenwriting is like ironing. You move forward a little bit and go back and smooth things out."
– Paul Thomas Anderson, *Punch-Drunk Love*

"My writing is a process of rewriting, of going back and changing and filling in. In the rewriting process, you discover what's going on, and you go back and bring it up to that point."
– Joan Didion, *True Confessions*

Some people would advise you against writing quickly without first writing a treatment, and/or making an outline or other guide.
Some people write a treatment, make an outline, and then write fast.
Some people hate writing treatments and/or outlines.

"I'm always very much concerned with outlining and giving a shape to it before I dive in. Whenever I've just tried to take a run at it, I find myself writing myself into impossible corners, and having to backup and rethink things. So, I tend to think very much about structure and organization. I do a lot of preliminary sketches and notes, and put Post-Its on the wall to figure out where certain scenes are, before I actually dive in."
– David Magee, *Mary Poppins Returns*

"I used to outline what I was going to do. I don't do that so much anymore. It's part of trying to loosen up the process and not know what's happening. But I think I'm a linear person, and when I write I don't write a quick draft and then go back. I don't like to leave anything behind me, because I'm uncomfortable with it. I tend to write a scene many times over before going on. The last time I was really doing drafts was when I was working for George Lucas. Now, I will sometimes revise and make little changes, but the essentials don't change. I take a lot of time and effort with the first draft, and I'd rather shoot that."
– Lawrence Kasdan, *Silverado*

Go back and read that draft, from the first page to the last. As you do so, give it a wave of rewriting – all the way to the end.
I advise people to avoid showing anyone the first draft of a script. A first draft is also not something you should bring to a screenwriting workshop.
Study David Trottier's *Dr. Format Tells All*. Underline what you think is important so that you can go back and do a speed read of those underlined passages.
Read award-winning screenplays in the genre of your script.

"At each level you reach, you have to tear up what you have done before, which costs an enormous amount of psychological and emotional energy. That makes the process of screenwriting very, very difficult. And I don't know any

screenplay that I have ever worked on where I did not go through ten to twelve or sometimes sixteen drafts before I showed it to anybody."
– Frank Pierson, *Dog Day Afternoon*

Read through your script.

Correct the scene headings.

Decide if each scene reveals something necessary for character and story progression.

Figure out the scene pillars – as in: What is important in that scene for the viewer to notice or hear in ways that progress the story and engage concerns?

If there are scenes that are not necessary for the story and character development, why are they there?

"Good dialogue comes from character development. The better you know your character, the more specific the dialogue will feel."
– Chris McCoy, *Good Kids*

Print out a copy of the script.

Perhaps do what many actors do to screenplays: In the left margin, next to each scene heading, write one, two, or three words that relate to the tone and mood of each scene.

"No matter how big or high-concept your story is, it only works if there's a small, personal story at its core."
– Chris Sparling, *The Sea of Trees*

In the right margin, write one, two, or three words having to do with what the character's motives, wants, needs, disappointments, expectations, and satisfactions are in that scene.

Consider what each character's contention is in each scene – including by what we see them doing. Depending on what their goals are, perhaps the words they speak hides their contention, because they need to hide something from – or simply lie to, or mislead – someone else in the scene. Their actions might be calm, when we know their heart is racing as they are on deadline, and are deeply afraid of not making it.

"What does this character want. And, more importantly, why do they want it? Those are what I look at as I'm writing dialogue."
– Brad Ingelsby, *Torrance*

Read through the script again. Do another wave of changes.

Get your script up to the point that you think it is ready to submit to agents, managers, producers, contests, and fellowship and mentorship programs. But, DO NOT submit it.

First timer scripts are rich in problems that trigger dismissal by managers, agents, producers, financiers, contests, fellowship programs, talent, and other people in the industry.

"Every script you write must be a sample of your talent on the page."
– Andrew Kersey, manager

"Realize that your script is a prospectus asking for an investment of millions of dollars. That is why it must be compelling.
Since tinsel town is into appearance, it is essential that your script look as good as it possibly can."
– David Trottier, author *The Screenwriter's Bible*

WORKSHOPPING

Hold off on submitting your screenplay to anyone. Take it to a screenwriting workshop, and spend weeks and months taking every page of the script through the workshop.

Be quiet during the workshop feedback – when the other writers tell you what they think of the script. Listen. Take notes.

The word listen has the same letters as silent.

If you want to have a career in screenwriting, get used to listening to comments on your screenplays – and stay silent as you listen to opinions that you don't agree with. It's part of the process.

You want to know when something in the script sounds untrue, is problematic, is illogical, is too reliant on the suspension of disbelief, is distractive, or otherwise what the readers "bump on." During the feedback, you might hear someone say, "I bumped on this bit of dialogue in this scene…"

Don't get defensive in a workshop. Don't take the feedback personally.

Be poker faced as you are getting feedback in the workshop. Don't facially react to guide their feedback. Of course, you might laugh, or have some other reactions. But do aim to avoid guiding the feedback. It doesn't matter if you agree or don't agree with what they say. Consider that, from their view, they are right. Don't correct them. Consider how the person may have factored their viewpoint.

Taking a script through a workshop will help get rid of formatting, story, grammar, tense, punctuation, spelling, factual errors, and other problems that could result in the script being dismissed by industry professionals.

"It's pretty essential that a script have proper format, because then as a reader I can relax and simply pay attention to the story – which is hopefully hooking me emotionally. If the script has a lot of errors – typos, grammar,

improper slug lines, or character intros, and confusing description – I'm going to have to work really hard to visualize the story in my mind's eye, and that's going to take me out (of the story) and frustrate me. So, rather than engaging in the narrative, I'm lost in the format – which means it is unlikely the script is going to work successfully."
   – Ruth Atkinson, Sundance Labs, Film Independent

Feedback in a workshop might be about everything from formatting to hearing comments about the story, backstories, pacing, tone, genre, style, energy, angle, dialogue, headings, descriptions, revelations, pillars, twists, tension, conflict, contention, motives, historical facts, reasoning, character professions, relationships, and the psychological profile of the characters.

"The beautiful part about writing is that you don't have to get it right the first time, unlike, say, a brain surgeon."
   – Robert Cromier, author *After the First Death*

The goal is to sharpen your script, which might mean giving it a whole other angle, eliminating characters, combining characters, creating new characters, cutting or shortening scenes, increasing the drama, tension, and conflict, making characters more likeable, hateable, loveable, detestable, contentious, primitive, grand, sophisticated, diabolical, frail, bold, strong, weak, obligated, resilient, pathetic, recalcitrant, dangerous, articulate, sloppy, intrusive, nasty, kind, hostile, creepy, inhibited, extroverted, introverted, threatening, clever, ambiguous, determined, persistent, regretful, sad, angry, or funny, making it into a TV series instead of a film, changing the era and genre, restyling the way you reveal the story so that it is more engaging, and so forth.

"The best, most amazing concept doesn't mean anything if you don't have characters that people want to spend time with. Circumstances and concepts are only interesting to me based on what the characters are doing within them."
   – Nikole Beckwith, *Stockholm, Pennsylvania*

A screenwriting workshop shouldn't cost much money. No matter how much it costs to take your script through the workshop, those expenses will be far less than wasting your time and money by submitting a script to managers, agents, producers, actors, financiers, contests, labs, and fellowship and mentorship programs when the script is not ready.
   During the months that it takes to workshop your script pages, engage your mind not only when your pages are the ones being workshopped, but also stay engaged in the workshop when feedback is being given on the scripts written by the other writers. You will learn faster that way. It will benefit your scripts.
   Do what it takes to write your script in a style that makes the characters interesting and engaging in a story that is compelling.
   If your script gets produced, millions of people might see it. The tricks are to manipulate the thought patterns of the viewers, trip their expectations, make

them want to know what happens next, and keep their reasoning engaged from beginning to end. Mess with your audience. Make them feel as if they are part of the main character's thoughts and motives. Take them to the brink. Bend their reality.

After you have done your homework, and workshopped your entire script, rewriting it and polishing it, and had it edited and covered (see the coverage section in this book), only then should you consider if it is something that you will want to spend the money to enter into a contest or fellowship or mentorship program, and/or if you want to use it to pursue getting a manager and then an agent. Or, if it is something that you want to film.

As I mention elsewhere, maybe your script won't sell, but will work as a way for you to get other work polishing scripts for producers, getting staffed on a series, getting hired to write a script.

If you land an agent or manager, don't expect them to hold your hand. Do expect to work, network, keep writing more scripts that can sell, and have meetings with people who you might end up doing business with. You might end up with a "blind deal" with a producer, production company, or network – which means that you will write something for them in a development deal, perhaps with an idea that they – or both of you – have, or with I.P. they own.

Know that, along every step of the way you take in this industry, as a writer you will continually hear people commenting about your scripts. And, hopefully, about your movies and/or series.

"A writer needs a pen. And artist needs a brush. A filmmaker needs an army."
– Orson Welles, *The Other Side of the Wind*

Before your script makes it to screen – and depending on how involved you are with its production (particularly if you are producing and/or directing) – you might be dealing with a variety of people, including financiers, distributors, producers, readers, agents, managers, actors, casting directors, entertainment attorneys, UPMs, directors, ADs, DPs, script supervisors, production designers, and on down the line. Each will have an opinion of your script. Their opinions are outside of your control.

"Even those who work for a company with a studio deal, or the network or the studio itself, have only so much bandwidth, and will have to fight the good for whichever project they select to bring onto their slate. They will have to sell it to their superiors, to other departments, to potential partners while competing with other projects from other executives. They will have to make a case for it again and again. If they are successful, it will help them keep their job; if they fail, there is someone in the wings already waiting to take their place. So, they better have the passion to fight for your project – or this writer they've take on – every day they go to work."
– Lee Jessup, screenwriting career consultant, LeeJessup.com

No matter how much some people like your script, some of the people working on producing it might not care for your script, but will work on the production as simply a job to make money... before they move on to their next job. It's a factory town.

As a screenwriter, you are the first person in the factory. Generate a script that will be free of common flaws and distracting elements that could trigger key people to dismiss it.

"I have a process where I eliminate dialogue and replace it with actions that can speak the same truth, if possible."
– Ki-duk Kim, *Rough Play*

Many scripts get into the hands of decision makers, and then the script's chances are lost because the script had not been polished, and/or is dull, unclever, unengaging, overwritten, one-note, rife with common errors, or otherwise only partially-baked. That situation might have been avoided if the writer had spent some months taking the script through a workshop consisting of other writers who are doing their homework.

When I worked at MGM/UA, John Calley said to me, **"Why should I spend time reading a script if the writer hasn't spent the time to polish it?"**

I saw Calley flip through scripts. If he saw lengthy paragraphs of description, rambling dialogue, pages of static dialogue lacking description or action (scenes lacking kinesis), and formatting errors, including wrong margins, etc., the script didn't get read. It failed **the flip test**.

"When industry folks open a new script from a writer they don't know, they often flip through the script (be it paper or digital) in search of tell-tale signs that the script is written by a novice. One of the biggest indicators of a new writer just figuring out his way is chunky action lines that quickly morph into action paragraphs, describing every prop in detail, directing the action and choreographing everything from fight scenes to love scenes on the page.

Success in screenwriting is very much about economy of language. Saying the most with the least. Making every word in every action line matter and count. It's the writers who succeed in this task, and even develop their own unique style, who often find success in their chosen profession."
– Lee Jessup, screenwriting career consultant, LeeJessup.com

Doing your homework, truly studying the books that I suggest, and workshopping every page, having it edited, and getting feedback from a coverage service – before showing your script to anyone in the industry – will help your script pass the flip test. Hopefully, your script will make it to the point of being produced. And it will help get you other work in the industry – perhaps including doctoring and writing scripts for producers and/or staffed.

"Being a writer is like having homework every night for the rest of your life."
– Lawrence Kasdan, *Star Wars: The Force Awakens*

"What really matters is what you do with what you have."
– H.G. Wells, *The War of the Worlds*

Copyright Your Scripts

No information in this book should be construed as legal advice. For such, consult with an intellectual rights attorney.

It is a good idea to copyright your screenplays. It allows for certain protections against plagiarism.

Your screenplay is your intellectual property (I.P.). It is an asset that should also be covered in your will.

"Ideas are not protected by copyright law. The essence of copyright law is that the protection granted to a copyrighted work extends only to the particular expression of the idea, and never to the idea itself."
– Stephen F. Breimer, Esq., author *The Screenwriter's Legal Guide*

Copyright law only protects the expression of ideas, not the ideas or concepts in the form of thoughts that have not been written. So, get that expression down on paper (a tangible medium) in the form of a screenplay, and register it.

To start, write a synopsis or treatment, which you can also register with the U.S. Copyright Office. As soon as you finish the screenplay, you also can then register it. Any of those steps are good to do, before you share your idea, concept, or document with people in the industry.

If your story has a character that is so dominant that they can be used in spinoffs, sequels, franchises, or otherwise "derivative works," you can write a document detailing the specifics of that character, and also copyright that as your intellectual property. However, if the character is too vague, don't expect copyright protection – such as: A leader of a nation is corrupted by foreign leaders, and works as a spy for that foreign government. There must be more specifics than vagueness. Consider the document as a character breakdown and backgrounder.

If there is a co-writer/co-creator, the co-creator of the material must be listed on the copyright. The percentage of the ownership should be detailed in a written agreement.

When you register your I.P. (In this case: A screenplay, treatment, or detailed character breakdown and backgrounder) with the U.S. Copyright Office, you will receive a copyright registration certificate – which you must have to defend your copyright in court.

When you sell or license the rights to your I.P. to a producer, production company, or studio, you are allowing them to limit what rights you are selling or licensing. An intellectual rights attorney can help you understand what that means, including the rights to perform, produce, distribute, publicize, and publicly display the work.

You can also limit what you sell relating to derivative works, including sequels, spinoffs, and franchises, and products relating to the screenplay and its character and theme or created world content (clothing, toys, games, amusement park rides, etc.). Each of those can be commercially exploited to create a different revenue stream. Discuss this with your attorney.

Even if you have an attorney, do yourself a favor and read up on copyright issues relating to screenplays.

If the script you wrote was a "work for hire," you were an employee of someone who owns the I.P., and you are not the one to file the copyright. That is up to your employer. Your name won't be on the copyright.

Your scripts are automatically copyrighted when you write them. But, it is always good to take measures to protect your I.P.

Look up the famous film plagiarism cases.

In the season that I wrote this, the trades reported that Guillermo del Toro allegedly stole the idea for his film *The Shape of Water* (suit dismissed). And, the Duffer brothers were being sued for allegedly stealing the idea for their show *Stranger Things*. Accusations were denied.

Take the steps necessary to protect your work.

Know that registering your script with the Writers Guild of America is NOT the same as filing a copyright with the U.S. Copyright Office.

(Search: Screenplay copyright information.)

(Search: Entertainment attorney or intellectual rights attorney.)

(Search: Branded entertainment licensing.)

(Search: U.S. Copyright Office.)

"As a writer without an active screenwriting career, you really have two jobs: The first one, obviously, is to write. Write a lot. Challenge yourself to keep getting better. The second one is to get your material read. If it doesn't get read, it will never garner interest. If it doesn't get interest, it won't gain you any industry advocates, be they executives, agents, or managers. By all means, register your material with the WGA and the U.S. Copyright Office, before you get it out there. Read all releases, before you sign them. Don't send your material to anyone you can't find with a quick IMDbPro search. And always make sure to have a paper trail."

– Lee Jessup, career coach, LeeJessup.com

Register Your Scripts with the WGA

In addition to copyrighting your scripts, register them with the Writers Guild of America. Do it before submitting your scripts to agents, managers, producers, directors, investors, actors, other industry professionals, and to labs, contests, mentorship and fellowship programs.

As mentioned elsewhere, in addition to your screenplays, you can also register your treatments with the WGA.

See the WGA site for more information, including cost.

Know that registering your material with the WGA does NOT mean that you are a member of the WGA. The WGA is a union, and that union allows anyone to register their screenplays with the service.

To become a member of the WGA, there are certain specific things that need to happen. However, you might not want to be in any hurry to become a member of the WGA. Consider that it might be better to work writing indie films, and to not join the WGA so soon that you would be limited to production companies that and producers who are signatories of the guild.

See the WGA site for more information about how to become a member.

"A screenwriter's currency is a finished script. Not an outline, a take, a beat sheet, a rough draft. A finished script."
– F. Scott Frazier, *xXx: The Return of Xander Cage*

"Once I've written the screenplay, and handed it over to somebody else, If I'm not directing it, it's their movie. If they want to change it, they can change it, and I support them and do everything I can to help them do that. I'm no longer about, 'Oh, I wrote the scene this way. It would have been so much better like that.'"
– Christopher McQuarrie, *The Way of the Gun*

WHO GETS CREDITED AS THE WRITER?

"As a screenwriter, I had sold four or five screenplays – two commercial scripts, which were food-on-the-table spec sales, and then three or four smaller movies – and they weren't panning out the way I wanted. They were getting shelved, or made into movies that were completely rewritten. It was a really horrific experience to be honest. One of those situations where you get rewritten and no one talks to you for a year, and you don't meet the director, and yet you go to the premier and see your name up on the screen with people you've never met and had no association with. I was questioning the industry and questioning my writing. I had to get down to basics and make my own little films."
– Shawn Christensen, *The Vanishing of Sidney Hall*

If you worked on your script with someone as a co-writer, who is your writing partner, you are a "writing team," then there should be an ampersand between your names: `Jill Havenhurst & Agnes Tosito`.

But, if you sell your script, and another writer does significant work on it (as determined by WGA guidelines: See the WGA Handbook), their name can be added as a co-writer. In that situation, there will be the word "and" between the names: `Jill Havenhurst and Agnes Tosito`. It also may include the name of a third writer who worked on the script (Depending on how much of it is their writing. The standards for that are in the WGA guidelines).

If you are a writer who was hired to completely rewrite a screenplay from page one (a "page one rewrite"), you can then receive the sole credit, even though the original screenplay was written by the original writer (again, see the WGA handbook). Then, the original writer gets a "`story by`" credit. A "`story by`" credit can include anyone who worked on the treatment or story outline.

There is also the "`screenplay by`" credit, which is given to up to three people, or three teams of people. Is that perplexing enough? (See the WGA handbook.)

The "`written by`" credit can include those who receive the "`story by`" and "`screenplay by`" credit. The "`written by`" credit is limited to two people. (Yes, again, consult the WGA handbook for details on all of that.)

When there is a dispute, the WGA arbitration process can determine who gets credit, and how the credits should be worded.

The WGA arbitration process can also end up giving a writer or creator of the ideas that resulted in the screenplay being written by other writers the credit of "`screen story by`."

If the screenplay was based on an article, blog, or other certain type of intellectual property, the writer of that other property then receives the credit of "`Based on` (Name of property: Article, etc.)." This all gets complicated. See the WGA for information.

For your spec script that was completely written by you, you will put this on the front page, beneath the title of the script:

`By`
`Your Name`

"Screenwriting is a craft based on logic. It consists of the assiduous application of several very basic questions: What does the hero want? What hinders him from getting it? What happens if he does not get it?"
– David Mamet, *Redbelt*

A TREATMENT

"Writing a treatment is essentially refining your story from 90 pages to five pages, to three pages, to one page to a paragraph, to a single sentence. Once you've done that, you'll be able to develop the pitch for your movie in a more effective way – since you'll know every view and length of it. Turning a script into a treatment teaches you what's important about your story."
– Ben Yennie, ProductionNext.com

Consider first writing the script story as a treatment.

A treatment is one-to-three pages – or more – in length. Try for three – or fewer – pages.

A treatment tells your basic story in an enticing way with the main beats that form the emotional engagement – or emotional through-line – of the beginning, middle, end, and resolution.

In a treatment, aim for telling the story in a way that readers then want to know more, and will end up reading the script.

A studio, manager, or agency might ask you for a treatment.

If you are hired to write a script, you might be asked to write a treatment.

Who is going to read the treatment?

Is the treatment simply for the assistant to read so that they can decide if they want to read your script? Does the assistant know anything about the screenwriting process that you went through? Are they asking for the treatment without the knowledge of their boss (an agent, manager, producer, director, or actor)? Are they being flip and dismissive, and not serious about ever reading your script?

Is the producer or agent going to read the treatment?

Is the agent only going to read the treatment, and try to help you option or sell the script based on the treatment – and not on reading the actual script from front to back? Don't be surprised by that situation.

Some variety of all of the above scenarios are likely the reality of what you will experience as you spend decades working in the film industry.

Investors, producers, and distributors could ask to see a treatment.

If you own the rights to a book, or the rights to someone's life story, and are seeking a deal, you might be asked to present a treatment.

Is it wise to have polished treatments available and ready for each of your scripts, in case someone asks for one?

"I never write treatments, because I hate them so much. I hate writing them, and I hate reading them."
– Emma Thompson, *My Fair Lady*

"I want an outline. I want a beat sheet. I just hired someone to adapt a book. He gave me a 50-page 'scriptment.' And this is an experienced writer-director. When I read it, I felt like I just saw a movie, except for the dialogue. I said, 'This is fantastic.' I really appreciated it."
– J. Todd Harris, producer

Some writers who read what J. Todd Harris says there will want to say something to him, or perhaps write a script where they do things to a producer who asks for a "scriptment." Even the word "scriptment" sounds like something that could trigger revenge torture.

Many writers say that writing a treatment is difficult, and they avoid doing it. Some say that they have never written a treatment.

"There is no rule on how to write. Sometimes, it comes easily and perfectly. Sometimes, it's like drilling rock – and then blasting it out with charges."
– Ernest Hemingway, *For Whom the Bell Tolls*

Some writers say that they didn't spend months – or years – writing a script to have someone then insist that they first present them with a treatment before they will read the script.

"Always and consciously, I try to hook the audience in the first five minutes. I want them right from the start to feel something – Boom! I want an explosion right at the beginning. I always want that."
– Gene Wilder, *The Woman in Red*

Hey, producer, how about listen to the pitch, and then ask questions? Or, read the first fifteen to twenty pages of the script. Consider that the writer might have a variety of good reasons why they don't want to write or present you with a treatment – including because a treatment would fail the script. You're dealing with a screenplay writer, not a treatment writer.

"Never write a treatment or outline, unless someone is forcing you to do so, or is paying you a lot of money to do so."
— James Schamus, *Indignation*

Requesting that a writer present their screenplay story in treatment form is considered by some – not all – to be pretentious, rude, kind of cruel, a waste of time, unnecessary, and something that only a person who doesn't understand the screenwriting process would insist. It is as if the writer is being asked to pass some sort of short story contest to get a script read.

A screenwriter may be great at writing scripts, but horrible at writing treatments. Those who insist on getting writers to present them with treatments should consider that as a possibility.

"I usually give a new script ten to fifteen pages. A lot of people call it a 'crack twenty' (read twenty pages). I've been doing this a while, so if it doesn't hook me in the first ten, I'm usually out."
— Jake Wagner, Good Fear Film + Management

Some writers say that a screenplay should always be presented only as a script, not as some sort of short novelizationesque-ish story in a treatment form – which can completely lack the inventive, cleverly subtext-, conflict-, and contention-rich, compelling style of an engaging screenplay that the writer spent months or years crafting.

It's understandable that some writers react harshly when they are asked to present a treatment of a script.

Then, there are those who ask: How do you expect to write a TV script of about 48 pages, or a feature script of about 100 pages, if you can't write a treatment that is one, two, or three pages?

Write the treatment without expectations. Allow it to suck. Go back and rewrite it.

Save the treatment.

Even if the treatment is lousy, and is filled with typos, bad grammar, and misspelled words, register the treatment with the WGA and the copyright office. Those are two levels of protection to establish the story as yours. The WGA and copyright office don't grade your treatment.

Yes, it doesn't matter if the treatment that you register and copyright sucks and is filled with errors. All that matters with those treatments is that they cover the bases and characters of the story – sort of like a light blueprint.

Don't be someone who continually copyrights a bunch of treatments, and never finishes any screenplays based on those treatments. That is one way to waste time, energy, electricity, calories, money, paper, and space in the universe.

It is a good habit, practice, and brain exercise to finish projects.

"The road to hell is paved with works-in-progress."
— Phillip Roth, *Total Reality*

Don't be the person who tells everyone that you wrote a treatment. Nobody cares about your treatment. It's not an accomplishment. It's one piece of thread in a huge fabric. Finish the script – also without telling everyone that you are writing one. Put your energy into and focus on finishing the project.

Yes, it is true that films have been funded based on treatments. That might be more likely to happen if you've written and/or directed films that have topped the international markets. Or, maybe it won't. Even directors of massively successful films have had problems getting their other films funded.

"The way to get started is to quit talking, and begin doing."
– Walt Disney, *Steamboat Willie*

Don't tell everyone – or anyone who doesn't need to know – that you are writing a screenplay. Yapping about it disperses energy. And, nobody cares – even if you think they do care. Your talent, skill, and existence are not validated simply because you wrote a treatment for a screenplay, or because you wrote a screenplay.

"Talent is a wonderful thing, but it won't carry a quitter."
– Stephen King, *The Stand*

While it may be satisfying to you that you have finished a screenplay, what matters to the outside world is finishing the job of writing the script, and then optioning or selling it, and that it gets produced.

"I spend a lot of time writing about the script, thinking about characters, getting ideas, lines of dialogue – before I actually write it. Anything that pops into my head I write it down and I start to organize that to shape the story. I spend months doing that. Sometimes before I write a scene I'll spend an hour writing about the scene, and I sometimes realize I'm stuck on something. So, what I'll do is start with the dialogue and see where it goes, and then I fill in the action and different elements."
– Scott Frank, *Minority Report*

Once you have written that treatment to register with the WGA and file with the copyright office, make a new document of the treatment. Break up each scene into its own paragraph. There, you have some sort of outline of your script.

"Creativity is allowing yourself to make mistakes. Art is knowing which ones to keep."
– Scott Adams, *Dilbert*

If you haven't yet written the script, take the outline and write a rough draft of the script focused on what each scene needs to reveal, and what sort of sparse dialogue would be helpful to include for advancing conflict and character contention in ways that engage the reader. Then, go back and adjust the treatment.

If someone insists that you submit a treatment, at least you will have that document.

Don't have your treatment include a detailed description of every single thing in the script. Write what will engage the reader in the conflict of the story, the contention of the characters in it, and what will entice the reader to want to read the script – and have a desire to watch the film.

(Search: Dov Simens Screenplay Treatment.)

"You cannot own an idea. But a treatment – based on your idea – is something you can own and sell.

Whenever you get an idea, type three-to-five pages. Put on a title page. Title it 'A Treatment for Feature Film.' Register it with the Writers Guild of America, and now it is no longer an idea. It is a thing that you can own with a date proving when you created it."

– Dov Simens WebFilmSchool.com

And here, I'll tell you a little trick that some screenwriters do: After you have finished your script, take it through a workshop. After your script has been workshopped, have it edited, then pay for a script coverage service to give you their coverage. You paid for the coverage. It is a "work for hire." You own it, and it only applies to your script, so it isn't like anyone but you can use it anywhere or in any way. You can then adjust that coverage, and use it as your treatment. (See the coverage chapter in this book.)

In *The Screenwriter's Bible*, Trottier advises having a "one-sheet," which is one page containing the script logline, and a brief but tantalizing story summary. In film marketing, a one-sheet means a film poster. But, in screenwriting, a one-sheet means that: One page containing the above info.

"If contractually obligated to doing a beat sheet or an outline, I will do it. And sometimes you are. And, what usually happens is you spend all this time on this beat sheet, and this outline, and it's the most bastardized thing in the world. Because, it's not a script, it's not a story, it's kind of this thing that exists halfway between a script and a story. But, I will do it, if contractually obligated to, I'll do an outline. I'll do a very detailed outline, and I'll do it always to the best of my abilities. I won't slum. But, I'll do it, and I'll hand it in, and the producers will go, 'We love this outline. This is a great outline. Now, go write the script.' And you'll go write the script, and you'll have your outline, and you'll say, 'Okay, here is what the outline is telling me.' And you'll start writing, and it will immediately start changing. And better ideas will emerge. And, the next thing you know, the outline is completely out the window."

– Larry Wilson, *Beetlejuice*

"Eighty percent of a motion picture is writing. The other twenty percent is the execution."

– Billy Wilder, *The Front Page*

"A story should have a beginning, a middle, and an end. But, not necessarily in that order."
– Jean-Luc Godard, *Breathless*

"Precisely imitating someone's surefire model without a strong application of creativity may result in a formulaic screenplay."
– David Trottier, author The Screenwriter's Bible

ACT STRUCTURE

"The more you adhere to some kind of screenwriting formula, the more likely you are to end up with a formulaic screenplay."
– Gary Whitta, *After Earth*

"When you impose yourself and a formula and you're not open to explore and to find what is right for the movie, I think you're doing a disservice to the story and what you're trying to express."
– Emmanuel Lubezki, director

"When I can see that somebody is following a system or some formula they've been taught, I completely lose interest. I prefer things that break the rules somehow."
– Michael Shannon, actor

Depending on who you listen to, there are three acts to the structure of a screenplay. They consist of the setup, the confrontation, and a resolution that includes the climax. Or, depending on who you listen to, a climax followed by a resolution, followed by a denouement. Or, not.

Or, there is a climax happening in the second act, and what we watch after that as the third act is the resolution. See *Writing Drama* by Yves Lavandier for more about that theory.

"You're writing a play, a play for the screen – a screenplay. What are the elements that make a play? I was trained by Howard Stein at the University of Iowa Writers' Workshop. He said that everybody had to read *Aristotle's Poetics*, which we did, in the Francis L. Ferguson translation. These are my antecedents. When I taught I would point out that in writing drama

for the screen, we first decide what drama is, then worry about how to put it on the screen. That sounds deceptively simple."
— Nicholas Meyer, *The Human Stain*

Some people mention the ancient Greek philosopher Aristotle as the architect of the setup, confrontation, resolution of Three Act dramatic structure. He philosophized that the whole of a causal chain has a beginning, middle, and end.

The Roman drama critic, Horace spoke of Five Act structure (See: *Ars Poetica*).

"I don't always believe in the formulas that they have on a 'page such and such' you should hit a certain mark. I think our instinct should drive that more."
— Nancy Meyers, *The Intern*

"The path to being a writer is littered with corpse-like scripts that contain all the supposedly necessary page marks/plot points that the confused, I-don't-get-it-I-totally-followed-the-rules writer has hit. In fact, that's almost every script written by new writers."
— Ed Solomon, *Bill & Ted's Excellent Adventure*

One popular screenwriting book is *Screenplay* by Syd Field. It has been required reading in many college screenwriting courses. Field's book covers his concept of a four-act structure. He taught that scripts have an initial "inciting incident," and that it and other story plot points tend to happen on certain pages. Plot points also include the initial confrontation with the antagonist (or that we know there will be one), a progression into that confrontation, a reversal of fortune testing the character's will, a final confrontation, a resolution, and an epilogue providing answers to and/or a wrap up of the main concerns. To get clarity on his teachings, read Field's book.

"To uncover the plot of your story, don't ask what should happen, but what should go wrong. To uncover the meaning of your story, don't ask what the theme is, but rather, what is discovered. Characters making choices to resolve tension — that's your plot. If your protagonist has no goal, makes no choices, has no struggle to overcome, you have no plot."
— Steven James, author *The Synapse*

"This 'by page X, Y has to happen' thing has destroyed many careers — before they even start, in my opinion. Same with so-called 'plot points,' whatever they are. Because it makes you think the structure of a screenplay is some externally-applied pam, when in fact it's not at all."
— Ed Solomon, *Men in Black*

"You don't learn how to write a screenplay by just reading screenplays and watching movies. It's about developing the kind of mind that sees and

makes drama. You can do this in a kind of holistic way by reading history and theology and psychology, reading great fiction and poetry, and plays. You develop an eye for the structures of everything and look for the patterns that help you become a dramatist."
– Robin Swicord, *Wakefield*

Some writers will mention late author Joseph Campbell's books *The Hero with a Thousand Faces* and *The Power of Myth* as valid books to study. Campbell is known for views on mythology and religion. His story structure concept is based on what he viewed as the structure of stories told throughout history. He recognized that mythological stories had similar things in common, including a person put into a situation that they can choose to engage in. If they choose, they will likely experience conflict that they will have to contend with, wearing them down, but making them stronger and wiser as they succeed, or fail. Then, they settle into the world with a different view than what they had when they first accepted the challenge.

"Who is your hero, what does he want, and what stands in his way?"
– Paddy Chayefsky, *Network*

In his book *The Writer's Journey: Mythic Structure for Writers*, author Christopher Vogler aimed Campbell's concepts at writers. Vogler goes into the issues relating to emanations of the hero archetypes, structure formulas, journey mapping, the polarized system of conflict, and other issues helpful for understanding character and conflict. (Search: *The Hero's Journey*.)

"So, what is structure? Really, it's just whatever you decide is the optimal way to tell this particular story – and that applies to pace, order, plot, tone, etc. And by optimal it can also – depending on the script – be just: What is the coolest way to do this?"
– Ed Solomon, *Men in Black*

If you are writing for TV, look up *The Harmon Circle*, which is an eight-part story structure developed by Dan Harmon, creator of the series *Community*. The eight segments include:
1) A character is in a zone of comfort.
2) But they want something.
3) They enter an unfamiliar situation.
4) Adapt to it.
5) Get what they wanted.
6) Pay a heavy price for it.
7) Then return to their familiar situation.
8) Having changed.
(Access: DanHarmon.tumblr.com.)

On YouTube, see Dov Simens, and listen to what he says about filmmaking. Watch ten of his videos. Get some ideas about how screenwriting,

215

filmmaking, and the film industry work. You might start to understand what you are up against as a screenwriter, and might apply his teachings to your scripts, and career. He is someone who has been around a long time, and people like Quentin Tarantino are known to take his advice.

"If you give an audience all the answers, they'll forget you as soon as they leave the cinema. But, if you ask the right questions, they'll think about you for days."
– Asghar Farhadi, *The Salesman*

Another popular book is John Truby's *The Anatomy of a Story: 22 Steps to Becoming a Master Storyteller*. It's a book that I suggest screenwriters study. You might find his "Twenty-two Building Blocks" to be useful.

"I discovered John Truby ten years ago, when a friend told me about his screenwriting course. I studied Truby's principles for a year. And, using them, I wrote the first draft of *The Thieves of Ostia* in two weeks. I go back to his teachings before each new book I write. Each time I study Truby, I learn something new."
– Caroline Lawrence, author *Queen of the Silver Arrow*

Often, people who go about sticking with a specific structure theory mention that something is to happen on about page ten. Or page twelve. Or page eleven. Or page nine. Or something like that. By page thirty, the First Act is somewhat blending into the Second Act (or Middle Act), which goes on for about sixty pages (in a feature film script). Then, there is the thirty-page climax. Or, is it a twenty-page climax, followed by a resolution, or a resolution and a denouement? It depends on who you listen to.

"The problem with supposed screenwriting 'formulas for success' – *Save the Cat*, etc. – is that they breed formulaic screenplays. They teach you to write and edit from plot rather than from instinct. You've been watching movies and television your whole life. Trust this now embedded visual storytelling instinct to offer answers to the sole question of 'What do we see next?'"
– Ken Miyamoto, *Hunting God*

Then, there are those writers who have converted to a certain concept, and who will blow their top because I'm being too loose and not so exact with my description of structure – because what they were taught is the one and only way, and anything else is sacrilege (to them). Maybe the overpriced screenwriting seminar they attended is something they mistook as some sort of gospel. However, it is simply opinion and commentary.

Or, depending on who you listen to, there are four acts.

Or, three acts and a denouement.

Or, is it that there are three acts, a resolution, and a denouement.

Or, was German novelist and playwright Gustav Freytag correct? The "Freytag Pyramid" or "Freytag's Triangle" was what he concluded about structure by studying Greek dramas and Shakespeare's plays.

The Freytag structure model has five acts, illustrated in a dramatic arc of:

1) **Exposition.** Basic information is provided, including determining the protagonist, setting, era, and premise, and the antagonizing character or element.

   Perhaps also identifying the philosophical and societal stance of the character is part of this – which plays into how the protagonist is challenged by their situation, and what choices they will likely make to get what is needed and/or wanted.

   Essentially, the goal is to try to engage the audience in the story.

2) **Rising action**. Consider how the story rises with tension, conflict, contention, concern, and other matters to the apex of the pyramid.

3) **Climax.** The highest part of – and the tipping point of – the action.

4) **Falling action.** This results in the final stage of the struggle of contention and conflict of the characters – or as much as we will know of it in the story being presented. It might purposely leave us with a sense of doubt of our own conclusion of what happened, and of where the characters will go from or within the situation.

5) **Denouement.** We see how the protagonist – and maybe the antagonist – functions in the view of their situation that is the result of what we saw them go through. Basically, it is some form of rearranged life philosophy of the characters, and of closure to the story – which doesn't necessarily mean a happy ending.

There are people who will argue with you if you so much as give a hint of not believing in sticking with the Freytag form of storytelling structure when screenwriting. Freytag developed his concept in the 1800s. (See: *Die Technik des Dramas*.) Maybe storytelling through film and TV allows for situations of more structural layers than the five in the Freytag Pyramid.

Perhaps there are eight sequences that are all about nine to ten minutes in length. This structure concept was based on the length of film reels (now largely replaced by digital systems). Within each of the sequences, there are identifiable Three Act stories. The first two being the First Act. The next four sequences being the Second Act. The seventh sequence being the resolution, and the eighth being the denouement.

The sequence paradigm was the theory of František "Frank" Daniel, who was dean of the USC School of Cinema, and taught at Columbia, and at the Academy of Performing Arts in Prague.

Or, there are simply twelve act sequences.

Or, there are innumerable sequences wound in and among themselves, with one being chief, and all playing out into some sort of resolution that will satisfy audiences.

David Trottier of *The Screenwriter's Bible* details his "Magnificent Seven Plot Points," which include:

1) Backstory.
2) Catalyst – where the balance is upset.
3) Big Event.
4) Midpoint / The Pinch / Point of no return.
5) Crisis.
6) The Showdown / Climax.
7) Realization.

Notice how Trottier lists the big event and the catalyst as two different things. The catalyst upsets the balance, and is not necessarily the big event or inciting incident. It can work separately to give the character a goal, crave, or mission.

"I was never conscious of my screenplays having any acts. It's all bullshit."
– John Milius, *Red Dawn*

Maybe you shouldn't cement your way of writing into one form of structure.

"If you take the occasional seminar and come away with one great tip you didn't know before, that's a good thing. But I've come to believe you only learn on your own by doing it, by trying to tell stories that work. When you write fourteen to twenty screenplays, you begin to internalize a sense of timing and movement of the story, structure, and dialogue. It's not somebody else's rules that matter, it's your own. If you do it by trial and error from the inside out, your work will find its own unique storytelling voice."
– Michael Schiffer, *Crimson Tide*

My theory is: Do what is best for each script. One script might end up along the lines of the Three Act structure, and others five – or more – acts.

Shakespeare [or perhaps Edward de Vere? Christopher Marlowe? John Fletcher? Philip Messinger? Mary Sidney Herbert? Queen Elizabeth? Research those names in connection with Shakespeare.] used Five Act structure.

"Actors and writers need to come back to the theatre, because it's a place where you can learn. You have to pay your dues, and people who haven't paid their dues in the theatre, I think, have a hard time creating a whole career."
– Joanne Woodward, actor

Playwright Henrik Ibsen didn't stick to one type of structure. Maybe you also should not. (At least, for film. See below for TV.)

"For me, knowing and being able to understand and respect the rules of dramatic structure frees me to be more adventurous, and take bigger risks, because I know I will always be able to find the way home."
– Alexander Dinelaris, Jr., *Birdman*

"In screenwriting, structure is the most difficult thing. I'm not a classicist about structure. I don't think there's a set number of acts that a screenplay has to have. I think each screenplay has to have its own structure. Sometimes the structure is very simple, and can be seen graphically."
– John Sayles, *Lone Star*

Maybe simply aim to write a film screenplay of around 90 to 100 pages (normal for comedies) to a maximum of 120 pages (for drama, but usually 100 to 110 pages for noncomedies). Edit it into what you find to be the most engaging form of the story – while not obsessively focused on structure.

Maybe your film script will fall into its own structure.

"I think one of the worst things that ever happened to screenwriting is this guy – what's his name? Bob, who wrote this book about?... Bob McKee – First Act, Second Act, that one. Well, you know, it doesn't work that way. It's not that simple."
– Paul Schrader, *The Last Temptation of Christ*

One film that people exemplify as being ruined by writers apparently sticking to the commercialized film structure recipe touted by the so-called screenwriting gurus to illicit audience response during specific time stamps is *Bohemian Rhapsody*. While Rami Malek's performance is landmark, and displays his obvious talents, so much focus seems to have been placed on hitting corny story tent pole points that vast chunks of the film are absolutely complete fiction. People say that the film ruins Freddie Mercury's story, distorting what happened, blatantly disregarding what did happen, and fabricating so much to the point that it is a perfect example of an unfortunate way to do a biographical piece, and one that isn't quite much of a biography, but more of a vaguely and solidly fictionalized offshoot of the real story.

The director, and others involved with bringing Freddie's story to screen, should have requested that the film be based more in his reality. The true story is far more interesting than what that film shows. The writers could have spent more time on it, and made a more clever, interesting, and worthy film. What they did do is canned commercialized fiction. I've heard Queen fans describe the film in scatological terms, and worse. That film's existence makes it so that it is unlikely that a more realistic movie about Mercury will be made, at least not one that gets the rights to the music, and has the budget needed to tell the more interesting, true story.

Fictional elements reign supreme throughout *Bohemian Rhapsody*. Mercury did not simply happen to present himself to the somewhat unknown to him bandmates after the previous singer dropped out, which is what the film shows. In real life, Freddie knew the band members for at least many months. He didn't happen to meet his future wife, he knew her because another bandmate had been involved with her. The character played by actor Mike Myers, and who plays a major role in the film, is completely fictional. The film has the band creating the *We Will Rock You* song years after it had been an

219

international hit. The film has Queen break up for at least years, after Mercury did some solo career work, then Mercury happens to find out about the Live Aid concert, and gets back with the band just in time to do the concert. And, just days before the Live Aid concert, the film has Mercury telling his band mates that he has AIDS. In real life, Mercury was not the first in the band to do a solo album, and his bandmates didn't care about that. In real life, the band did not break up for years – which is a major point in the film. In real life, they had finished a major tour just weeks before the Live Aid concert. Mercury wasn't diagnosed with AIDS until after the Live Aid concert. His band mates didn't know that he had AIDS until years later, shortly before his death. There are numerous other things in the film that are fiction. The film has excellent acting and production values, but doesn't represent reality.

"*Grand Canyon* is as loose a film as I've ever written, and when I was done with it I saw that I was following exactly the same kind of structure I had been using since I learned it in college. I hadn't thought about it once during the writing – which is what you're hoping for."
– Lawrence Kasdan, *The Accidental Tourist*

A one-hour TV pilot has a page count of about 45 to 55. (See the TV section of *The Screenwriter's Bible*). If the script is for a streaming platform with no commercial breaks, it might be 55 to 65 pages. (Some streaming platforms do have commercials). (Search: TV scripts, episodic scripts, anthology scripts, limited series scripts, and miniseries scripts. If you are in L.A., go to the WGA Library, and read some of their TV scripts.)

Depending on which form of delivery (network, cable, streaming, or web channel) you might need to adjust the script.

An hour-long network script contains an opening conflict teaser scene with a hook and/or mini-cliffhanger that usually displays character contention, or establishes a pre-set for it to jump into being present. There are three or four other acts (each with a mini-cliffhanger), and a wrap-up ending act. Each act is labeled at its start (TEASER, ACT ONE, ACT TWO, ACT THREE, ACT FOUR) and labeled at its ending (END OF TEASER, END OF ACT ONE, etc.). Each act starts on a new page. There is usually a main story, and two subplots.

Single-cam sitcom scripts are similar to hour scripts, aren't filmed in front of an audience, and are about 24 to 30 pages.

Multi-cam sitcom scripts are filmed in front of an audience, usually cost less to produce, have a different layout and pacing than hour-long episodics, anthologies, or limited series, have certain elements that are upper-case and underlined, and are 50 to 55 pages. The teaser is a COLD OPEN. The final scene is a TAG (also known as the epilogue). (Study: The sitcom chapter of *The Screenwriter's Bible*.) (Search: Multi-cam sitcom scripts.)

Then, there are soap operas, which are a different beast. (Search: Soap opera scripts.)

You might be interested in writing short films that will stick to the structure of your choice, or no specific structure. Make and use those to enter film festivals. And use them to try to land bigger jobs. And/or use them to get funding to make the full-length version.

Maybe your screenplay will be deconstructionist and nonsequential, which is called "nonlinear narrative." This structure is a cleverly disorganized puzzle that snaps together by – or during – the final scene. (See: *Memento, Snow Falling on Cedars, Sliding Doors, The English Patient, Celine and Julie Go Boating, Zabriskie Point, Belle De Jour.*) (Search: Nonlinear narrative films.)

"I read novels, and in a novel you can start in the middle of the story. They're doing something, and it's just moving in the forward momentum of what they're doing – they're taking place in the here and now. And now, it comes to chapter three, and chapter three happened two-years before. I always felt that if you did it the way they did it in novels, that would be inherently cinematic. The cross-cutting would be neat."
– Quentin Tarantino, *Once Upon a Time… in Hollywood*

You might choose to write your ensemble character script in multiple storyline structure, and mix that with a nonlinear narrative.

"Also known as the multiple protagonist/antagonist, or multiple storyline structure, parallel storytelling is essentially the story of a group. Various members of this group go through a sequence of events where a common problem reveals itself through a journey, and a central theme emerges out of the relationships that form between the various plots."
– Karen Lefkowitz, UCLA School of Theater, Film, and TV

"Movies don't look hard, but figuring it out, getting the shape of it, getting everybody's character right, and having it be funny, make sense, and be romantic, it's creating a puzzle."
– Nancy Meyers, *Something's Gotta Give*

Do a search for "film structure," and you will be hit with a vast number of articles, videos, and books expressing a variety of opinions about film structure. Read and watch some of them.

If you want to be a successful screenwriter, what you have to do is to write and finish and polish screenplays to the professional level expected by agents, managers, producers, directors, stars, distributors, and financiers, and that can be made into what will satisfy audiences… and bring in money to satisfy investors. Put your skills into doing that, above paying attention to a particular structure theory.

"If you're going to be a writer, the first essential is simply to write. Do not wait for an idea. Start writing something and the ideas will come. You have to turn the faucet on before the water starts to flow."
– Louis L'Amour, *Hondo*

If a production is so interesting that millions of people watch, it will satisfy investors. If that satisfaction takes place, it doesn't matter what structure you followed while writing the script.

"Writing a screenplay for me is like juggling. It's like, how many balls can you get in the air at once. All those ideas have to float out there to a certain point, and then they'll crystalize into a pattern."
– James Cameron, *Avatar*

"Keep in mind what your reader/audience already knows – and then just keep trying to make it interesting to them. Keep them drawn in, and going deeper. And that will serve you way better than trying to hit certain page marks or plot points."
– Ed Solomon, *Mosaic*

"Forget every rule Syd Field, Robert McKee, or any other screenwriting guru ever taught you. Except one: Never be boring."
– David Mamet, *Wag the Dog*

"I trust my judgement when I think it's boring, dull, tepid, and not interesting. That's important to listen to."
– Kenneth Lonergan, *Manchester by the Sea*

"I write scripts to serve as skeletons awaiting the flesh and sinew of images."
– Ingmar Bergman, *Sixty-Four Minutes with Rebecka*

"The writer's job is to get the main character up a tree, and then once they are up there, throw rocks at them."
– Vladimer Nabokov, *Lolita*

"I am extremely suspicious of dialogue, and consider dialogue to be a last resort, rather than a first wave of storytelling."
– Christopher McQuarrie, *Edge of Tomorrow*

THE FIRST ACT

"I always try to make the opening image of the film reflect the theme of the story in its entirety. I don't always succeed, but that is my goal when I write the opening."
– Danny Strong, *Empire*

"The goal for me is to have literally everything in the movie be – in some way, shape, or form – an exploration of the central theme of the story."
– Rian Johnson, *Knives Out*

For the next few sections, let's pretend that we follow the Three Act structure. Or, something like it.

I'm not advising you to follow the Three Act structure. I include contradictory information and quotations expressing varieties of opinions throughout this book so that you can be exposed to numerous views, and formulate what works best for your screenplays.

Maybe what works for your scripts will be Three Act structure, or maybe it will be something else that you find in the following pages.

What we should pay attention to when writing a screenplay is the story, the conflict, and creating a compelling world populated by interesting characters displaying their contention in a way that engages people to watch until the final scene of the play on the screen.

Use the script as a portal through which the reader will enter into the world you have created. Get the readers inside of the minds of the characters, and engaged in their predicaments, goals, drive, reasoning, and manipulation.

To start your story, have a premise, and that has to do with knowing what the main character is hoping for.

"The author using a badly worded, false, or badly constructed premise finds himself filling space and time with pointless dialogue – even action – and not getting anywhere near the proof of his premise. Why? Because he has no direction."
– Lajos Egri, author *The Art of Dramatic Writing*

"Audiences are harder to please if you're simply giving them effects, but they're easy to please if it's a good story."
– Steven Spielberg, *The Goonies*

"Make sure your first twenty pages kick serious ass. Hook that first reader, get them interested, then it's off to the races."
– Scott Neustadter, *The Fault in Our Stars*

The First Act is the exposition, during which important information about the world within the script is presented, setting up the audience to care about what they are seeing and hearing to the point that their anticipation is so strong that they want to watch the rest of the production.

"With your screenplay, you are creating a world. Consider everything – every character, every room, every juxtaposition, every increment of time – as an embodiment of that world. Look at all of this through that filter, and make sure that it is all consistent. As in a painting, every element is part of one whole composition. Just as there is nothing separate in the actual world, there should be nothing separate in the world you create."
– Charlie Kaufman, *Confessions of a Dangerous Mind*

Exposition

One purpose of polishing and rewriting your script will likely be to disguise the information behind the actions in the description and the words of the dialogue, while carving an emotional pathway.

Exposition is needed and important. It can be done well. Or, it can be done badly. It sets and manipulates the perception of the viewers. It provides puzzle pieces and informs the viewer so that they form anticipation and engage their focus to figure out the puzzle.

Exposition used wisely and cleverly uses the storytelling devices of visuals and dialogue to include the minimum snippets of information needed by the script reader and viewer to speed them into, understand, and be emotionally engaged in the:
- plot
- world
- societal constraints
- reasoning of the culture
- rules of the setting
- tension
- conflict

And the character's dynamics of:
- concerns and/or motivation
- goals/wants
- needs
- contention
- conflict – both internal and external conflict (persons or things)
- logic
- philosophical or moral challenge or burden
- choice to go on the adventure
- emotional through-line or tracking
- crucial things they need to focus on to complete their mission

And the necessary backstory of the character's:
- relationships
- prior mission, or lack thereof = their rise
- socioeconomic status, place, and presentation
- chosen life roleplay, concept, philosophy
- hopes
- wounds
- gains
- losses
- deceptions
- hates
- and/or joys

Don't give the reader a bunch of information that they don't need. That means: Don't overload the dialogue or description with unnecessary information.

"Don't write what they want. They don't know what they want. Just make it good."
– Nora Ephron, *When Harry Met Sally*

David Trottier's Seven Deadly Dialogue Sins:
1) Obvious exposition.
2) Overwriting.
3) Exaggeration.
4) Everyday pleasantries.
5) Unnecessary repetition.
6) No room for subtext.
7) Derivative dialogue and other original speeches.

"It's a gamble you take, the risk of alienating an audience. But there's a theory. Sometimes it's better to confuse them for five minutes than to let them get ahead of you for ten seconds."
– Paul Thomas Anderson, *There will be Blood*

A trick is to install just enough information in each scene so that it helps to form parts of a puzzle being gathered in the minds of the readers, but not so much information that it talks down to the reader, or is so distractive that it takes them out of the story.

- Include the information that keeps the reader on the path of the story.
- Include information that maintains the conflict, concern, and contention.
- Use side characters to deftly deliver information that is helpful to moving the story forward, and that includes roadblocks for the character to face and use logic to maneuver around – which is a way of providing information about the intellect, goals, needs. and wants of the character.
- Avoid monologues to deliver information, unless done so cleverly, without clogging the script, disrupting the flow, or providing information that is so obvious that the reader would figure it out without that dialogue.
- Serve information that maintains a consistency of viewer focus on the emotional tracking of the characters from scene to scene.
- Provide information…
  - at the best and most clever moments
  - in exposition beats
  - to land the aha! moments in the minds of the script readers.
- Give only the information that is needed in each scene. Then: Move along to the next scene.

That means using brevity to start as late as possible in the scenes in a way that eliminates wasted screen time, and provides the needed information, and then get out of the scenes as early as possible. Then, cleverly snap into the next scene at a point of what we need to see and/or hear.

"Never let the character tell me something that the camera can show me."
– Taylor Sheridan, *Without Remorse*

From the start, aim to avoid dialogue that simply exposes everything for the audience to know. As mentioned elsewhere, don't use dialogue to "talk at the audience." Instead, reveal things by the spoonful, with as little exposition in the dialogue as possible for understanding what is going on. Build audience expectations. Do what smartly engages the audience.

"You always want the audience wondering what's going to happen next."
– Taylor Sheridan, *Hell or High Water*

If there is expository dialogue, be creative about it. Perhaps if there is stuff that the audience needs to know, it can be presented in the form of an argument between characters, with each trying to prove their point – but not saying things that each already knows. Avoid talking to the audience.

"The trick that I learned from a friend of mine named John Rodgers – who is a feature and TV writer – John has always been good about nesting exposition, or framing it as an argument. And so, if you have some sort of

debate that happens among the characters, and use them as trying to defend their point by explaining why they think they are right, you are still explaining things. But, it's under the context that I think it makes it more digestible."
– Eric Heisserer, *Bird Box*

Be clever and elegant in teasing the audience with little bits of information. Give them puzzle pieces that they will assemble in their brains. Make them want more of the puzzle pieces so that they keep watching to factor the situation among the characters and how the characters are playing out their needs and wants that fuel and animate their motive actions. Then twist things to alter audience expectations, perhaps making them think that they are wrong – even if the audience is right, and finds out that they are correct.

"A great story isn't so much about the story as it is the character. What attracts me to a story is the characters involved. With *Secretariat* what makes the story work is the character. If you don't have good characters, it doesn't matter how strong your story is, it'll sink. For me, it's always been about finding that character that I could really sink my teeth into."
– Mike Rich, *Finding Forrester*

In the First Act, have you brought your characters into the story for the readers to focus on, in a way that those characters are the stars?
Know that when actors are reading screenplays, they are going to look for what they can do, how they can play the character, and what there is about it that is going to be interesting through acting to display it in the character's actions and words.

"Be exceedingly economical with your words. If you can show a concept, idea, or emotion, do it. Don't tell your audience about it if you don't have to. Think of the scenes in your script as little mysteries: Give your audience just enough information to be able to solve it, but not enough to solve it for them. For example, don't write dialogue that has your character telling someone that they're depressed at a party, give your character a thousand-yard stare as everyone around them enjoys the festivities.
Audiences are smart, and they don't go to the movies to be spoon-fed. They want to engage with your story. They want to wrestle with it. If you don't give them the opportunity to do that, they'll lose interest faster than you can say 'helicopter screenwriter.'"
– V Reneé, *Writing Exposition: Why You Should Stop Being a Helicopter Screenwriter*, NoFilmSchool.com

"I think with my films, if you see them once you see a film, but to really get it, you have to see it more than once. I think any good film should be seen more than once. Look at the great paintings: You don't say, 'Hey, we're going to go down and see the Rembrandt tomorrow.' 'Oh, I saw that.'"
– Robert Altman, *McCabe & Mrs. Miller*

"I've made up little mantras for myself, catchphrases from a screenwriting book that doesn't exist. One is 'Write the movie you'd pay to go see.' Another is, 'Never let a character tell me something that the camera can show me.'"
– Taylor Sheridan, *Sicario*

Starting from that first page, what are you visually feeding the audience in ways that are engaging, rich in subtext, and that also apply to the conflict, that, throughout the screenplay, draws characters to contend with their situation as they are set on a goal that – when aimed for through actions – puts the character through a threshold of mental, relationship, career, life, cultural, and/or other transformation?

"As you write, take a moment after finishing each scene and make sure you know what your main character is feeling. And then ask yourself if the audience needs to see what she's feeling."
– Kristina Reed, producer

Are you showing and not telling? Can we see dispute in what we seem to know that the character wants compared to what they seem to have or seem to know?

"In thematic structure, the purpose of the story is to take the main character – the protagonist – from a place of ignorance of the truth, or the true side of the argument you are making, and take them all the way to the point they become the very embodiment of that argument, and they do it through action."
– Craig Mazin, *Chernobyl*

While there should be some physical display of character purpose, have you gone too far in micromanaging the actor's movements and facial expressions to the point of puppetry direction?

The story and the dialogue should be strong enough that you aren't – or are not often – telling the actor when to raise a brow, to smile, to fold their arms, to cross their legs away from the other character, and other expressions and body language.

"I think one of the coolest things about the job is the level of trust we have for each other. The actors fully trust that the writers will write amazing episodes, and the writers trust that the actors will follow their instincts with the characters."
– John Krasinski, actor on *The Office*

While some actor direction might be useful, don't over-explain. Don't over-direct. Leave the acting up to the actors. (While in production, you may end up discussing things with the actors – especially if you are a staff writer on a series. In that situation, there will be collaboration, and styling the script for the actors – in combination with the directors, producers, and editors. But, for spec scripts, you are not in that situation.)

Leave the direction up to the director.

Leave the camera work up to the DP and camera operators.

"Good films can be made only by a crew of dedicated maniacs."
– David Lean, *A Passage to India*

Tell a story and tell it well, and let the dramatics play out on the screen.

It is highly unlikely that the final produced film or TV show will end up exactly as you thought it should be. So, forget about it being precisely as you envisioned it as you were writing it.

"When I'm imagining it, it exists on a piece of paper, and in my head. When other people come in – actors, the rest of the people, the designers – it becomes something else. It becomes an interpretation of a large group of people that kind of come together and create this thing. And so, it's expansive. People often say, 'Is this what you pictured?' Well, how could it be? In fact, if it were, it would be a disappointment – in a way. Because it becomes more. And that is what you are trying to do. You're trying to keep it alive when you're on the stage."
– Charlie Kaufman, *Anomalisa*

"Exposition is always something that I'm terrified of, terrified about, because I typically spot it very easily when I watch movies, and it usually pulls me out."
– Destin Daniel Cretton, *The Glass Castle*

"The hardest thing is always the same thing for every writer: Exposition.

Exposition is the bane of a writer's life, and how you can tuck it and hide it, disguise it. But, the things that seem tough – like speeches – are in fact much easier than exposition."
– Paul Schrader, *Light Sleeper*

"Each scene must be a drama in itself. The whole picture must be made up of a series of small dramas. This makes the completed picture a mosaic of little ones. Scenes that have no dramatic value in them, or say nothing, must be eliminated. So, the scenario writer must bear in mind at all times not what he can put into a picture, but what he can leave out."
– Jeanie Macpherson, silent film director, writer, and actor

Are the characters saying things that we don't need to hear them say, but that we should be able to understand simply by observing their actions and body language?

"I'd say the most common problem with scripts I'm asked to consider rewriting is that they aren't sufficiently dramatized – the characters explain who they are and what they're doing, rather than revealing it through their

actions. This doesn't mean you don't use dialogue, only that the dialogue is revelatory rather than expository."
    – John Sayles, *The Howling*

Expository dialogue is that which throws all sorts of information to the audience and dilutes or obliterates what could have been clever subtext. The writer us talking down to and over explaining to the viewer. It makes the production less interesting to watch, and likely slows down the pacing, and dumbs down the characters.

In expository dialogue, the writer seems to assume that the audience needs everything explained to them, including the political, cultural, religious, and societal rules so that the audience then knows what the characters are dealing with, what guidelines they are living under, and what they will contend with – what the conflict will be.

A popular sci-fi film from 2010 that made loads in the international box office is filled with expository dialogue. Less dialogue would have been better.

"Don't write people off as stupid, or as having too short attention spans. People are as good as what they're given. So, give them the best."
    – Stephen Beresford, *Pride*

"I think the problem today is that all films are dealt with in exactly the same way, and they're all basically made for the lowest common denominator, which is the fourteen-year-old boy."
    – Robert Altman, *Thieves Like Us*

Is the dialogue you wrote necessary for revealing the character's psychological profile, and their concerns, wants, and needs, and how those play into the conflict and display of contention?

"The worst crime you can commit with an audience is telling them something they already know."
    – Aaron Sorkin, *The Newsroom*

If we watch the film or TV show without sound, could we get a sense of the place, character psychology, need, want, motive, relationships, and situation?

If any part of the film is applicable to having no sound, perhaps the first act is that part. Will the audience be instantly enticed by what they see?

For a silent opening to a film that is an excellent display of story without dialogue, see: *Hell or High Water*.

"Don't bend; don't water it down; don't try to make it logical; don't edit your own soul according to the fashion. Rather, follow your most intense obsessions mercilessly."
    – Franz Kafka, author *The Metamorphosis*

Have you presented puzzle pieces that the viewer's want to factor and piece together?

Can we recognize some sort of conflict, friction, and hurdle within the first one to three pages that helps set up what will be the character's contention in relation to their wants, needs, and motive?

Do we know what the main character's life is about simply by seeing their surroundings?

Do we connect with the basic humanity of the character in a way that we understand their predicament, needs, wants, drive, and hustle?

"A filmmaker's most important tool is humanity. You want to be able to capture humanity in your stories, and bring out humanity in your characters."
– Ryan Coogler, *Black Panther*

Do we know why the character would want something different for themselves than what we see that – or perceive as being what – they have at the opening?

Would we want something different for that character – especially if we were placed in the same situation?

Can we identify what the character seems to want, and empathize with the feelings of frustration and loss they will experience if they aren't able to get it?

Are we able to identify with something so that we want to see what happens with it? It could be that we expected something, but then we were thrown by a reversal of our expectations, and there is an "uh oh!" moment that grabs us, tosses the character into terminal velocity, and makes us watch more to see what happens with their reasoning and actions, and our expectations.

"Your motivation is part of the relationship to your character. You don't write an inciting incident. You don't write: Push character out of safety. That gives you no real guidance to let something blossom. What you write is an ironic disruption of stasis. Ironic as in a situation that includes contradiction or sharp contrasts – that is: Genetically engineered to break your character's soul. You're going to destroy them. You are God, and you are designing a moment that will begin a transformation for this specific character. So, you have to make it intentional. It can be an explosion, or it can be the tiniest little change. But it's not something that would disrupt everyone's life, the way it's disrupting this person's life. You have tailored it perfectly – and terribly – for them."
– Craig Mazin, *Chernobyl*

Does that "uh oh!" moment – which some writers refer to as the catalyst or inciting incident that could change everything for the main character – happen somewhere around pages nine to twelve?

Inciting incident:
- Is considered a hook: It hooks the audience in to watch and anticipate what happens next.
- Happens in the first act.
- Is a dramatic element.

- Is a paramount event.
- Turns the adventure onto a certain path.
- Works as a hinge to open the window to the adventure.
- Thrusts the audience into being engaged with the story.
- Is key to the plot.
- Gives the protagonist a mission.
- Sends them on their quest.
- Sets off a bell in their mind.
- Is a dispute between what they want and what they see or are experiencing.
- Challenges their life philosophy.
- Ignites their courage.
- Triggers their plan.
- Escorts the emotional through-line into Act II.

See Syd Field's book *Screenplay*. Maybe you will agree with his structure concepts. Maybe they will work for your story. Or, not.

Maybe your script will work to be one in which shoving the character into a contentious situation won't happen until later than page ten.

"All drama is conflict. Without conflict, there is no action. Without action, there is no character. Without character, there is no story. And without story, there is no screenplay."
– Syd Field, *Men in Crisis*

"There's a common piece of advice that you should start the script in *media res* or 'in the middle of things' – meaning that something compelling, emotional, and filled with conflict and spectacle should happen right away."
– Erik Bork, *From the Earth to the Moon*

Can we identify characters as the protagonist and antagonist?

"I feel like in a movie, even if the movie is complex, I'll tend to limit it to two, or, at most, three points of view – the Omniscient point of view, which is the wide frame, and then, classically, there's a protagonist and the antagonist, you know, in thrillers, but usually there's a bunch of protagonists, and usually I pick one or two. So, generally, we're seeing the world from either the Omniscient point of view, or that of one or those characters."
– John Sayles, *Men of War*

Can we identify the hurdles that the main character faces?

Do we identify with or otherwise care enough about them to want to stick around and see how they handle their hurdles and intellect, and use their logic to get what they need?

Have you instilled a sense of being and tone of presence within the audience so that they emotionally engage in the world that you have created?

Do we care about the characters, even if we wouldn't want them in our home, neighborhood, or town?

Do we have some level of repulsion, disgust, or refusal with or about a person or thing in the first 3 to 12 pages?

"I always think that if you look at anyone in detail, you will have empathy for them, because you recognize them as a human being, no matter what they've done."
– Andrea Arnold, *American Honey*

Do we feel compassion or empathy – and a connection – with someone in the opening pages?

"For years, I've used the term audience identification. Something about your story, most particularly involving your protagonist, must resonate with a reader. What that boils down to is creating a sense of empathy on the part of the reader with at least one of your central characters. If you do that, you shrink the distance between the reader and the story universe you are creating. Indeed, the reader can begin to live vicariously through the experiences of the protagonist, the degree of empathy so strong as to pull the reader into the story.

It's not enough to create empathy. Empathy does not necessarily translate into a compelling story. To do that, we need to craft a narrative that involves some sense of tension. You've heard the saying, 'You can't have good drama without conflict'? That is the same sentiment as what is at work here. There have to be problems to solve and obstacles to overcome in order for a narrative to create a sense of tension in a reader. Of course, the presence of this tension presupposes a resolution to it which in turn provides a sense of emotional satisfaction."
– Scott Myers, GoIntoTheStory.BlckLst.com

If you are writing a film script, you are probably focused on one or two characters – unless it is an ensemble piece.

If you are writing an episodic, anthology, or limited series pilot, know that it is most likely – more or less – an ensemble piece. By the end of the first act, the characters have been introduced, and the audience should have a feeling of the world the characters exist in, their reasoning, the problems they face, and that we can relate to, what the characters want and need, and a sense of how the characters might be factoring and dealing with their situations, struggles, and needs: We see their logic and contention and motives.

"That's our job – to spark curiosity and emotion from an audience, for them to discover what's going on in their own heads."
– Seth Lochhead, *Hanna*

"The first ten pages can and should be filled with fun-to-watch, high-conflict material, but these should be examples of the kinds of things the main character is dealing with in their current status quo life. It should not usually be already changing that status quo in a significant way. That should be saved

for the catalyst. First, you have to compellingly dramatize what the status quo is, such that the reader is properly seduced."
– Erik Bork, *Band of Brothers*

Be aware that you are not only writing for the readers at the management company, agency, producer's office, production company, and studio, you are writing for the director, DP, and actors. You want them to engage in the story. Each one of them will be looking for different components within the script, in relation to the job they have to do. Satisfy them.

As far as the actors, you want them to desire to play the characters, and to even fight to play them. The roles should be something that the actors see as what will advance their careers. The roles could help the actors become who audiences want to watch, and who directors, producers, and studios want to have in their films.

"The more specific and compelling each image, each action, and each line of dialogue of your main character becomes, the more it reveals about the deeper themes that draw an actor to your character."
– Jacob Krueger, WriteYourScreenplay.com, *The Matthew Shepherd Story*

By the end of the First Act, we want to watch the Second Act, because we are left with a dramatic question that we want to see answered through the protagonist and antagonist characters manipulating and contending with their situations through internal and external conflict.

By now, you also should have the external conflict solidly established, even if it shows up BIG time toward the end of the First Act. That means, we are aware of what is manipulating the character in the form of a protagonist that is a person, or external conflict that is other outside forces, such as a weapon, bomb, creature, storm, mechanical problem, encroaching army, oppressive laws, religion, or society, or other concerns, threats, or potential problems that will trip the protagonist and keep the audience anticipating what will happen.

"If the proposition is that a screenplay should have three acts, I would say that's not rocket science, because you can't help but have three acts. You set up the premise. You challenge the status quo. Then you resolve this. Those are the three acts. That's all there is to it.

I personally believe in a well-structured film. I don't see the screenplay as something that should be separate from the film. I don't make a screenplay, I make a film. But it still has to be well-structured, there's no getting around it. It's essential and as important as having a well-structured building. But I have little time for the industry that has grown up around theorizing this."
– Mike Leigh, *Peterloo*

"When I go to the cinema, I'm often frustrated because I can guess exactly what is going to happen about ten minutes into the screening. So, when I'm working on a subject, I'm always looking for the element of surprise."
– Sergio Leone, *Aphrodite, Goddess of Love*

"The reduction of dialogue is what makes great movie dialogue. The best actors want less of it, and so give it to them."
– Brian Helgeland, *Man on Fire*

"By thinking of dialogue in musical terms – thinking of dialogue in terms of something that conveys an emotion, rather than information – it has changed the way I write scenes. When I find myself writing something that is purely informational, if I can't inject it with something like conflict, humor, tension, suspense, drama – especially conflict – then I know that what I'm doing is that I'm writing information, and information is the death of emotion."
– Christopher McQuarrie, *Persons Unknown*

THE SECOND ACT

What are you visually feeding the audience in a way that is engaging and applies to the conflict, but also triggers the character to contend with their situation in ways that reveal their wants, needs, logic, and philosophy while engaging our attention, concerns, expectations, reasoning, and anticipations?

Are you showing, and not telling?

Seek to show the story visually, rather than telling it through dialogue.

Does the situation become more of a struggle for the characters so that we hope and reason that they contend with it in certain ways?

"It's always a conscious choice to surprise people. That is always the mandate. Today, with all the wonderful – and sometimes not so wonderful – entertainment it's harder than ever to keep things interesting, so you have to surprise people."
– Vince Gilligan, *Breaking Bad*

Are there reversals of audience expectations that make them want to continue watching so that they see what happens?

Do you toss enough problems at the character to test their resolve – to keep them working, factoring, and trying through bold and/or subtle contentious actions to get what they want?

Is it interesting and engaging enough to hold the audience?

If the audience doesn't identify with the characters and conflict, or start psychologically going along with the character and their situation by the beginning of the second act, there is a script problem.

Are you sending the character through a maze that makes them use their intellect, words, and actions in ways that reveal motive? Do we want to root for and fight with them to get what they apparently need and/or want?

235

"You want to have the action and fighting. But, the most effective films have the emotional battle. The one-on-one battle is the one that affects us the most. We tried to balance the two, and there were a lot of characters to service. You want to give everyone their moment."
– Joe Robert Cole, on *Black Panther*

Are the characters experiencing things that they and we could have never expected, and are they sufficiently improvising their way through those situations?

Are the forces that the characters are fighting against so pervasive that the audience feels the frustration and wants to help the person get through the situation?

Are you maintaining intrigue and messing with audience perceptions and expectations while doing the same to your character?

"I think, when writing a script, you always ask yourself what a person's goals are. What are they after, and what do they want? There's a superficial answer with these three characters in the movie, and then there's the real answer. The movie is about the real answer: What these people really want. Then, what are they willing to do to attain that?"
– E. Max Frye, *Foxcatcher*

Is the character getting so tangled in their situation that they are moving deeper and deeper into a point of no return in which they are increasing their risks, and must both figure out a way and act to change things?

"I like it when you read a script and there's the part that you show to the other characters, and then there is the part that only the audience knows."
– Angelica Huston, actor, director, producer

Is it believable enough so that the characters behave as real people would behave when placed within the circumstances you have created in the script?

Is it unbelievable, contrived and/or boring nonsense that people won't care about?

Is the script too one-note, which is that it is all about one thing that isn't very interesting, and also played out by characters who most people won't care enough to watch?

A script that is all about an uninteresting person wanting something that most people wouldn't want, and wouldn't cheer for the character to get is likely a one note script. Perhaps the story would be better off as a side story, if it plays into another lead story that is more engaging, interesting, intriguing, and that is played out by watchable characters, and would keep an audience focused and hopeful.

"Every five to ten pages, I want a big fist to come out of the screenplay and punch the reader in the gut."
– Allan Durand, producer

Is the character's apparent reasoning and response through their actions and words unbelievable, stupid, ridiculous, or absurd – and therefore going to turn off the audience, because the audience doesn't care about the person or their struggles?

Is the audience going to leave their seats?

Do you maintain the personality and emotional journey of the characters so that they remain consistent, but also show an arc in which they learn and grow and become more determined to succeed at getting the thing or situation they want?

"At the top of my computer, in big, bold letters, it says, 'What is the simple emotional journey?' I look at that all the time."
– Billy Ray, *State of Play*

"Carl Jung asserted the process of individuation as the greatest calling of the human adventure and that process is fundamentally about metamorphosis – becoming who we are meant to be, indeed, in a way, become who we already are (as represented in the various aspects of our psyche).

Why is metamorphosis perhaps the single most universal narrative archetype? Again, we could talk about this for days, but if I had to name one reason it's this: People want to believe they can change. Stories that feature characters who do change reinforce that belief.

So, I think it's safe to say that in most movies, the protagonist does go through some sort of metamorphosis.

There are stories where the protagonist does not go through any significant metamorphosis. *Forrest Gump*, *Being There*, pre-Daniel Craig *James Bond* movies are a few examples. Forrest Gump and Chance are change agents. That is, they don't change – they change others. In the case of *James Bond*, that's more of a reflection how in some action movies the protagonist's story is not so concerned with their psychological journey, but rather the impact they have on others, most notably, nemesis characters. Of course, there are lots of action movies where the protagonist does change – *Lethal Weapon* and *Die Hard* spring to mind – but only if the filmmakers are interested in exploring that character's inner life."
– Scott Myers, GoIntoTheStory.BlckLst.com

Is there one more thing that finally gets to the character, and makes it seem that they will not succeed, which brings them to succumb to fear and doubt, but that leaves a tiny window of possibility that they can crawl and grovel through to get that thing or situation that they want?

Are we still rooting for the character? Or, have we given up on caring about them? Or, are we in the game with them, and committed to see how the character has an epiphany, breaks through being dragged down, and goes for the win?

At this point, we should want to stick around for the next act.

"The event that occurs at the second act curtain triggers the end of the movie."

– Billy Wilder, *Fedora*

"You ask a question, and then don't answer it. Keep that ball up in the air as long as possible. Once you answer the question, the dramatic energy is over."
– Danny Rubin, *Groundhog Day*

THE THIRD ACT

Breaking into Act Three, we get a sense that the protagonist's fate is being sealed as a result of what we saw them go through, as their actions and words formulate a conclusion. Maybe we hate them or love them, or want the opposite result, but we want to sit and watch and see if what we expect to happen is happening, or if there is going to be one final thrust that will give us what we do or don't expect.

"If I could ask for anything with my movies, the rest of my career, it's not that I be successful. There'll be movies that are successful, and there'll be movies that won't. But I'd like to hold on to the idea that my movies are mirrors. They're not going to tell you what to think but, rather, act like a mirror, so when you get to the end of the movie, you see yourself in it."
– Jason Reitman, *The Front Runner*

In every act:
What are you **visually feeding the audience** in ways that are:
- **engaging**
- **riveting**
- and **intriguing**

In ways that apply to the:
- **conflict** and **contention**
- **logic** and **reasoning**
- **intellect** and **skill**
- **goals** and **motive**
- **instigation** and **manipulation**
- and **roadblocks – and the intention to get through them**?

239

Throughout the previous two acts, all of that has likely been visually on display – in clever ways.

The Third Act plays into what has gone on in the previous acts.

"The most ordinary word, when put into place, suddenly acquires brilliance. That is the brilliance with which your images must shine."
– Robert Bresson, *L'Argent*

Are you using a minimalist economy of words in the dialogue?

"As a writer you try to listen to what others aren't saying, and write about the silence."
– N.R. Hart, author *Beauty and Her Beast*

Are you using deft brevity in the description to show how and why the characters are contending within the conflict?

"Description begins in the writer's imagination, but should finish in the reader's."
– Stephen King, *The Talisman*

"I try to be brief and evocative. I write in fragments. I try to paint a visual picture as efficiently as possible."
– Kira Snyder, *Incursion*

Is the scene description throughout the script visual? That is what the description is: The visual. It doesn't describe the thoughts of the characters. It doesn't describe the past or the future of people or things. Always remember that the people who watch the production are not going to see your script.

"I think part of being a good screenwriter is being as concise as possible."
– Eric Roth, *The Curious Case of Benjamin Button*

At this point, we should want to watch the end stages.

Have you concluded the backstories and shown arcs in the main character as well as in the secondary characters?

Are we able to identify with what the character has been through so that we are going to feel some satisfaction in their choices, and in what we see them get?

Even if they die, are we going to be satisfied with what was accomplished?

"The principal obligation you have as the writer is to get to a climax which interests and excites – and if it doesn't satisfy, it at least makes an audience sit up and take notice of it. It must also be valid. It must take the various traits of the individuals involved in your story, and make them do something or react to something as their nature dictates.
This is to say that, for example, if you're dealing with a Quaker pacifist who is constantly being beaten on the head by the neighborhood bully, and who suddenly at one given moment in his life says 'I will not turn my cheek

again. I will hit back,' and does so, you must absolutely believe that there is a moment when a man will turn his back on a fundamental belief and do something foreign to his nature.

Or, the reverse is true. You can show a bully who all his life has stepped on people, who does it out of a sense of sheer cruelty, who has no sense of the value of the dignity of other human beings – or the feelings of other human beings – and at a given moment in time, put into a position where he has a chance to save someone he couldn't care less about, but literally risks his life to do so. There must be a reason he does it, and a believable explanation as to why he does it, and the fact that you believe that he does it. This is the sort of thing you must do."

– Rod Serling, *Night Gallery*

"Writing should be about withholding. Write it all, first. And then see how much of it you can withhold. Because, that's the way you'll create your tension."
— Emma Thompson, *Last Christmas*

THE RESOLUTION

"I think I always approached film from more of a structural point of view of storytelling. I'm always finding a form, and often that form has a lot to do with the time element of the story versus the plot. There's a time element to all of our lives just inherently and the way we process every day, so I think in a lot of my storytelling methodologies time has largely replaced the notions of what a plot is, which to me feels kind of constructed. Not that life doesn't occasionally offer up a plot twist, but it's always offering you time linearity."
— Richard Linklater, *Last Flag Flying*

By the resolution, the ticking clock is fading, or has been muffled by all that we have concluded.

In the resolution, the audience looks for the completion of issues in a way that is somewhat what they had hoped. Those may not be exactly what they were expecting, but would be understandable as realistic to what the characters went through.

To be satisfying – even if left unclear – the resolution must be clear enough so that the audience could draw their own conclusions.

According to the structure you are following, is the resolution also the denouement? Or, is the denouement something that follows the resolution? It depends on who you listen to, and on your script. Some will say that the resolution and denouement are one and the same. Others will not agree with that stance.

Perhaps the resolution within your script and the production made from it will be interpreted differently by each reader and viewer, and that might be its perplexing, enticing, engaging brilliance.

The final product also depends on the director and editor, and perhaps also on the producer(s), and distributor(s).

"The conclusion of your story should be emotionally satisfying, in that:

1) The action culminates in something grand and creative (possibly with a twist),

2) The primary relationship(s) resolve in a touching or moving way, and…

3) The ending is meaningful.

This is just a guidance, but it implies that when you write or revise, you have some idea of your ending first so that you know what you are building to."

– David Trottier, author *The Screenwriter's Bible*

"There is no real ending. It is just the place where you stop the story."

– Frank Herbert, author *Dune*

"A great script creates an irresistible narrative flow that propels a reader to an inevitable dramatic conclusion."
– Javier Grillo-Marxuach, *Guardians of the Galaxy*

The Denouement / Conclusion

"At a fundamental level, stories are about change. Events change, circumstances change, locations change, time changes. But perhaps the single most important change in a movie is this: Metamorphosis.

Joseph Campbell said that at some level, the entire point of the Hero's Journey is metamorphosis (he used the term 'transformation'). Whose metamorphosis? The Hero, of course – a character screenwriters refer to as the protagonist."
– Scott Myers, GoIntoTheStory.BlckLst.com

The denouement is the very end of the script. It is the final scene or scenes in which we get a brief view of how things of the world we watched are changed and settled in a new way. It is the epilogue where loose ends are tied, or we get a feeling of how they are dealt with or viewed with what the character learned from their escapades.

"The script must keep you off balance. Keep you surprised, entertained, involved, and yet, when the denouement is reached, still give a sense that the story had to turn out that way."
– Sidney Lumet, *Find Me Guilty*

By the denouement, the unraveling is through. The arcs are complete. We have witnessed the character's catharsis, whether it be through or by catastrophe, failure, tragedy, repentance, marriage, restoration, heroic success, life release, sealing of fate, acceptance, changed culture, wisdom gained, reunion, letting go, apology, truths revealed, or other satisfactory final stages of the concerns we had during the previous parts of the story.

In the eight-sequence structure that Frank Daniel of USC's Graduate Screenwriting Program developed, the denouement consists of the final segment of a film that is broken up into eight sequences.

"One thing I found I really loved in certain movie endings is when it ends a little bit before you think it's going to end. In other words, it doesn't close in the traditional 'let's tie up all the loose ends' kind of denouement, but instead tries to end with a major sequence that gets your emotions up, and then gets out."
– Damien Chazelle, *10 Cloverfield Lane*

Is your ending true to the spirit of the story and character intellect, reasoning, and emotional journey that your script displayed?

Will the audience be satisfied enough with how the characters ended up? That doesn't mean that everything about the future of the characters and how they deal with what they went through has to be revealed. It means that you can leave the audience some guessing room. It could mean letting the audience draw their own conclusions – even if the audience members disagree with each other.

Likely, by the very last frame the protagonist has experienced an adjustment of their life philosophy, or has proved it to be true as they stuck to their concept of how things should be and have forced things to happen in tune with their philosophy.

"I guess what I like in my movies is where you see a character change by maybe two degrees as opposed to the traditional movie change of ninety degrees. I guess that always feels false to me in movies because that doesn't truly happen. Around me, at least in the life I live, I guess I don't see people change ninety or a hundred degrees. I see them change in very small increments. I think it's just a monitor I might have on myself as a writer to not make any false scenes."
– Paul Thomas Anderson, *Magnolia*

"With film, it's normal for the screenwriter to never be seen again after finishing (the script), until after the premiere."
 – Jane Goldman, *Kick-Ass*

"The first time you make a feature film, I don't care how prepared you are, it's terrifying, and you think you know what you're doing, and you don't find out until the editing room that you don't know what you're doing."
 – Christopher McQuarrie, *The Tourist*

Pre-Production Prep: Script Breakdown, Schedule, Budget, Scouting, Shot List, and Storyboards

Before a script can be filmed, a UPM (unit production manager) will need to go through and "breakdown the script." That is: To put the script into a technical format.

The technical formatted script will be slightly different than the spec script formatting, but will contain the same margins and other formatting parameters.

In both the spec script and the technical script, each page represents about one minute of screen time. That means that each line represents approximately a little over one-second of time (not that you should write your script with that sort of precision – and don't expect others to).

When a script is broken down:
• Scenes will be numbered.

Scene numbers are never to be included in a spec script.

The scene numbers are only to be included on the technically formatted production script – which is also used in post-production (after filming has ended and all of what was filmed, along with the continuity notes, then go to the editor, and other post-production craftspeople).

• The script will be broken into 8ths of pages.

Each day during production, a "call sheet" will be handed out to the cast and crew.

The call sheet is the daily schedule of what is to be filmed and what and who will be needed for filming that day.

The call sheet will list how many 8ths of pages will be filmed that day.

- Props and other needs of each scene will be noted and categorized depending on which department handles each element: Cast (each cast member is considered an element in the script), props, set dressing, wardrobe, camera, sound, FX, stunts, vehicles, etc.

- A shooting schedule will be made. That is a multi-page document.

    The preliminary shooting schedule will be sent to the producers, director, 1st AD, DP, gaffer, production designer, art director, set decorator, props master, transportation manager, location manager, and other department heads who are the ones in charge of the various teams of craftspeople (that might also include the post production team members: The editor, colorist, FX, foley artists, composers, and others) who will look it over. Each of those people might have suggestions for changes to the schedule.

- The cast and crew needed will be taken into consideration.

- A topsheet will be written detailing the needs of the production.

    The topsheet will list the estimated budget. A detailed budget will be attached to that – detailing how the money will be spent. (Then, during production, some of that planning is obliterated. But, hopefully, the production will be finished under budget, and on schedule – good luck with that adventure.)

    A line producer will help determine the budget, and oversee the production to make sure it stays at or below budget.

The breakdown might be shown to the writer, to see if the writer notices anything in the breakdown that could be confusing – such as a character was overlooked, or characters of similar names were mistakenly noted as one character. Or, a character was not included in a scene where they should be present. All of these details matter to scheduling, budgeting, cast, and crew.

Don't expect to be shown a breakdown of your script. But, don't be surprised if it is sent to you for you to look over.

If the breakdown is sent to you, pay attention to the details. Share any feedback information that you think might be helpful to the production. They also might not send you the breakdown, but will have some questions about certain scenes so that everything in the breakdown is clear and accurate for scheduling and budgeting. Be cooperative, helpful, and generous.

The breakdown, schedule, and budget will be required for a number of things, including:
- Investor concerns.
- Production loans.
- Production insurance.
- State or other government incentive programs.
- Location scouting.

- Location managers.
- The craft and skill needs of every department head and crew on the show.
- Equipment needs.
- Even the craft service people will need to know how much their department gets, so they know how much money they can spend for supplying snacks and drinks to the cast and crew each day.

   The craft services is in addition to the caterers who prepare the breakfast and lunch buffets for the cast and crew.

- **Matters which the breakdown, schedule, and budget determine include:**
  - The number of bathrooms that will be needed each day.
  - The number of transportation vans or shuttles that will be needed each day.
  - Cost of rental vehicles, and rented equipment and props.
  - The number of parking spots for cars and trucks that will be needed each day.
  - The location permits that will be needed, and the cost of each location.
  - The type of wardrobe changing facilities that will be needed for background actors.
  - Hair and makeup people
  - Production insurance (including for errors and omissions), and deductibles.
  - Legal consultants.
  - Etc. See below.

In addition to the breakdown, there will be the shot list.

   That includes the list of shots that the director wants to include in the film. Things considered in the shot list include:

- Location.
- Lenses, cameras, crew, and equipment, and the budgetary concerns relating to what is needed to get the shots.
- Dialogue.
- Framing.
- Composition of the shots.
- Tone and mood of the scene.
- Color and lighting.
- The framing, composition, tone and mood, color, and lighting of the previous and following shots and scenes.

   The shot list will be in alignment with the copy of the script containing lines drawn vertically by the director to indicate when each shot starts and where they end, including the insert shots (such as close-ups of the character's hands as they open a book, tie a knot in rope, type on a keyboard, cut fabric, knead dough, press a button, etc.).

   The preliminary shot list will be used during location scouting. That is when the director, DP, production designer, art director, producer, and some other key people (such as the line producer) travel to where the scenes might be filmed, and take photos, consider the light qualities, terrain, and other matters that would require certain adjustments, tools, vehicles, equipment, and crew specialists.

There might be a tech scout held after the location scout that includes certain crew department heads who will help decide what is needed for filming at each location.

The location scout photos and the preliminary shot list can then be used to create a more ideal shot list, and to help create the storyboards (unless the director doesn't use storyboards). (Storyboard might also be animated.)

"I have trouble working off things that are too preconceived, like storyboards. When things become too prepared, the life comes out of it."
– Terrence Malick, *A Hidden Life*

"I don't storyboard, because I can't draw well enough, and I don't like having another barrier: Hiring somebody to draw for me."
– Noah Baumbach, *The Squid and the Whale*

"I like to draw my storyboards myself."
– Bong Joon-Ho, *Barking Dogs Never Bite*

With all of that, the director, DP, production designer, art director, set decorator, wardrobe designer, and other key behind the scenes players work together to decide on how the whole thing will be filmed, and what equipment, crew, sets, props, and wardrobe will be needed – in tune with the budget.

"For Marty, the camera writes in a way. Every camera angle has a meaning to it. If the camera moves or doesn't, there is always a reason for that. He does extensive shot listings, and diagrams, and drawings, and shares those with me. And he pretty much sticks to it."
– Rodrigo Prieto, director of photography *The Irishman*. About working with Martin Scorsese

During the time that those decisions are made, the breakdown, shot list, storyboards, schedule (which – depending on the production – could be prepared by an assistant director, or the UPM, or the line producer), and script will go through changes. The crew will be hired by the line producer. (Each department head might be bringing in their own familiar team of people. And the producer's relative or lover will be given a job that they aren't qualified to do [maybe I'm kidding]), a final schedule is made (which is never actually final) in tune with the revised budget, and the film goes into production.

After filming (principal photography) is completed, the line producer's job will end and the records they kept of the production (called the "wrap book"), which contains everything from permits to contracts, rental agreements, insurance information, the list of cast and crew contact information, and other records, will be handed over to the producers.

The post-production supervisor then takes over.

(Search: How to breakdown a script.)

(Search: What is a film budget top sheet?)
(Search: Introduction to film budgeting.)
(Search: Film script shot list.)
(Search: Lining a film script.)
(Search: Film storyboard.)
(Search: What is a unit production manager? and What is a line producer?)

If you understand how to break down a script, it can help you write financially reasonable scripts.

Expenses taken into consideration during the breakdown and budgeting include… but are not limited to (and not in this order):

- Principal actors
- Child actor needs
    Including teachers, classroom, dressing rooms, safety equipment, food, parent/guardian needs, additional PA, children medic, special transpo, etc.
- Casting
- Background actors
- Standins
- Photo doubles
- Background car rental
    The background (extras) are often paid for use of their vehicles on film and TV shows.
- Props
- Props rental, purchase, or creation
- Mechanical effects
- Model maker
- Optical effects
- Prosthetics
- Blood
- Wardrobe/costumes
- Makeup
- Hair
- Stunts
- Medic
    A medic is on set of TV shows and films when on location. When filming is at a studio lot, there is a medic office on the lot that cast and crew can go to for various minor medical needs: Pain meds, bandages, eye wash, etc.
- Animals (livestock, pets)
- Animal handlers
    People who take care of the animals on set. They are usually the people who also own the animals.
- Wet scenes/rain
    If rain machines and other equipment are needed.
- Snow scenes

If snow machines are needed. I worked on *The Call of the Wild* set in Placerita Canyon (north of L.A.) during a heat wave. A small town was built, a tarp was suspended above the town, and snow machines were used to keep coating the town with snow. Enormous blue screens were at each end of the town so that snowy mountain views could be added in post. That all cost many millions. Oh, and we were dressed for Alaska. Yes, it was hot.

- Dusty scenes
    Could mean bringing in special equipment, including water trucks to keep the dust down on and around set.
- Cold scenes
- Hot scenes
- Indoor scenes
- Exterior scenes
- Night scenes
- Portable heaters
- Portable air conditioning units
- Sound equipment
- Sound crew
- Camera equipment
- Camera crew
- Video playback
- Lighting equipment
- Lighting crew
- Rigging crew
- Transportation equipment
- Transpo crew
- Greens rental (potted plants and trees, turf, parts of trees, etc.)
- Greens person
    Takes care of the plants that are used in scenes.
- Hotels, airfare
    When a crew works very long days (more than 12 hours) they can be offered free stay in a local hotel to prevent them from driving when they are too tired. Unfortunately, a variety of crew people have died after they fell asleep at the wheel while driving home from set.
    I know crew people who have demolished their vehicles when they fell to sleep while driving home from work. (See: The documentary by Haskell Wexler: *Who Needs Sleep?)* (Search: *Sleepless in Hollywood.*)
- Catering
- Craft service
    Provides the all-day snacks, coffee, tea, water, juices, kombucha, and sodas. Might also supply soups, salads, sandwiches, and other food.
- Crafty crew
- Porta potties
- Set construction and maintenance

- Production designer
- Art director
- Set decorator
- Set dresser
- Set painter
- Furniture rental
- Locations
- Sound stage rental
- Location permits
- Location supervisor
- Security staff
- Parking space rental
- Production insurance
- Workers comp insurance
    Could be handled by the payroll company.
- Agent fees
- Payroll
- Union fringes
- Production office
- Office equipment
- Office supplies
- Walkies
    Walkie talkies used during production for all the department heads to communicate with their crew.
- Assistant directors
- Production assistants
- Director's assistant
- Producer's assistant
- Principal actor's assistant
- Clerical staff
- Office production assistant
- Production secretary
- Accountant
- Office coordinator
- Payroll clerk
- Shipping
- Editing
- Colorist
- Audio mix
- Foley sound
- Music composer
- Soundtrack
- Music licensing

"At first glance, I always check the page count and formatting. I don't want this to make me sound pretentious in some way. Believe me, I've worked with screenplays that would make a professional screenwriter vomit, and that's okay with me. The thing is, these clues are just a couple early warnings about how experienced the filmmaker is, and how intense the project might be."

– Nathan Blair, *2nd Greatest*

"Prep is the movie you want to make. Production is the movie you think you are making. And post is the movie you've made."
– Christopher McQuarrie, *The Mummy*

"If you're writing a screenplay for a feature, you don't have any involvement with the casting process, the editing process, the set design, the costume design, or any of that stuff."
– David Benioff, *Game of Thrones*

"I generally think of myself as an author. The French have this beautiful word, *auteur*, to refer to filmmakers who are responsible for the content of their own films. I've never been interested in directing other people's works."
– Michael Heneke, *The Piano Teacher*

EDITING AND POST PRODUCTION

"Movies are pieces of film stuck together in a certain rhythm, an absolute beat, like a musical composition. The rhythm you create affects the audience."
– John Carpenter, *Dark Star*

"Once you've got the nuts and bolts of the story working, and you're down to time, and you know that all the big story beats are being hit, then you go in, perhaps in a bit more detail, and you play with the minutiae of looks and delivery, and the balance and rhythm. I suppose that's what we do all day long, sitting in a dark room."
– Gary Dollner, editor of *Killing Eve*

One essential person involved in making a film and who new writers seem to not consider is the editor. It appears that many writers don't quite have much of an understanding of the skills set of editors, and how editors can use those to alter a film or TV episode.

"Editing is the end of the writing process. I end up with a lot of footage. It's more like an archive. But, it's very nice to build the film in the editing, to combine things that I couldn't have directed. And the writing continues, even with the subtitles."
– Maren Ade, *The Forest for the Trees*

One way new writers disregard editors – or treat them as if the editors don't know what they are doing – is the writers include transitionary direction at the end of scenes. The transitionary direction is editing direction. That means the CUT TO: that naïve writers put at the end of scenes is a cue for the editor.

It is not needed to include CUT TO: at the end of a scene. Including it can be considered talking down to the editor.

It is obvious that there is a cut, because there is a new scene heading. Simply delete that transition direction.

There is also all of that other stuff newbie writers include at the end of a scene: WIPE CUT TO:, SMASH CUT TO:, CROSS FADE TO:, SPIN CUT TO:, SPLATTER CUT TO:, and so forth. The writer might consider that transition direction to be creative or cool, but it can all be viewed as… obnoxious and distractive. However, if it truly does go with the style, tone, and mood of the script, it might work. Or, it could be a distractive irritant.

Putting FADE TO BLACK at the end of a scene, or end of a script is perfectly fine. It could also be done cleverly, to fade to a color, other than to black – if it is in tune with the theme of the film. For instance, a film about a woman who picks up on younger men could FADE TO COUGAR PRINT.

"Any time you use "FADE OUT" at the end of a scene, remember that the audience can't see anything that's happening until you fade back in."
– The Onion, *Tips for Writing a Screenplay*

The transition information could also be considered director direction. The director also doesn't need it.

"Before you say 'cut,' wait five more seconds."
– Wim Wenders, *Until the End of the World*

Not that the editor necessarily will cut the scenes in the same place as the script indicates. The editor may cut earlier, or later – adding additional footage, or using a long take that included the actors improvising as the director waited a while to call "cut," or otherwise rearranging the scene visuals and dialogue through editing in ways that are more interesting and engaging. Hopefully, their choices will better serve the conflict, contention, tension, tone, mood, pacing, and other matters.

"I'm able in the editing process to make the choice. I may have you talking to your dinner mate, and if there's twelve of you at dinner there's maybe six of those conversations going on. I may feature two of them. I don't know what they're going to be until I come to that final edit."
– Robert Altman, *Gosford Park*

"With *Marriage Story*, what people don't necessarily realize is that every hesitation and every unfinished sentence is all scripted – the words are the words, and you have to stick to that. (Writer/director) Noah (Baumbach) is a real stickler about that, which is fine."
– Scarlett Johansson, actor

An editor can do so much work on a film that, in a certain way, the editor ends up being a co-writer of the film. They are.

"A film is never really good, unless the camera is an eye in the head of a poet."
— Orson Welles, *Don Quixote*

"Something that I say in virtually every class I teach at A.F.I.: Every frame matters. It must be there in support of the story."
— Matt Friedman, editor *The Farewell*

A skilled editor will do what works for the scene, a director will approve or suggest changes, and a producer – and studio suits – might be involved in how the cuts are done from one scene to the next.

"I love being in the editing room and playing with the tempo and with the rhythm of shots."
— Damien Chazelle, *La La Land*

If you are going to direct or produce your script, you can include any transition direction that you want. Otherwise, leave it out, or use that stuff sparingly, such as a `DISOLVE TO:`. Certainly, don't include transition direction after every scene.

Never include a `CUT TO:` at the end of a scene in a spec script... unless you want to irritate the reader, or want to appear as an amateur writer.

If you are a writer with a proven track record of writing scripts that get produced and bring in truckloads of money from around the globe, write your scripts any way you want.

The week I wrote this, I read a script by a major producer/writer/director. His script is filled with all sorts of small non-standard writing. But, he has massively successful shows on TV, has won numerous awards, and is directing the script he wrote.

"Cinematography and editing are at the very heart of our craft. They are not inherited from theatrical tradition, or a literary tradition: They are cinema itself."
— Guillermo del Toro, *Scary Stories to Tell in the Dark*

"The notion of directing a film is the invention of critics. The whole eloquence of cinema is achieved in the editing room."
— Orson Welles, *The Lady from Shanghai*

"I go to the set mostly to grab things, so I can go to the cutting room. Quiet. Dark. And then you can change the whole script. You change the acting. You change everything."
— Fernando Meirelles, *Maids*

While your film or series is being shot, there will be an editor – or editing team – getting the dailies (daily footage = what is filmed each day) and assembling a cut: Which is: One version of the film or show: And that is also called: "The first assembly." Or, assemblage.

"My favorite part of the whole filming process is the dailies. We serve drinks, nobody takes notes. These people work all this time, and by the time they see themselves on the screen it's edited and it's a year later and they've done four other films, three theater pieces; they never get the applause. In the dailies, they get the applause of their own peers. They cheer, and they start rooting for each other to do well."
– Robert Altman, *Beyond Therapy*

As the project is being filmed, the editing team is likely keeping a list of transition shots, close-up shots (inserts), and scenes that need to be refilmed. Some of that filming will take place during original photography (often by a "B-Unit" camera team and production team working at the same time as the original crew), and some scenes might be filmed weeks or months after the principal filming has been finished.

That "additional footage" and "reshoot" might be done by a different crew than those who worked during the original weeks or months of photography (but key people will likely be the same during the reshoots: Director, cinematographer, set design, etc.)

Along with the editing staff, the post-production team likely includes a post-production producer and/or supervisor, the sound department (including the A.D.R. [automatic dialogue replacement] techs, which involves re-recording some of the dialogue that can't be taken from the dailies/production sound recordings), the music or soundtrack craftspeople, and the D.I. (digital intermediate) team, who do color correction and/or colorize the film, adjust certain aspects of the images, and digitizing the final cut. There might also be a VFX team (visual effects techs that can be involved in a wide assortment of projects for various scenes of the film) involved in filming a variety of additional footage, and working to manipulate and digitize that footage. There also might be additional stunt footage filmed, using photo doubles, stunt doubles, and other talent – and puppets – with it all being directed by the main director and/or by another director – in tune with whatever is needed to piece the film together into a flawless mosaic.

When principal photography (filming) is completed, the editor (and typically an assistant editor and other team members – depending on budget and needs) does some finishing touches on their version (the editor's cut), which is then shown to the director, who may have a whole variety of suggested changes. Then, there is the producer's cut. Unless, of course, the director has a "final cut" agreement where the director gets to select what the final film will look like.

"No matter where I am working, I cannot make a film without one-hundred percent creative control and final cut. If there is such a guarantee, I can work anywhere."
– Bong Joon-Ho, *Sea Fog*

257

The "picture lock" final cut of the film is handed over to the sound department, which fixes the sounds (actors might be called in to re-record some of their dialogue = ADR [Automated Dialogue Replacement – also called looping]), add sound effects, and a composer adds music.

That rough final cut (which is an unfinished version of the film) might be shown to test audiences consisting of people selected from the general public to watch the film in a theater. If it is a film that will be marketed to college-age people, the test audience might be recruited from around a college campus, and shown in their local movie theater. Depending on how the audience responds to that test screening, and what they write on their feedback paper, the producers and/or director might decide on making some changes to the film – including by filming additional scenes, reshooting some scenes, adding a different ending, or recasting one or more of the roles with a different actor, and refilming all of the scenes containing that character.

Meanwhile, the marketing team is assembling a variety of materials (images [from freeze frames and the photos taken by the on-set stills photographer], advertising, trailers, posters, etc.), and arranging for the talent to be interviewed by various magazines, newspapers, radio shows, and talk shows, and appear at events and film festivals.

If the film is a tent pole for a big studio, the marketing could also include toys, fast food restaurant giveaways, and other junk that all adds to global air, water, and land pollution – which is meant for the studio to globally gather money to satisfy stockholders.

The months of post-production takes much longer than the principal photography (filming) process.

As mentioned, even after all of that post is finished, some additional footage may be ordered, which means that a crew is assembled and there might be days – or weeks – of additional filming – including to reshoot some scenes, and get other angles for scenes that had been filmed, or shoot another ending… or beginning, or middle. The additional footage then has its own variety of post-production as it is edited and altered, and added to the final cut – which could also include alterations to the soundtrack and other elements of the film.

But, for purpose of this chapter, I want to provide a view of what the editing entails.

"The essence of cinema is editing. It's the combination of what can be extraordinary images of people during emotional moments, or images in a general sense, put together in a kind of alchemy."
– Francis Ford Coppola, *The Outsiders*

"The film is made in the editing room. The shooting of the film is about shopping, almost. It's like going to get all the ingredients together, and you've got to make sure before you leave the store that you got all the ingredients. And then you take those ingredients and you can make a good cake – or not."
– Phillip Seymour Hoffman, actor

"We call it cutting. It isn't exactly that. Cutting implies severing something. It really should be called assembly.

Mosaic is assembling something, to create a whole.

Montage means the assembly of pieces of film, which, moved in rapid succession before the eye, creates an idea. Of course, the most elementary form is the juxtaposition of imagery in various sizes.

A lot of people think that cutting is – or, we'll say montage or assembly – is taking a man from one place to another and jumping into a close-up of him – which (D.W.) Griffith invented, it's true. But, to me it goes much deeper. And, as I say, the picture *Psycho* contained quite an amount of cinematic approach to its basic content. In the first place, we had in it the murder of a woman in a shower – of a nude woman.

Now, as you know, you could not take the camera and just show a nude woman being stabbed to death. It had to be done impressionistically. So, it was done with little pieces of film – the head, the feet, the hand, the parts of the torso. Everything, you see. The shower itself. I think in that scene there were 78 pieces of film in about 45 seconds."

– Alfred Hitchcock, *Champagne*

"Making a film is like adapting a screenplay. You adapt the whole thing to film, and then you take out the bits that work. You can't use the stuff that doesn't work. You have to cut it. And what is interesting about that is that you can shoot something that has been essential in the screenplay. Essential, and then you film it. You've adapted it to film, and you watch it, and you think, 'I've seen that, I can see it, so I don't need to have that scene.'"

– Emma Thompson, *Wit*

"Editing is the only unique aspect of filmmaking which does not resemble any other art form – a point so important it cannot be overstressed. It can make or break a film.

Writing, of course, is writing. Acting comes from the theater, and cinematography comes from photography. Editing is unique to film. You can see something from different points of view almost simultaneously, and it creates a new experience."

– Stanley Kubrick, *The Shining*

"After the film wrapped, I believed – foolishly, it turns out – that I didn't need to hire an editor because, well… I could edit the film myself.

This mistake – not my last during editing – would prove costly. Not only was I too close to the material – having written and directed it – but I also 'didn't know what I didn't know,' which made me – at least when I began – the worst person possible to edit the film. It would take over a decade laboring in my home studio – crafting and then re-working cut after cut of the movie – for me to learn what editing was all about. In thousands of tiny choices – what to leave in or take out, what to modify and hoe – I gradually made a discovery

I would not have anticipated: That, to me, editing was by far the most creative aspect of filmmaking."
    – Martin Garrison, *Jackson Arms*

Some screenwriters might take issue with Garrison's statement that editing is "by far the most creative aspect of filmmaking." However, he does have a clear and useful point. Perhaps it is better to not to try to do everything, and to hire someone with the skills already in place to edit a film. But also, perhaps – in a certain way – the editor is sort of a writer of the film.

An editor can alter the tone, tempo, tension, conflict, contention, structure, pacing, dialogue, wants, needs, motives, logic, relationships, and storyline – including in ways that the writer and director hadn't considered.

"You never know what you do that could be totally out of left field, which actually might work and give something fresh to the whole scene, to the character, whatever. If you have that with a director who then knows how to shape it, either in the direction, in the moment, or in the editing, then that's good."
    – Robert De Niro, actor

"When you're in the editing room, the dangerous thing is that it becomes like a joke again, and again, and again. Eventually, the joke starts to not be funny. So, you have to be careful that you're not throwing the baby out with the bathwater."
    – Ridley Scott, *Boy and Bicycle*

"The problems I have with a flawed script are always revealed in the editing room."
    – Xavier Dolan, *The Death and Life of John F. Donovan*

Write scripts knowing that it is unlikely that you will be present on the set, and that it will be even far less likely that you will be in the editing room.

Write a script knowing that you are going to hand it over to other creative people, including the director, cinematographer, gaffer, production designer, art director, sound techs, wardrobe designer, composer, editor, and people who do FX, colorization, title design, and other talent who do things that you are not going to be in control of. While you play a role in what they do with the material you wrote, it is unlikely that you will be around when they do their work. Be busy writing your next script that will sell and be produced. Hopefully, you will like what the other craftspeople did with your writing.

"I hate sitting around waiting. That's why I always have an editing suite on set."
    – Til Schweiger, writer, director, actor, producer *Head Full of Honey*

"Film, for me, is in two stages. One is when I write the script more or less on my own – that's the nice bit. And then comes for me the unpleasant bit

when they all go off, 100 people – actors and camera people and film and sound – and I stay away. When they go into the editing room, I come in again, and that's the bit I like."
– Ruth Prawer Jhabvala, *The City of Your Final Destination*

"I the very beginning, women were editors because they were the people in the lab rolling the film before there was editing. Then, when people like D.W. Griffith began editing, they needed the women from the lab to come and splice the film together. Cecil B. DeMille's editor was a woman. Then, when it became a more lucrative job, men moved into it."
– Thelma Schoonmaker, editor *The Color of Money, The King of Comedy, Cape Fear, Gangs of New York*

A time when you as the writer end up in the editing room is when you are also the director and/or the producer. There are some successful filmmakers who write, direct, and edit their films – and likely an abundance who try to do all of that, and would be better off taking on the job of writer, and leaving the rest to more skilled and experienced talent.

"Directors by their nature are control freaks and there is nowhere you have more control than in the editing room. Being on-set is fun. Casting a movie is fun. But it's a little out of control. You get to an editing room, you are finally in control."
– Todd Phillips, *War Dogs*

"I am in awe of directors like the Coen Brothers, who can shoot their script and edit it, and that's the movie. They're not discovering the movie in post-production. They're editing the script they shot."
– Spike Jonze, *Bad Grandpa*

"The excitement of wading into 'reality' and just finding out what happens – and then the challenge of selecting those things that happened and shaping them in the editing into a narrative that will have appeal and be engaging – is a great thrill."
– Jonathan Demme, *The Truth about Charlie*

"By the time the editor and the director come into the editing room, they're ready to really get down to work and really be able to focus on the film on a different level than they do when they're in production. And so, it becomes a very – hopefully – a safe place. Hopefully, a safe, creative place. It becomes a place where you want to be able to create an environment of trust. Where the director can trust you, and that you'll be honest with them, and that you guys are all working towards the same end."
– Terilyn Shropshire, editor *Love and Basketball, The Secret Life of Bees,* and *Eve's Bayou*

Editors are a major creative ingredient in the collaborative team of any film or TV project.

261

"Film editing is now something almost anyone can do at a simple level and enjoy it, but to take it to a higher level requires the same dedication and persistence that any art form does."

– Walter Murch, *Return to Oz*

"I learned to not separate writing, shooting, and editing. It's all sort of one big mess of creative output."

– David Lowery, *The Old Man & The Gun*

To get an idea of how important the other creatives are on the team that will be making your script into film – including how they will use technology to bring it all into the play on the screen, consider the words of Tom Cross:

"We definitely cut the IMAX material with a different pace in mind. Damien Chazelle wanted the scenes on the moon to feel different in every way. He always intended to have this striking transition where you're inside the lunar lander in 2.40, and then the camera moves outside through the hatch into full IMAX. The aspect ratio grows taller, but also the resolution changes and he wanted this great sound moment when the sound gets sucked out. All of a sudden there's complete silence. So, he likened it to the transition in *The Wizard of Oz*, when we go from black and white sepia to Technicolor. He really wanted to throw the audience off their feet and make them feel like they were plopped into another world. The IMAX photography helped this a couple of different ways. The detail in the large negative invites you to hold on the shots longer. That helped us double down on the subjective point of view that we had tried to set up in earlier parts of the film. We lingered on the POV shots climbing down the ladder so that the audience would feel like it was their hands on the rungs."

– Tom Cross, editor of *Whiplash*, *La La Land*, and *First Man*

Communication between the editor and director can make or break a film. Of course, there might also be the studio suits who request the film to be screened before "test audiences" who then give feedback in questionnaires. As mentioned earlier, depending on how those audiences respond, the studio can request that the director alter the film. That could involve additional filming days. Stuff like that – having the studios take charge of what is in the film – can drive directors – and editors – bonkers. If the film doesn't perform well at the box office, every one of those people will likely be pointing blame at the other.

That above scenario is what can create an unsureness during principal photography, and get directors to film an abundance of footage, including additional scenes, scenes that can be edited into an alternative ending, scenes that can alter the conflict, contention, pacing, mood, tone, and other elements of the film, and scenes that may not make sense to the cast and crew who are on set.

Experienced crews know when it is time to be quiet and do their jobs, even if they think that what is being filmed doesn't make sense – or seems like a complete waste of time and money. They can also like the overtime pay that results from filming all of that stuff. The sleep deprivation from working overly long days is what they don't want (But then it helps pay the mortgage, alimony, children's tuition, childcare, credit card debt, medical bills, student loan debt, etc.).

I've been on plenty of sets where I've seen things being filmed that don't seem to make sense, or that seem like a waste of time. But, I wasn't the director, producer, writer, or editor. So, I keep my mouth shut, aim for being cooperative, agreeable, and mannerly, and otherwise simply do my job. Then, you see the film, and either none of that is in there, or when it is it could be perfectly edited together, and makes sense. (Then, you learn that it is a good thing that you kept your mouth shut, stayed in your lane, and did your job.)

On set, do your job, and do not interfere in the jobs of others.

I did work on a TV show where they had to reshoot part of a scene that was filmed weeks earlier. The second unit crew that was brought in to film that scene thought they had everything set up correctly. I was the stand-in and photo double of the star, and I was there when the original scene was shot. Because I knew that crew, I knew that I could talk to them openly. I told them that the lighting was on the wrong side of the room, as was the furniture. The second unit director and D.P. thanked me. They switched everything around, and then we shot the scene with me as the double (I was in the clothing of the character, did everything he did during the original filming, but my face wasn't seen). It would not have worked if they had filmed it the way they had set it up. It would have drove the editors up the walls with no way to match cut.

"You just don't know when you get in the editing room what you will need as a link or a tool for a transition. If you're in a room, and there's a kettle boiling, get a shot of it. Don't worry if people think you're nuts."
– Angelina Jolie, *First They Killed My Father*

On one of the TV shows I worked on where I did all of the hand doubling for the star of the series, I often was instructed by an editor telling me what they needed as far as how my hands should move, how fast or slow they should move, and at what angle they should be in, including the position of my fingers and thumbs.

Hand doubling can get micro specific. If the actor is shown in a medium shot holding a cell phone with his fingers in a certain position, as you are doing the job of the photo double you want your fingers to be in the same position.

On one show, I had to double doing handwriting for an actor who is left-handed. I am right handed. I found out the night before, and practiced what he writes during the scene. We got the shot in two takes.

The editors want things to match as doing so simply looks better, and is less distractive. You want the hand doubling to be as flawless as possible, and to not alert the viewers that the hand close-ups (inserts) were done at a different time, or by a different set of hands. You want the editors to be happy.

"It's hard for people to understand editing, I think. It's absolutely like sculpture. You get a big lump of clay and you have to form it – this raw, unedited, very long footage."
– Thelma Schoonmaker, editor *The Departed, Raging Bull, Goodfellas*

"Sometimes when you're heavy into the shooting or editing of a picture, you get to the point when you don't know if you could ever do it again."
– Martin Scorsese, *Casino*

"I liked filmmaking. But the most difficult thing was the editing. I found it tormentingly difficult."
– Vanessa Redgrave, actor

Don't underestimate the influence of and creative work done by an editor on a film or series.

Write your script. No matter who you hand it over to, it is going to be changed. It's not going to end up exactly as you wrote it. Get over it. And move on to your next writing project.

"Movies become art after editing. Instead of just reproducing reality, they juxtapose images of it. That implies expression. That's art."
– Alejandro González Iñárritu, *Biutiful*

"You always discover a lot in the editing room. Particularly the action, because you have to over-shoot a lot, and shoot an enormous amount of material, because many of the sequences have to be discovered in the editing and manipulation of it."
– Christopher Nolan, *Dunkirk*

"Editing is where movies are made or broken. Many a film has been saved and many a film has been ruined in the editing room."
– Joe Dante, editor *Grand Theft Auto*

"It takes a certain type of person to be comfortable in the field of editing. The ability to work long days, long weeks, and long months in a small, crowded room with the same small group of people is a necessity. You must be able to concentrate on the tiniest detail, and keep working until it is right. Editing can be an obsession – good editing almost certainly is."
– Norman Hollyn, editor *Heathers*

"When I tried to get into the industry, there were only certain jobs open to women. Things like hairdressing didn't really interest me. I might have been interested in photography, but women couldn't do that in those days. I found

the most interesting job a woman could do – other than acting – was editing. I didn't know much about editing when I went into it, but I learned to love it."
 – Anne V. Coates, editor *Lawrence of Arabia*

"I was always begging work on a movie by reading the script, often several times, looking at storyboards, and talking to the director, a lot, trying to get her or her vision clear in my head. Then, I work with the material that is filmed. I can't edit what was not filmed, but there are chances to bend the material to stay true to the story, and a director's vision."
 – Elisabet Ronaldsdottir, editor *Shang-Chi and the Legend of the Ten Rings*

"I'm not a person who believes in the great difference between women and men as editors. But, I do think that quality is key. We're very good at organizing and discipline, and patience, and patience is fifty-percent of editing. You have to keep banging away at something until you get it to work. I think women are maybe better at that."
 – Thelma Schoonmaker, editor *The Aviator, Casino*

John Sturgis directed some of the most well-known American Western films, including *The Magnificent Seven, Bad Day at Black Rock*, and *The Great Escape*. In his early days, he made instructional and documentary films for the U.S. military. He worked his way up in Hollywood as an editing assistant, became an editor, and then a director of feature films.

Something Sturges said is what I think screenwriters should keep in mind as they write: You are writing scenes to be staged. They are then filmed as they are staged. Then those bits of filmed scenes are handed over to an editor.

"It really comes down to the bottom line.
The bottom line is cutting that film.
The big trick in a movie is to create the illusion that it is happening. Make people forget that they're looking at a whole bunch of pieces of film: This is happening. So, staging is preparation for cutting. You stage it in such a way that you cut it. The final job is the way that film is put together. That is what makes the scene come alive. You got to do it in a way that people don't realize that you're doing this. It's just happening."
 – John Sturges, director

Not only are you writing for a director, D.P., a variety of craftspeople, and actors, you are writing for an editor.

Write elegantly with as few words as are needed to portray the story in a clever style rich in relevant layers and subtext, and involving interesting characters who carry out the story in a way that keeps us watching.

But, don't write as if you are writing an instruction manual for the people making the project.

Consider that each paragraph is a different piece of film: an angle.

(Search: The Russian filmmaker Lev Kuleshov and The Kuleshov Effect. On YouTube, look up: *The Kuleshov Effect - Everything You Need to Know*.)

"Our (with cinematographer Kseniya Sereda) main concept was all about color. It is a common stereotype that the films about war should be mainly black and white. That's why we decided to re-introduce color back to this period. While reading war diaries, and looking at pictures from the period, we realized that people sometimes used color – having things be colorful – as a defense mechanism against the war."

– Kantemir Balagov, *Beanpole*

COLOR GRADING

Finalizing the look of a film could include recoloring, colorizing, color correcting (color grading) some – or all – of the scenes (done by a colorist), which can fix some issues caused by or adjust concerns relating to:

• Lighting
• Lenses
• Exposure
• Visual identity, tone, warmth, and coolness
• Background and foreground separation
• Subject isolation and viewer focus
• Brightness of the sun, fire, explosions, etc.
• Shadows
• Improve, alter, or eliminate reflections
• Set, prop, wardrobe, hair, makeup, and eye color variances
• FX blending
• Visual continuity in tune with the chosen color palette
• Aesthetics

The colorization of a film or TV show is one area that the screenwriter is not likely going to be involved. But, they can write in a way that helps convey tone, mood, tension, revelation of story, conflict, contention, and other components that will play a role in how a film is colorized.

Some productions don't pay much attention to colors, and go for more of whatever sort of drab or rambunctious colors happen naturally. That might be because they have a limited budget, or the filmmakers haven't developed those kind of skills, or don't have the sort of awareness about how colors can subtly manipulate audience perception and engagement.

266

Lower budget productions might want to consider that colorists could have an appreciation for the project to the point that the colorist will discount their rates – especially if it will be a project that can help advance the skills and career of the colorist. And, if they see promise in the filmmaker.

A colorist should be involved before principal photography begins, before set colors are chosen, and before wardrobe is selected. Camera and lighting equipment choices also matter, and a skilled colorist and post production company can help a filmmaker with the best choices for their budget.

Even short film filmmakers would be wise to consult with a colorist, and to do so in the early stages of pre-production. It's all about achieving conformity of mood, tone, and vision throughout the project.

If you are going to make a film, consult with a post-production house as you start pre-production.

Many projects involve having a variety of people in tune with the color palette goals of the project. Those include the production designer, art director, set decorator, set dresser, set painter, props, wardrobe designer, makeup artist, hair stylist, the greens department (those who take care of the plants being used in the scenes), food stylists (yes, even the foods that are seen on screen can be specially selected and platted/arranged in tune with a color palette), and the DP, gaffer, and director.

Some films and TV shows hold a test shoot before they start principal photography. That could include calling in the actors, the stand-ins, the production designer, art director, the set dresser, the props master, the wardrobe designer, makeup and hair people, the gaffer, the director, the producers, editors, and colorist for a day or two of camera tests and test grading using colorist software (Baseline, DaVinci, and Nucoda). This will help set the tone, mood, and color palette of the production. It might include choosing the hair color of the principal actors, and sometimes dying the hair of the standins, who could also work as photo doubles. Or, the standin might have a hair color that the production likes, and the actor's hair is then dyed the color of the standin. (I worked on a show where they dyed the actor's hair my color.)

Commercials and music videos often pay keen attention to every color that ends up on screen. Some directors and others working in film and TV started out working in color-obsessive commercial and music video production, and carry that awareness to their projects.

Even when films were black and white, attention was paid to the colors of the sets and clothing, because certain colors can be problematic when they are in gray scale. Red next to black can simply end up being black when in black and white. And that also plays into how people who are color blind see things.

The masters of early films knew that the contrast between the various shades of black and gray could play into the manipulation of the viewers.

The Wizard of Oz is a good example of how gray scale and color can play into story and audience perception. Dorothy goes from the humble, mild life of a farm girl that is seen in black and white, and then is transported into the brilliant colors of her dreams. It's a massive transition into dream time. The color choices play big into psychological associations. The transitions of color schemes throughout the film combine with the characterizations and soundtrack to trigger emotional responses. The good witch has a light, safe personality, and her colors play into that. The evil witch is dark and moody and threatening, as are her associates, the nightmarish flying monkeys. There are also transitional colors, when Dorothy is in scenes that aren't quite emotionally one way or the other, or she isn't sure of the things and people around her, where danger may lurk. When her emotional shift goes to afraid or happy, the colors and sounds are in tune with those feelings. A variety of people working on that film had to work in coordination with all of Dorothy's emotional baggage, including those who chose the camera lenses and set lighting.

The Wizard of Oz was shot during a time when films were transitioning into color. That transition meant filmmakers also had to learn how color played into audience engagement, emotions, perceptions, expectations, and anticipations.

The colors on screen play a role in eliciting the conflict, contention, tension, theme, mood, tone, era, genre, pacing, and characterization, and the story and character arcs. All of those are reasons why productions have approved color palettes, including those that might change from the early scenes to the latter scenes, and to how the scenes in flashbacks, flash forwards, dreams, memories, fantasies, hallucinations, and other parts of the film can have their own color palettes.

Warren Beatty had his *Dick Tracy* film shot using certain lighting techniques and with sets, props, costumes, makeup, hair coloring, and prosthetics in tune with Chester Gould's 1930s comic strip palette that featured seven primary colors. The process was a major challenge for the production. No computers were used as the film was made using old techniques of actual sets, matte paintings (including some on glass), and scale models – all in tune with the color palette.

While older films may be used as examples of how colorization was used to manipulate audience focus and perception, many modern films are put through post production colorization. Pretty much, if a film has a big budget, it gets colorized in post.

Color value, hue, brightness, saturation, and desaturation can impact how the audience perceives everything from how the characters are viewed, to how the characters feel, and what they dread, need, want, crave, love, and hate, and what they are enamored or nurtured by.

Colors play into the psychology of both the characters on screen and the viewing audience. A horror film might have colors that are stark and that duel and clash with each other. An intense film with scenes of characters exhibiting drugged-out, frantic behavior may have a chaotic, intense color palette that is like a headache. A romantic comedy or children's movie will likely feature a friendlier, kinder color pallet. The color choices are all part of the emotional symbolism and audience manipulation.

"One of the things you do as a writer and as a filmmaker is grasp for resonant symbols and imagery without necessarily fully understanding it yourself."

– Christopher Nolan, *Interstellar*

A scene to be perceived as dreary and claustrophobic will have color schemes that are different than scenes that are happy, safe and welcoming, warm or cool, or somber, austere, dangerous, menacing, nurturing, comforting, or amorous. When colorization is done well, it works well. When it is done badly, the colorization can end up as corny, over-the-top, and absurd, and can distract viewer focus.

Colors can also reveal the racism and ugly views of the filmmakers, and/or the characters within a film.

An example of how color is used as metaphor, watch for the color red in *American Beauty*. Also, look up semiotics, the study of symbols or signs, and the interpretation of them. In film, semiotics not only apply to colors, but to tone, mood, lighting, camera angles, props, setting, sounds, wardrobe, makeup, hair, and editing. Signs and symbols can be infused into each one of those with connotative meanings. The dialogue can also play into connotations, or associated meanings. In dialogue, words can play differently than their denotation, but have vastly different connotations, especially within certain cultures, religions, governments, clubs, and their inherent ways.

Color schemes communicate messages. If you are a filmmaker, consider what your color choices are communicating, including through the colors of the sets, dressings, gack (various set dressing stuff on set), props, makeup, and wardrobe. Know about the complimentary, monochromatic, triadic, and analogous color schemes.

Each part of a film may have its own mood board, which are the approved colors, tones, shades, tints, warmth, coolness, vibrancy, duality, harmony, contrasts, discordance, and juxtaposition for the scenes. That all starts in preproduction with the director, production designer, art director, set decorator, costume designer, hair and makeup heads (department bosses), and DP, and plays out in the drama that ends up on the screen.

Mood board templates can be found online. They are also used in storyboard software.

To learn more about this topic, do searches for: "Film colorization," "movie palette," "film color scheme," "film color theory," and "Technicolor history." Also, read up on Natalie Kalmus, who ran Technicolor with her husband, and worked as the color consultant on many films.

"Only after post-production is complete do I feel like my script is finished."

– Bong Joon-ho, *Barking Dogs Never Bite*

"By excising something, not only from a screenplay, but also from a film – this works on both pieces of work – you can make the juxtaposition of the two remaining scenes so much more powerful – by leaving something out."
– Emma Thompson, *Effie Gray*

"Bad exposition is like bad lighting. It exposes more than it illuminates."
– Josh Friedman, *Avatar 2*

COMMON SCRIPT ISSUES

"Regarding getting past the reader, don't think about the reader. Just keep trying to make the script the very best it can be. Do not have typos. If there are typos, that means you have not gone through it with the care you need to. Theoretically, you should be writing draft after draft after draft for a project. You hear stories about people writing a draft in three days. That's an anomaly."
– Chris Salvaterra, producer

There are many little things that can be problems for your screenplay. The more of these distractions that there are, the less likely a management, agency, studio, mentorship, or fellowship reader will finish reading it – or will read it at all. If the script doesn't get read by the reader, it doesn't advance to the manager, agent, producer, development executive, director, or other decision maker.

The following is a list of things to consider, before submitting your script to the industry. They are based on notes that I wrote while running hundreds of workshops.

The notes are each numbered for reference when giving feedback to writers.

"Understand that it's not about getting a scholar to declare that your screenplay is worthy of consideration – it's about entertaining someone with your cinematic story. It's about engaging them to the point where they can't put the script down until they reach the final page with anticipation. It's about moving someone enough for them to put their reputation on the line by typing *recommend* on that script coverage cover page."
– Ken Miyamoto, *Blackout*

- **NOTE 1: TITLE: The title doesn't match the script. If it does, it still isn't good because it isn't enticing, and won't do much for the marketing of the film.**

Consider the hit films of recent years. What were their titles, and how did those titles both relate to the film and/or otherwise provide a way for the film to gather the attention of audiences?

Is the title you gave your script something that people will identify with? Are they going to recognize it as something they want to see? Is it boring? Does it fail to paint a desirable or curious image in the minds of the potential viewers? What would be a more enticing title?

I heard someone say that a film title should be more than one word. They said it with such a tone that it was as if their word were gospel. Wrong.

A single-word title isn't a bad thing. Consider: *Dunkirk, Birth, It, Okja, Room, Coco, Birdman, Frozen, Arrival, Scream, Logan, Moonlight, Deadpool, Boyhood, Interstellar, Whiplash, Minions, Doubt, Fences, Nebraska, Carol, Spotlight, Brooklyn, Titanic,* and *Wonder*. They did well at the box office.

Don't adjust yourself to every rule you hear in Hollywood. They are often simply opinions. Sometimes, you have to make your own rules. But, those also can be a hindrance.

Don't let the opinion of one person stop you from achieving your dreams.

"Visions are worth fighting for. Why spend your life making someone else's dreams?"
– Tim Burton, *Edward Scissorhands*

If you take your screenplay through a workshop, and one person says something discouraging about the title, that is one opinion. That is what you are there to hear and consider. But, that doesn't mean that you should alter your script based on that opinion. If numerous people in a workshop tell you that your title doesn't represent your script, consider changing it.

Know that, no matter what title you choose, and how best you think it serves your script, the studio, producers, and/or director might change the title. Also, the product could end up with a different title in other regions of the world. Get over it, before it happens. By the time the script goes into production, you will already have moved on to writing your next variety of hit screenplays – and you should not concern yourself with the title they choose. It's out of your control.

- **NOTE 2: COVER PAGE: There is unnecessary information on the cover page.**

Use the courier type face for all cover page wording.

The cover page of a spec script should have the title of the script centered on the page, with the name of the writer(s) below the title.

On the bottom left or bottom right corner, there should be simple writer contact information.

By contact information, I mean: At least an email address. Maybe a phone number – if you feel safe sharing it.

A street mailing address is NOT something you need to share on the cover page of your script. The email should be good enough.

It is unlikely that someone reading your script needs your street mailing address. So, why share it? Consider that the script, and your contact information, might end up on the Internet.

If you must share a street address, consider getting a P.O. box at your neighborhood U.S. Post Office (if you live in the U.S.), rather than a P.O. box at a commercial mailing center. But, a U.S. Post Office is open fewer hours than a commercial mailing center. However, having your P.O. box at a U.S. Post Office can speed up your mail delivery by one day, as it won't have to be sent out to be delivered to a P.O. box at a commercial mailing center.

I have been using a P.O. box mailing address most of my adult life.

If you have an agent, manager, and/or an entertainment attorney, you can also use that as your contact information. I suggest that you at least include a personal email address.

"Hey, screenwriters. I see a lot of you putting your street address on your cover page. This worries me as a security issue – especially for women. No one is going to mail you. They don't need to know where you live. Phone and email for unrepped writers is fine."
– Shaula Evans, *The Ascension of Ava Delaine*

Some people will correct me and say that the contact information is always put in the lower left corner. Others like it on the right. It doesn't matter if it is on the lower left or lower right. Choose one side.

If you want, you can put the WGA registration number with your contact information on the cover. But, that is not necessary.

(Search: How to register a script with the WGA.)

You can include the © symbol and year that the script was copyrighted, if you want. Not that you need to. Some people say that you must include it. Others say that you don't need it. But, do copyright your script with the copyright office. (Search: How to copyright a screenplay.)

An attorney might advise you to include the © symbol with the year that the script was copyrighted.

Don't put anything else on the cover.

Don't put a date on the cover – unless you really, feel the need to put the © symbol with the year on the cover. Consider what the copyright office directives state.

Don't put a fake production company name on the cover. Anyone can do an internet search for the name, and find that it is nothing. Why would you put a production company name on a script that you are trying to sell? It's not going to impress anyone valid – at least, not in the ways that will benefit you.

Don't put a draft number on the cover.

Don't put a synopsis of the script on the cover.

Don't put a list of character names on the cover.

Don't put a quotation, drawings, or a photograph on the cover.

Don't put song lyrics on the cover. Especially if you don't own the rights.

Don't use any fancy paper for the cover. Only use white paper, or white card stock for the cover. If you do choose to use a color of cardstock for the cover, know that the WGA Library uses red covers for film scripts, and blue covers for TV scripts. Perhaps stick with those choices.

Know that you might only need a PDF to be emailed.

(Search: Screenplay cover images.)

- **NOTE 3: BINDING: The script is bound with more than two brass brads, or uses some other type of binding.**

The industry standard is to use two brass brads to bind the script. Not three. Leave the center hole open. (Search: Screenplay cover brads images.)

Don't bind your script in any other manner.

These days, you will likely submit your script to people as a PDF (portable document format) sent via email – and will never print it.

In the old days, you would send printed scripts. Homes in and around Hollywood were built with wide-mouthed mail boxes so that scripts could fit into them. Years ago, I knew a successful TV writer who had his door built with a special mail slot that held his script deliveries.

Agents, managers, production companies, contests, and others might ask that you send your script as a PDF.

Learn how to convert your script into a PDF.

- **NOTE 4: PAPER COLOR: The script is printed on color paper.**

As mentioned, you will most likely be emailing your script as a PDF, or as a Final Draft document. But, if you print your script, know this:

Use plain white paper for your screenplay. Including the cover page.

If you put a card stock cover on your script, also use white. Leave the cardstock cover blank. Then, have the cover page of the script as the second piece of paper, not numbered.

The first page of the script containing the opening scene is the first page.

The page numbers start on page 2.

Color pages in scripts should be reserved for shooting scripts, and updated pages within a shooting script.

The revision colors of scripts are likely to be standard, no matter which union film or TV show you work on. This is done so that writers, directors, producers, and others will know what to expect on the various productions that they work on. The colors have been set by the WGA as:

- Unrevised pages: White.
- First revised pages: Blue.
- Second revised pages: Pink.

- Third revised pages: Yellow.
- Fourth revised pages: Green.
- Fifth revised pages: Goldenrod.
- Sixth revised pages: Buff.
- Seventh revised pages: Salmon.
- Eighth revised pages: Cherry.
- Starting with the tenth revision, the colors repeat, starting at Blue.

On some productions, I have seen rainbow colored pages of certain tones. Blue tone rainbow. Pink tone rainbow. Yellow tone rainbow. And, so forth. Or, there are other colors they use past the eighth revision. That way, they are sure to avoid confusion. You don't want confusion or filming errors during production, as mistakes can cost thousands – even millions – of dollars.

If you work on a major TV or film production, you will get used to the revised script pages being handed out, sometimes they replace pages more than once per day. A production assistant might give you a single page that is from somewhere in the script. Simply tear out the old page, and replace it with the revised page (which will not be white). Later in the day, they might hand you revised pages from different parts of the script. You will need to replace the pages in your script. Do it as soon as possible – or else you will be out of tune with what is being filmed.

It is important to replace your pages whenever the revised pages are handed to you. Study the new pages to note the changes, and know what to expect during filming.

When you print your spec script, print it on white paper. White with black lettering in the Courier font.

- **NOTE 5: PDF: The script was sent as a PDF (portable document format), but wasn't accessible on the agent's, manager's, or producer's system.**

Not including .PDF at the end of a file name when you send a PDF could be problematic for some systems. Without the .PDF at the end of the file name, the person getting your script might not be able to open your script.

You might name your script this way:

Name of script, date, draft number, .PDF

That means, draft 7 of a script named `Joe Bob Billy Sue` completed on May 17, 2020 would be this:

JoeBobBillySue05.17.2020D7.PDF

Or, if that PDF is meant for only one person to see, such as if you are sending it to Alfred Hitchcock, you can include the name in the file name:

JoeBobBillySue05.17.2020D7AlHitch.PDF

The week I was writing this, I spoke with a staff writer on a series who said one of the producers couldn't open a script file that the writer had sent, and the producer said it was because the writer hadn't included .PDF at the end of the file name. Apparently, it caused some problems. I'm not a computer person, and don't know how all of that works, but good to know.

- **NOTE 6: PAGE COUNT: The script contains too many pages.**

A one-hour TV script is about 47 pages. There are reasons why it could be slightly shorter, or slightly longer – including for cable, streaming, web channel, and other forms of content delivery.

A film script is typically anywhere from 90 to 120 pages. Comedies are often fewer than 100 pages, and dramas are often more than 100 pages.

It's probably good to avoid going over 110 pages, unless there is a valid reason to do so.

Many screenplay contests have a limit of 120 pages, some limit scripts to 110 – or fewer – pages.

If one page of a script might be around one minute of screen time, a 90-page script would result in an approximately 90-minute film.

Fanatical time estimate:

Considering that one page might be roughly one-minute of screen time.

And that one script pages is about 55 lines.

A person might say that each line of a script page is a little over one-second of screen time. (But, in reality, it could be much longer, or shorter, than that.)

So, with that in mind, some people say that you should not include a sound as a single line or single paragraph, as in:

```
Breathless, sweaty Sheila weakly picks up the gun.
Aims it at Evil Thang and...

BANG!

Evil Thang glances at his chest, where his skin
deflected the bullet. Laughs mockingly.
```

However, in sitcom scripts, sounds are sometimes their own paragraph.

People say that using the gun blast sound as one line would mean that the gun sound took more than one second of screen time, and that would mean it is in slow motion.

But, don't be that person who gets fanatical about the time count per page. It doesn't really work that way – it only sort of does.

Do consider that a single paragraph likely represents a camera angle, so why use a single line for a sound? Simply include the sound in the scene description:

```
Breathless, sweaty Sheila weakly picks up the gun.
Aims it at Evil Thang, and BANG!
```

The opposite of sound is silence, which has different rules. It might be useful to include silence as a single paragraph, as it could effectively indicate that there is both silence and no motion. But, if so, say so:

275

```
Ralph angrily turns off the radio.

Silence. Nobody moves.

Agness steps over, pushes Ralph away, flicks the
radio back on. She and Hildegaard continue to disco
dance.

                    Ralph
              (covers eyes)
          Your sinful movements soil my
          thoughts.
```

There could also be silence with action or expression, followed by a sound:

```
Silence. Bertha's eyes well with tears. Then, the
sound of a dog lapping water. Bertha looks across the
room...

Where Fido happily drinks from his bowl.
```

Films that have won major awards have been more than 120 minutes. *Dances with Wolves* is three hours, fifty-six minutes. The extended version of The *Lord of the Rings: The Return of the King* is four hours, twelve minutes. *The Last Emperor* is two hours and forty-three minutes. *Malcolm X* is three hours and twelve minutes. *Watchmen* is two hours forty-two minutes. *Nixon* is three hours and twelve minutes. *JFK* is three hours and nine minutes. *The Godfather: Part II* is three hours and twenty-two minutes. *Titanic* is three hours and fourteen minutes. *Apocalypse Now* is two hours and twenty-seven minutes. *The Irishman* is three hours and thirty minutes. All of those films engaged their audiences, and made massive quantities of money. But, those films had majorly successful people involved with them, which helped get the films funded, produced, and distributed.

"*Hateful Eight* was already a long movie anyway, and the way I looked at it was, "Well, this is a play." I haven't been to the theatre in years where the play wasn't at least three hours long. That's the standard for a real play. I figured that for this movie as a play – especially the way I was doing it with an intermission and everything – that was par for the course."
– Quentin Tarantino, *The Hateful Eight*

"I think a story should take as long to tell as it is appropriate to that particular story."
– Frank Darabont, *The Shawshank Redemption*

Maybe you are the next master screenwriter who will write a produced, multi-award-winning film that is three – or more – hours long. It's probably a good idea to write several common-length scripts, in addition to your epic, four-hour masterpiece. (Maybe you really want to write a limited series.)

"So, by the time I got to my tenth or eleventh script, I just started writing whatever I felt like writing – regardless of genre, and trusted that I had the skill and craft to do it well."

– Michael Werwie, *Extremely Wicked, Shockingly Evil, and Vile*

- **NOTE 7: MARGINS: The script does not have the correct margins.**

It's probably a good idea to have the Final Draft software. You might be asked to email your script as a Final Draft document.

If you don't use Final Draft, make sure your script is written and formatted in ways that are in tune with what the agents, managers, directors, stars, producers, studios, and financiers expect.

For the specifications on margins, see *The Screenwriter's Bible*.

- **NOTE 8: FONT: The script uses a font other than 12-point Courier.**

Use 12-point Courier typeface in your screenplay, including on the cover page. Anything else may be viewed as ignorance. Courier makes it so the script length is in tune with all other scripts in Courier.

The cover page may contain a title that is larger than 12-point. But, it is probably best to stick with using Courier font for the title of a spec.

You may say that you saw scripts online that used fonts other than Courier. Don't go by what you see online. Those could have been typed up by anyone.

- **NOTE 9: SCENE HEADINGS INCORRECT: The script contains scene headings that are not standard, or are distractive.**

A scene heading starts with either INT. for interior, or EXT. for exterior. Then the location, and if it is night or day (or, sunrise, sunset, or twilight).

All words in a scene heading are capitalized.

If you want, you can underline the scene headings. But, that isn't needed.

If there is a scene that takes place both inside of and outside of a truck, car, hut, house, cabin, or other structure (such as on the porch at the doorway of the living room), you can list both INT. and EXT. at the start of the master scene heading (the "establishing shot" that establishes the location in which a scene or series of scenes will take place). List INT. first if the first shot or angle of that scene is indoors, or EXT. if the first shot or angle of the scene is outdoors.

```
INT./EXT. DEBBIE'S TRUCK/PARKING LOT - NIGHT
EXT./INT. HEATHER'S BACKYARD/OUTHOUSE - NIGHT
INT./EXT. LUANDA'S FOYER/PORCH - DAY
```

Or, some people use this – possibly distracting – style, using IN. instead of INT. and EX. instead of EXT.:

```
IN./EX. LUANDA'S FOYER/PORCH - DAY
EX./IN. LUANDA'S PORCH/FOYER - DAY
```

There are times when it is important to indicate if it is dusk or dawn, or sunrise or sunset, or twilight.

```
EXT. MONIQUE'S TIRE STORE — DUSK
EXT. LISA'S FARMHOUSE — DAWN
```

EXT./INT. ANNIE'S CLUB/LOW RIDER - SUNRISE

Some scene headings need more clarity, such as if they are a flashback, flash-forward, dreams, daydreams, visions, hallucinations, series of shots, montages, flash-forward montage, and flashback montage. To understand how to format those, refer to *The Screenwriter's Bible*, and *Dr. Format Tells All*.

This book can't cover everything – it's already nearly 600 pages.

- **NOTE 10: SCENE LOCATION: The script contains scene headings that lack a defined location.**

I read a script with this scene heading:

EXT. DAY.

What? Where are we? Floating in deep space? Then, it should say EXT. DEEP SPACE - LIGHT (or DARK = if in a planet or moon shadow.)

Each master scene needs to have either EXT. or INT. at the start of the scene heading. This should be followed by the name of the location, such as: BERTHA'S GUEST HOUSE. That is to be followed with DAY or NIGHT (or DUSK or DAWN or SUNRISE or SUNSET).

EXT. BERTHA'S GUEST HOUSE - DAY

I recently saw a scene heading worded this way:

EXT. SAN FRANCISCO — DAY

Are we seeing the city from a birds-eye-view?

No, the scene description then went on to say something like: Bobby knocks on Andrea's apartment door.

If Bobby is knocking on Andreas's apartment door in San Francisco in the daytime, then the scene heading could be:

EXT. ANDREA'S APARTMENT DOOR — SAN FRANCISCO — DAY

Or, if you choose to flip the macro to micro in the style that some people use for all scene headings, and some use for only the master scene headings:

EXT. SAN FRANCISCO - ANDREA'S APARTMENT DOOR - DAY

Master scene headings mention the master location (large = macro), then the smaller location (small = micro) of that master location. Then the situation of the sun (DAY, NIGHT, DUSK, DAWN, SUNRISE, SUNSET, TWILIGHT, or when necessary – and if clear for the viewers in the story situation: MORNING, AFTERNOON, EVENING [But, it is unlikely that the crew needs to know the time of day, as they only need to know the lighting situation. So, avoid using MORNING, AFTERNOON, EVENING]). (If the audience needs to get a sense of time, that chronoception should be obvious in the tension of the scenes.)

If we already know that the film is based in San Francisco, you don't need to keep mentioning the city in the scene headings. Say it once, in the first scene heading at the start of the script. If we go to another city in a scene later in the script, then mention that city (if we need to know) in that scene heading. Otherwise, throughout the script, we know that we are in San Francisco, because the first scene heading of the script says so.

- **NOTE 11: SCENE HEADINGS, TO BOLD, OR NOT TO BOLD: The scene headings are bolded. Or, some are bolded, and others aren't (and that's irritating – and makes the script look as if it is not finished, or is written sloppily).**

If you choose to **bold** the scene headings, be consistent. Be sure to **bold** every single one of them throughout the entire script – including the master scene headings and the subheadings (also called secondary headings).

Bold does not mean UPPERCASE. **Bold** means thicker lettering.

Scene headings are always to be in UPPERCASE.

You probably want to go with what managers, agents, producers, and studios are used to seeing. If you vary from it, you may irritate the readers.

Some people say that bolding the scene headings seems odd, since they are not more important than other elements of the script – the scene description, character cues, and dialogue. They say that nothing in the script should be bolded.

Or, maybe consider going with the theory that bolding the headings makes the script clearer to read. It will be more obvious when a new scene starts, or when there is a change in location. And, bolding the scene headings makes them easier to find. And, it makes the subheadings clear and defined.

It is easier to write without having to go and **bold** the scene headings. Otherwise, you have to go through the script and manually **bold** every scene heading, and every subheading (make sure that you don't skip any).

Nobody is going to toss your script if you don't **bold** the scene headings, or if you do **bold** the scene headings.

Don't choose to only **bold** the master scene headings, but not bold the subheadings. That, too can be an irritant and a distraction.

Some people advise against bolding other things in the script, including words in the scene descriptions, the character cues, or words in the dialogue.

I have gotten to like bolded scene headings. Sit-coms use that style.

Some people also underline the scene headings. Why put in all that effort? However, some TV series do underline the scene headings. If you are writing for those shows, follow their guidelines.

- **NOTE 12: SCENE HEADING CAPITALIZATION: The scene headings aren't in all uppercase lettering.**
Scene headings should be in UPPERCASE lettering.

- **NOTE 13: SCENE HEADINGS INCONSISTENT: The scene headings are inconsistent throughout the script**

If you have a scene in the gift shop where scenes take place throughout the script, and define it as `GIFT SHOP`, and later in the script you are again in the gift shop, then you should continue to refer to it as `GIFT SHOP` in the latter scene headings, and not `GIFT STORE`, or `MARY'S STORE` (or the name of whichever character might own the gift shop). Stick with one name.

If you have a car, and in the first scene of something going on with or in the car, and you refer to the car as MARY'S CAR in the scene heading, then, continue to identify it as MARY'S CAR throughout the rest of the script.

Don't give a thing a different name later in the script, unless there is good reason to. To be clear of the switch in name, you could mention it like this, such as if it then becomes owned by a character named Charlie: Charlie's car (formerly Mary's car).

- **NOTE 14: SCENE HEADING INFORMATION REPEATS IN THE DESCRIPTION: The scene description repeats information from the scene headings.**

If the scene heading tells us that we are in Rebecca's bedroom, the scene description shouldn't then say things like: Drew leaps through the doorway into Rebecca's bedroom, and scampers beneath Rebecca's bed.

We already know that he is entering Rebecca's bedroom, and we know that it is Rebecca's bed, because the scene heading says "REBECCA'S BEDROOM." Cut out the ownership wording.

The description would be: Drew leaps in through the doorway, and scampers beneath the bed.

- **NOTE 15: SCENE DESCRIPTION KEEPS MENTIONING ITEM OWNERSHIP: The description keeps repeating the obvious of who things belong to.**

If the scene heading indicates that we are in Rebecca's bedroom, don't keep mentioning ownership of the items in the bedroom. Don't say: Drew sits on Rebecca's bed and opens the drawer of Rebecca's side table, and pulls out Rebecca's Bible, and turns on Rebecca's lamp, and tiredly reclines back onto Rebecca's pillows.

Instead, because the scene heading tells us where we are, and we would assume that everything in her bedroom is Rebecca's, the description would be: Drew sits on the bed, opens the drawer of the side table, pulls out a Bible, turns on the lamp, and tiredly reclines onto the pillows. (Notice the deletion of the word back before reclines, as there is no reason to say reclines back onto... Simply say reclines onto...)

Also, there is no need to indicate ownership when it is obvious who owns something. It gets tedious reading stuff with ownership indication like this: Hilda checks the recipe on her laptop screen, picks up her ladle from the hook on her wall, steps up to her big boiling pot of stew at her stove, and uses her ladle to stir her stew.

What happens is:

Hilda checks the recipe on the laptop screen, takes
the ladle from the wall hook, steps to the stove, and
stirs the pot of stew.

- **NOTE 16: SCENE HEADING TIME OF DAY: The scene headings indicate a time of day.**

Each master scene heading should include the word NIGHT or DAY. Some scenes, for very specific reasons, might be listed as DUSK, DAWN, or SUNRISE, SUNSET, or TWILIGHT, but not 1:37 IN THE AFTERNOON.

If it is necessary, you can use MORNING, AFTEROON, or EVENING in the heading. But, only do so while knowing that it is far less common to use – and it might appear as if you didn't do your homework. Do so if the scene absolutely needs a specific tone. Know that it is largely for the crew to know if it is dark/night or light/day. So, DAY or NIGHT usually is what is needed – or DUSK or DAWN or SUNRISE, SUNSET, or TWILIGHT.

The people viewing the film will not see your script. They will only see what is on the screen. (The sense of time passing is chronoception, and the audience will likely pick that up, without you noting the exact time.) If it is important for the audience to know the time of day, you must have a clock in the scene that the audience can see, OR have a character say the time, OR have voiceover that says the time, OR indicate that the time needs to be superimposed on the screen, which is indicated on its own line in the script, flush left (do put the words that viewers are to read in quotation marks):

SUPER: "1:37 p.m."

Or, some people use the complete word:
SUPERIMPOSE: "1:37 p.m."

You might also see this, instead of SUPER::
CHYRON: "1:37 p.m." Or, CAPTION: "1:37 p.m."

However, an attentive audience will likely pick up on what time of day it is – if it is important to the story, and if the scenes are filmed in a way that communicates that information… if it needs to be understood.

- **NOTE 17: CONTINUOUS: The script incorrectly uses CONTINUOUS.**

If a scene is a continuation of the prior scene, but in a switch of location (such as to the next room), it is a continuation.

If a scene outside is of a character talking to someone who won't open a door, and we then see the person inside standing in the foyer at the door while listening to what the outdoor character is saying, it is helpful to put the word CONTINUOUS or the abbreviation CONT. at the end of the first interior scene heading. INT. FOYER — CONT.

If the scene continues to switch back and forth from the doorstep to the foyer, there is no reason to keep including – CONT. or – CONTINUOUS after the subheading of DOORSTEP or FOYER, or INSIDE or OUTSIDE.

Often, it is obvious that the scene is a continuation, and therefore the CONT. or CONTINUOUS can be excluded from the scene heading.

• **NOTE 18: USE OF SAME: The script incorrectly uses SAME.**

If the scenes switch back and forth from one location to the next, to show what is going on at the exact same time, use the word SAME at the end of the scene heading.

SAME is not used to indicate that the scene is in the same location as the previous scene.

If the scene takes place directly after the previous scene with no time lapse, use the word CONTINUOUS or the abbreviation CONT. at the end of the scene heading – because it is a continuation of the prior scene.

The camera and editing direction (technical direction) cue called INTERCUT is okay to use when writing scenes that are taking place in two locations at the same time, and both of those locations are to be switched back and forth on screen. Or use SPLIT SCREEN. It will give the camera crew an idea of how to frame the subjects so that they can play into the angles of the subjects in the intercut or split screen scenarios on screen. The script supervisor will note the intention in notes that go to the editor. The intercut or split screen would also be noted on the production script.

*Lois Weber used a triple screen shot in her 1913 silent film, *Suspense*.

• **NOTE 19: SUBHEADINGS AND TIME LAPSES: The script does not use secondary headings or subheadings.**

There are master scene headings that include EXT. or INT. at the start of them.

INT. JEFF'S KITCHEN — DAY

And, there are secondary headings or subheadings that continue the story from one room to the other within the same structure, or master area, such as from one area outside to a connected outside area.

NEXT TO TREE, and BEHIND THE BUSHES, could be two subheadings in a scene taking place at a family party in a backyard.

If we have been established within a house or other building, and we are simply going from one room into a hallway, or other room in the structure, simply use a subheading to tell us that we are in a different area of the same building: HALLWAY. Not: INT. HALLWAY – DAY, or INT. HALLWAY – DAY – CONT. If they move to the bedroom or office within the same structure, the subheading would simply be one word BEDROOM or OFFICE.

You can include CONT. or CONTINUOUS, if the switching to connected places is one continuous scene. But, if it is already clear enough that it is a continuation, you can omit the CONT. or CONTINUOUS.

With subheadings, you don't include the lead INT. or EXT., because the master scene heading has already been established that we are inside (interior) or outside (exterior).

With the subheadings, you don't include DAY, or NIGHT (or DUSK, DAWN, SUNRISE, SUNSET, or TWILIGHT) at the end of the subheading – because the master scene already established that.

If we have been established at a house or a car, and there are scenes that continue from the interior to the exterior of the house or car, then it is okay to use subheadings to indicate the switch in locations. LIVING ROOM, BACKYARD, TIM'S BEDROOM, DRIVEWAY, IN THE GARAGE, and ATTIC, are all subheadings that can be used without having to keep typing INT. or EXT. when multiple scenarios take place in and around the house or car in a continuous fashion without a lapse in time – such as during a house party, or a police raid.

A time lapse indicator can also be used as a subheading, such as when we are in the same location, and we advance to moments later, minutes later, or hours later. Simply type MINUTES LATER, MOMENTS LATER, or HOURS LATER as a subheading. Then, start with at least one sentence of scene description, such as the character awakes from a nap, a candle has burned out, their ice cream has melted, or they awake to find that their dog ate their food.

If a time lapse happens in the same location, extending from day to night, and you are simply using a time lapse as a subheading, you can end that subheading with DAY or NIGHT. As in, LATER – NIGHT.

A person's name can be used as a subheading or secondary location. Especially if there is something going on in a large setting, such as a backyard party.

BERNADINE

dances with Charlie. They fall into the pool.

PATRICIA AND CLAUDE AT THE TABLE

laugh and guzzle their drinks.

Notice how the name Bernadine is being used both as a subheading, and as the first word of a sentence. That is why the word dances doesn't begin with an uppercase D. The same with PATRICIA AND CLAUDE AT THE TABLE being used as both a subheading, and as the beginning of a sentence – which is why the L in the word laugh is not in uppercase.

A time lapse scenario in a single location can be formatted this way:

INT. NATALIE'S LIVING ROOM - DAY/NIGHT/DAY

TIME LAPSE

-- Natalie sits before a blank canvas.

-- The window light fades as she's half done painting a sunflower.

-- By candle light, she paints as Bob places a sandwich beside her.

-- In daylight, she eats as she considers the finished painting, which now has a child's face in the center of the flower.

-- Natalie is gone. The child's face painting smiles.

Then, go into a standard formatted scene.

- **NOTE 20: FORMATTING: The writer apparently didn't study script formatting.**

Stop allowing your lack of knowledge of basic formatting to hold back and clutter your script – which is also likely to be so filled with grammatical, punctuation, spelling, and other errors that it won't advance.

Don't be one who models their script on a screenplay that they found online. A script that you found online might be some mix of a pre-production script, a shooting script, a published script, and a script typed up by someone who doesn't understand correct formatting – and who also doesn't understand spec script formatting, or the difference between spec script formatting and production script formatting.

Study this book, and *The Screenwriter's Bible* and *Dr. Format Tells All*. Make them your own. Write notes in them. Underline what you find to be helpful for your writing so that you can later go back and speed read through the underlined parts of the books to refresh what you learned.

- **NOTE 21: SCRIPT PROOF EDITING: To proof the script, the writer relied on people who know NOTHING about screenwriting**

Depending on friends and family to proof your script isn't going to be of much help. What do they understand about the craft of screenwriting? They might be entertained by the story, and that is good. But, they are likely to be unskilled in recognizing what the script needs, and will be a waste of your time in relation to sharpening the script for industry submission. They are unlikely to recognize the problems in formatting, pacing, story, character psychology, and other matters – that will be noticed by industry professionals.

Many years ago, an agency wanted to see one of my scripts. Before I submitted it, my girlfriend sat and read through it to proof it. Did she know anything about screenwriting? Nope. That wasn't a good idea.

Screenwriting is not something that a person can learn in a month, or several months. After years of studying it, there is more to learn.

While it may be fun and interesting, and may be helpful, to have friends and relatives read your script, do not rely on them – or anyone who hasn't studied screenwriting – to help you polish your script to prepare it for industry submissions.

"Unfortunately, people believe that their first thing should be great. Writing is like anything else. You're not supposed to write a page and expect it to be good. You have to write a thousand pages and expect it to be good. It's as if we were training for the twenty-yard-dash, and instead of waiting until we'd trained before we ran, we invite everyone to our first practice, and of course, we fall flat on our face."

– Akiva Goldsman, *The Dark Tower*

Find ways to network with other screenwriters. Read each other's work. That might mean connecting with screenwriters online, attending or forming a screenwriting workshop, attending college courses in screenwriting, including online classes and seminars. Zoom has opened up the possibilities here.

Don't ask other screenwriters to read your screenplay – until after you have studied the books *Dr. Format Tells All*, *The Screenwriter's Bible*, and perhaps *The Art of Dramatic Writing*, and *The Anatomy of Story*, and several other screenwriting books of your choosing. If you are writing for TV, read books about writing for television. Watch YouTube videos about screenwriting. Read articles about screenwriting. Read scripts that have won awards for best screenplay (see the WGA list) – and watch the films made from those scripts.

"I will watch a movie that I love, and I sit there and pause and unpause it and basically diagram it out, time wise. I basically make an outline of the film with the time code of when stuff happens."

– Rian Johnson, *Looper*

Having other screenwriters read your work should not be about them fixing common mistakes. First, do your homework. Study the books. Do your best to polish the script. Then, have other screenwriters read your work.

- **NOTE 22: SLOPPY, DILUTED SCRIPT: The script is so filled with errors, inconsistencies, and overwritten scenes lacking conflict, tension, subtext, an emotional through-line – and void of an engaging story played out by interesting characters – that it simply is not engaging.**

If you have glaring mistakes throughout your script, it means that you have not taken the time to study screenwriting. People who read scripts for a living will notice.

"A builder who does not know the material he is forced to work with courts disaster."

– Lajos Egri, author *The Art of Dramatic Writing*

Learn what you can about correctly writing scene headings (also known as "slug lines"), sub headings, scene description, parentheticals, dialogue, series of shots, and other matters – all within the correct margins.

A studio, agency, or management company reader likely has dozens of screenplays to read every week. Don't give them the chance to dismiss your script based on it being filled with incorrect formatting, typos, rambling scene description, pointless dialogue, boring scenes, uninteresting characters, or a lack of motives, conflict, contention, tension, and so forth.

Submitting an unready script to a contest, manager, agent, producer, development executive, or other decision-maker in the industry is a waste of time. You may only get one chance to get your script to people who can send it on the path to being produced.

- **NOTE 23: DULL SCRIPT: The scenes are boring, and it's unclear what they are meant to communicate.**

If you bore the management, agency, studio, contest, lab, fellowship, mentorship, or other industry reader, it is unlikely that an audience will ever see your film in a theatre or series on a screen.

"Want drama? Ask a character: 'What do you fear the most?' Then, put them in a story where they have to confront that fear."
– Scott Myers, GoIntoTheStory.BlckLst.com

Push the lead character off of a psychological cliff. Increase the conflict. Pump up the contentious drama. Infuse subtext. Punch up the comedy. Decrease the tell. Increase the show. Don't over explain. Do those even in subtle ways to improve the pace and make the scenes, the story, the dialogue, and the characters compellingly engaging and interesting.

"Screenwriting is about condensing."
– Nick Hornby, *An Education*

Work every word of the scenes so that the only words left on the pages are the ones that are needed, matter, and help the reader to pay attention.

Delete words that don't add anything to the story or play into creating the world we are to see and the characters we are to watch and hear.

"If you're reading through and stop, something is wrong. Cut it. Cutting leads to economy, precision, and to a vastly improved script."
– Paddy Chayefsky, *Network*

Maybe it's not as easy or simple as Chayefsky says there, but consider it when reading your script.

"I tried to write in an extremely spare, almost haiku style – both stage directions and dialogue. Some of it was a bit pretentious – but other times I thought it worked pretty well."
– Walter Hill, *Aliens*

"I've been writing screenplays now for twenty-five years, and it's taken me all this time to see even a glint of where I should be heading, which is to aim for a certain simplicity, and stop trying to pack the screenplay with as much as I can."
– Lawrence Kasdan, *The Big Chill*

Perhaps successful scripts are not about the characters in the story. Maybe they are formulated for what people might experience in their own lives, in some relatable form, in a universally subconsciously identifiable journey played out by characters by proxy. Read the *The Hero with a Thousand Faces*.

Maybe the successful scripts are about commonly relatable issues, such as the fear of loss, the desire for connection, or the mystery of death, and having a hero or savior – even if that figure is the self.

People tend to favor the savior figure, or the wise ones who inspire the saving of self – even if simply by having self-faith, and being less afraid to face the unknown and feel secure. (Search: Horus, Mithra, Krishna, Odysseus, Romulus, Heracles, Dionysus, Glycon, Buddha, Attis, Zarathustra, and Jesus.)

Maybe a screenplay isn't about getting a reader into the lives of the characters, but is more about getting the characters into the life of the reader.

Screenplays are more like novels than films. That is so because – similar to a novel – a screenplay has to engage the reader's imagination so that they can visualize the actions, the characters, and the stories, and so that they can mentally hear the characters and the sounds. But, a screenplay isn't to be written in the novel-style of prose, it's to be written in screenplay form, including with the correct formatting elements in place – and without distractive issues.

Write sparingly, clearly, meaningfully, and with the intention of engaging the mind of the reader. Grasp the reader's interest, mess with their reasoning, play with their imagination, subvert their expectations, and don't let go of their psychological engagement. Get your script to be the one that they encourage their bosses and talented filmmakers to read.

"The most ordinary word, when put into place, suddenly acquires brilliance. That is the brilliance with which your images must shine."
– Robert Bresson, *The Devil, Probably*

- **NOTE 24: CONFLICT DILUTED: The conflict in the scenes is diluted, and the scenes are overly long, to the point that the conflict and contention – if they are even present – are a mere elusive vapor of what they could be.**

One of the main problems in scripts is that the writer has not clarified what message they need to communicate in each scene. Even to the point that the writer doesn't seem to know what they are presenting to the audience, and are sort of tossing things on the page that might have meaning – or are too vague.

"First, find out what your hero wants, then just follow him."
– Ray Bradbury, *The Picasso Summer*

It is helpful for scenes to be written with a purpose of revealing character need and want, and conflict and contention, in a timely manner. Do so elegantly, with slick, engaging pacing – even during calm scenes, and without being overly long or wordy. Character is story.

Write scenes deftly. Grasp the audience's attention. Trigger them to emotionally engage with the character's reasoning, manipulation, and motive through ongoing contentious acts in scenes with good pacing and that are rich in subtext and that reveal intention. All in a relevant tone and mood.

"Mostly when I think of pacing, I go back to Elmore Leonard, who explained it so perfectly by saying he just left out the boring parts. This suggests cutting to speed the pace, and that's what most of us end up having to do."
– Stephen King, *Carrie*

If you are the only one who understands the conflict, and the only one who finds the actor's display of contention – or lack thereof – compelling, interesting, and/or engaging, your script is unlikely to get made. Unless you make it. And the people in your life might be the only ones who will (suffer to) watch it.

"The idea was born out of financial necessity. It had been several years since I directed a feature, and I wanted to write something I could afford to shoot with almost no budget. This meant cutting back on cast, crew, lighting, locations, props, wardrobe, and just about everything else – which basically left me with nothing. And then one day I came up with a very challenging concept: A guy buried alive for an entire movie. No other actors appearing on screen, no cutting away from this one location."
– Chris Sparling, *Buried*

- **NOTE 25: SCRIPT IS UNREADY FOR PRESENTATION: The script was submitted before the script was ready.**
  It's a waste of your time, money, resources, and potential to submit unpolished screenplays.
  Other people who are entering their scripts into the contests, mentorship, and fellowship programs are doing their homework. They are making sure that they are doing their best that they can with their scripts – before they submit them. Your script will be competing with theirs. The time they spent on doing their homework and on polishing their scripts will be obvious.
  Be among those who submit polished scripts. Anything less is not sufficient in the highly competitive screenplay marketplace.

- **NOTE 26: SCRIPT IS UNPOLISHED: The script hasn't been thoroughly polished, and every page reveals that.**
  I read the scripts that go through Screenwriting Tribe. It is clear which writers pay attention, do their homework, and work to improve their skills in the craft during the weeks and months it takes to workshop every page of their scripts. I notice the improvement of their skills displayed both in their scripts, and in the feedback that they give to the other writers.

There are those who don't like the feedback process during a workshop. They get defensive. They try explaining the script. One thing they will not be able to do is explain the script to the agency, management, studio, contest, or mentorship readers who will read that script when the writer is not present.

Not that a sloppy script will advance that far.

What is needed for a script to survive the highly dismissive path to being optioned and produced is for that script to be sharp, self-explanatory, engaging, clever, and to stand on its own.

If you can't put up with the feedback you are going to get in a workshop, how do you expect that you are going to deal with the feedback you get in meetings with managers, producers, directors, and others in the industry?

"Constant revision teaches you not to be too precious. It can be very humbling, but it makes you a better writer. Know when to defend something you've written, and know when to let it go."
– Kira Snyder, *Moonlight*

Be a collaborator. That doesn't mean that you have to agree with everyone, or change your script according to every bit of feedback you get on it. But, do listen, consider how the person giving you the feedback factored it, and take some time to think about how the feedback could improve your script.

A screenwriting workshop can help get you up to speed on reading scripts quickly, and deciding ways to fix and polish them. It's a good practice to get into. Especially if you want to be a staff writer on a TV series – where things happen quickly, and with many people involved.

Don't only attend a screenwriting workshop when it is your turn to present pages. Attend the workshop when others are workshopping their pages, read those pages, and listen to the feedback. You will learn faster that way – even when you don't agree with the feedback, and don't favor the scripts.

- **NOTE 27: UNPREPARED WRITER: The writer may have read only a few screenwriting books, as if believing that all of the books are the same. Their skill – or lack thereof – reveals it.**

There are a number of screenwriting books that are similar, but others provide helpful information in ways that others don't.

I know that this book is unlike the others, as I wrote it while running workshops and doing my own research – while helping a wide variety of writers – and some producers and directors – with their screenplays. Thank you for choosing this as one of the screenwriting books to study.

Go to your local library and see which screenwriting books they have in their collection. Read them.

When people ask me which books to read, and I name specific titles, I often get this: "But, I've already read (name of some other screenwriting book)." As if the book that they read is the one and only book that they need to read, and now they know everything, their screenwriting studies are finished, they are a screenwriter, and the books I suggest are simply more of the same – even though they have not read them. Good luck with limiting yourself.

- **NOTE 28: SCRIPT HAS SLOW START: The initial pages do not reveal conflict and character, or build toward what a well-written script would display in conflict, pacing, contention, and other matters.**
  While using correct formatting, and sharp writing, do your best to bring the reader straightforward into an emotional through-line and character philosophy, manipulation, and motive in and interesting world for the story.

  From the start, trigger the reader with a sense that things are not as they appear, and that the reader is about to go through an engaging adventure.

  Take the reader out of their life and into the world you created, and keep them there. Mess with their expectations. Twist, entice, turn, and hook them in. Make them want things for the characters enough so that the reader is going to keep reading to see if the character gets something resembling what the reader wants them to get.

  "I don't care if a reader hates one of my stories, just as long as he finishes the book."
  – Roald Dahl, *Willy Wonka & The Chocolate Factory*

  "The strongest human emotion is fear. It's the essence of any good thriller that, for a while, you believe in the bogeyman."
  – John Carpenter, *Halloween*

  Give the reader every reason to want to keep turning those pages until they have read to the final word at the end of the script.

  "Write something unique that showcases your voice. Readers read so much – at times four or five scripts a day. So many of those scripts become one blob in your head – a singular voice. It's the scripts that really strive to do something unique, whether it works or whether it doesn't, that stick with you. As long as you're writing something that is representative of your voice and your experience, I think you can't go wrong."
  – Justin Kremer, *White Noise*

  Make the script so good that the reader is going to tell their boss that they must read the script.

  "There is no terror in the bang, only in the anticipation of it."
  – Alfred Hitchcock, *Dangerous Virtue*

- **NOTE 29: SCRIPT START IS UNENGAGING: The script doesn't get the reader involved in the story by page 10, 7, 5, 3, or... 1.**
  Granted, not every great script will be so engaging on the first page. But, there should be reasons why the reader wants to turn to the next page, and the next, and the next.

The script should have a certain something showing that you mean business in telling a story that is so engaging that large numbers of people will sit for hours to watch what will be produced from it.

One of the quickest ways to lose the reader in the early pages is to bore them with dullness. Other ways are to write a script filled with errors, redundancies, rambling scenes, elaborate scene description, seemingly pointless and wordy dialogue, and sloppy formatting.

"If a hundred words of meaning can be expressed with five words, the story is moving twenty times as quickly."
– Amnon Buchbinder, author *The Way of the Screenwriter*

An occasional lengthy block of wordy dialogue isn't necessarily a bad thing. It works well as a monologue during the scene in *A Place in the Sun*, when George Eastman (Montgomery Clift) speaks with Mr. Vickers. But, that is one finely-written scene that plays into a buildup of soul-twisting consequences. There are good reasons why actors study that scene and its tender delivery.

If you are going to have a character talk a lot, there better be a good reason for it.

"One day I will find the right words, and they will be simple."
– Jack Kerouac, *On the Road*

While you may have written one of those great scripts that starts out slowly, at least be sure to have those pages polished and free of wordy description, formatting problems, grammatical issues, formatting and other distractive issues, and dullness.

- **NOTE 30: THE SCRIPT IS FLAT: The script is flat, is devoid of subtext, and lacks an intriguing story, engaging conflict, and an interesting character worth watching and who is contending with their situation and hurdles in compelling ways.**

"You can dress it up, but it comes down to the fact that a movie is only as good as its script."
– Curtis Hanson, *L.A. Confidential*

This can be a book right here. But, this book you hold is about everything in this point, and about getting your script to contain the qualities that agents, managers, readers, producers, directors, actors, investors, distributors, and audiences want.

"If all you have is that big game, you're lost. The film has to be about something else. Take *Seabiscuit*, for example. It's a story about loss and healing that just happens to be set against the backdrop of horseracing. Jeff Bridges' character lost his son. Tobey Maguire's character lost his family. Chris

Cooper's character lost his way of life. Working with the horse and each other helped to ease those losses."
– Eric Guggenheim, *Parenthood*

Does each scene end with the reader thinking, "But, what happens next?"

"You know, my problem with most screenwriting is it is a blueprint. It's like they're afraid to write the damn thing. And I'm a writer. That's what I do. I want it to be written. I want it to work on the page, first and foremost. So, when I'm writing the script, I'm not thinking about the viewer watching the movie. I'm thinking about the reader reading the script."
– Quentin Tarantino, *From Dusk Till Dawn*

Immerse the readers, take hold of them, and entice them with the story. Write clearly, cleverly, brilliantly, sharply, at a good pace, and visually with subtext, conflict, and engaging contention. Make them forget they are reading.

- **NOTE 31: EMOTIONAL AND SENSORY ENGAGEMENT: The script doesn't play with the senses and emotions of the audience.**
Write for the complete set of senses of the audience: Not only sight, sound, smell, taste, and touch, but also the sense of duration of time perception (chronoception), the sense of basic needs of hunger, thirst, warmth, and coolness (interoception), the sense of possible pain or harm (nociception), the sense of the body parts, their positions, and what they are doing (proprioception), and the sense of temperature perception (thermoception).
Then, there is the relationship desire that is limerence (search that).
Beyond seeing the visuals and hearing the sounds, get the audience to feel as if they are smelling, tasting, and touching the things in the scenes.
Make your audiences laugh and cry, fidget in their seats, hold their noses, cover their mouths, want to look away, grab onto their lover, hug their children, or verbally respond. Reread the chapter *Consider Film a Drug* (pages 10-16).

"The play was a great success, but the audience was a disaster."
– Oscar Wilde, *The Importance of Being Earnest*

See *American Pie*. There is the scene when Stiffler picks up the ale, which is a play into the self-identity of his character. It's a scene that makes you want to slap that ale out of his hands, or want to look away, but you can't look away – and you are repulsed as you watch what happens.
One shocking scene is when something pours onto Carrie. That plays with all of the senses. (See the 1976 film, *Carrie*.)
Watch *The Shining*. If that doesn't trigger you to have physical reactions, I don't know what will. It strongly plays with audience nociception.
In *Billy Elliot*, there is a scene when the Father runs to see something. It plays with audience proprioception. You so badly want him to run faster that your breathing changes, you can feel your legs want to move. You want him to get where he is going to see what he is going to see. And it's a tear jerker.

"One of the things that I've always been interested in doing is actually invading your comfort space. Because that's what we're supposed to do. Get under your skin, and make you react."
– Stephen King, *Creepshow*

When a friend saw *Halloween*, she had her foot on her knee. When something awful happened in the film, she jolted in her seat, accidently kicking the head of the guy sitting in front of her. That sure surprised him.

If a character opens a door, and a rotting corpse covered in bugs falls onto them, it can make the audience squirm, as if they can feel and smell the slime and stench of that corpse, and those bugs.

Think of the films you have seen. Which scenes in those films triggered you to respond physically? Consider how you can write scenes that do similar things to an audience.

- **NOTE 32: CHARACTER REACTION: The characters don't react to what is happening around them, or the characters are overly reactionary to the point that we don't care for them as they are simply drama queens who make too much out of nothing, or they do react when it would be more impactful and in tune with what they are going through – and their motives – if they don't react – or they hold off on reacting.**

All throughout the script make sure the setups have a payoff, including within scenes when something happens. Have the characters react in that scene, or, if it would have more of an interesting payoff, give a delayed reaction in a future scene. Or, have them privately react, and reconfigure their plan.

When something happens to a character:
- Does the character's reaction equal that of the stimulus?
- Do we feel the need for the character to react that way, or to hold off?
- Do we understand why the character reacts that way?
- Do we know the character is reacting that way based on something they went through, or their hopes or needs?

Will the reason they react that way play into the parameters of:
- Who the character is?
- What the character's goals are?
- What the character has been and is going through?
- How the character treats others?
- What will happen to the character?

Maybe the character is so burned out and so let down by life that they don't react when someone tells them some awful, terrible news, or when they see something heinous happen. Or, they are so unaccustomed to expressing themselves, or maybe they refuse to allow anyone to see them react, so they do not react there – they remain poker faced. It is only when they get outside, walk

293

into a forest, and finally break down into tears that we see their emotions take hold and overwhelm them.

Sometimes, it could be interesting for a character to have no reaction. Maybe we know a character is so burned out on life, and has given up so deeply, or is so intent on something happening or not happening that they don't react to some event that the audience does react to.

See the oddly hilarious war zone scene with the character played by Robert Duvall simply carrying on a rambling conversation with the freaked-out young soldiers in *Apocalypse Now*.

- **NOTE 33: REVERSALS: The script lacks reversals.**

If the story and the characters in it are simply going along one path, and not experiencing gains and setbacks to those gains, letdowns, disappointments, advances, and other reversals, what is it that we are supposed to feel, want, hold onto, hate, be disappointed by, or otherwise feel for the character and about the story?

I saw a student film in which a character wants something, and simply goes about getting it without any sort of hesitation, no apparent contention, problems, threats, antagonist, worry, fights, arguments, hurdles, losses, life storms, family or friend drama, begging, robbery or cheating. There was only happiness along the path to getting what she wanted. Yawn.

That film was about as interesting as watching a character walk into a room with a can of paint, say they are going to paint a wall, then paint the wall and exit the room.

"Your bad guy must always be taking action. He's always plotting, planning, stealing, killing, wounding, belittling, or scraping cheese off your pizza. If the bad guy isn't constantly making more clever moves, he's not much of a bad guy."
– William Akers, author *Your Screenplay Sucks*

See *The Wizard of Oz*. There are wants, needs, expectations, gains, setbacks, twists, turns, mysteries, suspicion, fear, and uncertainty. There is an engaging protagonist, and engaging antagonists, and engaging supporting characters all around. So much so that even a small child will stay tuned to watch the entire film from beginning to end. Or, like my sister did when she was four years old. The poor girl stood in front of the TV crying madly and became an entire emotional mess about everything that was going on in *The Wizard of Oz*, refusing anyone who tried to get her away from the TV, or who tried to talk to her. She was mesmerized.

- **NOTE 34: LEAD CHARACTER SEEMS TO BE WRONG CHOICE: The lead character is not as interesting as other characters in the script, or is not in the situation that is the most compelling in the group of characters populating the story.**

If what we are paying attention to in the first dozen or so pages is a different character than the one you chose as the lead, consider why we are doing that. Maybe you are doing it on purpose, and then there will be a switch to another character in a way that serves the story. Or, maybe what you thought is working is exactly what is not working.

The story may quickly turn so that we then are most engaged with the character who you chose as the lead. If so, you might want to make sure that happens in a way that best serves the story – and reader and viewer focus.

If your script is about a bunch of people with money, maybe the best point-of-view is that of a character who isn't the wealthiest or who isn't considered to be the most powerful in the group. Maybe a poor relative is the most interesting. Or the rebellious child. Or the relative who gives large amounts of money to nonprofits. Or the relative who is considered the failure. Maybe the housecleaner is the most interesting, engaging, and potentially rewarding character to watch.

Maybe instead of focusing on the drugged-out bank robber who holds the bank employees in a back room while cops gather to negotiate outside, it is the mousy, shy, apparently boring bank secretary who would be the most interesting person in the group. Maybe that quiet, seemingly shy lady knows things, and does things, has contacts, and has an unexpected history and view of life that we would not have expected – and she ends up being the hero of the film.

"I'm interested in finding extraordinary moments in otherwise normal people."
– Mark Boal, *The Hurt Locker*

Instead of the captain of the spaceship, maybe it is the manipulative actions and communication of her blind and clever daughter using robotic technology who would be more interesting and engaging, and enthrall the audience.

"What does this character want, and more importantly: Why do they want it? Those are what I look at as I'm writing dialogue."
– Brad Ingelsby, *Torrance*

- **NOTE 35: ANTAGONIST ISN'T ANTAGONIZING: The antagonist isn't that much of a threat or hindrance to the safety, position, hopes, needs, and/or goals of the protagonist.**

"The single most important question, I think, that one must ask one's self about a character is what are they really afraid of?"
– Robert Towne, *Mission: Impossible*

Consider making the antagonist more warped, clever, devious, driven, manipulative, unpredictable, and interesting. Then, a little bit more. Make them a bigger threat, a more troubled creep, a manipulative beast, a diabolical lunatic that might appear normal to outsiders, but who is so deviant that they are the one who the audiences want to help the protagonist to fight, outwit, confuse, undermine, trip, and outmaneuver.

- **NOTE 36: ANTAGONIST CHOICE: The antagonist isn't who you seem to think it is.**
  Maybe you are thinking of your antagonist as a person, when the antagonist is actually a thing: A nonentity.

  "To my mind, the movie *Adaptation*, the main character in that movie is screenplay itself. And the evolution of the screenplay from its initial intents to its ultimate kind of corruption, and to me that's kind of the tragedy of this creature – is the screenplay that never was able to reach their fruition, that Charlie had hoped. He never was able to make a movie about flowers."
  – Charlie Kaufman, *Adaptation*

  An antagonist or external conflict could be something like abuse, bullying, societal rejection, repressive religion, an unrighteous government, poverty, or the elements (tornado, a storm, a flooding river, a potential landslide or avalanche, etc.), or whatever the main character is fighting, or what is externally stopping them from getting what needs to be had for them to break free of the thing holding them back from what they want and need. (Internal conflict would be how they deal with what they are facing – and that is displayed through actions and words.)

  "The threat of violence is stronger than the violence."
  – Alfred Hitchcock, *Psycho*

  To have the antagonist be that of a nonentity, rather than a person, make sure that you understand the threat posed by the antagonist, and what it does, how it can impact the life of and stall or harm the protagonist, and how the audience can engage with the story involving a nonentity antagonist.

- **NOTE 37: CHARACTERS ASK TOO MANY QUESTIONS: The characters continually question and answer each other.**
  Don't make your dialogue an ongoing set of interviews with one character asking a question, and the other person answering.
  Go out in public and listen to the way real people converse.

  "If it's a good movie, the sound could go off and the audience would still have a perfectly clear idea of what was going on."
  – Alfred Hitchcock, *Champagne*

  Consider showing more through action, and telling less through dialogue. But, do it without extraneous action – that which is irrelevant to the story.
  Watch silent films, and films that contain little dialogue (*Tuvalu, Wall.E, All is Lost, Rambo, A Quiet Place*).

- **NOTE 38: BLATANT STRUCTURE RECIPE: The structure is too obvious, and isn't a good choice for the story.**

Consider that all of the things you learned about structure have overwhelmed the execution of your story. You have latched onto some sort of so-called ideal structure theory, and you are striving to stick within it.

Write more freely, and see what the results are from that.

Maybe the inciting incident you chose is so blatantly evident on that certain page – which the structure gods said it must be on – that it works out to be base and corny. And, predictable.

The arbitrary rules of structure that you studied could limit your script to being some lesser piece that is not as engaging or interesting as it could have been – if you had simply not tried to force that structure into your script.

"The screenplay is so well-written in a scruffy, fanzine way that you want to rub noses in it – the noses of those zombie writers who take 'screenwriting' classes that teach them the formulas for 'hit films.'"
– Roger Ebert, film critic (about *Pulp Fiction*)

Many successful screenwriters don't pay attention to structure when they write a script. They simply write the story, and things fall into places that work best for the story. If it happens to fall into a form of structure that has been taught by the so-called script gurus, then it is fine that way. If it works in another way, then that is the way it is.

"It doesn't appeal to me to have kind of a formula for writing anything. I think some people like it, and it's helpful for some people, and I wouldn't tell people not to do it – if they want to do it. But, I'm not interested in sort of going in with a framework. I think it inhibits the possibilities – for me."
– Charlie Kaufman, *Being John Malkovich*

The main thing is to write an engaging script, one that studio readers will advance to their bosses, that their bosses will want to produce, directors will want to direct, actors will want to act in, financiers will want to finance, distributors will want to distribute, and, most of all, that a broad number of filmgoers will want to watch, and will be satisfied by – which will satisfy investors and advance the careers of the filmmakers – and, you.

"On *Wind River*, I ran out of money in post-production, so I had to submit it to festivals to try to get a distribution deal to get more money to finish it. *Sicario* nobody wanted to touch, but it wound up getting sent to a producer who was doing *Prisoners* with Denis Villeneuve, who read it and said, 'I have to do this next.' So, we very luckily stumbled into a desirable director, which put us in a position to get actors, which allowed us to get a good budget. *Hell or High Water* was fortunately in a really competitive situation in terms of selling it, so we were able to get a commitment for a budget of $12 million. That was enough to get an actor that garners you good foreign-sale projections – which

helps move things forward. Getting a movie made is a fascinating, complicated process. You could write a movie about it."
– Taylor Sheridan, *The Last Cowboy*

"On the day that Patty (Jenkins) and I were going to sign the contract for a straight-to-video with Blockbuster on *Monster* – because no distributor would pick it up – literally, the lawyer was coming to the editing room (to sign the straight-to-video contract) – we got a call from (distributor) Bob Berney.
Those things happen where you stop trying, you almost give up and surrender. But then magic happens. It is a little bit like we work in a business where we are trying to constantly capture that lighting in a bottle."
– Charlize Theron, actor/producer

"The market that existed, that took me under its wing and actually gave me a platform to do my movies – that market doesn't exist anymore."
– Quentin Tarantino, *Reservoir Dogs*

- **NOTE 39: IMAGERY: The script doesn't utilize imagery.**
Not that you should be blatantly and novelistically describing imagery. But, do consider the imagery that your scene description paints in the minds of the readers.

"Cheat your landlord if you can and must, but do not try to shortchange the Muse. It cannot be done. You can't fake quality any more than you can fake a good meal."
– William S. Burroughs, *Drugstore Cowboy*

Film is both a visual and sound medium. Utilize the media to tell your story through imagery, more than through dialogue. There will also be a soundtrack.
Use the imagery of the setting. Imagine yourself there, and notice what you see, smell, and hear. Consider what your characters are seeing, smelling, hearing, feeling, and considering in relation to the setting.
How does the setting play into the character's wants, goals, needs, perception, anticipation, reasoning, and philosophy? How are those things challenged, and possibly changed?
Use sparse wording to describe the arrangement and movement (kinesis) of objects and people, and the character's structural condition and affliction, the visual aspects of their mental state, and also their wardrobe, and actions.
Always be careful of not being overly wordy in scene description. If you have to over explain, perhaps what you are describing isn't working.
Realize that the reader has a brain, and their imagination will likely pick up on what you are communicating. Don't hit them over the head with grand, wordy descriptions. Especially avoid description that repeats messages that the audience already clearly understands.
Some writers go for an overdone form of what is called pathetic fallacy. It could be a black cat running across the path of a character who also happens to

walk beneath a ladder, and then experiences all sorts of bad luck. It could include the "dark and stormy night" sort of thing where audiences are supposed to get the feeling that there is something ominous lurking about. Rain could also be reflective of a character being depressed. There could be imagery that could be considered subtly sexual. Pathetic fallacy could be blatantly comical or dramatic.

Conflicting pathetic fallacy could be used by having characters dancing in the rain, instead of being depressed in it. Conflicting pathetic fallacy could also be a rigid religious sect holding a meeting in which the pious characters who are seemingly opposed to all things sexual do something that is subtly reflective of sex in what might appear to be innocent to the participants, but blatant to the observers.

Imagery of irony could be a college girl character eating a luscious dessert at a family picnic. The local parish priest, who we know has had some morality issues, and who has been invited to the picnic, appears to avoid looking over to her. As the priest experiences a change in his breathing, the girl asks him if he is experiencing indigestion, and if he would like a dessert, or something else.

Ironic imagery could be a silent scene of an apparently proper and pleasant, large family enjoying a day at the zoo while the caged gorillas they watch suddenly engage in aggressive sex. Then, a voiceover of the mundane teenage daughter says that she never discussed the birds and the bees with her parents who homeschooled her. But then, there is that awkward moment.

Conflicting pathetic fallacy imagery could be combined with music. Such as happy music while a character is dreadfully depressed. Or high-intensity, frantically cheerful dance music being played while a character slothfully crawls to the toilet to try to vomit up the pills they took.

It is also common in films to use metaphorical imagery. Such as in *The Wizard of Oz*, when Dorothy goes from black and white into color, as her mind opens to a whole new world.

Some scenes combine imagery containing many layers of revelations or expositions relating to the main story. An old dancer clearly dreading the state of his progression into limited physical capacity as he sits in a wheel chair while mourning the death of his lifelong lover… while he watches happy children leaving ballet class and dancing along the sidewalk… as a happy love ballad plays… and nearby, a couple of young lovers' kiss on a park bench… and a pregnant woman passes by... while a young Father plays ball with his son. And it is all reflective of the various stages of the elderly man's life.

- **NOTE 40: COMMAS: The writer misuses commas.**
Learn the proper use of commas. Perhaps a little refresher on correct grammar and punctuation will sharpen your writing.
Study *The Elements of Style*, by Strunk and White.
Know that commas are rarely used in scene headings, or in parentheticals.
Screenwriting differs from other writing.

- **NOTE 41: SPACING AFTER PERIODS: The script contains inconsistencies of spacing after periods.**

Little things like missing punctuation – or punctuation that changes from sentence to sentence – can be like little, distractive pests to a reader.

Spacing after periods is inconsistent is one of those pests.

I have worked on loads of TV and film sets. They are filmed in all sorts of weather, in all varieties of lighting. Some writers say that it makes it easier for the cast and crew to read the scripts by placing two spaces after a period – both in scene description and in dialogue.

I've seen scripts with one space after the periods, and others that use two spaces. To me, it makes no difference.

On set, the mini script pages they use (called the "sides," which are printouts of the scenes that are being filmed that day) are usually printed on half the size of a normal sheet of paper, which means the type face is half the size of normal. Two spaces after a period shows up more clearly on pages that are half the size.

When I get the sides on set, I read the through them while using my pen to bold all of the periods, commas, apostrophes, hyphens, and other punctuation. Doing that makes it easier to read in any lighting condition, helps me to memorize the script, and makes it easier to read if I glance at the sides during rehearsals.

In non-script writing (such as in this book), I use one space after a period.

Use the *search and replace* feature on your computer to replace period/space with period/two spaces.

- **NOTE 42: HYPHEN MISUSE: The writer misuses hyphens.**

There are ways of using hyphens in screenplays that are correct, and there are ways of using hyphens that will stick out like a sore thumb – and reveal that you have not done your homework.

Avoid misusing hyphens, and don't leave them out where they should be in the script. That is one way to irritate the studio or agency reader.

A person isn't a three year old. The person is a three-year-old. But, they aren't three-years-old, they are three years old.

(Search: Use of hyphens.)

Study the book *Dr. Format Tells All*. Also, get a reference book – or bookmark pages on the Internet – about punctuation and grammar.

Double hyphens are also used as a way to indicate that a character's dialogue is interrupted by another character, or by some sort of action.

```
              ANDREW
     Lisa, will you marry --

              LISA
     Andrew! Don't be ridiculous.
```

Double hyphens can also be included before the dialogue of the character who is doing the interruption. This can help the actor know that they are to speak up to interrupt the other actor.

```
                    ANDREW
        Lisa, will you marry --

                    LISA
        -- Andrew! Don't be ridiculous.
```

Some people go nuts with hyphens, putting them all throughout the script in various ways, using them as continuations of thoughts -- and continuation of dialogue. Stop with the overuse of hyphens – especially when it is more accurate to use a period, comma, or ellipses.

You can use a double hyphen when a character interrupts their own dialogue stream, and switches to another thought, or to say something else. Don't use ellipses (three dots…) for that.

```
                    CONNOR
        I was about to put the bottle on
        the -- Oh, wait! Before that, I
        removed my shoes.
```

- **NOTE 43: HYPHENS WHEN CHARACTER SPELLS SOMETHING: The writer uses periods after letters when a character spells something aloud, when the correct format is to place hyphens between the letters.**

When a character spells a word, put hyphens between the letters.

```
                    HENRIETTA
        Darling, the condition is insomnia.
        It is spelled i-n-s-o-m-n-i-a. And, I
        suffer from it.
```

- **NOTE 44: ELLIPSES AND HYPHEN MISUSE: The writer misuses ellipses and hyphens.**

One of the things… that will quickly… irritate… a reader… is… the overuse… of… ellipses.

Learn how ellipses are used in screenplay dialogue. It can be different from what you are used to in other forms of writing.

Ellipses can be used to glide the scene from one angle to the next, without saying "we see," "the camera glides to," "P.O.V. on," or "we pan to see.

Klutzy writing with acknowledgment of the camera movements:

```
Eliza glances over her shoulder as the camera pans
off to:
```

ANGLE ON: Damian as he enters and puts away his cell
phone and looks over to wink at her.

Better:

Eliza glances over her shoulder to see...

Damian enter as he puts away his cell phone and winks
at her.

Or, you can omit the ellipses after the word "see."

Eliza glances over her shoulder to see

Fewer words with no acknowledgement of the camera gives us what we
need.

If a character wanders off in thought, use ellipses.

> CLARENCE
> I thought she would be there.
> But, she said that...

If another character then finishes that sentence, start the second character's
dialogue with ellipses:

> MEGAN
> ... she would never fly again.

If a character shifts thought during dialogue, they are essentially
interrupting themselves. So, use double hyphens for that situation.

> JEANIE MAE
> I was about to tell -- You
> lied to me!

Don't use ellipses for when a character's dialogue is interrupted. Use
Double hyphens for that.

> TAQUIFA
> (holds up a small box)
> Stookie, will you --

> STOOKIE
> -- Yes! Yes, I will marry you!

> TAQUIFA
> It's a pill box. I can't figure out
> how to open it. I need my meds.

As mentioned earlier, including double hyphens at the start of the dialogue
that interrupts the previous dialogue can help signal the second actor that they
are to jump in with their dialogue, to overtalk the other actor.

Use hyphens also when a sound or action interrupts dialogue.

```
                    BOB
        When you touch it here --

BOOM! The tire explodes. Bob falls backwards.
```

- **NOTE 45: ITALICS: The script contains words in *italics*.**

Don't use *italics* in a script. (Except: See ** below.) Unless the rare time in dialogue when you might use italics when a character uses a foreign word. But, it might be better to use an underline (or, use dual dialogue when there is an abundance of foreign language). Some scripts will bold dialogue that is in a foreign language. Dual dialogue is more clear.

However, consider that the tension, conflict, contention, and subtext of the scene should speak for itself, and the actor would know the inflection, without you micro-managing the dialogue delivery by underlining words.

It's doubtful that anyone will dismiss your script because you use italics. If you do use them, do so sparingly – maybe a few times in an entire script.

Don't be that person who italicizes or underlines every word on which you think the actor should place influence. That is obnoxious, and distractive.

"Don't use italics or bold to set apart anything in narrative description."
– David Trottier, author *The Screenwriter's Bible*

Putting passages of dialogue in italics is essentially putting a sign on the page saying, "My script is written badly, and the subtext is weak, and the tension, conflict, and contention are so diluted that I have to put some of the dialogue in italics – or underline it – to try to tell the actors how to say stuff, because they obviously won't get the inflection from reading my screenplay – so, I need to micromanage their delivery.

You might say that you saw italics all over in a (name of grandly globally successful filmmaker here) film script. Go look in the mirror. Do you see that filmmaker looking back at you? If so, go back to keyboard and write any which way you wish – because you are going to direct that script. If you don't see that director in the mirror, then simply follow spec script formatting.

**Trottier lists the following as incidents when italics could be used in a screenplay:
- For dialogue that is a text message.
- For foreign words, but that isn't required – and could be noted in a wryly. Or dual dialogue could be used, with the foreign language on the left, and the English translation on the right.
- For words that absolutely must be noticed – but rarely do that. Underlining would be more noticeable.
- For sign language as dialogue.
- For song lyrics.
- For poems.

You will always find screenplays written in different styles that work for those scripts. Go for what is clear, not confusing, and not distractive.

- **NOTE 46: FOREIGN LANGUAGE IN DIALOGUE: The writer's style of indicating when a character uses foreign language is confusing, taxing to read, and/or distractive.**

Foreign language spoken when most characters are speaking English can pose formatting issues, and confusion as to when the character is or is not speaking in one language.

One way to clarify when a character is speaking a different language is to use dual dialogue, which is a format available in Final Draft and other screenwriting software. Place the language being spoken in the left dialogue block and the English translation in the right block. In parenthesis next to the character cue, include the name of the foreign language. I prefer this:

```
       CINDY (French)                   CINDY
French dialogue here.       English dialogue here.
```

Another style is to use a wryly to note that a character is speaking a language other than English.

```
                 CINDY
          (in French, subtitled)
      But, the dog!
```

I've seen scripts where they foreign language dialogue is **bolded**.

You can also make a note within the scene description, in parenthesis, that a character is speaking in a different language, and that their dialogue is to be in subtitles. At the end of the scene, put the words (END OF SUBTITLES).

```
INT. TAXI - NIGHT

Stanley gets in, considers the driver, who appears
Persian. (The dialogue in this scene is in Farsi,
subtitled in English.)

                 STANLEY
      To the airport, please.

                 DRIVER
      You look familiar.

                 STANLEY
      Well, I live in London.

                 DRIVER
      I go there. My sister --

                 STANLEY
      -- Oh, the wedding!
```

```
                    DRIVER
     Thank you for getting my parents
     the hotel room.

They laugh, as if at a memory.

                    STANLEY
     It was my honor. They are
     wonderful.

                    DRIVER
     This ride is on me.
```

(END OF SUBTITLES)

- **NOTE 47: PARENTHETICALS / WRYLIES: The writer misuses parentheticals.**

Many writers go overboard with the parentheticals.

There are specific reasons to use words in parentheses on a line between the character name (cue) and the dialogue.

Parentheticals generally are used to direct something an actor does (especially when saying the line of dialogue), or to indicate the inflection the actor is to use when saying the dialogue, or to indicate who they are speaking to when they are in a setting containing three or more characters.

Basically, parentheticals are used for clarity, and/or to indicate that something is being implied or done (even if it is a look to a certain character) when the dialogue is being said.

"I feel I do my best work when it's all there on the page, and I feel that the character is very vivid as I read the script and I'm not having to create stuff and trying to cobble together something. If I have to do that, then I don't entirely trust what I'm doing."
– Guy Pearce, actor

One reason you would direct an actor by using a parenthetical beneath their character cue, but above their dialogue is because they need to say something with a certain accent that they wouldn't normally use, such as they suddenly speak (`in a Boston accent`). But only use a parenthetical for that if there is a good reason for that to happen pertaining to the character, tone, mood, tension, drama, comedy, and the story.

One reason to use parenthetical actor direction is to indicate that they do a specific thing while they are saying the dialogue.

```
                    MANDY
               (slices the cake)
     I hate birthdays.
```

305

Don't write in a parenthetical: (`she slices the cake`). We know that Mandy is a she. (`slices the cake`) is correct.

Don't write a parenthetical with a period: (`slices the cake.`) The period is not needed.

Another reason to use a parenthetical is to indicate that the character is speaking directly to a particular person when there are a number of other characters in the scene. Such as, a mom who scolds one misbehaving child (`to Bobby`), when there are several other children in the scene.

I recently read part of a script in which nearly every character cue was followed by one or more lines of parenthetical direction. Don't do that.

Parentheticals are good to indicate that a character is to sing a line of dialogue.

Parentheticals are good to indicate if the character says the dialogue in an ironic, snarky, mocking, cynical, pretentious, or ridiculing manner.

Parentheticals are good for clarifying how a certain piece of dialogue is to be said so that the intention isn't misunderstood.

```
            Anne
         (laughs)
    I am going to kill you!
```

Parentheticals are good for clarifying that a character (`whispers`), or says something that only they can hear (`to self`), or otherwise says the dialogue in a specific way (`mockingly`) that is needed for the character intention to be revealed, and for the conflict and contention to move within that dialogue.

Parentheticals are good for when it is absolutely necessary to direct an actor so that the subtext of the scene reads well.

Here is one example of how to use a parenthetical:

```
            Sheila
         (runs to the doorway)
    The spider ran under the thing.

            Bob
    The chair?

            Sheila
    No.
         (off his perplexity)
    The table.
```

That parenthetical also helps guide the actor to be perplexed.

Avoid the overuse of actor direction in parentheticals.

Use parentheticals sparingly, and smartly.

Simply tell the story through sparse scene description, needed actor direction, and excellent dialogue rich with subtext.

"The challenge of screenwriting is to say much in little, and then take half of that little out, and still preserve an effect of leisure and natural movement."
– Raymond Chandler, *Double Indemnity*

- **NOTE 48: OBVIOUS DIRECTION IN PARENTHETICALS: The script states the obvious in the parentheticals.**

An example of a parenthetical that isn't needed is the following, because it is likely said as the character is upset:

```
            BONNIE
         (upset)
He lied to me about being married!
```

Because her tone is obvious, the above parenthetical isn't needed.

But, if her response is supposed to be completely the opposite of the obvious, then do use the parenthetical:

```
            BONNIE
         (cynical smile)
He lied to me about being married!
```

Indicating something for the actor that they should already know – because it should be blatantly obvious – based on the wants, needs, tone, mood, dynamics, conflict, and contention of the character and a scene is one way of "micromanaging the actor." Avoid doing that.

- **NOTE 49: ACCENTED LANGUAGE: There is overuse of accented language description in dialogue – to a painful level.**

If you have to keep repeating how a character is to say their dialogue, you also might keep removing the reader from the script.

Establish the character distinctions the first time they appear in the script.

Learn how to introduce characters. Study the *Screenwriter's Bible*.

Don't feel as if you have to keep reminding the reader that a certain character is from a particular region or country.

Do write the dialogue as that person would say it in their regionalism, but don't go overboard with the inflection and accent in the dialogue.

Don't be the writer who writes every line of dialogue so intricately accented that it is difficult for the reader to understand.

"I've spent quite a lot of my life in America, so I consider myself reasonably familiar with America and its ways. If I write an 'American' screenplay, I always get various American friends to read it. They might say, 'We wouldn't say or do that.' They give it an 'American sound.' There is a particular rhythm to the way English is spoken in America.

I also ask people who are familiar with the content of my screenplay to read it. For instance, if I wrote a story about a ship at sea, I'd ask a sailor to

307

read it to see where it jars with what would really happen at sea. In the end, you need advice from people who live the life you're writing about."

— Julian Fellows, *Downton Abbey*

- **NOTE 50: ACTOR DIRECTION: There is actor direction in scene description that would work better or be more helpful and clear as a parenthetical.**

  If one bit of scene description directly applies to how a character is to say dialogue, or if they need to say that dialogue to a specific person in a group of people, or they absolutely need to be doing something during the time they say their dialogue, it is okay to use a parenthetical for actor direction. But, do so only when it is necessary to be clear and specific with what the actor needs to do when they say that dialogue (`lowers the plunger`), or how they need to say that dialogue (`tiredly`), (`slurs`), (`whispers`), (`drunkenly`), (`perplexed`), (`disinterested`).

- **NOTE 51: PARENTHETICAL LENGTH: There are parentheticals that continue for two, three, or more lines.**

  If the information contained in a parenthetical goes on for more than one line, make sure that you have good reason for doing that. Otherwise, consider that it isn't needed, or is something that would be better off reduced, or placed in the scene description.

- **NOTE 52: PARENTHETICAL CASE: There is capitalization in the parentheticals.**

  In the parentheticals, the words are all in lower case, unless, they are commonly capitalized, such as names of people (`to Connie`), product names (`points to the Honda`), and so forth.

- **NOTE 53: PARENTHETICAL NEATNESS: There are periods, uppercase letters, other punctuation, and unnecessary gerunds ("ing" words) in the parentheticals.**

  The following is not correct. Notice the uppercase "W," the period, and the gerund:

```
                JENNY
           (Whispering.)
     The key is beneath the table.
```

  This is correct.:

```
                JENNY
           (whispers)
     The key is beneath the table.
```

- **NOTE 54: PARENTHETICAL MISPLACED: There are parentheticals on the same line as dialogue.**

Parentheticals get their own line, and should never be put on the same line as dialogue. (Unless it is a multi-cam sitcom script. In the Screenwriting Tribe workshop, we don't do multi-cam sitcom scripts.)

This is not correct. Unless it is a multi-cam sitcom script:

```
                    GARY
     (To Ed) Stop kicking me!
```

This is correct. Unless it is a multi-cam sitcom script:

```
                    GARY
               (to Ed)
     Stop kicking me.
```

The above scene would be when there are more than two people in the scene, and we would have to know that Gary is speaking to Ed, and not to another character in the scene.

- **NOTE 55: PARENTHETICAL ORPHANS: There are parentheticals after the dialogue blocks.**

Parentheticals go before the dialogue, not after it.

A parenthetical placed after the dialogue is called an orphan.

Rid your script of orphan parentheticals.

```
                    DILLON
               (parenthetical goes here)
     Actor dialogue.
               (not after dialogue)
```

- **NOTE 56: TORNADO DESCRIPTION: The scene descriptions are tornadoes of unnecessary information mixed with helpful details.**

Don't give a tornado of information in one paragraph of scene description. The scene description is what is seen on screen.

Scene description is not about the history of the characters, things, or places, and does not contain memories. `It was the seventeenth anniversary of when Marcus landed on the island where flocks of parrots flourished. Their color reminded him of his grandmother's shoes.`

Scene description is not to contain the memories, plans, or other thoughts of the characters. `As she entered, Tabitha remembered when the frog leaped onto her in second grade.`

Scene description is not to tell about the reasoning of a dog or other animal. `Barky thought he should return the ball, but didn't.`

Scene description is not to over-direct the actors (puppetry direction). `He reached for the bowl, picked up the bowl, looked at the bowl,` etc.

309

Scene description is not to charm us with your novel-writing skills. As her soft hand lovingly caressed his rough skin, he finally looked to her with remembrance.

Scene description is not to describe the dialogue that we are then going to read.

He then said that he was going to turn off the light.

>   DILLON
>   I'm going to turn off the light.

Scene description is not to repeat what is in the scene heading.

INT. SHENAI'S ROOM - NIGHT

Kevin climbs in through the window of Shenai's room.

Scene description is not to give intricate technical instruction to the camera operator.

The camera shakes as it pan's to the left as it glides into a close-up of the snake.

If you are going to include camera direction in your script, do so rarely, and only when absolutely useful, clever, and necessary to revealing something in a way that plays into the story and/or character and/or audience realization.

Using camera direction when it isn't necessary is lame.

Scene description is not to include long paragraphs of useless information.

Always remember, the viewers of the finished project will not have your script in front of them. So, don't talk to the viewers in your scene description.

Scene description should be brief, and to contain a prudent economy of words that keeps the focus on what is seen happening in the scene, and with a pace that does not bog down the energy of the read.

Aim for having almost a haiku sparsity in the wording of the description.

"It's about allowing the audience to figure it out without shoving it all in their face."

– Nat Faxon, *Downhill*

- **NOTE 57: PUPPETRY DIRECTION: The script gives over-the-top actor direction, even detailing intricate facial movements.**

I'm being over-the-top in mentioning this, because it is so common in beginner scripts.

Telling every facial expression and physical movement of the characters quickly dulls the script, slows the pacing, clutters the read, and will make it unlikely that the pros will finish your script – and more likely that they will not refer it to their boss.

Don't fill scene description and parentheticals with things like:

"She blinks and itches her nose while thinking
about..."

Or even far more ridiculous:

"She reaches with her left hand to take the wand.
Holding it in like a sword, her face contorts into
anger as her brows raise while she smiles slyly, then
her nostrils flare as anger crosses her face and she
sneers..."

I've read that sort of direction – and worse – in scene description.

I read a script in which there was scene description written something like this:

"With a crinkle of her nose, Carla raised her hand
and reached across the table to take up her lace
purse, which she unzipped, digging around among the
coins, lipstick, keys, mascara, compact mirror, and
candy to find her sunglasses, which she pulls out,
unfolds, looks at the lenses, and decides to polish
them using the table cloth. She gave Tom a dastardly
glare as Debbie up and ran quickly from the room."

What? That's not screenwriting. It's a detailed mess. It's an information dump. It's tornado description.

How would all of that be shown, unless the camera goes into her purse?

Only present what we need to know to reveal character and conflict and contention. Be clear and prim.

Displeasure crosses Carla as she picks up her lace
purse, pulls out sunglasses and cleans them with the
table cloth as she glares at Tom.

Debbie runs from the room.

Don't micromanage the actors, or over describe their expressions and movements.

"You don't want a screenplay to be too complete. Because, if a screenplay is utterly complete, there's no room for the performers. You are creating something with enough air in it that a performer can come in and fill it up. That's the trick.

You don't want to overwrite a screenplay. There has to be those gaps – and I think that that's something one really gets through experience more than anything else."
– Rebecca Miller, *The Ballad of Jack and Rose*

Simply tell an interesting story with spare, clear description, and that is rich in conflict and subtext played out by engaging characters. The actors should be able to interpret what is needed to convey the meaning of each scene through adequate displays of contention. Let the actors act.

"I learned that you really don't have any control as a writer. Waah, waah, waah. Big deal. Unless you're the director on the movie, or putting up the money for the movie, you really don't have a lot of control. As someone who's just writing scripts, you just kind of have to shrug. I have no problems or issues with screenwriting in general. It is what it is."
– Bret Easton Ellis, *The Informers*

- **NOTE 58: ANIMATRONIC DESCRIPTION: The scene descriptions are repetitive, overly detailed, and redundant.**

Clarice reaches over and grasps hold of the bottle of water and picks up the bottle of water and pours water into the crystal glass and puts the bottle of water down and picks up the crystal glass of water and drinks from the crystal glass of water...

Writing like that makes it so that your script is unlikely to be read by anyone relevant in the industry.

"Stage directions are very important to me. Very, very important to me, as the reader of scripts. If they're witty, and well written, then I know I'm in good hands. If they're cursory, or indeed banal, then I am very unwilling to read the bloody dialogue. Because, if you can't be bothered to make your screenplay the most beautiful thing you can make it – every word."
– Emma Thompson, *Sense and Sensibility*

- **NOTE 59: BODY LANGUAGE: The description unnecessarily details the body language of characters.**

While it might be tempting to include the posture and movements of characters as a way to describe their body language, don't go overboard with it. Do it sparingly, and only when truly necessary.

Let the conflict of the scenes be enough to help the actor interpret how the thing should be acted.

Sparingly describe facial movements. You might say things like, the stress draws on her face. But, going into how many times a character blinks, or that their left cheek shivers, or that one side of their lip curls – and so forth – is going overboard into micromanaging the actors with puppetry direction.

The tension, mood, and tone of the scene in relation to the story is likely enough to give the actors ideas of what emotions to display.

It may be helpful in some instances to describe how a character sits or stands, such as that they are faced away as they speak, not wanting anyone to see them cry, or that they fall to their knees.

There is a helpful way of giving some facial and body direction. However, it is easy to cross the line into overkill. It is a tender balance.

As with all other description, leave body language spare, clear, but dramatically well painted using few words.

"Writing is a form of herding. I herd words into little paragraph-like structures."
– Larry McMurtry, *Brokeback Mountain*

```
Andrew approaches the window. Pushes the curtains
aside. Stares out at the city view. Tears glide down
his cheeks.

Nancy enters. Throws a suitcase on the bed. Pulls out
a drawer. Dumps the contents into the suitcase.

Andrew opens the window. Jumps out.

Nancy falls to her knees. Claws her hair. Screams.
```

There, you have a scene rich in subtext, free of dialogue, but dramatically tells a story – or part of it – visually. With spare direction of body movements.

- **NOTE 60: DEXTERITY IN DESCRIPTION: There are descriptions of which hand a character uses to do things.**
  Unless we absolutely must know why a character is using a certain hand to do something, don't mention it.
  I write this on a night when I had read a script containing scene description indicating which hand a character was using to do things. And none of that direction was needed.
  Even if a character does things with their right or left hand, is the audience going to notice?
  Also, don't litter the script with other hand details, such as they bite at the pinky finger on their right hand. If we don't need to know the exact fingernail they bite, simply mention that the character bites a finger nail, or – more dramatically – gnaws on their thumbnail and spits out a piece.

- **NOTE 61: EXPRESSION BAGGAGE: The script is clogged with emotional expression baggage.**
  If you find it necessary to tell us every time a character laughs, smiles, blinks, scrunches their nose, rolls their eyes, frowns, licks their lips, touches their hair, takes a deep breath, squints, or otherwise uses any muscle in their face or body, you are going to lose the reader with that puppetry direction.
  Write a compelling, engaging, interesting, script filled with conflict and populated by challenged characters contending with their situations in manipulative ways that display their intentions to get what they want and/or need. If you do so, it will be clear to the actor what sorts of mindset and related expressions they will need to engage for each scene. Likely, the actor will

313

simply act, and various expressions will happen in tune with what is going on in the scenes.

If an actor has a particular physical movement that we must know about, and it plays a role in the story, mention that. For example, if one character notices that an elderly character's hand is shaking, which is an indication of physical decline, that would need to be mentioned, if it is part of the storyline. Or, some boy walks with a limp, which other children make fun of – until they are scolded, and are told that the boy has that limp because he was in a terrible car accident that killed his father and sister.

"One rule in screenwriting: Does the reader want to turn the page?"
– Leslie Dixon, *The Thomas Crown Affair*

- **NOTE 62: MIRACULOUS ACTOR SKILLS: There is description that is impossible for the actor to act out in a script that likely will not get the budget necessary to create the special effects.**

Zack gets so angry that steam rises from his forehead and the veins in his eyes intensify.

As Nancy giggles, every hair on her head turns into varieties of cosmic colors.

Tamara picks up the cat, and stares at it as her face begins to resemble the cat's face.

Don't expect to have those in your film, unless there is a CGI budget.
Be aware of the budget necessary to film what you write.

If you are writing ridiculous stuff that you think will be interesting to watch, but that doesn't do anything to make the story worth sitting through, and won't play into bigger box office returns to make up for the cost of filming them, it is unlikely that your script is going to be produced.

If you continually try to make each scene visually interesting to watch in ways that have nothing to do with the conflict and don't display the character's manipulative acts in relation to an emotional story through-line, consider that you are simply wasting your time writing a script that won't sell, and that may be too expensive to make – especially compared to how much the film is likely to bring in at the box office.

"Big budget movies can have big budget perks, but small budget movies have no perks, but what the driving force is, of course, is the script."
– Morgan Freeman, actor

"I wrote a science-fiction movie for James Cameron. The fun with that was that anything I could think up, if he liked it, he would invent it. Even if the technology didn't exist. He's so good at that stuff that there were no restraints in the storytelling."
– John Sayles, *Eight Men Out*

- **NOTE 63: DESCRIPTIONS UNTEATHERED: The scene descriptions need to be tamed.**

On one end, scene description can be much too complicated, and on the other end, it can be too vague.

Use as few words as possible to clearly describe the visual, while not trying to be overly controlling, allowing some breathing room, and knowing that the various craftspeople involved in making the film will interpret the description in their own ways. Everyone from the production designer, art director, set dresser, prop master, and the wardrobe designer, hair and makeup heads, camera, and lighting departments will work under a director with a certain budget set by producers.

"You don't necessarily have to do the job of the costume designer and the prop master and the set designer. It's more just about finding the visuals and finding these characters through dialogue."
– Jonathan Tropper, *The Micronesian Blues*

Avoid – or rarely include – technical direction in a spec script. It easily becomes clutter. Use it only when absolutely necessary for a particular scene in a way that is important for the conflict, the contention, and the character progression. Otherwise, write unencumbered by technical direction.

"Screenwriting involves an often impersonal process. Cowriters, directors, producers, everyone has a say in what you put on a page, and stories are constantly changing according to budget, actors, and commercial needs. Films are a collaborative process and are also inherently narrative and structured, so you are always working within very tight parameters."
– Chiara Barzini, *Into Paradiso*

Leave the acting up to the actors.
Leave the camera angles up to the D.P. (director of photography, who is also called the cinematographer) and their team.

"You have to understand what the story is about and then find out how to make images that work for the story."
– Michael Ballhause, cinematographer

"We all want our movies to look great visually, to be beguiling and enticing, but I think that what really defines a great cinematographer is one who loves story."
– Seamus McGarvey, cinematographer

"I believe that the best cameraperson is one who recognizes the source, the story, as the basis of their work."
– James Wong Howe, cinematographer

Leave the lighting up to the gaffer.
Leave the editing up to the editor. Simply tell the story.

315

Know that the technicalities of editing are not likely to be your choice. If you want to edit your script, you also likely have to direct and/or produce it.

Leave the directing to the director. Read a book or three about film directing.

Largely, leave the micro details of the set design up to the production designer. What they do will play into what the art director does, which plays into the hair and makeup staff, prop masters, set dressers, and other people in charge of the appearance of the production – in tune with a color palette.

Leave the wardrobe details up to the wardrobe designer, who works to stylize the wardrobe in combination with the production designer and art director.

You might mention the type of clothing a character wears, but avoid going into the types of fabrics, cuts, and textures – unless it is absolutely necessary for the story.

"You are not the costume designer. Every time you describe a piece of clothing or something in a room – any thing – ask yourself: 'Is this essential, or is it an option? Is Mary's red coat necessary? If the coat is blue, does her character change or the story fall apart?' Get rid of the options, letting our collaborators make the decisions, and retain the essentials."
– Charles Deemer, author *Screenwright: The Craft of Screenwriting*

Leave the prop specifics up to the prop master.

Do mention that there are certain necessary things in a scene, but go into detail about their color, year made, and other specifics only if it is absolutely needed for the story.

"I usually write very few stage directions. I think a lot of that is a waste of time. The art of screenwriting is in its terseness, saying a lot with a little. I have no patience when I read a script where the writer describes this guy and what he's wearing and his glasses and his hair."
– Scott Frank, *The Lookout*

I read a script that detailed the types, textures, and colors of fabric of the clothing, and also mentioned with which hand the character did things. I asked the writer if there was a reason why she included such detail. She said that is the way she saw it. I told her that it would be better to be less controlling in the scene description, and that the details of the wardrobe are best left to the wardrobe department. Unless there is a solid reason to describe which hand the character uses to do things, leave out the dexterity specifications.

Who is going to watch a movie and pay attention to if a character is right or left handed? Unless it matters to the story, don't mention it in scene description. It might matter in a sports or criminal story

"You do not have to explain every single drop of water contained in a rain barrel. You have to explain one drop – H2O. The reader will get it."
– George Singleton, *Perfect Attendance*

- **NOTE 64: SCENES LACK KINESIS: While some scenes work well as static (no or little movement) visuals, having too many scenes with little to no movement can end up being dull or uninteresting.**

While it can be good to indicate character movement in scenes, such as characters doing something like folding laundry, sweeping a floor, fixing a car, building a bonfire, playing tennis, cutting their toe nails, or other movement while dialogue or silence takes place, don't go overboard in describing every little movement.

Give us more of a general idea of what the characters are doing, rather than describing their actions in such detail that the description gets overly wordy, mechanical, and novelistic.

The opposite of scenes being too static are scenes with so much kinesis that it is difficult to follow the story.

An activity that a character is involved in, and how they do it, can have something to do with what they are thinking (but don't mention what they are thinking), what is stressing, frustrating, exciting, motivating, and otherwise engaging them, and how they relate to, contend with, and deal with their past, their present situation and relationships, and their view of the future.

Movement can also be done cleverly from scene to scene. Perhaps there is a scene that is oddly static, followed by a scene that is comically frantic. A young woman casually eating a large meal as her self-impressed date tells her that he likes his woman to be fit and active. She mildly asks the self-impressed date if he would like to go for a jog. The next scene is the young woman easily running at extreme speed as he struggles to keep up with her.

Movement "floats" from one scene to the other could include clever imagery and movements of shapes. Such as a woman is in a sports store looking at basketballs, testing one by bouncing it in the store. The next scene is a basketball being dribbled along a court by the woman in a scene of a group of people playing basketball.

Transition Floats:

Floats carry a shape, color, motion, or expression from one scene to the next scene.

A color float would be a child playing with a pink balloon. In the next scene the mother wears a pink coat. In the next, a grandmother pulls up in a pink car. But, it should all have some relevance to the story.

A stuttered float is when there is one scene between the two scenes that contain the float of a shape, color, motion, or expression.

Don't get obnoxious with trying to make floats happen from/to every scene. Maybe you will, and it will be elegant, brilliant, dramatic, comical, and/or play into the emotional through-line. Or, maybe it will come off as distractive and as trying too hard, and as obvious and clutzy.

On set, they factor ways to do floats. So, don't be overly concerned with floats while writing your script. If anything, they happen naturally – without you having to overdescribe them.

- **NOTE 65: TECHNICAL DIRECTION CLUTTER: The script is cluttered with camera and editing direction = technical direction.**

You are not the director or cinematographer. Leave the camera angles and technical specifics up to them.

"I don't put any stage directions that tell like, 'pan left,' and 'pan this way.' No. I try to write the stage directions as very descriptive of imagery, and leave the directing to the director, and the camera work to the camera guy. And just tell what you see and what you hear, and try to make the prose as telling of the tone and place as possible. So, it's a real palpable sense of where we are."
— Taylor Sheridan, *Sicario: Day of the Soldado*

You are not the editor. Leave the editing up to them.

Don't put the sound, prop, and FX in caps (flagging the words for the crew). Leave the flagged word annotations for the shooting script.

Simply write a clever, engaging script containing a story played out by interesting characters cleverly manipulating their situations.

"Camera directions isolate the reader from your protagonist. They remind us that we aren't there."
— Jeff Richards, Allied Alchemy Studios, and The Script Forge

Don't clutter your script with the technical intrusions that are camera direction (see * and ** and *** below). If you use any, be sparse.:
ANGLE ON:
BIRD EYE VIEW:
CA: or C.A.: (cutaway)
CAMERA SHAKES:
CLOSEUP ON:
CRANE SHOT:
CU: or C.U.: (close-up)
CUT-IN: (angle on one detail)
DRONE SHOT:
DUTCH TILT: (slanted angle)
ECU: (extreme close-up)
EWS: or E.W.S.: (extreme wide shot)
EYE LEVEL:
HIGH ANGLE:
LOW ANGLE:
MCU: or M.C.U.: (medium close-up)
MS: or M.S.: (midshot)
NODDY SHOT: (shows a character nod their head in agreement)
ONE POINT PERSPECTIVE:
OSS: or O.S.S.: (also over the shoulder)
OTS: or O.T.S.: (over the shoulder)
OVER THE SHOULDER:

PAN TO:

POV: or P.O.V.: (point of view) *** see below when P.O.V. (or: POV) might truly work for a scene.

PULL BACK TO REVEAL: (But, this is one camera direction that could influence a scene, and might be worth using – under certain circumstances.)

SLANTED ANGLE:

TIGHT ON:

TILT:

TRACKING: (a tracking shot)

TRACKING SHOT:

TWO-SHOT: (two characters in the frame)

VWS: or V.W.S.: (very wide shot)

WIDE SHOT:

ZOOM IN ON:

*Animated scripts can include camera direction. As Trottier points out in *The Screenwriter's Bible*, "They are being written for a storyboard artist, rather than a director."

Only include specific camera direction if it is very much absolutely positively truly necessary for the cleverness of that scene. As in: There likely will be very few times that you will indicate camera direction in a spec script.*

***Except: When including camera angles will help convey what is going on, and especially to amplify external conflict. That could include a horror movie, in which you see things through the point of view (P.O.V.) of the unseen, mysterious lurking person or creature who spies in windows, sneaks into houses, hides, or swims beneath water... killing people (See: The original [1978] *Halloween*). In other words, when you need to show a scene from a mysterious character's point of view, which is called a "phantom P.O.V.," or "phantom angle," format it as that in description:

EXT. SHEILA'S HOME - FRONT DOOR - NIGHT

PHANTOM P.O.V.: Through binoculars: Tom fails to unlock the door. Steps back to look at the upstairs bedroom window. Looks around the yard. Runs to the door, bashes through.

INT. SHEILA'S FOYER - CONTINUOUS

Tom falls in through the broken door. Smashes into a small table. A vase shatters.

Sheila points the squirt gun at him.

> SHEILA
> Why don't you knock, first?

"Here's my rule of thumb: Use an editing direction when it is absolutely necessary to understand the story, or when its use helps link two scenes in a way that creates humor or drama, or improves continuity."

– David Trottier, author *The Screenwriter's Bible*

Do not include editing direction/scene transitions (transitionary direction) in your spec script, including (see * below):

CROSS DISSOLVE TO:
CROSS FADE TO:
CUT TO:
DISSOLVE TO:
FLIP:
IRIS:
JUMP CUT TO:
MATCH CUT TO:
SCATTER CUT TO:
SHATTER CUT TO:
SMASH CUT TO:
SPIN CUT TO:
SPLATTER CUT TO:
SPLINTER CUT TO:
WAVE CUT TO:
WIPE TO:

… or whatever other imaginative term you can use for the scene transition = transitionary direction = editing direction.

*Unless, it is something like FADE TO BLACK, after a scene. Which would require another FADE IN to start the next scene.

And there may be other reasons to include a certain type of transition direction = editing direction. But, do so when it truly serves the script. And, don't go overboard with it – use it sparingly.

Saying that there is a cut, or some grand, subtle, or whimsical wording to indicate a style of a cut is not needed.

You are not going to flatter anyone, or reveal that you have deft skill in the craft of screenwriting by being creative with how you write cut, or that you include some version of the unnecessary editing direction CUT TO: after every scene – or any scene.

Including camera angles and editing direction doesn't improve your script, or make it more interesting, creative, or professional.

The management, agency, and studio readers don't need your technical direction, and might consider it an irritant, a distraction, and amateurish – and ridiculous.

The viewers aren't going to see your screenplay. All they will see is that one scene ended, and another scene started, and they will see the images framed in whatever way the camera person framed them.

Do write scenes in a way that you don't need to indicate camera or editing direction.

Don't write:
CLOSEUP ON: A drop of blood lands on the spoon.

Or:
EXTREME CLOSE-UP: A drop of blood lands on the spoon.

Simply delete the camera direction. We know that it is a close-up, because we are seeing a drop of blood land on a spoon. Obviously, it isn't a wide shot.

Do write:
A drop of blood lands on the spoon.

You also don't need to write: INSERT: before that obvious insert, which also is an E.C.U. or ECU (extreme close-up). The experienced script readers who read the script will understand it, without the technical direction.

The term "insert" has largely taken the place of the phrase E.C.U. On set, you will hear that they want to do an insert. You likely won't hear them say that they need to do an E.C.U.

I have been a hand double many dozens of times for principal actors on various TV shows, movies, and commercials. The production saves money by having a lower-paid hand double fill in for the high-paid stars. I mean, when they need to do a close-up on a character's hands doing something, such as typing, opening a lock, tying shoes, dialing a phone, etc.

If you are a grandly successful writer/director with a global following, and you are writing a script that you are going to make, and major studios want to do business with you, write the script any way you wish, Mr. Tarantino.

Two directions that could be considered editing and camera direction, and that could be used to clarify a scene that is taking place at the exact time as another scene is the INTERCUT: direction and the SPLIT SCREEN: direction used when there is a back-and-forth between or side-by-side of two locations that the audience needs to watch at the same time. If it is important that the intercut or split screen styles are to be used, the camera might need to film the scenes at particular angles while framing the subjects in a way that will make the intercut or split screen styles work. The lighting of the scenes also might need to be set up in tune with the intercut or split.

It is okay to use the intercut and split screen camera and editing direction in a spec script. But, is it needed?

Unless it's used cleverly, I'd avoid, or very sparingly use the intercut or split screen scenarios that show things going on in different locations at the same time. It does work in some films. Some films have screens that break into three, four, or more segments to show multiple locations. But, use that style when absolutely necessary and/or helpful for the story, for clarity, and for dramatic, comical, clever, or time crunch impact.

Aim to write scripts that are engaging and entertaining. If it means using the camera and editing directions to make the script work, go for it. But, make sure it is a choice that suits your script.

Otherwise, for those writing spec scripts, don't clog your script with camera and editing "technical direction." It can remove the reader from the script, remind them that they are reading a screenplay (written by an amateur), and get them into thinking about the technicalities of filming the scenes.

- **NOTE 66: INSERTS AND CLOSUEP: The script contains close-ups that are confusing, distractive, or otherwise not formatted correctly.**

  In addition to the information provided in the previous notes, learn how to format a cutaway, also called an insert or close-up of an object or thing.

  If you want to show what characters in a scene are seeing on their TV, do this:

T.V. SCREEN: Grandmother Stinson's mug shot on the news.

                   NEWSCASTER
    The suspect was last seen speeding
    from the bank in a chrome Tesla.

THE KITCHEN STAFF

collective dumbfounded stare at the T.V.

                    MELBA
    Doris, your grandmother got herself
    a reputation.

                    DORIS
    She's only trying to get my college
    tuition.

                    SHAWN
    Ten years in the state pen is more
    likely.

- **NOTE 67: CAMERA ANGLES: The writer says that they need camera angles to get their style across, and they've seen scripts online from TV shows that contain the types of camera direction that they want to put in their script.**

  Each TV series – especially those that have been in production for many seasons – has its own way of writing and formatting their scripts.

  Reading scripts from various episodic, sitcom, procedural, limited, and anthology series will show you the style of each show. It doesn't mean that the style displayed in their script is industry standard, or acceptable by anyone – other than the people who work on that show. Nor does it mean that people who read your script will understand a style that you are going for – especially if it is unique to one script that you had read.

Do what works for your script. But, know that the camera and other technical direction can also hinder the read, slow the pacing, displace the attention from the story, bury the clarity, and otherwise distract the reader.

If including the technical direction works for what you are going for, do it – if it truly is needed for the tone, mood, pacing, and style. Otherwise, consider leaving it out, and see how it reads without it.

Including technical direction could end up seeming as if the writer is over-explaining, and talking down to or trying to micro manage the D.P. (director of photography), director, and other craftspeople – and "directing from the page."

Or, not.

Maybe you are correct, and the technical direction enhances the fun of the read.

Maybe being different will help distinguish you. Limiting yourself to only what everyone else is doing might work, but maybe it will be like everyone trying to crawl into the same box. Only a certain number will fit in.

But, maybe doing things differently than industry standard could be seen as assuming and pretentious, and will turn off the decision-makers who you need for getting your script sold, filmed, edited, and distributed.

If you decide to include camera direction in your script, it's good to keep the camera direction to an absolute minimum.

The script of the film *A Quiet Place* is probably the most unusual one that you will find for a film that was produced and became a grand success. There are pages with barely any words. There are pages with large text. There are drawings.

A script containing a single graphic is that of *Arrival*. Writer Eric Heisserer wanted to be clear about what the written language of the aliens should look like, so he included a small graphic in the script. (Search that.)

- **NOTE 68: WE SEE: The script uses the term "we see,' "we now see," or other direct reference to "we" in scene description.**

Avoid using the phrase "we see" in scene description (or as editing direction). Scene description is what we are seeing. It is redundant to tell us that is it what "we" are seeing.

Using terms like "we now see" in the script might remove the reader from the story, and remind them they are reading a smarmy script.

The people who watch the film are not going to have the script in front of them to read. They will see and hear the movie.

If it is important to know that the audience sees something, but that one or more of the characters don't see that thing, simply state "Nikita doesn't see: The vampire bunny creeping up near his leg." (That could be worded: Unnoticed by Nikita: The vampire bunny creeps up to his leg.)

323

Don't put the focus on us or "we." Put the focus on the story involving the characters and things we are watching.

I read a script with the words `We clasp eyes on Henrietta sitting at the bar.` Don't write stuff like that. It would be written: `Henrietta sits at the bar.`

If you do happen to use some variety of the term `we see,` be certain that it is helpful, and not pretentious or distractive. Otherwise, delete that bedtime story phraseology.

- **NOTE 69: ADDRESSING THE SCRIPT READER: The script addresses the reader.**

Don't talk directly to the reader with author intrusions, as in:

`"Oh, reader, you are about to read a story..."`

Leave that sort of verbiage for novels. Or, if it serves the script, for clever voiceover: `"What you are about to see is something you may find hard to believe, but my grandma told me..."`

If your name is Shane Black, you can do it. (Search: Shane Black screenplays.)

Or, maybe you can do it, and it will be clever and work quite swell, and your script will be sold for millions, and you will be the next celebrity screenwriter that others will want to emulate. Or, not.

- **NOTE 70: GERUNDS ING ING ING: The writer overuses "ing" words/gerunds in description.**

Reduce the use of gerunds – and words – in description.
`Sherry is slowly walking on the sidewalk while wearing tattered clothing while passing by the mansions.`

There can be a cleverer micro to macro (small to big) visual of what we are to see first, widening out to what we see as the camera backs away – but, without mentioning camera movements – and without the gerunds:
`In tattered clothing, Sherry mozies along the sidewalk past the mansions.`

Look up: Gerund.

"–ing verbs are blah; they are boring expressions that an action is taking place. The simple present ('walks') is more immediate (than "walking"). The whole point of a film, and therefore a script, is to give us an experience; anything that distances us from that experience is bad and should go. 'Is walking / crouching / shooting / burping / assassinating' is passive and dull. Axe it."

– Jeff Richards, Allied Alchemy Studios, and The Script Forge

- **NOTE 71: PASSIVE VERBS: The writer overuses passive verbs.**
  This book can't teach you everything.
  (Search: Passive verbs.)

"There was a girl who came to me with her first screenplay. It was a good first shot. I gave her some advice. I told her, 'I want you to go home and take a yellow Marks-A-Lot, and highlight every verb in this 120-page screenplay, and then I want you to read them out loud and ask yourself, 'Can I find a stronger verb?' Characters should never enter. They should storm in, they should skulk in, they should tremble in. These are the only chances you have to create visual pictures in people's brains."
– Larry Ferguson, *The Hunt for Red October*

"The master chooses his verbs with precision and obviates the need for adverbs – 'charges,' 'lopes,' and 'scuttles' are verbs that are more than functional; they add character. Similarly, adjectives should be used sparingly, and most of all with precision."
– Amnon Buchbinder, author *The Way of the Screenwriter*

- **NOTE 72: ADVERBS: The writer overuses adverbs.**
  (Search: Adverbs.)
  Did you know that Stephen King was once a high school teacher? Read the book he wrote titled *On Writing*.

"I believe the road to hell is paved with adverbs, and I will shout it from the rooftops. To put it another way, they're like dandelions. If you have one in your lawn, it looks pretty and unique."
– Stephen King, *Children of the Corn*

- **NOTE 73: INTERJECTIONS: The script contains too many interjections in dialogue (um, ah, eh, er, um, sooo, yeah, mmmm, um,…).**
  Interjections are words or sounds that convey feelings, emotions, or attitudes, such as laziness, disappointment, surprise, nervousness, hesitation, inadequacy, and so forth.
  Don't overuse interjections in scripted dialogue. They get to be irritating and tedious to read.
  It may be best to simply let the tone and urgency of the scene dictate how the dialogue is said.
  Maybe include an interjection here and there to set a character tone and mood. But, leave the acting to the actor, and the directing to the director.
  Maybe the interjections could help, in specific situations. Such as a hilarious scene during which a fumbling character feels awkward that they are being seduced by someone vastly out of their league.
  (Search: Interjections in dialogue.)

- **NOTE 74: NAME CAPITALIZATION: Character names are in uppercase every time a character appears in a scene.**

The character name should be in uppercase one time in scene description, and that is: The first time the character appears in the script. Usually followed by an age or age range and comma, and often with some sort of simple visual description that indicates personality or character attitude and social status:

```
Across the conference table from Louella sits ANDREW
(early 40s), smirky-faced lawyer in an ill-fitted
suit.
```

To be more specific: Only capitalize the character names who have dialogue, or who are very much key to the story. Only the first time they appear in the script.

There are lead characters who do not have dialogue, such as Elisa in *The Shape of Water*. She is mute. Even though she does not have dialogue, her character name should be in uppercase the first time she appears in the script.

After the initial appearance of the character, their names are not in all uppercase in any following scene description throughout the rest of the script. Of course, only the first letter of their name remains in uppercase throughout the rest of the scene description: `Andrew`.

In character cues (where the name is above the dialogue), all of the letters of the cue names are always in uppercase:

```
                    ANDREW
          Andrew's dialogue goes here.
```

- **NOTE 75: BOLDING CHARACTER NAMES: The character names are bolded in the character cues (the names that appear above the dialogue).**

It's not necessary to **bold** the character cues.

Some writers **bold** the names of the principal characters the first time those characters appear in the script. Other writers say that doing so can be an irritant, a distraction, and unnecessary.

However, I doubt if anyone is going to dismiss your script if you **bold** the names of the principal characters the first time they appear in the script.

But, it can then be odd to some people that only some character names are **bolded** the first time they appear, and lesser character names are not bolded.

Perhaps make it easier, and simply do not **bold** the character names – anywhere in the script.

When I say **bolding** the character names the first time those names appear in the script, I mean **bolding** them in the scene description. Which, again, I advise against.

The character names absolutely should be in UPPERCASE the first time they appear in the script – but, I mean in the scene description. Do not **bold** or CAPITALIZE the character names when those names appear in the dialogue.

(To be clear: **Bold** does not mean UPPERCASE. **Bold** means thicker lettering. I've had writers confuse the meaning.)

- **NOTE 76: CASE OF CHARACTER NAMES: The character names are in uppercase in the dialogue.**

Do not put the character names in UPPERCASE when the names appear in the dialogue.

Of course, the character cues (the character names above the dialogue) should be in uppercase.

As mentioned, the names of the principal characters should be in uppercase the first time those names are mentioned in the script, in the scene description, and only the first time the character appears in the script.

Never put character names in caps/uppercase in the dialogue.

Also, don't **bold** the character names in dialogue.

- **NOTE 77: CHARACTER NAME CHANGES: The character names change halfway through the script, and it's difficult to follow.**

If you want to confuse and/or lose the attention of the reader, partway through the script, change the name of one or more of your characters.

If you have a character that changes names later in the script, when that new name starts to be used, as their character cue, put the previous name in parentheses after the new name:

TOM (ANDREW)

In the scene direction of the scene in which the new name begins to be used, it would likely be a good idea to briefly clarify that the character has a different name in that scene. TOM (formerly Andrew).

Notice that the first time that name change is clarified in the scene description, the new name is in uppercase.

I likely will be a good idea to continue with the name change clarification in the character cue throughout the rest of the script:

TOM (ANDREW)

Make sure that (if you are involved in making the film) name changes are also clear in a script that will be used to break down, schedule, and budget the script. One thing that is done during the breakdown is that a list of characters will be made, and that will help determine how much is going to be spent on the needs of the cast, including how many dressing rooms will be needed, how many makeup, hair, and wardrobe people will be needed, how many people will be eating at catering, how many on-set chairs will be needed, and so forth. Everything factors into production costs.

- **NOTE 78: CHARACTER DESCRIPTION: A character's description is deep into a scene, when the character appeared for the first time on camera earlier in the scene.**

The first time your character appears in a scene, especially if it is the first time they appear in the script, be sure to give some sort of visual that represents their physical condition, and in a way that relates to their personality or status.

```
Skipping into the room is DAISY (11), delicate and
bright as a spring flower, she sees the puppy. Stops.
Giggles unsurely...
```

Often, I read beginner scripts that describe a character deep into a scene, after the character has been in the scene, and even after the character has had dialogue.

Learn to correctly introduce characters. Reference *The Screenwriter's Bible*.

Know that when you describe a character's home, office, bike, car, clothing, and other belonging, and their neighborhood and associates, you likely also are providing clues at the character, their status, culture, education, practices, tone, mood, undercurrent, and goals – or lack thereof.

- **NOTE 79: CHARACTER IS HEARD BEFORE BEING SEEN: A character's description is included before they are on screen.**

If we hear a character who has yet to be visually present in the screenplay, only describe their appearance the first time we see them. In the description, because it is their first time appearing in the script, put their name in upper-case.

```
INT. GREENBERG LIVING ROOM - DAY

Cracking sounds are heard, plaster dust and chips
fall onto the coffee table. A large crack opens in
the ceiling. Plaster falls.

                    MARLON (V.O.)
                (gravelly voice)
          These are so good.

More cracking. More plaster dust and chips fall to
the coffee table. KABAM! To the coffee table falls
MARLON ARNOLD (40s), obese, in pajamas, bed hair,
donut in hand.

Lucy rushes in from the kitchen.

                    LUCY
                (aghast)
          You promised you'd stop eating
          donuts!
```

```
Marlon wipes plaster dust from the donut. Continues
to eat.
```

- **NOTE 80: MULTI-CAM SITCOM CHARACTER NAMES: In a multi-cam sitcom script, the writer didn't capitalize and underline the first time the character names appear in the script, but they should be.**

Sitcom scripts are formatted differently than film, short film, and one-hour drama scripts, and also differently than single-cam sitcom scripts. Upper-case and underlining is used differently. (See the sitcom section of *The Screenwriter's Bible*.)

Because there are so many formatting and time stamp issues specific to multi-cam sitcoms, the Screenwriting Tribe workshop doesn't workshop multi-cam sitcoms. Tribe does workshop single-cam sitcoms.

- **NOTE 81: SIMILAR CHARACTER NAMES: Character names are too similar in spelling and/or sound, and it is confusing.**

In April, Andy went to Arthur's wedding, where he was marrying Andrea, the sister of Annessa, who works for Annabelle, who is related to Arthur's dog sitter, Alise, who robbed Andy's Aunt Ann's liquor store to pay for the vacation she went on with Amanda's husband, Antonio, who was officiating at Arthur's wedding at Amanda's house.

Avoid using names that are of similar sounds, or start with the same letters… or that contain too many of the same letters. It confuses the reader. You don't want to confuse the reader.

If you need to find a variety of names, there are baby name books and web sites that you can use to find names. Or, open any newspaper or news site and simply choose names from the articles.

- **NOTE 82: UNNAMED CHARACTERS: The speaking characters lack names.**

Unless you have a good reason – playing into the core of the story – to use general names for speaking characters to be identified in general terms (`Man`, `Woman`, `Boy`, `Girl`, `Detective 1`, `Detective 2`), do give proper names or nicknames to the characters.

If you have an apprehension to giving the characters proper names, at least call them something that reveals more about them than a job title and a number (`Manager 1`). Consider calling them by a name that reveals their personality, stance, or attitude (`Apprehensive Manager`).

The first time that speaking character appears in the script, do put their name in uppercase (`APPREHENSIVE MANAGER`) in the scene description. After that, in scene description, do capitalized the first letters of their name (`Apprehensive Manager`). That way, the name is a bit more memorable, and applies an image, personality tone, and body language to the character.

Giving your characters names relating to how they behave and/or their intellect can also help guide the way the readers visualize your script.

Just as in life, first impressions count.

Which of the following provides a more interesting visual COP 1, or MUSTACHE COP? How about COIFED OFFICER, SLOB OFFICER, DAPPER OFFICER, OFFICER DUMB WILLY.

You can also name characters after some oddity that you see in their appearance. Or, a personality trait. That worked comically well for STIFLER'S MOM in *American Pie*, and for LARGE MARGE in *Pee-wee's Big Adventure*.

What provides more opportunity for casting guidance, without intruding on the job of the casting director (but, makes the casting easier to do), and also tells something about the character's personality that an actor can play into: WOMAN 1 or BEEHIVE HAIRDO? How about ACCOUNTANT 1, or MR. CONSTIPATION FACE? Or, DELI CLERK 3, or LOUD CLERK?

The script reader will see the characters better if you use the quirky names: A college boy named BED HAIR BOY. A door guard named BUZZCUT BADASS. A makeup saleslady named GARISH MAKEUP. A questionably unclean and perpetually smiling hippie chick named CREEPY SANDY. A cousin named BIG RED. A neighbor named DERANGED EYES. Those all work better than giving some side character a name like Bob, Lisa, Ken, Andrew, or Polly.

- **NOTE 83: OVERUSING NAMES: The dialogue is name happy.**

> BIFF
> Oh, Barbie, how are you today Barbie?

> BARBIE
> Oh, I'm good Biff. How are you today, Biff?

> BIFF
> Oh, Barbie, you wouldn't believe.

> BARBIE
> What do you mean, Biff?

> BIFF
> Well, Barbie, my car fell into a sinkhole, and my wife, Bambi, who I am divorcing, was in it.

> BARBIE
> Oh, Biff, that's terrible.

> BIFF
> Oh, Barbie, I know. Hey, Barbie, do you want to get a drink later?

```
Bambi enters, hair askew, lipstick smeared,
dress soiled. Laughs crazily. Falls to her
knees.
```

In real life, most people don't use names so often in conversation.

Next time you are around a group of people, listen to how they converse, and how often they use each other's names.

- **NOTE 84: GREETINGS: The script contains numerous scenes that unnecessarily have characters entering and greeting each other.**

```
                    FRED
        Hi, Donna, how are you today, Donna?

                    DONNA
        I'm okay, Fred. Did you have a nice day,
        Fred?

                    FRED
        Oh, yes, Donna. I tied up our boss and
        locked him in the closet. And how was your
        day, Donna?
```

No.

Unless you are writing for comical effect.

Or, maybe the way they converse has to do with how people are forced to speak a certain way in some sort of distorted culture.

Otherwise, if you don't have a good reason for the script to have numerous scenes containing greetings, avoid them.

See the comical impact of greetings in the film *Muriel's Wedding*. There are specific reasons why the characters greet each other using a certain wording and tone. It's not simply coincidental. It's no coincidence, at all. (If you saw the film, you know what I mean.)

- **NOTE 85: USELESS CHARACTERS: There are unnecessary speaking characters who don't do anything to help reveal the thoughts, desires, needs, wants, plans, expectations, contention, or other aspects of the main characters, and do nothing to move the story forward.**

If there are principal characters (characters who have dialogue) who aren't necessary for the progression of the story, delete them. If they need to be in the scene to populate it, take away their dialogue. They can be a featured background actor, void of dialogue, but still play a role in the scene. The fewer speaking roles there are, the less it will cost to film the script.

However, if a character is very involved in action, such as they have to wrestle with or retrain another character, or they are doing things like jumping up on or off of a horse, or they have to perform any sort of risky action, that would be considered a stunt – and stunt performers cost more money than background actors. Write with an eye on budgetary concerns.

331

- **NOTE 86: OVER-DESCIBED CHARACTERS: The characters are overly described to a fault, and in ways that limit casting.**

```
Debbie, a rather shapely woman of about 5 feet
five who has one crooked tooth, elfin ears, and rosy
cheeks like Santa Clause, puts shoes on her feet that
are so small they look like little girl's feet.
```

```
Daryl, who is six-feet-three-and-a-half and has a
body like a Greek God, a V-shaped back, a 30-inch
waste, 34-inch legs that are well-proportioned to his
torso length, tapered fingers, the face of a 1980s
supermodel, one blue eye and one brown, and a smile
with an amazing set of teeth...
```

No.

Give a general tone of character. Don't go into character description that adds nothing to the storyline.

Don't go into physical characteristics that would require a global casting search.

Don't be ridiculous by giving exact body measurements – unless it is absolutely truly needed for the story.

- **NOTE 87: TORNADO CHARACTER DESCRIPTION: The script is filled with tornado descriptions of the characters.**

Tornado description = a cluttered paragraph of description swirling with all sorts of details that aren't needed.

A tornado description of a character is this sort of thing:

```
In walks half-German, half-Brazilian, blue-eyed,
brunette, 6'7" LEON (35), with his chiseled jaw,
aquiline nose, $7,000 Brioni suit, $2,700 Berluti
slip-ons covering his imported silk socks, and
diamond-encrusted $28,000 Altiplano watch that was a
gift from his fiancé. He stops and looks around the
restaurant.
```

The casting director doesn't need to know that much detail about a character. Who is cast in the role is less up to the writer, and more up to the casting director, director, producer, investor, studio, and others. So, skip the micro-description that only results in a tornado of useless information. The script might also be restyled for a certain successful actor.

Hint: We wouldn't know how he obtained that watch, unless we saw it being given to him, or he mentions where he got it, or another character mentions where he got it, or there is voiceover telling us where he got it. It isn't likely that we will need to know that his socks have been imported, or that they are silk – or anything about his socks.

That same character description can be reduced to this visual:

```
In walks stunning LEON (35), tall, exotically
handsome, expensively dressed. He scans the
restaurant.
```

That's less than half the length of the tornado description, and likely provides all we need to know to formulate the character's appearance in our imagination.

If it is truly necessary to the storyline, mention his nationality, hair color, eye color, etc. – especially if it is important that he appear to be of a certain mix and coloring. Such as: One character is waiting for an arranged dinner date who she has never seen, but she was told that the date is tall, half-German and half-Brazilian, with blue eyes, a chiseled jaw, and brunette hair, etc.

Two of my scripts do mention character hair color. In both cases, it plays into plot twists and confusion about who is who as in some scenes their face isn't seen. In one case a character is seen from a distance in a certain location, but the viewer would not be sure which character it is – until late in the script, which reveals something important about an event, trust, motive, and other matters. In the other case, the hair color has to do with a specific twist in the audience perception about one of the other characters.

- **NOTE 88: WARDROBE: There are unnecessary and lengthy descriptions of the character's wardrobe.**
  Give simple character descriptions. Enough to create a visual in the mind of the reader.

  If a character is wearing something that needs to be mentioned in relation to the story, do that. Otherwise, use few words when describing what a character wears.

  Consider that it isn't necessary to mention details of character clothing. The reader will pretty much guess what a haggard, punker coffee house worker is wearing, what a disco-era roller skater is wearing, what a 1950's business person is wearing, what a car mechanic is wearing, what a contemporary-era judge is wearing, and so forth.

  If a character needs to wear something unusual, and it relates to the storyline, mention that. For example, if the pilot of a jetliner is in anything other than standard pilot wardrobe, mention that. But only if it is necessary for her or him to be in out-of-the-ordinary wardrobe.

  I read a screenplay that mentioned how many weeks a character owned a hat – as if that mattered to anything at all. The only way we would know how many weeks he owned the hat is if he said so, someone else said so, or there was voiceover saying so. Or there was some sort of visual that indicated how old the hat was, perhaps – for some specific reason – the hat featured a tag with a date on it from September, and it was obvious that the scene was happening on Halloween. Or, the man is trying to return the hat to the store where he purchased it, and the store worker mentions that they discontinued those hats last season – and that reveals a story twist.

"While some writers may opt to insert some thoughtful, choice novelized lines into their feature spec or original TV pilot script, for the most part I prefer keeping action lines just for that: Visuals. Economical. Action. Therefore, refrain from providing backstory in your action lines, telling us what a character thinks or feels, or explaining to the reader something that took place at some point in the story, but wasn't included in the script."
– Lee Jessup, screenwriter career consultant, LeeJessup.com

I read a script that mentioned the type of fabric that a character's dress was made of, and that it had something to do with her grandmother. That detail had nothing to do with the character, conflict, contention, goal, need, or want. It had everything to do with the writer over-writing, over-describing, and writing novelistically – and, amateurishly.

"As a producer and script consultant, I continually remind my clients that scripts cannot read like novels, because they are a visual medium and must rely on images, action, dialogue, etc. – more so than lengthy paragraphs of prose. Scripts must include detail in order to transport the reader to a specific time and place, but finding the right balance is key. Excessive details, if not modulated, can reveal a lack of discipline where the writer has become too enamored of his or her descriptions. Frequently, less seasoned writers will include a preponderance of minute details and stage directions throughout their screenplays, which become distracting and prevent the potential buyer from immersing him or herself in the characters and situations."
– Wendy Kram, LAForHire.com

If it is important for the reader to know that a car mechanic is wearing a tutu – or that any character is wearing some unusual bit of clothing – mention it.

Maybe that mechanic lost a bet, or his daughter made the tutu, and asked him to wear the tutu to work, so the he did. It would work to reveal what sort of person that car mechanic is – that they would do such a thing for fun. Or, maybe that mechanic is challenging local culture, or community standards, or is protesting something that a local homophobic, closet-case preacher said. Or maybe they spent all night at a rave, where they dressed oddly, and felt like going in to work that way.

Or, the car mechanic is female, and she heard some other worker say something negative about having to work next to a female mechanic, and that fixing cars isn't a job for women, and that women should be doing stuff like being waitresses or teaching ballet classes.

- **NOTE 89: OVERDESCRIBED SET: The script contains lengthy descriptions of a room or setting.**

Unless there is a specific reason to go into detail about certain types of furniture, rugs, chandeliers, moldings, planters and the plants in them, and so forth, leave out the details.

Rather than detailed setting description, provide brief details like "sleek office," "ramshackle furniture," "fancy, eighteenth century American antiques," and "sparsely furnished ghetto apartment," and the reader will get the idea.

Don't clutter scene description with stuff we don't need to know.

I recently read a script that described the type of wood that the office furniture was made of. There was no reason for us to know that.

A cherry wood cantilevered end table, a maple counter top, an amber-stained pinewood dresser. What? Why is that in the scene description?

"Not a wasted word. This has been a main point to my literary thinking all my life."
– Hunter S. Thompson, *Fear and Loathing in Las Vegas*

I read a script that not only described the colors of furniture, but mentioned who bought the various pieces of furniture. There was no reason for us to know the colors of the furniture. And there was no reason for us to know that the kitchen table was purchased by the grandmother before her first baby was born. We wouldn't know when the table was purchased by the grandmother, unless a character says so. If we do not need to know that sort of detail, delete it – and save it for the novel.

You are not the production designer, art director, set decorator (scenic designer), wardrobe designer, hair stylists, or makeup artists. Leave micro details of the appearance of the production up to those who have those jobs.

Use simple, clear, basic wording to give an idea of a setting.

This is simple and clear:

```
A threadbare, filthy sofa sits among claustrophobic
clutter. Fruit rots on the battered coffee table.
Plastic grocery bags are taped over the broken
windows.
```

- **NOTE 90: OVERDESCRIBED SCENERY: Scenery is described to no end to create a cinematic vision that reads more like a novel written by a delusional person with grand ideas of how their script is going to be made exactly as they write it.**

Again, be basic – but clear – with the setting description. It's unlikely that the location scout, production designer, art director, set decorator, and set dresser will need to know much more detail than that.

This is simple and clear:

```
The half-burned, one-room schoolhouse and a charred
oak tree are all that remain on the scorched land.
Distant smoke nearly blocks out the orange sun.
```

"The script is what you dreamed up. This is what it should be. The film is what you end up with."
– George Lucas, *The Mandalorian*

- **NOTE 91: VEHICLE DESCRIPTION IS OVER-THE-TOP: Excessive description of a car/truck model, make, paint, tire brand, year, wear and tear, and so forth.**

I once read scene description that went something like this:

```
Biff exits the diner and approaches his 1978 cosmic
blue Ford Camaro with yellow-tipped red flames
painted along its side and the shiny spokes on the
tire rims and the white lettering on the tires are
slightly dusted from his earlier trip through the
dirt road up to his uncle's house
```

What?

Ford doesn't manufacture the Camaro. It's a Chevy. Do your research to make sure that you do not make those types of errors.

Why do we need to know the colors of the flames?

The description could be cut down to this:

```
Biff exits the diner and approaches his dusty 1970s
mint Chevy Camaro hot rod.
```

- **NOTE 92: SONG TITLES: Exact song titles are listed playing in each scene.**

Unless you are assured that you can get the rights to a certain song that must be playing in a scene, don't mention an exact song.

If we need to know that type of music is playing, mention that. 1970s disco. 1950s Cuban jazz. 1980s boy band tunes.

```
Bossa Nova plays as Don smiles and slow dances while
cuddling the stuffed toy dog.
```

"A writer client of mine made the mistake of using established song lyrics in his script, basically quoting the whole song. The song was an integral part of the script. He then asked my opinion. I told him that, depending on the context, a songwriter might well be outraged at such use. You should be aware that it is customary to license song rights for movies. It is quite a business, so you should not plan on making use of someone else's song or any other material, for that matter, as a key part of the script, or any other material you're planning to copyright. That is not to say that you won't be able to get permission. But, if someone else's work is the basis of your script,

such as 'Ode to Billie Joe,' and you use only the words from the song in the title, be sure to get permission, first. Otherwise, your writing may be for naught. If the lyrics are incidental, on the other hand, then you can always change the song if you run into trouble. For purposes of showing the script (not selling it), you are probably not going to get sued – although, technically, it is infringing. Beware of the problem."
– Stephen F. Breimer, Esq., author *The Screenwriter's Legal Guide*

"You should know that people in the Hollywood script development community – all the way from top executives to interns and script readers who provide coverage – have been trained to think this when they see a spec script which includes an existing recorded song: Amateur writer."
– Scott Myers, GoIntoTheStory.BlckLst.com

"The negation of song rights is an arduous, unpredictable, expensive process. It is doubtful that Led Zeppelin will give up their song rights for your cheeseburger scene.
No one should get so attached to a particular song that it becomes essential to the film. It's much cheaper and much less trouble for the producer to hire someone to write original music."
– Pamela Buchmeyer, Lone Star Screenwriting Competition

- **NOTE 93: VOICEOVER / OFF SCREEN / OFF CAMERA: The script misuses V.O and O.S. and O.C.**
V.O. (voiceover) is when a character's voice is heard over the scene, as in narration. The voice is heard as if we are to hear them think, read us a letter, or tell us things that we need to know to understand the story, or the history of blatantly or subtly manipulative contentious acts of the character – or other characters – and their experiences in ways that will get us up-to-date, build the conflict, advance the story, and engage us.

"The whole purpose of screenwriting is to convey everything through action and dialogue and not explanation and exposition. To me, there are movies where voiceover works really well because it does something more than exposition; it actually becomes a tonal element of the movie."
– Jonathan Tropper, *Harvey*

Don't include voiceover, unless it is truly needed. Limit the voiceover to what we need to know. Don't tell us what we already know, or what we will know by watching the scene.

"Bad dialogue tends to spray out information in every direction, whereas smart dialogue sneaks the facts in while you're otherwise entertained."
– John August, *Aladdin*

V.O. can also be used next to a character cue when they are being heard over a telephone, walkie talkie, intercom, doorbell speaker, or other device.

337

```
                    JOAN (V.O.)
          Darling, did you get the aged sour dough?

Heidie eyes the loaf of rye bread.

                    Heidie
          What if we used a darker grain?
```

O.S. (off screen) is when a character is at the location, perhaps around the corner in a hallway, or taped inside a cardboard box, and we can hear them talking, but we can't see them. This could be when someone sits in their kitchen, and they hear another character who is outside in the yard shouting at a neighbor, but we can't see the person whose voice we hear – because, they are off screen. But, you can also use V.O. for that.

O.C. (off camera) can be replaced with O.S., including when a person is only heard on a phone, but is at a different location. O.C. is considered archaic.

Writers mostly use V.O. for the dialogue said over a phone or other electronic device. Do that.

- **NOTE 94: CLICHES: The script is filled with clichés like, "The thought hits her like a ton of bricks," or, "He freezes like a deer stopped in front of headlights."**

I have read more than one script in which one character gives or offers another character some sort of meat. And the other character – who happens to be a vegan – says something about meat being murder.

Don't have your characters say clichés that put them in such a stereotypical hole that you lose the audience.

Avoid dialogue that plays into stereotypes – unless you are going for social commentary, or using it for other reasons. Or, it is a biography, and you are using exact words – such as from what was said in a court hearing.

- **NOTE 95: STEREOTYPES: The script is filled with all sorts of stereotypes that don't work for the genre.**

"The fundamental problem of a stereotype, beyond the fact that it is usually a cliché and often offensive, is that it obliterates the distinction between outer characteristics and inner life. It is a kind of annihilation of character. I find the example of the decrepit old fart emblematic, because it sees age purely as a process of decay, rather than a refinement of character – which age also is, for better or worse."

– Amnon Buchbinder, author *The Way of the Screenwriter*

Is it going to work for your script, or cheapen it, by including a hippie in a tie-dyed shirt, having a Beverly Hills woman carrying a tiny dog, putting a nylon stocking over the face of a bank robber, having a pot-smoking Jamaican spewing philosophy, describing a person with a certain accent as "cheap" or "trashy" (be careful about stereotyping nationalities), or having a blond woman character say blatantly dumb things while she is apparently unaware of what her ample cleavage is doing to the menfolk?

Unless you are going for social commentary, eccentric displays, ridicule, or using stereotypes in some other specific characterization that serves a purpose, be careful of cheapening your work with stereotypes.

"When trying to create authentic characters, remember that specifics are the kryptonite that destroys stereotypes."
– Robin Swicord, *The Curious Case of Benjamin Button*

- **NOTE 96: SUBJECTIVE AND OBJECTIFYING GAZE: The script lacks an understanding of its scopophilia.**
If all of your female characters are objectified as they are described as "pretty," "sexy," and they seem only to be there for some simplistic potential sex conquest way, reconsider how you are describing the characters, how they are to be portrayed, and why they are there. (Search: "Laura Mulvey, *Visual Pleasure and Narrative Cinema*," and "scopophilia.")

Similarly, if you are reversing the situation, and only presenting male characters as sex objects, eye candy, breeding samples, dumb hunks, or one-note coifed things, consider that your script is flatlining.

You know that scene describing the sexy, smoking hot waitress, receptionist, secretary, cashier, stewardess, nurse, etc.? That cinematic representation of females has already been in thousands of other scripts.

Why would you write a principal character who is only in the scene for appearance? What is their relevance to the story? Write valid characters.

"When I watch a movie, someone's beauty isn't what engages me, it's what's going on internally. And I imagine it's what the audience thinks, too."
– Toni Collette, actor

The objectified character that has been used in so many scripts is something like this: A smoking hot darling with ample breasts challenging her blouse buttons, and who happens to wear RPGs (rape prevention glasses [a term that could be considered offensive, or plain pathetically humorous – and should only be used if everyone knows it is obviously meant to be that stupid way – or is part of the story]) that disguise her hotness. Now, all they need is to cast a perceived young bombshell. She is put there for her shell. Her mind doesn't matter. Put her hair in a bun, put her in the glasses, a tight blouse and a body-hugging skirt. There you have the objectified librarian, secretary, doctor, teacher, or cashier. Be sure to have that hair bun unravel at about the same time she removes the glasses. And cast a male actor who is twenty-five – or more – years older than her to play her love interest... because that's always (not) believable. (Search: Age gaps in movies.)

An objectified male character might happen to lose his shirt, revealing his 8-pack abs, and is unaware of the attention his physique triggers.

Objectified characters would work in a comedy ridiculing Hollywood, as social commentary, as a comical diversion, or otherwise blatantly mocking the situation.

"There has always been an obsession with youth and beauty. What's missing is the equal obsession with respect for older people and their wisdom, knowledge, and courage."
— Julie Christie, actor

"Women of a certain age are underrepresented on our screens, and I'd like to change that."
— Bruna Papandrea, producer

- **NOTE 97: SEX AND NUDITY: The script contains random or meaningless make-out or otherwise sex scenes, and/or blatant nudity.**

If you are relying on sex scenes and/or nudity to hold the audience's attention, reconsider how your story is going to hold an audience.

If your script calls for nudity and/or sex scenes, consider what you are asking of the actors, and how it could limit both the film's distribution and the audience's level of comfort.

Don't try to compete with porn. If people want to see that, they will. They don't need your movie to satisfy their desire for elicit imagery.

If your film's main draw is the sex or nude scene, you must not be much of a writer.

Having nudity and sex scenes can limit where your film is distributed. You are eliminating the family market, and certain cultures.

By including nudity and sex scenes, your film marketing will be to get those who can see it. Certain countries won't allow it, and that could be a problem in the global marketplace – limiting who will distribute your work. If you don't know by now, the global market is where the big movies make their money.

A film containing sex and nudity is automatically a *segmented film*, as it will be for a certain segment of theatergoers – while others are shut out. Consider that a *four-quadrant film* could be more marketable. That is, a film that can be viewed by young, old, males and females, and families.

With nudity and sex scenes, you aren't going to get certain actors – or a certain level of talent.

If you want to make something ugly, and blatant, and crass, and degrading, and gross, consider what it might do to your career. Will you be proud of it later in life?

"I don't write fights or eye-stretching sex scenes. On the whole, I'm interested in what's going on in their minds, rather than in their beds. It's all about people's mental journeys. That's what interests me. How did they get from A to B?"
— Julian Fellowes, *Vanity Fair*

I can think of one case where the nudity worked along with the story, and it wasn't blatant nudity. It was on network TV. It was tame, but disturbing. It was in the 1970s miniseries *The Holocaust*. It had to do with how the Jewish people were treated in extremely disgusting, dehumanizing, and horrifying ways, having to line up naked before they were sent into the gas chambers.

- **NOTE 98: NOVELESQUE DESCRIPTION: The scene description contains all sorts of words that don't need to be there.**

If you are over-describing things, and writing wordy/novelistic scene description, you are displaying how amateurish you are. You are not giving the reader the benefit of the doubt that they are capable of understanding the scene. You are filling your script with description that slows down the pacing, dilutes both the conflict and acts of contention, and obliterates subtext.

"Whenever you write, whatever you write, never make the mistake of assuming the audience is any less intelligent than you are."
– Rod Serling, *Requiem for a Heavyweight*

Write precisely and clearly, with only the words needed to paint the visual of the scene in the reader's mind. Do so while believing that the reader is at least as intelligent as you are.

If you are writing a scene that needs some explaining to get what needs to be conveyed, again: Do it with as few words as possible: Simple, clear, visual scenes rich in subtext and with contention in response to the conflict.

- **NOTE 99: EXCESSIVE BUDGETARY NEEDS: The script contains badly-written, complicated description that would take days – and loads of money – to film.**

```
Louis and ChiChi sling from the bar and onto the
crowded dance floor, where they dance a little, then
say hello to their neighbors sitting at a table, then
go make their way through the crowd to get outside
and have the doorman call a taxi, and realize they
left ChiChi's purse in the bar, but they can't get
back inside. So, the doorman has to call the bar
manager, who isn't answering his phone. Suddenly, a
car crashes into a nearby fire hydrant, washing away
ChiChi's makeup and wig, and a 50-foot lizard
approaches.
```

What?
No.
Unfortunately, that isn't too much of a stretch from what I have read in what some people call a screenplay.
Don't write like you're a rambling drunkard getting lost in a story that seems to lack meaning.

Filming that paragraph would require a dozen camera and lighting setups, would take days to film, require a variety of background actors, need stunts and FX, a street closure, and a car to crash, and CGI (computer-generated imagery – unless you can find a trained 50-foot lizard agreeable to what you need for the scene). But, what does it all mean to the conflict and contention, and for conveying whatever that story is with an emotional through-line?

If you want to see a well-done, conflict- and subtext-rich bar scene with a couple caught up in a contentious-saturated mess of a relationship, see the nightclub scene in Spike Lee's *Summer of Sam*.

- **NOTE 100: FLAGGING WORDS: The script contains capitalization of set dressing, props, FX, and foley sounds (post production sound effects) – also known as "flagging the crew" who handle those needs.**

A spec script is not a shooting script. You don't need to flag certain words by putting them in uppercase.

A shooting script (not a spec script) contains props and sounds in uppercase because it is meant to cue the props and sound departments to take notice of what is needed for that scene. Flagging by uppercasing certain words is also a way to help factor the budget of the film, by highlighting what is financially needed to film each scene.

Don't litter your script with the shout outs to the sound, props, set dressing, and FX crew. The crew will not be reading your spec script.

Capitalizing the set dressing, props, and sounds might only serve to irritate the management and other readers, and reveal that you are a beginner.

Don't consider putting the sounds in uppercase to be a style, as if you are writing a comic book with the BAMs and the PUNCHes and the OUCHes and the SMACKs and the SLAPs and the EXPLOSIONs in uppercase. You might think that it appears clever and fun (like the 1960s *Batman* series). But, it only makes your writing appear amateurish. If it is an important sound, sure, go ahead and put it in upper-case. But, don't overdo it.

Simply write spec scripts in spec script formatting, as detailed in *The Screenwriter's Bible* and *Dr. Format Tells All*.

- **NOTE 101: SOUND EFFECTS INDICATED WITH SFX: The script contains "SFX" before sounds, as if the sound, foley, and FX crew need to take note of that, and are going to be reading your spec script (they aren't).**

It is archaic to tag a sound with SFX. Leave that out.

The script will be formatted for sound cues when the production script is annotated. That is when the sounds will be (flagged by putting them) in uppercase (and they won't be tagged with SFX).

Rarely should you put sounds in uppercase. Only do so when a sound is very important or must be noted. Otherwise put the sounds in lower case.

Also, don't put the sounds in italics. And, don't underline the sounds.

That said, if you really, REALLY need to influence a word in description, underline it – rather than italicize it. Be prudent about it. If you do too much of that, it ends up losing its effectiveness, and becomes a distraction.

- **NOTE 102: DISTRACTIVE CAPITALIZATION: The script is littered with unnecessary and distractive capitalization.**

As mentioned, don't put props, set dressing, and (rarely, but only important) sounds in uppercase lettering.

I read a script yesterday that had all of the sounds, all of the props, some set decoration or dressing (chairs, coffee table, etc.), and certain words in dialogue in uppercase. It wasn't easy to read. Stuff like that takes the reader out of the film, and breaks the fourth wall, as in: "Here we are reading a screenplay, written by someone who has some work to do."

"All readers come to fiction as willing accomplices to your lies. Such is the basic goodwill contract made the moment we pick up a work of fiction."
– Steve Almond, author *William Stoner and the Battle for the Inner Life*

Other than the FADE IN, the scene headings, the first time a speaking character's name appears in a script, the character cues (where the character name is above the dialogue), certain formatting needs, and THE END at the end of the script, there are very few reasons to use uppercase lettering.

One of the few reasons to use capitalization is to indicate where words are to appear on the screen, which means that the words are to be superimposed. In that case, on its own line, you indicate it with:

SUPER: "Waikiki, April, 1973."

Or, for those who like to use the entire word for clarity:

SUPERIMPOSE: "Waikiki, April, 1973."

Or, for those who like using this word, instead of SUPER::

CHYRON: "Waikiki, April, 1973." (Or, use CAPTION: instead of CHYRON:)

Note: As in the examples, any words that the audience is meant to read should be put inside quotation marks.

Some people put the superimposed words in uppercase. Why? It's not necessary. Formatting them as they are in the above example is sufficient.

Don't include capitalized words in the parentheticals – other than the first letter of character names, and things that would otherwise have letters in uppercase.

                    DAVINA
              (whispers to Maude)
         We need to do this.

343

If you must put any word in dialogue in uppercase to indicate inflection, do it sparingly – and consider underlining, instead. The scene conflict and reasoning of the characters displayed in subtle or bold expressions of contention should speak without you having to capitalize or underline dialogue. If you indicate inflection in dialogue more than sparingly, it gets to be obnoxious, and appears as if you are trying to micromanage or direct the actors ("direct from the page," or engage in puppetry direction).

To clarify the issue of what is correct to capitalize, underline, or italicize in a script, see *The Screenwriter's Bible* and *Dr. Format Tells All*.

- **NOTE 103: OPENING ON BLACK SCREEN WITH OR WITHOUT SUPERIMPOSED WORDS: The opening is confusing in how it seems to indicate that words are to appear on screen.**

If you want the film to open with a black (or color, haze, or pattern) screen with words on it for the audience to read, you can format it in one of the following ways, which all mean the same thing. As always, whenever there are words for the audience to read, put them inside quotation marks.:

```
ON BLACK: "Dublin, 1943"

OVER BLACK: "Dublin, 1943"

BLACK SCREEN: "Dublin, 1943"

SUPER OVER BLACK: "Dublin, 1943"

CHYRON OVER BLACK: "Dublin, 1943"
```

If you want the black screen to be present for a moment before the words appear, skip a line, then the put the words that are to be read by the audience.

```
BLACK SCREEN

SUPER: "Dublin, 1943"
```

Or, use CHYRON:, or CAPTION:, and add any sounds or V.O. dialogue:

```
CHYRON: "Dublin, 1943" or, CAPTION: "Dublin, 1943"
```

```
                    CONNOR (V.O)
          Every night, another bottle.
```

Then, put:

```
FADE IN.
```

Then, write a standard formatted scene, such as:

```
EXT. DOLAN'S PUB - NIGHT

Relentless drizzle soaks the façade of the old pub
and sidewalk. A bottle shatters against the door.
```

If you are not going to superimpose words on the black screen, but want a pause, with sound, write the sound to be heard during the black screen:

```
BLACK SCREEN

An echo chamber of a woman's laughter gets loud.
Then, fades to…

Silence.

PRE-LAP: Whimpers of a dog.


FADE IN:

EXT. DEXTER'S BACKYARD - DAY

The feet of a whimpering golden retriever dig into
dry dirt next to a distressed wooden fence.
```

The term `PRE-LAP:` is meant for hearing the sound of something that – or a character's voice who – is then going to be part of the next scene.

- **NOTE 104: UNDERLINING: The script contains underlined words.**

Rarely – if ever – do you underline a word in a script – unless it is a TV sitcom script, which has a different set of formatting rules (see *The Screenwriter's Bible* and books about writing sitcoms).

One case that could be acceptable for underlining is when you absolutely must indicate that a word in dialogue is stressed more strongly than other words. Do that rarely, or never.

Otherwise, avoid underlining anything in a script. (Unless it is a TV multi-cam sitcom script – which do contain specific underlined words.)

Avoid underlining words in dialogue to stress that actors are to say them in a particular manner. The tone, mood, stress, conflict, contention, motives, and concerns within a scene should be obvious enough to indicate that the words are to be said with a certain inflection.

Leave the actors alone to do their acting. Don't try to micromanage them. You aren't the director. Again, don't "direct from the page."

Let the director direct the actors.

Do not expect to see your script filmed exactly the way it appears in your brain. It won't be. But, you might be pleasantly surprised by the final product.

"It's not so much that I enjoy screenwriting, though mostly I do, but the difference is, with adaptations, somebody else has done the hard part – made up a story, provided the characters."
– Tom Stoppard, *Empire of the Sun*

Consider the time when Anne Rice was appalled when she heard that Tom Cruise had been cast to play Lestat in the film adaptation of her book *Interview with the Vampire.* Rice said, *"The Tom Cruise casting is so bizarre. It's almost impossible to imagine how it's going to work."* But, when Rice saw the film, she wrote, *"From the moment he appeared, Tom was Lestat for me."* She said that the film is *"What I dreamed it could be."*

"A movie is not a book. If the source material is a book, you cannot be too respectful of the book. All you owe to the book is the spirit."
– Richard Price, *The Color of Money*

Be careful about what you say relating to how your story is being made into a film. Don't go around trash talking the producers, director, or actors to paint grotesque views of them, as your words will be remembered, and how you deal with the situation can impact your career. Hopefully, you will be quite satisfied. If you aren't pleased with the film, don't get stuck in your disappointment, keep busy writing, polishing, and selling other scripts. Otherwise, you will be stuck in the past – and might spoil your future.

- **NOTE 105: BOLDED WORDS: The script contains bolded words in scene description, dialogue, and/or parentheticals.**
  Don't **bold** words in description or dialogue in a spec screenplay.***
  Ever.* (*see below)
  Unless you want to appear as an amateur.
  You might say that you saw a **bolded** word in a script that you saw online, or in a script that someone else wrote. Leave it up to others. Leave it up to certain TV shows to **bold** words in scripts of shows that are currently in production, as it might be the style used on that particular set.
  Don't **bold** the scene headings in your spec script.* (*see below)
  Don't **bold** words in the scene description of your spec script.
  Don't **bold** the character cues in your spec script.* (*see below)
  Don't **bold** the parentheticals in your spec script.
  Don't **bold** words in the dialogue in your spec script. (If you feel that you must put inflection on certain words in dialogue, consider underling them, and do so sparingly.)
  Don't **bold** words in your spec script.* (*see below)
  If you want to, you can **bold** the title on the title page, and…* (*yes, see below)
  *If you like, you can **bold** the scene headings and the subheadings, as that is one style. Doing so could make it so that the reader can easily tell when a scene begins and when there is a location change within a scene (subheading). However, if you choose this style, make sure that every scene heading and every subheading is bolded so that the entire script is consistent.
  You can also, if you bold the scene headings and subheadings, also bold the character cues, and the superimposed words tag (either use SUPER: or CHYRON:).
  And, with that, you can also bold FADE IN: and THE END.

If you bold `FADE IN:` and the headings, subheadings, character cues, the `SUPER:` or `CHYRON:` or `CAPTION:,` and `THE END`, make sure you do it right, and everything that is supposed to be bolded in that style is bolded. I tend to like that style, as it looks sharp and clear. However, it is more work to go through the script and bold them all. Know this: Some people don't like it.

- **NOTE 106: TEXT MESSAGES: The text messages for the audience to read are not formatted correctly.**

Another reason to italicize dialogue is when the dialogue is of the words in a text message, as italicizing is one style to indicate that dialogue words are text messages. The production can decide if they will also be voiceover.

But, format the text messages as they are below, and skip italicizing.

Be sure to put the on texted wording inside of quotation marks. (Whenever words, headlines, dates, times, or words from a note or letter appear on screen for the viewers to read, include quotation marks.)

`Marian tries the door. Locked. Pulls out her cell phone.`

`PHONE SCREEN: TEXT FROM AMBER: "Key beneath potted plant."` (or, you can also delete the words: `PHONE SCREEN:`)

`Marian tilts the pot. Gets the key. Unlocks the door.`

You can also format the text this way (deleting the `PHONE SCREEN:`):

`AMBER'S TEXT: "Key beneath potted plant."`

You don't need to type "`BACK TO SCENE`" after showing the text. Use of `BACK TO SCENE` in such cases is nothing but clutter, a distraction, and unnecessary. It's obvious that we are then going back to showing what Marian is doing, because there is scene description telling us what we see.

How that text appears on the screen is up to the director, likely in cooperation with the editor – and producer. They might show a close-up/insert of the cell screen. Or, they might show Marian looking at her cell phone while a "text bubble" or chyron appears on the screen with the texted words. Or, it could be that the text words are superimposed on the screen:

`SUPER. AMBER'S TEXT: "Key beneath potted plant."`

I wouldn't get too technical in the script about how the text appears on the screen. If it is truly in tune with the tone of the film, you can indicate:

`BUBBLE OF AMBER'S TEXT: "Key beneath potted plant."`

Or, use the term `CHYRON:` or `CAPTION:,` instead of `BUBBLE OF...`

`CHYRON: AMBER'S TEXT: "Key beneath potted plant."`

I like the one above, rather than the following:

CHYRON OF AMBER'S TEXT: "Key beneath potted plant."

The same can be used for on-screen messaging: when two people are sitting at screens in different locations. Replace the word TEXT with the words SCREEN MESSAGE. (You can always use CAPTION: instead of CHYRON:)

If the text or messaging is lengthy, format it like this with fewer indicators:

CHYRON: SHAWN'S TEXT: "Waddup?"

CHYRON: LEO'S TEXT: "UR awake?"

SHAWN: "No. I'm sleep txtg. Haha."

LEO: "Eye got the job. I'm moving 2 Cleveland."

SHAWN: "Brown's fan now?"

LEO: "Go! Browns!"

SHAWN: "U bish."

You can also format a text as dialogue, like below, using italics, but not putting quotation marks on the texted words. But, the following can be less clear than if you had formatted the texts as they are above. Also, because italics are not so obvious in the various types of lighting where things are filmed, it can be pretty useless to italicize dialogue.

> SHAWN (TEXT)
> *Waddup?*

For more on this issue, see David Trottier's books.

- **NOTE 107: CHARACTERS COMMUNICATING THROUGH SCREEN TECHNOLOGY: The script's formatting of screen communication is confusing.**

For Skype, Zoom, or Facetime, or otherwise scenes in which characters are communicating through screen technology (computer screens, cell phone screens, etc.), and one character is seen on the screen technology during a scene, format their character cue this way:

> TIMOTHY (ON ZOOM)

Or:

> TIMOTHY (ON SCREEN)

If the conversation switches around, from one location to the other as they communicate through screen technology, use subtitles to indicate the switch in location:

TIMOTHY'S BEDROOM

He tilts his wrist to the screen so that Charmichael can see the lesion.

```
                    DR. CHARMICHAEL (ON SCREEN)
        Yes, that does appear to be a lesion. When
        did you first notice it?
```

DR. CHARMICHAEL'S OFFICE

She looks through a chart on the desk.

```
                    TIMOTHY (ON SCREEN)
            Two days ago.
```

She pulls a paper from the file, holds it up to the screen.

```
                    DR. CHARMICHAEL (ON SCREEN)
        The chart does note a past occurrence.
```

- **NOTE 108: TITLE CARD AND TITLE CUES: The script has title card and/or indicates credit cues.**

There is likely no reason to include where to place the title card, or for when to roll or end the movie credits. Doing so is usually stepping out of bounds.

Title cards and credit cues –and the opening sequence of them on screen – are technical directions to leave out of a spec script.

If you include a title card, have a good reason for doing so. Otherwise, doing so can be distractive, and be viewed as controlling, out-of-bounds, and breaking the fourth wall.

When the film is edited, there will be decisions made as to where and how the credits will appear on screen. That is not your job.

A friend did write a script that indicated where the title sequence started and ended. But, he was also the producer, had funding, a director, and star attached, and a big hand in what ended up on screen.

- **NOTE 109: SCENE NUMBERS: The script contains scene numbers.**

Do not number the scenes in a spec script.

Scene numbers are for scripts that are formatted for production so that the script can be budgeted and scheduled.

After the script is purchased, and it is being prepared for production (the "break down" is being done), each scene will be numbered.

In addition to being used on the shooting schedule, the scene numbers will be used when there are updates and/or rewrites done to portions of the script.

The scene numbers will also be listed on the daily call sheet. The call sheet is handed out on set every day to show the cast and crew what will be filmed the next day. (On YouTube, search: What is a call sheet? Also, search on YouTube: How to make a call sheet.)

Prior to the first day of filming, certain crew (department heads) will be given the filming schedule. Those who receive the schedule include the producers, director, assistant director (and the production assistants), office staff, editors, writers (on the small screen productions), script supervisor, head of sound, boom operator, D.P. (director of photography), the camera operators, the focus puller, the camera assistants, the gaffer, key grip, wardrobe department, hair and makeup departments, location scout, location manager, transportation managers, drivers, the prop master, FX, production designer, art director, set decorator, set dresser, greens person (they provide all of the potted plants, and other plants used in the scenes), medic, craft service (so they know how much food to have on set each day), catering (so they know how many people they will be feeding), stunts, lead standins, and so forth.

When scripts are filmed, scenes are often not filmed in order. The final scene of the movie might be filmed first – on the same day when a scene from the middle of the script is filmed, on the same day that the third scene of the script is filmed. This might be done because all of those scenes take place at the same location.

Because certain actors, locations, weather patterns (such as snow or rain), and so forth will only be available for a week, all scenes that need those actors, locations, and weather patterns might be filmed during that week. That means that the first scene, a few scenes in the middle of the script, and one or more scenes toward the end of the script will be filmed during that week.

If you put scene numbers in a spec script, it only reveals that you do not understand the filmmaking process.

Scene numbers are not needed in a spec script. It is not your job, concern, or place to add them.

- **NOTE 110: INSERTS: The inserts are done wrongly or distractively.**

If you need to show a close-up on a certain item, such as a watch to show what time it is, or a cell phone screen to show what is being texted, don't put:

ANGLE ON:

Or:

CLOSE-UP ON:

Or:

EXTREME CLOSE-UP ON:

Or:

E.C.U.:

Or the bedtime story phraseology:

NOW WE SEE:

A close-up on an item is called an "insert."
An insert should be on its own line.

Here is one style:

`INSERT: BOB'S WATCH: "1:37 a.m."`

As always, put anything that the audience is to read inside quotations marks.

You can forget the technical stuff, delete the camera direction (`INSERT:`), and simply put on one line:

`BOB'S WATCH: "1:37 a.m."`

That is clear and simple. No need for camera or "technical" direction.

Don't put `BACK TO SCENE:`, because it isn't needed. We never left the scene time or location. It wasn't a flash forward, flash backward, dream, daydream, or fantasy sequence, hallucination, or memory.

Skip one line after that insert, which is also called an extreme closeup.

Continue with the scene description or dialogue.

It is okay to continue right on with dialogue after an insert, because we are still in the same scene setup.

I like the simple version, as it is less technical, less wordy, is clear, and is easy to understand. It doesn't remind you that you are reading a screenplay, and it doesn't suddenly give you the feeling that you are supposed to be arranging cameras and lights, and focusing lenses. The director, D.P., and crew are going to film it in their way, and you don't have control over that.

Please see *The Screenwriter's Bible* for clarity on inserts. There are ways to do them that either reveal you did your homework, and ways to do them in ways that make your script confusing and/or unprofessional.

- **NOTE 111: WORDS ON SCREEN: The writer doesn't correctly format when words are to be on the screen (superimposed).**

When the words, date, or time are on screen for the audience to read, it is called superimposed.

To indicate when words, dates, or times are to be superimposed on the screen, format it like so by abbreviating the word superimpose.

`SUPER: "Little Italy, Cleveland, 1957."`

Or, you can use the word `CHYRON:` or `CAPTION:`. A chyron or caption is superimposed lettering on a TV or film screen.

`CAPTION: "Little Italy, Cleveland, 1957."`

When the audience is to read something on screen, put what they are to read inside of quotation marks.

As a pause before the superimposed words appear on screen, an image can be described, and then provide the words to then be superimposed:

```
INT. CARLA'S KITCHEN - DAY
```

```
Hair a mess, Carla, in a wrinkled bed dress,
deliriously stares out the window at the vivid sunset
above the distant mountains.
```

```
SUPER: "Six months later."
```

```
She clicks out of the stare. Gathers dirty dishes
from the table.
```

```
The dishes slip from her hands and shatter.
```

```
Halted, she steps to the chair, sits, and cries.
```

Some screenwriters use the term TITLE CARD:. But, a <u>title</u> card is the <u>title</u> of the movie, nothing else.

SUPER:, CAPTION:, or CHYRON: are the contemporary ways of indicating that something to be read by the audience is to appear on screen.

If you have seen the original Star Wars film, the scroll of words that appear on screen for the audience to read is also superimposed. In that case, a scroll of words can be indicated this way (you can also format the scroll so that it is as narrow as a dialogue block):

```
SUPER. SCROLL:
"In a medieval forest, where turtles once ruled, one
proved to be the greatest of all…"
```

If it is necessary for the tone and mood of your script, you can indicate the color of the words to appear on screen, such as blood red, if it is a vampire film. But, don't type them in anything but black 12 pt. Courier font.

- **NOTE 112: TIME REGISTER: The scene headings and/or direction contain exact times of day, when that isn't needed. When time register is needed, it isn't done correctly.**

The viewers of the film are not going to see the scene headings or the scene description. They will not be reading your script.

They are going to see the setting, and see what the characters do, and they are going to hear what the characters say, and they are going to hear the other sounds in the scene, and, if there is one, they will hear the soundtrack.

If it is necessary for the audience to know the time, you will either have to include dialogue of a character saying the time, or you will have to show a clock in the scene, or a character in voiceover needs to say the time, or you will have to show the time on the screen by superimposing the time on screen:

```
SUPER: "1:30 p.m."
```

Or:

```
CHYRON: "1:30 p.m." Or, CAPTION: "1:30 p.m."
```

If the viewers do not need to know the exact time, then skip out on making any effort to indicate the time.

The audience will likely factor the time constraint simply by watching what is taking place on screen.

Most scene headings will be listed as either NIGHT or DAY.

EXT. MOLLY'S POOL - DAY

If it is important, a scene can be listed as SUNRISE or SUNSET, or DUSK or DAWN, or TWILIGHT.

- **NOTE 113: CHARACTER ENTRANCE: The use of the word "enters" isn't being used when a character walks into a room.**

Drew "enters" is the correct stage direction script wording when a person is simply walking into a room. Not, "walks in," "comes in," "walks into the room," etc.

But, if Drew is doing something other than walk in, then you would clarify that for subtext dealing with the mood of Drew. Drew leaps in, fumbles in, skips in, crawls in, dances in, runs in, summersaults in, backflips in, is tossed in, or meanders in are ways to display the internal mood or energy of the character. Otherwise, if a character simply walks into a room, write: "Drew enters."

There also could be personality- or mood-establishing action involved in his entry:

Drew laughs as he enters with a rope he pulls attached to a cow that enters behind him.

Or:

Drew falls through the doorway, laughs hysterically, cries ferociously, and babbles indecipherably.

Similarly, with exits: If a character is simply walking out of a room, they exit. They don't walks out, or goes out of the room, or goes out, or leaves. Or, maybe they do. It's your script. Write what works best.

But, if they are exiting in some way that is indicative of their personality, mood, thoughts, and intentions, then describe the way they are exiting that is not simply walking, such as: hesitantly exits, or tiptoes from the room, or stumbles to and out of the doorway. Or, Blustered, Jim storms out.

Or:

Shauna pulls out her gun. Aims it into the hallway. Listens. Exits.

- **NOTE 114: MONTAGE AND SERIES OF SHOTS: The montages and series of shots are formatted incorrectly.**

Montages and series of shots need to be written correctly, including so that the breakdown, scheduling, budgeting, and one-sheet of the script can be done efficiently. The director of photography needs to be able to see what they will be filming. The production designer, art director, set decorator, set dresser, props master, sound techs, grips, locations manager, assistant directors, and others need to be able to decipher what is needed for each shot.

For a detailed description of how to write and format montages and series of shots – and the differences between a montage and a series of shots – see *The Screenwriter's Bible*. This book is meant to be studied with that book.

- **NOTE 115: FLASH, FANTASY, DREAM, AND VISION SCENES: The script is not clear about starting and ending a flashback, flash forward, fantasy, hallucination, vision, dream, daydream, nightmare, imagining, and distorted or other out-of-present-day scenes.**

To start one of the above, tag it on its own line before the scene heading:

BEGIN FLASHBACK.

Or, BEGIN FLASH FORWARD, or BEGIN ANGELA'S FANTASY, or BEGIN OBSCURE FANTASY, or BEGIN ANGELA'S DREAM, or BEGIN OBSCURE DREAM, or BEGIN DAYDREAM, or BEGIN ANGELA'S VISION, or, BEGIN ANGELA'S HALLUCINATION.

You could also put those on the same line as the scene heading:

EXT. TOWN FIREHOUSE — DAY (ANGELA'S FANTASY)

For clarity, do put it inside parenthesis, as shown above.

At the end of a flashback or dream sequence, or other jump forward or backward, or nonlinear scene, be clear to put the words END OF FLASHBACK, or END OF DREAM SEQUENCE, or END OF DAYDREAM, or END OF FLASH FORWARD, or END OF HALLUCINATION, or END OF VISION, or END OF FANTASY SEQUENCE, etc. Or, use BACK TO LINEAR STORY. Or, BACK TO PRESENT DAY. Or, BACK TO SCENE.

Be clear in as few words as possible so that you don't confuse the reader. Don't take them away from their focus. Keep them engaged in the story.

- **NOTE 116: TENSE USAGE IN OUT-OF-LINEAR OR OUT-OF-PRESENT-DAY SCENES: The script uses past or future tense in flashbacks, flash forwards, dreams, daydreams, hallucinations, fantasies, visions, imaginings, nightmares, and other distorted or out-of-present-day scenes.**

Use present tense in all scenes. Not future tense, or past tense. (Search: Future and past tense.)

- **NOTE 117: SERIES OF SHOTS USE IN OUT-OF-PRESENT-DAY SCENES: The script uses confusing format in uses of flashbacks, flash forwards, dreams, daydreams, hallucinations, fantasies, visions, imaginings, nightmares, and other out-of-present-day scenarios.**

To start a series of shots that are out-of-present day, and that don't contain dialogue, simply list the shots after indicating what sort of variety of state it is. You can use numbers or letters.:

BEGIN CASANDRA'S DREAM SEQUENCE

A) Casandra in a prom dress surfs on an ocean wave.

B) Casandra in a different prom dress mans a lunar module, the distant Earth seen through the window

C) Casandra in a different prom dress builds a brick wall.

D) Casandra in a different prom dress drives a firetruck.

E) Casandra in a different prom dress mountain bikes down a forest pathway.

END CASANDRA'S DREAM / BACK TO PRESENT DAY

Or:

BACK TO PRESENT DAY

Or, this might be better:

BACK TO CASSANDRA'S OFFICE CUBICAL

Or, whatever location she is in during the present day.

That is how to list a series of shots that do not contain dialogue, even if the characters are seen – but not heard – speaking.

When characters are seen talking, and we can't hear their voices, you can include the letters M.O.S. in the description. That stands for "mit out sound." It is a term coined by Austrian director Eric von Stroheim. (Search that.)

NEAR THE POND

The ducks swim about as Lindy and Karl talk and giggle M.O.S.

If there is dialogue in any of those shots, they need to be written like a normal scene with a heading, description, and dialogue. (For clarity on this, see: *The Screenwriter's Bible*.)

• **NOTE 118: NONLINEAR: The script does not clearly indicate when the scenes are nonlinear. Or doesn't include when the nonlinear scenarios continue for more than one scene.**

Nonlinear is when the scenes are not in the order in which the story plays out. The scenes are cleverly presented in a way that is a puzzle of flashback and flashforward and present day twists and turns for viewers to put together in their minds – preferably with rich subtext and a strong, satisfying payoff.

If the nonlinear scenario goes into more than one scene, be sure to note in the scene heading that it is still taking place by noting it in the scene heading.

```
EXT. TOWN FIREHOUSE — DAY (FLASHBACK CONTINUES)
```

Or: FANTASY SCENARIO CONTINUES, or DREAM SCENARIO CONTINUES, or FLASH FORWARD CONTINUES, or NIGHTMARE SCENARIO CONTINUES, or DAYDREAM SCENARIO CONTINUES, or VISION SCENARIO CONTINUES, or DRUG HALLUCINATION SCENARIO CONTINUES.

Be clear. Don't confuse or distract the reader. Keep them engaged.

Consider studying the script of one of the most popular nonlinear films, *Memento*.

For the standard way to format all of the above sequences, see the books *The Screenwriter's Bible*, and *Dr. Format Tells All*. Go with the books, rather than with any unusual formatting that was used in scripts found online. It is likely best to stay with the type of formatting that managers, agents, producers, directors, D.P.s, and others are used to seeing.

"Novelists have always had complete freedom to pretty much tell their story any way they saw fit. And that's kind of what I'm trying to do. Now the thing is for both novels and films: 75% of the stories you're going to tell will work better on a dramatically engaging basis to be told from a linear way. But there is the 25% out there that can be more resonant by telling it this way. Both *Reservoir Dogs* and *Pulp Fiction* gain a lot more resonance being told in this wild way."
– Quentin Tarantino, *Once Upon a Time... in Hollywood*

• **NOTE 119: BACKSTORIES: The script lacks backstories weaved throughout the script.**

Don't make the mistake of thinking that backstories are introduced and play out all within one page. Some might. Most won't. Maybe none will.

There might be a backstory that plays out within one scene of the script. But, it is likely part of a larger reason to reveal character and conflict.

"The sun, along with its other activities, creates rain. If it is true that the characters are secondary in importance, there is no reason why we should not use the moon instead of the sun."
– Lejos Egri, author *The Art of Dramatic Writing*

Backstories can play out as undercurrents to boost the main story. It is similar to the weather, with fluctuations in temperature, humidity, atmospheric pressure, wind, cloudiness, precipitation, and condensation. Backstories can help to reveal and intensify the weather of the story, or part of it. Use backstories to play with tone, mood, hooks, twists, motivation, anticipation conflict, irony, tension, emotional through-line, and contention.

"You go deep into the backstory so you know why they have the responses they have. What is the personal cost of those responses? The more you know, the more they challenge your assumption and the less risk of a cliché."
— Melanie Marnich, *Big Love*

"Interesting things happening to interesting people is basically the only rule of screenwriting."
— Brian Duffield, *Insurgent*

Backstories prevent scripts and the characters within them from being flat, mundane, and one-note.

Learn to weave backstories throughout a script, and to give the backstories beginnings, middles, ends, and resolutions.

There are different views on backstory concepts.

"In Hollywood, they always want to know about the character's backstory, which is the stupidest damn idea. It's like asking what kind of underwear the guy in the painting is wearing."
— David Mamet, *About Last Night*

"Even if you have two lines, you have to do the same complete work as if you're number one on the call sheet. If you get in an elevator and somebody gets on, rides two floors and gets off, that person has a reality that goes back to when they were born. They have memories, they have people, they have a life. They are doing something right now that the camera is on them in their space. We live in our own close-up all the time."
— Alfre Woodard, actor

"I'm not a method actor. I don't really have to go live in a hut in the tundra to play an accountant. People tell you that's what you should do because it's what De Niro does. It never worked for me. I've always been able to learn what I need to learn from the script."
— Tim Roth, actor

- **NOTE 120: SIDE CHARACTERS: The script does not use side characters in ways that serve the conflict of the main or backstories.**
The subtle or bold display of contention of the secondary characters could help reveal the inner workings of the minds of the antagonist and protagonist, helping to reveal motives, reasoning, and conflict that engage the audience.

357

If a side character doesn't serve a purpose relating to the conflict of the main or back stories, consider deleting them. Does it improve the script if they are not there?

- **NOTE 121: OVERPOPULATION: There are too many characters.**

Identify the characters who are needed for the progression of conflict and engagement of character contention and viewer intellect.

If characters aren't needed for story progression, why are they there?

"Each writer is born with a repertory company in his head. Shakespeare has perhaps twenty players. I have ten or so, and that's a lot. As you get older, you become more skillful at casting them."
– Gore Vidal, *Suddenly, Last Summer*

The more actors that are needed, the more expensive it will be to film and edit the script.

Be aware of how much money your script will need for production. The more money it costs to make, the less likely that it will get made.

Too many characters might confuse the reader, and the audience. It dulls and dilutes the conflict and subtext, alters the pacing, muddles the story, and clutters the screen with too many people to focus on. Especially if those characters are too similar, including with similar wardrobe, ethnicities, displays of culture, and names, and if how they display their intentions isn't engaging. Having too many characters is one of the easiest ways to lose the audience, and removes their focus.

If you have so many characters that you lose the audience, consider what is important for the audience to know from the actions and/or words of each of those side characters. Then, combine one or more of those characters into one character who is needed for engaging story, motive, wants, needs, internal and external conflict, and contention.

Make a list of each speaking/principal character. Go through each scene and decide why each of the characters is there. Cut what isn't needed.

- **NOTE 122: ONE-NOTE ANTAGONIST: The antagonist is simply a one-sided, flat shade of evil (or of good), with no indication that there is anything good (or bad) about them.**

"How can I be substantial if I do not cast a shadow? I must have a dark side also, if I am to be whole."
– Carl Jung, founder of analytical psychology

Contention within character is good to reveal. Especially if it is done in a way that gets the audience to see a different side of the character that they didn't expect, and that might change the view of the audience, or make the audience guess and doubt, expect, compare, consider, reflect, and want. If it makes the audience feel compassion, empathy, or the opposite for the character, play with those feelings.

Build contention within the minds of the audience in relation to how they are dealing with the predicament, philosophy, and motives of the protagonist.

"Everything about me is a contradiction, and so is everything about everybody else. We are made out of oppositions; we live between two poles. There's a philistine and an aesthete in all of us, and a murderer and a saint. You don't reconcile the poles. You just recognize them."
– Orson Welles, *Touch of Evil*

Consider that there is a character who behaves so terribly that the audience may solidly hate the character. But then, you see that character do something nice, like save an old lady from a mugger, buy a bike for a poor child, help a duckling find its mother, feed a stray dog, or avoid killing a spider by covering it with a glass and tenderly taking it outside to let it be free.

"If your dark, gritty movie contains no humor or joy, it is most likely not a true reflection of the world. Even in the darkest times, there's almost always humor and light to be found. It's a survival instinct."
– Gennifer Hutchison, *Breaking Bad*

"Character is destiny. Change, growing from within and forced from without, is the mainspring of character development."
– Rita Mae Brown, *The Woman Who Loved Elvis*

Consider that even the worst character once was someone's baby. Maybe they were loved as a child. Maybe they weren't, and that is why they are so terrible. People who are emotionally hurt or often are the ones who go about hurting other people. But, not always. Sometimes they're gullible and clingy.

For every motion and word of a character, there is an inner reason. A motive.

What is causing them to behave the way they are behaving, and say the things they are saying?

If they are simply doing things that don't make sense, perhaps they are mentally ill, or drugged, or have an undetected condition, or have suffered a brain injury. But, even those are the reasons why they do what they do.

If there is turbulence, why is it happening? There are reasons when storms take place. What is causing the underlying issue of the storm. Even if it isn't revealed in the script, understand it for yourself as you write.

"Whenever I write any character for any script, I like to have all of the backstory and history and everything about the character."
– Ana Lily Amirpour, *A Girl Walks Home Alone at Night*

"I don't think of my characters being bad or good, or bleak, but I rather try to find what motivates them, how they operate."
– Kantemir Balogov, *Beanpole*

What is it that makes your characters do and say what you have them doing and saying? If you don't know that answer, perhaps you have not thought out your characters.

Not that you have to know and show everything about your characters, and you certainly don't have to reveal everything about their history or thoughts.

There are some things that we will know about certain characters, such as that they are driven by greed, that it is likely that they were not loved, that they are embarrassed by the condition of their spouse, that they favor one of their children, that they are frustrated by their financial situation, that they are in a predicament that they don't want to be in, that they feel physically and emotionally inadequate, and so forth. But, deeper than that, why are they behaving in ways that, perhaps unbeknownst to them, reveal traits of their past?

- **NOTE 123: ANIMAL CHARACTERS: The animal characters in the script are one-note, flat, and overused.**

Animals can play out as secondary characters – especially in a child's or animated series or film.

Make the animal characters more than one-sided. Consider a vicious animal, which is a danger to the protagonist – or to other characters who we care about. To give the dangerous animal more of a personality, show it caring for its young, or even caring for the young of another species. Perhaps the animal was only vicious because the animal perceived a threat to its young.

- **NOTE 124: NAMING CHARACTERS: There are important characters who lack names. And/or, there are characters with names who are not important enough to have names, and/or are not principal. Or, they have a name that does not suit them, and perhaps tells us nothing about them.**

If there is a character who continually appears throughout the script, has numerous speaking lines, and is key to the story, that is likely to be a character who is needed. They should be given a name, or a relevant nickname having to do with their appearance, personality, philosophy, job, perceived position in life, or actions.

There are times when giving a character some sort of nickname works for the script. Do it in a way that is helpful, and not in a way that causes confusion, or otherwise hinders the script. Avoid cliches and offensive stereotypes.

Some will say that you should give every character a name because actors like playing characters with names.

Do what is right for the script, and don't worry about the actor egos.

If there is not strong enough reason to give a character a name, then don't give them one. Maybe it is better that they remain the `Piano Man`, or `Drunken Preacher`, or `Grouchy Boy`, or `Stud Muffin`, or `Meth Madness`, or `Bearded Woman`, as that talent, addiction, or visual, or physical identification will be more clear and easy to follow throughout the script, and less confusing than if you gave the character a proper name. Especially if they only appear a few times, and they have a strong visual, status, action, philosophy, or personality identification helpful to the story.

When giving a character an identification, such as a nickname, do use uppercase in the first letters: `Bank Robber`. And do put the name of that character in all uppercase letters only the first time they appear in the script: BANK ROBBER. Of course, their name in the dialogue cues should always be in all capital letters.

Do what is clear, keeps a good pace, doesn't confuse the reader, adheres the reader to the story, and works best for the script.

- **NOTE 125: COMBINING CHARACTERS: The script contains a number of characters who can be combined into one character in a way that better serves the story.**
Go through your script and consider if there are two or more characters who can be combined into one character. Especially if doing so helps the script to be more engaging, clarifies audience attention, improves the pacing, concentrates the displays of contention, and defines or highlights conflict.

- **NOTE 126: GENRE FAIL: The script falters in its apparent genre.**
The script seems to be weak in the genre you set it in.
Why did you select that genre?
How does the conflict play out in and engage the gears of that genre?
Consider that the story may play out better if you switched it to a different era with concerns and a timeline more consistent with another time, place, terrain, culture, socioeconomic status, and character background.
Consider that a dual-era or multi-era script might work better to tell your story. That is, dual timelines of two or more similar stories taking place in different years. That involves a lot of clever switching back and forth between eras, settings, and characters.
One such multi-era script is *The Hours*, which follows three generations of women dealing with a similar issue.
A dual or triple era script doesn't have to keep each era of characters one gender, race, religion, or financial situation. It could show the commonality of humanity dealing with similar issues and concerns, from an ancient warrior, to a WWI soldier, to a bullied girl in 1990s Ecuador, to a South African surfer girl. Mix it up, layer it, make it riveting, engaging, and brilliant.
Consider setting your western far in the future. *Star Wars* is a space western.
Consider that *Westside Story*, which is set in 1957, has similarities to *Romeo and Juliet*, which was set in the 1500s.
The conflict in your script might be heightened if you changed the financial background, education, careers, life conditions, and family and friend situations and philosophies – or lack thereof – of the characters.

Consider turning the modern courtroom drama into a situation in which, instead of so-called proper people in nice clothing, they are in a post-apocalyptic setting decades after war and global financial collapse had eliminated most of humanity.

Consider taking the neighborhood drama you set in the modern world, and turning that into a group of people on a ship stuck in a dead zone, in the 1700s.

Take that quirky comedy you wrote about high school seniors preparing to live their last month of high school, and set it among senior citizens living in a retirement home in a beach town in Florida, and how they might be dealing with the same issues of knowing that they will soon never see each other again. Have the elderly people misbehave, cheer each other, gossip, fight, laugh, become frightened, cry, and make up and comfort each other in the same manner as teenagers in their final weeks of school.

Take the spaceship drama, and put the characters in a mental hospital, where they are in various stages of believing they are traveling in an alternative universe, led by a deranged nurse who gives them different concoctions of pills to see how the drama plays out – and is recording it all on hidden cameras.

Why is the hostage drama set in the modern day? Could it work in the 1500s, or in early Aztec culture? Could it be set among the homeless living in tunnels beneath Las Vegas (search that), or in West Virginia coal mines?

Why is it a rock and roll flick? Would it work better in the jazz world of the 1920s? (Read the autobiography *Really the Blues*, by Mezz Mezzrow.)

Why is it a group of upper-crust friends having relationship problems, when it might be more interesting to set it among struggling migrant farm workers in the modern-era.

Why are the characters in the wedding comedy so polished, as if they walked out of a magazine advertisement? Would it be more interesting, and the fights, comedy, and drama more interesting for the audience if the characters were poor people living in the woods of Maine?

- **NOTE 127: DESCENT INTO HELL: The script is depressing, tragic, and lacks any sort of hope.**

In the 90s, I was in a video store looking for movies to rent. One-after-another, the story descriptions on the video cases said something like this, "One man's steady descent into hell." After picking up several films with that sort of description, I laughed. How many films are we supposed to watch about someone's descent into hell? Why would we find that interesting to watch numerous times for 90 to 120 minutes of our life?

"I'm not interested in characters who aren't broken. I'm not interested in happy people. It just doesn't draw me as a writer. Theater people say you are either a comedian or a tragedian, and I'm a tragedian. And the vexing, dark characters, the ones where I don't understand their pain or their anguish, they are the characters that appeal to me."
– John Logan, *Skyfall*

While I sometimes watch films about someone's descent into hell (if done well, such as the harrowing true story in *The Pianist*), I like to take a break from that and watch films that make me laugh, uplift me, motivate me, make me feel good about humanity, reveal historical events, or generally don't leave me feeling the dreariness I felt for days after watching *Leaving Las Vegas*.

Watching *Leaving Las Vegas* was like suffering a gunshot wound to the soul. I worked in the publicity department of the studio that distributed *Leaving Las Vegas*. I helped arrange the press screenings, and the cast and crew screening, and I attended those screenings. And, I worked on the awards campaign for the film. A week of repeatedly seeing that gloomy film was a bit far too much dreariness.

"In the early days, especially writing the *Breaking Bad* pilot, I worried so much that Walt wouldn't be likeable. It's funny, I bent over backwards to give the audience reasons to sympathize with him. I was nervous – anxiety-ridden, as I typically am – that what I was saying in that script wasn't interesting enough for the audience. Watching that first episode, I probably overdid that a bit. In hindsight, I've learned the audience will go along with a character like Walt so long as he remains interesting and active, and is capable about his business. People like competency. What is it people like about Darth Vader? Is it that he's so evil, or that he's so good at his job? I think it might be the latter. All the fears I had – 'Boy, no one's gonna sympathize with this guy'– turned out to be unfounded, which was a very interesting revelation."
– Vince Gilligan, *Better Call Saul*

If someone is going to write a movie that is about a dark night of the soul, with someone slamming against the bottom of their life, and feeling hopeless about it, they may want to consider doing it in a way that isn't corny about the uplift, but does have a realistic payoff (even if depressing), or isn't going to leave the audience in a funk – unless maybe that is the way the story would be most realistic.

It appears that there is a market for the sort of film that leaves people feeling miserable. It's likely not the most marketable movie that will fill theatres, or that will do best at satisfying distributors or investors.

Writing a film based on misery might not be the worst idea, but it is probably a good idea to write a variety of other films for your portfolio – so that you improve your possibilities of selling scripts.

"One thing that I think holds back many creative people – and thus holds back our art forms and culture – is that they keep doing the same thing and thus keep delivering the same results. How do you break out of your box?"
– Ted Hope, Amazon Studios

"You don't want to spend your life repeating yourself. It's true of any kind of artist. You want to explore as wide and as far as you can go."
– Toni Collette, actor

363

While some screenwriters do make a living by writing the same sort of films over and over again, it might be a good brain exercise to explore writing a variety of films based in different eras, genres, and cultures.

Someone I know won awards for a screenplay. Then, he felt as if he were stuck being expected to write follow-up films, or films in the same genre, that had the same sort of impact, and would be watched by the same audiences who viewed his award-winning script. He wanted to break out of the one-hit-wonder situation, and escape the single genre type of career.

It might be good to keep the question in mind when writing a script: "Is this what I want to be remembered by?"

"Twenty years ago, screenwriter Larry Marcus (*The Stuntman*) told me that if you have a great script it may take a week, a year, or even ten years, but if you've written something undeniably fantastic, someone will find it. Why? Because there simply aren't that many great scripts out there. It's straight-up supply and demand. This is the real key for any aspiring writer – 'It only takes one buyer.' That's what my first agent told me, and it's just as true today. You can hear a thousand 'No's,' have a million doors slammed in your face, but just one simple 'Yes' validates everything. As a writer, I've always found strength and inspiration in that. You don't have to conquer Hollywood, you just need to find that one buyer out there who gets it."
– John Jarrell, *Romeo Must Die*

Choose to write at least one script that will impact people the way you want to be remembered, and that may impact humanity for generations. It happens.

"Say who you are. Really say it in your life, and in your work. Tell someone out there who is lost, someone not yet born, someone who won't be born for 500 years. Your writing will be a record of your time. It can't help but be. But, more importantly, if you are honest about who you are, you'll help that person be less lonely in their world – because that person will recognize himself or herself in you, and that will give them hope – and it's done so for me. And I have to keep rediscovering its profound importance in my life. Give that to the world, rather than selling something to the world."
– Charlie Kaufman, *I'm Thinking of Ending Things*

The dark night of the soul film doesn't have to be as dreadful as it sounds. Rather than the end of humanity, and being stuck in hell, a dark night of the soul is relative to a character's background, setting, relationships, and expectations. In a comical way, a dark night of the soul might be that someone wanting to live a certain way, counts on living that way their entire life, but their life ends up being not the way that they had expected. They might be the spoiled person. While they might view their situation as their darkest days, we might see them as pretentious, and find humor in their being thrust into their perception of misery.

"Most of our lives are basically mundane and dull, and it's up to the writer to find ways to make them interesting."
– John Updike, *The Witches of Eastwick*

Raising Arizona could have been a dark, edge-of the-seat film about the kidnapping of a baby by an x-convict and his police officer wife. But, the filmmakers twisted it in every direction aiming for laughs with the hyped-up characterizations, and did so successfully. It helped that they also cast a variety of excellent actors, and a talented crew.

The same could be said about the film *I, Tonya*, but it would probably be difficult to get an audience to care much about the story the way it was presented in the media: Some poor white trash chick and her team of goons attacking her proper competition. Instead, the filmmakers took a far more interesting route, and made that story into a twisted, dark comedy, and one with scenes that made us laugh at the vastly wrong behavior of the characters. Audiences even laughed at the mother's harsh treatment toward her daughter.

Probably the most common path of a dark night of the soul movie is for there to be an uplifting, inspiring, or otherwise triumphant ending. You don't have to write what is common.

Then, there are films that go downhill, continue downhill, and remain at the very bottom of dread. But, they might be landmark projects for the filmmakers and actors – who go on to get nominated for a variety of awards. The film could open career doors for all of the talent.

Personal revival films don't have to be about falling into misery, but can be about feeling left-out, burned-out, or otherwise living a life cluttered down or shoved aside by society, family, coworkers, classmates, contemporaries, or others.

After establishing that a character isn't where they want to be in life, and revealing what they are contending with, for the film to be more marketable, there probably needs to be something that instills hope, inspiration, an unwavering want, or a drive to find a more satisfying way of living – and it might be best to present it within some sort of pressure cooker timeline. Maybe the thing they have always wanted will only be available for a short amount of time, and for the character to get that thing, they must take the steps necessary to get it, which means they might have to do something they have never done, exercise talents or powers they have never used, or have neglected to use, communicate in ways they have not practiced – or have refused to practice, or have neglected to practice, and otherwise go about making sure to get what they want.

Then, something happens that seems to assure that all of their efforts will go to waste – unless they do something very specific to make something happen. We and they know that they will be taking a risk, and we are all for them taking that gamble to get that thing. The actions they have to take and the words they have to speak to attain that thing are what engage the audience as they feel as if the character's actions and words are being forced by the audience. The audience is so invested in the story that they are on the edge of their seats, so badly wanting that thing for the character that the audience will want to push the character into getting it. The character has to use every skill they have, every bit of knowledge they have gained, and every spec of wit, charm, wisdom, and muscle in their being to get that thing. Along each twist and turn, the audience is ready to pounce on any barrier, break through any wall, jump over any hurdle, and argue and fight with anyone to get the thing. The audience could be so engrossed that they will not get up to go to the bathroom, will not pause the film, and will delay everything and anything to watch until the very last frame.

"What does the character want? What is the conflict? To me, that is ultimately how it breaks down into three acts. And that is what keeps you in your seat. You want to find out if the character will get what they need or what they want."
– Lauren Shuler Donner, producer

By the end of Act Three and into the conclusion, there should be a believable lamination of what the character wanted and what they got. The characters actions and words – and what has gone on – have synthesized into what is manifested. It could be the opposite of what the character started with, what the character was, and what the character wanted at the opening of the film, in ways that satisfy the audience. That doesn't necessarily mean a happy ending. It could mean that the character has a new philosophy of life.

- **NOTE 128: GUNS AND WEAPONRY: The script relies on guns – or other weaponry – as an external conflict crutch to hold up the tension and internal conflict of an otherwise weak presentation.**

  If the character's contentious acts rely too much on weapons, consider the possibility that you are using weapons as a crutch in a script that lacks engaging displays of intention, conflict, contention, and tension.

  How many scenarios can there be in which the person needing that gun – or other weaponry – gets hold of it just in time, and uses it in a way that solves their perceived problem?

  How many film posters have we seen featuring a character holding a gun, or other weapon?

  Everything from medieval to science fiction films are promoted using images of the characters holding a gun, or the equivalent sort of weaponry from the era – be it a spear or a laser gun. Maybe those images can be viewed as absurdism, or social commentary.

  Consider that having guns – or similar weaponry from the era of the story – weakens the script. Of course, if the script takes place in a battlefield, or is a true story about something involving a weapon, perhaps the weapons aren't something that can be missing. But, maybe you will be the clever person who writes a battlefield drama or corrupt cop script that happens in a unique way.

Consider writing scripts containing no guns, and no other structural weaponry.

Manipulation of perception can be a weapon.

"If a whole lot of films have used automatic weapons and there's been a lot of slaughter or supernatural powers, then you can counter program with a film where someone has issues with rent, where they can't shoot their way out of it.

There are loyal cinephiles around the world that will show up for social realism. It's not everyone's cup of tea, but that's why you've got to make the films pretty cheaply."
– Debra Granik, *Leave No Trace*

- **NOTE 129: ENTRANCES AND EXITS: The script contains unnecessary scene openings and endings during which the characters enter a setting at the start of a scene, and exit the setting at the end of the scene.**
If the script contains scenes during which the characters enter scenes, instead of already being there when the scenes begin, have a good reason for that entrance to be happening. A rule: Does it help the presentation?

"Come into the scene at the last possible moment."
– William Goldman, *The Princess Bride*

If you do not have a good reason for characters to enter a location, consider cutting to later, when they are already at or in the location – when action is taking place that we need to see, and/or dialogue is being said that we need to hear.

Similarly, if you have scenes during which characters exit locations at the end of scenes, have a good reason why the scenes are written that way.

End a scene at the time that we have finished getting the information that we need from the scene.

"Most beginning writers – when I read scripts – their biggest mistake is that their scenes begin too early and end too late. So, they just stretch out things where they feel like they gotta show the guy turn on the light switch and come into the room, when you don't. Every scene should just be moving forward"
– Derek Haas, *3:10 to Yuma*

There may be action scenes, such as car chases that go on from inside and outside a car, and filmed from cranes, helicopters, and drones, and other shots of the car being chased. Then, we cut to a scene in a room where there are walls of monitors showing the chase from security cameras mounted around the city. We see characters run into the room. In that case, maybe it is good to show the characters rushing into the room to watch the monitors. But, it depends on what action and dialogue are needed for manipulating the audience.

- **NOTE 130: EARLY SCENE STARTS: Scenes start too early, before stuff happens that we need to see, and before dialogue is said that we need to hear.**

Again, start the scene at the point of the scene where something is happening or being said that we need to see and hear.

"Start the scene as close to the end of the scene as possible."
– David Trottier, author *The Screenwriter's Bible*

Rid your scenes of dead zones. Even if you are going to lose something that you enjoyed writing. If it doesn't advance the conflict, if it doesn't have anything to do with what we need to know about the characters and their situations, and the way in which they subtly or boldly contend with their situation to get what they want or need, delete it.

"There is only one type of scene that should be in your movie: Scenes that move the story forward and illuminate character. If a scene doesn't do one or both of these chores, then that scene doesn't belong in your screenplay."
– Paul Chitlik, *The Wedding Dress*

- **NOTE 131: LATE SCENE ENDINGS: Scenes end far too late, after what we need to know from the scene has been communicated to us.**

End the scene when we have seen and heard what we need to see and hear during the scene. Doing so improves pacing and energy, and concentrates the focus on the essentials of the story.

- **NOTE 132: MEDITATIVE SCENES: The script contains too many meditative scenes that do nothing, other than to dilute the conflict, fill space, don't display contention, and put the audience to sleep.**

Yes, contemplative pauses could be good to give the audience a rest from massive amounts of action and dialogue, and let them simply absorb a setting, such as a scene of the setting sun over the paradise-like farm where the story takes place. This can give the audience a sense of why someone would want to live there. Or, show a freezing cold setting with a bunny shivering in the snow, to reveal why even wildlife would not want to be there.

If you have too many meditative scenes in your script, there are likely good reasons to cut them, including to not bore the audience. If the audience gets bored, falls asleep, or exits early, they will likely tell others about it – including by posting about it on social media. Social media quickly impacts everything from politics, to medicine, religion, immigration, stocks, education, energy, technology, food, sports, travel, the environment, and entertainment.

"There are no rules in filmmaking. Only sins. And the cardinal sin is dullness."
– Frank Capra, *Boobs in the Wood*

- **NOTE 133: SOUNDTRACK: The script is written in a way that makes it seem as if the writer doesn't realize there will be a soundtrack.**

"Music does a lot of things for a lot of people. It's transporting, for sure. It can take you right back – years back – to the very moment certain things happened in your life. It's uplifting, it's encouraging, it's strengthening."
– Aretha Franklin, singer

"To me, movies and music go hand-in-hand. When I'm writing a script, one of the first things I do is find the music I'm going to play for the opening sequence."
– Quentin Tarantino, *Pulp Fiction*

Remember when you are writing the script that there most likely will be music added to the film.

"Rhythm and harmony are essential to the whole of life."
– Plato, Athenian philosopher

Listen to various types of music while reading your script, and see if that would make you want to rewrite any of the action or dialogue.

Don't go through your script and write in the exact names of songs, or go overboard with indicating which type of music should be playing during each scene. Unless, you want to be considered naïve, controlling, and/or pretentious. But, if the script is about music, such as the life story of a composer, or you have the rights to use certain songs, then go at it and include the music cues.

Often, it isn't until a film is being edited that music choices will be made for the scenes. Leave that up to the director and composer.

"If I were not a physicist, I would probably be a musician. I often think in music. I live my daydreams in music. I see my life in terms of music."
– Albert Einstein

"Music has a way of ineffably penetrating our hearts and minds and souls. Perhaps, then, it should not be surprising that the most recent theory concocted to explain the universe is string theory, which posits that the smallest, irreducible element at the core of any piece of matter is a single, vibrating string. In other words, according to this theory, music is the essence of the universe: The cosmos is one massive symphony of vibrations and waves pulsating at myriad frequencies, tempos, and rhythms.

The capacity of humans to relate to music may be simply an innate means for people to comprehend and connect with the cosmos at the most profound level."
– Randall Grass, in his book *Great Spirits: Portraits of Life-Changing World Music Artists*

Do your job of writing a great script that engages the senses through sight and sound – including potentially through a soundtrack.

369

If you want to indicate that a certain type of music is playing during certain scenes, do that – if it works best for the script. Don't name exact songs.

"Sometimes when I'm writing I'll play Cole Porter, just because the rhythms and the lyrics are so perfect that it's like having a smart partner in the room. I have a huge collection of music that I listen to when I'm writing, and I also prepare a lot of music before I start directing. I put it all onto an iPod that I have with me on the set. It's helpful to the actors, because for an emotional scene, I'll play it and say, this is how it feels, to keep us in the zone."

– Nancy Meyers, *Private Benjamin*

I've been on the sets when directors plug in their cell phones to play particular songs to help set the mood of a scene. It is something that Andrea Arnold does. She's wonderful to work with.

"I always make a soundtrack when I'm working. I think of songs that pertain to the script I'm writing. I start to make lists. I start to make CDs. I play the music when I'm writing. Sometimes when I'm in the car. And it creeps in and seeps in. It's invaluable."

– Brian Helgeland, *Legend*

- **NOTE 134: VOICEOVER REDUNDANCY: The script uses voiceover (V.O.) narration to tell things that the audience would already know simply by watching the film.**

If your script contains narration, aim to feed into the character, the conflict, the tension, the perception, the pacing, the subtext, and emotional through-line.

Much – or all – of the narration might be unnecessary, irritating, or a distraction. But, might be brilliant.

If the narration says what would be better displayed through visuals, or bold or subtle acts of contention, consider that you might be relying on voiceover in ways that fail your script.

Give the audience something to factor. If they are going to realize something without the narration, consider deleting the narration.

Read your script while skipping over the narration. Consider if there is something missing with the narration omitted.

For successful use of voiceover, see *Fight Club, The Shawshank Redemption, The Usual Suspects, Apocalypse Now, Jules and Jim, Stranger than Fiction, Ferris Bueller's Day Off, A Scanner Darkly, The Big Lebowski, Trainspotting, Badlands, Double Indemnity, Y Tu Mama Tambien, Taxi Driver, All about Eve, Goodfellas, Barry Lyndon, Sunset Boulevard,* and *Raising Arizona.*

"In doing voiceovers, be careful not to describe what the audience already sees. Add to what they're seeing."

– Billy Wilder, *Sunset Boulevard*

- **NOTE 135: VOICEOVER MISUSED: The script uses voiceover narration of a character who the audience doesn't need to know about, and/or who isn't necessary to revealing anything about the antagonist or protagonist, conflict, or contention.**

Is the character whose voice we hear in the narration the best person for the narration? Would their narration confuse the audience? Is their narration needed? If you omit the narration, would the conflict suffer or be reduced because of it?

If, by some twist of your imagination, the narration done by a non-essential character works, such as that it is a way to contain a quirky, odd, funny, dark, scary, or otherwise entertaining backstory within the film, do it. But, make sure that it doesn't hinder or negate the film – but makes it more engaging.

Maybe using narration in an unusual way will make your script brilliant.

"David (Fincher) had said, 'The narration should not help the audience. It should be its own disembodied thing.' So, then I just changed it all to commentary that either did not move the story forward, but moved the character forward, or contradicted what you're seeing."
– Jim Uhls, *Fight Club*

- **NOTE 136: PRE-LAP MISHAP: The formatting of the sounds of the next scene heard before the current scene ends is not done correctly.**

(The opposite is a post-lap of sounds from the previous scene)

If you want the audience to hear the sounds or the voices from the following scene, before that scene is on screen, do this (in the following scene, we see Bertha in one scene, but hear sounds from the next scene that she is in).:

```
EXT. BERTHA'S HOUSE - DRIVEWAY - DAY
```

```
The German shepherd stands still as Bertha clips the
leash to the collar.
```

```
PRE-LAP: Sounds of car tires screeching to a halt as
a dog barks.
```

```
Bertha opens the back door of her car. Guides the dog
to hop inside.
```

```
EXT. ANNETTE'S GUN SHOP - DAY
```

```
Bertha runs from her car, and into the gun shop.
```

```
The German shepherd barks from the back seat of the
car.
```

While we are still in one location, if it is a person speaking who is heard talking in the next scene, do this:

INT. AGNESS'S FUNERAL HOME - WAKE ROOM - DAY

The knitting needles are arranged in the clasped
hands of Mildred's corpse in the coffin.

Agness steps back to consider the arrangement.

> LAWRENCE (PRE-LAP V.O.)
> Agness, have you seen my knitting needles?

Agness giggles and closes the casket.

INT. KLINE RESIDENCE - BEDROOM - DAY

The clutter on the desk is shuffled about by Lawrence
who is in pajamas.

Disinterested Agness reclines on the bed, her eyes
focused on a newspaper. She barely hides a smile.

> AGNESS
> Maybe Mildred took them.

His face traces with perplexity as he considers her.

> LAWRENCE
> No!

She bursts into cruel laughter.

As mentioned, a post-lap is the reverse: Sounds from the previous scene.

- **NOTE 137: DESCRIBING ABSENCE OF DIALOGUE: There is
  scene description that tells us when a character doesn't say anything,
  that a character doesn't verbally respond, or otherwise is quiet.**
  It is clumsy writing to say in scene description that a character is silent, or
  doesn't say anything, or is quiet, or doesn't respond.
  If we see that there is no dialogue for a character, we know that the
  character is silent.
  Always remember: The viewers won't have your script in front of them
  when they see the film.

- **NOTE 138: STATIC DIALOGUE: The script contains pages of
  dialogue without any scene description.**
  It's a screenplay, not a radio play.
  Film largely is a visual medium. Provide description of the static (stillness)
  or kinetic (movement) of is seen in each scene – especially when it can help us
  discover something about the character motives, reasoning, and struggles
  within the situation.

Almost always, avoid static scenes, which are long scenes of dialogue with no description of what is going on during the verbal exchange.

What are the characters doing while they speak with each other?

What is it about their stance or movements that will help reveal character psychology, status, contention, tension, motive, conflict, and subtext?

What are they doing while they are talking that will reveal their thoughts and composure, and the manipulation and anticipation of their situation better than how their dialogue does?

Show, don't tell.

Write description in a way that helps to reveal the inner workings of the character's minds.

Be true to the intellect of the characters within the tension.

Avoid having characters explain too much through dialogue. You probably don't want your script to sound like a soap opera, with on-the-nose dialogue.

Get the film *Soapdish* and listen to it without watching the film. It's meant to sound like a soap opera. You might find it hilarious.

Turn on a TV soap opera, listen to it without watching it.

Get a recording of a radio play, and listen to how the story is revealed through dialogue. It should be easy to find *The Prairie Home Companion* radio theater on the Internet.

(Search: Mystery Play Internet Radio. Search: Classic radio dramas.)

Listen, and understand how radio play dialogue also reveals just enough of the story and characters to engage the listeners.

Know that within stories of plays on screen, certain things don't need to be said for the audience to understand the story, or the concerns, wants, needs, motives, expectations, and troubles of the characters.

- **NOTE 139: RAMBLING DIALOGUE: The script contains rambling dialogue.**

The longer the dialogue, the more each word needs to be important to what the audience needs to hear.

"Dialogue should simply be a sound among other sounds, just something that comes out of the mouths of people whose eyes tell the story in visual terms."
– Alfred Hitchcock, *The Ring*

Decide what the dialogue needs to reveal about character motive, anticipation, manipulation, intellect, and the contention, conflict, mood, tone, and tension in ways that the visuals do not.

The audience sometimes benefits by not knowing what is or was said. We don't know the final words exchanged between the characters in *Lost in Translation*. We didn't need to hear them for the scene to have meaning. We are left to decide for ourselves what might have been said. It can be far more interesting that way.

373

"I like telling the story in a visual way. I don't like explaining a lot in dialogue."
– Sofia Coppola, *Lost in Translation*

Play with and manipulate viewer imagination, perception, and expectations. Give us what we need, and move along to the next scene.

"The trick about dialogue is it's about rhythm. You want to say it out loud. You want to say it often. You want to repeat it over and over again. And above all, you want to shorten it."
– Brian Helgeland, *42*

- **NOTE 140: CONTINUED COMPLETE SENTENCES IN DIALOGUE: The characters always speak in complete sentences, which is unnatural for most real-life conversations.**
While some people do speak in complete sentences, many do not. But, that's not to say that you should fill the dialogue with interjections (um, er, eh, well, hmm, etc. Usually, leave those up to the actors). It is odd and unnatural for every character to always speak in complete sentences. Go for natural-sounding speech patterns.

In a job interview, or other pressured professional exchanges, or in an academic situation, a person might strive to speak in complete sentences.

On the campaign trail – which is basically one long job interview – politicians often don't speak in complete sentences. For instance, Sarah Palin was known to ramble on and on in carry-on sentences saturated with dysfluency and anacoluthon. Other politicians speak so well that they could be considered stiff and unrelatable. And others blurt out whatever bombastic ramblings that their delusional minds think up.

Listen to how people speak in public. Write dialogue that sounds as real. Even educated people don't always speak in complete sentences, or use correct wording.

You don't need to follow the rules of grammar and proper sentence structure when writing character dialogue.

Clever dialogue is often shaded by one or more things like intention, motive, calculation, denial, defense, idiosyncrasies, traits, logic, tension, mood, urgency, stress, manipulation, foreshadowing, perception, presumption, belief, fear, grace, purpose, education, flaws, quirks, inflection, doubt, fascination, anticipation, theory, morals, fortitude, elegance, needs, wants, regrets, celebration, capability, favor, disfavor, temperament, skill, ignorance, suspicion, cleverness, stubbornness, repulsion, courage, passivity, commitment, weakness, inhibition, hope, inadequacy, and ten thousand other things. It all plays into subtext: Which is what is not said. And that is in tune with wants, needs, anticipation, and motive.

Don't unnecessarily explain anything through dialogue. Give us action to watch, and fewer words to hear.

"The screenplay is the child not only of its mother, the silent film, but also of its father, the drama."
– Terrence Rattigan, *The Winslow Boy*

For an idea of what can be done with no or little dialogue, watch the films *Ida, Tuvalu, The Artist, Silent Movie, All is Lost*, and *A Quiet Place*. Also, watch some of the silent films made by Alice Guy-Blaché, Mabel Normand, Charlie Chaplin, Lois Weber, Buster Keaton, Dorothy Arzner, D.W. Griffith, and Jacques Tati.

"A good film script should be able to do completely without dialogue."
– David Mamet, *Phil Spector*

Consider the silent scenes in *Jaws, Mudbound, Alien, Halloween, Terminator II, Get Out, Trainspotting, Requiem for a Dream, Hell or High Water*, and your favorite films. How does the silence convey story?

Watch the film *Japan Story*, and notice how parts of that film work without dialogue, and we understand what is going on, the feelings being expressed, and the impact that the situation has on their lives.

Having your script read aloud in a workshop can be helpful for deciding which dialogue can be deleted, and what would benefit by being shortened and/or rewritten.

- **NOTE 141: UNNECESSARY DIALOGUE: The script contains dialogue that explains things that we don't need to know.**
  There should be a reason behind every word of your dialogue.

  Give the audience the benefit of the doubt, and avoid stating unnecessary things in dialogue that will only slow the pace, dull the story, muffle the emotional through-line, and dilute audience focus.

  Know how unnecessary dialogue can be for conveying intentions and story when the visual does the job. Sometimes, no dialogue can work better.

"You'd be hard pressed to remember dialogue in some of the great pictures that you've seen. That's why pictures are so international. You don't have to hear the dialogue in an Italian movie or a French movie. We're watching the film so that the vehicle is not the ear or the word, it's the eye. The director of a play is nailed to the words. He can interpret them a little differently, but he has his limits: You can only inflect a sentence in two or three different ways, but you can inflect an image on the screen in an infinite number of ways. You can make one character practically fall out of the frame; you can shoot it where you don't even see his face. Two people can be talking, and the man talking cannot be seen, so the emphasis is on the reaction to the speech rather than on the speech itself."
– Arthur Miller, *The Crucible*

- **NOTE 142: DIALOGUE OVERKILL: The script contains dialogue that states things that are so obvious that it is monotonous, and would be better off being deleted.**

"How do you convey things without being explicit? Don't be expository about them. How do you talk about things without talking about them? Formally, I focused on how stories can be told visually. Dialogue is a support system for the cinematic experience – that includes sound and so on. Try to give as much thematic information – not explicit, but thematic – inside the frame as possible."
– Alfonso Cuarón Orozco, *Gravity*

"I think half of a writer's job is usually trying to come up with innovative ways of delivering an idea or an emotional beat. You want to avoid sentences like, 'You know what I think about you?' and stuff like that, and try to get across how someone is feeling without having them state to another person how they are feeling."
– Cesar Vitale, *Counting by 7s*

Having a character shivering and saying "It's cold."
Or having characters walking in the rain and saying that it is raining.
Or having a character wearing a fancy gown with a yellow belt, and having another character say, "You look good in that fancy gown with the yellow belt."
Or having a character removing lint from their pants, and say, "I have lint on my pants."
It is a form of *on-the-nose dialogue*. It dumbs down your script – unless it somehow sounds natural for that character, and is something that a person would say while experiencing what the character is experiencing in the world and society that you created.

"As an actor going into screenwriting, I was able to understand what type of dialogue feels natural. A lot of the time, as an actor, you don't have the freedom to change what your lines are, and they can often be very unnatural or difficult to portray in a real light."
– John Francis Daley, *Spider-Man: Homecoming*

"A common mistake I see in screenplays by new writers is giving us information that would not be available to someone watching a movie. They tell us what a character knows, thinks, feels, realizes, etc. They give us backstory in description. They tell us what a character is looking for, waiting for, or trying to do. They describe a character in terms of their profession, or what relationship they have to another character. Whenever we go to the cinema, no one steps in from the wings to give us that information. It must all be conveyed through the characters' actions and/or dialogue. That's not to say the characters must wear their hearts on their sleeves, and openly express their thoughts and feelings. That's called being 'on the nose,' and it's another common mistake."

– Michael Ray Brown, known for his *Screenwriting Structure Checklist*

- **NOTE 143: NUMBERS IN DIALOGUE: The dialogue contains numbers that should be spelled.**
  Most – but not all – numbers should be spelled in dialogue.
  As David Trottier clarifies in his book *Dr. Format Tells All*: "*All numbers – except years and proper names (such as C3PO [the robot character in* Star Wars]) *– should be written out as words in speeches.*"
  If a character says a year, the year should remain in numbers:

                    ANTONIO
        I was born in 1980.

  If a character says their age, some people say that you should spell it:

                    CLARICE
        I'm thirty-seven,

  Some people say that the age stated in dialogue should not be a number. But, does it matter when it is obvious and clear?:

                    CLARICE
    I'm 37.

  If a character indicates the number of items, spell it:

                    BELINDA
    I would like thirty-two green marbles.

  But, you won't be sent to screenwriter purgatory if you use numbers (I'm guessing):

                    BELINDA
    I would like 32 green marbles.

  If a character says a time of day, you can spell the numbers, OR you can use the numbers. Choose one style to use throughout the script.:

                    TESSA
    We left the scene at seven-thirty-three p.m.

                    TESSA
    We left the scene at 7:33 p.m.

  Notice, there are periods in `p.m.`, because the letters are pronounced individually.
  WD-40 is a common product that is to be typed just as the name appears on the label, not: `W.D. Forty`.

In scene headings, and in superimposing (when words appear on the screen), you can use numbers:

SUPER: "Abigail's 3rd day in Cleveland."

As always, when something appears on screen that the audience is to read, put it inside quotations marks.

In scene description, it is okay to use the actual numbers. (In dialogue 3rd would be spelled: third.)

- **NOTE 144: ABBREVIATIONS IN DIALOGUE: The script contains words in dialogue that are abbreviated, but they should be fully spelled.**
  In dialogue, Dr. Sherlock should be spelled:

LADY AGNESS

Doctor Sherlock.

But, it is okay to use the common abbreviation for doctor in scene headings:

INT. DR. SHERLOCK'S DEN - DAY

... and in scene description:

Dr. Sherlock's car races by.

Don't abbreviate cities and states like "Cleve., OH" in dialogue. The dialogue should be written as the character says it:

MRS. DELACRUZ

My dog was born in Cleveland, Ohio.

- **NOTE 145: ABBREVIATIONS IN SCENE HEADINGS: Abbreviations are misused in the scene headings.**
  It is okay to use common abbreviations in scene headings:

EXT. L.A., CA. — DOWNTOWN STREET - DAY

But, if it isn't so common, such as when not everyone would know the abbreviation:

EXT. CLEVE., OH. CITY HALL - FRONT STEPS - NIGHT

... don't abbreviate it. Instead, spell it:

EXT. CLEVELAND, OHIO CITY HALL - FRONT STEPS - NIGHT

Notice that a comma is used in that scene heading.
When in doubt, it is probably best to spell the word in scene headings.

- **NOTE 146: PRONOUNCING LETTERS: The writer doesn't use periods to indicate when letters are to be pronounced individually by the actor.**

CIA in dialogue should be typed `C.I.A.`, because the letters are pronounced individually.

Do not use periods when an abbreviation is said as a word or acronym. Because NASA is said as a word, do not use periods in NASA.

But, IBM is pronounced as the individual letters. So, in dialogue, IBM should be typed `I.B.M.` (to indicate that each letter is to be pronounced individually).

<pre>
                    TIFFANY
          I said, I'd like it ASAP.

                    RALPH
          Do you mean, A.S.A.P.?

                    TIFFANY
          I simply want it done, pronto.
          NASA is waiting.

                    RALPH
          Then, why did you say to send
          it to the F.B.I.?

                    TIFFANY
          I meant to say S.S.A.

                    RALPH
          The Social Security Administration?

                    TIFFANY
          Yes.
</pre>

If a character is to spell a word, don't put periods after the letters. Put hyphens between the letters.

<pre>
                    HEATHER
          How is individual spelled? Well,
          let's see. I-N-D-I-V-I-D-U-A-L.
</pre>

- **NOTE 147: DIALOGUE DESCRIPTION: The scene description describes what the character says.**

Keep the dialogue in the dialogue.

Do not write scene description that tells what the character is going to say, or considers saying – or what the character thinks or remembers.

I read a script in which the scene description was something like this:

The dinner party is in full swing. Davis brings up
that he won't be available for the meeting, because
he is going on a vacation.

>   DAVIS
>   I won't be available for the
>   meeting. I'm going on a vacation.

There is no reason for the scene description to describe what the character
says. Simply provide the dialogue in its correct place.

- **NOTE 148: SOTTO: The term "sotto" or "sotto voce" is used in the
  parentheticals (below the character cue [character name], and above
  the dialogue).**

Use "sotto" or "sotto voce" if you want to irritate the reader.

You don't suddenly need to use Italian in an English script.

If you want the character to say something that only the character hears, as
a parenthetical, put the words:

>   RIALTO
>   (to self)
>   That can't be my son.

Or:

>   RIALTO
>   (quietly)
>   That can't be my son.

Or:

>   RIALTO
>   (under breath)
>   That can't be my son.

But not:

>   RIALTO
>   (says quietly to himself)
>   That can't be my son.

Don't:

>   RIALTO
>   (sotto)
>   That can't be my son.

- **NOTE 149: NONLANGUAGE SOUNDS: The dialogue contains
  grunts, groans, screams, sneezes, burps, and other nonlanguage
  sounds.**

Put the screams, and other vocalized non-words in the scene description,
not in the dialogue.

- **NOTE 150: ANIMAL VOCALIZATION: The script has dialogue blocks for cat mews, dog barks, etc.**

Don't make dialogue blocks for animals that are simply making their typical vocalization, unless the animals are speaking a human language.

Unless it works for the script, or it is an animated character, avoid:

```
                FIDO
           (eagerly)
     Bark. Bark.
```

Simply write that the dog barks in the description block:
```
Fido eagerly barks to alert Sheila. She sees the
rabid raccoon approach, and she runs.
```

If you have an animal character who speaks human language, put that dialogue in a dialogue block, as you would for human character dialogue:

```
                FLUFFY
           (displeased)
     She bought generic cat chow?
     Pillows will tear. Curtains will
     shred.
```

- **NOTE 151: CROWD SCENE DIALOGUE: The dialogue for nonprincipal characters in a crowd is given their own dialogue block.**

When there are people who are shouting in a crowd, and those people are not principal characters (they only will appear in that crowd scene) put their suggested dialogue in the description to give them a variety of ideas of what to say.

The assistant director will assign suggested lines to the (probably background) actors, all to be shouted out during the scene.

In your script, if you want to indicate that people in a crowd are saying a bunch of jumbled and indecipherable dialogue, write:

```
              CROWD VOICES
          (indecipherable shouts)
```

Or, you can write description that indicates their tone:

```
The frustrated crowd shouts indecipherable things.
```

Normally, you wouldn't describe dialogue in description. But, the above is okay, since it is not a principal character speaking, and it isn't understandable words, but is important only for indicating the tone of the crowd.

If it is a union production, and one or more of those background actors says something that is clearly heard as they are seen saying it on camera, they would be given a day player contract, and "upgraded" to the higher pay rate. If the production doesn't voluntarily do it, the actor can file a claim with the union to get the pay owed to them.

```
EXT. MAURICE BAKERY - DAY

Tired Maurice and Claudia push through the front
door. They halt to see that...

an eager crowd of happy customers clogs the street.
Some with signs "Your bagels are orgasmic,"
"Maurice's donuts are love machines," etc.

Others shout over each other: "I sleep with your
cookies." "Can you make our wedding cake?" etc.

Laughing, Maurice and Claudia scamper back inside.
```

If you want any line of dialogue to be clearly heard during the crowd scene, then give that character a name – or descriptive name – and that line of dialogue its own dialogue block.

```
                WOMAN WITH POODLE
             (lunges forward)
       Why don't you make doggie biscuits?

Burst into laughter, Maurice and Claudia rush back
inside.
```

- **NOTE 152: BEAT PAUSE: The script is speckled with the word "beat."**

A beat is a length of time. A pause is an actor taking a moment to consider or wait for something.

Using the word "beat" in a script might be viewed as you talking dumb to the actor. As if they are too clueless to understand the scene, so you are going to direct their every inflection = you are micromanaging the actor / directing from the page.

Maybe you don't mean "beat," maybe you mean "pause." If so, and if truly necessary, use the word "pause," as in: `Antonia pauses to factor that.` That is, if you want the actor to do so. But, why are you micromanaging the actors?

Consider that, in the mind of the reader, a "beat" could be thought as a freeze frame. Do you want the reader to not know what is going on during that time of that a so-called pause, which really isn't a pause?

Perhaps you could add something after the word beat, such as this as its own paragraph for a character recalibration pause:

```
Beat. How could Tommy not understand?
```

Use that character recalibration pause style device sparingly in a script. If you use it abundantly, it might become equally distractive. I'm currently reading a script that uses the device dozens of times. It's like a pest.

The word "`beat`" could be deleted. And the question could be left as its own paragraph, as we then figure that the character talking with Tommy considers that question.

`How could Tommy not understand?`

Then, go on with the next bit of dialogue, or action. Or, into the next scene, leaving us there in the past scene with the character in a state of realizing that Tommy doesn't understand.

That might be a touch of novel writing, but maybe it works. Maybe it gives us that moment to visualize the character as being confounded.

Do what works for the script.

But, know that…

`Beat.`

… does about nothing helpful or clever for your script.

A beat by itself is nothing. It's not a visual.

A pause is more visual, but what is going on during that pause? What are we seeing take place in that space of time that isn't a beat?

Why is that beat taking up one line of the page? It's not a camera angle. It gives us no emotion or description. It is essentially a blank space.

Maybe there is something nonverbal that could happen in that part of the scene.

The character shuffles through a book.

The character turns away in their chair.

The character smirks, then corrects. Too late, the nun saw her.

The character stares at a photo.

The character ignores another character.

The character pretends to fall to sleep.

The character glares at the other.

Suspicion grows on their face.

The character considers their finger nails.

The character dusts their desk.

The characters who is fighting with their spouse, fidgets with their wedding ring. (But, is that a cliché that is seen too many times? Or, something realistic that married people do during relationship strife?)

The character dealing with a business partner who they have grown to dislike wants to be rude, so they pick their nose in front of the other.

The character spins in his seat to gesture toward the great city view.

Using the word "beat" – or the word "pause" – could be an easy way to break the fourth wall for the reader. That is, remove their focus from the script. It reminds them that they are reading a script by a writer who is using the word "beat" – or the word "pause" – because the writer didn't know what else to put there as a visual scene description. And, it could leave the reader wondering what is happening during that blank space.

Use "beat" if you want to show that you don't know the psychology, motive, and actions of your characters, or the conflict, contention, tension, and subtext of your script.

Use "beat" if you think you are the director telling the actor to pause, or are the actor thinking that you are going to pause. Don't.

"There is no point in having sharp images when you've fuzzy ideas."
– Jean-Luc Godard, *Breathless*

In other words, using "beat" or "pause" kind of indicates that you are not done writing the scene, and that you are not sure what is going on in a scene that you wrote.

It is likely that you can simply delete the word "beat" or "pause" anyplace that it appears in the script, and it won't negate the script in any way – but could improve it.

If there is a pause that should happen in a scene, let it happen naturally as the actors act out the scene. Don't try to micromanage the actors by telling them to pause – especially by writing the word "beat."

If you believe there should be a pause in a scene, what is the visual answer? By visual answer, I mean: What is going on with the image on the screen, or with the actor?

A visual answer is:
A description of something that we will see on the screen. Even if it is that the actor stares at the other, as their tears well.

When your movies start making hundreds of millions at the box office, you can then write your scripts any which way you want. But, until then, follow the spec script guidelines. And, don't give the reader, manager, agent, director, financier, contest, lab, or fellowship or mentorship program a reason to dismiss your script for being vague and elusive – or filled with micromanaging jargon.

You might say, "Well, (name of globally successful writer/director) includes pauses in their script." Go look in the mirror, do you see that (name of aforementioned globally successful writer/director)? Nope. You see a writer who wants to establish a career by writing sharp scripts that get made.

Keep writing. Sharply. Cleverly. Fascinate the readers with engrossing stories weaved throughout with engaging drama saturated with conflict, contention, subtext, tension, character arcs, and clever plot twists played out by interesting characters.

"If you don't have something that glues the audience to the screen, you're in trouble."
– Neill Blomkamp, *District 9*

Write scripts that the readers can't put down until they read the final word.

"All good writing is swimming under water and holding your breath."
– F. Scott Fitzgerald, *The Great Gatsby*

"Writing movies is like surgery. Every moment needs to be crafted. Threads need to be implanted early, and woven throughout. It needs to be tight, and lean, and agile, and full of diverse, authentic bits."
– Elizabeth Chomko, *What They Had*

- **NOTE 153: BEAT ACTION: The script tells the actors to do something for a beat.**
  Don't write something like:

```
Claude brushes off his sweater for a beat.
```

Or:

```
Antonia takes a beat to adjust her belt.
```

Or:

```
Latifa looks at David for a beat.
```

Do write:

```
Claude brushes off his sweater.
```

Or:

```
Antonia adjusts her belt.
```

Maybe Latifa has a certain expression as she looks to David. She glares, or stares, or lividly eyes David. If there isn't some defined meaning why she is looking at him, why mention it?

There is no need to write that characters do something `for a beat`.

Write visual scene description that reveals intention, character, and contains meaning for the story with suitable pacing.

Provide a visual solution to "beat," or simply delete the use of "beat." It is unlikely that your script will suffer – especially if you have written a script rich in conflict, contention, tension, and subtext with interesting characters at the center of an engaging story.

- **NOTE 154: EXCLAMATION POINTS: The script contains exclamation points all over the place!!!!!**
  Leave the overuse of exclamation points for excitable youth, their classroom notes, their texts, their social media postings, self-serving adults who tweet nonsense, and delusional, sniffling, inept, self-impressed politicians.

  Refrain from using more than one exclamation point!!!

  Use exclamation points sparingly.

385

Often, an exclamation point can be replaced with a period. If the scene is strong with implications, the inflection remains.

The conflict and contention of the scene should speak for itself, without you pushing it with exclamation points.

If you absolutely need to be clear that a character says something in a specific way, provide parenthetical direction before their dialogue:

```
                    EDWINA
                  (shouts)
         I have always loved you.
```

That is clearer than using an exclamation point.

- **NOTE 155: HISTORY OR FUTURE IN DESCRIPTION: The description tells the history or future of characters or of things.**

I read a script in which there was a scene in a kitchen containing a damaged table. The scene description told how the table had been damaged, and who had damaged it, and why – years prior. Why would we need to know that? Why would it be in the scene description? If we do need to know that, how could it be filmed in a way that we would know it?

Always remember that the people who watch the film are not going to see scene description in your script detailing the history and future of people or of things.

The details of the history of people and things in scene description are called "unfilmable." They are unfilmable because they aren't visual as the scene is written.

For the audience to know how that table was damaged, one of the characters has to say how the table was damaged, or there has to be voiceover dialogue telling how the table had been damaged, or there needs to be a flashback showing how the table was damaged.

If the scene was filmed the way it was described, we would see a damaged table, but we would know nothing about how it had been damaged, or who did it, or when they did it, or why they did it: The motive.

I read a script containing scene description telling how a character was sitting in a swing while thinking about her childhood, and about a specific situation that happened to her when she was a little girl.

If the scene were filmed as described, all that we would see would be a woman sitting in a swing. We would know nothing about what she was remembering.

The only way we would know what the character is thinking is either she verbalizes her thoughts, or there is voiceover telling us about what she is thinking of, or there is a flashback showing us what she is thinking of.

Be careful to avoid writing "unfilmables" in scene description.

- **NOTE 156: COUNTING OBJECTS: The scene description mentions the number of objects that have been handled, finished, worked on, accumulated, gone through, or otherwise subjected to something.**

I've read scripts containing scenes saying something like:

```
INT. CARLA'S BIKE SHOP - DAY

Carla works on replacing the 23rd flat tire of the
day.
```

We would not know how many flat tires Carla has replaced that day, unless Carla or someone else – possibly in a voiceover – says so. Her co-worker could pass by and say:

```
                    FELICIA
        That's the twenty-third flat tire you've
        replaced, today.
```

Or, there is a fast-motion segment quickly showing her fix 23 tires. Or, there is some chart that we see on which Carla is recording how many flat tires she has replaced that day. Or, there is a stack of flattened inner tubes – but who is going to count a stack of inner tubes in a scene? We wouldn't know how many inner tubes are in the stack, but would get the idea that she has been busy replacing flat tires. Perhaps it is part of a storyline that she clandestinely puts tacks in the nearby road, so that bikers get flats, and they come to her financially strained bike repair shop to have their tires replaced.

If Ricardo who works in a bakery is trying to teach himself a new way of making flowers on birthday cakes, we could understand how many cakes he has screwed up – if we can see those screwed up cakes on the bakery table. The scene description could say that there are several screwed up practice cakes. The image on screen is the "visual answer."

Don't write something like:

```
Darla is in the hat store trying on her thirteenth
hat as her poodle watches.
```

All we would see is that Darla is trying on hats. We wouldn't know how many hats that she has tried on – unless she or someone says so.

Instead, simply write (the scene heading would tell where she is):

```
Darla tries on hats as her poodle watches.
```

Don't write:

```
Darla tries on numerous hats as her poodle watches.
```

…unless we are going to take the time to watch her try on numerous hats. The "s" in hats already indicates that she is trying on more than one hat.

But, why would we take the time to film all of that, and why would it be necessary? Maybe we see her quickly try on two or three hats, or she is wearing one while holding two. Maybe there is a put-upon sales assistant also holding hats next to a chair where other hats are stacked, and that visual gives us the impression that Darla has been there for a while, trying on hats.

But, don't write:

```
Darla tries on the 13th hat.
```

Maybe… Darla did a "do-or-dare" game, and was challenged to go to a store and try on 13 hats. Then, we cut to the scene in the store where she is standing amongst the clutter of hats, and we get the idea – because of a previous scene in which we found out about the dare – that she completed the dare.

Mentioning a specific number of objects that a person has made, or practiced on, or finished, or worked on, or otherwise been concerned or involved with in a scene is an unfilmable. We have to see it, or there has to be a character mentioning the number, or there has to be a visual indication of it in the scene.

- **NOTE 157: CHARACTER THOUGHTS: The scene description goes into character decisions, preferences, anticipation, and reasoning.**
  We can't film thoughts. We can only film images of things and animals (including humans), and record dialogue and sounds.

  Avoid writing scene description that describes character thoughts, such as:

```
Kendra decides to call her divorce lawyer.
```

How would we know what Kendra is thinking that thought by filming her? We would only know what she is thinking it if she has dialogue that expresses the thought, or there is voiceover dialogue telling us what she is thinking, or maybe it is a science fiction film and electrodes are attached to her skull, and her thoughts are being read by a robot, or they appear on a monitor displaying words that we can read, or the monitor shows scenes of her thoughts.

Do not use scene description to tell us character decisions, preferences, memories, plans, ideas, or reasoning – which are all thoughts.

Don't tell us that a character is listening to their favorite song. We wouldn't know that it is their favorite song, unless there is dialogue that tells us so, or there is something written or printed in the scene – perhaps on a CD cover – indicating that the song is their favorite.

The people watching the film or series will not be reading the scene description. They will be watching and listening to the film or series.

- **NOTE 158: LOOKING FOR: The script contains scene description telling us what an actor is looking for, or what a character wants.**

```
Clyde drunkenly wanders into the room looking for the
shoe.
```

If we filmed that scene description, all we would see is a character looking around a room. We would have no idea that they are looking for a shoe, unless there was something said or done in a previous scene indicating to us that he would then go into the room looking for a shoe (but, you would still not mention his thoughts in the scene description). Or, we would know if he were looking for a shoe if he has dialogue saying that he is looking for a shoe. Or, there is off screen dialogue of someone in the other room – or we can hear the voice over a phone speaker – asking him if he found the shoe. Or, there are words that appear on screen (superimposed on the screen) telling us that the guy is looking for a shoe. Or, there is voiceover telling us that he is looking for a shoe.

Otherwise, we might know he is looking for a shoe if he is clearly only wearing one shoe, and we can see that his other foot is bare. Or, he is holding one shoe in his hand, and we might get the impression that he is looking for the other shoe.

We would also know he is looking for a shoe if he finds the shoe, picks it up, and is apparently satisfied with, or angry about, or has some other emotional display relating to – or says something about – finding the shoe.

Scene description should not contain character thoughts about what they are looking for, or what they want, or what they need, remember, or plan.

- **NOTE 159: SMELLS AND SCENTS: The description tells us what a character is smelling, or that the character is smelling a specific scent.**
  We would only know what a character is smelling if it is quite obvious, such as we have seen what they are smelling (a skunk, a fire, burning toast, a diced onion, rotting garbage, a decomposing body, a bouquet of flowers, etc.), or the actor says that they are smelling a specific thing, or another character says or asks them what they are smelling – and the character answers, or there is voiceover that tells what the character is smelling.
  Saying:

```
Darla walks in the room and smells the distant fire.
```

... is not going to work, unless we know there is a fire (based on a previous scene), someone says that there is a fire, or we see her actions indicating that she is smelling something, and she runs to the window to see that there is a fire outside.

- **NOTE 160: TELLING CHARACTER REASONING: The script contains scene description with a variety of unnecessary information.**

I read a script containing scene description telling why a character is wearing a certain color of clothing.

The only way we would know why she is wearing that color of clothing is if one of the characters in the scene mentions why the character is wearing that color, or there is a voiceover telling us why the character is wearing it, or there is a scene that somehow conveyed why the character is wearing that color.

Writing scene description that tells us why a character is doing something should be worded in a way that it can be filmed as an image of action. The action should reveal the character's reasoning – or we eventually will understand the character's reasoning for doing that action as the film progresses.

Don't say something like the following in scene description:

```
Kyle places the plank from Beverly's truck next to
the garage door so that Beverly can pick it up to fit
it into her pickup truck bed.
```

How would we understand all of that story by filming Kyle putting a plank next to his garage? We wouldn't.

Do say:

```
Kyle places the plank next to the garage door.
```

Later, we will see Beverly take the plank and fit it into a slot on her pickup truck bed. Show, don't tell.

In other words, having scene description telling us why a character is doing something isn't going to mean anything, unless we hear in dialogue why they did it, or see action relating to why they did it.

Avoid including unfilmables in scene description of a spec script.

- **NOTE 161: CHOREOGRAPHY FANATICISM: The scene description is overly controlling with its choreography.**

Choreographing scenes in ways that clearly are not necessary do nothing to sway the audience through conflict, don't convey anything about the character's subtle or bold acts of contention, and simply bogs down the script is unnecessary detail.

Micromanaging scene choreography could mean describing how characters move around a room, what objects they are passing or pausing near, telling how someone pulls out a chair and sits in it unusually, or any specific action that doesn't matter to revealing what we need to know about character and conflict to advance our understanding and improve our perception of the story. Those and other ways of micromanagement of the actors, props, and setting is elaborating, slows the script, and loses the simplicity that is helpful for a script to display.

Imply what is needed to help the audience engage with story.

I have read numerous scripts containing scene description that tells the actors exactly how to pick up or put down things, how to open and close drawers, open locks, arrange things on desks, set dinner tables, and so forth – including detailing which hand they use to do things. Don't write puppetry direction. If you do, there should be good reasons for it, such as a character is neurotic to the point of it overtaking their life. Otherwise, writing overly choreographed description doesn't serve your script.

- **NOTE 162: FIGHT SCENES, ACTION SEQUENCES / SET PIECES: The action and fight scenes are clogged with unnecessary details, and otherwise wording that dulls the scenes, and makes the read tedious.** An action sequence is also called *a set piece*.

Especially during fight and action scenes, don't write in information dumps with so many tornadoes of detail in every sentence that it is tedious to read.

"A sequence is, in a sense, a huge scene that has been cut down to its essence, defined by disruptions in time and space, and which connects a series of actions around a particular idea."
– Amnon Buchbinder, author *The Way of the Screenwriter*

Break up action sequence into beats with each beat having its own paragraph. However, do not describe every single twist, turn, grimace, flinch, duck, hit, grab, smack, trip, shove, sweat bead, blood drop, and other micro-detail.

Pick any five successful action films, find the screenplays for them, and read the action sequences. Consider the dexterity of the writing.

Simplicity, sparseness of wording, and elegant description are especially necessary for keeping a brisk pace going in action, chase, and fight scenes.

For instance, in a boxing scene, when the blood spews from the broken nose – unless you want a slow-motion shot, or it is absolutely necessary for some sort of artistic something or other that you are aiming for – don't go into detail about how the blood spews from the boxer's nose like a flock of angry bees escaping a hive, splattering across the sweat-dampened ring, through the ropes, and out onto the audience, where it stains their clothing… and so forth and so on. Unless… it really works for your script.

I read a script with a fight scene that detailed every character move, including which hands and which feet the characters favored while they fought. That might work in a radio play.

"The only formula needed to edit action is the constant teamwork, not least with the choreographers. Action sequences are an art-form, an alpha dance. Of course, my approach changes with the choreography and how it's filmed, but I aim to be precise. Unless there's good reason for it, I do not enjoy repetitive beats."
– Elisabet Ronaldsdottir, editor *Atomic Blonde*, and *John Wick*

391

"It's very important for an audience to know where they are and why they are there in a musical. It allows them to relax and follow this form that operates in shorthand. So, the economy of the form, in many respects, is why a lot of screenwriting is so sleek. Because the visuals are where the explosions happen."
– George C. Wolfe, *The Immortal Life of Henrietta Lacks*

Especially important in fight and action scenes is that, if it isn't necessary and meaningful for the reader to know, if it doesn't play into the brisk, brutal intensity, and the conflict, and advancement of the character, leave it out. If it is necessary, describe it in a way that is clear, uses a conservative variety of words, and keeps up a good pace for the reader.

"When your story is ready for a rewrite, cut it to the bone. Get rid of every ounce of excess fat. This is going to hurt; revising a story down to the bare essentials is always a little like murdering children, but it must be done."
– Stephen King, *Carrie*

"The main thing is to use whatever means at hand to tell stories that mean something to you on a personal level. And often, again especially in the action field, what is personally interesting to you may be invisible to others. In the end, of course, when reviewing the result, the person you have outsmarted is very often yourself."
– Walter Hill, *Aliens*

- **NOTE 163: VISUAL DISPLAY OF THOUGHTS: The writer seems to have forgotten that a purpose of a scene is to visually reveal the workings of the character's mind, especially in relevant displays of manipulative contention in ways that are valid for and move the story forward within the situation of conflict.**
Decide what each scene is meant to reveal in manipulative puzzle piece messages communicated to the audience through action and dialogue.

If a scene is not moving the story forward, and getting the viewers to understand and engage with the conflict and concerns of the characters, why is the scene in the script?

To understand the conflict, concerns, reasoning, needs, wants, intentions, anticipations, and motives of the characters, we need to see actions, and sometimes hear words and other things that get us to understand what is going on, in ways that move the story forward, engage us, and keep us watching until the final scene.

What you do not want to do in your screenplay is to detail the character's thoughts in the scene description. Don't write what the character wants, hopes, regrets, plans on doing, is looking for, is remembering, or otherwise is thinking. That is one of the common mistakes in the screenplays of new writers. Put that novelistic wording in novels, not in screenplays. The screenplay is what we see characters doing, and what we hear them saying.

- **NOTE 164: PAST TENSE: The script contains the use of past tense in scene description.**
Write scene description in present tense. The description is what we see happening as it happens, not before or after it happens.

"A screenplay is written in the present tense. Novels and short stories are almost always written in the past tense. By being in the present tense, a screenplay has a more immediate sense of time – these events, these actions are happening now! They unfold in a hurry, they move, move, move!"
– Scott Myers, GoIntoTheStory.BlckLst.com

Write scene description as if it is happening, not as if it did, or will happen. Wrong:

```
Grandma Agnes spat, turned on the jackhammer and used
it to break apart the sidewalk.
```

Correct:

```
Grandma Agnes spits, turns on the jackhammer. Grips
tightly. Proceeds to shatter the sidewalk.
```

- **NOTE 165: JUST OR SIMPLY: The script uses the word "just" when a better choice would be to use the word "simply."**
Go through your script description and consider each instance of the word "just." Would it be better to use the word "simply"?

```
Martha just grasps the bumper and flips the car.
```

```
Martha simply grasps the bumper and flips the car.
```

However, in this case, the word "`simply`" can be eliminated:

```
Martha grasps the bumper and flips the car.
```

In dialogue, the use of "just" instead of "simply" could be the better choice – to reflect how people use the words.

- **NOTE 166: HARD OR DIFFICULT: The scene descriptions use the word "hard" when a better choice would be to use the word "difficult."**
Concrete, marble, and granite are hard. A task could be difficult.
Consider that you would say:

```
With some difficulty, Lisa picks up the elephant.
```

You would not say:

```
With some hardness, Lisa picks up the elephant.
```

You also wouldn't say that a rock is difficult. You would say that a rock is hard.

393

Is that difficult to understand?

Look through your scene descriptions and find if there is the use of the word hard where the word difficult would be a better fit.

In the dialogue, keep the wording reflective of the way people naturally speak. They are more likely to use the more correct word choices if they are someone who is a science journal editor, English teacher, librarian, or literature professor. Not that highly-educated people always make the best word choices.

- **NOTE 167: SLANG OR PROPER: The characters don't speak within their realistic culture or socio-economic status.**

Not that it is always more realistic to have university professors speaking correct English, and to have poor people speaking as if they are uneducated. Doing the direct opposite could be more interesting – especially if there is a good reason for doing so that serves the story.

Maybe the professor is trying to prove something to her students by speaking as if she doesn't know proper English.

Maybe the woman who grew up poor didn't know how to read. To compensate for not being able to read, she is especially sure to use correct English. Maybe, to have a mind that is like a reference library of history, music, art, science, industry, and the stories contained in books that she never read, she gleaned information by listening to and watching news programs and documentaries, and listened to endless interviews on public radio and public television.

- **NOTE 168: BREAKING DESCRIPTION PARAGRAPHS: The writer doesn't seem to know where to break scene description into new paragraphs – even if those paragraphs would be one-sentence long.**

One of the problems with scripts written by beginners is that they tend to have long, wordy paragraphs in the scene description. (Long description blocks.)

Scene description written by new screenwriters often contains information that doesn't need to be in the script.

If you know how a scene is filmed, you will have an idea of how to break scene description into a new paragraph when a new camera setup is needed (when the camera, lighting, and sound equipment is rearranged).

A new camera setup is likely needed when a new angle of the scene takes place. Breaking the script description into paragraphs can also be called breaking the scene into beats.

Pay attention to the beats of the scene, and that could be where to break the paragraph. By doing that, you may not have to pay attention to the probable camera setups. (When it is filmed, the director and cinematographer won't necessarily film it in the same way that it is written.)

Mostly, scripts will contain scene description paragraphs that are fewer than four lines, and often one line. But, not always.

(Search: Free screenplay downloads.) You will find that you can download the scripts of recent award-winning films. Get an idea of how the scene description consists of short paragraphs.

"Know your literary tradition, savor it, steal from it, but when you sit down to write, forget about worshiping greatness and fetishizing masterpieces."
– Allegra Goodman, author *The Chalk Artist*

Be aware that the scripts you read online are often shooting scripts (containing a variety of things not to be contained in a spec script, including camera angles, props and sounds put in uppercase [flagged, as in: to alert the crew what is needed for the scene], scene numbers, and descriptions that detail what the director and various crew working on the production need to know). Scripts that you find online also might be development scripts (which could contain notes and incomplete scenes), or published scripts (which could have been typed up by anyone, contain all sorts of bad formatting and/or are condensed to reduce the use of paper).

"A film is a petrified fountain of thought."
– Jean Cocteau, *Orpheus*

- **NOTE 169: DIRECTOR'S JOB: The writer doesn't seem to understand the director's job.**

"Ninety-percent of directing is casting."
– Milos Forman, *Valmont*

"A team effort is a lot of people doing what I say."
– Michael Winner, *Death Wish*

"There is a lot made of this sort of adversarial relationship between directors and writers – which I don't believe in, personally. And I have had a lot of luck with four different directors I've worked with more than once. You need them, and they need you. You're kind of lost without each other. A secure director wants to hear what you have to say – whether he or she agrees with you, or not. The kind of more push and pull and tug there is between you the better the film will probably be."
– Brian Helgeland, *A Knight's Tale*

Some scripts are worded as if the screenwriter is explaining everything the director needs to understand and do, in a baby spoon-fed kind of way.
Don't write a script that micromanages the director, or as if it is an instruction manual for a less-intelligent director.

"Screenplays don't have to read like an instruction manual for a refrigerator. You can write them as a pleasurable read."
– William Goldman, *Chaplin*

395

"I think movies are collaborative. You can't escape that if you are a screenwriter. People have come in and they're all going to start talking about the script. It just is the way it is. A suggestion isn't writing, even a line of dialogue. You still have to write the movie, and take these notes, and put it all through your point-of-view, and then when you have a director on, you have to make sure you are supporting their point-of-view. Because you can't force a director to do something they don't understand – even if you hold a gun to their head, they'll do it poorly. You hope you and the director have the same point-of-view."
– Scott Frank, *Minority Report*

"It's the actors who are the main element. Let's equate it to a wall. I'm a painter and you give me a wall, and you say, 'Oh, it's a seventy-foot wall, and you can paint the whole wall, but you've got to have horses in it.' I'll say, 'Oh, okay.' Then I get the paint – and the actors are the paint and it's living pigment, and each person who's added to that bleeds through to the next person and causes reaction after reaction, and it moves and finds its own composition. That's the way it seems to me. Everybody doesn't work the same way, nor should they."
– Robert Altman, *Short Cuts*

If you are directing the script you wrote, you will likely go about doing things differently than if you are writing a script that someone else will direct. One of those things is that during casting you might not use scenes from the script when you audition actors. You might use scenes from other scripts that you didn't write. You might write new scenes that aren't included in your script – but that will give the actors things to do during the audition so that you can see how they might portray the character, and display their talents.

"I never use the script for the casting. I think it's very dangerous. Actors prepare for casting differently. For me, it's always good when they are open and able to react. I always write completely new scenes for the casting."
– Maren Ade, *Everyone Else*

No matter who is going to direct the script, remember that audiences go to films for escapism, to feel things, to see characters do and express things that they can't do or express, to see people live lives the audience members wish they could live – or not live. But mostly, to experience their senses.

"Audiences go to movies to feel. When the movie becomes too mechanical – instead of organic – audiences detach from the film."
– Simon Kinberg, *Fantastic Four*

Not all film or series sets welcome the writer. It could be an expense matter, an issue relating to safety, time constraints, director request (so the director can be left to do their job), a producer or studio standard, or other reasons.

"I don't think screenplay writing is the same as writing. I mean, I think it's blueprinting."
– Robert Altman, *Short Cuts*

"Writing is like when the generals are in the war room, with maps spread out on the table, making their grand plans, and then when you're directing, you're actually in the trenches with the troops, trying to actually make it work. You just have to take the hill. At the same time, when I'm writing, I am directing in my head. I can't write a scene unless I can see it visually, and also have a sense of tonality and otherwise how it's going to play."
– Rian Johnson, *Knives Out*

Think of yourself as an architect who drew up the plans for a building. You hand them over to a contractor, who works with a construction crew to build the structure. As a screenwriter, you are the architect of a production. The script is the blueprint for a film or series – hopefully with much more personality than a blueprint. You hand that to the producers and/or development execs, and/or the director, who then work with the DP, actors, crew, editors, and post-craftspeople. They turn it into a structure that is seen on a screen. Maybe they make it into something that people will want to watch.

"It's a thing. It has to be perfect. It has to be as perfect as it can be. And then, you do hand it over to other people's art. And that's a privilege."
– Emma Thompson, *Last Christmas*

By the time the film you wrote is ready for the screen, you are far out of the process of being involved with it, and you are working on and selling your next best script – and maybe working for hire for producers as you doctor the scripts of other writers, are writing scripts on assignment, and/or are working as a staff writer on a series.

Don't freak out if something you wrote got made into something that is not watchable, and is a complete financial failure. It's finished. You aren't. Keep moving forward.

"It's the falling in love with the first thing that comes out of your head that is what will take you down. It will make you impossible to work with, and it will result in things often not being as good as they could be."
– Paul Feig, *Ghostbusters*

Don't freak out if the people who are making your script into a show don't want you on set. Concern yourself with your next projects.

Maybe they don't want you on set because you are unpleasant, needy, cross lines, and like a thorn in human form. Maybe they find you to be intimidating.

Be glad that you won't have to be on set. Your job is done. You aren't going to be in control of the production. That's why there is a director, A.D., producers, D.P, sound techs, grips, electricians, and other hardworking crew – and hopefully a talented cast who will help make your work shine.

"I look for a director with a script he likes a lot, but I'm probably after the directors more than anything. Because of the way the business is structured today, I have sometimes turned down scripts that I might otherwise have accepted, had I known who was directing them. *Witness*, for example."
– Jack Nicholson, *Head*

"To be a filmmaker, you have to lead. You have to be psychotic in your desire to do something. People always like the easy route. You have to push very hard to get something unusual, something different."
– Danny Boyle, *Hamish Macbeth*

"You're following your track, the story, your only plan, your map for the audience, and all the other stuff is the fun stuff: The costumes, the locations, the set-dressing, and the actors. They can all be as variable as you like if you stick – however roughly – to the path."
– Gus Van Sant, *Drugstore Cowboy*

Even if you are going to direct your script, don't write your script as if it is an instruction manual for a director, DP, and editor. That is: Don't saturate it with technical direction, and over-explaining, and puppetry direction and parentheticals for the actors. Skilled craftspeople will read your script, and recognize what you have done – and may not be interested in working with someone who is that naïve, as it might be like a babysitting job for them.

"Make your own stuff. Whether it's short films or whatever you can do, my advice is to make your own stuff. I'm a real believer in preparation meets opportunity."
– Annie Mumolo, *Bridesmaids*

"Writing and editing aren't support skills, they are the job. You can't become a director until you master the art of screenwriting. If you want to make narrative films, you're gonna have to write for yourself. You're making a film in your brain, and a screenplay is the written record of your imagination."
– Alexander Payne, *Citizen Ruth*

"It seemed to me that the writers have done a large part of the visualization of the film. You know how every line is supposed to sound; you've pictured the set so you imagined the blocking, so why not shoot it? How far wrong can you go?"
– Harold Ramis, *Groundhog Day*

"Find people who are as passionate about filmmaking as you, that complement what you want to do. So, if you want to be a director, you find someone as passionate about editing, or as passionate about lighting, or as passionate about acting. If you can team up with them, it just gives you so much more momentum to get things done. Especially if you're working on the very low-budget side of things, and you're trying to put together a short film – or even a very low-budget feature. I think if you can find just a small team, it

makes people take you more seriously, and it gives you much more chance of trying to do it, as opposed to trying to do it on your own."
– Duncan Jones, *Moon*

"Most directors, I discovered, need to be convinced that the screenplay they're going to direct has something to do with them. And this is a tricky thing if you write screenplays where women have parts that are equal to or greater than the male part. And, I thought, 'Why am I out there looking for directors?' – because you look at a list of directors, it's all boys. It certainly was when I started as a screenwriter. So, I thought, 'I'm just gonna become a director, and that'll make it easier.'"
– Nora Ephron, *You've Got Mail*

"I first came to cinema as a passionate filmgoer, when I was a child. Then, when I was a very young man, I became a film critic, precisely because of my knowledge of cinema. I did better than others because of this. Then, I moved on to screenwriting. I wrote a film with Sergio Leone, *Once Upon a Time in the West*. And then I moved to directing."
– Dario Argento, *Deep Red*

"When you start shooting, anything can happen. The nature of a shoot is that there are going to be problems, and the director's job is not to let them get out of hand. Truffaut used to say that shooting a film was like having yourself and your whole team on a train, on a fast track, and with no brakes And that it was the director's job to make sure the train didn't derail."
– Pedro Almodovar, *Pain & Glory*

To understand what a director does, and what they can do with your script, study some books about film and TV directing. While you are at it, read books about producing, and books about editing.

"When I first meet with the scriptwriter, I never tell him anything, even if I feel there's a lot to be done. Instead I ask him the same questions I've asked myself: What is the story about? What did you see? What was your intention? Ideally, if we do this well, what do you hope the audience will feel, think, sense? In what mode do you want them to leave the theater?"
– Sidney Lumet, *Night Falls on Manhattan*

The better you are prepared with an understanding of the various aspects of production and the people involved with it, the more likely your skills in the screenwriting craft will improve. The more you know how to deal and communicate with talented, skilled, and experienced people in the industry, the more you will know your place. With all of that, the more likely your scripts – and you – will be a success.

Understanding the director's role in making a screenplay is key to working with them.

"Screenwriting is a much more collaborative effort. When you write a novel, it's just you with input from your editor."
– Meg Cabot, *Avalon High*

Don't disregard the director's input.

Know that directors may see something in your scripts that you didn't expect. Be patient in understanding their perceptions.

"A lot of times you get credit for stuff in your movies that you didn't intend to be there."
– Spike Lee, *BlaKkKlansman*

It is not uncommon for writers to be at some level of disappointment with how their script was turned into a film or series. But, once it is done, it is time to take the lessons learned, and move on to other projects.

"When you're directing a movie, you're always deficient. When you're a writer, you can always fix it – until they take it away.
I think if you ask any director, they'll say there's no film they've ever worked on that they're completely satisfied with. I think that's universal."
– Tony Gilroy, *Armageddon*

"I'm not really a writer-writer. I'm a director who writes out of necessity. But once another writer comes on to polish it, it's like 'Oh, my god! This is exactly what I wanted to do.'
For me, I thrive on collaboration."
– Hasraf Dulull, *The Beyond*

Do learn how to be collaborative, and to discuss things in civil ways – especially when there are disagreements. Keep your cool, even when the other person behaves badly. You are not their brain, their life experiences, their manners, their choices, their mood swings, their substances, or their career.

One benefit of attending a screenwriting workshop is that you sit at a table of writers, read script pages that you didn't write, and then discuss them with other writers. The process helps prepare you for discussing scripts with managers, agents, development executives, producers, directors, and actors.

"A good script – or a great script – can become a bad movie. It takes execution. And it takes a lot of people having the same vision for it to do well."
– Taylor Sheridan, *Those Who Wish Me Dead*

It's not in your best interest to get combative with development executives, producers, or directors – unless you want to burn bridges, and limit yourself.

It is a relatively small industry. News of who is involved with which projects – and how that progresses or regresses – travels fast. Especially with social media, and texting. People in the industry communicate, quickly. If you don't know that, you will learn it.

"If you put someone in a room with no script to direct, they're just going to sit there. Writing scripts is the execution for a show. Then the director takes that and hires people. It's like trying to build a house without any bricks. You need a great script."
– John Patrick Shanley, *Doubt*

Know that you can't control all aspects of your film's path to being financed, cast, scheduled, filmed, edited, scored, and marketed.

Know that sometimes – and maybe every time one of your scripts is produced – the scripts will go through massive changes, including rewrites, which may include other writers being credited with writing what ends up on the screen.

"Many screenwriters think they have the Holy Grail of scripts, and cannot face requests to rewrite elements of their screenplay, or even an entire rewrite. I have found that when a writer is actively working with the producer to make the script better following the director and producer's notes, there is a bigger chance that the script will actually end up being produced."
– Markus Linecker, Dedicated Talent Management

"My biggest compliment is how the viewer might think it's improvised. Like, 'Oh, you just turned on the camera, and that happened.' That's a compliment, because we work really hard to make it feel that way.

Between the actor and myself, my biggest compliment is for the actor to feel like they wrote the scene, or they contributed so much that's it's them, you know.

To me, the most magical moment is when these words on a page meet performer, and where that goes is kind of – to me – that's the essence of what you're gonna be experiencing in the film. But, actors tell me that I'm very Zen and relaxed and give them a lot of leeway, and I'm like, 'good!' Because that's what I'm trying to be.

I think it's the director's job to create an atmosphere where you can do your best work."
– Richard Linklater, *Boyhood*

Filmmaking is a collaborative business. You can't do it alone.

Only a person with unrealistic expectations would think that what they write in a screenplay will be exactly what ends up on screen.

"I'm not against improvising certain scenes, if they are compatible with the character, but my greatest preoccupation is for the actors to forget that they're acting, and to find something fresh, to truly give something to the characters."
– Kantemir Balogov, *Closeness*

"(Bob) Rafelson's shooting the goodbye scenes; the wind blows, and a bird flies through. It's the oddest thing of all time. Not planned. The audience may

not realize it consciously, but, somehow, they know that is what made the scene right. The written seen is 'I love you.' The bird is on his own."
— Jack Nicholson, about filming *Five Easy Pieces*

"Steven Spielberg had purchased my script *Continental Divide*, which was very different from the film which resulted. The script had a kind of Hawksian speed, momentum – hopefully – about it. I don't think the film turned out that way, which was one of those painful experiences I had early on. But Steven's enthusiasm for it was what got me involved with him and George."
— Lawrence Kasdan, *The Empire Strikes Back*

"The only validation you have as a writer is to yourself, that you've written something good that you really cared about, that you can look at and read it and say, 'This is my script. This is what I really wanted to say.' If your friends like it, then you're really pleased. What your dream is that an audience gets a chance to see your vision. I mean, that's why you write movies. But you have to move to grips with the reality that the chances of having a movie made are so slim. That it's so, so difficult."
— Laurence Dworet, *Outbreak*

As you work in the industry, you will likely notice many things that you would rather have happen differently, especially with how your scripts are treated. Get used to it. And, get over it. Always be involved in writing, finishing, and polishing your next script – and your next best script after that.

"Film is thought of as a director's medium, because the director creates the end product that appears on the screen. It's that stupid auteur theory again, that the director is the author of the film. But, what does the director shoot – the telephone book? Writer's became much more important when sound came in, but they've had to put up a valiant fight to get the credit they deserve."
— Billy Wilder, *Double Indemnity*

Many screenwriters don't like that both the advertising for a film and the credits at the start of a film can say that it is a film by the director. The writers say it should be a film by the writer, directed by the director.

"A "Film By" credit is ugly. It is ego. It is elitist, and excludes all the people who work hard on a movie."
— Katherine Fugate, *Valentine's Day*

"We spend six months crafting this thing, and then the director is given all the credit. Of course, the Writers Guild has been trying to fight that, but it's a common feeling we as screenwriters have."
— Jane Anderson, *The Wife*

"I have always credited the writer of the original material above the title: *Mario Puzo's The Godfather*, *Bram Stoker's Dracula*, or *John Grisham's The*

Rainmaker. I felt that I didn't have the right to Francis Coppola's anything, unless I had written the story and the screenplay."
– Francis Ford Coppola, *Apocalypse Now*

"The truth is, a director wins an Oscar for a writer's script and actor's performances."
– George Cukor, director

"I think maybe there is the auteur theory that kind of confused everybody for a long time. But, I do think that writing in – especially in Hollywood – is not important. And, you know, it's proven again and again. I mean, the people who market movies and make movies don't need writers. The worse movies with the most problematic scripts become the most successful movies. And so, I think when you see that, then writers aren't important. But, directors have names, and they have visual styles, and you can sell movies with them, because they got this sort of celebrity – sometimes – quality to them. But, it's very different in theater. It's the opposite in theater. At least in the United States. I don't know how it is here (in Goteborg, Sweden), but it's the playwright who is the famous name, and it is the playwright who owns the material and has the copyright, and you can't change anything without the playwright. It's not the same with writers in Hollywood."
– Charlie Kaufman, *Eternal Sunshine of the Spotless Mind*

When there is a remake of a film or TV series, the story basically stays the same, and a different person directs it. Taking that into consideration, shouldn't the films be credited to the writer, and directing credited to the director?

"Well, Jack Warner may have been celebrated for calling writers schmucks with underwoods, but twenty years earlier Irving Thalberg said, 'The most important person in the motion picture process is the writer, and we must do everything in our power to prevent them from ever realizing it.'"
– Steven de Souza, *Judge Dredd*

It is probably not in your best interest to try to control what is going to end up on the screen. You can share your opinion, and then the producers, director, D.P., set designer, art director, set dresser, wardrobe designer, actors, editors, and others will do what they will.

"As a screenwriter, you have to let go, and you have to hand your baby over and let it go off into the world, which is entirely appropriate."
– Philippa Boyens, *The Lord of the Rings: The Return of the King*

Settle for being happy that someone paid you for your script. As your career advances – if you continue to sell screenplays that end up being produced and that then make significant money – you might have more of a say in what ends up on the screen.

"I wrote screenplays as a way to get into production. I wrote six or seven before I sold one. That was *The Bodyguard*. I thought if I started selling these screenplays, I'd get a chance to direct. I thought that was the way in."
– Lawrence Kasdan, *Raiders of the Lost Ark*

Maybe you will also direct one or more of the screenplays that you wrote.

"Directing was easy for me, because I was a writer-director, and did all my directing when I wrote the screenplay."
– Preston Sturges, *The Great McGinty*

Until you have established a career, write scripts that are compelling, engaging, commercial, and that will sell. Always be glad they did.

"I always claim that the writer has done ninety percent of the director's work."
– Harold Ramis, *Groundhog Day*

If you want complete control of a writing project, write a novel, and publish it on Amazon, through Amazon's print-on-demand platform, Kindle Direct Publishing – so that you won't have to deal with a publishing company.

(Search: Amanda Hocking self-published.) Read about how Amanda Hocking self-published her novels, sold over a million copies, and attracted a major publisher. While she has had some books published through a publishing company, she also has continued self-publishing some of others.

- **NOTE 170: BUDGETARY WRITING: The writer didn't seem to take budgetary issues into consideration when writing the script.**
  Consider the amount of money each scene in your script will cost to film. Will it require a kitchen and table, or are there car chases, explosions, flocks of animals, massive numbers of children, crowds of people engaged in fighting, rain, mud, burning buildings, flooded villages, crashing airplanes, a train derailment, sinking ships, and other expensive scenarios throughout the script?
  Consider one expensive element, such as the flock of animals scenario. Where are you going to get all of those animals, how are they going to be stored between takes, how many people are going to have to be involved in feeding them, protecting them, guiding them in and out of the filming location, and cleaning up after them? Are the animal scenes needed to tell the story? Could the animal scenes be cut from the script without negating the story? Could they be done with CGI, which means they can do exactly as needed?
  Even if you have a single animal, such as a horse that will need to run at certain moments, jump at others, and otherwise behave on cue, there will be a number of expenses associated with getting all of that on film, while also feeding and caring for the horse.
  I was on the set of a TV show about a zoo. They had a number of large animals. There was a giraffe who was clearly not in a healthy condition. That poor, sweet creature seemed scared, nervous, confused, and otherwise

uncomfortable. Don't do that to an animal. Exotic animals are better off in the wild, or in sanctuaries with adequate space to move around, and receive the care they need to remain healthy. They shouldn't be used as props on movie sets, or freaked out to film them for audience manipulation.

Consider not including animals in your script. Or, if the film has a significant budget, any animal can now be created with (CGI).

If you have children in your script, know that there are laws governing the use children in TV shows, films, commercials, music videos, and other productions. Children must have a parent or guardian on set at all times. There will need to be a set teacher. A quiet, safe place to hold class will need to be provided. There needs to be certain safety measures taken when children are used in scenes, including having a medic present. The children will be limited to working for a certain number of hours, and they must take breaks at specific times. In other words, using child actors requires money. One way to reduce production costs is to use actors who are at least 18 years old, but who appear to be younger.

The more expensive your script is to make, the less likely it will be to make it into production, through editing, and onto the screen.

Consider the recent films that have been successful at the box office and on cable and streaming services. Make a list of them. Label them as high-budget, medium budget, low budget, and very low budget.

Consider the global marketplace for film and TV, including the U.S., China, Germany, Australia, India, Korea, Japan, Brazil, Mexico, the U.K., South Africa, etc. Will your production play well in those countries? Can it attract actors who are famous in those regions so that audiences in those regions will have a familiar cast member to interest them?

One reason that many films feature actors who are famous in various countries is purely for the reason that their fame increases the chances that the film will make money in that region of the world.

Consider this specific issue: The investors want the greatest return on investment (R.O.I. = "Good Roy").

Will the film play well on cable? This could include HBO, Showtime, TLC, FX, Syfy, A&E, Bravo, B.E.T., Oxygen, The History Channel, Hallmark, or Lifetime.

Will the film play on streaming platforms? Streaming services include Netflix, Hulu, Amazon, Quibi, and YouTube.

Could the project play on network TV? Those include NBC, CBS, ABC, Fox, and The CW.

Will the project play well on TV stations in Australia, New Zealand, Korea, Japan, South Africa, Nigeria, Brazil, India, Canada, England, Ireland, Scotland, Germany, and other countries and regions?

Will the film play on airplanes? Yes, the airline industry also is a form of revenue for the film industry. They have to keep those millions of passengers satisfied during long flights.

The more places that a production could be shown, the greater its chances for long-term financial return.

Some films play so well at the theatres that there isn't as great of a concern that they will be viewed on cable, streaming, and other forms of display.

Will your script require a budget within reasonable expectations of a satisfactory box office return on investment?

Low budget movies that were successful at the theatres include *Lady Bird, Napoleon Dynamite, I, Tonya, Moonlight, Get Out*, and *Saw*.

Consider series that have been successful in many countries, including *Game of Thrones, Stranger Things, Westworld, Ray Donovan, The Crown, Breaking Bad*, and *Baywatch*. How does your script stand up to those for international interest?

Does your script have the potential for sequel material, like *Star Trek, Star Wars, Sharknado* (yes, *Sharknado* has been a huge success for investors), *Jason Bourne, Harry Potter, Rocky, Mad Max, The Lord of the Rings*, or lower budget films that have spawned sequels and/or remakes, including *Trainspotting, Before Sunset, The Best Marigold Hotel, American Pie, Halloween, From Dusk Till Dawn, Cruel Intentions, Wild Things, Poison Ivy, Roadhouse, Dirty Dancing*, and others?

Could your project result in theme park rides, toys, clothing, video games, and other money-making ventures for the investors? Film merchandising is a multi-billion-dollar global industry (and then it all ends up as global trash).

(Search for the article: *Movie Merchandising* by Mark Litwak.)

The more you understand about the money-side of the film industry, the more likely you can write films that cater to investor interests.

"I think about the audience in the sense that I serve as my own audience. I have to please myself that way, if I saw the movie in theatre, I would be pleased. Do I think about catering to an audience? No."
– Shane Black, *Last Action Hero*

Maybe all of the considerations of money and merchandising nauseates you, and you simply want to write films that matter, that make a difference in the world, that are socially valid, that raise the awareness of important issues, and that can be cherished for generations. Go for what moves you. But, know that your script also has to carry some promise that it will generate a return on investment – or it is less likely to get produced.

Perhaps you want to make a documentary to explore and reveal important issues that you think people should know of. There are books and videos that will help you understand the documentary process. Search that topic.

- **NOTE 171: SCRIPT END FORMATTING: The script ends in an unusual way.**

It is common to end your script with these words centered on a blank line after the final scene:

                    THE END

Or, you can put:

                                        FADE TO BLACK

              THE END

You can choose to also put **THE END** to the right.

                                        THE END

If the director or producers – or editor and/or title designer – want something unusual or fancier than that, they will do it.

See the film *Wild Things*, and watch the additional entertaining shots throughout the credits. It is unlikely that all of that was written into the script. It's a director, editor, and/or producer decision.

"I'm not under too much of an illusion of how smart – or unsmart – I am, because filmmaking ultimately is about teamwork."
– Guy Ritchie, *The Gentlemen*

"What is the overall through-line of the play, what is the spine, what does everything kind of hold on to?"
– Horton Foote, *Tender Mercies*

Considering Your Script

"What makes screenplays difficult are the things that require the most discipline and care and are just not seen by most people. I'm talking about movement – screenwriting is related to math and music, and if you zig here, you know you have to zag there. It's like the descriptions for a piece of music – you go fast or slow or with feeling. It's the same."
– Robert Towne, *China Town*

"Every scene should be able to answer three questions: Who wants what from whom? What happens if they don't get it? Why now?"
– David Mamet, *The Postman Always Rings Twice*

Excavate your scenes. See what lies beneath. Recognize and explore the underlying structure of each scene. Identify what the pillars and beats are of the scenes. Factor ways for it to work elegantly to convey story and the inner workings of the character's minds, including their hopes, fears, repulsions, happiness, sadness, wants, needs, perceptions, anticipations, disappointments, and love – or lack thereof – and many other things.

Make your script into what directors, actors, producers, and other industry professionals would like to be a part of, to advance their careers… and yours.

"Today's films are so technological that an actor becomes starved for roles that deal with human relationships."
– Natalie Wood, actress

- **NOTE 172: BROADLY APPEALING: Is the story engaging, and told in a way likely to be interesting to a broad number of people?**
Investing in films is all about getting a return on investment. Anyone putting money into a film who doesn't have this in mind is failing.

If the script doesn't hold the likelihood that the final product will fill a theater and/or get significant distribution on various platforms (TV, cable, streaming, etc.), it is far less likely to get financed, produced, and distributed.

- **NOTE 173: STORY PATH: Does the story have a beginning, middle, end, and a denouement (final conclusion)?**

If it is flat, rework it. Pump up the conflict. Use clever, thoughtful acts of manipulative, subtle, or bold contention so that the scenes are more likely to be interesting, engaging, and satisfying to a broad number of viewers.

Or, put aside the script, and move onto writing one that holds more promise.

Even screenwriters who have already written scripts that were produced and resulted in films that were globally successful have had to abandon scripts that weren't working. They don't want to waste time. Don't waste your time.

The more screenplays you write, the more likely it will be that you will start one that you first thought was a grand idea, but realized wasn't worth your time, energy, or resources.

Keep a copy of your abandoned scripts. Maybe one day you will factor ways to make them compelling and marketable – or maybe another generation will find them and do so.

- **NOTE 174: SCENE REVIEW: Have you reviewed each scene to consider if the main story remains dominant or an undercurrent?**

What is the conflict, contention, threat, and concern of each scene that stakes it into the script, and hooks into the through-line and emotional trail?

Even if the scene is a pause in all of the action – of the sun rising above the city, or a farm, or a forest, or a war zone, or other place – the tension and concerns of the central driving story is to be maintained, is present, and continues for the rest of the script. The audience is to know that something is unsettled, and some other important thing for the ultimate outcome is nigh.

- **NOTE 175: DIRECTOR ADVANCEMENT: Will the film advance the career of the director?**

If the gig isn't something that is going to look good on a director's resume, what kind of director do you think the script is going to attract?

- **NOTE 176: NAME ACTORS: Will top actors want to play the roles?**

Not that the script must attract the so-called biggest stars in the world, but recognizable actor names can help get scripts funded and distributed, and bring in audiences – and money.

If you attach one actor who is famous in each region of the world, that casting can help get your script funded. Distributors and financiers like recognizable names. It could be much more difficult to try to sell a naked script, which is one that has no recognizable, established talent attached to it.

But, if those recognizable actors are miscast, or the script isn't good, or the production values falter (bad sound, camera, lighting, editing, etc.), the project could end up being a waste of time and money.

- **NOTE 177: BUDGETARY NEEDS: Will the film get the budget needed to attract the talent you want – preferably talent who can help land significant distribution?**

Having a low budget doesn't mean that you can't get the level of actors you wish to see in the roles. You simply need their level of script.

Write characters that are so interesting that major actors will want to play the roles. Even if it is a chance to redesign their career, and to break away from the types of roles they have been offered.

If the role is so revolutionary for an actor to play, they may accept minimum union scale rates. Especially if it will advance their careers. Charlize Theron did it in *Monster*. Halle Berry did it in *Monster's Ball*. Mickey Rourke did it in *The Wrestler*. Cher did it in *Come Back to the 5 & Dime Jimmy, Dean Jimmy Dean*, and in *Silkwood*. Robert Pattinson did it in *The Lighthouse*.

Hilary Swank revolutionized her career trajectory by starring in *Boys Don't Cry*. She was paid a few thousand dollars. She won every major acting award.

Top actors appear in both low-budget and high-budget films. Michael B. Jordan, Julianne Moore, Kristen Stewart, Woody Harrelson, Alec Baldwin, Johnny Depp, Miranda Otto (she's terrific to work with), Kate Winslet, Viggo Mortensen, Denzel Washington, and Meryl Streep are known to do low-budget films. Stars need to prove their skills. Write the material they need. If you write high-quality screenplays, they need you just as much as you need them.

- **NOTE 178: DISTRIBUTOR PRE-SALE: Would distributors be interested in knowing about the project and team of attached talent – before filming?**

There have been films fully or partially financed by distribution deals. Some say that era is over. But, that opinion isn't a rule.

- **NOTE 179: TITLE MESSAGE: Does the film have a title that speaks to the audience, and provides a clue as to what it is about?**

Saw and its grim sequels are films with visual name recognition.

The films *Interstellar, Moon, Fight Club, Sleeping with the Enemy, Rebel Without a Cause, Pulp Fiction, The Usual Suspects*, and *The Perks of Being a Wallflower* have names that trigger a visual. So does *Sharknado*. Mixed with interesting marketing images, they attracted audiences that satisfied investors.

- **NOTE 180: DOMINANCE OF STORY: Does story rule each scene?**

Have you ever watched a film that you completely got so lost in that you could not stop watching it, and every scene held your attention to both the main story and layers of backstories?

Write scripts that succeed in holding audiences in their seats.

"I just try and decide what I'm interested in and what excites me. I don't worry about how it's going to be perceived."
– Yorgos Lanthimos, *The Lobster*

- **NOTE 181: PARAMETERS OF THE WORLD WITHIN THE SCRIPT: Does the world that you created in the script establish societal parameters that can't be crossed, and within which the characters must function?**

In *The Wizard of Oz*, Dorothy lives as a member of a humble farm family. Every day of her world is about the same: Work and family, school, chores, errands, dinner, and sleep. Those are the parameters of her reality. But, in her dream, she enters a surreal world in which everything is fantastical, and the parameters of her experiences there are vast, wild, and fascinating, and with characters living lives grandly different than what she is used to. Once she awakes, she is back in her humble family situation, and tries to explain the vastness of what she experienced – which is all outside of her family's reality.

What are the societal parameters of the world in which your characters live and that they are bound by? Do they serve the story that you are trying to tell?

- **NOTE 182: TIMELY CHARACTER INTROS: Do you introduce each character in ways that serve an interesting visual and increases the conflict, even external conflict (monster, virus, tornado, fire, etc.)?**

Write an excellent character setup.

Here is how to not introduce a character, as it says about nothing at all:

```
People dance on the lighted dance floor. Sally (24),
blonde, pretty, in a pink lace dress with high heels,
enters the bar. Some people notice, including Ted.
She sits near him.
```

That's bland. Do we need to know the color of her hair? Pretty? Subjective and says little. Pink lace? Why? High heels? Do we need to know? Unless there is a specific reason for us to know the color of her hair or details of her clothing, leave it out, and leave it up to the casting director, director, producer, wardrobe designer, or whomever is going to make those decisions.

One reason we might need to know the color of her hair is because there was an early scene in which Ted says something about how he could never date someone with the same color of hair as his high school prom date, who was a brunette. And maybe he has a thing for pink lace dresses. If those details have – for some reason – been established in an earlier scene, then, mention the hair color and the clothing details. Maybe his friends arranged it all to wake up the guy's love life… with their female friend who likes shy guys.

411

How about:

```
The speakers blast a disco/hip hop remix.

The lighted floor is packed with dancers. Some do
impressive and others silly moves.

At the empty bar sits Ted. Swigs a beer. Takes out
his phone, scrolls the screen. Yawns.

Blonde SALLY (20s), dressed to party in a pink lace
dress, takes a seat, swings around to watch the
crowd. He eyes her. She looks. He diverts his eyes.

                    SALLY
            So. Do you dance?
```

Introduce characters in a clever and visual way. Serve up some subtext. Challenge people in the scene, then show how they shy away from, or approach, contend with, and manipulate the situation – and each other.

If they aren't challenged in ways that can stumble them and lead them to make choices that the audience wants to see the impact of, why are they a lead character? That can all start from the moment they enter the screen.

As an exercise, with a notepad, go to a park, beach, coffee house, office campus, train station, or other public place and write intros for the people you see around you – as if they are characters in a screenplay. Try for wording that gives personality to the intro in ways that immediately plug the reader into what the character is about.

- **NOTE 183: CHARACTER PURPOSE: On which page are we sure or unsure who the antagonist is, and who the protagonist is?**
This doesn't mean that the initially perceived protagonist has to remain the protagonist, or that the initially perceived antagonist has to remain the antagonist throughout the story. We might end up hating the character who we thought we were going to be cheering for, and liking the character who we thought we were going to be cursing. Our perceptions also might switch back and forth during the film.

Shifting and manipulating the attention and expectations of the audience is one way to keep them engaged and in their seats.

- **NOTE 184: CHARACTER PREDICAMENT: Do we know enough about the character's situation early on so that we understand them and their predicament in an engaging way?**
This doesn't mean that you need to use dialogue to inform us about the characters. Much can be said without dialogue.

Consider the first scene of a script as this:

An obviously drunken young man asleep on a filthy sofa in a ramshackle apartment; three children cry as they sit in front of empty plates at a dirty table; a young woman on her knees silently prays with a rosary in front of a plastic Virgin Mary statue. The woman takes out a scratcher lottery ticket, scrapes off the numbers, wrinkles it, and angrily throws it at the head of the man passed-out on the sofa.

Without words, we understand the predicament of all of those characters.

Use imagery to portray character history, position, wants, needs, and undercurrent. Film is a visual medium – with sound. Always remember that while you are writing a screenplay. But, also know that there likely will be a soundtrack, and the tone and inflection of the actor's delivery also plays into manipulating the audience, and their perception, anticipation, and desire.

- **NOTE 185: ATTENTION GRAB: By page eight or nine, do we have an understanding of what the character wants and/or expects so that we know how deeply frustrated, humored, exhilarated, motivated, excited, terrified, let-down, or otherwise emotionally involved they will likely be when whatever happens somewhere around page nine-to-twelve impacts their expectations?**

Set us up and get us emotionally involved in the story. Then give us a big twist (inciting incident that starts the character's journey) somewhere around pages nine to twelve. Keep twisting it – and the backstories. Take us on a manipulative roller-coaster ride of anticipation with rough twists, turns, jolts, and roll-arounds. Mess with audience perception and anticipation.

- **NOTE 186: AUDIENCE SATISFACTION: Near the end of the script, will we know enough to be satisfied, or satisfied with guessing what will happen with the character?**

Think of the ending as you write the beginning.

This does not mean that we have to know everything that the character has concluded, or how they settled into the changes, but maybe we are able to make conclusions about how the character will carry on into their existence.

- **NOTE 187: HUMOR: Are the funny parts truly funny?**

This issue is one reason why it is good to workshop a script, to see and hear how a room full of writers and actors responds to the parts of the script that you think are funny.

If your script is funny to you and only you, consider rewriting it, or consider letting it rest a while. Write another script. Then, return to the previous one.

"What's the trick to writing a genuinely funny comedy? The trick is therapy. Take notes."
– Lake Bell, *I Do… Until I Don't*

"First and foremost, when you're doing comedy, you gotta be relevant and applicable to the times that you're living in. When you try and just do comedy about who is dating who, and lifestyle jokes, it gets tiring after a while. It's hard to be funny in that realm."
– Adam McKay, *The Big Short*

- **NOTE 188: STORY SETUP: Do you satisfactorily setup the story, backstories, lead characters, and secondary characters, and mix it all with conflict, interesting twists and turns, hurdles, and an emotional through-line in ways that we stay tuned to see what happens?**
Workshop it. Listen to the feedback. Take notes. Consider. Rewrite. Then, send the script to an editor. Do another polish. Then, get it to a coverage service, and consider the coverage (see the coverage chapter in this book).
Do a table read of the script with a group of actors (perhaps from a local theater company).

- **NOTE 189: SCENE LENGTH: Could the scenes be shortened by cutting out the first part and/or end, and being more succinct in the description – while still presenting us with what we need to know from the scene?**
Remove the dull from the scenes.
Only include the description and dialogue that are critical to the scene and that promote an engaging, contention- and subtext-rich forward tracking motion of the story.
Concentrate the conflict, and have the characters cleverly manipulate their situations within it.
Likely, each scene is a set-up or a payoff, or a mix of the two intertwined with the main story and the backstories in tune with an emotional through-line.

- **NOTE 190: STORY REVEAL: Could the scenes be presented in a different order, such as in a nonlinear style so that the viewers become more engaged in figuring out the puzzle?**
Or, if you already have your script in nonlinear style, would it work better if the script were linear?
(Search: Linear screenplays vs. nonlinear screenplays.)

"A tip from (Ernst) Lubitsch: Let the audience add up two plus two. They'll love you forever."
– Billy Wilder, *Double Indemnity*

- **NOTE 191: LOVE PLUNGE: If characters are falling in love, is it happening in a way that we feel it, and want it?**
If the characters bore us, are unappealing, or simply don't engage us, or we simply don't care to spend a second of our life watching them, it is likely that we would also not be interested in their love life.

Even if the script features characters who are dull, and otherwise what might be considered unwatchable, maybe you will do a good job of connecting us with their humanity, and basic needs, including their need to be loved. Perhaps your script could be surprisingly satisfying in unusual ways.

I heard someone say that you cannot have the villains fall in love with each other. Why not? That might be more interesting than the good people. As long as it pulls at the base emotions, and perhaps gives us some empathy and compassion for the villains, it could sustain viewer interest. Perhaps one of the villains has an ulterior motive.

Maybe the antagonist falls in love with the protagonist. Or, the protagonist manipulates it into happening as a form of defense, and then retreats at the right moment.

Twist it up and play with audience perceptions and anticipations.

Surprise us.

- **NOTE 192: AMOROUS ADVENTURES: If there are heavy make-out or sex scenes, are they needed for the story?**
Throwing sex and nudity into a script because you think that more people will watch it if it contains those is one way to cheapen your project.

Consider what you are asking the actors to do. The more blatant it is, the more you will also limit the project's ability to land a certain level of talent.

If people want to watch porn, they will do that. And your sex scenes will not compete with it.

Be less blatant, and more suggestive and tantalizing. Don't throw everything in our faces. We have imaginations. Let us use them.

"If you have your movies so that everyone understands everything, I think that's probably not a very good movie."
– Alexander Payne, *The Descendants*

Just as it could be good to refrain from telling us other things about the character, and letting us guess and factor our own conclusions, do the same with their most private moments. Refrain from being explicit.

By including nudity and sex scenes, you also limit the project to a narrower market. It is unlikely to play in certain countries, or on airplanes, or certain platforms that could end up making significant money for investors.

- **NOTE 193: TWIST, TANGLE, MANGLE, AND PUZZLE: Are you complicating things enough to provide a variety of twists and expectations throughout the story, and that are relevant and concerning enough within the story to engage us?**
Puzzle us.

Raise questions in our minds to make us reason, factor, anticipate, and want answers.

415

Keep us watching, unable to look away, and wanting to hear and see all of it.

Answer our concerns. Or, at least give us enough information to make our own conclusions.

- **NOTE 194: SECONDARY CHARACTERS: Are the secondary characters relevant, and more than simply there to fill space?**
  Work on making the side characters more real, less stereotypical, and more believable, interesting, and part of what stirs the story.
  Write the characters so that they aren't flat, but are multi-dimensional. Figure out what makes up the fabric of their reality in ways that validate their presence within the story.

  "The cinema I make is about people, emotion, humanity, and passion. It's not just about what they struggle through, but what they live for. That's what I love. The music they love, the people they love, the clothing, the hair, and the life that they love."
  – David O. Russell, *American Hustle*

  People have complex personalities. They live life for their own purpose, or they stick to people who and situations that they feel validate them, or they live for their children or others, or they are burned out and have given up on their life, interests, skills, and talents. Sometimes they lead secret lives, or a variety of secret lives – perhaps out of shame, or so that they are able to hold onto some other part of their soul and desires. But, mostly, they live in a way that seems to provide them with some sort of validity, or that they hope gives them meaning and safety, and contains a pathway to a better, more satisfying life. They join up with others who they perceive as like-minded, and on the same path, or who will help them obtain the life they desire.

- **NOTE 195: MOTIVES: For every chosen action and word of dialogue, there is a motive. Does your script display characters who are taking actions and saying words based on desires, intentions, perceptions, anticipations, hopes, and plans?**
  If your characters are so elusive that the audience finds them unbelievable, does not connect with them, or simply is not concerned enough with them to watch them, that will not sustain an audience's attention.
  What is the character about in the form of their hopes and needs, which we would want to watch as they pursue something with a strong enough incentive or payoff – even if through a terrible struggle, a quest to obtain something, or a hilariously comical catastrophe?

- **NOTE 196: CHARACTER JEOPARDY: What is the crisis of each of the characters, and how do their problems and concerns play into the storyline?**

Why do we care enough about them to watch them work toward their solution?

Do we dislike them enough to want them to fail? Maybe that could be worked into a script that is so engaging that it ends up as a hit.

"A good character always has a crisis lurking inside them like a ticking time bomb. Once I'd decided who the characters would be in *Little Miss Sunshine*, it was just a matter of figuring out when those crises would happen. You also want those crises to happen in ascending order of importance. It all fell together pretty easily in the outlining process. The only really noteworthy choice I made, I'd say, was to kill off grandpa at the midpoint, rather than hold off until the end of the second act. I hate seeing characters die in the late second act, or early third act—it's just such a clichéd time for a character to die. There's a lot more shock value in a midpoint death, because audiences aren't used to losing a major character that early in a movie."
– Michael Arndt, *A Walk in the Woods*

- **NOTE 197: BACKSTORIES: Are the B, C, and other backstories identifiable?**
Are there things about the backstories that the audience can pick up on, want answers from or for, and become emotionally engaged in? Consider one or more of the following: Fearing, hoping, wanting, detesting, being abhorred by, or expecting a funny, sad, tragic, motivating, triumphant, or romantic outcome.

Do the backstories build anticipation, play into the twists and turns, hurdles or successes, and serve as valid and relevant puzzle pieces?

"Sometimes romantic comedies can come off as almost a little bit cynical. Like, willed from the outside. For me, the rule is that there always has to be a law of causality where, internally, the triggers all make sense. Even if you end up with the most surreal situation ever, there's got to be a kind of internal logic that's obeyed or honored. Then you won't feel tricked and used the way you sometimes do in a movie."
– Rebecca Miller, *Proof*

- **NOTE 198: INTERSECTION OF BACKSTORIES: Do the backstories remain in their own lane, or do they intersect and weave in clever ways in which they play off each other, and perhaps flip-flop and play a role in the character arcs, the conclusion, and denouement?**
Lonely Joe, who is afraid of flying, has borrowed a car from his forgetful grandmother, who, without Joe knowing, had stored her life savings in a secret compartment of the car.

Joe desperately needs to get somewhere to accomplish a task – on the other side of the continent.

Joe doesn't know that weird Isabel – the lady who he avoided at the bar the night before he left – had bought the car from his forgetful grandmother.

Joe sees that Isabel is chasing him across country using planes, trains, bikes, roller-skates, scooters, wind surfing skateboards, and by hitch hiking on motorcycles and in 18-wheelers.

Joe doesn't know that Isabel is after the car. He thinks that she is fixated on him.

Joe gets to his destination, where he accomplishes his goal.

But, he then finds that Isabel is the actual owner of the car.

Therefore, he doesn't have to drive all the way back to return it to his grandmother.

After realizing that Isabel is not after him, but only wants her car, he feels better. But...

Joe finds out that his grandmother is deathly ill.

And, he needs a ride back to see his grandmother.

He swallows his queasiness and takes the ride back with Isabel.

On the returning trip, he finds that he starts to fall for Isabel.

During a pit stop, while Isabel is using a coffee house bathroom, Joe notices something in the car, a compartment containing a load of money.

And, so forth and so on. You can fill in other story pieces.

Those are back stories that intersect, even to the point of a bait and switch, where what you thought was the main story possibly becomes the back story.

Twist up things. Play with perceptions. Make what the characters think of as improbable the probable. Interject the trickster elements mixed with some misunderstandings and deceptions. Realign the character perceptions. Give them arcs and unexpected outcomes.

Intersect the stories, plot, character, wants, needs, secrets, motives, perception, conflict, contention, manipulation, and outcome.

- **NOTE 199: TRUTH OF CHARACTERS: Is there truth in the characters?**

Do the characters behave and communicate in ways that stay within their truth, life view, status, reasoning, hope, and expectations? Even within their secret life that they are hiding from others.

Does the conflict challenge their life philosophy, and push them deeply out of their comfort zone? Maybe it is what pushes them toward their truth.

Do they seem to be living within the financial constraints of their town, family, profession, and situation?

Do they speak in a way that is reflective of their past and present social and economic situations?

Does their behavior reflect the way they may have been educated by their schooling, surroundings, relationships, jobs, interests, and the political situation and the views and apparent standards and rules of their culture?

- **NOTE 200: WANTS, NEEDS, AND DRIVE: Is there reasonable motive behind the words and actions of every character to drive them to do and say what they are doing and saying?**

There is always a motive behind everything that people say and do.

Mostly with an understanding gained through the visuals, and less through the character dialogue, get the audience to factor and/or be involved in factoring the motives of the characters – and anticipate what they might do.

Learn what other filmmakers have done without dialogue. Watch some silent films. Watch *A Quiet Place*, and Jacques Tati films.

"I believe you must be madly in love with cinema to create films. You also need huge cinematic baggage. That is, the awareness of film history and techniques."
– Jean Pierre Melville, *The Good Thief*

- **NOTE 201: AUDIENCE ANTICIPATION: Can the audience detect what it is that the characters love and hate?**

Do the love and hate of the characters come across in relatable, concerning, or otherwise engaging ways?

Could the audiences be mistaken? Do the characters sometimes act outside of our expectations of what they would like and hate, making us question them, doubt them, reconfigure our expectations in relation to them and to how the main story and backstory lines are to play out?

Will the audience relate, and be drawn in to what is happening on screen in a way that the characters act in relation to audience anticipations?

- **NOTE 202: DIALOGUE, THEME, TONE, AND MOOD: Does the dialogue help establish the theme, plot, mood, tone, society, and world, and the rules of the game?**

"Theme is a pattern of meaning revealed within the storm and strife of human experience. It is an idea about life that is proven through the action of plot."
– Amnon Buchbinder, author *The Way of the Screenwriter*

The first words spoken by the characters are keys for us to understand their interior situation. A key is to stay within that personality, life philosophy, and what we would believably expect – including the way they would grow or adjust in tune with what we see them experience.

That doesn't mean that the person who first comes across as nice always then has to remain nice in every scene. Perhaps we will see that they live a double or triple life, adjusting their personality – and even their accent – to deal with the situations they are in, and the people they are with. Maybe they are compulsive liars, which plays into everything about them.

A character can be a wife taking care of a disabled husband and their children. From what they know, she's a sweet mom. Little do they know that

419

the nice church lady is hellbent obsessive in her plants to kill the person who caused her husband to become disabled. She's involved in illegal activities to get what she needs to carry out her plan. And that may surprise her friends at church. But, they might be in on it, assisting her plan.

The first dialogue a character speaks can lead us to be surprised by the various personalities they adjust to throughout the script to manipulated the twists and turns in their life.

- **NOTE 203: FORMING QUESTIONS: Is your story likely to form questions in the minds of the viewers in ways that they want to factor solutions and stick around to watch if their anticipations manifest in the life of the characters?**

If you aren't forming questions in the minds of viewers, playing with their perceptions, and having them continually reconfiguring those perceptions, there are reasons why your script might be considered flat.

- **NOTE 204: AUDIENCE CALCULATIONS: Are there elements in the story that will trigger the audience to conduct inner debates about what would be the reasonable and unreasonable choices of the various characters?**

Getting the audience to adapt to the reasoning of the characters brings them to escape into the story. That is the escapism that you likely want the audience to experience.

Screwing with audience expectations, and giving to, and encouraging, and taking things from their expectations, which frustrates and manipulates the audience can keep them engaged until the ending scenes.

- **NOTE 205: CHARACTER CHALLENGE: Is the character being challenged enough to mess with their self-worth, belief, expectations, skills, wisdom, or otherwise, so the audience gets into the character's reasoning, philosophy, and emotional path?**

Has the character reached their darkest moment, their wall, an unsurmountable thing that seems impossible to overcome, which will stop them from attaining that thing they want, that something that they had been fighting for, the position that they aim to be in, that relationship that they had been desiring?

What is it that would crush their drive, but that somehow could be gotten through, over, under or otherwise past – with struggle, cleverness, manipulation, and fight – to get what they want?

Maybe the boat to the next island that they need to get to has left the harbor, or it has sunk, or it is dangerous, or they know that it is impossibly problematic. But, there is a tiny speed boat, or they can kite surf, or, the ocean is on fire with an oil slick that cannot be crossed by water vessel. Giving up, the character goes to a bar. They overhear some old drunk woman bragging about how she knows how to fly her granddaughter's helicopter. The protagonist character REALLY needs to get to the next island. They must somehow get the old crazy drunk woman to fly them in that helicopter to the next island – even if it means that the character has do something or give up something that they don't want to give up or do. The possibility is there, but, can it happen? Make it as twisty, turny, and entertaining as possible.

- **NOTE 206: CHARACTER'S CHANCE TO PROVE: Is this the character's final chance to prove their worth, meaning, existence, value, worthiness, love, commitment, or belonging, or to validate their life, place in society, position in their family, or how much someone means to them?**

Has the character always been a mess, a disaster, a pushover, a failure at everything ever expected of them, and they know that there is something that they can do to save the day, to accomplish what seems impossible for them, to gather their courage, to believe in themselves, to make a jump in some way to get what drastically needs to be done to save someone's life, give someone happiness, or otherwise make the audience stand up and cheer?

Could it be that the character knows that if they do the thing that needs to be done, it will result in their death, but they do it anyway, because they know it will save a variety of other people? Even if the people to be saved have had the wrong view of the person, and treated the person terribly?

It could be something like a kidney transplant to save the life of someone who did them – and a number of other people – wrong. But, it would save that person's life, even if we don't think that person deserves it. And, the character who donated the kidney dies. But that causes such a revolutionary change in the person who received the kidney that they then do something that prevents something extremely bad from happening.

Do whatever it takes to manipulate and engage the reasoning and concerns of the audience, and take them on the adventures within the story. Challenge, transfix, and perplex them. Make it comically or dramatically riveting.

"Sometimes films ignore other points of view because it's simpler to tell the story that way, but the more genuine and sympathetic you are to different points of view and situations, the more real the story is."
– Ang Lee, *Eat Drink Man Woman*

- **NOTE 207: CHARACTER HOPE: Does the character have a complete loss of hope?**

After we see the character striving to obtain something, or make something happen, they experience so many problems that – toward the end of the second act – everything the character worked for seems to be lost, and their hope is lost, and their life meaning seems to have collapsed, leaving them destitute.

What could it be that keeps them holding onto one molecule of hope, that makes them keep trying, that reignites and triggers their drive and determination to go into overdrive, and that will put the audience on the edge of their seats, to make the audience want to jump into the screen to help the character gain and keep control and manifest their solution?

- **NOTE 208: CHARACTER PHILOSOPHY AND REALITY: Is there a disintegration of time, resources, options, belief, communication, ground, and relationships that threaten the character's quest in ways that test them so deeply that their life philosophy is challenged?**

Is there a time in the script where certain options simply will no longer be available, and the audience, the good guy, and the bad guy(s) know it? How is it that you are playing with the possibilities in a way that will most effectively manipulate the audience perception and anticipation?

How can the audience get the feeling that a time window fuse is burning, and getting shorter, and in a way that makes the audience squirm in their seats as their concerns engage with the conflict, constraints, and display of character concerns and contention?

- **NOTE 209: TICKING CLOCK: Do the story's time constraints work for the pacing, characterizations, and all that takes place?**

Does the audience get a strong feeling that something must happen within a certain amount of time, or else there will be great dissatisfaction, trouble, loss, or other alterations in the life of the main character?

A time constraint could be that we know a cruise ship is going to leave the dock at a certain time, and the main character needs to get there, or else lose the chance to be on that ship to plead with the person they love so that they don't agree to the proposition planned on during that cruise with the person who has been their significant other.

A time constraint could be that Antonia's child has been kidnapped. To pay the ransom by a certain time, Antonia needs to get to the bank before it closes, or she needs to pawn something in enough time to get to the agreed-upon location, or else her child will be harmed. For some reason, she doesn't trust the authorities to get involved – perhaps because she is in a foreign country, or is living in the country illegally, or the police are looking for her because she has been falsely accused of something terrible. She can't risk anything that would interfere with her getting the money she needs so that she can do the drop off at that agreed-upon location. Maybe the kidnappers have locked a recording and tracking device to her body, and the kidnappers can hear everything she says, and know where she goes. But, the kidnappers can't see everything she does, and that detail provides an option for a big twist: Absolute silence on the part of the people she gets to help her.

"Our primary function is to create an emotion, and our second job is to sustain that emotion."
– Alfred Hitchcock, *Blackmail*

- **NOTE 210: ENCROACHING DANGER: Is the character unaware of some sort of danger that the audience does know of?**

Is there a time in the film when the audience knows that the bad guys are honing in on the good guy, and the good guy doesn't know of the danger? That could keep the audience on the edge of their seats – hoping that the good guy gets out of that location, before it is too late.

Perhaps the character is aware of the danger, and is working to avoid or take care of some other matter. Then, they get an inkling that they must take an incredible risk to get to where they need to be to escape from the bad people. They realize that they are being followed, and they know that the person is so close that it is almost impossible for them to not get caught, but they know something that the bad people don't, such as that they can jump off the train at a specific moment that allows them to take a short fall into deep water, or that the office building they designed contains a flaw, allowing for a certain wall to be broken through – and so forth.

- **NOTE 211: ORIGIN OF POSITION: Do we know why the character is in the situation?**

If the character's situation seems random, the audience might need to know how and/or why that happened.

It is likely that the audience needs some sort of connection to or understanding of why and/or how the character is in their situation.

If you make things too convenient for the characters, that also is a way to lose the audience. The audience should be factoring ways in which the character can get out of their situation. Make the struggle real.

Let the audience in on the primal human need of the character.

Engage the audience so that they know what the characters are battling, thinking, feeling, wanting, needing, reasoning, or otherwise the motives driving the characters to say and do what they are saying and doing. Mix that with what we want for the character.

- **NOTE 212: REMOVING PERCEPTION OF SECURITY: Is it likely that the audience expects a guaranteed solution?**

Does the script keep hinting that the solution is secure, but pull that sense of security from beneath the audience?

"I always want the audience to out-guess me, and then I double-cross them."
– Buster Keaton, *Go West*

Have you somehow made a contract with the audience that if they continue watching, they will be satisfied – even if it means that they will be grabbing onto their seats, biting their nails, pulling out their hair, and wanting to look away as you mess with their expectations, perceptions, wants, and basic concept of how life should play out?

Do you undermine the audience's reasoning and expectations? That is, do you give the audience satisfaction here and there, especially in ways that you then take away, reinstate, and again remove that satisfaction so that they lose and gain hope, become frustrated, disappointed, and maybe even angry, sad, fascinated, or possibly laugh? Do you do that in a way to engage the audience so they continue watching, anticipating, wanting, and then being satisfied by the answers, expectations, and/or perceived resolutions you provide at the conclusion of the script?

Do you maintain that guarantee by a string so as to not lose the audience's hopes, wants, expectations, and concerns?

"Grab 'em by the throat, and never let 'em go."
– Billy Wilder, *The Seven Year Itch*

- **NOTE 213: CHARACTER ARCS: Do the characters have noticeable arcs?**

Do the characters have realization arcs in which they end up not being the same as when the script began? Does it happen believably through the challenges that we see them go through?

If, by the end of the script, the main characters are simply the same people they were at the beginning of the script, it is likely that the characters are flat. (Some say that Harrison Ford's character in *Raiders of the Lost Ark* has no character arc. That movie worked, especially at the international box office.)

Have you explored the possible backstories of the characters in ways that would explain their behavior?

"There's magic to being present when you're writing a character. Just spit it out, then go back and edit it later."
– Reid Carolin, *Magic Mike*

Do you know the psychological background of each character, and how they philosophically view life? If you don't, how will the audience reason the action and/or dialogue of those characters as role players in the story?

Perhaps you are missing out on opportunities to make your characters far more complex, interesting, relevant, challenged, driven, clever, afraid, cautious, and otherwise engaged and engaging.

It might be too much to create backstories of each character before you write the script. But, character backgrounds could be something to keep in mind as you write – and rewrite – the script.

Even if you do create character backgrounds, you don't have to stick with them. Do what works best to create layered characters in an engaging story rich in conflict, tension, and subtext.

After you have written a significant first draft of the script, maybe working out the backgrounds of the characters could be a helpful thing to do. It might give you ideas of how to layer the script with interesting and clever twists, turns, psychology, dialogue, motives, desires, relationships, and so forth.

"First drafts are for learning what your story is about."
– Bernard Malamud, *Der Gehilfe*

Character background might include how they ended up on the planet, how their parents got along, the character's relationship to their parents and relatives, their school, sports, and neighborhood friends, their education, health issues, and the experiences of the characters during the days, months, or years before the script story takes place. Character background includes things that formed their traits, reasoning, responses, manners, caution, expectations, views of life and the world they live in, and ways of communicating.

"I think everything I do is to try to get my characters as rich as possible. To try and understand them as much as I can. To really go into their perspective. With screenwriting, it's really good to put yourself into each character – even if it's just a side character. To think about their personal needs in a situation, even if on the surface it doesn't serve the plot too much."
– Maren Ade, *Everyone Else*

Read through the script, and consider what type of backstories apply to each character, and how that plays out in their desire, caution, motives, words, and actions.

The tiniest little life experience could turn a flat character into one that is far more interesting.

In a drama about a group of young thugs holding store employees and customers hostage, it would be interesting to know the back stories of the thugs, employees, and customers. The way the backstories are revealed makes all the difference. Maybe it turns out that one of the hostages is the birth mother of one of the thugs who was adopted as a baby – but the thug doesn't know it. And, one of the cops who shows up is the adopted father of that thug, who the cop hasn't seen in several years. And, the cop's wife, the adopted mother of that thug, is one of the customers being held hostage – which is not something the thug had planned. As the night wears on, the birth mother and adopted mother begin to share their life stories, and realize their connection.

Taylor Sheridan speaks of one of his scripts in which a character doesn't really have an arc. They are impotent, and remain the same. Sheridan is one sharp writer. Doing something like that has to have a purpose in serving the story. Maybe a character is stuck, and that serves the story. But, only do something like that if it truly works, and serves the story.

A character without an arc is probably going to be a side character, rather than the main character. Maybe that is how that character serves the story.

A stuck character could be the parent adhered to their ways of consistent racism and terrible behavior, which motivates the main character to live life completely differently, and learn a better way – likely by going through rough life experiences to learn what their lousy, neglectful, abusive childhood didn't teach them.

- **NOTE 214: PUSHING THE CHARACTER: Is your main character living out of context with how they would need to live to provide an understanding of how to get what they want and need?**

What would transform their view of life to open their mind to their solution?

How do they engage in making their solution happen – or how do things happen in a way that forces them to form the solution?

How does the character create their solution in a way that is entertaining, engaging, and/or concerning to the audience?

Do we understand what the character is opposed to, what they don't want, what will displease them, what will make them feel frustrated, drive them up the wall, make them happy, and satisfy them? How does that play into what they do, what they say, and how they occupy the storyline?

There are writers who hire psychologists to analyze the psychological profiles of their screenplay characters. Perhaps doing that is something that would help you write a more psychologically engaging script.

- **NOTE 215: THE CATALYST: Is there a catalyst for the audience to recognize and emotionally engage with?**

Is there an event, verbal exchange, emotion, agreement, need, want, fight, victory, failure, or loss that changes everything?

Are their sub-catalysts that twist and turn the story and the backstories so that there are multiple levels of conflict and expectations that engage and manipulate the audience's perceptions, reasoning, anticipations, and senses?

Have you workshopped the script, and did the other writers recognize the catalysts?

"I often attribute my screenwriting to journalism because they drill in the who, what, when, where, and why – but we really need to land on that why. That's what I've been exploring in my writing for many years, and trying to get better at."
– Mara Brock Akil, *Being Mary Jane*

- **NOTE 216: BINDING THE AUDIENCE: Do you take the audience with you along the twists and turns on the road of the conflict?**

Is the break from the first act into the second act detectable by the audience? Does it need to be?

Is there a turn of events, of expectations, of reasoning, of action, of dialogue that makes us want something so badly, to stay tuned to see how the drama plays out, to be compelled to watch how the characters manipulate their situations, and want for there to be a satisfactory conclusion?

- **NOTE 217: SUSTAINING THE ROLLER COASTER: Is the primary concern built early to manipulate an anticipating audience and get**

**them on board with the adventure, and to remain present in their seats
and pay attention throughout the story?**

Do the scenes continue on a path that plays with and takes the audience on
a trip into and through the conflict, contention, concerns, motives, irony, hooks,
tension, twists, turns, reversals, gains, losses, and final accomplishments?

"The beginning is when the audience is most susceptible, the most
vulnerable, the most fertile. How much do you maximize that moment? And
then the other most important moment is when the lights come back on and
people exit the theater, because that last scene is going to roll through their
heads right afterwards."
– Damien Chazelle, *Whiplash*

- **NOTE 218: PACING: Does the pacing maintain momentum in
  relation to how the story is being played out?**
  What is the impact of each scene?
  Does each scene play into providing messages and advancing the story, and
  then cut as soon as the needed information is given, and in a way that is at a
  good pace for the story?
  Concentrate the energy of the scenes by eliminating unnecessary words –
  including overdescription and redundancies, and messages that may be
  overdone or repeated.
  Once an audience gets a message, they likely don't need to repeatedly hear
  and see that message. They might need to know that symptoms are worsening,
  and the solution needs to be found, and that there is a timeline that limits how
  long a character can take to accomplish something. Doing so will maintain
  pressure. But to have a character keep repeating the same message dulls the
  concerns, slows the pacing, and clutters and dumbs down the script.

- **NOTE 219: MIDPOINT: What is the midpoint of the story?**
  What do you view as the midpoint of the main story? Does it twist the story
  in ways that engage the audience so that they care what happens to the
  characters and within the theme, plot, conflict, reasoning, and contentious
  behavior that you have been displaying among the characters?
  The midpoint is likely where the character seems to be getting what they do
  want – or relentlessly going for what they want – with a strong knowledge of
  the fragility of the situation, and knowing that, despite all of their
  manipulations, they might not get it, or may lose it, or that everything can go
  drastically wrong, or right – if they don't do or say the right things.

- **NOTE 220: BACKSTORY MIDPOINT: Are there also midpoints in
  the backstories?**
  What do you view as the midpoint of the backstories? Do they happen in
  ways that play with audience reasoning and expectations?
  Are the backstories needed, and relevant to the main story?

Could there be more engaging backstories that truly play into the dramatic or comical tension?

- **NOTE 221: BACKSTORY PLACEMENT: Are the backstories truly backstories, or are they so strong that one of them is the story that the audience will focus on?**

Do you maintain your backstories in ways that don't overpower the main story?

If a backstory does overpower the main story, maybe that backstory is what should be brought to the front as the main story. But, what would that do to the main characters? Would it realign the importance of the characters in the story? Would the side characters then become lead? Maybe the script would work better – and be far more interesting – to switch it all up.

- **NOTE 222: MAIN NEED: Is the main character's need handled?**

Even if your main character unexpectedly dies, did they do what the audience would want them to have done – or cause to happen – before they departed? For instance, the character of Jack in *Titanic* makes sure that his love survives the terrible tragedy. He succeeds, leaving her devastated, but also leaving her knowing that she broke free of things in her life that would have constrained her. (But, she could have moved over and shared the debris.)

- **NOTE 223: CHARACTER RELATIONS: Will the audience be able to detect the bonds between the various characters?**

Are the characters bound through being neighbors, coworkers, students, community members, in a religion, in sports, politics, belief, or through crime, corruption, scandal, marriage, illness, addiction, disease, a transplant, contamination, victimhood, investments, invention, a hunt for something, knowledge of a treasure, suspicion, or understanding of a concept, conspiracy, or witnessing something like a similar crime, paranormal activity, or other situation?

What do they need or want from each other?

Is one cheating the other?

Who is manipulative, clingy, distant, dominant, submissive, abusive, loving, trusting, suspicious, accepting, unwilling, crass, restrained, desperate, nurturing, sincere, infatuated, taken, closed, deceptive, the caretaker, fixer, planner, task maker, doer, gossiper, player, liar, underminer, enabler, weak link, or strong link?

If they are not in some sort of good, bad, distracted, escapist, doubting, or other type of relationship, why are they relating to each other? Why is their relationship interesting to viewers?

Do we understand what the character is resolving to do in their relationships, or hope to understand it in a way that is engaging and will keep us watching to see what happens?

Perhaps we don't detect a bond between two or more characters, which could play into the story. Especially if one is so desperate that they will accept anyone into their life, or is infatuated with someone out of their league – but we know that a character is being played for something that the other can get. (See: Trophy wife.) Maybe the one being played ends up being better at the game, and trashes the deceiver.

- **NOTE 224: CHARACTER CHALLENGE: Do you make it so that the characters have enough struggle and difficulty in their quest?**
Are there ways to make the burdens the characters face more difficult?

You want to set a puzzle for the audience to solve. Get and keep the audience engaged so that they want something to happen in the story as badly as the characters who struggle to get what they want and/or need.

Have you placed enough hurdles, snares, bumps, and barriers in the way of the main character so that their getting what they want is a true struggle and fight that challenges their relationships, resolve, philosophy, perception, belief, safety, or trust at every turn?

Can it be done in a way that makes them more obsessed, focused, resilient, and determined to work for and get what they want in a way that the audience is going to stick with them on the journey?

- **NOTE 225: SUBJECTIVE PERSPECTIVE: Are you providing the audience with a subjective perspective?**
Will the audience become engaged in wanting the character to attain something and experience the satisfaction, even if risking treasure, career, health, safety, family, relationships, and love?

Get the audience to see the story from the perspective of the character and their want and need. Get the audience to agree with the character, and to feel the risks that the character takes.

"Put yourself in the place you've designed for your principal characters. Ask yourself, 'If this was really my problem, would I do what I'm having this character do? Would I say what he or she is saying?'"
– Stephen J. Cannell, *21 Jump Street*

- **NOTE 226: SUSPENSION OF DISBELIEF: Are you asking the audience to believe something that is so unbelievable that they will consider it silly and unengaging?**
If you stretch things so far away from what could occur in reality, consider that you will also be pushing the audience too far from rational belief, and they will not be interest in watching it. They might describe it as preposterous, stupid, or worse. Then, they will tell people how unbelievable the film or show is. And the reviewers will likely also trash it.

(Search: Action films that bombed at the box office.)

- **NOTE 227: CONVENIENT COINCIDENCES: Does your script include solutions to problems that are too convenient, that only take place for the storyline to proceed, and that are too convenient for you as a writer to get a character from point A to point B?**
Convenient coincidences weaken a story.

An absurdly convenient coincidence would be if a character can't get something because that thing is behind a locked gate, and one of their keys just happens to fit the lock. Or, a child gets locked inside a safe, and the mother panics, runs outside, and happens to find a passing locksmith who can open the safe before the oxygen runs out. That isn't too much of a stretch from the sorts of convenient coincidences that are in some movies and TV shows.

"You are allowed one coincidence per script. Otherwise your story feels like too much 'writer's convenience.'"
– Scott Myers, GoIntoTheStory.BlckLst.com

- **NOTE 228: RESOLVES: Are the main character's unresolved problems the issue?**
What are the characters problems? Do they get resolved? Or, is it more emotionally satisfying to the audience – and more realistic – to see that the character doesn't get their concerns resolved?

Some films are so clear by the end that it isn't necessary – and far more satisfying – to avoid showing the final stages of how the characters deal with things, and what the outcome will be. By the end of the film, it is likely that we have factored the character's reasoning and philosophy, and we can guess what steps they will take to resolve their situation.

Leaving character problems cleverly unresolved – and the audiences guessing – can leave the door open for a sequel. It can also be what gets audiences to argue and disagree after they view the film or show.

- **NOTE 229: PREDICTABILITY: What is predictable and unpredictable in your script?**
Not that all predictable films are bombs. For instance, we pretty much know that the troubled Kate Winslet character in Titanic is going to survive. However, we don't know about the somewhat daring Leonardo character, and that is one thing that keeps us watching. While we expect the ship to sink, we are not sure how the love story and lives will play out.

There are films where it apparently is obvious that something will happen at the end: The guy will get the girl, or vice versa. The sports team will win. A person will be redeemed. A cure will be found. A person will escape the unrighteous imprisonment. A wrongly accused person will prove their innocence, or have it proved. A war will be won. And so forth.

A predictable story doesn't mean that the film is bad or good. How the story is delivered, the quality of the acting, the production values, and how it engages, manipulates, and satisfies the audience helps to determine its success.

"If your ending is predictable, maybe you should start asking some 'What if?' questions, or do some completely off-the-wall brainstorming."
– David Trottier, author *The Screenwriter's Bible*

- **NOTE 230: EXTERNAL CONFLIT: Do you use external conflict in clever ways to manipulate the audience and drive the story?**

  External conflicts are the looming outside forces that manipulate character motive and reasoning, put them in a bind, constrain their time and resources, and trigger their actions. They conflict with the character's needs and goals, and drive the story. They fuel and instigate the character's internal conflict.

  External conflict can be a person, weapon, bomb, creature, virus, fire, approaching tsunami, a volcano, a sinking boat, a leaking damn, war, an encroaching army, abuse, bullying, poverty, oppressive laws, religion, or society, or other threats or problems that interfere with the protagonist's goal.

  External conflict can come off as predictable. Aim to cleverly write it so that it is less so, and done in ways that play with audience anticipation, and help engage them to stay watching to see what will happen next.

- **NOTE 231: STORY DRIVE: What drives the story from start to finish?**

  If you can't answer this question, how do you expect the audience to? How do you expect them to be involved in the emotional through-line? How do you expect to get actors to hook into the character philosophy, need, want, irony, discovery, manipulation, conflict, contention, tension, and all the rest of it?

  Consider what Jen Grisanti says:

  "The mistake that the writer makes that they can't recover from is having a weak setup. If the writer fails to define a clear goal – and we don't know what the character wants, and why they want it – the story fails. When the goal is clear, the actions, obstacles, and stakes link back to it. When the goal is undefined, there is nothing for these story points to link back to, and this creates a story with no momentum."
  – Jen Grisanti, screenwriter career coach, JenGrisanti.com

- **NOTE 232: RELEVANCE OF SETTING: Is the scenery of the world you created the best choice in relation to the story?**

  Explore the possibilities of setting your story in a different era, country, culture, world, or socioeconomic and political setting. But, know that the more sets, props, period clothing, and FX you will need, the more expensive it will be to produce the script.

  Always remember: The cost of producing the script has to be rationalized with the potential box office take, and the return on investment for financiers.

  "The way I tend to approach a film is that character and background are equally important: One informs the other."
  – Alfonso Cuarón Orozco, *Ascension*

"If the dialogue makes you sit forward a little, and listen a little bit more, that's a good thing. It makes the audience active in the experience."
– Aaron Sorkin, *The Newsroom*

TABLE READ THAT SCREENPLAY

"I like something that you can do that is active, that is cheap. And, that is: Have a table read.

I have always had a table read for anything I've ever written – all the way back to my very first 'nobody should have read that.' It's super easy. You literally just invite some actor friends over, and nowadays you don't even have to print out the script. You can just have everybody bring an iPad, or a laptop. Don't let people read on their phones, that's weird. But, send them the script, and have them sit around and read it. I would advise you: You (the writer) don't read anything. You only listen. Have someone read all of the stage directions out loud, don't skip over those parts – because that is part of the script. And, you will hear so much. It's not even about getting feedback that you get from those people. It is about the experience of hearing it."
– Marlana Hope, *Grey's Anatomy*

After you have workshopped a script, and had it edited, consider holding a table read. That is, before you send the script to a coverage service. And, before you send the script to a manager, agent, development executive, producer, director, financier, or a contest, mentorship, fellowship, or lab.

A table read is when a group of people gather and read through the entire script, out loud.

To have a table read, you will need a place with enough seats for however number of characters are in the script. Although, you might have some of the actors read more than one role.

Doing the table read online could be convenient, but something is lost in the energy and pacing there, and you don't get to experience the audience reaction.

Do try to get actors to do the read – so that you get some trained, dramatic voices in there.

Simply because someone has what you consider to be a great voice doesn't mean they will be good for a table read. If their voice and delivery is wrong for the role, pacing, tension, mood, tone, setting, era, and story, it can ruin the table read.

It could be easy to find the actors you need if you live in a big city, or a town like Ashland, Oregon, which has a summer-long Shakespeare Festival.

Have someone as the narrator who reads the scene headings and description. That's an important part as their energy and pacing will guide the read. The wrong narrator can ruin the table read. One table read I attended had a narrator who read as if she were reading a kind, nice bedtime story to a child. It was an action script. Her pleasant, slow delivery ruined that table read.

You don't want to hold the table read in a public place where outside noises and people can interfere. But, a quiet, shaded area of a park could be a good place – depending on the script. If someone has sufficient seating in their home, or backyard, that could work.

Some community theaters will rent their space to writers wanting to hold a table read. Actors associated with the theater might be available to read the roles, which is an added benefit of using a community theater.

For the table read, you might provide some pay to the actors, and have snacks and drinks (if the venue you use allows that). You can also have a free raffle among the actors, so that someone wins a gift certificate.

You might also invite managers, agents, directors, potential financiers, other writers, actors, associates in the industry, and friends to sit in the audience. That way you can see and hear how an audience reacts to hearing your script. You might also give them copies of the script so that they can follow along – email them a PDF of the script, and invite them to bring a laptop or other screen device to read the script during the table read.

Do arrange so that you can simply observe and listen to the table read. Take notes.

"I believe myself that a good writer doesn't really need to be told anything, expect to keep at it."
– Chinua Achebe, *Things Fall Apart*

"Contrary to popular belief, studio script readers and assistants are not one and the same.

True script readers read scripts, novels, and other forms of intellectual property, and then write script coverage. That's it. No answering phones, no fetching coffee, no making copies, or any other such office jobs delegated to assistants and interns.

However, assistants and interns are usually asked to write script coverage as well, primarily because there is so much material to go through."

– Ken Miyamoto, @KenMovies. *A Simple Guide to Formatting and Writing Studio Script Coverage*, Screencraft.org

Script Coverage Services

"Coverage started out in studios where readers were employed to read countless scripts so that the producers didn't have to. These reports were purely for internal use, with the readers marking a script with a pass, recommend, or consider at the end. Scripts that were marked recommend would get passed up the food chain. The writer would never be privy to these comments.

Coverage services like our own are different. Our sole intention is to help a writer create a better draft of their work: To get it to a point where it's ready to be sent out to people in the industry. We are honest over what we feel does and doesn't work, giving clear reasons for our opinions.

When analyzing a screenplay, our readers focus and write on the premise, structure, character, dialogue, pace, visuals, believability, marketability, and provide a conclusion. We make suggestions throughout the coverage as to how the writer can improve their story."

– ShoreScripts.com

After you workshop an entire script, it is a good idea to then get script coverage and analysis from a script coverage service.

A typical coverage service will likely give you:
- **About three to five pages of material, including:**
  - **A logline**.
  - **A synopsis or summary**. Usually a page, or up to two pages.
  - **A critique**. Including the strengths and weaknesses of the script.
  - **A cover page that includes:**
    - Listing the title of the script, the writer(s), format (film or type of series), genre, setting, and sometimes an estimated budget.

- **A scoresheet**. Includes a check box grid to rate the following as excellent, good, fair, or poor.

    Agencies, management companies, production companies, and studios have their own variety of elements they list on their grid, but usually it is some combination of these:
    - Plot or story
    - Characters
    - Dialogue
    - Structure
    - Pacing
    - Theme
    - Contention
    - Conflict
    - Catharsis
    - Originality
    - Marketability… And perhaps other components of the script.
- **And a level of recommendation that includes either:**
    - A pass: The script is not ready, and likely has a variety of problems. Most scripts will be in this category.
    - A consider: The script might be material that is worth sharpening.
    - A recommend: The script is sharp, interesting, clever, engaging, would likely interest a broad audience, and is worth purchasing.
- **Coverage will also include a separate rating on the writer:**
    - A pass: The writer doesn't display sharp skills in the craft.
    - A consider: The writer could be worth working with.
    - A recommend (the script might get a pass rating, but the writer displays such skill that they get a recommend rating): The writer displays sharp and clever skills in the craft and storytelling.

The Screenplay Readers (ScreenplayReaders.com) script coverage service also rates scripts on how they treat the gender and diversity of the characters.

If you have an agent, it is likely that you can get a copy of their script coverage. If your script makes it to a production company, studio, or industry professional, they also may have done coverage on your script, and you may – or may not – be able to get a copy of their coverage. A nice assistant might slip you the coverage. Or, they might be risking their job by giving you a document that is meant only to be seen by people working for that company.

I once was given coverage by an agency that said the main character in my script engaged in incest and commits suicide at the end of the script. But, the script did not contain any incest or suicide. I have no idea what happened there. Perhaps the assistant with at the agency read many scripts over a weekend, and confused the ending of another script with my script. Whatever happened, the agency apologized for that, and said they would have someone else read my script and do coverage.

Do not expect the script coverage to be all nice and pretty. Do expect it to (hopefully) provide realistic and helpful feedback about your script.

There is a coverage service that says it will give you excellent coverage that will help you get your script read by producers. You shouldn't be paying to get coverage that makes such promises. I don't list that company below.

Coverage isn't what you would get from a script consultant, but there are people who do script consulting and also provide script coverage.

Be wary of people who market themselves as script consultants, and are only out to make money with little to no benefit to you. They might have no valid experience in the industry. Some quite scammy "script consultants" have approached me, as if I'm going to refer people in Tribe to them. Nope.

A person who is a script consultant might have experience as a studio development executive, a college professor, a literary manager, a series staff writer, a successful screenwriter, or a screenwriting book author (don't ask me to read your script, and don't send it to me).

If your script deals with a character who works in a particular specialized field, you can have someone who works in that profession read through the script and advise you on how to make it more realistic – such as by hiring a real private detective to read through your script that is centered on a character who is a private detective, hiring a jetliner pilot to read your script that takes place on a jet, hiring a real estate agent to read a script based in that profession, or hiring a psychologist to advise you on your script that is about a psychologist.

If your screenplay is deeply psychological, you might want to consult with a psychologist to help formulate the personalities of the characters.

If you get coverage from a couple of different coverage services that say your script has a variety of problems, consider that feedback. It might inspire some adjustments to your script. Consider reworkshopping the script.

Know that you eventually have to submit that script to the industry, or abandon it, and move on to writing other screenplays – using what you learned from writing the previous scripts.

"I treat absolutely everything as practice. No matter whether I'm sitting down to write, or rewrite – or rewrite again for the five-hundredth time. I always ask myself, 'Okay, this is practice for the next thing I'm going to write – that I couldn't possibly write, if I didn't learn whatever I have to learn writing this thing.'"
– Sera Gamble, *Aquarius*

Getting coverage from a coverage service will cost you money, but it will likely increase the chances that your script will be polished and also improve the chances that you will have a marketable script.

You can include a copy of the coverage when you submit the script to an agent, manager, producer, development executive, director, or investor.

When you are asked for a synopsis or treatment of your script, instead of writing one, you might instead simply give the person a copy of your coverage

– or make adjustments to that coverage to include the beats of the story, and use that as the treatment. You own the coverage, because you paid for it.

Because you own the coverage, you can adjust it any way you want to make it into a treatment. But, do not change the coverage if you are submitting it as coverage, and saying that the coverage service wrote what you wrote.

People might ask if your script has coverage from an agency, manager, production company, studio, or service. Give it to them. Hopefully, it will entice them to read your complete script.

Managers, agents, development executives, and producers might read coverage from a wide variety of scripts, and they then choose a script to read based on what they find from reading coverage.

Even if you get great coverage, and your full script gets in front of the eyeballs of a major decision-maker, such as a studio president, your script still might be dismissed based on them glancing through the pages, and deciding that the script doesn't look polished. That is what I saw when I worked for a studio. I was surprised by how quickly screenplays were dismissed – simply because the scripts looked overly wordy and/or had formatting issues noticeable by flipping through the pages.

I encourage you to take the time to put every page of your script through a workshop consisting of writers who do their homework, and then polish the screenplay based on the feedback, before you pay for coverage from a script coverage service.

Professional script coverage services (for a broader list, do an online search):
- **Austin Film Festival:** AustinFilmFestival.com/submit/coverage-program
- **Bulletproof Script Coverage:** See: Indie Film Hustle below.
- **Coverage, Ink:** coverageink.com/standard-analysis/
- **Indie Film Hustle:** IndieFilmHustle.com/script-coverage-service
- **Industrial Scripts:** IndustrialScripts.com
- **Launchpad:** Launchpad.tracking-board.com/script-coverage/
- **Christine Macedo:** Christine@ContinuedEvolutionMedia.com
- **Screencraft:** ScreenCraft.org
- **Screenplay Coverage:** ScreenplayCoverage.com
- **Screenplay Readers:** ScreenplayReaders.com
- **Scriptapalooza:** ScriptCoverage.com
- **Script Gal:** ScriptGal.com
- **Script Pipeline:** ScriptPipeline.com/shop/development-notes
- **Script Reader Pro:** ScriptReaderPro.com/our-script-coverage-services
- **Shore Scripts:** ShoreScripts.com
- **Spec Scout:** SpecScout.com
- **David Trottier:** KeepWriting.com
- **We Screenplay:** WeScreenplay.com

"If you're not prepared to be rejected, don't try to write films."
– Peter Hyams, *Beyond a Reasonable Doubt*

SCREENPLAY COMPETITIONS

"You have to try your hardest to be at the top of your game and improve every joke you can until the last possible second, and then you have to let it go. You can't be that kid standing at the top of the waterslide, overthinking it. You have to let people see what you wrote."
– Tina Fey, *Unbreakable Kimmy Schmidt*

"You can literally change your life by entering these competitions and festivals."
– Steven DeBose, Austin Film Festival, Director of Script Competitions

In the era of silent films, so many people were submitting scripts to studios that competitions were held to award cash prizes for well-written scenarios (as screenplays were once called). The goal was to find talented writers for the booming industry. The competitions were held by studios, and also by *Photoplay* magazine.

As the film industry developed, a variety of screenplay competitions came and went.

One of the earlier screenwriting competitions was funded in the 1950s by Samuel Goldwyn, Sr., and was limited to students or graduates of UCLA.

Over the years, some of the screenplay contests were not quite valid. Scam artists learned that they could place ads in writing and trade magazines – and other publications – promoting a screenplay contest, which required a fee to enter. Cash prizes and career-enhancing contacts – and sometimes contracts – were promised. The scam artists knew that there was no regulation, they could get hundreds – or thousands – of entrants, with each writer paying an entrance fee. Then, the scammers could close shop, keep the money, and nobody knew much about what to do about it.

Luckily, with the Internet, it became easier to research screenwriting contests, and find out which ones are more likely to be legitimate. This has greatly reduced the scams. But, you may learn there are still those that are more relevant than others – and some pretty much mean nothing at all to managers, agents, producers, and studios.

What many consider to be the top screenplay competition is the Nicholl Fellowship, which the Academy of Motion Picture Arts and Sciences began in 1985.

As word got out that Hollywood was paying fortunes for screenplays, there was a surge of interest in screenwriting. Magazines and books focused on the industry of screenwriting were published. Screenwriting seminars sold out. And many people were wasting money on the hopes of becoming the next millionaire screenwriter (Search: Shane Black and Joe Eszterhas).

As the Internet was established, it also became a source for information about screenwriting contests, books, seminars, retreats, pitch sessions, and hollow promises of meetings with industry leaders – or people claiming to be.

As various film festivals started, they also began holding screenplay competitions. These include the Austin Film Festival, Slamdance Film Festival, Nashville Film Festival. (Search: Film festival screenplay contests.)

There are also screenwriting fellowships run by some networks and or studios.

As I'm writing this, there is a screenwriter mentorship accepting submissions, and that is called Imagine Impact. It is backed by director/producer Ron Howard and his producing partner Brian Grazer.

While the current situation of selling screenplays to Hollywood is not what it was in the 80s and 90s, during which screenwriters selling scripts for millions of dollars was the reality for a few people (but also vastly blown out of proportion compared to the reality of most screenwriters), there are legitimate ways to enter into the industry through entering legitimate screenplay competitions, fellowships, mentorships, labs, and by networking at certain film festivals, and other events. (In addition to making your own material – preferably with high-quality production values, and in ways that legitimately display your talents.)

I know of writers who have submitted screenplays to various competitions, and won, conducted themselves honorably and smartly at meetings, signed with managers and agents, and established careers.

Below is a partial list of some of the many screenplay competitions and fellowships. You can find others online.

Before you enter a contest, research it. Consider who started the contest, know who runs it (a film fest, group, industry company, or other entity), and who is on the judge panel.

Does that judging panel consist of successful writers, and/or legitimate producers, directors, agents, managers, development executives, or producers? Research each of their names on IMDbPro.

Don't simply enter every contest. Consider the type of screenplays you have written, and if the genre, budget, and tone coincides with what is most likely to win those contests.

If possible, look into who previously won the contest that you would like to enter. Perhaps do an IMDb search for what their career has turned into.

You might be surprised to learn that scripts that have won contests often end up never being produced. But, those scripts could have led to the writers getting other work in the industry, including script doctoring, writing assignments, and being TV series staff writers.

Before entering a script into a contest, take the time to polish your script.

Do not enter a script before it is ready. Doing so is a solid waste of time and money.

Of course, ways of polishing your script is to take every page of it through a workshop, then have it edited. Maybe do a table read with actors. Then, send the script out to one or two coverage services to see what they have to say about it. Polish it more. Do all of that, before entering the script into a competition. Your script will be up against other scripts that have been put through those types of processes.

It seems blatantly obvious that some screenplay contests chiefly exist simply to bring in money. The contests engage in massive promotion to bring in the most amount of entrants possible. The people who run them know that a large number of scripts entered will be unpolished, and easily dismissible. They feed off of the entry fees that the naïve writers give them.

To be more ethical, the contests should at least provide a list of books for writers to study – before the writers spend money to enter their scripts into the contests.

If your script isn't absolutely polished to the bone and so tight that it bleeds conflict, contention, and subtext played out by interesting characters in an engaging story, don't waste your time entering your scripts into what are considered the top contests.

No matter the script contest, only enter a script when it is ready. To enter a script before it is ready, you may as well take the money that you spent entering the contest and burn it.

Simply because your script wins a contest does not mean that the script will be produced. The contest may simply work as a way for you to network and meet people who might help you in your career, including managers, agents, producers, development executives, showrunners, and directors. But, you have to continue to hustle, and be engaged in formulating a career.

Simply because I list a contest here does not mean that you should enter it. Do your research to find the best contests for your script.

- Academy Nicholl Fellowship
- American Zoetrope Screenplay Contest
- Atlanta Film Fest

- Austin Film Festival Screenplay Competition
- Black Screenplays Matter
- BlueCat Screenplay Competition
- Cannes International Screenwriting Competition
- Cinestory Feature Retreat
- Creative World Awards
- Cynosure Screenwriting Awards
- Edinburgh Screenwriting Competition
- Faith in Film
- Fantastic Horror Film Festival
- Film Independent Screenwriting Lab
- Final Draft Big Break Contest
- Finish Line Script Competition
- Fresh Voices Original Screenplay Competition
- Hamilton Film Festival Screenplay Competition
- Kairos Prize for Spiritually Uplifting Screenplays
- Latino Screenwriting Competition
- Launch Pad
- LGBTQ Screenwriting Competition
- Nashville Film Festival
- Ojai Film Festival Screenplay Competition
- Page International Screenwriting Awards
- ScreenCraft Action/Thriller
- ScreenCraft Pilot Launch
- ScreenCraft Sci-Fi
- ScreenCraft Screenwriting Fellowship
- Screenplay Festival
- Scriptapalooza
- Script Pipeline
- Shore Scripts
- Shriekfest Film Festival
- Slamdance Screenplay Competition
- StoryPros Awards Contest
- Sundance Screenwriters Lab
- Sundance Episodic Storytelling Lab
- Sundance Feature Script Contest
- Toronto International Screenwriting Competition
- TrackingB Feature and TV Script Contest
- Tracking Board's Launch Pad Competition
- VisionFest Screenwriting Competition
- WeScreenplay
- Women Who Write in Film

(Search: Screenplay contests.)

"I realized screenwriting was a real art form. I had to prostrate myself before it and study it – if I wanted to be good."
– Stephen Gaghan, *Traffic*

"I do truly believe that the smallest stories can wind up being the biggest, because it's through the specific that a writer can best access the universal."
– Damien Chazelle, *Babylon*

Screenwriting Labs

Screenwriting labs are held for days in a row at one location, sometimes on a campus, other times at a retreat center, and others at a conference center, hotel, or other location. Lodging and some meals might be included in the price. Or, they might have deals with nearby hotels. You will likely have to cover your transportation costs.

Labs will have instructors and/or mentors of some sort, usually people established in the industry: directors, writers, producers, managers, and college professors.

Labs may involve writing, analyzing the writing, workshopping the script pages, panel discussions, guest speakers, mentoring, group meals, one-on-one meetings, and assignments.

Some labs go on for up to a week, and then they are finished. Others require attending a lab intensive weekend (or week), followed by a fellowship program that lasts months – or a year – involving mentoring, meetings, and networking opportunities, which could mean that you will have to relocate.

Some labs may be associated with film festivals, university programs, professional organizations, or a sponsorship of sorts.

Here are some of the screenwriting labs you may want to consider. Compare these with the fellowship programs.

- **Athena IRIS Screenwriting Lab**. For women writers. Held in New York. Associated with the Athena Film Festival. AthenaFilmFestival.CAthena-IRIS-Screenwriting-Lab.
- **Black List / Women In Film Feature Lab**. Held in Los Angeles. BlckLst.Com/Education/Opportunities/48
- **Cinephilia Shorts Screenwriters Lab**. Held for ten days in various cities. Sessions are conducted in English. CinephiliaProductions.com/ShortsLab.

- **European Film Lab**. Held in Brittany, France. LeGroupeOuest.Com/EN/Script-Lab
- **Film Independent Screenwriting Lab**. A five-week workshop, during which you work on one script. FilmIndependent.org.
- **Hamptons International Film Festival Screenwriter's Lab**. East Hampton, New York. HamptonsFilmFest.org/ScreenwritersLab.
- **Hedgebrook Screenwriter's Lab**. For women writers. Whidbey Island, Washington. Hedgebrook.org
- **Imagine Impact**. Los Angeles. Started by Brian Grazer and Ron Howard in 2018. A "global content accelerator program" and a "global boot camp." Imagine-Impact.com. This has been evolving in how it functions.
- **Keep Writing Retreat**. Sundance, Utah. *The Screenwriter's Bible* author David Trottier's annual retreat. KeepWriting.com/Sundance
- **Middlebury Script Lab**. Middlebury, Vermont. Fellows are chosen to attend this tuition-free week-long lab. Middlebury.EDU/Script-Lab
- **Missouri Stories Scriptwriting Fellowship**. Held in Missouri. Stories must be based in Missouri. MOFilm.Org/Made-in-Missouri/MOStories
- **New Voices Fellowship**. India. AsiaSociety.Org/India/New-Voices-Fellowship-Screenwriters.
- **The Norman Mailer Center Workshop**. NMCenter.Org.
- **Outfest Screenwriting Lab**. Associated with the LGBTQ Outfest Film Festival in Los Angeles. Includes year-long mentorship. OutFest.org/SWL.
- **Praxis Screenwriters Lab**. Whistler, British Columbia, Canada. WhistlerFilmFestival.com/Talent/Praxis-Screenwriters-Lab.
- **The Stowe Story Lab**. Stowe, Vermont. StoweStoryLabs.org.
- **Sundance Institute**. Offers labs, intensives, and fellowships. Sundance.org.
- **Sun Valley Film Festival Screenwriters Lab**. SunnValleyFilmFestival.org/screenwriters-lab.
- **Write/LA Screenwriter Lab**. Two-day lab that is part of the Write/LA Screenwriting Competition. Write-LA.Com/#Why-Us.
- **The Writer's Lab**. For women over 40. Held in a rural area outside of New York City. TheWritersLab.NYC.

"For a screenplay or television pilot to gain traction in the professional space, it has to be read and well received by many, many people. Whether it's about moving forward in a screenwriting contest, landing a coveted television writing program spot, or getting a manager or an agent, the quality of the material has to be agreed upon by any number of people. So, how do you make sure that your material is received as you had hoped? You get notes. You expose your work, early and often, to people whose opinion you trust, whose story savvy you can rely on, and who will be demanding of the work and help you push it to its best, strongest place possible. Only when you get feedback on what's bumping your reader, what logic is failing to track, and what characters are hard to like or invest in, can you dig back into the work and make it as strong as you need to be to garner the reception you are looking for."

– Lee Jessup, career coach, LeeJessup.com

"Film school was often seen as a place to evade adulthood or even avoid the draft, but many there took their studies seriously. Shooting their 8mm student films on shoestring budgets, the most deeply smitten gave off the ardor of novitiates, believers in a new religion of film that could change the world at twenty-four frames per second."
    – Marc Norman, *What Happens Next: A History of American Screenwriting*

"When people ask me if I went to film school, I tell them, 'No, I went to films.'"
    – Quentin Tarantino, *Once Upon a Time… in Hollywood*

"I learned more from music videos than I did from film school, without a doubt."
    – Hiro Murai, director

FILM SCHOOLS

"I've had students who are lazy. And laziness is something that I really can't tolerate. Because of laziness, I think that speaks of a sense of entitlement. That's just not a good look, in this industry, where you think that you are entitled to something. That you deserve something, because you're wherever you think you are. It doesn't work like that.

Another thing I'd like to add is that – and I'm talking about my school – a lot of people come out of NYU thinking that because you have this degree from this prestigious institution – NYU, or USC, or AFI, Columbia – in the real world, they don't really give a shit. If you don't have the talent, that (having the degree) to me doesn't mean a thing. If you come out of school, if you are a director, you should have a film. If you are a D.P., you should have a reel. Editors should have a reel. If you are a screenwriter, you should have scripts. People really want to see the work you have done."
    – Spike Lee, *He Got Game*

Since the 1960s, film schools have multiplied across the globe, including in special high schools, and in junior colleges, universities, and trade schools.

Consider how much time and money it takes to attend film school. Compare that with how much it might benefit you to spend years making a variety of films – without attending school, but learning by making mistakes.

Instead of spending money and time on film school, would you be better off diving in and spending that time and money on making one low budget, full-length feature film per year that you can enter into various film festivals, and try to sell to distributors who cover various regions of the planet? Or, would you be better off diving in and spending that money on and time in film school, and networking with the students in what could amount to life-long professional relationships?

444

"Every inch of my writing career has been influenced by my screenwriting education. I was lucky enough to go to film school at USC, and I got a crash course in how to tell a story efficiently. I learned structure, pace, my style, how to know your audience, and most importantly, how to take criticism and edits properly."

– Victoria Aveyard, *Red Queen*

"The real trouble with film school is that people teaching are so far out of the industry that they don't give the students an idea of what's happening."

– Brian De Palma, *Raising Cain*

"You don't need writing classes or seminars any more than you need this or any other book on writing. Faulkner learned his trade while working in the Oxford, Mississippi post office. Other writers have learned the basics while serving in the Navy, working in steel mills, or doing time in America's finer crossbar hotels. I learned the most valuable (and commercial) part of my life's work while washing motel sheets and restaurant table cloths at the New Franklin Laundry in Bangor. You learn best by reading a lot and writing a lot, and the most valuable lessons of all are the ones you teach yourself."

– Stephen King, author *On Writing*

What becomes of your career is more up to you than anyone else – regardless of whether or not you went to film school.

"When I was sixteen or seventeen, I wanted to be a writer. I wanted to be a playwright. But everything I wrote, I thought was weak. And I can remember falling asleep in tears because I had no talent the way I wanted to have."

– Francis Ford Coppola, *Youth Without Youth*

"The first day of school, they gave you a camera, and a daylight spool of film. They taught us how to load these cameras, and they would send you off without a light meter, just to film. And every week they would give you a bit more of a tool. The second week you'd get a light meter. The third week you'd get a little bit more footage. The fourth week you'd have to do a certain amount of dissolves. It was very 'learn by doing.' And over the course of that first semester, I knew nothing about making films – the actual craft – the technical tools, the technical skill, I would say I needed. And so, I took a year off after that first semester. I asked myself a question. That question was: Am I not good at this because I'm black, and I'm poor, and my mom was a drug addict? Or, do I not know how to utilize these tools.

I guess the first lesson I learned in filmmaking was: No matter how strong your voice is, if you don't have a mastery of the tools, that voice is going to be suffocated. Now, you can work with people who do have a mastery of the tools, but I wanted to control the way my voice was going to be filtered through the craft. So, I took a year off, and I started watching foreign films. What I realized was everybody in film school was mimicking what they were watching. So, if all you watch is Steven Spielberg – and there is nothing wrong with watching nothing but Steven Spielberg – your work is going to come out in the voice of Steven Spielberg. And, so I thought, well, I'm going to start watching everything else. Everything that nobody else was watching, which was Asian New Wave cinema, French New Wave cinema, and then I also started reading film criticism. I got a subscription to *Sight & Sound* magazine. And then, I took a 35 millimeter still photography course. I wanted to make my own 35 millimeter prints."

– Barry Jenkins, Moonlight

Certainly, there are people who attended film school and then experienced great success in the industry. And, there are people who have experienced similar success in the film industry without going to film school. It depends on how you work the game, self-study, learn from mistakes and failures, and persevere, network, aim forward, and refuse to be lazy.

"If you are talented and you go to one of these schools – USC, UCLA, Chapman, or something – and you're sitting in a room, a seminar, where a professor has 15 students, and he's reading your writing, if you are talented, that professor is going to fall in love with you and help you and connect you to someone like me. Because for people who are that incredibly talented, someone is going to help them and invest in them along the way."

– Jewerl Ross, Silent R Management

Some companies will not hire people who don't have a college degree. That is one motivating factor to get that degree – even if you don't make it in the industry.

"I didn't sell my first screenplay until 1977 – the seventh feature-length script I had written. I also had written dozens of short film scripts and filmed several of them myself. That's one of the first lessons I will pass along to you. Don't ever stop writing. So, I had served a ten-year apprenticeship teaching myself how to write scripts before I became a professional."

Joseph McBride, *Rock 'n' Roll High School*

Even if you do go to film school, you still have to engage in self-education to polish – and continually maintain and update – your skills in the craft.

"I was at a film school not that long ago, and some of the students had never seen *Dr. Strangelove* and didn't know who Andrei Tarkovsky was. I found that actually chilling."

– Roger Deakins, director of photography *1917, Skyfall, Doubt*, etc.

To me, Roger Deakins is one of the people who film students – and anyone in the film industry – should know of.

Don't expect to learn everything that you need to know about film by going to film school. It is beneficial to self-educate. There are numerous books to read about the film and TV industry, and the various aspects of filmmaking. Reading *Sight & Sound* magazine is also a way to learn things.

"I never took any writing classes, or seminars, or anything like that – read pamphlets. My whole thing was: Everything I learned as an actor – studying acting for six years – I basically applied to my writing."
– Quentin Tarantino, *Once Upon a Time… in Hollywood*

"What I tell young screenwriters is, 'Take responsibility for your work.' Collaborate with friends who want to make films, and with them produce your work on whatever scale your filmmaking team can afford. Digital video has brought down the cost of making your own films. Don't wait for permission. Create your own opportunities. In terms of your craft, be as mentally free as you can be while you are writing – and then be ruthless in your assessment of your need to rewrite. Find readers you can trust, whose notes and advice trigger an 'Oh, you're right!' response of self-recognition about the revisions that remain to be done.

And just keep writing.

Malcolm Gladwell in his book *Outliers* pegs the time commitment at ten thousand hours before you begin to achieve expertise.

Write a script and put it away. Write another. Put it away. Go back and look at the first script again and rewrite – you'll see that you already know more about writing, just from having written."
– Robin Swicord, *The Curious Case of Benjamin Button*

Successful screenwriters who didn't attend film school:
• Paul Thomas Anderson
• Wes Anderson,
• James Cameron
• Ethan Coen
• Terry Gilliam
• Peter Jackson
• Stanley Kubrick
• Akira Kurosawa
• Christopher Nolan
• Ridley Scott
• Steven Spielberg
• Quentin Tarantino
• Lilly and Lana Wachowski

They learned by self-education, by engaging in the craft, by working on projects with other craftspeople, by making mistakes, by learning from failure, by experiencing success. After one project, they moved along to their next project – and used what they had learned along the way.

"Every human being needs an outlet for his inborn creative talent. If you feel you would like to write, then write. Perhaps you are afraid that lack of

447

higher education might retard you from real accomplishment? Forget it. Many great writers, Shakespeare, Ibsen, George Bernard Shaw, to mention a few, never saw the inside of a college."
— Lajos Egri, author *The Art of Dramatic Writing*

Tarantino's film education could partially be considered that he worked at the now closed Video Archives rental store in Manhattan Beach, California. What better way to learn about film than to surround yourself with films all day long, watch them play on the store monitors, and talk with people about films? He likely saw vastly more films than any film school student, while he was also taking acting lessons for six years.

"Trying to make a feature film by yourself with no money is the best film school you can do."
— Quentin Tarantino, *Death Proof*

Luckily, I live in a city with two well-stocked video stores that continue to operate: Cinefile in West L.A. and Videotheque in South Pasadena. The Cinefile staff has been particularly helpful and engaging, and I'm always telling Tribers to go check out Cinefile.

As I'm writing this, it has been announced that Vidiot's – which had been my favorite video store – where it had formerly been located in Santa Monica – is going to reopen with its own film theater in Glendale.

"Even with college, the reason I wanted to go so badly is because I wanted to major in film. I want to take screenwriting classes and learn more about behind the scenes stuff, because I love people like Steve Carell and Kristen Wiig – who are able to write a lot of their own material and be so involved in everything they do."
— Miranda Cosgrove, actor

A friend of mine attended film school at a major university. She ended up with a whole lot of student debt. Stuck with that debt, she works a regular job – outside of the film industry.

What did spending over one-hundred-thirty-thousand dollars – and her inheritance – on years of film school do for her?

Would she have been professionally and financially better off – and learned more about making movies – by spending massively less money by not attending that university, but instead taking the film classes at Santa Monica College (a community college with a mini film and TV studio), and making a variety of ultra-low-budget films? Maybe Ghetto Film School could have been part of her learning (yes, it's a real thing. GhettoFilm.org) – in addition to joining an intensive screenplay incubation workshop, being involved with New Filmmakers L.A., and with Women in Film, and taking other steps to self-educate, network, and improve her skills in the craft by being a writer/director/filmmaker – and not simply a student at an expensive university.

"I worked for very many years in and around our elite universities. I am able to report that their admissions policies are an unfortunate and corrupt joke.

Harvard was once sued for restricting admissions of qualified Jews; a contest currently being waged by Asians.

The unqualified may be accepted for many reasons, among them, as legacies, and on account of large donations made by their parents."

– David Mamet, *The Unit*

"I went from wanting to be a novelist, to wanting to be a playwright, and somewhere – probably in my sophomore year of college – I started thinking about film.

I bought a book on the technical aspects of filmmaking. That was a couple of years of just reading. I dropped out of college, and then started watching three or four movies a day, bought some equipment a little bit later. After that, started the Austin Film Society, kept making films, and here I am."

– Richard Linklater, *Slacker*

You don't have to attend a film school to be able to read the text books that are used in film schools (some film schools use this book that you hold in your hands as one of their texts). You don't have to be in film school to have access to filmmaking equipment, and to watch instruction videos on YouTube.

But, perhaps you are one who would greatly benefit by attending a legitimate film school.

"I had a wonderful teacher, Irwin Blacker, and he was feared by everyone at the school because he took a very interesting position. He gave you the screenplay form, which I hated so much, and if you made one mistake on the form, you flunked the class. His attitude was that the least you can learn is the form. 'I can't grade you on the content. I can't tell you whether this is a better story for you to write than that, you know? And I can't teach you how to write the content, but I can certainly demand that you do it in the proper form.' He never talked about character arcs or anything like that; he simply talked about telling a good yarn, telling a good story. He said, 'Do whatever you need to do. Be as radical and as outrageous as you can be. Take any kind of approach you want to take. Feel free to flash back, feel free to flash forward, feel free to flash back in the middle of a flashback. Feel free to use narration, all the tools are there for you to use.' I used to tell a screenwriting class, 'I could teach you all the basic techniques in fifteen minutes. After that, it's up to you.'"

– John Milius, *Clear and Present Danger*

There are film schools in many countries. To find them, do a search for: (name of country) film schools.

"I was interested in writing, and when I got to Ann Arbor, I started writing theater and fiction, and was able to see my plays get produced. I didn't

get into the film program for a while. I was never formally part of it – I was an English literature major – but I eventually started taking film courses. Very quickly, I began writing feature-length screenplays."
– Lawrence Kasdan, *Body Heat*

Before paying tuition to any film school, conduct a search for online reviews of the school. Consider who teaches at the school. Find out if anyone successful in the film industry graduated from the school. Factor how much it will cost you to go through the film school. Try for grants and scholarships, while avoiding student loans.

Consider going through at least one or more years of film school, during which you live and breathe doing everything you can to learn about filmmaking. It's not a time to be lazy. Be active. Hustle to make things happen. Live as absolutely cheaply as possible with only the basic things that you need to get by – no restaurants, new clothes, or vacations. It's a time to network, to make films, and to gain working relationships that might last decades.

A person can learn a whole lot about making films by using free online sources.

Learn all you can about the new technologies used in filmmaking by watching online videos – such as the numerous videos on YouTube that explain and demonstrate film equipment.

Consider getting a job at a film equipment rental company.

Make a film guerilla style, with a rehearsed cast to steal shots without permits, using your smart phone with filming attachments. You say that is difficult? Consider that there are 13-year-olds making short films, and posting them on YouTube. Maybe you would consider their short films lousy. But, they've made more films than you have – and their mistakes might be advancing them in the craft faster than what a dismissive and doubtful person will gain by waiting for that ever-elusive prefect time to make a project.

The money you spend on making your guerilla project might never be regained. But, maybe that will be your tuition of learning by doing it that way – so that your next film will be better. On the other hand, if you put the costs associated with that project on a credit card, consider that it might be at a higher interest rate than school loans. If you rented the equipment, you can return that. If you had been in film school, that equipment would be available to you without rental charge through the school. Any crew you might have paid could have been had for free through fellow students.

Before you make your own film:
- Read books and watch online videos covering producing, budgeting, directing, editing, sound design, colorization, and otherwise, the processes and skills you will need to know.
- Know how to breakdown a script. There are at least several worthwhile YouTube tutorials on that topic. Articles about breaking down a script also can be found. Filmmaking books also describe how to do it.

- Do your homework, whatever that means for making the sort of project that you want to make. There is a whole bunch of free information about filmmaking on the Internet.
- Gain the skills in the craft that you need to succeed. That might mean volunteering to work on film projects done by other people, so that you can get hands-on experience.
- Know that it all starts with the screenplay. So, make sure it is all that it could be, and shoot it within a budget that likely equates with the type of money that genre brings in.

"I think the point of film school is the same as the point of law school, or in the case of some undergraduate majors, earning a specialized degree that trains you well to do a very specific job. The mission is to provide an intense, focused, and safe training space for students to learn their craft and build well-honed, professionally scrutinized portfolios. Students also come away with a deep understanding of the business, as well as a life-long support network consisting of their classmates, their faculty, and the industry contacts they make through internships and programs.

I went to USC for an MFA in screenwriting, and earned a rare 'Distinction' on my thesis script. That script went on to be produced, and was successful, but nobody in Hollywood cared at all that I was a USC grad, or what award that script had won. What they cared about was the product: My skill on paper and in the room, which I completely developed in film school. I have four produced movies, have performed twice as many writing assignments, and most importantly, I have great training, better-than-average discipline, and a fantastic network in place across all facets of the business – and that all began for me in film school."

– Brad Riddell, DePaul University, and USC School of Cinematic Arts. GoIntoTheStory.BlckLst.com

"I often joke, when people ask if I went to film school I say, 'Oh, I went to the Stanley Kubrick film school,' which means you just buy a camera, and you learn how to use it, and you start making movies, and that's as good as anything else. I mean, I lived near the University of Texas Film School, had a lot of friends who went to school there, and I would sit in classes, I'd go to student films. I felt I had some connection there. Even though I was never enrolled, I'd go to student short screenings, and certainly watch thousands of films on campus. But, as far as my own stuff goes, I had a personality, I think I just wanted to do it on my own. I really didn't want to be judged. I was naturally very shy, and I think for film you don't really need necessarily that – if you're a self-motivated person. But, you need to be for film anyway. That's lesson number one.

It's not like you get your degree and then the industry gives you this, or that. You know, if you're ever really gonna write and direct movies and get your own movies to make, you have to be a hustler. You got to be kind of obsessively motivated. School is not going to teach you that, or give you those skills. You just kind of have to do it. And I was lucky enough to fall in with some like-minded friends. We were all sort of raging with the ideas of film. It was a great period of my life. Myself, roommates, in a music town like Austin, we were film guys. We showed films and promoted them, and talked about film. And went to every film, and that was life. It was pretty damn great."

– Richard Linklater, *Where'd You Go, Bernadette*

In addition to the schools listed below, there are other universities and community colleges offering film studies.

This list is not an endorsement of the schools. What works for some people, doesn't work so well for others. Do your research. Be careful how you spend money. Live inexpensively, not as a replicant of advertising imagery. Second-hand stores, garage sales, and used item sites (CraigsList, etc.) can be your shopping options – including for barely used film equipment. Never buy a brand new car (certified used hybrid or electric is smarter). Avoid student loan debt. Try for grants, and other funds that you don't have to pay back.

• American Film Institute, Los Angeles
• Art Center College of Design, Pasadena, California
• Australian Film, Television, and Radio School
• AUT University, New Zealand
• Beijing Film Academy, China
• Biola University, La Mirada
• Boston University, Massachusetts
• Bournemouth University, UK
• California Institute of the Arts, Valencia
• California State University Northridge
• Centro de Capacitacion Cinematografica, Mexico
• Chapman University, Orange, California
• Cleveland State University, Ohio
• Colorado Film School, Denver
• Columbia College, Chicago
• Columbia University, New York
• Cuyahoga Community College, Cleveland
• DePaul University, Chicago
• Dongseo University, South Korea
• Edinburgh University, Scotland
• Emerson College, Boston
• FAMU International, UK, Prague, Czech Republic
• Film & Television Institute of India
• Florida State University, Tallahassee
• Full Sail University, Winter Park, Florida
• Galway Film Centre, Galway, Ireland
• Ghetto Film School, New York and L.A.
• Goldsmith's University of London
• HFF Munich, Munich Film Academy, Germany

- Hollins University, Roanoke, Virginia
- International Institute of Modern Letters, New Zealand
- Irish Film Academy, Cork, Ireland
- Ithaca College, New York
- La Femis, Paris, France
- L.A. Film School
- Lodz Film School, Poland
- London College of Communication
- London Film School
- Los Angeles City College
- Loyola Marymount University
- Met Film School, UK
- Mount St. Mary's University, Los Angeles
- National Film and Television School, England
- National Film School of Denmark
- National Film School, Institute of Art, Dublin, Ireland
- New York Film Academy
- New York University Tish School of the Arts
- Norwegian Film School, Norway
- Pepperdine University, Malibu, California
- Pratt Institute, New York
- Rhode Island School of Design
- Ringling College of Art & Design
- Sam Spiegel Film & Television School, Israel
- San Francisco State University
- Santa Monica College Film Program, Santa Monica, California
- Sarah Lawrence College, Bronxville, New York
- Satyajit Ray Film and Television Institute, India
- Savannah College of Art and Design
- Stanford University, Palo Alto, California
- Sydney Film School, Australia
- Syracuse University, New York
- Tel Aviv University, Israel
- Toronto Film School
- University of British Columbia
- University of California Berkeley
- University of California Los Angeles
- University of California Los Angeles Extension
- University of Melbourne, Victorian College of the Arts, Australia
- University of Michigan, Ann Arbor
- University of North Carolina, Winston-Salem
- University of Pittsburgh, Film Studies
- University of Southern California, Los Angeles
- University of Television and Film, Munich, Germany
- University of Texas, Austin
- University of the Arts, Philadelphia, Pennsylvania

Screenwriting Tribe
- University of Wisconsin, Milwaukee
- Vancouver Film School, Canada
- Vanderbilt University, Nashville
- Vassar College, New York
- Wesleyan University, Middletown, Connecticut
- Yale University, New Haven, Connecticut

"You'll gain a lot more knowledge by studying editing than you will by studying screenwriting.

Screenwriting is something inside of you. It's what you are going to do, and it's gonna be dictated by so many other things.

Watch how movies are built. That's where it really comes together. Watch how movies evolved through the process of editing."

– Christopher McQuarrie, *Jack Reacher*

"I think you can study too much. I've seen that happen. Young people get immersed in the work of other directors, and end up imitating them – rather than finding their own identity. It's important to see the work of as many directors as possible, but you must not become self-conscious. You have to accept that your first attempts are going to be quite rough, compared to the finished works of great masters."

– James Ivory, *Quartet*

"As a representative, I feel it's my responsibility to be an objective eye."
– Tony Gil, manager

"What a general meeting for a writer is: It's a meeting with someone (usually an exec at a studio, network, or production company) after they've read your material. The exec liked your material and wants to get to know you. Sometimes showrunners will do generals with writers, as will actors or directors."
– John Zaozirny, manager

Agents and Managers

"Writing is a lonely job. Having someone who believes in you makes a lot of difference. They don't have to make speeches. Just believing is usually enough."
– Stephen King, *The Gingerbread Girl*

Agents and managers need writers skilled in the craft of writing broadly marketable films. The agents and managers make money when the scripts of the writers they represent sell.

"I always write the movie that I want to go see, and just assume someone else will want to go see it, too.
Trying to guess what someone else is going to like or want: That's such a moving target. You'll find yourself trying to write something that's false."
– Taylor Sheridan, *Yellowstone*

The agents make ten percent of the sale, and the managers make fifteen percent of the sale. So, they want writers with scripts that can and will sell. It's about money. If you can't make them money, they won't have any use for you. You need to be part of their money-making process. If your scripts aren't sellable, and aren't selling, they don't need you.

"It's very important to keep producing material because the months fly by and you need new samples for your agents to circulate. It can be tempting, but it's important not to feel competitive with other writers. It's really unproductive."
– Nora Nolan, *Paradise PD*

"A great client is one who is hungry and just keeps writing."
– Steven DeBose, Austin Film Festival

Preferably, screenwriters will have a variety of scripts written – and polished – before they search for representation.

"Mostly, you write a script and someone's gonna rewrite you. They get hundreds of – not hundred, but they get ten writers to write something. If you have a big budget, you can go and get a lot of people to write one script. I just actually heard that somebody said, 'Well, your screenplay got bought and now someone like Carrie Fisher will come in and rewrite you.' And I feel terrible, you know, because that's not what I mean to do. My idea was never to raid something and trash it, you know. Because that's more work for me."
– Carrie Fisher, *Postcards from the Edge*

Agents and managers also like writers who are willing and are skilled enough in the craft to take on writing assignments. That is, to get paid to write scripts that are based on an idea, or to adapt a book or news story into a screenplay, or to rewrite scripts written by other writers and that are going into production.

There are many writers who make the bulk of their income from writing assignments.

Agents and managers want writers who can give great pitches to producers.

Agents and managers want writers who are "good in a room" – as in, good in a room of writers and producers working on a project. That means, they want writers who communicate well with others – including when there are disagreements and unclear concepts that will need to be worked out so that the projects get written efficiently, and can keep moving forward.

"The first mistake people make is thinking they have to impress. That instinct combined with nerves means they may talk more than they usually do and are overly effusive in their praise of the show/pilot, and the showrunner's past work. Please don't do that. For starters, if we think you're a person who talks too much, you're not getting the job. That's not the vibe a showrunner wants or needs in their writers' room.

All you really have do in the meeting is two things:

1) provide evidence that you're not a sociopath, and…

2) be thoughtful about the material.

If you're meeting a showrunner, it means they like your writing. We don't take meetings to take meetings. We don't have the time. We might ask about your script, but what we're really curious about is who you are and what kind of talent and energy you're bringing to the room."
– Amy Berg, *Leverage*

Agents and managers want writers who understand the business. Included in that is knowing that film financiers and distributors want films that will bring a good return on investment. Without satisfying financiers and distributors, it is unlikely that you will have a financially satisfying screenwriting career.

Agents and managers want writers writing screenplays containing characters that will be desirable for star actors to play. Attaching recognizable names to the project helps satisfy investors and distributors.

Agents and managers want writers who write scripts that are hugely entertaining. It helps if the screenplays can be made into sequels and prequels, and/or turned into an episodic, anthology, limited, or other series (see: *Fargo*).

Big studios like screenplays containing elements that can be turned into merchandise, including toys, games, T-shirts, and other crap that sells at stores like Target and Walmart, or as giveaways at toxic fast food restaurants – which helps pollute the planet.

Agents, managers, and producers want writers who are easy to work with, who can take script notes, and utilize those notes when overhauling the script – before it goes into production. Sometimes, those changes will be requests by not only the producers, but the directors, the stars, the financiers, and the distributors. All of that can be an ego festival. Welcome to the industry.

"Whoever's giving you notes also wants what you want – a great project. People who give notes well will give constructive notes and be leaning into it. Sometimes you'll get a strong tone, which is hard, but what you have to try to do is get the tone out of your head and find what's behind it. What's the intention behind this note? Say, 'Thank you.' Then, go off and think about it to see what sticks with you."
– Chris Salvaterra, producer

"The people who make movies are actually desperate for good material. They're desperate. And, honestly, if you write a brilliant script they really wouldn't care if you were a 95-year-old grandmother from Duluth. They really want something that's brilliant on the page. And it's actually one of the main reasons why I chose it, is that it's very subject to elbow grease, subject to hard work."
– Aline Brosh McKenn, *Crazy Ex-Girlfriend*

Agents "field offers," push scripts, close deals, and package projects.

Managers help grow a writer's career. They give professional advice, and guide you on how to deal with the various people in the industry, with the goal of selling your work so that they can make 15% of your pay.

While managers may read your script, and give you advice on it, agents will (probably) read it, and do what they do with it. That is: Try to sell it.

Agents want to send out scripts that also build on the agent's reputation for representing high quality, producible scripts.

What agents don't want are scripts that are not ready to sell, that aren't the type of scripts they want to send out, and that aren't the type of scripts that advance and maintain their career as reliable sources for marketable, commercial scripts.

Not that you should only concentrate on writing what might be viewed as broadly commercial and therefore marketable. Hopefully what you write will also be something that will draw people to the screens in the quantity that satisfies investors.

"Isn't there a risk you run if you preoccupy yourself with audience reaction at the expense of either your own integrity, or your own artistic judgement? I'm convinced that ninety percent of the writers who walk around laying claim to the honored soverkit of a writer are thinking in a sizeable portion of their mind, 'Will they love it in Des Moines? Will they understand it in New Orleans?' And, consequently, they will deliberately prostitute and write downward to what they believe is the lowest common denominator. And when you start to preoccupy yourself, I think, you're in trouble. This is not to say that I wouldn't share the Fellini feeling (who claimed to only make the art for himself, and didn't care if anyone else saw it) — if indeed that's the way he thinks — that I will only write for dirty old Rod, and that which pleases me must please you, and if it doesn't: The hell with you. But, the reverse, I think, concern should also be extant — that I must realize that because I am writing in an art form, the whole function of the art form is to be translated to other people. There's an emotional experience to be shared. Consequently, it isn't just me in my tower. It's how people will react to what I write.
— Rod Serling, *The Loner*

Agents are likely to have far more clients than the number of clients that managers have. That also plays out in their income.

Many managers also get involved with producing films, which can make them far more money than representing writers whose scripts sell. Thus, some managers are more centered on producing scripts, and less on selling.

Both agents and managers will likely make more money from you if you become a writer on a TV series, rather than sell an occasional feature film script. The longer you work on a series, and the more series' that you work on, the more you will become a commodity, and a source of income for them. With that, they will be sure to help your career keep rolling.

Your relationship between you and your agent and manager is a business relationship. They are not there to be of service to you. They are not your parent or caretaker.

Agents want to make things happen. They can only do that if you have marketable scripts that are ready to be sold, and scripts that gain the interest of producers, directors, stars, financiers, and distributors. Because of that, only submit scripts to the industry after you have polished them.

I strongly advise that you take every page of your scripts through a workshop, and spend weeks or months doing so, and have them edited and covered, before you send the scripts to a manager or agent.

As you look for representation, I encourage you to familiarize yourself with Lee Jessup, who is a career coach for beginning and emerging screenwriters.

Her blog contains helpful information for beginning screenwriters, including interviews of writers, agents, managers, and others in the industry.

"How do they work with new emerging writers? How much do they develop with you? Are they hands on or off? Do they give you notes, or not? Do they have a strategy for your career? Can they be honest about your strengths and weaknesses, and is their plan to correct bad habits?"
– Moises Zamora, *Selena*

Managers develop careers. They look at the portfolio of scripts you have written, and they strategize with what you have. They want to turn your scripts into what you will need for getting out there and selling scripts, and writing scripts for producers and stars, directors, and showrunners.

Managers may read your script and help you develop it into something that is marketable. They might hook you up with co-writers, and connect you with producers who need writers to turn an idea into a script, turn a book or news story into a script, or rewrite a script that is already financed.

Managers can advise you on what to expect at meetings with agents, producers, directors, and others. If you have questions about your career, ask your manager. If you have questions about how marketable your script is, and how marketable your writing is, speak with your manager.

Having a valid agent and a manager gives you credibility in the industry. But, it doesn't mean you can be lazy. It means that it is time to be the best writer you can be, and too be proactive in your career choices.

A problem associated with not having an agent and manager is that you have lack of access to many doors in Hollywood. These are doors to production companies, directors, studio development execs, and others who will look at your script only if you have it submitted through an agent or manager.

Some studios, producers, and production companies will not accept scripts that are submitted by entertainment attorneys. Some require that all scripts be submitted by an agent or manager.

If you are a new writer, an agent or manager impressed with your work might "hip pocket" or "backpocket" you. That is, not officially representing you, but perhaps giving feedback on your script from one of their readers or assistants, and doing some initial introduction of your script to the market (sending it "out to market" by getting it to some contacts at production companies or studios, or to directors or actors who might be interested) to get a feel for the potential of your writing. It might result in a sale, and spike an interest in more of your work – or get you a writing assignment. If this happens during pitch season (July through October for network TV), you might end up being considered for a writing gig on a show – as a staff writer. A producer, star, or director might also become so interested in your script that it results in a "shopping agreement," which allows them a certain amount of time (likely months) to try to set up the project with a production company, studio, network, or other party. Explore your possibilities.

Your agent can help negotiate your deal. With their knowledge and experience and contacts, they are likely to get you a better deal than you can on your own.

The quality of your material is key. Without quality "hot" scripts, it doesn't matter what you look like, what you say or do, or any other aspect of your being.

Agents, managers, production companies, screenwriting contests, and fellowship programs want material that is polished, formatted correctly, clear to read, and written in a way that is self-explanatory.

By a self-explanatory script, I mean that the script will represent itself as the writers can't be there to explain the script to the agents, producers, studio readers, and others as they read it. What is needed for them to like your script is an engaging and marketable, compelling story that is rich in conflict, contention, and subtext, with clever, sharp dialogue said by interesting characters, and with other beneficial qualities.

Your script needs to stand on its own, and it needs to be convincing from the first page. You want the decision makers to see it as a script that will make money for everyone, including agents, managers, producers, directors, financiers, distributors, stars, and you.

One thing to remember when you meet with producers is that you are to maintain the reputation of your manager and agent. Be good in the room. Be a person who listens to and considers notes. Don't be defensive. Know how to collaborate. Be professional. Don't say nonsense. Your agent and manager are representing you, and you also need to represent them.

"Writing a screenplay with a group of collaborators is like the Lennon/McCartney collaboration. Sometimes one or two people do more than others on certain parts of the process, and vice versa."
– Peter Jackson, *The Lord of the Rings: The Return of the King*

Before you go to meet a producer, do some research. Look them up on IMDbPro.com. Do a search for their name on the web. Look at what they have produced. See if you can find their career profile. See if you can find interviews they have done on YouTube. See if they have been mentioned in *The Hollywood Reporter* and *Variety*. See if you can find out what school they went to, and where they were born. Maybe they are related to someone in the industry, people you know, or you have similar backgrounds or interests.

Don't cause drama between your agent and manager and the people they connect you with. The big drama should be on the page – not in your meetings with the producers. Maintain a professional business composure. And don't appear to be defensive or eager. Especially don't act as if you are desperate.

Don't try to impress the producers when you meet with them. Since this will only make you look naïve. It's okay to be nervous, it's part of being human. It could be helpful to have a pen and notepad handy – as there are things you might want to write down, and a list of points to cover. Breaking out your laptop or other device might be over-the-top.

All they want is a script that can be turned into a successful project.

"A general (meeting) is basically a first date between the writer and a producer or executive. The room will be warm because the executive or whomever will be familiar with the writer's work, and the writer should know about the executive's projects, studio, company, etc. Generals are very informal, and really about the executive getting to know the writer as a person. This is why it's so important for screenwriters to be able to sell themselves in a one-on-one situation.

Sometimes specific projects will be discussed, and sometimes generals end without any specific future work discussed. Leave it to your reps to follow up and cut through the subtext with the executive."
– Andrew Kersey, manager

Let them know that you are someone they can work with.

Know that there is always more to learn, and that what you previously learned might not be what is accurate, wise, or best for you.

Continually work on your craft and learn the business side of the industry.

"I'm trying to empower writers to be a more necessary and involved part of the process. Writers are taught to take themselves out very early on.

Writers are taught that you write a screenplay, and you sell that screenplay, and then – miraculously – a producer gets a director attached to it, and then – somehow – they find financing, and they shoot the movie that you wrote – which sounds to me like hitting the lottery many, many, many times in a row.

The problem with that is that writers are neither taught how to engineer movies, and, more importantly, they're taught a lot of bad habits by executives in terms of executing stories that are based on plot – and reasons, and answering the question 'Why?' Executives tend to be like children in that phase of life who just keep asking why, why, why, why, why?

Why things are happing is not really important. Why the big events of the story are happening are much less important than: Why is the character acting out a certain way within that. I'm much more interested in why characters are doing what they are doing than what the plot of the movie is."
– Christopher McQuarrie, *Top Gun: Maverick*

Simply because you don't land representation is not evidence that you lack the talent needed to succeed in the industry. There are other ways of entering the business, such as by becoming an editor, a script supervisor, a camera operator, or other film and TV craftsperson. Many successful screenwriters have worked in other areas of the industry. Explore your options.

"Absence of evidence is not the evidence of absence."
– Carl Sagan, *Contact*

"I love my rejection slips. They show me I try."
– Sylvia Plath, *The Bell Jar*

"A successful manager is someone who has the client's best interests in mind while staying true to the writer's goals and the stories they want to tell. Also, it's like asking, 'What is the key to a successful marriage?' The manager-writer relationship should be built on trust, commitment, patience, and constant communication."
– Matt Dy, Lit Entertainment Group

Finding and Dealing with a Manager

"Screenwriters should look for a manager who has the time to invest and really believes in you as an artist."
– Zach Cox, Circle of Confusion management

"I like working with writers who I get along with on a personal level. We're going to be spending a lot of time together – mostly on the phone – so, it's important that our personalities align to an extent.
   In terms of qualities that are desirable, I would say the most important one is being resilient. It takes a really long time to be a successful, working writer, and there are usually tons of pitfalls and detours along the way. Resilience is key."
– Jonathon Hersh, Housefire Management

"Managers are not WGA-affiliated, so they are not obligated to use WGA-approved contracts. Carefully look at any contract they offer. By law, they can't negotiate contracts, or find you employment, but that law (the California version is called California Talent Agencies Act) is seldom enforced."
– David Trottier, author *The Screenwriter's Bible*

Research managers. Make a list of those who might possibly represent you.
   You can meet managers at events, conferences, seminars, film festivals, and through contests, fellowship or mentorship programs, labs, and studio writing programs. If you are in an active writers' group, perhaps you will have proved yourself as a dependable, sharp, talented writer to the point that you will be introduced to managers by the repped writers in the group.

"I always look for two things: An original voice, and commercial instincts. The voice is more important though, as that is not something I can teach, whereas I can guide them to more commercial ideas and concepts. Also, they have to be hungry, humble, and willing and able to take meetings in L.A. and generate new ideas and specs consistently. Writers write, if you're not too busy with writing assignments, everyone should be generating something new every six months."
– Jake Wagner, Good Fear Film + Management

"The screenwriters I am most excited to work with are those who have clear convictions of what they want to do with their career, and understand that they wield a creative tool that requires focus and care. I usually look for them to be prepared with ambitions for the future, with knowledge of the industry's projected trajectory, and with a willingness to calibrate and strategize on their career ahead. I want to know that we're going to work together towards their goals, and that it will be a long-term, professional relationship."
– Daniela Gonzalez, Circle of Confusion management

Managers will like if you have a variety of polished scripts. They will like it if any of your scripts have placed high (were quarterfinalists or semifinalists) in valid screenwriting contests and/or have won awards. It will interest managers to know if you have gone through a mentorship, fellowship, lab, studio writing program, or attended a film school, and if you are a member of a workshop or writers' group. They will like if you are active in improving your skills in the craft, if you are up-to-date on the business of the business (read the trades), and can continually turn out new, sellable scripts.

"Nobody has it easy. Just know that you're in good company when you get that rejection letter. So, just keep going. Commitment is so important."
– Nikole Beckwith, *Stockholm, Pennsylvania*

Query Letters
• Know how to write a sharp, sparsely worded query letter that…
  • Won't take much time to read.
  • Probably takes less than a couple minutes to read.
  • Contains only the words that are needed.
• Keep it to one-page.
  • Don't try to stuff it with everything on this list…
  • Do include plenty of white space on the page – not dense, like a page from a book.
• Choose a standard business font, such as Times New Roman.
• Don't be flowery, or use compliments to try to flatter the manager.
• Don't brag or use hype ("Top actors will want to star in this film," etc.).
• Do mention if you were referred by someone who the manager already represents, or who is a significant person in the industry.

- Include a compelling, short, enticing logline of one of your screenplays – preferably your script that is most likely to sell.
- Mention:
  - If any of your scripts have placed high in or won competitions.
  - If you have been in a mentorship, fellowship, or studio writing program,
  - If you have had a film made that was screened at a known film festival.
- Include a sentence about if you have had any true involvement in the entertainment industry:
  - Not simply your hopes, or your weak or unfounded claims.
- Knowing that it is easy to find out if you are lying about your so-called career, be honest with managers. Mention if you:
  - Are a film school graduate, or attended a film school for a year or more.
  - Are a member of an industry union.
  - Are an editor, director, etc.
  - Are established in other areas of writing – journalist, author.
  - Are a long-term member of an established screenwriting workshop, etc.
    - If they have not been, don't say that your scripts have been put through a screenwriting workshop. I've been contacted when a person was falsely claiming to have workshopped scripts with Screenwriting Tribe. Their lie was easily exposed, and didn't work in their favor.
- Do include an email address and phone number.
- Don't include a home address. They aren't going to be paper mailing you anything. It's the electronic age.

Maybe the manager will request to see one or more of your screenplays.

The following should be about as obvious as could possibly be: Only present a screenplay to a manager after the screenplay has been polished. As in: Do what is suggested in this book to get your script up to industry standards. Presenting an unpolished, flawed, half-baked script to a manager is not wise.

"Always be polite and to the point in any correspondence, and do take no for an answer. You will get rejected way more times than you get accepted. If you don't deal with that gracefully, you'll get a reputation for being difficult, and no one will want to work with you. Listen to feedback, and take criticism on board."
– Chris Lindsay, *River City*

Use IMDbPro to research any manager, before you meet with them. Also, search to see if the manager has been mentioned in the trade publications, including *The Hollywood Reporter* and *Variety*, and in other film and TV industry magazines, and on film and TV industry sites.

When you do have a meeting with the manager, see if they ask you to sign with them. If they don't want you, they won't ask you to sign with them. Their choice might be because they feel as if you are not ready, they might not be the right manager for you, or for other reasons. Do send them a short, written note thanking them for the time and consideration.

If they do ask you to sign with them, respond positively. But don't overdo it. Don't go off on a tangent. Maintain your professional agenda to be the writer who they want to represent.

Don't tell them that you need days, or weeks, or months to think about it. You aren't represented. Simply accept their representation.

You can always – in months or years – go with another manager.

If they do ask to represent you, ask them what they expect from you.

Don't talk over them. Let them finish their sentences.

Ask them what they typically do to help writers advance in their careers.

Listen to what the manager says.

"It is a symbiotic relationship; there is give and take, a negotiated exchange of ideas. The money is a side-effect of a situation where I can guide the client to his or her best screenwriting potential and capacity."
– Markus Linecker, Dedicated Talent Management

Ask the manager what they want you to do within the following weeks or months.

Ask them how often they would like to communicate with you.

Ask them if they have specific ideas that would help you in your career.

Ask them if there are specific books that you should read.

Do as they advise.

Remember that the manager can also drop you, if you are not creating the work that is worthy of being sold, if you are problematic to deal with, if you are not professional in business meetings, and – for whatever reason – if you don't engage in advancing your career.

Once you land a manager, your career is not set in stone. It means it is time to work and hustle.

Work daily on writing a variety of polished, marketable scripts.

Work daily on improving your skills in the craft.

Work daily to get to know the industry, know who the key players are, and know who is producing the types of films and TV shows that you want to write.

Work daily to create the career you want to have.

Do not expect your manager to do everything for you. It won't happen.

You must make your career happen, in tune with the manager's guidance. Don't be lazy about it. Be active and present in the screenwriting community.

"Know the players: If you're smart, you'll be able to assign names to key development execs at the studios. Also, big producers. And, while you're at it, top agents and managers. These are the people who dominate the script world. Everyone you meet with in Hollywood will know these players. If you can do more than stare blankly into space when a name is mentioned, two points for you.

Note: I know what you're thinking. If I don't know a name, I can just nod my head as if I do know who they are talking about. This is dangerous

territory, my friend, the equivalent of Russian roulette. When a studio exec or producer meets with a writer, they are sizing you up. Would you rather get caught in a lie, or simply admit, 'Sorry, don't know the name'? Opt for the latter. Your excuse? Smile sheepishly, shrug, and say, 'I pretty much focus on writing stories.' As long as you convey a modicum of what The Biz is about, the 'My job is to write stories' card is an ironclad defense."
– Scott Myers, GoIntoTheStory.BlckLst.com

The next time you speak with the manager – and every time you speak with the manager – show advancement in writing marketable scripts, in your networking, in your understanding of the industry, and in your professionalism.

Keep a journal of what you spoke about with the manager so that you have a record of the meetings. Take actions in relation to what was discussed. Be in the habit of doing what you say you will do.

The manager will likely check in with you to consider what is going on with your various scripts, your rewrites, connections, and ideas. They will be giving you notes, and sharing ideas about what can happen with your career, and they might suggest events for you to attend and networking opportunities to engage in. But, don't wait for them to tell you everything. Engage in advancing your career.

"Sometimes a really strong script isn't enough to want to work with a screenwriter. When I meet with the person, I want to feel that this could be a compatible relationship – that our personalities vibe together and that our goals and vision for shaping the writer's career are aligned. I also want to know if the person is a strong idea generator, and has a lot of interesting and distinctive projects living inside them that we can develop together."
– Matt Dy, Lit Entertainment Group

The key to a career as a scriptwriter is to write a variety of marketable scripts that the manager can help you sell, or that land you writing gigs.

Keep your fingers typing better scripts, a variety of scripts, and keep your mind open to the possibilities of your career.

When dealing with pros in the film industry, remember this:

"You can't just ask someone who's never met you to read your script. When you walk up to a total stranger with a 110-page screenplay in your hand, shove it at them and say, 'Would you please read my script?' it's like asking a stranger, 'Hi, you don't know me, but would you help me move this weekend?' You're asking for five hours of somebody's time – time to read it, to prepare notes, and the time they'll spend with you over the phone trying to talk you off the ledge. When it comes to connecting with others who are in a position to help you, you should look at it this way: It's an imposition to be asked for a favor, but it's flattering to be asked for advice."
– Bill Marsilii, *Courage the Cowardly Dog*

"You have to put your best foot forward as a screenwriter. It's got to be your best work, the best version of your script."
– Jake Wagner, producer

"As an author and a burgeoning screenwriter, the fact of the matter is: I can't do this alone."
– Taylor Jenkins Reid, *Resident Advisors*

MANAGER LIST

It is probably a good idea for a screenwriter to first get a manager, before getting an agent. But, do what is best for you.

Look up management companies on IMDbPro, see who is on the current staff, and which talent they represent.

• 3 Arts Entertainment
• Anonymous Content
• Apostle
• Bellevue Entertainment
• Black Box Management
• The Cartel
• Cheng Caplan Company
• Cinetic Media
• Circle of Confusion
• Code Entertainment
• DMG Entertainment
• Echo Lake Entertainment
• Energy Entertainment
• Epicenter
• Good Fear Film + Management
• The Gotham Group
• Grandview
• Heretic Literary Management
• Heroes & Villains Entertainment
• Hollander Entertainment
• Hopscotch Pictures
• Hung Entertainment Group
• Industry Entertainment

Screenwriting Tribe
- Jeff Ross Entertainment
- Kailey Marsh Media
- Kapital Entertainment
- Kaplan/Perrone
- Luber Roklin Entertainment
- Madhouse Entertainment
- Magnet Management
- Manage-ment
- Management 360
- Management SGC
- Manus Entertainment
- Mindframe Films & Management
- Mosaic Media
- MXN Entertainment
- New Wave Entertainment
- Oasis Media Group
- Pollinate Entertainment
- Principato Young Entertainment
- Rain Management Group
- Rosa Entertainment
- Scoot Woop Entertainment
- Sentient Entertainment
- The Shuman Company
- Silent R Management
- Skyway Entertainment
- Station 3
- Lee Stobby Entertainment
- Think Tank Management
- Untitled Entertainment
- Writ Large Management
- Zero Gravity Management

"Managers tend to serve as, to use a sports analogy, scouts for the agencies."
— Jeff Portnoy, manager

"Management has a responsibility to find the diamonds in the rough – to cultivate new talent – because agencies aren't doing it."
— Zodac Angell, agent

"Never submit a script, unless you're sure the manager or agent specifically is interested in everything about your script. Otherwise, it's a waste of everyone's time. Agents are so busy. You'll never really understand just how busy someone can be, until you work in an agency. It's unbelievable."
— Rob Gallagher, manager

"Agents want a polished script. Screenplay agents are closers. Closers. They are not script whisperers who will take the time to patiently nurture your script to its fullest potential over a period of months."
– Stephanie Palmer, *20 Screenwriting Terms You Must Know*

"Don't worry about getting an agent. When you have enough quality work under your belt, they will come calling."
– Stephany Folsom, *Toy Story 4*

AGENT LIST

Do not concern yourself with getting an agent, until you are ready.

So many people think that when they have finished their first script, they immediately need an agent to help them sell that script – which likely isn't ready to be submitted… to anyone. Don't pester agents when you are at that stage. You won't impress them in ways that will benefit you, and they will remember you as another person who bothered them with unpolished work.

Before a screenwriter gets an agent, it would probably be good to get a manager. But, only when the writer is truly prepared.

Just as it is probably better to start with a boutique management company (a smaller management company), it is likely also probably better to start with a boutique agency, and not with a big, bustling top agency – where you will be lost among the stars.

"No reputable agent charges a reading fee. Be wary of requests for cash for referrals to specific script consultants. However, an agent may legitimately ask you to cover the cost of photocopying your script."
– David Trottier, author *The Screenwriter's Bible*

If you are starting out, consider the agencies that have fewer employees. The large agencies that have dozens of employees may be best for established writers. But, that isn't a rule, or how it works for every new screenwriter.

Contact the WGA and find out which agencies are signatories.

Do a search on IMDbPro to find out more about each of these agencies, including who works there, and which talent they represent.

- Abrams Artists Agency
- Agency for the Performing Arts. APA.
- The Alpern Group

469

- Brant Rose Agency
- Don Buchwald & Associates
- Callamaro Literary Agency
- Creative Artists Agency. CAA.
- The Dravis Agency
- Featured Artists Agency
- The Gersh Agency
- Innovative Artists
- International Creative Management. ICM.
- Jim Preminger Agency
- Kaplan Stahler Agency
- Maggie Roiphe Agency
- Original Artists
- Paradigm
- Preferred Artists
- Rothman Brecher Kim Agency
- RWSG Agency
- Verve
- William Morris Endeavor. WME.
- United Talent Agency. UTA.

"The whole business of selling it – ideas – is all about concept. Even in the TV world, it's all about the two or three sentence idea that's fresh and original. Like my agents would never say, 'This is bad.' What they would say is, 'This doesn't have a hook, and it's hard to sell.'"
– Erik Bork, *I Got This*

"If you believe in your screenplay, be relentless. Don't give up."
– Diana Ossana, *Brokeback Mountain*

"Once a writer has dedicated serious time and effort to reading scripts, writing scripts, sought out whatever education serves their process, and broken well past the point of those cursory insular drafts, they should seek out honest, actionable feedback on their material, before they start exposing it to representatives."
– Scott Carr, script supervisor

In other words, join a screenwriting workshop, follow its guidelines, do the work. Get your scripts polished, and ready for industry submission. Be the one who gets it done.

"Make lots of mistakes. Be ambitious. Don't compare yourself to others. Protect your creative voice and your passion for the work at all costs. Drown out the noise, and do the hard work."
– Natalie Erika James, *Relic*

"You can't know what the industry expectations are of screenplays in today's marketplace, if you're not reading other TV pilots or feature scripts. You won't know whether or not what you are writing has already been done (or had a version of it done), if you're not watching TV shows or movies actively. And you will never be able to hold up your end of a meaningful conversation with anyone else working in the industry, if you can't comment and provide your opinion on other material in the space. No one wants to be an educator. So, if you do want to move your screenwriting career forward, be sure that you are able to hold your own."

– Lee Jessup, career coach, LeeJessup.com

"You have to build a tribe around yourself, but you also have to be willing to do everything yourself."
— Mark Duplass, *Room 104*

ENTERTAINMENT ATTORNEYS

There is no way that this chapter could possibly contain all that you need to know about the legalities of the screenwriting profession. Nor is this book meant to cover all that you need to know about screenplay sales. Research the various things you are going to be dealing with when selling a script, doing rewrites, and other issues relating to script sales and contracts.

Do study the WGA contract (it's on the site of the Writers Guild of America). Study Stephen F. Breimer's book *The Screenwriter's Legal Guide*. Look on YouTube, Google, and other sites and search engines for information about screenwriting contracts.

"When you're a content creator or owner, you really want to make sure that you date and meet (with) potential lawyers so that when you have a deal on the table – before you sign something, or before you truly collaborate with people – that you have a lawyer involved to protect your interests."
— Elsa Ramo, entertainment attorney

Do you need an entertainment attorney? It depends on what you are doing, who you are dealing with, what your goals are, if you don't want to be taken advantage of, and if you want things to go in your favor in ways that can be satisfactory to each of those impacted by the deal – in the long-term.

Consider that the person you are dealing with when selling a script also might not know how badly they are doing business, or how faulty their requests are. An entertainment attorney can help pave a better path for everyone. What works in your favor might also be good for the other side.

You probably want to familiarize yourself with entertainment attorneys who deal with screenwriters, and protecting the intellectual property that is your screenplay.

You might hire an entertainment attorney to help you deal with one project, or be associated with one to help you deal with all of your script sales, hired writing gigs, and other matters relating to your career.

Some screenwriters have a manager, an agent, and an entertainment attorney. This is especially common for the highly successful film and TV writers. For instance, those involved with a film or series that could have spinoffs, sequels, or prequels, and toys, video games, and other products associated with the project (and with global trash).

A fledgling writer may need an attorney, even more than what is needed by an experienced writer – who already knows many of the ins and outs. But, the more experienced writers are likely to be sure to use the services of an intellectual rights attorney, and to be involved in understanding each provision of the contract they are being asked to sign – especially since they likely have learned the hard way how things can easily not go in their favor.

Do yourself a favor and have an attorney look over any contracts, before you sign them.

Some producers find script option and purchase agreements online, and use those as a basis for their own contracts. Consider that to be not the wisest choice for them – or for the writers involved.

Perhaps study the various option and purchase agreements that you can find online, and learn what is a better choice for you, while having an attorney look over any contract that you are considering signing so that it contains the necessary provisions to take care of your I.P. (intellectual property) rights. You want the contract to memorialize your intent while protecting your interests, and provide an exit strategy. Any contract that you sign will also be vetted by others with interest in the project, including producers, studios, and financiers.

Although the film and TV industry could not exist without writers, the writers are often treated as some sort of burden when it comes time to make the deals. Maybe the current situation is left over from when studios used to keep groups of writers on contract, and many of those laborer writers could be used on one production.

It is interesting that when awards shows take place, the actors and others who win awards thank all sorts of people, from the crew to their hair and makeup artists, and the camera operators, wardrobe designers, and their spouses. But, they forget to mention the writer who created the project. Also, directors are put up on the pedestal as the film is considered to be their film. But, where would the directors and stars be without the persons writing the scripts that the directors direct and the stars star in?

As negotiations take place, things like net profits and other matters can become tricky and distorted. An attorney experienced in film and TV contracts can help interpret a contract for you – so that you understand what it means, and how it will bind you, obligate you, and how and when the options, bonuses, and other matters are calculated and paid. Then, there is the issues relating to sequels, ancillary distribution matters, reversions, and so forth.

What about any sort of toys, video games, clothing, and other materials that may result from your screenplay? Do you know how to deal with those issues in your contract?

Do you already feel lost? Well, then, perhaps you may want to consult with an experienced entertainment attorney.

It's a good idea to read up about entertainment attorneys, before you meet with one. And to meet with one, before you get to any stage of negotiating a screenplay sale. In addition to a phone call, perhaps they will do a screen chat with you.

What you don't want is to get burned by signing some contract that is lacking in your interests – to the point of working against you.

You want an attorney to be with you along the negotiations path. Don't leave it all up to your attorney to handle without your understanding the process. Take efforts to understand the process, and to read over any part of the contract as it is altered in relation to the negotiations.

You also want an attorney who isn't going to make unrealistic demands, such as requesting absurd perks and extraordinary provisions. That likely means that you want an attorney who has worked in the field of film and TV contracts, and understands what can be requested by either side, and how that can be altered to benefit you, but also satisfy the other party or parties.

Also, have an entertainment attorney look over any agreement you might be presented with that covers being a writer for hire. (Never post your contract on social media and ask for advice about it. I've seen that happen.)

While you might not have to deal with a contract in relation to doctoring a script, and payment might be a cash transaction when you hand over your notes and otherwise alterations to the script, do make sure that you are not being bound to any sort to situation that does not serve your interests. Matters can get complicated if you end up being more than a script doctor, but do rewrite so much of the script that you become one of the writers who will then be dealing with being given writing credit.

With contracts, always remember that it is your name on the contract, and not the name of your manager, agent, or entertainment attorney. It is you who is being bound by the contract.

Never sign an agreement or contract that you do not understand. The provisions within the agreement can be tricky, and especially in relation to how, when, how much, and why you are going to be paid.

Also know that when you option a script, your option may only start after you have finished the rewrites, and that extension in the length of your option may not be monetarily rewarded. You might have an option for 18 months. But, you took four months to do the rewrites that were agreed upon, and then that option for 18 months starts after you finished the rewrites. What you thought was going to be an 18-month period is then a 22-month period.

Contracts can include provisions requiring your exclusive writing services. That is, you are only to be working on material for that producer, production company, or studio, until you have delivered the contracted material. Working on other material during that contracted time could mean that you have breached your contract.

Do not be intimidated into signing something that you don't understand, and/or that you don't agree with. Ever.

Know that they cannot use your screenplay that you wrote and that you own the copyright, until you agree to allow them to use it. But, of course, if the screenplay was one you were paid to write, as in, you were hired (commissioned) to write a script, the copyright is then owned by the person who hired you to write the script – the person who has rights to the story.

I know someone who was paid by a guy to write a script based on the wealthy guy's idea. The writer for hire never owned the copyright of that material. He was paid an agreed-to amount, and was done with it.

Done with it is also something writers should consider when they sell their screenplay to a producer, production company, or studio. After the financial transaction takes place, the writer gives over their script to that producer or company, and what happens to the script thereafter is out of the writer's control. As the script goes into development, many more writers might end up working on the script. Some of them might be paid more money than you were paid for the script – because they are likely established writers. One writer might be brought in to punch up the comedy, another writer may be brought in to make the dialogue sound more natural, another writer may be brought in to make the fight and action scenes more dramatic, another may be brought in to make the romantic scenes more believable and enticing, another writer may be brought in to tone the script so that it favors the actor who was hired to star in it. The script might be given a new title, the character names also could be changed. Other characters that you didn't write might be added. Some of the characters that you wrote might be reduced, or combined, or eliminated. The setting might be moved to a different town, city, country, or era. The script might undergo so many changes that the final produced film may have little resemblance to what was originally written.

Keep a copy of the original script that you wrote. Because, even after all of the "development" that the script went through under the producer, production company, or studio, they might not make it. Then, you get the rights back. You don't own the changes that they did to the script. What you own is your original script with the words that you wrote. And you can then try to option or sell your original script to someone else.

"The reality in Hollywood is that very few screenplays that are optioned actually get purchased and/or made. I don't know if anyone could give you an exact percentage, but it is fairly low. Given that reality, the question you should be asking yourself is: 'What happens to my rewrite if my script is only optioned and not purchased? Remember that writing services fall under the category of a 'work-made-for-hire.' In other words, the person who pays for it owns it. Thus, if your script is optioned but it is not purchased (that is, the

475

option expires), you get your original script back, but the person who commissioned the rewrite owns the rewrite!

Suppose this happens to you. An option expires, and now you want to option your screenplay to someone else. You can only option the original screenplay without the rewrite and all the good work that you put into that rewrite. Remember: Someone else owns the rewrites, and you cannot touch it – any of it – except those portions that existed in the original screenplay. If you do use any of the rewritten material, you or whoever uses the rewrite can be sued for copyright infringement by the owner of the rewrite."

– Stephen F. Breimer, Esq., author *The Screenwriter's Legal Guide*

The above quotation is only part of the things you might like to know about screenplay sales and contracts. In his book, Breimer covers many varieties of situations that those in the field of screenwriting likely should consider – including what a reversion is, and why you want that in your contract. Hint: It has to do with being able to sell your screenplay to another person or company, after you have done rewrites on it under a previous contract.

Somewhere in all of that cluster of writing and rewriting, you want your interests to be taken care of, so that you at least are reimbursed in a way that is satisfactory.

How do you find valid, experienced entertainment attorneys? One way is by accessing IMDbPro, where you can look up a variety of writers, and see who is listed as their representation. Also, if you have an agent or manager, ask them about entertainment attorneys who they have dealt with. Ask other writers.

"It's getting harder than ever to convince a producer to read your script. You have to draw upon all your contacts. Some producers respond to a tantalizing query letter or a synopsis. If the story sounds intriguing, they may agree to read your script, provided you sign a release, or submit it through an attorney."

– Michael Ray Brown, *Screenwriting Structure Checklist*

Before you sign a "submission agreement" or "release form" from a producer or production company, you might want to have an entertainment attorney look it over. For a sample of a release form, see *The Screenwriter's Bible*.

"Look books can be comprised of mood boards, overlays, lines of text, character studies, photos of actors in character, essentially anything that allows you to create a point of entry for an investor. The best look books begin discussion and engage potential investors. The worst underscore the level of risk involved for any investor, and end the conversation. But, be warned, there is a fine line between providing prospective investors with creative insights to your vision and making business representations of economic expectations. If you have any mention of the business side of the investment opportunity, make sure to have entertainment legal counsel review the material, to avoid any wanton misrepresentations, which can easily end you up on the wrong side of the SEC for fraud or other securities violations."

– Bianca Goodloe, managing partner at Goodloe Law and Kines Global; *The 7 Dirty Secrets to Film Financing*, IndieWire.com

THE PRODUCER QUAGMIRE

This book isn't meant to cover every aspect of the film industry. But, here is some advice for those writers who might want to also produce their film.

Read a variety of books on film financing, film production, and film editing. Know what each person on the crew does.

The following is likely only less than a calorie of the information that you will need to consider when producing a film.

If you are positioning yourself as a producer, and have signed "recognizable name" actors to star in the film, to satisfy investors (including if you presold distribution rights to various regions of the world, accepted loans from entertainment lenders [that usually means: Banks], completion bond companies, territorial distributors, foreign pre-sales agents, and so forth), those stars then have to book out time to work on the project.

To a star, time is money – including because they likely employ a number of people, and are an income source for other professionals, including agents, managers, and lawyers.

That means, if your project gets delayed, you will likely still have to pay a full paycheck to that movie star – even if they never worked on the project.

For a star to commit to the project, you likely had to pay them a nonrefundable deposit.

In addition to lenders, to stars, and to a line producer, you may also end up spending money on and/or owing money to a foreign sales agent, producer rep (and covering their expenses to be at one or more film market [such as AFM in Santa Monica, Cannes in France, TIFFCOM in Tokyo, IFP in New York, CineMart in Rotterdam, the Toronto International Film Festival/TIFF, FILMART in Hong Kong, the EFM in Berlin, and other film markets] – even if they are also submitting expense reports to other producers, and making money off of that situation), an entertainment attorney, and a securities attorney.

If an early cut of the film shown to any of the investors is not satisfactory to them, or is faulty in its production qualities, they might back out of the deal, and default on their final payments.

In other words, producing is not simply organizing a bunch of people and getting them to toss a film together.

"As a director or producer, you're no different from any other leader. Yes, you need to have a clear vision of what you want, but you don't need to be an expert in every facet of the process. Instead, it's more important to be able to communicate what you want to those whose expertise in a given area outshines yours."
– Ron Cicero, *Happy Happy Joy Joy: The Ren & Stimpy Story*

"Try to make the cheapest possible film you can first off. Do this and you give yourself the greatest chance of artistic freedom, and this enables you to find your voice – before others can tell you who or what you are."
– Romola Garai, *Amulet*

"Don't settle or compromise too much while making your film, because you won't enjoy or be fulfilled by the end result. And if you have a bad feeling about something, in pre-production, or otherwise, speak up. Also, prepare diligently so you can step foot on set completely confident and sure of what you need to accomplish that day."
– Emily Wilson, *Danny's Girl*

A friend landed partial financing for his film by featuring a product from a company that paid him for that product placement. Consider if there is a product that can be in your production, such as a drink, automobile, kitchen utensil, sports equipment, or fashion item. The manufacturer might pay you, especially if you have a character mention the product by name.

"Don't burden yourself early on with financing challenges or festival exposure. Find a cheap, low friction way to create as much content as possible with other artists in your orbit. Make shorts for you and the people around you. A period of low-risk experimentation is essential for building your own relationship with the medium."
– David Bruckner, *Southbound*

Follow sites like NoFilmSchool.com and others that will help give you an angle on how to make films on the cheap.

"I think it's one of the great myths propagated out there that movie stars don't matter. I would argue the opposite. I would say, movie stars in the right role with the right property matter more than ever before."
– Tom Rothman, Sony Motion Picture Group

Online Resources

Check out the screenwriting pages on Facebook.

There is a Facebook page for Screenwriting Tribe.

Look up various screenwriting resources on Twitter.

There are a wide selection of videos on YouTube having to do with screenwriting. Watch a variety of them so that you can gather as many opinions about how things are done by a broad collection of screenwriters, and hear about how they went about establishing careers.

(Search: Screenplay download links.)

- **AdelaideScreenwriter.Blogspot.ca**.
- **AFI.com. American Film Institute**.
- **AmericanFilmMarket.com**.
- **AnonymousProductionAssistant.com**.
- **AnonymousProductionAssistant.com/UTA=JobList**. UTA job list.
- **TheArtOfScreenwriting.com**. Don Macnab-Stark.
- **ASCMag.com**. American Cinematographer.
- **AtlScript.org**. The Atlanta Screenwriter's Group.
- **AustinFilmFestival.com**.
- **AWG.Com.AU/View/Event/Script-to-Screen**. Australian Writer's Guild.
- **Bang2Write.com**.
- **BBC.co.uk/WritersRoom**.
- **BerlinAle.de/en**. Berlin Film Festival.
- **BigIdeas.com**. Barri Evans, consultant.
- **TheBitterScriptReader.Blogspot.ca**.
- **BlckLst.com**. The Black List. Research what others say about the site.
- **BlckLst.com/Podcast**. Ojai Film Festival.
- **BlcklLst.com/Cassian-Elwes**. Independent Screenwriting Fellowship.
- **BluecatScreenplay.com**. Screenplay Contest.

- **BoxOfficeMojo.com**.
- **BreakingInTheBiz.com**. Manny Foncesca and Cheryl Diffin.
- **BreakingIntoHollywood.org**
- **Catalinafilm.org**. Catalina International Film Festival.
- **Celtx.com**. Software used for screenwriting.
- **CineStory.org**.
- **ClevelandFilm.org**. Cleveland International Film Festival.
- **ComplicationsEnsue.Blogspot.ca**. Alex Epstein.
- **CoreyMandell.net**.
- **Coverfly.com**. Familiarize yourself with that site.
- **CrackingYarns.com.au**.
- **TheCreativeIndex.com**. Lists producers.
- **CreativeScreenwriting.com**. Online version of the former magazine.
- **CreatorUp.com**.
- **DanielMartinEckhart.com**.
- **DannyStack.com/Blog**. UK screenwriter and director.
- **Deadline.com**. Industry news.
- **DenVog.com/app/index-card**. Program for storyboarding with index cards on the iPad.
- **Dichosis.com/Blog**. Dichosis Studios.
- **DoneDealPro.com**.
- **Draft-Zero.com**. Chas Fisher and Stuart Willis.
- **DubScript.com**. Screenwriting software ap.
- **EIACE.org**. Entertainment Industry Association of Consultants & Educators.
- **EmergingScreenwriters.com**.
- **FadeInOnline.com**.
- **FadeInPro.com**. Software.
- **FilmFreeway.com**. Get to know this site.
- **FilmIndependent.org/LA-Film-Festival**. Los Angeles International Film Festival.
- **Filmaka.com**.
- **FilmmakerFreedom.com**. By Rob Hardy.
- **FilmmakerMagazine.com**.
- **TheFilmSchool.com**. Writing and directing classes. In Seattle, Washington.
- **FilmStudies.cal.msu.edu/resources/grants**.
- **FilterApps.Wordpress.com/ScriptWrite**.
- **FinalDraft.com**. Screenwriting software. For the iPad, get Final Draft Reader.
- **FlyingWrestler.com**. Erik Bork script consulting.
- **FourStarFeedback.com**. Doug Davidson.
- **FreemanGames.com**.
- **FunLittleMovies.com**.
- **GetMade.net.** Evan Littman.
- **GoIntoTheStory.blcklst.com**.
- **GoodInARoom.com**.
- **HUScreenwriting.com**. Hollins University Screenwriting Blog.
- **HollywoodReporter.com**.
- **IFP.org**. Independent Film Week.
- **IndieFilmHustle.com**.
- **IndieWire.com**.

- **InfoPlease.com**.
- **InkTip.com**. Considered a "script broker."
- **IMFDB.org**. Internet Movie Firearms Database.
- **IMSDb.com**. The Internet Movie Script Database.
- **JasonArnopp.com**.
- **JenGrisanti.com**. Consultant.
- **KalBashir.com**.
- **KeepWriting.com**. David Trottier, author of *The Screenwriter's Bible* and *Dr. Format Tells All*.
- **KenLevine.Blogspot.ca**.
- **LA-Screenwriter.com**. Angela Bourassa.
- **LAWritersGroup.com**. Los Angeles Writers Group.
- **LeeJessup.com**. Career consulting.
- **LessonsFromTheScreenplay.com**.
- **LFS.Org.UK**. London Film School.
- **Logline.it**.
- **MarilynHorowitz.com/Blog**.
- **MckeeStory.com**. Robert McKee.
- **Mentorless.com**. About writing, editing, shooting, and producing.
- **MovieBytes.com**.
- **MovieOutline.com**.
- **MoviesByHer.com**.
- **MyPDFScripts.tumblr.com**.
- **NantucketFilmFestival.org**.
- **Nerdist.com/Podcasts/Nerdist-Writers-Panel-Channel**. Ben Blacker
- **AsiaSociety.Org/India/New-Voices-Fellowship-Screenwriters**.
- **NoBullScript.net**.
- **NoFilmSchool.com**.
- **OjaiFilmFestival.com**. Ojai Film Festival.
- **OnThePage.TV**. Pilar Alessandra, consultant.
- **ProducersGuild.org**. The Producers Guild of America (PGA).
- **PSFilmFest.org**. Palm Springs International Film Festival.
- **ReadWatchWrite.com**.
- **Reddit.com/r/Screenwriting**.
- **RedSharkNews.com**.
- **Registry.ScreenCraft.org**.
- **RoadmapWriters.com**. Learn this site.
- **Rocliffe.Com/index.php**.
- **RuthAtkinson.com**. Script consultant.
- **SandlerInk.com**. Ellen Sandler of *The TV Writer's Workbook*.
- **SBIFF.org**. Santa Barbara International Film Festival.
- **ScottishScreenwriters.com**.
- **ScreenCraft.org**.
- **Screenplay.com**.
- **ScreenplayCoverage.com**.
- **ScreenplayInc.com**.
- **ScreenplayReaders.com**.
- **ScreenplayScripts.com**. Industrial Scripts.
- **ScreenplayStory.com**.

- ScreenwritersColony.org/Blog.
- ScreenwritersDailyDose.com.
- ScreenwritersUtopia.com.
- ScreenwritingCommnity.net.
- Screenwriting.info.
- Screenwriting.io.
- TheScreenwritingProcess.com.
- ScreenwritingResearch.com.
- ScreenwritingSpark.com. Screenwriting-related sites.
- ScreenwritingU.com.
- ScribeMeetsWorld.com.
- Scriptapalooza.com.
- ScriptButcher.com.
- ScriptChat.Blogspot.ca.
- ScriptGal.com.
- ScriptReaderPro.com.
- ScriptRevolution.com.
- ScriptShadow.net.
- TheScriptLab.com.
- ScriptMag.com.
- ScriptNotes.net. John August and Craig Mazin.
- Script-O-Rama.com.
- ScriptPipeline.com. An online script broker.
- ScriptPitch.com.
- ScriptReaderPro.com.
- ScriptwritersNetwork.com.
- SellingYourScreenplay.com. Ashley Scott Myers.
- ShoreScripts.com.
- SimplyScripts.com.
- SingleScreenwriter.com.
- Slamdance.com. Slamdance Film Festival.
- SnarksScriptNuggets.Blogspot.ca.
- SoCreate.com.
- SpecScout.com.
- Stage32.com. An industry social network.
- TheStoryDepartment.com.
- StoryMastery.com. Michael Hauge the author.
- StoryPlanner.com.
- StorySkeleton.com. For the iPhone and iPad.
- StoryTouch.com. Screenwriting software.
- Storywriter.Amazon.com. Amazon Storywriter.
- StoweStoryLabs.org.
- StudioBinder.com.
- StudioPitchFest.com.
- Sundance.org. Sundance Institute.
- Talentville.com.
- TellurideFilmFestival.org.
- TIFF.net. Toronto International Film Festival.
- TimeToWrite.Blogs.com.

- **TheTinyProtagonist.Wordpress.com**.
- **TrackingB.com**.
- **Tracking-Board.com**.
- **TribecaFilm.com**.
- **TVTropes.com**.
- **UniFrance.org**.
- **UrbanDictionary.com**.
- **Variety.com**. Industry news.
- **Voyagemedia.com/blog**.
- **WeScreenplay.com**.
- **WGA.org**. Writers Guild of America.
- **WGAe.org**. Writers Guild of America East.
- **WGC.CA**. Writers Guild of Canada.
- **WheresTheDrama.com**.
- **WiSceenwriterForum.org**. Wisconsin Screenwriters Forum.
- **WomenInFilm.org**.
- **WordPlayer.com**. Ted Elliott and Terry Russio.
- **TheWorkingScreenwriter.Blogspot.ca**.
- **WriterDuet.com**. Screenwriting software.
- **WritersStore.com**.
- **Writers911.com**. Screenwriter 911.
- **WriteSoFluid.com**. Michelle Goode.
- **WriteToReel.com**.
- **WriteYourScreenplay.com**.
- **YourScreenplaySucks.Wordpress.com**. From the author of the book.
- **ZacSanford.com**.

Online sources can help you learn about and get into the industry. But, don't get stuck on the internet when you should be finishing screenplays – and taking actions to get them optioned, sold, and produced.

"Film is a distributor of dreamers, and of dreams."
– Ingmar Bergman, *Sixty-four Minutes with Rebecka*

"The role of a writer is not to say what we all can say, but what we are
unable to say."
– Anais Nin, *Henry & June*

SHORT FILMS AND FILM FESTIVALS

Many people will tell you that making a short film to display your skills is a smart thing to do. It can help people see what you are capable of. With a short film, you can get into film festivals, and network with people who can advance your career.

Many successful screenwriters and directors started their careers by making short films. They include: Spike Lee, Kathryn Bigelow, Rian Johnson, Steven Spielberg, Alfred Hitchcock, Ava DuVernay, Jafar Panahi, David Lynch, Francois Truffaut, Barry Jenkins, Tim Burton, Guillermo del Toro, Kasi Lemmons, Antoine Fuqua, Aisling Walsh, and many, many others.

A short film can help you gain funding to make the full-length version of the story.

Consider the history of the film *Whiplash*. Writer/director Damien Chazelle struggled to gain funding for the feature. He then turned fifteen pages of the script into an 18-minute short film starring actor Johnny Simmons as the student. Johnny is no relation to J.K. Simmons, who played the music conservatory instructor. J.K. Simmons has a degree in music from the University of Montana – where his father was director of the music department. For the short film, Chazelle wanted actor Miles Teller to play the role of the student, as Teller knew how to drum, but Teller was not available during filming. That short film was shown at the 2013 Sundance Film Festival, where it won the short film Jury Award for fiction, which attracted funding for the feature project. The feature was filmed with 19 days of principal photography. J.K. Simmons remained as the instructor, but the student in the feature is played by actor Miles Teller. The feature won a variety of awards – including the Audience Award and Grand Jury Prize at the 2014 Sundance Film Festival. It was nominated for a Best Picture Academy Award. It won for

Best Sound Mixing, Best Editing, and Best Supporting Actor for J.K. Simmons.

Some people advise against making short films. One of their reasons is that there is likely to be no money in shorts. The reality of that depends on the quality of your short, and who sees it.

Unless you have other motives for making a short – such as using the short film as a trailer for a larger project, or you feel it will adequately display your talents – you don't need to make a short film. It might not bring you much of anything. You aren't likely to get a distribution deal. You might be able to sell them to some sites that show short films. But, will that compensate you for what you spent to make the thing? Will it advance your career? Maybe. Will it help you understand the filmmaking process? Yes. Will making multiple short films help you understand the process even more? It depends on if you actually learn, or if you keep making the same mistakes.

Ben Watkins made a short film called *Quest to Ref*, which he also starred in. That role brought him to the attention of a casting director, and he landed a regular role on the soap opera *The Young and the Restless*. He turned the short script into a feature script, which sold. He wrote a pilot, which then worked as a writing sample, and that landed him a job as a junior writer on the series *Burn Notice*. On that series, he worked up to being an executive producer. He then created and became the showrunner on the series *Hand of God*. (A showrunner is an executive producer, but not every executive producer is a showrunner.)

Mark Sinclair was a troubled teen who broke into a New York theater and ended up taking classes there. He participated in his step-father's theater company. He landed acting gigs in Off-Off-Broadway productions while working as a bouncer at New York clubs. Sinclair ended up moving to Hollywood to try his hand at film acting. When he returned disappointed to New York, his mother gave him a copy of Rick Schmidt's book *Feature Films at Used Car Prices*. Sinclair then wrote a short script called *Multi-Facial*. He directed and starred in the film, which he shot in three days. The short was accepted into the 1995 Cannes Film Festival. Steven Spielberg saw the short and cast Sinclair in *Saving Private Ryan*. Sinclair has since starred in some of the most successful action films in history, including *The Fast and the Furious*. For *Fast and Furious Seven*, he was paid about $47,000,000.00. Sinclair's films and other productions have collectively made billions of dollars. Oh, at some point in his young adult life, Mark Sinclair changed his professional name to Vin Diesel.

So, yes short films sometimes are the mothership of someone's career.

"I'm interested in new worlds, new universes, new challenges. I always said the only reason to make a film is not for the result, but for what you learn for the next one."
– Alfonso Cuarón Orozco, *Roma*

Making short films can be practice; can teach you about making a film; can be fun; can be a headache; can be a waste of your time (depending on what you expect from, and what you do with them), resources, and energy; can be a way to spend time with friends and family; can end friendships; can leave you with something that might be worth watching; can be entertaining to your friends and family; and can get you into film festivals – because film festivals need content.

Getting your short film into a festival might not amount to much – other than, your film gets screened. The film festival might give you an award. That might not amount to anything. Or, it might help you land a manager and/or an agent – if you have other scripts written that the manager and/or agent can help you sell, and use to land you writing assignments.

"My thing was going to the movies a lot and educating myself about European cinema. Then having the opportunity to make a low budget film, and getting festivals to invite you across Europe, and meeting other filmmakers, and seeing their work."
– Sara Driver, *Sleepwalk*

There are many hundreds of film festivals. (Search: List of film festivals.) Some of them might provide situations that can help your career. (Access: FilmFreeway.Com/Festivals)

Some of the top film festivals include:
- Berlin, in Germany
- Canne, in France
- Lincoln Center, in New York City
- Palm Springs, in California
- South by Southwest, in Austin, Texas
- Sundance, in Park City, Utah
- Telluride, in Colorado
- Toronto, in Canada
- Tribeca, in New York City
- Venice, in Italy

Don't dismiss other film festivals attended by industry people who might recognize your talents.

Consider film festivals that are close to Los Angeles, including the film festival held in Santa Barbara. Many successful people attend that.

Film festivals in what you might consider unlikely cities could also be key to your career. I know someone who made significant deals at the Cleveland Film Festival, in Ohio.

There are also film festivals screening films in certain languages, or that are centered in particular cultures or countries. There is a Brazilian Film Festival held in Los Angeles. The Pan African Film Festival is also held in Los Angeles.

If you have a script that might apply to a certain culture, or that could be of interest to people of a certain descent, do your research to find opportunities to meet producers, actors, directors, financiers, and distributors who might be interested in your script.

Consider that getting into some film festivals might be a waste of time, energy, and money. They are often sponsored by the city they are held in. It's beneficial for the tourism industry of that city, including the hotels, restaurants, ride share drivers, the people who make money through vacation rentals, and the local film theatres. But, how much is it going to benefit you?

The larger film festivals can bring tens of thousands of people into a city, throughout the days of the festival. Each person spends money. Film festivals are held because they make money. It's about the city having a cultural event. And the local people might feel as if they are part of the so-called glamour of Hollywood.

Instead of making a short film and spending all of what it takes to get into and experience a film festival that screens your short film, consider that it might be better to save your money and resources, and make a full-length feature film. You say that you don't have that sort of money? Look up the films *Slacker*, *Jamon Jamon*, *Primer*, *Clerks*, *Night of the Living Dead*, *El Mariachi*, *The Blair Witch Project*, *The Brothers McMullen*, and *Paranormal Activity*.

Be wise about how you spend your time, money, resources, and talent.

"The bigger festivals have more of an industry presence. So, if you're looking to meet an agent, or make various types of film business connections, that can happen at those types of festivals.

With that said, don't write off the smaller, local, and regional festivals. Because, along with industry contacts, it's equally important to have a strong network of ambitious local filmmakers on your side.

So, even if you're not screening a film of your own, I still recommend going to those types of festivals – because you're going to meet people who are making things and getting those things out into the world.

And those are the people you want in your corner. Those are the people you want strong relationships with. Filmmaking is a team sport, and especially in the indie world, you have to do it as a community.

Film festivals offer such fertile ground for building those communities, so don't pass them up."
– Rob Hardy, FilmmakerFreedom.com

Do what builds a career in screenwriting: Write marketable scripts, polish them, and get them to the right people who can get them sufficiently financed, and produce them with high-quality talent and a skilled production team.

"To make a film is easy. To make a good film is war. To make a very good film is a miracle."
– Alejandro González Iñárritu, *Biutiful*

On the day that I'm writing this chapter, a member of Screenwriting Tribe is in pre-production on a short film that he is making with the goal of being able to attract financing for the feature version.

"I had gone around for those seven years with screenplays, asking for permission to make movies, or asking someone to make my movie – which is not even asking for permission to make a movie. It's asking someone if they would kindly take my dream away from me, and make it into their dream."
– Christopher McQuarrie, *Mission: Impossible*

Consider the possibility of making your own film that you write and direct, and possibly work on in other ways – maybe as an actor or editor. Perhaps that is your future, and will be the career that you create.

People with less than what you have – and likely in far worse situations than what you have experienced – have worked for and created successful careers in the industry. Consider Tiffany Haddish, who experienced a terrible childhood, during which her step-father tried to murder her, her siblings, and her mother by causing their car to crash, which resulted in her mother experiencing a life-altering brain injury. Haddish ended up living in foster care. Statistically, Haddish should have been another casualty of a life of tragedy. Even as an adult, Haddish ended up living in her car. Despite all of that, Haddish worked her life into being a successful writer, producer, comedienne, and actor, and the first African-American comedienne to host *Saturday Night Live*.

Either you can work for and create the life that you want to experience, or not. It's up to you. As a screenwriter, you are a creator, and you can create the life you dream of having. Get busy with it. Making a short film might be the key to your success.

"Do not feel that you are required to write about yourself and your world. Write about any world you want. You're making the world. You are not confined by any guardrails."
– Aaron Sorkin, *The Social Network*

"If there's a specific resistance to women making movies, I just choose to ignore that as an obstacle for two reasons: I can't change my gender, and I refuse to stop making movies."
– Kathryn Bigelow, *Undertow*

"When Denzel Washington and Halle Berry won his and her Oscars he was only the second African-American man to win best actor, and she was the first African-American woman to win best actress."
– Manohla Dargis, A.O. Scott, *Hollywood's Whiteout, New York Times*

"Do I participate in stereotyping, or maintain my cultural integrity?"
– Brian Young, *Why I Won't Wear War Paint and Feathers in a Movie Again, Time* magazine

DIVERSE FILMMAKERS, AND MEDIA PORTRAYALS OF WOMEN, PEOPLE OF COLOR, AND THE DENIED

"I look at the way the film begins, with me in bed with Liam Neeson, and we're kissing – and it's a sexualized kiss. And, here I am: I'm dark, I'm 53, I'm in my natural hair, and I'm with Liam Neeson. I'm with what American would consider to be a hunk. And, he's not my slave owner. I'm not a prostitute. It's not trying to make any social or political statements. We simply are a couple in love. And, what struck me about that in the narrative is that I've never seen it before. And you're not going to see it this year. You're not going to see it next year. You're not going to see it the year after that. And most people who look at it, most critics – most critics, I will say – most cinephiles, will probably not even acknowledge that as anything novel. They'll say, 'Okay, so what, it's not making a political statement.' So, if it's not making anything, then why isn't it done?

If we are indeed committed to inclusion and diversity, and we actually do see people of color as the same as us, as our counterparts, then why can't you consider a character that maybe is not ethnically specific, why can't you consider someone like me for it – if it's not a big deal? Why hasn't it been done? You know? And sometimes, I feel like the biggest political statements are the simplest."
– Viola Davis, in reference to her role in *Widows*

"I got sent a screenplay once where the character was described as '37, but still attractive.' That pissed me off."
– Kathleen Turner, actor

Other than Screenwriting Tribe, all of the workshops that I have attended have been dominated by Caucasian men. Maybe Tribe is different because I've reached out to varieties of people – including womens' organizations and minority and diversity writers' groups.

It would be helpful for more women, diverse, misrepresented, denied, and underrepresented people to attend screenwriting workshops. Their input, views, voices, and life experiences are needed in the film and TV industry.

"I would love to see more women directors because they represent half of the population – and gave birth to the whole world. Without them writing and being directors, the rest of us are not going to know the whole story."
– Jane Campion, *Top of the Lake*

One way of correcting the misrepresentation and underrepresentation of women, minorities, and the overlooked and denied on screen is for them to write polished, engaging, marketable scripts that get produced.

"If you want more diversity in the industry, you need diverse people writing scripts and developing them."
– Patty Jenkins, *Monster*

"Don't be ashamed if the name Madelyn Pugh (1921-2011) doesn't ring any bells. Most people aren't familiar with the legendary TV writer, even though she helped create the most enduring show of all time. Women were a rare sight in writers' rooms during television's infancy in the 1950s, but Pugh not only sat at the head of the table during the *I Love Lucy* production meetings, she's also partly responsible for Lucy's becoming a star at all. She and collaborator Bob Carroll, Jr. – with whom she worked for five decades – helped Lucille Ball develop her radio show into a vaudeville act and then a TV pilot, and were involved in every episode of her 1951 to 1957 classic sitcom."
– Jennifer Armstrong, *The Secret History of Women in Television*, Bust.com

How tiring, uninteresting, and even obnoxious is it to commonly see typical stereotypes, racial distortions, sexist portrayals of women (and men), and hyper-distorted characterizations of a variety of people, including of the handicapped and/or physically or psychologically challenged?

Why are so many on-screen portrayals of everything from minorities, LGBTQ, and handicapped so over-the-top?

Of course, there are some real people who are similar to media stereotypes. But, they seem overly represented in TV and film.

There is a wide variety of humanity that is not being represented on screen. At the same time, the stereotypical portrayals are overdone, and stale. They are an assault on the intellect of the viewers, and on the misrepresented.

Of course, there are films and TV shows that are about the experiences of having to deal with the nonsense shoveled out to women, minorities, the denied, diverse, and the handicapped. For instance, a script about someone like Rosa Parks would be largely about her experience of having to deal with the awful behavior she was subjected to, and about how she dealt with it. But, if there is a script that has a doctor who happens to be African-American, does the script have to feature so many references to him being African-American? Of course, he may experience racially-tainted, ugly situations in his daily life (which, unfortunately continues to be reality), but does it have to contain references to his race? It is common for African-Americans to be doctors, and to hold other well-paying jobs requiring university degrees.

Other than for specific story reasons (including biographies), do most scripts need to point out which characters are meant to be played by a non-Caucasian or a handicapped person, a person of a certain shape, or a woman? It doesn't seem so. But, also, it is odd to have characters who are meant to be of a certain culture to be forced into a script in a way meant to be more marketable and acceptable to another culture.

"I was just like, 'I'm not gonna do that anymore,' and it sorta changed things for me. I no longer feel like I have to amend to their culture anymore. Our culture is just as worthy as theirs. I do that on the page, in the film. I wanted a movie that was one where it didn't appeal to a broader audience. I really wanted to appeal to us, then if white people wanted to come and listen in, they could."
– Lena Waithe, *Queen & Slim*

I live in Los Angeles County, a region that is rich in diversity, but when you turn on a series, or watch a film set in L.A., where are the realistic portrayals of Asians, Persians, East Indians, Latin Americans, Pacific Islanders, Indigenous peoples, other cultures, or people with disabilities? If they are there, they are often played up, super stereotypical, or overly obvious about being of a certain heritage. The characterizations are distorted. The person who has a handicap is all about their handicap. It's old, stale, and often in bad taste.

"How hard it is to portray a three-dimensional woman of color on television or in film? I'm surrounded by them. They're my friends. I talk to them every day. How come Hollywood won't acknowledge us? Are we a joke to them? Now, having been in the industry for a couple of years, I'm not entirely sure it's blatant racism, as I had once assumed. It's more complicated than that."
– Issa Rae, *The Misadventures of an Awkward Black Girl*

Of course, the casting directors play into this – by casting the Caucasian actors in the so-called "normal" roles, then casting other races and heritages in the other roles. And perhaps having to make an effort to get a physically diverse or handicapped person in there. I saw a casting notice today asking for non-white actors to submit for the role of a gas station attendant. Maybe there was a good reason for it. Or, not.

"I think that young women and little girls need to see that they don't have to be the damsel in distress. They don't have to not show their strength. They

491

don't have to be whatever the stereotype is, or the tropes that we go to in our minds."
— Octavia Spencer, actor

"Despite all the movements, and despite everything we read now, why don't creative writers find women interesting? It hasn't changed at all in my direct experience. Women have made huge strides, and yet we're still seen as being a mere adjunct to whoever is the great dramatic engine of a play."
— Glenda Jackson, actor

"Everyone always thinks it's an anomaly when it works. The truth is, there's a huge audience, a huge thirst, not just for female-led stories, but for big female ensembles."
— Bruna Papandrea, producer

Women actors often have been limited to being the girlfriend, the wife, or the victim. Jodie Foster has commented about being tired of reading scripts in which the female character has rape as part of her life experience. How about writing scripts that don't feature women whose chief role is to be the girlfriend, wife, or victim? Or the sleek power woman, or the hyper-emotional female, or the dame who is all about hair, makeup, and clothing, and happens to be slutty, or presented as dim?

Why, when a production is between takes, must the makeup, hair, and wardrobe people rush out to make sure the actress has her makeup touched up to be flawless, her hair perfectly arranged, and the clothes fitted just so? It all plays into the distortion, similar to airbrushed magazine covers. I've seen it on set many times: Even when they are playing cops, fire fighters, military personnel, and others in active jobs, the actresses playing those roles are put through the ringer of makeup, hair, and wardrobe, often between most takes, as if they are going to be featured in some sort of cosmetics advertisement.

"We're not waiting for the rest of the world to catch up with us; we're leading. We're persisting."
— Jane Rosenthal, producer

Writers can help craft scripts that don't play into stereotypes with the hyper-ethnic characterizations, heightened gay characters, helpless handicapped characters, over-referenced short people, narrowly characterized, one-note women, dimwitted hunky men, or the sort-of spiritual guru indigenous peoples. Yes, some stereotypes do exist in real life, but have been blatantly overdone on film and TV.

Consider the possibilities of having a character who is physically challenged. Not in a stereotype way. But in a way that is clever and could play into the story in ways not previously seen. Consider that they may have developed ways of doing things that others would not think of. The invisibility of the unique is partially the fault of screenwriters.

Don't be afraid to write characters who have physical differences, or to write characters who have not been seen on screen. Maybe that is one way your script will be brilliant, and awaken people to a realistic view of life.

"I had to bump heads with a lot of men in the industry. They were not comfortable with showing a progressive black female in an action role. As a strong woman, I was seen as a threat. I thought 'We don't need to walk behind you. We should walk beside you.'"
– Pam Grier, *Foxy*

"I'm convinced that we black women possess a special indestructible strength that allows us to not only get down, but to get up, to get through, and to get over."
– Janet Jackson, actor

Alien is a cool movie, because of the storyline. It also happens to feature a strong female protagonist played by Sigourney Weaver. But, how many other movies are there in that category? It's often a man hero, and then a woman who needs the man hero – because, you know, women are helpless without men. Or, actually, not.

"In mainstream movies, the woman's role is mostly just to prove that the leading man is heterosexual. I'm not good at that, and I'm not interested in that."
– Jennifer Jason Leigh, *The Anniversary Party*

There are scripts in which the overused characterizations work for what the film or TV show is going for. It might be a comedy, or some twisted take on reality, a view on socioeconomic circumstances, or a distorted or revised historical piece, or a commentary on society and culture, and that is all fine – if it works for that TV show or film. Go for what works cleverly to tell the story in that situation, setting, and era, and with that tone, mood, and genre.

"I read a lot of comedy screenplays, and the reason why most of them don't work is they're not about anything. If your story isn't about anything, or your character just wants a pretty girl and the bag of money, then it's not going to add up to anything."
– Michael Arndt, *Little Miss Sunshine*

Watch out for the stereotypical, sexist, phobic, and over-pronounced characterizations. Your audience might prefer an untypical hero. That may rock your audience in satisfying ways they had not previously experienced.

"No one is born hating another person because of the color of his skin, or his background, or his religion. People must learn to hate, and if they can learn to hate, they can be taught to love, for love comes more naturally to the human heart than its opposite."
– Nelson Mandela, author *Long Walk to Freedom*

493

To help create change, a script doesn't have to grandly showcase ways in which women and minorities have been shoved into certain perspectives, or to use some hyped up tactic to reveal how women and minorities break free of the nonsense. Little scenes and subtle exhibits of women, minorities, the denied, the handicapped, and the physically different simply living their lives free of the garbage that society shovels onto them can help break down societal norms and stereotypical views. It can also help reveal truths to and inspire future generations.

"During the (*Broad City*) episode *St. Mark's*, Abbi and Ilana are dressed up for a night out to celebrate Ilana's birthday when they pass a stranger on the street who informs them that they should smile. Without missing a beat, the two friends swing around and pull their faces into smiles using their upturned middle fingers. The scene came at a time when street harassment had become a vital part of the national conversation.

While countless articles mistakenly identified it as a new phenomenon, street harassment has always been a part of the female experience. At its mildest, it's a daily inconvenience for women, and at its deadliest, it has cost women their lives. It's also the subject of a stunning public art project by Tatyana Fazlalizadeh, which explores the danger of assuming women exist to please the male gaze."
— Naomi Elias, *A timeline of feminist history – making TV moments you need to know about*; HelloGiggles.com

Meanwhile, where are the women, minority, and people of diversity writers, and why are they not going to workshops? With so much talk of not enough relevant roles for them, it would be helpful for them to be writing scripts with realistic portrayals that don't play into the victim, sexist, racist, and other stereotypes, and scripts that are engaging and marketable, and, through workshopping, are made ready to submit to the industry.

"We need originality. We need new stories. We need stories from different ethnicities and different cultures, which animation is doing really great at. We need to do that in live action as well, I think. I'm talking about the world, not just necessarily Disney. I don't think we need to be remaking anything else. Let's create things. Creation, that's what women are best at. We create, right? We bring life.'"
— Linda Woolverton, *Maleficent*

"I would have producers sit down and say, 'The script is great, but who do you want as the male lead?' I would say, 'It's called *Two Serious Ladies*.'"
— Sara Driver, *You are Not I*

The conversations at the 2017 Cannes Film Festival were about the number of films screening that year containing unfortunate representations of women. In Hollywood, actor and director Elizabeth Banks called out Steven Spielberg for at least rarely making films with female leads. Banks called for more women screenwriters to help solve the issue. Some people criticized her for using a prominent figure as an example. She could have made a general reference to the lack of female leads in films. Spielberg isn't the problem.

"All members of a dominant, entrenched majority have a moral responsibility to transfer some of their power to members of minority groups. That means casting, hiring writers, hiring directors, choosing which stories to tell, choosing whom to support and back as new showrunners. I personally have been, I'd say, decent at this – and am trying to be better every year."
– Mike Schur, *The Good Place*

The DGA and the Golden Globes both didn't nominate a single woman director for the 2018 awards to be handed out in 2019. That carried on the situation of women being denied or overlooked. Globally, women who aren't Caucasian have more experience of being denied opportunities.

As I'm writing this, it is awards season, and the nominations once again favor the Caucasians. Of the 20 slots for best actress, best actor, best supporting actor, and best supporting actress, only one Oscar nominee is not Caucasian, and that is Cynthia Erivo, who was nominated for her brave portrayal of Harriet Tubman (Erivo didn't win). The best director nominees are all men – again.

The Internet has provided a way to find out how many women pioneers in film and TV have been overlooked, discredited, denied, or otherwise nearly washed out of consideration for their contributions to the craft.

Women have been working behind the scenes since the earliest years of cinema. Mabel Normand was a multi-talented creator of early films. She wrote, produced, and directed films, and is credited on over 200 films. She headed her own studio, Mabel Normand Feature Film Company, and was a mentor of Charlie Chaplin.

Lotte Reiniger: One of the overlooked and unappreciated women in film history

Many people have never heard of Charlotte "Lotte" Reiniger.

As a child, Reiniger created fanciful silhouette puppets and put on shows for friends and family.

As a young adult, Reiniger worked making title cards for the films of Georges Meilies, and cutout animation for the films of Paul Wegener.

She studied film at the Institute of Cultural Research, where she met her filmmaker husband, Carl Koch.

Years before Walt Disney was making animated films, Reiniger and Koch turned their home into a studio, where she developed stop motion silhouette animation using paper cutouts photographed on her own creation of backlit layers of glass, and turned them into short films.

Disney, and his team of creators, including animator Milicent Patrick, used Reiniger's techniques in the 1940 film *Fantasia*.

In 1922, Reiniger and Koch produced the animated film *Aschenputtel*.

While being sponsored by Louis Hagen, in 1926, they finished the animated film *The Adventures of Prince Achmed*, which director, screenwriter, and actor Jean Renoir sponsored for its premier in Paris. The popularity of the film allowed her to make others, including the 1928 feature *Doctor Doolittle and His Animals*, based on Hugh Lofting's book.

In 1929, Reiniger co-directed the live-action film *The Pursuit of Happiness*, which costarred Renoir and filmmaker Berthold Bartosch.

In 1935, she made the full-length animated feature *Papageno*, and dozens of other films. (Her films are on YouTube.)

During Hitler's rule, Reiniger was forced to make propaganda films.

Eventually moving to London, Reiniger and Koch made commercials, but also made animated shorts for the BBC under Primrose Productions, a company which she and Koch founded with Louise Hagen, Jr.

Shortly after her 82nd birthday, Reiniger died in Germany in 1981.

"Women were the main workforce in photographic manufacturing before the advent of motion pictures – in photo-finishing laboratories, photographic plate manufactures, and drying, cutting, and retouching film – and assumed similar work in the early motion picture industry."
– Erin Hill, *Never Done: A History of Women's Work in Media Productions*

To get an idea of women's contribution to film, consider seeing the 14-hour documentary *Women Make Film: A New Road Movie Through Cinema*.

Alice Guy-Blaché: The dawn of narrative film.

On March 22, 1895, Alice Guy had been working for a year as a secretary for a camera manufacturing and film supply company in France when she attended Auguste and Louis Lumieres' demonstration of film projection, which involved a simple scene of workmen exiting their father Antoine's film factory in Lyon.

On December 28, 1895, the Lumiere brothers first sold tickets to their films shown using their Cinematograph, a name they stole from Frenchman Leon Bouly, after he failed to maintain the patent on his invention of a film camera and projector. The grifter Lumiere brothers also took Georges Demeny's idea for a motion picture camera that he had patented in 1893.

Alice came up with the idea of filming a simple story in a single scene.

At age 23, in 1896 Alice made her first film *The Cabbage Fairy*, which is considered the first narrative film.

"My youth, my lack of experience, my sex all conspired against me."
– Alice Guy-Blaché, writer, actor, director, and producer

In 1907, Alice married Herbert Blaché, and they moved to Cleveland, Ohio, where Herbert worked for the Gaumont film equipment company. In 1908, they moved to New York. In 1910, they opened Solax Company, a film studio based at Gaumont's facility in Flushing, New York. In 1912, they moved to new facilities that Alice had spent a reported $100,000 to build and equip in Fort Lee, New Jersey. So that she could concentrate on writing and directing, in 1913 Alice let her husband preside over the company they named Blaché Features, Inc.

Herbert left Alice in 1918 to work in California.

In 1919 Alice made her final film, *Tarnished Reputations*.

Alice joined Herbert in California, but worked as his assistant director, and the two lived in separate homes.

From 1896 to 1920, Alice made or was involved in making over 1,000 films of various lengths. During her career, she experimented with special effects, made silent films, films that were hand-tinted with color and that featured dancers and that played along with music using the Chronophone sync-sound system that used music recorded on vertical-cut discs. She also made travel films, and feature films. She made a film with a cast that was all African-American, *A Fool and His Money*.

In 1921, Alice sold her New Jersey studio in bankruptcy, and returned to France the following year.

In 1964, Alice moved to New Jersey to be close to her daughter, and died there in 1968.

(Search: *The Lost Garden: The Life and Cinema of Alice Guy-Blaché*. And *Be Natural: The Untold Story of Alice Guy-Blaché*.)

Search the following names, and you will learn some things about the history of women filmmakers: Marion Fairfax, Tressie Souders, Elinor Ince, Jennie Louise VanDerZee, Alma Reville, Ida Lupino, June Mathis, Clara Beranger, Anita Loos, Adelina Barrassa, Lois Weber, Julia Crawford Ivers, Jeanie Macpherson, Mary Pickford, Alla Nazimova, Maria P. Williams, Elvira Notari, Esther Eng, Frances Marion, Marion Wong, Florence Lawrence, Dorothy Arzner, Mary Blair, Maya Deren, Milicent Patrick, Bianca Majolie, Joan Harrison, Katharine Hepburn, Monica Vitti, Carmen Santos, Margaret Booth, Jessie Maple, Elaine May, and Thelma Schoonmaker – to name a few.

(Search: Columbia University Women Film Pioneers Project. WFPP.Columbia.edu.)

(Read: *Nobody's Girl Friday: The Women Who Ran Hollywood*, by J.E. Smyth.)

"Directing is a way of looking at something and then communicating it. It would be hideous to think that either sex took a script and in any way pushed it toward any point of view other than the author's. I don't think it's important whether you're a man, a woman, or a chair."
– Elaine May, *Tootsie*

"Cinema is an opportunity to take audiences on unexpected journeys and to give them a deeper understanding of what it means to be a human on the margins. And, I think women are very much on the margins in our country."
– Eliza Hittman, *Never Rarely Sometimes Always*

"By coming together, we are lifting each other up and amplifying our voices into a powerful chorus that cannot be ignored."
– Julianne Moore, actor

"I asked the censor what was wrong with my film. He said, 'The female protagonist is immoral, she sleeps around for money, and what's more, she comes out of it alive. Film me a version where she's killed at the end, and your film will be authorized.'"
– Nelly Kaplan, *A Very Curious Girl*

"I don't think we're anywhere near the comfort zone of equal representation to have the luxury of not reminding people: This was directed by a woman. 'Woman directors' certainly shouldn't be a genre, but we don't live in a world where women's work is viewed with the same reception or financial support – with the same amount of frequency – as men's. That's the reality."
– Caryn Coleman, FutureOfFilmIsFemale.com

"I have my own theory that for years gay writers – male gay writers – spoke through the voices of women because they weren't free to write their own stories. And those fabulous creations that were the product of repression actually gave us an opportunity."
– Meryl Streep, actor

"The world has always been full of sheep. You want to be a sheep, okay, this is a democracy. But if you want to find your own way, this is the time to do it. It's not harder to be yourself, it's just more obvious that it's hard. Really hard. It's always been hard. It was for Keats."
– Jane Campion, *Bright Star*

In response to the concerns about how women have missed out on opportunities, Meryl Streep began supporting a screenwriting program for women writers over 40. The Writers Lab was established by New York Women in Film and Television along with IRIS and the Writers Guild of America East. It also has had financial support from Oprah Winfrey and Nicole Kidman.

"One of the most important keys to acting is curiosity. I am curious to the point of being nosy. What that means is you want to devour lives. You're eager to put on their shoes and wear their clothes and have them become a part of you. All people contain mystery, and when you act, you want to plumb that mystery until everything is known to you."
– Meryl Streep, actor

"I'm not an actor because I want my picture taken, I'm an actor because I want to be part of the human exchange."
– Frances McDormand, actor

"Nora Ephron was 51 when she directed her first movie. Nancy Meyers was 49. There kids were grown. If you're a woman who writes, acts, edits, A.D.s, etc. and you're ready to direct, you're not too old. I was 47."
– Aline Brosh McKenna, *The Devil Wears Prada*

It seems clear that women and minority film directors are held to a different level of exam. As it is pointed out which films have been directed by them, too much focus is placed on the box office. That doesn't seem to be the case with TV, where many shows are directed by women.

"There's no forgiveness. Oliver Stone could go wreck a car and get arrested for being on drugs, and then do *Alexander* (a major flop). But we can't do that. Women can't make mistakes."
– Penelope Spheeris, *Suburbia*

"The explosion of TV series has really benefitted female writers. Many women I know who got spat out from movies when the studios became tent pole factories have found happy purchase telling stories for the small screen with way less creative interference. And younger women I know are breaking into the biz more quickly. Including women of color. So, when people say there is too much TV and not enough qualified writers, don't worry, women from all backgrounds are rising up the ranks, and they are ready."
– Aline Brosh McKenna, *Crazy Ex-Girlfriend*

"Women of my generation, we've been taught that you don't show anger – that you make nice. I think there's a reason why you've – up until really recently – seen very two-dimensional, 'nice-washed' characters."
– Liz Feldman, *Dead to Me*

"I think it's very important to show women who don't fit in and who don't care if society judges them. Let other people be upset, but let these women speak out."
– Monika Treut, *Ghosted*

For the first Screenwriting Tribe workshop of 2018, we featured only female writers. I put out the call saying that we need their input, voices, experiences, and feedback in the workshop. Luckily, that helped bring in more women writers. Since then, there have been many more women of a variety of ages and backgrounds attending Tribe. Diversity has benefited the workshop. I also want Tribe to be part of the solution.

"I grew up never seeing myself on screen, and it's really important to me to give people who look like me a chance to see themselves. I want to see myself as the hero to any story."
– Sandra Oh, actor

"There is a genuine urge for audiences to want an industry that represents their life. That's why I'm very positive about the direction that we're going in. I

don't think that having people of different cultures or women will be a trend, because I think that it's what people want. We're changing as a culture."
   – Awkwafina, *Awkwafina is Nora from Queens*

Diversity in film and TV seems to finally be making headway. Sandra Oh is one onscreen talent who consistently gets work. But, Asians remain massively underrepresented in mainstream productions. Maybe the successes of *Crazy Rich Asians* and *Parasite* will make a difference. Time will tell.

Korea is one of the top film markets. Consider that as you write scripts.

In film and TV history, Caucasian actors were often cast to play non-Caucasian characters. One example that is often noted is Mickey Rooney playing Mr. Yumioshi in the 1961 film *Breakfast at Tiffany's*.

More recent films have had similar "Caucasian playing another race" casting choices. One example is Emma Stone playing Allison Ng, a character meant to be one-quarter Chinese, and one-quarter Hawaiian, in the 2015 film *Aloha*. Perhaps a character with such a genetic background could appear Caucasian. However, Stone said that the controversy relating to her casting opened her eyes to the issue of whitewashing in films.

As opportunities are opening in the U.S. film and TV industry, it is also empowering the overlooked, discredited, abused, and neglected people in other countries, including some using new and less expensive and accessible film technology to make their projects.

In India, women filmmakers are making things happen for themselves. Meghna Gulzar gained attention for her film *Chhapaak*, that she co-wrote with Atika Chohan, and that is about an acid-attack survivor. Juhi Chaturvedi, who had experience in commercials is writing and directing films. Female screenwriters are making significant careers in India, including Shibani Bathija, and Gazal Dhawliwal.

Iran cinema is also seeing in influx of women filmmakers, but, that is not new as women there had been making films for decades. Poet Forough Farroghzad, who made the 1963 film *The House Is Black*, about a leper colony, is known as the founder of the Iranian New Wave. In the 1980s, Rakshshan Bani-Etemad began making documentaries, before making narrative films centered on social and cultural issues. Marjane Satrapi, who wrote the graphic novel *Persepolis* loosely based on her life, turned it into the 2007 film, and won the Cannes Film Festival's Jury Prize.

In 2019, *Bed of Thorns*, a film written by, crewed by, and starring women in Uganda was awarded the Africa Focus Award at the London Art House Film Festival.

Also, in 2019, a group of Nigerian teenage boys calling themselves "ThE cRiTiCs" gained international media attention by making films using their phones, free editing apps, and unpredictable Internet service, and posting the results on YouTube. The boys collectively saved their money to be able to purchase equipment to make their projects, including a short they titled *Z: The*

Beginning. Their work has attracted the attention of Los Angeles agents, managers, and producers. They are creating the change they want to see.

"We want to do something crazy. We want to do something great, something that has not been done before, and from what has been going on now, we believe quite well that it is going to happen soon enough."
– Godwin Josiah, *Z: The Beginning*

"As Ralph Ellison once posited, we're invisible to them. We're simply not on their radar. As long as the people who are in charge aren't us, things will never change."
– Issa Rae, *Insecure*

If you want to see women, minorities, handicapped characters, and the denied to be realistically represented on screen, do something about it.

Complaints without action are simply commentary. Formulate answers.

Use your power in your writing. Write what you want to see on screen. Don't expect others to do it. Others with much less than you have done quite a bit more. Get busy.

"I would like to be the one to whom the other person is saying, 'No, don't go out and do that. Stay here at home, with me. Don't go out there and do the brave thing.' That drives me mad, it's always the woman saying to the man, 'Don't go and be the hero. Stay here.'"
– Emma Thompson, *Bridget Jones's Baby*

"A lot of times you see female characters in service of the man's plotline. A lot of times when I write the first draft, it feels boring, so I flip the genders of the characters."
– Melanie Marnich, *The Big C*

A producer once hired me to overhaul a script. It featured three female leads who were not wimpy, not exploited, and who were clever and interesting. One was evil. One was trying to find her way in life. And one knew what she wanted, and wasn't going to settle for less – and especially not for anyone's nonsense. They weren't delicate lovelies seeking man help, or overly emotional, or hyper power women, or victims, or stuck in the wife or girlfriend roles. It also wasn't a blatant feminist piece. It was a script that happened to have realistic female leads. It was an interesting script doctoring job, and refreshing to read and be a part of.

"Tired of films about women that seem to deeply despise women. I'm not talking about women characters being likable. I d.g.a.f. if a woman on screen is likable. I do care that she feels like a genuine, dynamic, flawed person with a real drive and point of view."
– Gennifer Hutchison, *Better Call Saul*

"I'm really interested in trying to tell stories about women that don't involve romantic components. It feels like it's built in, but I'd like to find a way that it's not. There are so many more stories than that."
– Greta Gerwig, *Little Women*

"I like to direct because I believe a woman, more or less intuitively, brings out many of the emotions that are rarely expressed on the screen."
– Lois Weber, *White Heat*

One of my favorite films about a woman living her life, and not living within the boundaries that people were trying to constrain her in, and about her connecting to and practicing her talents is *Artemisia*. It is based on the story of Artemisia Gentileschi, a painter who was born in 1593 and who is portrayed in the film by Valentina Cervi.

Two other films based on true stories of woman painters also stand out for their portrayal of women doing their thing and refusing conformity to societal expectations. One is *Frida* starring Salma Hayek as Mexican artist Frida Kahlo. The other film is *Séraphine*, about the tragic life of French artist Séraphine Louis, brilliantly portrayed by Yolande Moreau.

To find films directed by women, access: MoviesByHer.com.

"What's the trick to writing a great female character? Make her human."
– Nicole Holofcener, *Can You Ever Forgive Me?*

"The discussion of representation is one that has been repeated over and over again, and the solution has always been that it's up to us to support, promote, and create the images that we want to see."
– Issa Rae, *Insecure*

"It's irrelevant who or what directed a movie. The important thing is that you either respond to it, or you don't. There should be more women directing. I think there's just not the awareness that it's really possible. It is."
– Kathryn Bigelow, *Undertow*

"I'm very glad that today there are more opportunities for young women. I don't think it's a useless endeavor at this point, by any means. I almost feel jealous that I was not able to take advantage of this movement. Because, it's one thing to be a woman in this business, but, let me tell you something, it's another thing to be an older woman in this business. Because then you've got two strikes against you from the start."
– Penelope Spheeris, *The Little Rascals*

"In my films, I always wanted to make people see deeply. I don't want to show things, but to give people the desire to see."
– Agnes Varda, *Cleo from 5 to 7*

"When my film went to the Venice Film Festival and won the best script writing, the jury prize, it didn't go to my head. I know how many black

filmmakers that I am operating with whose names will never be mentioned. But, I'm part of them in that silent existence."
– Haile Gerima, *Teza*

From the origins of the industry, African-Americans were making films. (Search: Maria P. Williams, Noble and George Johnson, Hattie McDaniel, William Foster, Tressie Souders, Spencer Williams, Paul Robeson, Fredi Washington, Oscar Micheaux, and Pioneers of African-American Cinema.)

"We need to keep an eye on the other human experiences to give ourselves the fullness and the breadth of our own humanity. Our humanity is served back to us through the eyes of those who have diminished us. And they serve back to us a view of ourselves that is incomplete. If we don't look to the bigger picture, our view will narrow to that which is constantly fed to us."
– Sidney Poiteir, *For Love of Ivy*

"What we are learning from, what we're exporting out into the world and what we're seeing are stories that are overwhelmingly told from just one perspective. You may have heard about the (2012) statistics of female filmmakers working in Hollywood. On average, out of the 100 highest grossing films per year, 96% are directed by men, and 4% by women. And that's despite film school graduates having a ratio of about 50% men, and 50% women. These statistics have not changed in many years. And in 1975 there was a film theorist (Laura Mulvey) who coined the term 'male gaze' to talk about what happens when you see art – popular culture and film – through the lens of just one gender. How does that shape our experiences of the world or opinion of ourselves, or each other? People may say, 'Well, it's entertainment. It's movies. It's just good fun.' But, there are so many research studies which link things like body image and self-esteem to what we see on the screens. Particularly, children.
Geena Davis says, for young girls watching entertainment, 'If they can see it, they can be it.' Representation matters. And the way characters are portrayed on screen, or sometimes completely erased from stories has a huge impact on us as viewers."
– Alicia Malone, *Movie Trivia Schmoedown*

"There's more to all of us than we realize. Life is so much bigger, grander, higher, and wider than we allow ourselves to think. We're capable of so much more than we allow ourselves to believe."
– Dana Queen Latifah Owens, *The Cookout*

"It used to be that you had to make female TV characters perfect so no one would be offended by your portrayal of women. And now, thankfully, it's completely different."
– Mindy Kaling, *Late Night*

"Whenever I am asked what kind of writing is the most lucrative, I have to say, 'A ransom note.'"
— H.N. Swanson, literary agent

IF YOU MAKE
THE BIG HOLLYWOOD MONEY

"Security is a kind of death, I think, and it can come to you in a storm of royalty checks beside a kidney-shaped pool in Beverly Hills – or anywhere at all that is removed from the conditions that made you an artist, if that's what you are or were intended to be. Ask anyone who has experienced the kind of success I am talking about, 'What good is it?' Perhaps to get an honest answer you will have to give him a shot of truth serum, but the word he will finally groan is unprintable in genteel publications."
— Tennessee Williams, *Sweet Bird of Youth*

I'm covering this issue in the book because I've known people who had major success in Hollywood, then wasted all of their money – and ended up broke. Unfortunately, it's not uncommon for someone in showbiz to lose their fortune – for a variety of reasons.

I once had a long conversation with a suddenly globally famous rap star. Money and fame were flowing his way. I told him, "Now that you have all this money coming in, don't blow it." He said he knew what I was talking about. He was seeing other famous people throwing money around, buying elaborate gifts, extreme cars, over-the-top jewelry, expensive watches, and other future junk – as if the flow of money into their accounts would never end. I told him, "Don't buy a mansion." He said he doesn't need a mansion, because he's never home. I told him that he should buy an apartment complex – or more than one. He said he was already looking for apartment complexes. I told him, don't rent the apartments to friends, workers, or relatives. And that they don't need to know about his investments. He laughed and said that he knew what I was saying. Keep it a business. Hire a management company to take care of the apartment complex. Keep an eye on the numbers. Do the visits to the property to see if it is being taken care of, that the roof isn't leaking, that there are no health code violations, that the landscaping is maintained, that the insurance coverage is adequate. Be a smart business person. He said that is all part of the plan.

I would give the same advice to screenwriters who hit it big. They might have more money than anyone in their family has had. And, they have no skills relating to what to do with the money. Suddenly, they are buying stuff that they don't need, staying at expensive hotels, overspending on food, clothing, housing, and entertainment – as if the money will be never ending.

There was a young guy who sold a script for a bunch of money. He promptly bought a new Range Rover. Why would anyone need a vehicle like that? A luxury car is not and never will be an investment. It's a money hole. A smarter move would be to – if he even needed a car – buy a certified used hybrid or electric vehicle. I know rich people who won't buy new cars. Even they will only purchase certified used cars. They can take the thousands they save, and toss it into their investment portfolio. I know a wealthy woman in the industry who only buys certified used cars.

Consider that you don't need a car. You can use ride share services, a bike, and take public transportation. That way, you will not have to pay for car insurance, registration, parking, repairs, fuel, oil changes, tire rotations, new tires, and other maintenance. You won't spend time looking for a parking space, or for a gas station, or have to deal with anything else relating to owning a car – including vandalism.

One successful screenwriter I know doesn't own a car, because he doesn't need one. While not owning a car, he does own rental property. Smart moves. He sometimes walks miles to get to meetings – which is a healthy choice for a writer who spends so much time sitting.

If you get enough money to buy an apartment complex, consider doing that. Don't buy a house. If you do buy a house, get one with a guest apartment that you can rent out, or live in the apartment, and rent out the house. You likely don't need a house. Buy income property. Maybe purchase a fourplex. I know a writer who did that. He lives in one of the units, and rents the other units to people who aren't his friends, co-workers, lovers, or relatives. He maintains business as business.

Read some investment books. Watch a variety of YouTube videos about setting up an investment portfolio. Listen to a wide range of opinions.

Do not hire a stock broker. You might be amazed at how little many of them know. I know two people who work as stock brokers. One didn't graduate high school (not that every successful person does). The other went to school to be a phlebotomist. I recently spoke with a neighbor who has been working at a brokerage. His uncle got him the job. While speaking with him, I used the term O.T.C. He didn't know what it meant.

You can use any of the online brokerage firms to handle your own transactions – and avoid filling the bank account of a stock broker with your cash. Consider Vanguard.com, Fidelity.com, and Calvert Investments.

Be cautious of – or avoid – buying individual stocks. If you do purchase stocks, first research the company.

Consider investing in an index fund. An index fund owns stocks in a wide variety of companies, including some that pay dividends. On YouTube, watch a variety of videos about index funds.

Go to Vanguard.com or Fidelity.com, choose one of their index funds. Throw some money in it. Set up your account so that all dividends and capital gains get reinvested into the index fund. Set up the account to have at least $100 (preferably, a larger amount) automatically transferred from your checking account into the index fund every month. Leave it alone and let it grow for your retirement (and/or for a way to save for buying rental properties).

Through Vanguard.com or Fidelity.com, you can also buy into a 401(K) plan. Continue putting money into it every month for your retirement. Educate yourself about 401(K) plans by watching YouTube videos, and by doing other research.

Open a Roth IRA with a credit union, such as First Entertainment Credit Union. Deposit the maximum amount into the Roth IRA, every year. Leave it alone.

Research and look into investing in REITs. Those are Real Estate Investment Trusts. But, that will likely be only about 10% of your portfolio.

You can buy into a REIT fund run by Vanguard.com. The Vanguard REIT fund invests in a wide variety of REITs. Be sure to set it up so that the payouts are automatically reinvested. Again, no more than 10% of your portfolio.

If you buy into individual REITs, choose those that own assisted care facilities. The elder care industry is going to continue growing. Some people would advise that you avoid individual REITs that own office buildings, commercial buildings, hotels, or shopping malls.

Learn about bonds. Consider having a small percentage of your investment portfolio in bonds – perhaps 10% of your portfolio. Again, for long-term investment.

Learn what a SPAC is (Special Purpose Acquisition Company). Research those. There are plenty of videos about them on YouTube, and articles about them on the Internet. Consider investing in SPACs that seem promising. Do so before, or very soon after, they announce their merger intention. Sell when they gain value, then transfer the money into your index fund.

"Keep a good heart. That's the most important thing in life. It's not how much money you make, or what you can acquire. The art of it is to keep a good heart."
– Joni Mitchell, musician

Whatever you do, if you end up making significant money in the screenwriting industry, be smart about how you treat the money. Don't waste it. It might be your only chance for you to set up yourself for long-term financial stability.

One guy who succeeded in Hollywood into the stratosphere is writer, director, producer, author, documentarian, and film school professor Tom Shadyac. Some of the films he directed include *Liar Liar*, *Ace Ventura: Pet Detective*, *The Nutty Professor*, and *Bruce Almighty*. He had the massive mansion, and all the expensive things. Then, he suffered a bike accident that nearly killed him. He sold his mansion, moved to a small home, donated money to help unhoused people, and to the environment. He moved to Memphis – where he opened a rock climbing and workout gym and yoga and health center. His documentary *I Am* tells his story, and explores the problems related to materialism addiction.

Know that most people who sell scripts in Hollywood only sell one script during their entire life. So, be sure to maintain other income sources, as in: A job, or jobs.

Consider taking one evening class per semester at your local community college to keep improving your job skills and artistic talents. If screenwriting doesn't work out for you, there will be other skills that you have learned and can use.

Take care of your physical health.

Exercise and eat several colors of fruits and vegetables, daily. Avoid fried and sautéed foods, clarified sugars, bleached grains, bottled salad dressings, and fast food restaurants. Know how to make salads containing a variety of raw vegetables, and don't slather them with unhealthy dressings. See ForksOverKnives.com and NutritionFacts.org for nutrition and health information.

"When I'm asked for 'the secret of my success' (an absurd idea, that, but impossible to get away from), I sometimes say there are two: I stayed physically healthy, and I stayed married. It's a good answer because it makes the question go away, and because there is an element of truth in it. The combination of a healthy body and a stable relationship with a self-reliant woman who takes zero shit from me or anyone else has made the continuity of my working life possible. And I believe the converse is also true: That my writing and the pleasure I take in it has contributed to the stability of my health and my home life."

– Stephen King, *The Talisman*

"You should not have too many people waiting on you, you should have to do most things for yourself."

– Tennessee Williams, *Cat on a Hot Tin Roof*

"I use Final Draft on my laptop. I know some people write in long hand, but I find it helpful to sort of see it in the format of a screenplay as I write."
– Sofia Coppola, *The Beguiled*

Screenwriting Software

Final Draft is the most common screenwriting software used by studios, production companies, agents, managers, producers, and screenwriters.

There are other screenwriting programs, including Celtx, KIT Scenartist, Adobe Story, Fade In, Highland, Writer Duet, Movie Magic, Screenplay Markdown, Slugline, StudioBinder, and Fountain.

You can also write scripts by formatting a document using Microsoft Word – which can be more trouble than you might want to deal with, and leave your script looking as if it was an attempt to make it right (for the margin settings, see *The Screenwriter's Bible*).

Cell phone screenwriting apps include Final Draft, Writer Duet, Slugline, Fade In, Index Card, Highland, Scrivener, Contour, and Celtx.

What will you do when you have not used and do not own Final Draft, and an agent, or manager, or production company asks you to send your script as a Final Draft document, including for annotations? Maybe a regular PDF would work. Ask your nearest computer geek. Or, simply get Final Draft, and watch the online tutorials to get up to speed on the functions of that software.

"The intuitive ease of Final Draft allows the writer to focus on what's truly important – story."
– Robert Zemeckis, *Welcome to Marwen*

"Final Draft has eclipsed all of its competitors, because it is the best."
– Matthew Weiner, *The Romanoffs*

"I've tried a variety of scriptwriting software, and Final Draft is without question my favorite."
– Alan Ball, *Towelhead*

"It's not the writing part that's hard. What's hard is sitting down to write."
– Steven Pressfield, author *The War of Art*

"Writing and travel broaden your ass, if not your mind – and I like to write standing up."
– Ernest Hemingway, *The Old Man and the Sea*

Write Standing

Modern day people sit too much.
Sitting is the new smoking.
The body needs movement.

"Editing film is like a combination of being a short-order cook, a brain surgeon, and an orchestra conductor. Each of those three people stand to do what they do."
– Walter Murch, *Return to Oz*

Simply standing engages a variety of muscles. Using muscles is good for the cardiovascular, lymph, and nerve systems, hormonal and blood sugar balance, the digestion, the bones, and the brain. And, it is better for the spine.

Try standing as you write, instead of sitting. See if that makes a difference in your writing. Put your laptop on a box on top of your desk. Or, get – or make – a standup desk.

Ernest Hemingway wrote with his typewriter on top of a bookcase, and edited outside on a slanted lectern set on a table on his porch.

Henry Wadsworth Longfellow had a small desk that he kept on top of a table so that he could sometimes sit and sometimes stand as he wrote.

Virginia Woolf wrote at a standing desk that had a slanted top and a book shelf built in the lower part with a brass bar below that to rest a foot on.

Soren Kirkegaard kept a standing desk in each room of his home.

Vladimir Nabokov wrote while standing at a lectern.

Philip Roth had a broad, lectern-like desk with a slanted top, much like a drafting table.

Stan Lee was known to write outside with his typewriter on a picnic bench set on top of his patio table.

509

I put my headstand inversion bench on my desk, and I place my laptop on top of that. The bench is the perfect height for me to have on top of my desk. It's also nicely padded – so I can lean on it with my elbows. Every once in a while, I take down the bench and use it for its purpose: To do head stands.

I use a yoga brick to keep one foot up so that one leg is bent – which prevents lower back stress. I'll also use the brick to step up and down on as I'm at my desk. Instead of a yoga brick, you can be like Tom Brady, and use a slightly deflated football.

Besides Hemingway, Longfellow, Lee, Nietzsche, Roth, Kirkegaard, Woolf, and Nobokov, writers and others known for standing while writing include Rainer Rilke, August Wilson, Thomas Wolfe, Lewis Carroll, Fernando Pessoa, Edward R. Murrow, Albert Einstein, Nikolai Gogol, Charles Dickens, John Henry Newman, Victor Hugo, Thomas Jefferson, and Napoleon Bonaparte.

Some people buy a treadmill desk, or make their own treadmill desk. Used treadmills can be low-cost: Search online.

Getting movement in several times a day will likely improve your writing, and your sleep, as well as your brain and mood. Having a yoga ball to roll around on and to use to do crunches during breaks helps get some movement in, and gets the blood and lymph moving. I also have dumbbells for doing lunge steps on a yoga mat. I also have a couple of exercise resistance cords to do various arm exercises. Doing calisthenics and vinyasa flow yoga helps. I have a chin-up bar, and use that to do hanging leg lifts – feet to ceiling, and back down. I usually bike to get around town, or to a nearby canyon where there is a flight of stairs with about 170 steps that I go up and down several times. I also jog up the canyon, or I jog in the soft sand at the beach.

A writer shouldn't simply sit.

Exercise every morning to break a sweat. It's good for everything about you.

Cut out the junk food, fried and sautéed food (sautéed is a fancy word for fried), and other unhealthful food that clogs your brain and body, dulls you, and triggers degenerative and autoimmune diseases.

See the variety of healthy recipes and the *Forks Over Knives* documentary on ForksOverKnives.com. The site was put together by cardiovascular and cancer doctors, and a nutritional biochemist.

(See the documentary *The Game Changers*.)

Avoid foods rich in polycyclic aromatic hydrocarbons, acrylamides. glycotoxins, aldehydes, heterocyclic amines, and free radicals, and that contain the Neu5Gc molecule. Research those on NutritionFacts.org.

Increase your consumption of green vegetables. Consider adding a green powder to your diet, such as Infinity Greens (InfinityGreens.com).

Look into the nutritional benefits of maca, lucuma, mesquite, chia seeds, raw hemp seeds, and raw pumpkin seeds, and other whole plant substances that you can use in salads and smoothies. Get a vegetable juicer.

Go for organically grown foods as they are safer for you, for the farmers, for the environment, and for wildlife. Farming chemicals are known to trigger a variety of health problems, including cancer, birth defects, and learning disabilities. Farming chemicals kill the animals that help to keep us alive: Birds, bees, butterflies, bats, and other pollinating creatures that not only help to provide our food, but help the growth of plants that provide the oxygen that we breathe.

"I am writing this at my standing desk, which is against the window. The window offers a pleasant prospect over the lime trees and sun-bathed hills – delightful, natural scenery."
– Friedrich Nietzsche, *Road to Rio*

"The seed out of which everything for a film comes is the script. Even though there are so many important things, the script within it – as it does in theater, or in written music – contains all the possibilities that those other talents can then bring to flower."
– Francis Ford Coppola, *Distant Vision*

"It's unquestionable that how people experience films and entertainment is changing, not only as a business but as a culture. I consider it a mistake as a filmmaker to say, 'Well, they will adapt to smaller screens.' I think it's the opposite. Smaller screens have to adapt to cinematic visions."
– Alfonso Cuarón Orozco, *A Boy and His Shoe*

INT. YOUR PLACE - DAY
ADVICE TO A SCREENWRITER

"A lot of writers try to get approval and love way too early. Get the script right, first."
– Allison Burnett, *Autumn in New York*

- **You are writing a screenplay to be made into a movie (or series). Use your imagination. It's a movie. Emotionally move us.**
    Don't bore us – or else you will lose us, and we will move out of our seats.

"A screenplay is movement. It is written in time, and it expresses a passage of time. It is made in time, and it is viewed in time. It's a movie, it moves."
– Charlie Kaufman, *Chaos Walking*

"Film is important; it can be more than reportage or a novel. It creates images people have never seen before, never imagined they would see, maybe because they needed someone else to imagine for them."
– Steve McQueen, *Widows*

- **Know what the characters need and want.**
    Reveal how characters cleverly use bold or subtly manipulative actions to go about getting what they want and need in an interesting story mixed with backstories, all rich in subtext and engaging conflict.

"Dialogue is used to reveal not what we want to say, but what we are trying to hide."
– William Monahan, *The Departed*

This does not mean that the dialogue has to tell us what the character wants or needs. You can see the image of a person in a terrible situation, and know what they need, and probably guess what they want. Leave out the repetitive messages – especially duplicate messages in dialogue linked to the visual messages (which end up being on-the-nose dialogue).

- **Remember: Just as real people do – believable characters have flaws.**

  Perhaps the characters have defects that are part of the problems that keep them from attaining goals and accomplishing their glory. It could mean that the person who is revered and celebrated has a secret life that is a hindrance, or a private matter they simply like to hide – and maybe reveals their brilliance, or their charity, love, or compassion, or their crime. Maybe they have one last chance to do what is right, and they almost make the wrong choice, but they refuse anymore to participate in the behavior and language preventing them from doing what they need to accomplish.

  Maybe the character is so adored that anyone who finds out about their addiction to heroin would be shocked, and they might be kicked out of the position that we want them to stay in, because what they are doing at their job is helping someone who we know desperately needs their help. Maybe there is one last time that they need to do something to help that person all the way through their problem, but, instead of doing what they need to do, they purchase heroin. But, just before they inject, they stop themselves, and they do what they need to do, and they accomplish the goal – which makes them a hero. But then they go into such deep drug withdrawal, that they die anyway. Bittersweet, and harsh. But, that is somehow what life is.

  In reverse of that, maybe the villain has flaws in being bad, and they secretly do good things. Maybe they do so because they know how bad they have been, and are trying to make some sort of spiritual correction.

  "The stories that I like to tell are always interesting, because the good guys have really serious flaws, and the villains are very compelling."
  – Ken Burns, documentarian

- **Don't clog your script with camera angles, which is "technical direction." The D.P. and director will decide the camera angles.**

  Simply, avoid acknowledging the camera in your scene direction. (*Unless, see below.)

  Decide what is the most visually interesting part of each paragraph of description. Consider writing the first words of the description focused on the visual that you think is an interesting way to start the scene.

  If the sentence in description is worded as the following sentence is, it is clear that the shot goes from an extreme close-up of a blood drop forming, and widens out to show the cat lick up the blood. There is no need to say that it starts out as an extreme close-up, or that the camera follows the drop to the floor, or that the camera widens out to see the cat. The sentence is simply written cinematically.

513

```
A blood drop forms on Morgan's fingertip and falls
to the floor, where the cat sniffs it and licks it
up.
```

*There are situations when acknowledging a camera angle or movement works well in a script – especially: to intensify conflict. Do so sparingly. `WIDEN TO REVEAL` might be one camera direction. `THROUGH THE EYES OF A MASK` is another (also called "phantom angle" or "`PHANTOM P.O.V.`" See: The original *Halloween*, 1978.). Look at award-winning screenplays, and see how they use camera direction. But, don't write your scripts as if they are instruction manuals for camera operators.

- **Never put CUT TO:, SMASH CUT TO: – or other editing direction (known as transition cues) – in the spec script.**
  It's not needed. It's a distraction. It breaks the reader's focus. It's redundant. It dumbs down the script. It reveals your naiveté. It's assumptive, and it talks down to the editor.
  Don't talk down to the editor.

- **Use the correct font, margins, and format.**
  Use 12 point Courier font. Accurately write scene headings. In other words, learn how to format your script, and format it correctly. Anyone worth dealing with in the industry will quickly be able to tell if your script is – or is not – correctly formatted.
  Study: *The Screenwriter's Bible* and *Dr. Format Tells All.*

- **Don't repeat the heading information in the scene description.**
  The following is wrong, as it both repeats what we already know from the scene heading (we are in Brenda's bedroom) and it repeatedly assigns ownership to items that we would naturally assume are hers. (She is in her room, so there is no reason to keep saying "her."):

```
INT. BRENDA'S BEDROOM - DAY

Brenda is in her bedroom and sits on her bed and
opens her bed stand drawer, pulls out her cell
phone, dials her phone, and leans over onto her
window sill to look outside her window.
```

The following is one possible corrected version:

```
INT. BRENDA'S BEDROOM - DAY

Brenda sits on the bed, opens the bed stand drawer,
pulls out the phone and dials. She looks out the
window.
```

- **Know how to correctly introduce characters.**
  It matters. Study: *The Screenwriter's Bible* and *Dr. Format Tells All.*

- **Avoid writing elaborate or novelesque scene description.**

  Keep the unfilmable scene direction limited to when you introduce a character, if even then.

  If you are working on a series that has been in production, you might see more than the normal amount of unfilmable scene description in those scripts. Each show does things slightly differently. Do what the showrunner likes.

  "My scripts have always been a bit terse, both in stage direction and dialogue. I think I've loosened up in the dialogue department, but I still try to keep the description fairly minimal, and in some cases purposefully minimalist. I still punctuate to effect, rather than to the proper rules of grammar. I occasionally use onomatopoeias now, a luxury I would certainly never have allowed myself when I was younger."
  – Walter Hill, *The Getaway*

- **Do not write your scene description as if you are writing an instruction manual for an unintelligent director, D.P., gaffer, editor, wardrobe designer, production designer, art director, prop master, or other craftsperson.**

- **Use sparse wording to describe what is seen, without vast details, over-explaining, information tornado dumps, or talking down to a reader.**

- **Do not use the terms "We see" or "We hear" in scene description. It could be considered dumbing down the script.**

  Simply write what is seen and what is heard.

  Scene description is what is seen and what is heard.

  For sounds, simply put them in the scene description: The baby CRIES. A dog BARKS. A door SQUEAKS. A pig SQUEALS. The motorcycle RUMBLES past. The monster's stomach GRUMBLES.

  Yes, it is okay to use uppercase with some of the sounds ("flag" the sounds). But, flag the sounds only when it is truly needed, helpful, and relevant to the scene. Otherwise, put the sounds in lower case.

  For multi-cam sitcom formatting of sounds, see: *The Screenwriter's Bible*.

- **Avoid unfilmables in spec script scene description,**

  Yes, this again. But, it is a common mistake in spec scripts.

  Unfilmable scene description includes using scene description to tell us what a character remembers, wants, hates, regrets, plans, thinks they need, what they are looking for, etc.

  Unfilmable description also includes telling the history of things: She drives the car that her father once drove across the border to Mexico. Or, They moved the table to the other side of the room, where their grandmother used to keep it.

The way we know the history of things that are in a scene is either we see that history happening (maybe in a flashback or dream sequence), or a character tells the history in dialogue – even if it is voiceover.

- **Always remember that the audience will not have your script in front of them to read.**

  The viewers will only see what is on the screen, and will hear the dialogue and sounds (including the soundtrack). Engage them, and keep them engaged.

- **In scene description, only describe what is being seen and heard, not what any character thinks, remembers, plans, or desires.**

  The camera can't film thoughts. It can only film animals (including people), things, and their movements.

- **Don't use scene description to tell us the thoughts of what a character is looking for.**

  All we will see is that they are looking around. We will only know what they are looking for if they verbalize it, another character verbalizes it, there is voiceover telling us so, or when they find it – or if we can figure out what they are looking for based on the visual, such as: They are barefooted, holding one shoe, and looking around their bedroom. Or, in a previous scene something was mentioned or happened that would clue us in to what the character would then be looking for.

- **Omit scene description that tells the history of people, other animals, objects, or events.**

  Including the history of animals and things in description is unfilmable.

  History can be shown in flashbacks, or told in dialogue – including in voiceover.

  If you read a script of a series that has already filmed one or more episodes, you might find all sorts of unfilmables in those scripts. But, they are there for a reason – including to remind the director, actors, and crew of how to handle things, people, and situations in relation to how they were handled in the previous episodes – or in reference to future episodes.

- **Do not explain things in description that the viewers know.**

  It's repetitive, and it slows, dulls, and dumbs down your script.

- **Do not explain things in description that the dialogue tells us, or that the imagery clues us in on.**

"I've made up little mantras for myself, catchphrases from a screenwriting book that doesn't exist. One is, 'Write the movie you'd pay to go see.' Another is, 'Never let a character tell me something that the camera can show me.'"

– Taylor Sheridan, *Sicario*

- **Do not explain things in description that the viewers can figure out on their own.**

- **Do not explain things that the viewers don't need to know.**

  As previously mentioned, that also means: Don't do it in voiceover. Unless, the voiceover is some quirky side story on its own that plays its own games of manipulating the audience, and of creating a puzzle with a payoff.

- **Do not misuse voiceover.**

  Only use voiceover (`V.O.`) when it is truly helpful to the story. Or, be so clever with it that is it like an entertaining side show. (See Trottier's *Bible*.)

- **Know the difference between voiceover (`V.O.`) and off screen (`O.S.`).**
  Voiceover dialogue is when a character can be heard speaking, but is not at the location. The character could be...
- Heard on the other end of a phone line
- Heard over an intercom or loudspeaker
- Heard as part of a memory
- Heard as part of a hallucination
- Heard describing a situation
- Heard introducing characters or events
- Heard overlapping from the previous scene. That is a `post-lap`.
- Heard before we get to the next scene where the character is then both seen and heard (such as a child is in their bedroom and can hear the voice of their teacher, then we go to the classroom and we see and hear the teacher continuing with what they are telling the child.) That is a `pre-lap`.

Off screen dialogue is when a character...
- Can be heard, but is not seen, even though they are at the location – perhaps simply in another part of the room (maybe hiding behind the curtains)
- Or is outside of the room
- Or they are heard talking before they enter the room
- Or the scene takes place outside, and the character can be heard saying something inside of a house, tent, car, or outhouse

  Some people use `V.O.` to indicate what others would clarify as `O.S.` Choose one style, and stick with it through the entire script.

- **Rarely – if ever – <u>underline</u> or *italicize*.**

  If you are underlining and/or italicizing dialogue to cue the actor into saying that word in a certain way, what you are doing is micromanaging the actors – or directing on the page. The conflict and contention, mood, tone, urgency, pacing and other elements of the scene will already cue the actor into how they will likely say their lines.

  One reason to italicize a word is when a character uses a foreign word when they are speaking another language. The scripts of the Starz series *Power* has foreign dialogue in bold lettering.

517

Or, you can italicize dialogue that is to be said in a different language, as you write it in English, but the first time you do it in the script put in a note in the script:

```
(From here on out, all italicized dialogue is to be
said in the indigenous Southern California Tongva
language with subtitles in English)
```

Or whatever language your character is speaking.

But, you can also use dual dialogue when a character speaks a different language, with the dialogue on the left as the spoken language, and the dialogue on the right in what would be the subtitled English.

One reason to italicize dialogue is that a character is singing the words. But, there should be a parenthetical (`sings`) above the dialogue.

(If you don't own the rights to a song, poem, or book or play excerpt [or exact scenes from them], don't use any of them in your script.)

Poems and lyrics both can be in italics. But, it could be clearer if you wrote the poem or lyrics in stanza form.

Dialogue that is said as sign language could be in italics, as long as you note that the character is using sign language.

See the books *The Screenwriter's Bible* and *Dr. Format Tells All*.

- **Don't indicate the language to be spoken before every bit of dialogue.**

If the dialogue in a scene is spoken in a different language, in uppercase at the end of that scene's description – just before the first bit of dialogue for that scene – note that the scene is IN SPANISH WITH ENGLISH SUBTITLES. (Or, whatever language is being spoken in the scene.)

Don't put multiple parentheticals before every bit of dialogue in the scene that the words are to be said in a different language.

At the end of that scene, put the words END SUBTITLES.

```
INT. CLAIRE'S BIKE SHOP - NIGHT

Claire watches Beth adjust the spokes on Harley's
bike. IN HINDU WITH ENGLISH SUBTITLES.
```

Or, use dual dialogue blocks, with the spoken language on the left, and the English subtitles on the right. (That is a feature in Final Draft.)

- **Do not bold anything in your script. Unless…**

If you want to **bold** the scene headings, that is a style choice. If you do, be sure to bold all of them, including the subheadings (secondary headings).

Bold does not mean UPPERCASE.

Of course, the scene headings and the subheadings should always be in uppercase.

- **Don't type props or set decoration or dressing in UPPERCASE.**

Leave that for when the production prepares the shooting script.

You are writing a spec script, not a shooting script. The crew is not going to see your spec script. There is no reason to flag words for them to notice.

A shooting script is formatted with the props in uppercase both to help them factor the budget and schedule of the film, but also to cue the prop master as to which props will be used in that scene.

- **Rarely, if ever, put sounds in UPPERCASE.**

    Leave that for when the production does the shooting script. If you do put the sounds in uppercase, do so sparingly.

    It is okay to use uppercase in description when a dog BARKS or another animal makes a vocal noise: The Lion ROARS.

    It is okay to use uppercase for sounds if it is important for us to know that the door in the horror movie SQUEAKS, or in a comedy when the sound of both a JACK HAMMER and SCREAMING BABY awakes a character who has a hangover, and who had spent half of the night trying to get their baby to go to sleep. That sort of thing plays into the comedic rise you want the reader to get from the scene.

    But, do be careful that you aren't going overboard with using uppercase with noises. Only use uppercase for noises that we really truly need to take note of. The writer who cries wolf too often gets ignored.

- **Be careful how often you use UPPERCASE for dialogue.**

    Avoid using uppercase in dialogue. If it is truly helpful to the scene, you can put the dialogue in uppercase when a character shouts.

    But, don't go overboard with using uppercase in dialogue. That device should be used sparingly.

- **Do not number the scenes in your script.**

    Spec scripts do not contain scene numbers.

    Scene numbers will be added when the script is broken down to prepare and format the shooting script for scheduling and budgeting.

    If you really truly want to be seen as a writer who doesn't know what you are doing and who has not done their homework, include scene numbers. It's like putting blinking red lights all over your script that say "I don't know what I'm doing here."

- **Don't micromanage the actors by detailing their every move, expression, bend, reach, blink, eyebrow movement, and breath, or with the overuse of parentheticals. It's puppetry direction.**

    Use parentheticals sparingly. Usually, when someone is doing something while they are specifically saying that dialogue, or the parenthetical applies to how they say their line (which, when overused, is about you micromanaging and talking down to the actors = directing from the page).

    However, a multi-cam sitcom script has different formatting standards, including where actor direction is more acceptable. Each sitcom that has been in production also has some of their own rules.

- **Refrain from using the term `beat` in scene description or in a parenthetical to indicate a pause in the action or dialogue.**

  What is happening during the pause? What are we seeing?

  Using the term `beat` to indicate a pause could be viewed as you not knowing what is happening in a scene that you wrote. You also miss an opportunity to reveal character by telling what they do at that time.

  Some say the term `beat` is to indicate a recalibration. But, is it needed?

  I read a script containing the term `beat` hundreds of times, in either description or in parentheticals. I told the writer to take out all of those uses of `beat`, and then I would read her script. She never got back to me.

- **Use only the dialogue that is needed to cleverly move the drama forward in an emotionally engaging story rich in subtext, contention, and conflict with twists, turns, and backstories that cleverly play out.**

- **Get in the scenes late. Leave the scenes early.**

  Learn what that means. Hint: Only what needs to be seen and heard.

- **Limit the incidents of characters entering and then exiting scenes – unless it is beneficial to the conflict, or other components of the scene to have the characters enter and/or exit.**

- **Limit the use of "ing" words (gerunds) in description – especially in parentheticals.**

  Use few gerunds in descriptions. They are okay to use in dialogue.

- **Don't use the names of songs in your script.**

  Because you don't own the copyright to a song, and the rights to the song are unlikely to be available – or will be too expensive to obtain, in your script – simply indicate the type of music being played: Pop rock, classical, flamenco guitar, Brazilian jazz, blues, 1990s boy band, opera, 1960s surfer music, New Age yoga, 1980s hip-hop, rhythm and blues, acid rock, etc.

  If anything, there can be a songwriter, composer, or other musician hired to create music for the scene. But, that is also not up to you.

  Simply write interesting scenes.

  I once worked for a producer who purchased a script that was written not only with the title of a popular song as the title of the film, but also that told a story based on the song. The studio was unable to obtain the rights to use the song. The project died.

- **When a number is in dialogue, it is usually spelled, unless it is a year or a product name.**

  The year 1892 would be in numbers in dialogue: `1892`.

  If a character says that something happened 17 times, then the number should be spelled out: `seventeen`.

  If a character says they are 18 years old, the number in the dialogue can either be spelled out: `I'm eighteen years old`, or you can use the number 18. Decide on a style, and use that consistently through the entire script.

WD-40 is a product name, so it should not be spelled out. It should appear just as it is: `WD-40`.

- **Study this book (the one in your hands).**
    Underline what you find helpful.
    Go back and read through what you have underlined.
    Apply it to your scripts.

- **Knowing the craft increases your chances of succeeding in it.**

    "I make writing as much a part of my life as I do eating or listening to music."
    – Maya Angelou, *I Know the Caged Bird Sings*

- **Consider these books. Study some of them, and take notes:**
  - *The American Cinema: The Directors and Directions*, Andrew Sarris
  - *The Anatomy of Story*, John Truby
  - *The Art of Dramatic Writing*, Lajos Egri
  - *Cinematography: The Classic Guide to Filmmaking*, Kris Malkiewicz
  - *Cinematography: Theory and Practice*, Blain Brown
  - *Dialogue Editing for Motion Pictures*, John Purcell
  - *Directing Actors*, Judith Weston
  - *Directing: Film Techniques and Aesthetics*, Michael Rabiger and Mick Hurbis-Cherrier
  - *Dr. Format Tells All*, David Trottier
  - *The Elements of Style*, William Strunk, Jr. & E.B. White
  - *The Emotional Craft of Fiction*, Donald Maass
  - *Film Directing: Shot by Shot*, Steven Katz
  - *The Five C's of Cinematography: Motion Picture Filming Techniques*, Joseph Mascelli
  - *Getting it Write*, Lee Jessup
  - *The Hero with a Thousand Faces*, Joseph Campbell
  - *How Not to Write a Screenplay*, Denney Martin Flinn
  - *Inside Story*, Dara Marks
  - *In the Blink of an Eye*, Walter Murch
  - *Into the Woods*, John Yorke
  - *Man and His Symbols*, Carl Jung
  - *Masters of Light: Conversations with Contemporary Cinematographers*, Dennis Schaefer
  - *The Nutshell Technique*, Jill Chamberlain
  - *On Directing Film*, David Mamet
  - *On Film Editing*, Edward Dmytryk
  - *On Filmmaking*, Alexander Mackendrick
  - *The Power of Myth*, Joseph Campbell

521

- *Producer to Producer: A Step-by-Step Guide to Low-Budget Independent Film Producing*, Maureen Ryan
- *Rebel Without a Crew*, Robert Rodriquez
- *Screenplay*, Syd Field
- *Screenplay Story Analysis*, Asher Garfunkle
- *The Screenwriter's Bible*, David Trottier
- *Screenwriter's Compass*, Guy Gallo
- *Sculpting in Time*, Andrei Tarkovsky
- *The Seven Basic Plots*, Christopher Booker
- *Shakespeare for Screenwriters*, J.M. Evenson
- *Sight, Sound, Motion: Applied Media Aesthetics*, Herbert Zetti
- *The Soul's Code: In Search of Character and Calling*, James Hillman
- *Story Maps: TV Drama: The Structure of the One-Hour Television Pilot*, Daniel P. Calvisi
- *The TV Showrunner's Roadmap*, Neil Landau
- *The TV Writer's Workbook*, Ellen Sandler
- *The 21ˢᵗ Century Screenplay*, Linda Aaronson
- *Understanding Movies*, Louis Giannetti
- *Visual Story, The*, by Bruce Block
- *The Way of the Screenwriter*, Amnon Buchbinder
- *What Happens Next: A History of American Screenwriting*, Marc Norman
- *The Writer's Journey*, Michael Vogler
- *Writing Screenplays that Sell*, Michael Hauge
- *Your Screenplay Sucks*, William Akers

- **On YouTube, watch dozens of videos about screenwriting.**

- **Read dozens of articles about screenwriting.**

- **Read back issues of the WGA magazine *Written By*.**

- **Read back issues of *Sight & Sound*, the international film magazine.**

- **Read back issues of *Film Comment Magazine*, which is published by the Film Society of Lincoln Center.**

- **Read back issues of *Filmmaker Magazine*.**

- **Read back issues of *Screenwriting Magazine*.**

- **Read back issues of *Creative Screenwriter Magazine*.**

- **Read award-winning screenplays, and watch the films.**

- **Write no less than seven spec film and/or TV spec pilot scripts.**
  Make one of them a low-budget short. One a low-budget feature. One a TV pilot. One a production that a family can watch. One of them something that you could consider your masterpiece.

If you want a broadly successful screenwriting career, aim for broadly commercial in several regions of the international film marketplace, and turn out a new, polished script every season – as that is what agents, managers, and producers like, and need.

- **Workshop every page of your scripts in a screenplay incubation workshop consisting of other writers who are strong links at the table as they have been doing the homework to improve their skills in the craft.**

  Do so before submitting the scripts to managers, agents, producers, directors, financiers, actors, state film commissions, contests, writing labs, studio writing programs, and fellowship and mentorship programs.

  "Persistence is the main key for anyone in this business, because you never know when that luck is going to strike."
  – Matt Tinker, *Goliath*

- **Register your scripts with the WGA, and also copyright them.**

- **After you workshop a script, do have it edited, then have coverage from at least one of the script coverage services.**

  I often read scripts containing so many errors that it is distractive. Make that script as sharp and error-free as possible, before submitting it to anyone.

  (See this book for the list of script coverage services. Also, do a search for: Screenplay coverage services.)

- **Open an account on Stage32.com.**

- **Join the Facebook page of Screenwriting Tribe.**

  "Be passionate and move forward with gusto every single hour of every single day, until you have reached your goal."
  – Ava DuVernay, *Middle of Nowhere*

- **Visualize, work for, and create the career that you wish to have.**

  "You might never fail on the scale I did. But some failure in life is inevitable. It is impossible to live without failing at something, unless you live so cautiously that you might as well not have lived at all. In which case, you fail by default."
  – J.K. Rowling, *Harry Potter*

  "Do not worry about failure. Failure is a badge of honor. It means you risked failure."
  – Charlie Kaufman, *Eternal Sunshine of the Spotless Mind*

  "Everyone in this business is looking for the next new hot script and writer. We want it so bad. So, if you're talented, and you believe in yourself, just keep writing – because someone will find you, eventually."
  – Jake Wagner, Good Fear Film + Management

"There is not a singular path to becoming a working screenwriter. Ignore any naysayers and others who think they know what the path should be. Of course, do your homework, and understand the nature of the business. But ultimately, figure out how you can make it work for you and the stories you want to tell."

– Matt Dy, Lit Entertainment Group

"Even if the work is a big success, some reviewer somewhere will always hate what you've done. But, you just keep going. Do the next thing. The next thing."

– Lucinda Coxon, *The Danish Girl*

"Never get down on yourself for a day of bad writing. Every day, every hour, every minute you spend writing, even the worst, builds craft."

– John Vorhaus, *The Sentinel*

"People too weak to follow their own dreams will always find a way to discourage yours."

– Bob Mayer, author *Area 51*

"You are the champion of your own career. No one has more to gain than you do, so it is in your best interest to make the most of every opportunity."

– Lee Jessup, screenwriting career consultant, LeeJessup.com

"Have the resilience to keep at it. Pick yourself up when you get told no. Your job is keep replenishing your tool kit and building your resume."

– Kira Snyder, *The 100*

"The harder I work, the luckier I get."

– Samuel Goldwyn, producer

"Getting ahead in a difficult profession – singing, acting, writing, whatever – requires avid faith in yourself. You must be able to sustain yourself against staggering blows and unfair reversals.

When I think back to those first couple of years in Rome, those endless rejections, without a glimmer of encouragement from anyone, all those failed screen tests, and yet I never let my desire slide away from me, my belief in myself, and what I felt I could achieve."

– Sophia Loren, actor

"So many screenwriters have ambitions, but they're not very defined. They simply want things to get better. They aren't clear about what they need to do to bring this about. The clearer you are in your head about what it is that you want, the more likely you are to get it."

– Julian Fellowes, *Piccadilly Jim*

Write down your goals, review them every morning to align your thoughts and actions with those intentions, and be involved in accomplishing them.

Today and every day, position yourself closer to where you wish to be.

"When I write, I feel as though I'm honoring the innate gifts that God gave me. I feel like I really can do the shit at a high level. And that's a feeling that I've never had in my life before, in any regards. I feel like we all have one or two innate talents, and a task of life is to identify those, and then do that as much as you possibly can. Because that's where the joy and the presence is going to come from. That's where the grace is going to come from."
– Charlie Hunnam, actor

Engage in your talents. Daily. Make that your habit.

"The biggest gratification is when you're sitting at the back of a movie theater and you see the audience feel the energy of something you created on screen. That feeling is unparalleled."
– Phil Volken, *Extortion*

"Any path you choose will likely be long and full of ups and downs, so choose the one that brings you the most joy and makes you feel the most alive."
— Hilary Swank, Actor

BECOME FLUENT IN THE CRAFT

I consider screenwriting a sort of language. It is complicated to make it simple and clear, and to communicate the imagery, tension, conflict, and the subtext of the situation within the world of the script, and also the psychology, concerns, wants, needs, and emotions of personalities, and convey the reasoning, logic, philosophies, heritage, culture, and the subtly or boldly contentious behavior of the characters in a compelling and interestingly engaging way. It is like magic for a script to deftly communicate the inflection and tone and mood and elegance and energy needed for what can amount to brilliance. Then, there are the formatting tricks and ticks, and ways to word things, and ways to not word things so that they aren't distractive to – but do entice – the people who read scripts for a living.

When you think you know the craft of screenwriting, there is more to learn.

I have facilitated hundreds of screenwriting workshops, wrote this book, have dealt with hundreds of writers, have been a reader for producers, have helped doctor scripts for producers and directors, and every day – for years – have searched for, read, and listened to stuff about screenwriting.

I have no doubt that I have plenty more to learn about screenwriting, and I am light years away from being a master in the craft.

In screenwriting, I think it is good to keep an open mind to learning more about the craft.

One man who wanted to workshop his script with Screenwriting Tribe crossed his arms and asked with such an attitude, "Why should I read your book, when I've already read a screenwriting book?" Was I supposed to explain the book to him? It was as if he thought that I was out-of-place for requiring participants in the Screenwriting Tribe workshop to own the *Screenwriting Tribe: Workshop Handbook.*

The man read "a" screenwriting book? One? And that is all he thinks he needs to read? The book that he read covered every single thing about screenwriting? He's got it all down, and his screenwriting skills are now flawless? That's quite an achievement. Or, not.

I read part of his script. If anyone had things to learn about screenwriting, it was him. I write while knowing that some people might also say the same thing about me.

A screenwriting workshop does not owe someone like him anything. Why should that attitude be allowed in a workshop? We have plenty of writers who are doing the process, who are helping each other, who are studying a variety of books, who are taking other measures to improve their skills, and who know that they have much to learn about the craft – and are willing to do the work to learn it, as they are working on their screenplays.

I often read or listen to interviews of people who I would consider masters in the craft of screenwriting, and they seem to say that they also are continuing to learn skills in the craft. If those successful screenwriters are still learning, then any other screenwriter also has room for improvement. I know that I do.

A workshop works when the members know that they don't know everything, and they each are willingly working to improve their skills in the craft, and they are bringing that attitude of learning to the workshop to work together to engage in helping one another improve their scripts.

At Tribe, there is no teacher. It is not a class. I am not the teacher. I'm simply the one who founded it, who organizes it, who grew the membership, and who guides the workshop along, and watches the clock. It's a facilitated workshop with everyone in it learning from and teaching one another.

Someday, maybe there will be stories of the members of Screenwriting Tribe, and the screenplays we polished together – either in person in Los Angeles, or on screen, globally.

Since I've been holding virtual workshops using Zoom, writers from a variety of countries have participated. Virtual meetings aren't the ideal way to hold a screenwriting workshop, but I do what I can for the writers.

I always meant for Tribe to be about writers encouraging each other to improve their skills in the craft. Luckily, there have been very few people who have been disruptive and problematic to the point of having to be banned.

What we are doing is working on our dreams of turning the worlds within our imaginations into screenplays for films and TV shows.

"Never stop. Never stop fighting. Never stop dreaming. And don't be afraid of wearing your heart on your sleeve – in declaring the films that you love, the films that you want to make, the life that you've had, and the lives you can help reflect in cinema.

For myself, for a long time, maybe I felt inauthentic or something. I felt like my voice wasn't worth hearing, and I think everyone's voice is worth hearing. So, if you've got something to say, say it from the rooftops."
– Tom Hiddleston, actor

"One of the wonderful things about film is that it allows us to see a reflection of ourselves and who we are as people. It also allows us to see each other from an angle we might not have otherwise understood."
– Martin Scorsese, *Silence*

I encourage screenwriters to write at least one script that is more about important issues than it is about entertainment. That might mean what people call edutainment, that is: a cross between education and entertainment.

"I've been very careful and deliberate about finding things that really matter to me, and not, 'Wouldn't this be a cool movie?' Because, I don't have the technical skill to write a film that I'm not deeply passionate about. Emotionally passionate about. Intellectually passionate about. I'm trying to do things hopefully that are somehow reflective and bring some awareness to issues in an interesting, new way."
– Taylor Sheridan, *Without Remorse*

"A big part of movies has always been cutting through the crap and showing something that expresses a human truth we all can connect with."
– Adam McKay, *The Big Short*

As I say at the beginning of the book, screenwriters are cultural engineers.

Films and TV shows are watched the world over, and can function as educational tools for helping people to understand issues that matter.

"First and foremost, you have to entertain because you have to get people into the theater. But for me, this is almost a pulpit, and there are messages that I want to get into the world that I think are important, that will inspire people, that will maybe even change somebody's life."
– Debra Martin Chase, producer

Write a film or series that is socially valid, works to help create a culture and society in which you wish to live, that will uplift and inspire, that might reduce sociological oppression, and that will resonate with people wanting to protect the health of the environment, wildlife habitat, and wild animals.

With increasing ocean acidification, melting ice caps, melting permafrost, global climate change, rising seas, plastic pollution, pharmaceutical and chemical pollution, food shortages, corporate control of food plants, damage to the environment by the feed grain, cattle, fishing, fossil fuels, and various extraction industries, as well as from oil palm plantations, and also the loss of wildlife habitat, and the extinction of species, there is no shortage of important topics that can be cleverly exposed in a film or series.

"I don't think it's the job of the filmmakers to give anybody answers. I do think, though, that a good film makes you ask the questions of yourself as you leave the theater."
– Paul Haggis, *Letters from Iwo Jima*

Write a variety of films that you would like to watch.

"People at the top are extremely passionate about what they do. You cannot sustain that level if you're not passionate."
– Ron Howard, *Far and Away*

When you watch a film, know that scenes on the silver screen were once thoughts unseen.
Know that what is on screen will influence the thoughts of others.
Consider the types of thoughts that you would like your work to propagate.

"Don't forget, no one sees the world the way you do, so no one else can tell the stories that you have to tell."
– Charles De Lint, author *The Dreaming Place*

It is easy to become discouraged while pursuing the craft of screenwriting.
Chin up. Focus on the goals. Move forward. Persevere.
Write those scenes and manifest your dreams. Your favorite films are the result of other writers who have done it, too.

"Don't listen to those who say, you are taking too big a chance. Michelangelo would have painted the Sistine floor, and it would surely be rubbed out by today. Most important, don't listen when the little voice of fear inside you rears its ugly head and says, 'They are all smarter than you out there. They're more talented, they're taller, prettier, luckier, and they have connections.' I firmly believe that if you follow a path that interests you, not to the exclusion of love, sensitivity, and cooperation with others, but with the strength of conviction that you can move others by your own efforts, and do not make success or failure the criteria by which you live, the chances are you'll be a person worthy of your own respects."
– Neil Simon, *The Odd Couple* (The quotation originally mentioned "blonder," but he later apologized for listing that as an ideal.)

Don't bow to discouragement, bullying, jealousy, or fade your engagement in your talent because some blowhard said negative things. They are dealing with their own disbelief. What is going on in their mind has to do with their life experiences and how they have been treated, how they have decided to treat others, and how they choose to live their life. It is self-amplification.

"If someone tells you the odds are slim, just keep walking. Just do whatever the hell you want to do, because they don't know what they're talking about. When you love something, and you work really really hard at it, you can do it."
– Melissa McCarthy, *The Boss*

"Talent is helpful in writing, but guts are absolutely necessary."
– Jessamyn West, *Friendly Persuasion*

"If you are lucky enough to find a way of life you love, you have to find the courage to live it."
– John Irving, *The World According to Garp*

Do your homework, prepare, and do the work. Pursue success, and manifest the life you want.

"You've gotta be original, because if you're like someone else, what do they need you for?"
– Bernadette Peters, actor

"There is a vitality, a life-force, an energy, a quickening that is translated through you into action. And because there is only one you in all of time, this expression is unique. And if you block it, it will never exist through any other medium – and be lost. The world will not have it. It is not your business to determine how good it is, nor how valuable it is, nor how it compares with others' expressions. It is your business to keep it yours, clearly and directly, to keep the channel open.
Above all else, keep the channel open."
– Martha Graham, *Appalachian Spring*

Know that your only valid competition is yourself.
Be absolutely impervious to discouragement. Do not let it penetrate your mind or alter your focus on achieving your dreams.

"The world will provide you with every imaginable obstacle, but the one most difficult to overcome will be the lack of faith in yourself. Leave it to others to have doubts about you."
– Callie Khouri, *Thelma and Louise*

Be ravenous in your quest to sharpen your skills in the craft of screenwriting, to finish and polish scripts, to submit them to the right eyes, to get a manager, to get an agent, and to get your screenplays produced.

"It took me over eleven years from the time I left college to get my first job in writing. It's just what happened. I think tenacity is really the only thing. And what happens with tenacity is that the more people that see your stuff, the more times that you get to talk to people, the greater the chances that you'll hook up with somebody who gets it, and wants to do it. So, perseverance and believing that you can do this thing that you want to do – I think it's important. And, if you believe in your stuff, then you should continue to do it. You should continue to push for it."
– Charlie Kaufman, *Human Nature*

Work so hard in the craft that people are awed by your screenplays.
Make your life accomplishments reveal your critics as irrelevant.

"Dreams are lovely. But they are just dreams. Fleeting, ephemeral, pretty. But, dreams do not come true just because you dream them. It's hard work that makes things happen. It's hard work that creates change."
– Shonda Rhimes, *Grey's Anatomy*

Do the work that will create the life that you want to experience.
Astonish yourself in the expression of your intellect and talents.

"I like writing because it's introspection. It's a serendipity kind of thing when you're really in a place that no one else can be but you at the time. And it's your decision to share with the world if you want to."
– John Singleton, *Baby Boy*

"If you look at most of the success stories in our business, it's writers who have achieved that from never taking no and never stopping and never saying, 'This is not for me.' They believe this is what they should be doing in life, and they've chased it."
– David Boxerbaum, agent at Verve

Be your best advocate and coach.
Be the one who makes your career in screenwriting happen.

"The best thing you can give yourselves is the gift of possibility. And the best thing you can give each other is the pledge to go on protecting that gift in each other as long as you live."
– Paul Newman, actor

Know the power of your words that are spoken as dialogue by characters in a film or series. Also, be aware of the imagery you are helping to create, as images briefly seen can have long-term impact.
Understand that what you write in the form of a screenplay can help alter human culture.

"The artist, since the beginning of recorded time, has always expressed the aspirations and dreams of his people. Silence the artist and you silence the most articulate voice the people have. Destroy culture and you destroy one of the strongest sources of inspiration from which a people can draw strength for a better life."
– Dalton Trumbo, as read by Katharine Hepburn at a political rally for U.S. President candidate Henry Wallace held at Gilmore Stadium in Los Angeles during the Blacklist era

Be glad that you have the freedom of speech, and you can write important works not dictated by a suppressive government. Use that freedom.
There are people the world over who are living desperately as they are stuck existing in disadvantaged, repressive, neglectful, or abusive situations. One character on screen might awaken them to their possibilities, and motivate them to break through into a better life, altering the trajectory of their life

adventure. Because of it, that person can then end up helping many other people. In that way, screenwriters can be heroes.

Know that your screenplays might influence the lives of many. Do some good with that power.

"The pen is mightier than the sword."
– Edward Bulwer-Lytton, *The Last Days of Pompeii*

Thank you for reading my book. I hope that you have found it helpful. If so, perhaps you will let other writers know about this book.

I wish you of all the best.

Daniel John Carey

"The successful warrior is the average man with a laser-like focus."
– Bruce Lee, *The Way of the Dragon*

"Being like everybody is the same as being nobody."
– Rod Serling, *The Twilight Zone*

"Don't ever give up. There's better, smarter, more talented people who will give up. But if you're the one who sticks it out, then you might just complete your hero's journey, and get the mighty reward at the end. Don't give up."
– Pat Higgins, *Powertool Cheerleaders vs. the Boyband of the Screeching Dead*

"It's a terrible thing, I think, in life to wait until you're ready. I have this feeling now that actually no one is ever ready to do anything. There is almost no such thing as ready. There is only now. And you may as well do it now. Generally speaking, now is as good a time as any."
– Hugh Laurie, *Dragons of New York*

"Don't wait for permission to tell the stories you want to tell. Find the way. But don't ruin your life while you're at it. Don't let your filmmaking allow you to go broke. Take vacations. Try to have some fun."
– Elan Bogarin, *306 Hollywood*

GLOSSARY OF NAMES

A: GLOSSARY OF NAMES

B: GLOSSARY OF NAMES

C: GLOSSARY OF NAMES

Screenwriting Tribe

Coppola, Francis Ford, 1, 2, 88, 144, 258, 403, 445, 512; **Coppola**, Sofia, 374, 508; **Cosgrove**, Miranda, 448; **Costner**, Kevin, 47; **Coulam**, Daisy, 63, 135; **Cox**, Zach, 45, 100, 462; **Coxon**, Lucinda, 524; **Craig**, Daniel, 237; **Cranston**, Bryan, 119; **Cretton**, Destin Daniel, 229; **Cromier**, Robert, 200; **Cron**, Lisa, 187; **Cronenberg**, David, 26; **Cross**, Tom, 262; **Crowell**, Thomas, 91, 122; **Cruise**, Tom, 345, 346; **Cukor**, George, 75, 403

D: GLOSSARY OF NAMES

Darwin, Charles, 171; **Davies**, Marion, 23; **Davis**, Geena, 503; **Davis**, Viola, 489; **De Laurentis**, Dina, 48; **De Lint**, Charles, 529; **De Niro**, Robert, 42, 260; **De Palma**, Brian, 445; **de Souza**, Steven, 31, 403; **de Vere**, Edward, 218; **Deakins**, Roger, 446; **DeBose**, Steven, 438, 456; **Deemer**, Charles, 316; **del Toro**, Guillermo, 44, 63, 66, 204, 256, 484; **DeLapo**, James, 133; **Delpy**, Julie, 31; **Demeny**, Georges, 496; **DeMille**, Cecil B., 261; **Demille**, Cecil D., 24; **Demme**, Jonathan, 261; **Depp**, Johnny, 410; **Deren**, Maya, 497; **Desmond**, Norma, 28; **DeVito**, Danny, 146; **Devlin**, Lindsay, 65; **Dhawliwal**, Gazal, 500; **DiCaprio**, Leonardo, 430; **Dickens**, Charles, 36, 510; **Didion**, Joan, 35, 197; **Diesel**, Vin, 145, 485; **Dinelaris**, Alexander, Jr., 218; **Dionysus**, 287; **Disney**, Walt, 40, 114, 211, 495; **Diver**, Sara, 486; **Dixon**, Leslie, 314; **Dmytryk**, Edward, 521; **Dolan**, Xavier, 260; **Dollner**, Gary, 254; **Dolman**, Glen, 21; **Donner**, Laura Shuler, 366; **Doran**, Lindsay, 10; **Douglass**, Frederick, 5; **Douglas**, Kirk, 154; **Down**, Lesley-Ane, 124; **Driver**, Sara, 494; **Dubus**, Andre III, 41; **Duffer**, Matt and Ross, 204; **Duffield**, Brian, 357; **Dulull**, Hasraf, 400; **Duplass**, Mark, 139, 472; **Durand**, Allan, 236; **Duvall**, Robert, 294; **DuVernay**, 19, 49, 158, 185, 484, 523; **Dworet**, Laurence, 402; **Dy**, Matt, 63, 462, 466, 524

E: GLOSSARY OF NAMES

Ebert, Roger, 297; **Edison**, Thomas, 22; **Efron**, Zac, 80; **Eggers**, Dave, 56; **Egri**, Lajos, 52, 61, 64, 176, 224, 285, 356, 448, 521; **Einstein**, Albert, 369, 510; **Ejiofor**, Chiwetel, 14; **Elias**, Naomi, 494; **Elizabeth**, Queen, 218; **Ellis**, Bret Easton, 312; **Ellison**, Ralph, 501; **Emerson**, John, 25; **Emerson**, Ralph Waldo, 8, 37; **Emmerich**, Toby, 63; **Eng** Esther, 497; **Englander**, Nathan, 130; **Ephron**, Nora, 189, 225, 399; **Erivo**, Cynthia, 495; **Estabrook**, Helen, 181; **Eszterhas**, Joe, 28, 152, 439; **Evans**, Shaula, 272; **Evenson**, J.M., 64, 522

F: GLOSSARY OF NAMES

Fairfax, Marion, 497; **Farhadi**, Asghar, 34, 216; **Farroghzad**, Forough, 500; **Faulkner**, William, 40, 119, 156, 158, 187, 194, 445; **Favreau**, Jon, 196; **Faxon**, Nat, 137, 310; **Feig**, Paul, 34, 180, 397; **Feirstein**, Bruce, 188; **Feldman**, Liz, 499; **Fellini**, Federico, 21, 187; **Fellowes**, Julian, 160, 194, 308, 340, 524; **Ferguson**, Francis L., 213; **Ferguson**, Larry, 325; **Fey**, Tina, 31, 180; **Field**, Sally, 166; **Field**, Syd, 64, 232, 522; **Fincher**, David, 371; **Fisher**, Carrie, 456; **Fisher**, Mickey, 115; **Fitch**, Janet, 36, 171; **Fitzgerald**, F. Scott, 30, 48, 164, 385; **Flahive**, Liz, 138; **Fleming**, Ian, 38; **Fletcher**, Dexter, 178; **Fletcher**, Geoffrey, 147; **Fletcher**, John, 218; **Flinn**, Denney Martin, 64, 521; **Fogelman**, Dan, 193; **Folsom**, Stephany, 469; **Foote**, Horton, 408; **Ford**, Harrison, 424, 150; **Forman**, Milos, 395; **Fornés**, Maria Irene, 47; **Forster**, E.M., 181, 187; **Foster**, Jodie, 492; **Foxx**, Jamie, 42; **Frank**, Scott, 184, 211, 396; **Franklin**, Aretha, 369; **Frazier**, F. Scott, 206; **Freeman**, Morgan, 314; **Freytag**, Gustav, 217; **Friedman**, Josh, 256, 270; **Frye**, E. Max, 236; **Fugate**, Katherine, 402; **Fuqua**, Antoine, 484; **Fusco**, John, 94, **Fyffe-Marshall**, Kelly, 48

G: GLOSSARY OF NAMES

Gaghan, Stephen, 442; **Gaiman**, Neil, 43, 188; **Gallagher**, Rob, 468; **Gallo**, Guy, 64, 522; **Gamble**, Sera, 436; **Garai**, Romola, 478; **Gardia**, Liz, W., 190; **Garfunkel**, Asher, 64, 522; **Garrison**, Martin, 260; **Gentileschi**, Artemisia, 502; **Gerima**, Haile, 503; **Gervais**, Ricky, 31; **Gerwig**, Greta, 163, 502; **Giacobone**, Nicolas, 71; **Giannetti**, Louis, 522; **Gil**, Tony, 455; **Gilbert**, Elizabeth, 171; **Gillette**, Goulas, 167; **Gilliam**, Terry, 447; **Gilligan**, Vince, 235, 363; **Gilmour**, David, 12; **Gilroy**, Dan, 153; **Gilroy**, Tony, 39, 44, 123, 400; **Gioia**, Dana, 7; **Gladwell**, Malcolm, 447; **Glass**, Ira, 67; **Glenn**, John, 32, 67; **Glycon**, 287; **Godard**, Jean-Luc, 6, 14, 164, 213, 384; **Godefroy**, Christian, 178; **Goethe**, Johann Wolfgang von, 1, 39; **Gogol**, Nikola, 510; **Goldman**, Jane, 246; **Goldman**, William, 18, 28, 35, 56, 85, 105, 114, 175, 395; **Goldsman**, Akiva, 50, 285; **Goldwyn**, Samuel, 526; **Goldwyn**, Samuel, Sr., 438; **Gonzalez**, Daniela, 51, 463; **Goodloe**, Bianca, 148, 477; **Goodman**, Allegra, 395; **Gordon**, Bruce B., 16; **Gosselaar**, Mark-Paul, 119; **Gould**, Chester, 268; **Graham**, Martha 530; **Granik**, Debra, 130, 367; **Grant**, Richard E., 74; **Grass**, Randall, 369; **Gray**, James, 60; **Gray**, Julie, 52; **Grazer**, Brian, 439; **Grier**, Pam, 493; **Griffith**, D.W., 23, 25, 259, 261, 375; **Grillo-Marxuach**, Javier, 244; **Grisanti**, Jen, 431; **Grishham**, John, 402; **Grisoni**, Tony, 194; **Guay**, Paul, 157; **Guggenheim**, Eric, 292; **Gulzar**, Meghna, 500; **Guy-Blaché**, Alice, 28, 375, 496, 497

H: GLOSSARY OF NAMES

Haas, Derek, 367; **Haddish**, Tiffany, 488; **Hagen**, Louis, 496; **Haggis**, Paul, 4, 528;

B

C

F

GLOSSARY OF FILM AND TV PRODUCTIONS

10 Cloverfield Lane, 130, 245; **100, The**, 524; **12 Years A Slave**, 73, 144; **1917**, 189, 446; **21 Grams**, 61; **21 Jump Street**, 429; **2001: A Space Odyssey**, opening pages; **2nd Greatest**, 253; **3:10 to Yuma**, 367; **30 Rock**, 180; **300**, 12; **306 Hollywood**, 532; **42**, 374; **48 Hours**, 30; **52 Pick-Up**, 95

A: GLOSSARY OF FILM AND TV PRODUCTIONS

A.I. Artificial Intelligence, opening matter; **A.P.E.X.**, 157; **About Elly**, 34; **About Last Night**, 357; **Above the Law**, 188; **Accidental Tourist, The**, 220; **Ace Ventura: Pet Detective**, 506; **Adams Family, The**, 103; **Adaptation**, 296; **Adventures of Prince Achmed, The**, 496; **Adventures of Tom Sawyer, The**, 88; **Affair, The**, 188; **After Earth**, 213; **After the Rain**, 155; **Age of Innocence, The**, 3; **Aladdin**, 337; **Alexander**, 499; **Alice's Restaurant**, 77; **Alien**, 375; **Alien: Covenant**, 42; **Aliens vs. Predators: Requiem**, 144; **Aliens**, 286, 392; **Alita: Battle Angel**, 16; **All About Eve**, 370; **All is Lost**, 296, 375; **All-Star Weekend**, 42; **Alligator**, 132; **Aloha**, 500; **Alpha Blonde**, 391; **American Assassin**, 182; **American Beauty**, 71, 269; **American Crime**, 105; **American Honey**, 159, 195, 233; **American Housewife**, 51; **American Hustle**, 416; **American Night**, 54; **American Outlaws**, 187; **American Pie**, 80, 292, 330, 406; **Amulet**, 478; **An American Werewolf in London**, 26; **An Education**, 286; **An Unmarried Woman**, 8; **And then We Danced**, 164; **Anniversary Party, The**, 493; **Anomalisa**, 11, 229; **Any Given Sunday**, 185; **Apartment, The**, 113; **Aphrodite, Goddess of Love**, 234; **Apocalypse Now**, 82, 276, 294, 370, 403; **Appalachian Spring**, 530; **Apt Pupil**, 41; **Aquarius**, 436; **Area 51**; 524; **Armageddon**, 400; **Arrested Development**, 101; **Arrival**, 271, 323; **Artemisia**, 502; **Artist, The**, 375; **As Good as It Gets**, 80; **As I Lay Dying**, 187; **Ascension of Ava Delaine, The**, 271; **Ascension**, 431; **Aschenputtel**, 495; **Assistant, The**, 81; **August: Osage County**, 43; **Autumn in New York**, 512; **Avalon High**, 400; **Avatar 2**, 4, 33, 222, 270; **Aviator, The**, 265; **Awkwafina is Nora from Queens**, 499

B: GLOSSARY OF FILM AND TV PRODUCTIONS

Baby Boy, 531; **Back to the Future**, 17; **Bad Day at Black Rock**, 265; **Bad Grandpa**, 261; **Badlands**. 370; **Bal Canto**, ii; **Ballad of Jack and Rose, The**, 311; **Band of Brothers**, 234;

Bang: You're Dead, 10; **Barking Dogs Never Bite**, 249, 269; **Barry Lyndon**, 370; **Basic Instinct**, 28; **Battle of Versailles**, 185; **Baywatch**, 80, 113, 406; **Be Natural: The Untold Story of Alice Guy-Blaché**, 497; **Beanpole**, 266, 359; **Beautiful Mind, A**, 50; **Beauty and Her Beast**, 240; **Bed of Thorns**, 500; **Bedbugs**, 58; **Beetle Called Derek, A**, 192; **Beetlejuice**, 212; **Before Sunset**, 406; **Beginners**, 80; **Beguiled, The**, 508; **Being John Malkovich**, 297; **Being Mary Jane**, 426; **Being There**, 237; **Bel Canto**, 144; **Bell Jar, The**, 45, 462; **Belle De Jour**, 221; **Beloved**, opening pages, 5, 6; **Beowulf**, 188; **Bernie Mac Show, The**, 55; **Best Exotic Marigold Hotel, The**, 190, 406; **Best in Show**, 80; **Best Little Whorehouse in Texas, The**, 45; **Better Call Saul**, 49, 169, 363, 501; **Beyond a Reasonable Doubt**, 438; **Beyond Therapy**, 257; **Beyond, The**, 400; **Big Bang Theory**, 51; **Big C, The**, 139, 501; **Big Chill, The**, 54, 286; **Big Fish**, 135; **Big Lebowski, The**, 82, 370; **Big Little Lies**, 31; **Big Love**, 139, 357; **Big Short, The**, 414, 528; **Big Sleep, The**, 158; **Bill & Ted's Excellent Adventure**, 214; **Billy Elliot**, 80, 292; **Birch-Tree Meadow, The**, 2; **Bird Box**, 227; **Birdman**, 71, 160, 162, 218, 271; **Biutiful**, 264, 487; **Black Bodies**, 48; **Black Friday**, 104; **Black Hearts Bleed Red**, 159; **Black Panther**, 151, 195, 231; 236; **Black-ish**, 51; **BlacKkKlansman**, 14, 400; **Blacklist, The**, 74; **Blackmail**, 422; **Blackout**, 270; **Blade Runner**, 18, 156; **Blair Witch Project, The**, 487; **Blaze**, 140; **Blessings**, 42; **Blood Ties**, 60; **Bloom**, 21; **Blue Moon of Kentucky**, 173; **Boardwalk Empire**, 137, 157; **Bob and Ted and Carol and Alice**, 8; **Body Heat**, 450; **Bodyguard, The**, 404; **Bohemian Rhapsody**, 219; **Boobs in the Wood**, 368; **Book Tower, The**, 44; **Booksmart**, 70; **Borat**, 49; **Boss, The**, 529; **Bourne Identity**, 123; **Boy and Bicycle**, 141, 260; **Boy and His Shoe, A**, 512; **Boy Who Harnessed the Wind, The**, 14; **Boyhood**, 80, 271, 401; **Boys Don't Cry**, 410; **Brady Bunch, The**, 113; **Bram Stroker's Dracula**, 402; **Brave One, The**, 154; **Breakfast at Tiffany's**, 500; **Breaking Bad**, 113, 235, 363, 359, 406; **Breathless**, 213, 384; **Bridesmaids**, 398; **Bridget Jones's Baby**, 148, 501; **Brief Encounter**, 113; **Bright Star**, 498; **Bringing out the Dead**, 35; **Broad City**, 494; **Broadcast News**, 182; **Brokeback Mountain**, 165, 313, 470; **Bronson**, 80; **Brooklyn Nin-Nine**, 165; **Brooklyn**, 96, 271; **Brothers McMullen, The**, 80, 142, 487; **Brothers**, 57; **Bruce Almighty**, 507; **Bucket List, The**, 34, 35, 37; **Buried**, 288; **Burn Notice**, 485; **Butch Cassidy and the Sundance Kid**, 28, 35; **Butterscotch**, 187

G: Glossary of Film and TV Productions

H: Glossary of Film and TV Productions

I: Glossary of Film and TV Productions

J: Glossary of Film and TV Productions

K: Glossary of Film and TV Productions

L: Glossary of Film and TV Productions

M: GLOSSARY OF FILM AND TV PRODUCTIONS

N: GLOSSARY OF FILM AND TV PRODUCTIONS

O: GLOSSARY OF FILM AND TV PRODUCTIONS

P: GLOSSARY OF FILM AND TV PRODUCTIONS

Q: GLOSSARY OF FILM AND TV PRODUCTIONS

R: GLOSSARY OF FILM AND TV PRODUCTIONS

S: GLOSSARY OF FILM AND TV PRODUCTIONS

T: GLOSSARY OF FILM AND TV PRODUCTIONS

U: GLOSSARY OF FILM AND TV PRODUCTIONS

V: GLOSSARY OF FILM AND TV PRODUCTIONS

W: GLOSSARY OF FILM AND TV PRODUCTIONS

X: GLOSSARY OF FILM AND TV PRODUCTIONS

Y: GLOSSARY OF FILM AND TV PRODUCTIONS

Z: GLOSSARY OF FILM AND TV PRODUCTIONS

INDEX AND TOPICAL GUIDE

F: Index and Topical Guide

M: INDEX AND TOPICAL GUIDE

N: Index and Topical Guide

O: Index and Topical Guide

P: Index and Topical Guide

Q: Index and Topical Guide

R: Index and Topical Guide

S: INDEX AND TOPICAL GUIDE

U: INDEX AND TOPICAL GUIDE

V: INDEX AND TOPICAL GUIDE

W: INDEX AND TOPICAL GUIDE

"There is no greater disability in society, than the inability to see a person as more."
– Robert M. Hensel, author *Writings on the Wall*

"I will write my way into another life."
– Ann Pachett, *Bal Canto*

THE AUTHOR

In the winter when I was sixteen – to leave brutality – I hitchhiked from Cleveland to California. I knew California was where I wanted to be, including because I wanted to be involved in filmmaking, wanted to live near the ocean with its wildlife and energy, and wanted to grow food year-round.

Most people call me John. It's the name that my father wanted for me, and I got it from my great-uncle who grew apples. Since I was a child, some people have called me Dijon. I thought the name was unique to me – until I met other Daniel Johns who also go by the nickname. Some people call me Daniel. I don't care which of those names people call me. On film and TV sets they sometimes go by people's nicknames, to avoid confusing cast and crew with the same first names. So, on sets some people call me by my nickname.

I grew up barely able to understand what I was reading. Maybe that is why I became interested in films, because I could watch them and understand.

When I was 13, something clicked as I listened to the radio while delivering newspapers. For the first time, I could comprehend what I read.

I dove into reading books. I thought that one day I would write one.

As an adult, I spent years as a ghost co-author, helping other people to write their books. After many books, I lost interest helping so-called "authors" write books that they didn't actually write. I felt as if I were participating in deception.

After being a reader for producers, working as a studio assistant, and helping producers and directors polish scripts, and doing a whole lot of other stuff in the industry (including being murdered on several TV shows, and in some movies), and helping to run some other screenwriting groups, I founded Screenwriting Tribe in 2016. The membership quickly grew into the hundreds.

The first edition of this book was published in 2018. After some film schools started using it as a text, I thought I better write a second edition that is more thorough, and helpful.

I continue to doctor film scripts for producers and directors.

Other than the workshop, I do not work with writers on their screenplays.

Do not send unsolicited scripts to me. I will not read them.

I hope you found my book to be useful, and that it will help you avoid making the mistakes that I made, and helps propel you into your dream life.

See you in the movies.

If you have found this book helpful:

Please, write a customer review on Amazon.com. That helps others to learn about the book.

Share a photo of the book on Facebook, Twitter, Snapchat, Instagram, Stage32, and other social media.

If you know screenwriters, tell them about this book.

Start a screenwriting workshop, and use the book as a guide. Others have.

"Often, when you think you're at the end of something, you're at the beginning of something else."
– Mr. Rogers

Begin and finish projects. It's a good habit.

•

Daniel John Carey

Screenwriting Tribe